D1613958

D-Day and the Cover-Up at Pointe du Hoc

D-Day and the Cover-Up at Pointe du Hoc

2nd & 5th US Army Rangers
1 May–10 June 1944

Volume 2

Gary Sterne

Pen & Sword
MILITARY

First published in Great Britain in 2018
by Pen & Sword Military
An imprint of Pen & Sword Books Limited
47 Church Street
Barnsley
South Yorkshire
S70 2AS

Copyright © Gary Sterne 2018

ISBN 978 1 47382 374 7

A CIP catalogue record for this book is
available from the British Library

Typeset in Ehrhardt
by Mac Style

Printed and bound in the UK
by CPI Group (UK) Ltd, Croydon, CR0 4YY

Pen & Sword Books Limited incorporates the imprints of Atlas,
Archaeology, Aviation, Discovery, Family History, Fiction, History, Maritime,
Military, Military Classics, Politics, Select, Transport,
True Crime, Air World, Frontline Publishing, Leo Cooper,
Remember When, Seaforth Publishing, The Praetorian Press,
Wharncliffe Local History, Wharncliffe Transport,
Wharncliffe True Crime and White Owl.

For a complete list of Pen & Sword titles please contact
PEN & SWORD BOOKS LIMITED
47 Church Street, Barnsley, South Yorkshire, S70 2AS, England
E-mail: enquiries@pen-and-sword. co. uk
Website: www. pen-and-sword. co. uk

Contents

Introduction

Volume 2 continues to follow the activities of the US Army 2nd and 5th Rangers each day as they head towards D-Day. Covering every day of May and then running into June 1944, it shows the daily Allied intelligence briefings and the evolution of the famous Pointe du Hoc and Maisy gun batteries, as well as other Ranger D-Day targets. Using period reports just as they were issued, for the first time this work allows the reader to assess the changes to the German coastal defence positions and monitor their threat level, whilst at the same time comparing them to the overall Allied invasion plans.

The closer it gets to D-Day, the more the intelligence intensifies and we see exactly what data was given to the Rangers' leadership. Preparations climax with the Slapton Sands dress rehearsal, followed by embarkation and D-Day itself – the Omaha Beach landings, the Pointe du Hoc battle and three days later the battle for Maisy.

Then the After Action Reports taken from everyone involved are presented, as the author uses dozens of previously unseen, recently declassified Top Secret files. With documents in their original forms there can no longer be any speculation as to the Rangers' orders and objectives, as all of the Rangers' D-Day battles are laid bare. Judge for yourself if a cover-up really did take place, and if so by whom and for what reasons?

This ground breaking book will challenge the way that historians look at the Pointe du Hoc battle from now on and it sets the benchmark for any serious study of the US Rangers in Normandy.

Chapter 8

May 1944 – Slapton Sands and Climbing Cliffs

---

1 May 1944
5th Rangers – Companies A – F, Medical and HQ – Dorchester, England.
B Co. Corporal Clayton Gardner was assigned and joined from HQ 10th Replacement Depot 874 US Army.
Alerted for departure – Fabius 1.

2nd Battalion Historical Narrative.

> On 1 May, Companies A/B/C embarked on the Prince Charles. Companies D/E/F embarked on the HMS Ben My Chree and HMS Amsterdam at Swanage, joining Companies A/B/C in Weymouth Harbor on the evening of 3 May. The above-named ships had previously been transporting the 1st Ranger Battalion in their actions in the Mediterranean theater. The troops slept in hammocks below decks and were fed American 10-in-1 rations prepared by the ship's cooks. Mealtime was not looked forward to with much eagerness. Time on board was spent chiefly in briefing and attending ship's Movies; games of chance were also much in evidence.
>
> "Fabius I" was a full scale rehearsal of the actual D-Day assault operation. Troops participating included the I/116th Infantry, the 2nd and 5th Ranger Battalions, and two Amphibious Tank Platoons. The terrain selected was near Dartmouth. The mission of the Battalion was as follows:
>
> Companies D/E/F were to land at H-Hour, ascend a slight cliff, and secure the assigned objective. Company C would also land at H-Hour with I/116th Infantry and would simulate clearing the beach. Companies A/B with the Bn Hq Det would land one hour later and, with company B acting as point and Company A as flank protection, would precede the 5th Ranger Battalion cross-country to the location of Companies D/E/F. For the purpose of control, Companies A/B were placed under the command of the CO 5th Rngr Bn for the operation.

A Company 2nd Rangers – Dorchester, Dorset. No change. Alerted for departure – Fabius 1.
B Company 2nd Rangers – Dorchester, Dorset.
The following seven enlisted men went from Duty to sick in Hospital: S/Sgt. Young, T/5 Bramkamp, Pfc. Davis, Pfc. Miles, Pfc. Paniaha, Pfc. Snedeker, Pfc. Bragg. Alerted for departure – Fabius 1.
C Company 2nd Rangers – Dorchester, Dorset.
Pfc. Hareff went from Duty to absent (sick) to US Naval Hospital Advanced Amphibious Base, Falmouth, Cornwall. Alerted for departure – Fabius 1.
D Company 2nd Rangers – Swanage, Dorset. No change. Alerted for departure.
E Company 2nd Rangers – Swanage, Dorset. Alerted for departure.
F Company 2nd Rangers – Swanage, Dorset. No change. Alerted for departure.
Medical Detachment 2nd Rangers – Dorchester, Dorset. No change. Alerted for departure – Fabius 1.
Headquarters Company 2nd Rangers – Dorchester, Dorset.

On 1 May the arrangements for troop flow from the Marshalling Areas to the ports were distributed and thoroughly explained.

The Rangers' route went from Dorchester Marshalling areas to the Portland and Weymouth embarkation points.

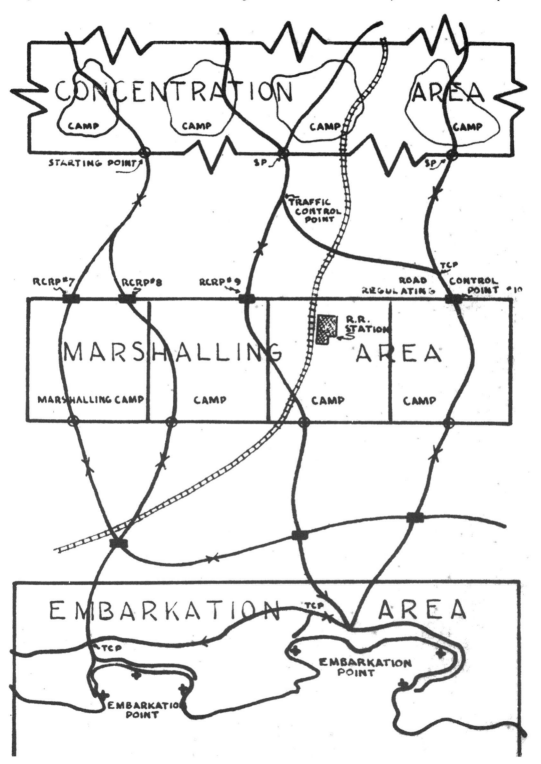

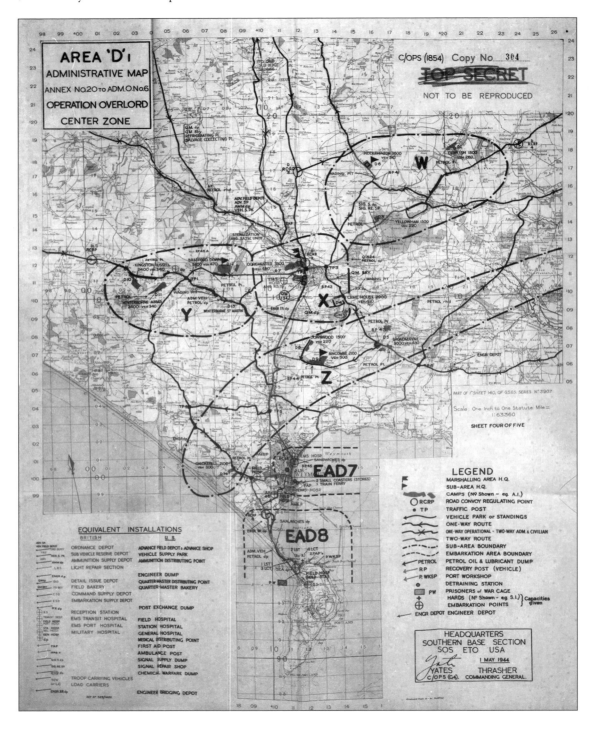

A blow-up of the 5th Rangers' Embarkation camp at Dewlish shows the camp headquarters and the wading pit for vehicle testing at Piddlehinton. It also shows the petrol supply points and the traffic flow indicators directing traffic towards Weymouth – their Port of Embarkation.

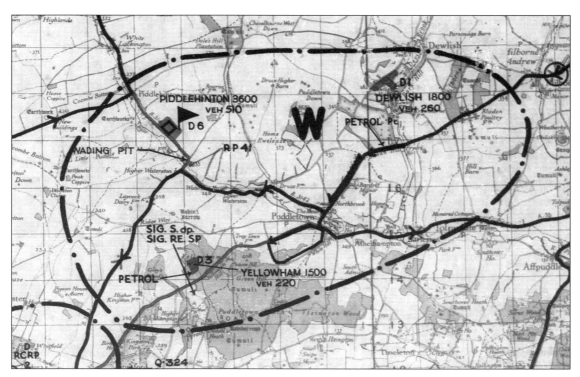

Dewlish Camp D1 had a capacity for around 1,900 men and 260 vehicles. The camp was situated in the woods and fields around Dewlish park in Dorset.

The vehicle wading pit for testing waterproofing.

A blow-up of the 2nd Rangers' camp at Broadmayne. Their Embarkation Headquarters was based in Dorchester.

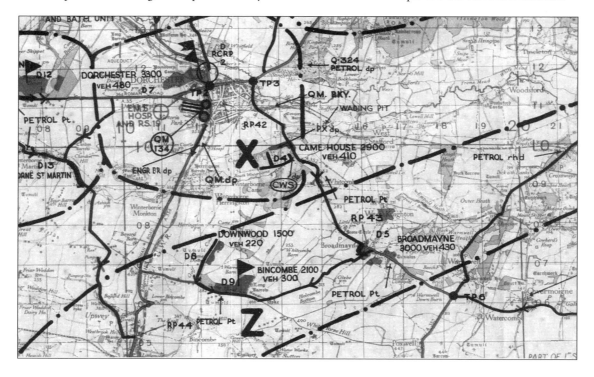

Detailed instructions were re-issued for the handing of personnel over to the Navy for embarkation.

Upon receipt of the Unit Sheet in the Marshalling Area, unit commanders will prepare Unit Party Embarkation Personnel Rosters for each Unit Party by merely ruling out the names of personnel on the original roster, not part of the Unit Party, and adding names not shown on the original roster. Eight (8) copies of Unit Party Embarkation Personnel Rosters will be prepared and turned over to the officer or NCO in charge of each such Unit Party. Upon formation of Craft or Ship Loads in the Marshalling Area, each Unit Party CO or NCO will deliver to the CO Craft or Ship Load the eight copies of the Unit Party Roster. The CO Craft or Ship Load will securely fasten all of the Unit Party Rosters so that he will have eight complete sets, which will then constitute complete craft or ship rosters (Passenger Lists). The distribution of the Personnel Embarkation Roster is as follows:

Three copies will be handed to the Embarkation Staff Officer at the Embarkation Point. The ESO will insure that Embarkation Personnel Rosters are collected for all Craft or Ship Loads embarking. The ESO will indorse on these Rosters the date and place of embarkation and the name or number of the craft or ship. Two of these copies will be dispatched to the Central Machine Records Unit, Hq, SOS, ETOUSA APO 887, and one copy to the AG at the Base Section in which the port is located.

The fourth copy will be retained by the CO Craft or Ship Load and will be corrected to reflect casualties, etc. enroute. Upon debarkation this copy of the Embarkation Personnel Roster will be turned over to the first available personnel administration section for forwarding to the servicing MRU.

The remaining four copies will be handed to the Commanding Officer of the ship.

A blow-up of Weymouth and Portland embarkation ports. Of note are the 'SANDWICHES' distribution points. For the men of the 2nd and 5th Battalions who were embarking their LCAs alongside the port in Weymouth, they were located on the seafront at the north end of the esplanade next to the beach. For the members of the Rangers who were accompanying vehicles – i.e. the half tracks and Ranger support vehicles, their refreshment and 'SANDWICHES' distribution point was along the beach road approaching Portland harbour.

2 May 1944

5th Rangers – Companies A – F, Medical and HQ – Dorchester, England.

5th Rangers 'Detachment A' – Saunton Sands – N. Devon.

A, B & C Companies 2nd Rangers – Dorchester, Dorset. Alerted for departure – Fabius 1.

D, E & F Companies 2nd Rangers – Swanage, Dorset. No change. Alerted for departure.

Medical Detachment 2nd Rangers – Dorchester, Dorset. No change. Alerted for departure – Fabius 1.

Headquarters Company 2nd Rangers – Dorchester, Dorset. No change. Alerted for departure – Fabius 1.

2 May Naval Report: *For purposes of full-scale exercise under code name FABIUS, A.N.C.X.F. assumed control of operations in the Channel in accordance with the arrangement for command during NEPTUNE.*

The Army took the threat of chemical weapons very seriously. This memo entitled *Chemical Warfare* is dated 2 May 1944.

1. *Object. The object of this memorandum is to establish the Chemical Warfare precautions within this theatre.*
2. *General. There is, at present, no evidence that the Germans intend to begin Chemical Warfare. They are, however, well equipped, both defensively and offensively for such operations and are in a position to initiate them on a major scale at any time.*

Offensive policy.
a) *Full sets of gas offensive equipment will be provided and held in the United Kingdom until gas warfare begins.*
b) *Toxic gas will not be employed, and offensive gas ammunition after delivery to the UK from the US will not be further moved into or through ports and port areas, until so ordered by this headquarters. Commanders responsible for the initiation of movement orders will insure that these orders are specific as to responsibility, control, markings, safety precautions, supervision and protective measures.*

C-O-N-F-I-D-E-N-T-I-A-L

DEBARKATION SCHEDULE: a. Debarkation stations are distributed forward to aft, by following designation; on starboard side, numbers 1, 3, 5, 7, 9; on port side, numbers 2, 4, 6, 8, and 10. They are further designated by color, numbers 1 and 2 being red; 3 and 4, white; 5 and 6, blue; 7 and 8, yellow, 9 and 10, green. Debarkation station number 5 may therefore, also be called Starboard Blue. Under most circumstances debarkation takes place on the lee side of the ship only.

b. (1) The information to be determined and recorded in the schedule is:
       (a) Type of boat to be brought to foot of the net at each
            debarkation station, for each team.
       (b) Time boat is to be alongside at station and time it is to
            shove off.
   (2) This information is based upon:
       (a) Time debarkation is to begin.
       (b) Debarkation stations available on the ship.
       (c) Length of time required for debarkation of various types of
            boat teams.

c. Generally, waves are successively loaded. However, some boat teams which include vehicles may be loaded at the same time as boats of other waves, if movement to shore would be otherwise delayed by slowness in unloading vehicles.

d. Teams are so scheduled for debarkation stations that they do not interfere with each other in moving from billets to stations. Teams which include vehicles must debark at nets adjacent to hatches from which their respective vehicles are unloaded. Teams should be billeted in such manner as to facilitate movement to their debarkation station. For short voyages it is obviously imperative to embark in the ship by boat teams, with proper consideration of routes to debarkation stations.

e. The battalion commander must influence the debarkation schedule in such manner as to reduce the time spent by troops in landing craft prior to H-hour. The motion of the boat and the fumes of the engine tend to make a certain portion of the troops seasick, seriously reducing their combat efficiency. Beginning the unloading of such vehicles and artillery pieces as are to be landed by the first trip of boats, before beginning debarkation of personnel boat teams is sometimes a primary measure. The assault rifle companies should be debarked last, loading them at the rail when practicable.

A copy of the Embarkation and loading Schedule in use by the Navy.

Defensive policy.
a) *Passive defence. Provision will be made in the UK for full-scale gas defence equipment for all troops to be engaged in operations. The guiding principles will be:*
    1) *One layer of protective clothing (outer) to be worn by all troops entering upon the continent during the assault phase.*
    2) *Not to separate the user from his personal protective equipment, except for a definite period or operation for which the risk can be accepted.*
    3) *To carry in forward areas only those unit or formation reserves of protective clothing and equipment that are considered necessary as indicated by gas intelligence, and to locate main reserves in such a way that they are readily available when required.*
        Inspections will be made of protective equipment with sufficient frequency to insure that this equipment is always serviceable.

Warnings.

a) *In the UK, the policy of the British government is to withhold general warning to the public until the first use of gas has been officially confirmed. Lower formations will give the first local warnings to civilians in the UK only if required to save civilian lives. British authorities will be responsible for the general warning.*

b) *General warnings of the presence of gas will be issued at all times during overseas operations and at all times in the UK after the issue of the general warning by the British government.*

On 1 and 2 May a set of tests on different types of automatic ladders were being undertaken by a small group of men from the 2nd Rangers. The story of the ladders spans many months and is a fascinating subject. This, along with an in-depth look into the rest of the Rangers' training will be covered in a future book.

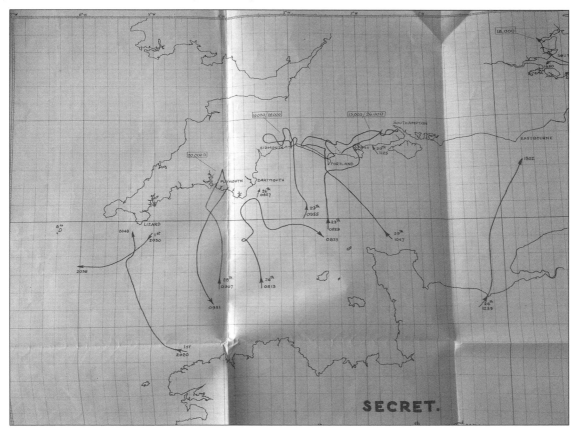

On 2 May the Allied Expeditionary Air Force produced a chart based on *'Enemy Overland Reconnaissance'* – which had been undertaken from the 26/4/44 – 2/5/44. The purpose of the study was to evaluate how much of the pre-D-Day build up the Germans could possibly have seen from flights over the embarkation areas. The results were drawn on a map showing the exact routes taken by those reconnaissance aeroplanes.

TOP SECRET.

HEADQUARTERS
ALLIED EXPEDITIONARY AIR FORCE,
KESTREL GROVE,   HIVE ROAD,
STANMORE,   MIDDLESEX.

ENEMY OVERLAND RECONNAISSANCE

Week – 26/4/44 – 2/5/44.

The map attached is based on Radar and Observer Corps plots and only shows reconnaissance flights which:

(a) were tracked overland,
(b) were tracked sufficiently near the English coast to render coastal cover possible,
(c) were heading for shore when tracks were lost at a range not exceeding 20 miles from land.

The map does not show sea reconnaissance.

The following comments are made in full cognisance of all available 'Y' information:

(1) Overland reconnaissance has been recorded in the PLYMOUTH, SIDMOUTH, PORTLAND, POOLE, SOUTHAMPTON and SOUTHEND areas. Further flights suspected of effecting coastal cover have been recorded in the LIZARD, DARTMOUTH, EASTBOURNE, DOVER and SHEERNESS areas.

(2) Considerable low level reconnaissance was carried out in Mid-Channel in the area due South of PORTLAND.

(3) The usual intensity of effort in the Western half of the Channel has been 4 operations daily by FW.190 or Me.109 operating in pairs.

(4) There is no record of overland reconnaissance over Scotland and Northern England.

AREA.	DATE.	TIME.	HEIGHT.	CONDITIONS FOR PHOTOGRAPHY.	WEATHER.
LIZARD	1/5/44	2030-2050	Probably very high.	Poor.	Half clouded at 2,000 ft.
PLYMOUTH	28/4/44	0920	20,000	Bad.	9/10 Cloud below 20,000 ft.
DARTMOUTH	26/4/44	0527		Good.	Almost clear sky.
SIDMOUTH	29/4/44	1015	16/28,000	Good.	Almost clear sky.
POOLE	29/4/44	1125	15/26,000	Bad	Overcast at 5,000 ft.
EASTBOURNE	26/4/44	1345	Probably very high.	Good.	1/4 covered with cloud at 10-20,000 ft.

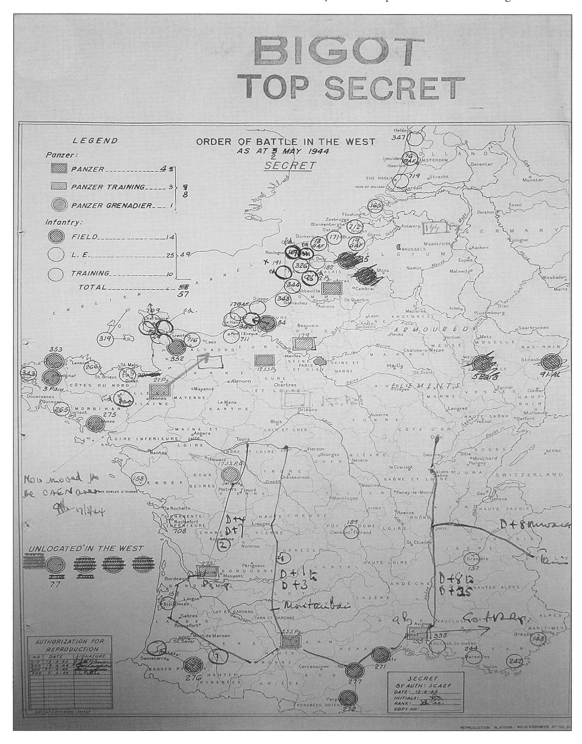

A regular update showing the German Order of Battle for the Normandy sector was produced and distributed. Of interest to the Rangers, it shows the 352nd Inf. Div. and the 716th in place in the Omaha area, again dispelling any myth that the Allies were not aware of the 352nd Inf. Div. in the area well in advance of the landings.

3 May 1944

US Army Report:

> Between April 27 and April 29, 1944, units of the VII Corps, including the 4th Infantry Division and other troops which were designated to make the eventual assault on Utah Beach, a part of the 101st Airborne Division, the 1st Engineer Special Brigade, naval shore fire control parties and other units participated in a full dress rehearsal in the Slapton Sands area. Between 3 May and 8 May 1944, the V Corps assault force designated to land on Omaha Beach held a similar rehearsal in the Slapton Sands area. Elements of the 1st and 29th Infantry Divisions, the 2nd and 5th Ranger Battalions, the 293rd and 294th Joint Assault Signal Companies, four air support parties and eighteen naval shore fire control parties participated in this exercise.

The Commanding Officer of USS *Slatterlee* wrote:

> **Naval Gunfire Support.**
>
> Many lessons were learned in the gunfire support mission.
>
> Our Shore Fire Control Party came aboard before the Fabius exercise. We worked with them in a later shore bombardment exercise. We had several communication drills. They came aboard again in Portland just before D-day. There was a complete and intimate understanding between the ship and the Ranger Shore Fire Control Party. As a result, during the close support firing, communications were uniformly excellent. It was as if the Shore Fire Control Party was in our C.I.C.
>
> Incidently, these fine young men were a great source of inspiration to the SATTERLEE. Everyone who had contact with them was greatly impressed by their enthusiasm, determination, and courage. They knew they had a tough assignment and were ready for it. And they had the ship ready to back them.

Navy War Diary entry:

> **May 3, 1944.**
>
> Admiral H. R. Stark, U.S. Navy, Commander U.S. Naval Forces, EUROPE; Vice Admiral Sir Geoffrey Blake, Royal Navy, British Liaison Officer for ComNavEu; Lieutenant General Omar N. Bradley, U.S. Army, Commanding General, FIRST U.S. Army; Lieutenant General Lewis H. Brereton, U.S. Army, Commanding General, NINTH Air Force; Rear Admiral M. L. Deyo, U.S. Navy, Commander Cruiser Division SEVEN; embarked on board the Flagship to observe Exercise "FABIUS I".

3 May Navy Report: *Exercise FABIUS.*

Berthing, loading and sailing of ships and craft of Forces Omaha, Sword, Juno, and Gold in exercise FABIUS continued through the day. The exercise embraced Port authorities and organisations, and communications generally. Covering forces were provided by Commanders-in-Chief, Portsmouth and Plymouth in lines of patrols to southward of the exercise areas.

5th Rangers – Companies A – F, Medical and HQ –
Dorchester, England.

5th Rangers 'Detachment A' – Saunton Sands – N. Devon.

A, B & C Companies 2nd Rangers – Dorchester, Dorset.
No change. Alerted for departure – Fabius 1.

D, E & F Companies 2nd Rangers – Swanage, Dorset.
No change. Alerted for departure.

Medical Detachment 2nd Rangers – Dorchester, Dorset.
No change. Alerted for departure – Fabius 1.

Headquarters Company 2nd Rangers – Dorchester, Dorset.
No change. Alerted for departure – Fabius 1.

Official Report on Operation Fabius (Slapton Sands D-Day practice) by the Historical Section European Theatre of Operations, US Army.

D-Day was only a month away, and most units participating in the exercise were to return, not to their home stations, but to the marshalling areas, there to await the actual invasion. No longer was there time for drastic revisions in plan or for retraining units. Minor deficiencies could be corrected, but FABIUS was primarily an exercise to give the troops experience in their tasks and to give the invasion machinery a chance to function as a whole before it would be called upon to perform its primary invasion. Every effort was made to duplicate the conditions to be met on the Normandy beaches, and planning orders called for the exercise to resemble NEPTUNE 'as closely as limitations of equipment and facilities will permit'. Approximately 25,000 troops were processed through the marshalling areas, embarked, landed [on] Slapton Sands, and then returned to the marshalling areas to await D-Day.

Units participating included the 16th and 18th regimental landing teams of the 1st Inf Div, the 116th regimental landing team of the 29th Inf Div, the 347th and 348th Engr C Bns of the 5th Engr Sp Brig, the 149th Engr C Bn of the 6th Engr Sp Brig, the 741st and 743d Tk Bns, and the 2nd and 5th Ranger Battalions, and other units attached either to the infantry divisions or to the Provisional Engineer Special Brigade Group. The overall plan was drafted by First Army headquarters, but the more detailed planning began with V Corps and continued through the various units to battalion level.

The tactical plan followed NEPTUNE closely. After a preliminary air and naval bombardment, the former simulated, two battalions of DD tanks were to land at H-Hour, followed by the first wave of infantry. Landing Team 16 was to land on the left and Landing Team 116 on the right. Engineers were to follow immediately, blow underwater obstacles, open up beach exits, and de-mine suspected areas. At H plus 3 hours, landing team 18 was to land and join the other teams in an attack inland.

Three Ranger companies were to land at Blackpool Beach approximately two miles north of Slapton Sands to destroy enemy artillery installations, precisely as Rangers were to land at Point du Hoe in Normandy. Another company was to land on the right flank of the regular assault beach, while other Rangers were to be landed with the infantry and were to make their way to the right to relieve the flanking company. Additional troops were to pour ashore, establish the beach, unload cargo, establish dumps, and set up supply installations.

Strictly speaking, the movement of the units into the marshalling camps was a portion of Operation NEPTUNE, since the troops returned there after FABIUS. In general, the movement was smooth and operation of the camps encountered no outstanding difficulties. Embarkation also went according to plan with the two 1st Div combat teams loading at Weymouth and Poole and the 116th landing team loading at Portland.

There were 168 craft in the convoy in addition to support vessels. Included were 100 LCTs, 8 LCT(A)s, 21 LCI(L)s, 23 LST(S)s, 3 LSI(H)s, 2 LSI(L)s, 3 XAPs, 4 APAs, and 1 LSH.

With most of the craft loaded, D-Day for all FABIUS exercises was postponed for 24 hours by 21 Army Group because of unfavorable weather.

The assault was launched on schedule. The convoy approached behind minesweepers and marshalled about 10 miles offshore. A bombardment group of craft laid down fire on simulated enemy defenses ashore, and gunfire support craft gave protection. DD tanks of the 741st and 743rd Tk Bn were launched 3000 yards from shore and assaulted the beach at H-Hour. These tanks did not leave the water's edge in the exercise. After the preliminary phase, they proceeded under their own power to Torcross and withdrew from the assault. Normal tanks which were loaded on LCT(A)s were so placed as to be able to fire when the craft were approaching the beach. Later, they were landed by normal means.

Maurice Prince: *We boarded our mother ship at the great channel port of Weymouth. It was the same ship we had during that overnight exercise at Braunton. We took our same places that we had originally to avoid new confusion and disorder. That completed phase one of the problem.*

Our ship was a modern Belgian passenger craft. It had been completed a couple of years before the war had started so that there had to be some work done on the boat in order to convert it into a Landing Craft Infantry. It held from 200 to

250 troops plus its crew in its two holds below the deck. Attached to the upper deck there were eight craft for assault landings (L.C.A's) which by means of pulleys and ropes, lowered and raised these craft to and out of the water. The ship was manned by a capable and experienced crew of English sailors who had already seen action with this very ship at Anzio, Sicily, and Africa and who had come out of these conflicts with very light casualties and no damage done to the craft, itself.

We spent three full days on the ship before we loaded into the LCAs to make the assault landing on the beaches somewhere off the southern coast of England. We hadn't moved, we had just lain anchored in the great bay of Weymouth, surrounded by similar craft and protected by an ever watchful and ever alerted line of cruisers and destroyers.

While on board ship, we didn't do much. Some physical training, a couple of boat drills and a lot

Rangers playing cards on deck of their mother ship before the exercise.

of gabbing and eating. Our chow was Limey food which wasn't exactly the best of nourishment, but was sustaining and satisfying. To supplement this, we had several cases of our own ten-in-one rations, which gave added balance to the diet.

A P.X. aboard ship received a good deal of our business, as there we could obtain chocolate, canned fruits, cookies, and other articles of eating that pleased our palates.

We managed to while away our leisure hours by sunbathing on deck, sleeping, reading, writing, shooting the bull or any other way we saw fit. Physical exertion was held down to a minimum as the days were too beautiful to be spent labouring.

We struck up friendships with the crew members and many hours were spent in exchanging tales and stories. They had a decided advantage over us in this relating business, as they had already tasted combat while we as yet were strangers to warfare.

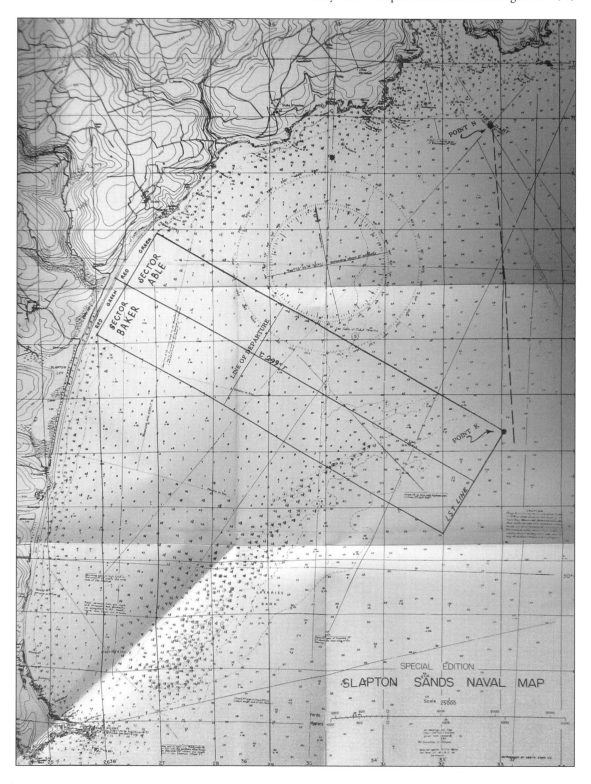

The Naval landing area plans for the Slapton Sands beach – these were used during the training operation.

SPECIAL EDITION
SLAPTON SANDS NAVAL MAP

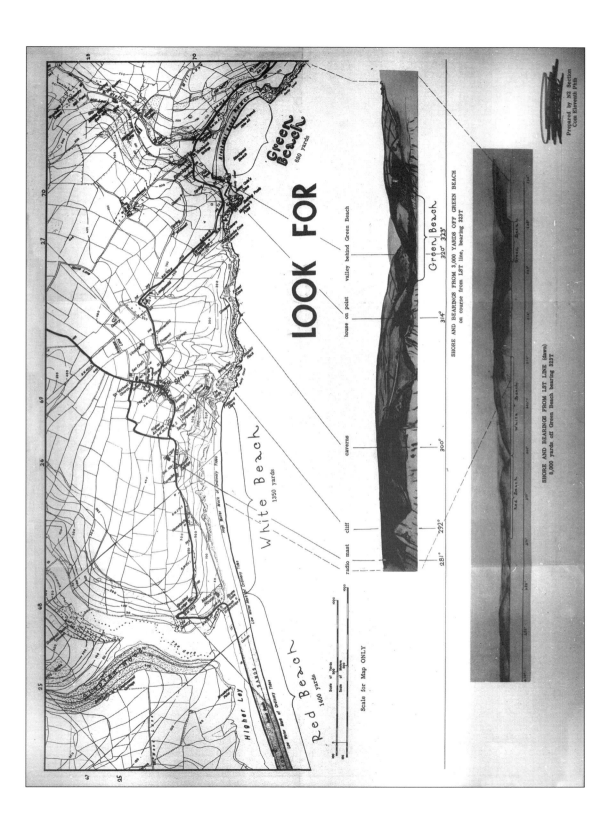

LOOK FOR

Green Beach
680 yards

White Beach
1350 yards

Red Beach
1400 yards

radio mast   cliff   caverns   radio mast   house on point   valley behind Green Beach

Green Beach
320° 323°

281°   292°   300°   314°

SHORE AND BEARINGS FROM 3,000 YARDS OFF GREEN BEACH
on course from LST line, bearing 323T

Green Beach

White Beach

Red Beach

SHORE AND BEARINGS FROM LST LINE (dawn)
8,000 yards off Green Beach bearing 323T

Scale for Map ONLY

Scale in Yards

Scale in Metres

Prepared by N2 Section
Com Eleventh Phib

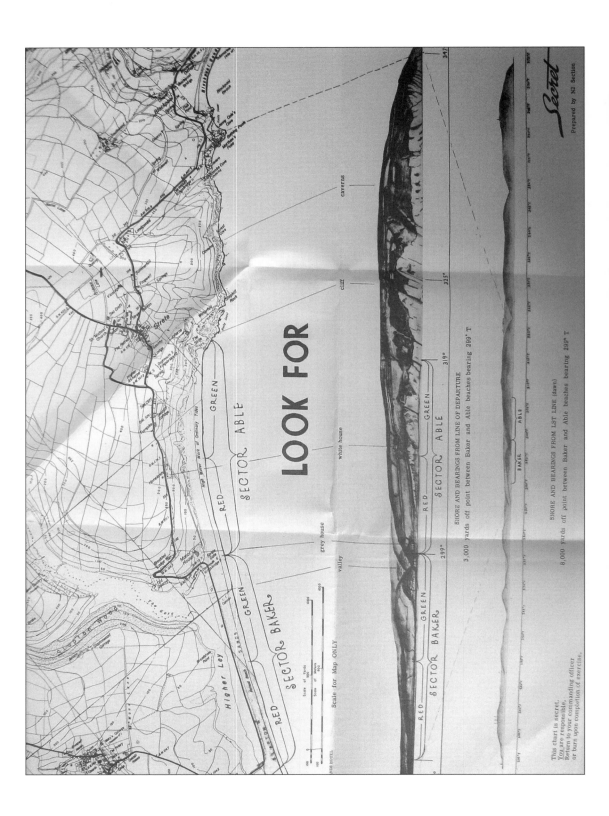

4 May – Amphibious Fleet Diary entry for the Slapton Sands operation.

```
May 4, 1944

                Operation Plan: Z-44.
          0800                    1200               2000
          50° – 12.5'N            Same               50° – 18 – 15'N
          03° – 26.5'W            Same               03° – 25 – 06'W
    Weather conditions: overcast with light intermittent rain, visibility 2-5 miles, sur-
    face wind 25-30 knots, state of sea rough.  Steaming in swept channel for exercise
    area, Slapton Sands, England.  0349 Anchored in 22 fathoms of water with 60 fathoms
    of chain out on the port anchor.  Anchorage bearings: Berry Head – 352°T; Start House –
    280°T; Tower – 328°T.  0445 Dispatched 6 LCV(P)'s to HMS JAVELIN for use in landings.
    0545 Went to General Quarters for morning alert.  0645 Secured from General Quarters;
    set condition Watch II MA.  0850 Lt. General BRADLEY, USA., Commanding General 1st
    Army; Rear Admiral KIRK, USN., C.T.F. 122, Lt. General BRERETON, USA., Commanding
    General 9th Air Corps, and Rear Admiral STRUBLE, USN., Chief of Staff CTF 122, aboard
    for a conference with Rear Admiral J.L. HALL, USN., Com. 11th Phib., 12th Fleet.  1120
    Lt. General BRADLEY, USA., LtGeneral BRERETON, Rear Admiral KIRK, USN., and Rear Admiral
    STRUBLE, USN., left the ship.  1245 Major General HUEBNER, USA., Commanding General
    1st Infantry, left the ship with all personnel of his command.  1250 Underway for an
    inshore anchorage.  1922 Anchored in 10 fathoms of water with 60 fathoms of chain out
    on the starboard anchor.  Anchorage bearings: Skerries Bank Buoy – 206°T; Day Beacon –
    156°T; Start Point Lighthouse 338°T.  2020 Major General GEROW, USA., Commanding
    General "V" Corps, and personnel of his command left the ship.
```

4 May 1944

```
May 4, 1944.

    Underway on board the Flagship to observe Exercise
"FABIUS I".  Conducted by Commander Assault Force 'O',
Rear Admiral J. L. Hall, U.S. Navy, in conjunction with
Commanding General, FIRST U.S. Infantry Division, Major
General C. R. Huebner, U.S. Army, as the Landing Force.

    Upon completion of the Exercise, returned to Port of
Plymouth and observers disembarked.
```

```
                U.S.S. DOYLE (DD494)

                THURSDAY, 4 MAY, 1944

    0800                   1200               2000

In exercise area       In exercise are     Off entrance to
Slapton Sands          Slapton Sands       Plymouth

    Enroute exercise area in company with transports of 11th
Amphibious Force and escorts.  At 0300 arrived in exercise area,
various units of Task Force 124 present, others arriving accord-
ing to exercise schedule.  0405 transports anchored in transport
area, proceeded to screening station in area "George".  0600
stood in towards beach to take station in fire support area,
arriving on station inside the Skerries at 0643.  Augusta, Tanat-
side, and Melbreak began shore bombardment on schedule at 0650.
0725 Doyle began firing shore bombardment, firing eight project-
iles and continuing simulated fire until troops reached the tar-
get area at about 0740.  Continued simulated fire on simulated
targets of opportunity.  Communications with Shore Fire Control
Party not being established.  Maintained very low rate of fire.
Reported 65% ammunition expended at 1005 but remained at area
hoping for communication with SFCP for training to be gained from
controlled fire.  1032 established communication by voice radio
with Shore Fire Control Party which closed down immediately and
without designating any targets.
```

```
                    U.S.S. SATTERLEE (DD626)

Thursday, May 4              Positions:
                                 0800      1200       2000
                         Lat.  50°-1830' N  50°-18' N  50°-18' N
                         Long.  03°-34' W   03°-34' W  03°-32' W

        Steaming as before.  At 0334 left screening station on convoy and commenced
patrolling screening station "Charlie".  Left screening station at 0558 and proceeded
to exercise fire support area, preparation to fire initial bombardment fire on pre-
arranges targets on beach at Slapton Sands, England.  Reached fire support area at
0650 and at 0721 commenced firing on beach target, ceased firing at 0722 having ex-
pended 8 rounds of 5"/38 caliber AA common ammunition.  Contacted Shore Fire Control
Party at 0905 and commenced simulated firing on various designated targets.  Completed
siluated drill at 1315 and commenced maneuvering on various courses and at a speed
of 25 knots (246RPM)leaving fire support area, having been relieved by U.S.S.
THOMPSON(DD627), and proceeding to outer screening area "Charlie".
```

5th Rangers – Companies A – F, Medical and HQ –
Dorchester, England.
Rangers 'Detachment A' – Saunton Sands – N. Devon

Seven Officers and 73 Enlisted men were assigned and joined from units as indicated. [Author: unfortunately this list is not legible and out of focus in the records.]

2nd Battalion Historical Narrative.

[Author: Note the distance inland that the Rangers were required to march. This corresponds exactly with the distance they were expected to advance to reach the D-Day Phase Line in Normandy before nightfall.]

```
    Landing at dawn, 4 May, the Battalion proceeded thru
the operation which, after contact with Companies D/E/F
was established, lengthened into a forced march of
about twelve miles.  Burdened as the men were with
their complete fighting load, the heat of the day made
the march a grueling task.  The Battalion was assembled
in the evening and Higher Headquarters dictated a non-
tactical night.

    The exercise was officially ended on 5 May and Compan-
ies D/E/F re-boarded their ships for the return to Swanage.
They were joined there on 7 May by Companies A/B/C and the
Headquarters personnel which made the movement by rail and
motor.
```

The USS *Frankford* in its War Diary notes on 4 May it *'conducted simulated shore bombardment, controlled by shore fire-control party No 1.'* NSFCP No.1 was assigned to accompany the Rangers on D-Day.

5th Rangers – Companies A – F, Medical and HQ –
Dorchester, England.
Rangers 'Detachment A' – Saunton Sands – N. Devon

Maurice Prince: *The third morning aboard saw us loading into our LCAs in preparation to make the assault run onto the shore. We were gently lowered into the water, with no motion being wasted. Our crafts then took off for the beach. We launched a successful attack as we overran the beach defences and took up positions on the flank of the 29th division. We co-ordinated our efforts, and continued to press forward. We had to hold up when the 29th Inf. stopped, as we had to await further orders from them. That evening found us bivouacked in a field some five miles from our point of landing. The first phase of the problem on land was now completed. The exercise was called off for the night and we became 'administrative'. We had done our part that day, and we had done it well.*

D, E & F Companies 2nd Rangers – Swanage, Dorset.
No change. Alerted for departure.

It was only during the training landings at Slapton Sands that 2nd Battalion Cannon Company Commander Lt. Frank Kennard and his men fired their guns for the first time. Before that, all operations had been done using blank training ammunition.

Frank Kennard: *'Except for firing the guns at Slapton Sands, we never had any "live" practice with any of the line companies.'*

Medical Detachment 2nd Rangers – Dorchester, Dorset. No change – Alerted for departure – Fabius 1.
Headquarters Company 2nd Rangers – Dorchester, Dorset.
Cpl. Daniel W. Chapman returned to Duty from Hospital. Alerted for departure – Fabius 1.

Photographs of the Rangers boarding their LCAs.

LCA coming in to land at Slapton Sands amid some very realistic explosions.

Note the marshal standing on the beach directing soldiers.

Below: Excerpts from the 1st Inf. Division radio logs concerning the advance of the Rangers on 4 May during the Fabius 1 exercise. It repeats the necessity for reaching the 'D-Day objective line'. NB: The Rangers are part of Regimental Combat Team 116 – 'RCT116' – but not the 116th Regiment.

HEADQUARTERS 1ST INFANTRY DIVISION
APO #1, U. S. Army

G-3 (JOURNAL*
~~(START)~~*

FWD CP
"FABIUS I"

Time : (From 0001
(To

Date   4 May 1944   CP Location   LOC CP 238668

TIME	NO.	FROM	SYNOPSIS	REC'D VIA	DISPOSITION#
0001	1		Journal opened		
0610	2		1st Wave debarked fr CHASE		
0625	3		2nd Wave debarked fr CHASE		
0648	4		3rd Wave debarked fr CHASE		
0710	5		Div Hq including Gen WYMAN ACG debarked fr CHASE		
0900	6	?Div Hq	Passed LD		
0918	7		Div Hq landed on beach EASY RED		
1050	8	G-3	CP opened at 238668 - 1045 hours	Rad	ANCON & J
1115	9		Lt Gen HODGES, Maj Gen ALLEN, Maj Gen HUGHES visited Div CP.		
1135	10	18th	Col Smith visited CP - informed G-3 all Bns of 18th landed as scheduled.		G-3
1136	11	16th	2nd Bn obj taken 1040		G-3
1150	12	116th	Regt Cp Loc 266685	In 0	G-3
1200	13	ACG	Gave info regarding sit on "FABIUS" I	M/C	CG & J

NOTES:
   *Delete one.
      "Rec'd Via" column will indicate how message was transmitted, i.e., Tp - telephone; Rad - radio; Tgp - telegraph; Tpe - teletype.
      #Following abbreviations only will be used in this column, other information will be written out: M - Noted on situation map; J - Appended to journal (applies to Overlays, Msg blanks, written orders, etc.); CG, C/S, etc. - indicates information passed on to Officer indicated; T- indicates information disseminated to units or troops, as indicated in text of message.
(Revised 3 Jan. '44)

- 1 -

G-3 Journal * ~~Diary~~ * for   4 May 1944   Cont'd.   Page 2

TIME	NO.	FROM	SYNOPSIS	REC'D VIA	DISPOSITION
1208	14	18th	CP closed at 237669	MC	G-3 & J
1209	15	18th	Instr requested relative employment 1st & 2nd Bns	MC	G-3 & J
1205	16	116	Initial beachead line secured. FWd ele 1st bn Y279704	MC	G-3 & J
1215	17	ACG	Request confirmation re instr to Mission fr Maj Grant, Hq Spec Trs.	MC	2d Bn 18th & J
1220	18	62d Armd	CP loc 240646, given by Capt McNamaro, DA		G-3
1235	19	ACG	Info given to CG re 1st Bn 116	MC	CG & J
1240	20	ACG	Closed old CP 041135 opened new CP Y232656. (16th)	MC	CG & J
1242	21	18th	Report of Sit - as of 1230 hrs - - - 3rd Bn CP loc 238674	MC	G-3 & J
1245	22	18th	G-3 Periodic report	MC	G-3 & J
1250	23	16th	2nd Bn loc 228669		G-3
1255	24	16th	CP loc 247647 (as of 0926)	MC	G-3 & J
1255	25	16th	Unable to contact Bn (CO) as of 0928	MC	G-3 & J
1300	26	16th	Reserve Bn landed 0935B	MC	G-3 & J
1302	27	116	2nd Bn Reached obj at 1055 hrs.	MC	G-3 & J
1309	28	16th	3d Bn vic Y232633 to Y239625	Ln O	G-3 & J
1310	29	37 Engr	CP loc Y252654 (as of 1025B)	MC	G-3 & J
1311	30	16th	2nd Bn on Obj	MC	G-3 & J
1315	31	149th	Opns proc on schedule as of 1100B	MC	G-3 & J
1315	32	16th	2d Bn 18th moving to contact 1st Bn 16th	Ln O	G-3 & J
1320	33	37th	Sit report	Ln O	G-3 & J

D-Day and the Cover-Up at Pointe du Hoc

G-3 Journal **Diary** for 4 May 1944 Cont'd.

Sheet 3

TIME	NO.	FROM	SYNOPSIS	REC'D VIA	DISPOSITION#
1330	34	16th	CP loc 231656	Rad	G-3 & J
1330	35	16th	Neg report	Ln O	G-3 & J
1335	36	16th	1st Bn passing thru 2d Bn	Rad	G-3 & J
1400	37	16th 37th 149th	Sit report – negative	Rad	G-3 & J
1425	38	16th	2d Bn 16th loc 224669. 2d Bn 16 & 2d Bn 116th are in contact. 3d Bn 16th is along line fr 242663 to 240619, and is moving forward. 3d Bn CP 233629. 1st Bn 213693 and on final objective.	Tel	G-3 & J
1428	39	18th	2d & 3d Bns moving fr initial assembly areas toward final obj. Adv elements 2d Bn at 223673 at 1330.	Run	G-3 & J
1430	40	116th	Rngrs knocked out Combe Point. 3d Bn adv on Blackawton. 1st Bn on line 291707, 286723 Adv CP CT 116 now at 259696	Rad	G-3 & J
1430	41	Hq 3d Armd	Sit overlay	Run	G-3 & J
1432	42	16th	1st Bn Lower Newton Obj taken, preparing defensive posn.	Rad	g-3 & J
1435	43	16th	A,B,D, Cos reached obj	Rad	G-3 & J
1435	44	16th	2d Bn at Y224669 – preparing def posns	Rad	G-3 & J
1440	45	116	CP at Y267697, bns have not rptd in	Rad	G-3 & J
1441	46	16th	E Co and L Co on obj	Rad	G-3 & J
1445	47	18th	Cr CP closed at 1410. All bns moving to final obj	Run	G-3 & J
1502	48	116	All bns final obj taken	Rad	G-3 & J
1510	49	G-3 Fwd	CG arr at Div CP	Rad	ANCON & J
1525	50	116	CP loc 259696	Rad	G-3 & J

THESE SPACES FOR MESSAGE CENTER ONLY

TIME FILED	MSG CEN NO.	HOW SENT

MESSAGE
(CLASSIFICATION)   (SUBMIT TO MESSAGE CENTER IN DUPLICATE)

No _____ DATE 4 May

To CG, 1st Div G-3

Rangers knocked out Combe Point. 3rd Bn advancing on Blackawton. 1st Bn now on line 291707, 286723. Advanced CP CT 116 now at 259696.

CO CT 116   1240B

OFFICIAL DESIGNATION OF SENDER   TIME SIGNED

SIGNATURE AND GRADE OF WRITER

GPO 16-20156

G-3 Journal* ~~Diary~~* for ___4 May___ Cont'd.

S E C R E T

Sheet 4

TIME	NO.	FROM	SYNOPSIS	REC'D VIA	DISPOSITION
1511	50	16th	3d Bn CP Y234629	Rad	G-3 & J
1530	51	16th, 116, 37th, 149th	Sit normal	Rad	G-3 & J
1600	52	16th, 116, 37th, 149th	Sit normal	Rad	G-3 & J
1604	53	16th	A.T. Cp at Y212682	Rad	G-3 & J
1610	54	62d Armd	CP loc 62d Armd 235628 (thru DA)	Rad	G-3 & J
1630	55	116	3d Bn on obj at 0345 hrs	Rad	G-3 & J
1630	56	116	3d Bn in contact with ey as of 1150 hrs	Rad	G-3 & J
1600	57	C/S	Conf between C/S, ACS-G-3, 116 (116) Last rpt Rangers cleaned out Combe Pt. They have been ordered to reorganize after completion of mission and patrol Dart R. No message since.(G-3) Recd msg at 1038 which was intercept saying 116 destroyed. Please check on that, it was fr 1st bn 116th, please call back.	Tel	G-3 & J
1615	58	18th	2d bn at E Allington, rr ele clring Coles Crossing. 3d bn adv on R passing through 1st bn 16th. 1st bn following 2d on L.	Tel	G-3 & J
1630	59	G-3	Rd between 238668 and 233659 traffic running both ways. Confusion betwn Regtl MP and Div MP. C/S said, he would straighten sit out.	Tel	18th & J
1630	60	Gen Cota ACG,29th	Plan for employment of 115 CT in case it came under control of 1st Div		G-3 & J
1635	61	116	Somebody must of decoded msg wrong in re to 116 being destroyed. (G-3) Your msg Ctr has not had any msg such as I read to you.	Tel	G-3 & J
1635	62	G-3	Ey plane down at 220703-31, Investigate and place guard.	Tel	V Corps & J
1635	63	16th	Loc of Co A 218695, Co B 212675, Co C 205684	Rad	G-3 & J

G-3 Journal* ~~Diary~~* for   4 May 1944 Cont'd.

Sheet 5

TIME	NO.	FROM	SYNOPSIS	REC'D VIA	DISPOSITION#
1645	64	CG V	Adv CP on shore, notify all units	Rad	CG & J
1700	65	1 Engr	CP opens 231676	Rad	G-3 & J
1705	66	116	2d & 3d bns digging in on obj. No recent contact with 1st bn.	Rad	G-3 & J
1705	67	G-3	Notify Range Comdt if range can be clrd in time to permit Navy to fire on the 8th.	Tel	ESB & J
1710	68	18th	Co I on objective.	Lno	G-3 &*J
1715	69	18th	3d Bn on obective.	Rad	G-3 & J
1720	70	G-3	Col Gibb, AC of ?S,G-3, left CP to go on Rcn		J
1725	71	116	No contact with Rangers	Rad	G-3 & J
1730	72	116	What is your loc?	Rad	G-3 & J
1800	73	G-3	REURAD our loc 238668	Rad	116 & J
1800	74	G-3	Situation overlay		J
1805	75	18th	Sit report - 2d & 3d on obj - 1st No rpt	Tel	G-3
1730	76	G-3	Would like posn? (16) 3d bn 233629, K Co 210605, L Co 218615, I Co 223615	Tel	16th & J
1745	77	DA	Loc A Btry 221649, B Btry 231675, C btry 500 yds NE of A Btry, 32d in posn 235666	Tel	G-3 & J
1825	78	G-3	in 2d Bn area there is bad rd corner that is bottle necking traffic. See Engrs about it. Coord 224668. (16) Have no Engrs, would have to got out and get them.	Tel	16th
1830	79	G-3	Inspect and if nec improve RJ at 224668	MC	1 Engr & J
1831	80	18th	Adv Regtl CP 203696, 2d bn on obj.	Rad	G-3 & J
1850	81	G-3	Under no conditions will bldgs be entered.	MC	Units & J
1900	82	CG	2d Bn 18th in position. Allington patrols. 2d to Kingsbridge at 1645B.	MC	J

G-3 Journal* ~~Diary~~ for ___4 May 44___   Cont'd.

Sheet 6

TIME	NO.	FROM	SYNOPSIS	REC'D VIA	DISPOSITION#
1930	83	18th	All units in posn - sending patrols forward	Tp	J
1932	84	Fwd CP	New CP opened.		V Corps
1935	85	16th	Negative Report	Tp	J
1942	86	G-3	Location new CP		V Corps
2030	87	G-3	All bns on initial objs		V Corps
2039	88	V Corps	2d Bn 16th Inf on obj. 116th CT advancing. No resistance by 041123B. CP loc at 267685	MC	J
2099	89	743d Tk	Arrived 265704 at 041300.	MC	J
2034	90	G-3	Correction in CP location		V Corps
2039	91	G-3	All bns are on initial obj	Tp	V Corps
2035	92	Ln O DA	Request info on 5th & 32d FA Bns. 5th not in yet - 32d still moving. Also request info on 111th FA Bn. They are looking for a position. Don't know location.	Tp	J
2045	92	18th	Nothing to report	Tp	J
2047	93	G-3	New CP open at 231673.		V Corps
2059	94	G-3	New CP open at 231673		16th, 18th, 116th ESB Gp, 16th AAA Gp, 3d Armd Gp&
2054	95	CO 116	Stream Rcn report on River Gara submitted by 112th Engrs.	MC	J
2145	96	GG	CP 1st Engr Bn at 231676		V Corps
2150	97		Corps Comdr visited Div CP		
2150	98	Air O Ancon	No change in situation. Rear CP now closed on forward CP	Rad	J
2230	99	18th	Overlay shown posns of 18th Inf units 1915hrs	Run	J
2312	100	V Corps	Location clm; Grip requested of front lines)		J
2312	101	18th	No change in situation. 3d Bn patrol to 172732 with negative report	Rad	J

G-3 Journal * ~~ooooo~~ for 4 May 44   Cont'd.   **Sheet 7**

TIME	NO.	FROM	SYNOPSIS	REC'D VIA	DISPOSITION
2202	102	116th	Rngr Gp moving forward to out post line fr Humphreys Combe on Dart River west to 255-752 along D-day objective line. CP 1st Bn loc 272738. CP 2d Bn loc 257698. CP 3d Bn loc 235723. All units preparing defensive positions and first plans.	Tgp	J
2202	103	116	3d Bn established patrol contact with 1st Bn on right and 18th Inf on left. 2d Bn maintaining contact with 16th Inf on left contact point. Number 3 situation otherwise unchanged	Tgp	J
2210	104	116th	Situation unchanged	Tp	J
2310	105	116th	Situation unchanged	Tp	J
2320	106	Ln O DA	Loc 5th FA Bn - 710142. 111th FA 768127	MC	J
2240	107	116th	Situation unchanged	Tp	J
2340	108	116th	Situation unchanged	Tp	J
2345	109	G-3	Div Arty CP loc at Y229679		V Corps & J
2355	110	G-3	Rngr Force CP at 287758. Rngrs outposted on 1st phase line fr 299769 to 255752		V Corps & J
2358	111	V Corps	Sit Report desired	Rad	J
2357	112	116th	Rngr Gp now outposting D-day obj line west from Humphreys Combe 299759 to 255752.	Tp	J
2133	113	18th	Report 2130 hrs contact patrols between 18th Inf. Bn being maintained for report	Rad	J
2236	114		Rd Block found at 215708. 2d Bn dispatching local patrols vic 20701. Parachute was discovered at 197706	Rad	J
2020	115	18th	Patrol to Kingsbridge returned 2015 hrs. Negative report	Rad	J
2055	116	16th	Report of situation 2100 hours - negative	Run	J
2400		G-3	Journal closed.		

Two overlay maps were produced for the operation, but these are difficult to understand without a map for context. I have placed a set of grid lines on top of them along with co-ordinates so hopefully they are now clear. The actions described above in grid reference numbers can now be seen on the overlays.

The grid references specifically involving the Rangers refer to the top right area of this overlay and the Rangers climbed the cliffs at Combe Pointe.

They then took that position and moved to the left on the map – patrolling the D-Day Line. The line, as it goes to the left, becomes indistinct on the original overlay, as are the further objectives.

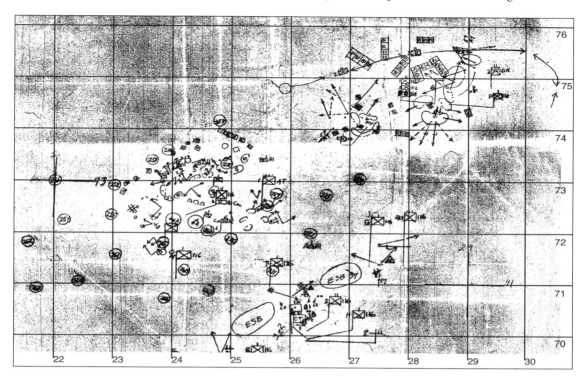

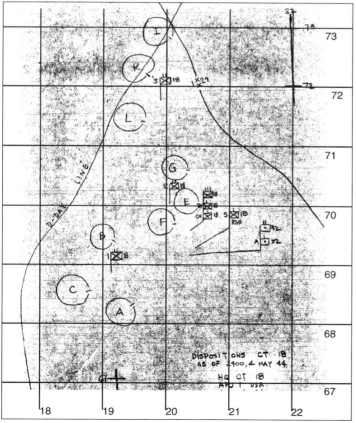

Navy Report for 4 May:

> *Assaults were carried out under conditions as realistic as possible by Force O at SLAPTON SANDS.*
>
> *Weather was favourable at the outset and the exercises, in so far as Naval forces were concerned, were generally satisfactory. Benefit also later accrued from Military personnel taking part in the exercise finding their way round ships and craft in which, in the event, they finally embarked for the actual operation.*
>
> *At 1300 weather commenced to deteriorate, with freshening South-Westerly wind which reached force 6 in the night, and the full programme had to be curtailed to avoid damage to landing craft.*

COMMANDER DESTROYER DIVISION THIRTY-SIX

May 4, 1944.

Aboard SATTERLEE steaming as before. 0400 Arrived in practice assault area (off Slapton Sands, England). Ships of DesRon 18 proceeded to designated Screening and Fire Support Areas. Prior to and during initial phases of practice assault ships exercises at simulated and real bombardment in assault area and drilled with Shore Fire Control Parties. Communications with latter found to be excellent; communications within Force "O" found to be poor, due to severe overloading of available circuits. As a consequence ships were slow in relieving in Fire Support Area and reports to Commander Force "O" were excessively delayed.

Below: A radio report stating where the Rangers were outposted.

An After Action Report for the day was written by Major Howie and he covers the first 24 hours of the mock invasion. He states that the Rangers were "*given the mission of outposting the D-Day Objective Line in the RCT sector of responsibility*".

G-3 REPORT

From: 0730/4 May 44

To: 2400/4 May 44.

Issuing Unit CT 116
Place Higher Fuge (259 696)
Date and Hour of Issue 2400/4 May 44.

No. ___1___

Maps: OSGS 3906, 1:2500, Sheets: 29/6 NW & SW, 32/6 NE & SE

1. OUR FRONT LINES : See Annex No. 1, overlay attached.

2. LOCATION OF TROOPS. : See Annex No. 1, overlay attached.

3. INFORMATION OF ADJACENT UNITS AND SUPPORTING TROOPS: Contact gained and maintained with 2nd and 5th Ranger Bns on right and 16th & 18th CT's on left.

4. WEATHER AND VISIBILITY: Variable, light showers and mist followed by clear weather and sunshine.

5. OUR OPERATIONS FOR THE PERIOD. See FO#1, Hq, CT 116, 18 Apr 44, "FABIUS I". Initial landing of assault troops and intermediate follow-up troops was accomplished as scheduled with the exception that no off-shore firing of 105MM SP guns was possible by reason of the failure of the USN to properly place the craft in firing positions on time. The ammunition trains and a portion of the 104 Med Coll Co were unable to land D-day as scheduled but will land at 0900 hrs D/1. The assaulting troops pushed rapidly inland, seized designated intermediate objectives and drove on to occupy final (1st & 2nd Bns 116th Inf) or initial (3rd Bn 116th Inf) objectives as ordered. See Annex No. 1. 2nd & 5th Ranger Bns, after accomplishing assigned missions and reorganizing, were given the mission of outposting the D-day objective line in the RCT sector of responsibility supplementing and reinforcing the defensive positions of the 1st Bn 116th Inf. The 111th 58th FA Bns are in support of the RCT (less 1st Bn) and the   1st Bn, respectively. Defensive positions have been and are being organized by all units and complete defensive fire plans prepared.

6 COMBAT EFFICIENCY : Excellent.

7. RESULT OF OPERATIONS: Attainment of all assigned objectives according to plan.

AC of S, S-3

THOMAS D. HOWIE,
Major, Infantry,
S-3

---

5 May 1944
5th Rangers – Companies A – F, Medical and HQ – Dorchester, England

A, B & C Companies 2nd Rangers – Dorchester, Dorset
No change. Alerted for departure – Fabius 1.

Prince and the rest of the 2nd and 5th Battalions were to advance to meet up with D, E & F companies inland.

Maurice Prince: *The next morning we resumed the attack. We continued our line of advance, by tactically advancing over a prescribed route using the roads as much as was permissible. The terrain was exceptionally hilly and the roads we traversed over were very steeply inclined. Our loads became burdens and difficult to carry. A blazing hot sun added to our discomforts. All the time during the march men were ridding themselves of their ammunition and equipment. At first, one would throw away* a clip of ammo, then a hand grenade, until finally full bandoleers were being discarded. By the time we reached our final objective, the men were only carrying the very essentials needed for a fight.

That night, when the problem ended, we were bivouacked in a field, several miles from our initial starting point. We were all tired and exhausted by the ordeal of that day and we were very happy that we had become administrative, as I doubt if we could have done any hint of importance that night. The exercise was a huge success, the teamwork and co-operation between the units had been good, the staff work and brain work responsible for this co-ordination had been brilliant, and the efficiency of the soldier himself who had participated was excellent. It is this combination of skills that marks victory in combat. The big brass and high officials responsible for this display could congratulate themselves for this operation.

The experience we had gained from this amphibious manoeuver was invaluable to us. Mistakes had been made and corrected so that we had benefitted from our errors. An idea was gained from this operation as to the greatness and immensity that such a problem entails, of all the planning, co-ordination and organisation that must be worked out and it showed the responsibilities of the individual to keep his place in the picture and not to add to the confusion and turmoil by getting lost or misplaced. We had spent five days in the running of this manoeuvre and now finally it was completed.

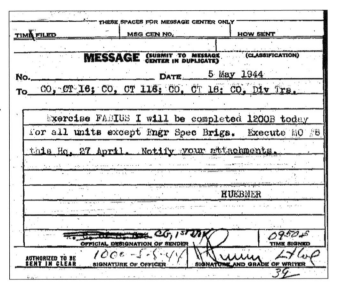

Shown is the 5 May end of exercise order from Major General Huebner, which was sent out by radio to all the participating units.

5 May – The commanding officer of the USS *Slatterlee* wrote the following to the Commander in Chief – US Fleet in New York. [the redacted words are 'FABIUS' and 'NEPTUNE'.]

> **Rehearsals.**
>
> The rehearsal exercise ████ and a shore bombardment exercise at SLAPTON SANDS were of the greatest value in preparing for the invasion. The general plan and the small details for exercise ████ were exactly the same as for operation ████ for this vessel. During this exercise communications with the Shore Fire Control Party of the Ranger unit were very good. The value of this rehearsal cannot be over emphasized. It was extremely well planned and executed, and provided many valuable lessons.

D, E & F Companies 2nd Rangers – Swanage, Dorset. No change. Alerted for departure.

Medical Detachment 2nd Rangers – Dorchester, Dorset. No change – Alerted for departure – Fabius 1.

Headquarters Company 2nd Rangers – Dorchester, Dorset.
The following three enlisted men went from Duty to sick in Hospital: T/5 Robert J. Cooper, Pfc. William Bass, Pfc. Roland J. Paradis. Alerted for departure – Fabius 1.

Shown on the next page are the Army Dispersal Orders for the distribution of troops back to the Marshalling Areas at the end of Operation Fabius. The highlighted sections show the specific Ranger timings for departure.

FROM: DRO EXETER

TO : DRO SALISBURY Marshalling Area "D"

INFO: CG, 1st Division; Regional Trans Office, SBS, G-4 SBS, Movement SOUTCO

DATE: 5 May 1944.

MDE 8436 SECRET DISPERSAL FABIUS 1 Move 7 May

(A) Spec Train No (B) Unit (C) Strength (D) Entraining Sta (E) Dep Time (F) Detraining Sta (G) Arrival Time. All reporting to home stations.

(A) 1UKS/49 (B) 1st Med Bn (C) 309 (D) Kingswear (E) 0001
(F) Maiden Newton (G) 0438

(B) 2nd Bn 16th Inf (C) 100 (D) Kingswear (E) 6001 (F) Bridport
(G) 0523

(A) 7/S/51 (B) Det Div Arty Hq and Hq Btry (C) 23 (B) 116th
Inf (C) 437 (D) Totnes (E) 0110 (F) Blandford (G) 0515

(A) 7/S/53 (B) 2nd Bn 18th Inf (C) 501 (D) Kingswear (E) 0215
(F) Dorchester (G) 0555

(A) 7/S/57 (B) 1st Bn 18th Inf (C) 401 (B) Co M 16th Inf
(C) 106 (D) Dingswear (E) 0230 (F) Weymouth (G) 0725

(A) 7/S/59 (B) Co B 1st Engr Bn (C) 271 (D) Totnes (E) 0310
(F) Corfe Castle (G) 0857

(B) Co C 1st Engr Bn (C) 95 (B) 2nd and 5th Ranger Bns (C) 138
(D) Totnes (E) 1310 (F) Swanage (G) 0934

(A) 7/S/55 (B) 116th Inf (C) 460 (D) South Brent (E) 0405
(F) Blandford (G) 0900

(A) 7/S/63 (B) Co M 16th Inf (C) 70 (B) Co K 16th Inf (C) 219
Co L 16th Inf (C) 219 (D) Kingswear (E) 0345 (F) Weymouth (G) 0840

(A) 7/S/65 (B) 1st Bn 16th Inf (C) 386 (B) Co A 1st Engr Bn
(C) 136 (D) Kingswear (E) 0630 (F) Axminster (G) 0910

(A) 7/S/67 (B) 116th Inf (C) 460 (D) Kingswear (E) 1030
(F) Blandford 1505

(A) 7/S/61 (B) 116th Inf (C) 460 (D) Totnes (E) 1310 (F) Blandford (G) 1700

(A) 7/S/69 (B) 2nd Bn 18th Inf (C) 407 (B) Cn Co 18th Inf
(C) 94 (D) Kingswear (E) 1500 (F) Dorchester (G) 1936

(A) 7/S/71 (B) 3rd Bn 18th Inf (C) 460 (D) Kingswear (E) 2115
(F) Dorchester (G) 0220 May 8

(A) 7/S/73 (B) 3rd Bn 18th Inf (C) 448 (B) 1 GR Plat 606th QM
Co Gr (C) 12 (D) Kingswear (E) 2245 (F) Dorchester (G) 0355 May 8

FROM: DRO Exeter.

TO : DRO Salisbury Marshalling Area D

INFO: CG, 1st US Inf Div

DATE: 5 May 44

Secret Dispersal Fabius moves 6 May. (A) Special train No. (B) Unit (C) Strength (D) Entraining station (E) Departing time (F) Detraining station (G) Arrival time. All reporting to home stations.

(A) 6S23 (B) 2d Bn 16th Inf (C) 400 (D) Kingswear (E) 0001
(F) Bridport (G) 0523

(A) 6S25 (B) 20th Engr C Bn (C) 487 (D) Totnes (E) 0110
(F) Blandford (G) 0515

(A) 6S27 (B) 112th Engr Bn (C) 487 (D) Kingswear (E) 0115
(F) Dorchester (G) 0555

(A) 6S31 (B) 1st Bn 18th Inf (C) 507 (D) Kingsear (E) 0230
(F) Weymouth (G) 0725

(A) 6S29 (B) 2nd and 5th Renger Bns (C) 510 (D) Totnes (E) 0310
(F) Swanage (G) 0908

(A) 6S33 (B) Hq and Hq Co 1st Inf Div (C) 201 (B) 1st Sig Co
(C) 201 (B) 1st MP Plat (C) 30 (B) Det 29th MP Plat (C) 24
(B) Det 29th Rcn Tr (C) 22 (D) South Brent (E) 0405 (F) Bland-
ford (G) 0900

(A) 6S37 (B) 320th AA Bar Bln Bn (C) 347 (B) 1st QM Co (C) 118
(B) 701st Ord LM Co (C) 50 (D) Kingswear (E) 0345 (F) Dorchester
(G) 0811

(A) 6S39 (B) 1st Bn 16th Inf (C) 522 (D) Kingswear (E) 0630
(F) Axminster (G) 0910

(A) 6S41 (B) Can and AT Co 16th Inf (C) 194 (B) Hq and Hq Co Med
Det (C) 254 (B) CIC Det (C) 3 (B) OB Unit (C) 1 (D) Kingswear
(E) 0955 (F) Crewkerne (G) 1250

(A) 6S35 (B) 121st Engr Bn (C) 386 (B) Co B and 1st Plat Co D
104th Med Bn (C) 127 (B) Hq and Serv Co 1st ESB (C) 72 (D)
Totnes (E) 1250 (F) Blandford (G) 1720

(A) 6S43 (B) Prov AA AW Batries (C) 261 (B) 85th Gp GCI and MUS
RAF (C) 30 (B) Serv Co 18th Inf (C) 91 (B) Hq and Hq Co Med Det
18th Inf (C) 120 (D) Kingswear (E) 1450 (F) Dorchester (G) 1936

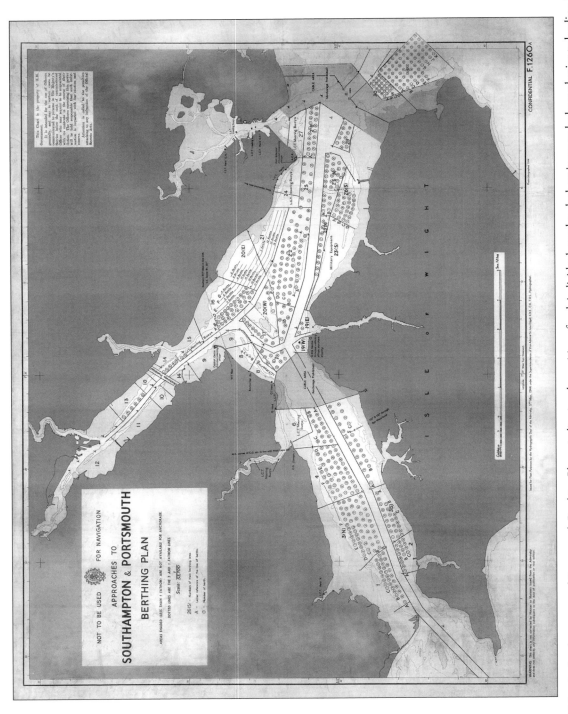

Issued on 5 May the Southampton and Portsmouth Berthing Plan – indicating the position of each individual vessel and where it was to be located prior to loading. The ships would leave all such berths along the south coast of England and proceed along designated paths to the Normandy coast.

MAP OF FIGHTER PATROL AREAS IN ASSAULT AREA AND OVER MAIN SHIPPING ROUTE

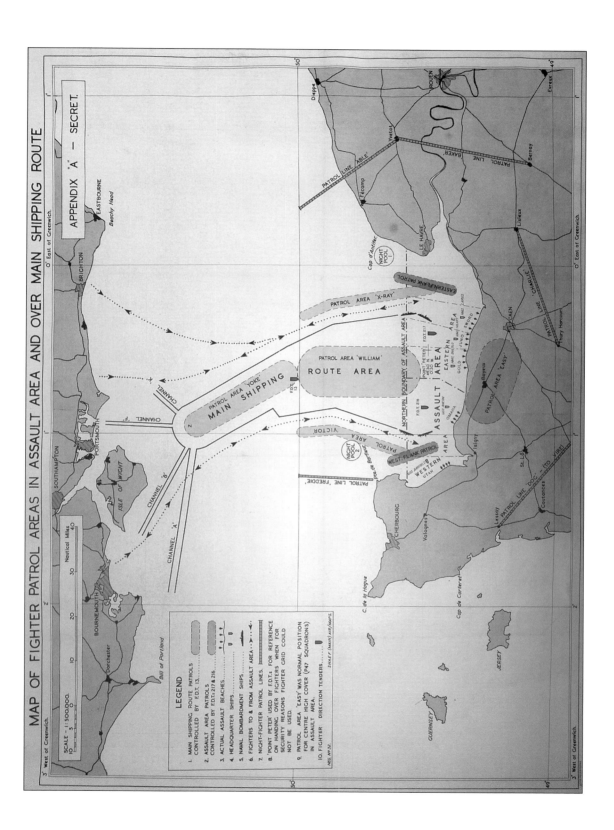

APPENDIX "A" — SECRET.

LEGEND

1. MAIN SHIPPING ROUTE PATROLS CONTROLLED BY F.D.T. 13.
2. ASSAULT AREA PATROLS CONTROLLED BY F.D.T.s 217 & 216.
3. ACTUAL ASSAULT BEACHES.
4. HEADQUARTER SHIPS.
5. NAVAL BOMBARDMENT SHIPS.
6. FIGHTERS TO & FROM ASSAULT AREA.
7. NIGHT-FIGHTER PATROL LINES.
8. 'POINT PETER' USED BY F.D.T.s FOR REFERENCE ON HANDING OVER FIGHTERS WHEN FOR SECURITY REASONS FIGHTER GRID COULD NOT BE USED.
9. PATROL AREA 'EASY' WAS NORMAL POSITION FOR CENTRE HIGH COVER (P47 SQUADRONS) IN ASSAULT AREA.
10. FIGHTER DIRECTION TENDERS.

SCALE — 1:500,000.
Nautical Miles

S.H.A.E.F. (MAIN) AIR/MAPS.
NEG. N° 32.

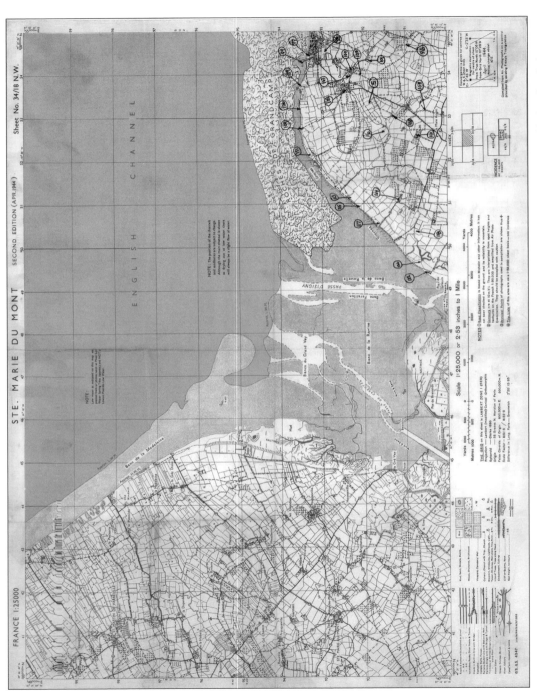

An intelligence map showing the Maisy Batteries area to the bottom right and Utah beach to the left. This particular map was annotated by hand with the target numbers by Captain John Raen of HQ Co. 5th Battalion. [Author: It is worth noting that the map he was given does not contain any detailed information relating to the Maisy positions. Without his notes having been added by him, there would be no mention of there being gun emplacements in this area. He has confirmed to me that he was NOT briefed that the batteries were there!]

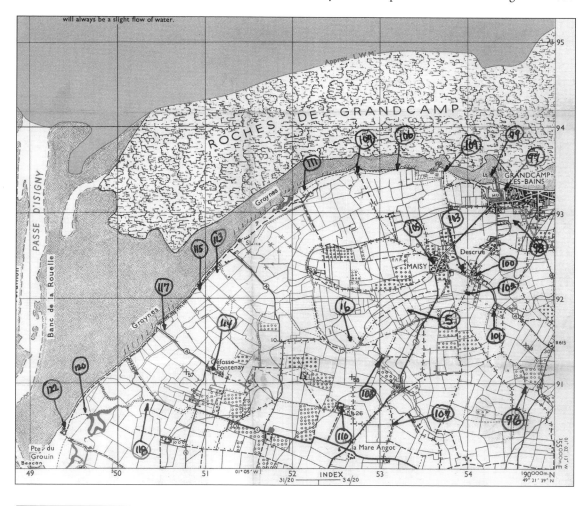

6 May 1944

5th Rangers – Companies A – F, Medical and HQ – Swanage, England.
A, B & C Companies 2nd Rangers – Dorchester, Dorset.
Pvt Armane Williams was assigned and joined B Company from HQ 10th Replacement Depot APO 874 US Army.
No change. Alerted for departure – Fabius 1.
D, E & F Companies 2nd Rangers – Swanage, Dorset.
No change. Alerted for departure.
Medical Detachment 2nd Rangers – Dorchester, Dorset.
No change. Alerted for departure – Fabius 1.
Headquarters Company 2nd Rangers – Dorchester, Dorset.
Alerted for departure – Fabius 1.

Above: A blow-up of the Maisy section of the map.

6 May USAF reconnaissance oblique low-level photograph showing differing types of beach obstacles.

7 May 1944
5th Rangers – Companies A – F, Medical and HQ – Swanage, England.
2nd Rangers – Companies A – F, Medical and HQ – Swanage, England.
Record of events. Alerted for departure. Arrived Swanage railway station, Dorset 1200 hours by rail. Alerted for departure – Fabius 1.

Navy Report 7 May: *A.N.C.X.F. gave permission for detailed plans of NEPTUNE to be discussed with officers of Captain's rank in destroyers attached to Eastern and Western Task Forces.* [thus ensuring at all Naval commanders in the area were made aware of D-Day land unit objectives].

Maurice Prince: *On the sixth day we boarded trucks which brought us to the local railroad station from where we entrained for a new station for our Battalion. Our train ride was spent in reviewing the results of the exercise and also in deep meditation. We began to realise that time was growing short for us. That things were beginning to add up and point in the direction of invasion. Our air offensive was sharply increasing in both volume and intensity. The weather was gradually becoming suitable for operations in the channel. And these large scale manoeuvers meant only one thing – a dress rehearsal for the coming real McCoy.*

Headquarters Company 2nd Rangers – Swanage, Dorset.
Twenty-one enlisted men returned to Duty from Detached Service. Seven enlisted men were assigned and joined from 234th Engineer (Combat) Battalion.
Travelled by train and arrived at Swanage railway station at 1200. Alerted for departure.

8 May 1944
5th Rangers – Companies A – F, Medical and HQ – Swanage, Dorset.
B Co. Pfc Ryan and Pfc Travers were both appointed to Tec 5. S/Sgt Herbert Hull and assigned and joined from HQ 10th Replacement Depot APO 874 US Army.
A Company 2nd Rangers – Swanage, Dorset.

Army Report: *At meeting at Supreme Headquarters A.N.C.X.F. gave his decision on naval considerations regarding D-Day. That 4th June was unacceptable, 5th and 6th June acceptable, and although 7th June had a number of disadvantages, it could be accepted in case of extreme necessity.*

Maurice Prince: *Our entry into the city of Swanage, county of Dorset, wasn't much of an affair, we detrained and proceeded to make our way to our new home, which was to be a school house that sat on the crest of the hill overlooking the bay at Swanage.*

Our brother Co.'s D.E & F, who preceded us to the town were on hand to welcome us. It was good seeing them, as we didn't get much opportunity in those days to see the other companies in the Battalion. Greetings and formalities were exchanged as we wended our way thru the town to reach our new billets.

We were rather well-billeted in our new home. The school house was a spacious building and it had all the facilities and accommodations of modern housing. We were comfortably quartered, so we made ourselves at home without making any fusses or wasting any time about it.

Battalion Headquarters was set up in a building at the foot of the hill, while our kitchen was situated in the same house. It was alright for us to go to town for chow, but the trip back caused many of us to cuss the fact that we had been chowhounds at the dining table.

I'll never forget our first run-in with the people of this town. It seems as though the American troops who had been billeted in this town before us and had just departed from the area had warned the local residents that The Rangers were a bunch of hoodlums, gangsters, and prisoners who were out on parole. They had said they had assembled us out of volunteers from state and Federal institutions and were letting us do the dirty and dangerous work of the Army. So that when we first started to walk around town during our leisure time, we began to receive funny and inquisitive looks. The weaker sex particularly didn't have anything to do with us, shunning us as though we all had B.O. Well finally the truth and reason for this snubbing leaked out, and it didn't take long until we straightened things out and proved to these people the kind of soldiers we Rangers were. Things were patched up and amended and the whole thing was written off as a farce. I have to chuckle to myself every time I recall this affair. Rangers being gangsters and prisoners – why it's a known fact that no member of the Armed services can enter our elite group, who even has the slightest mark or demerit on his service record.

B Company 2nd Rangers – Swanage, Dorset.
Paragraphs 1a and b of letter, HQ V Corps, subject, 'Desertion' dated 21st April 1944, were read to the members of B Company present at a formation of the Company at 1030 hours, on 9 May 1944.

C Company 2nd Rangers – Swanage, Dorset.
Paragraphs 1a and b of letter, HQ V Corps, subject, 'Desertion' were read to the members of C Company present at a formation of the Company at 1300 hours, on 28 April 1944. Alerted for departure.

D, E, F, Medical and HQ Companies 2nd Rangers – Swanage, Dorset. Alerted for departure.

A stark Army instruction was issued entitled *Action to be Taken on Receipt of Alert Order • WARNING.*

(1)   Every individual of the unit will be advised of the last sentence of the 28th Article of War, reading as follows:

'Any person subject to military law who quits his organization or place of duty with the intent to avoid hazardous duty or to shirk important service shall be deemed a deserter.'

(2)   a.   It will then be explained that combat duty is considered important service within the terms of the 28th Article of War and that any person absenting himself without leave is guilty of desertion in time of war, the extreme penalty for which is death, and all lesser penalties for which are severe and involve forfeiture of rights of citizenship.
*   b.   Personnel to be Cleared from Units.*
(1)   Officers recommended for reclassification. A Report will be made immediately to this headquarters thru channels of any officer against whom reclassification procedures have been instituted prior to receipt of alert order. Any intermediate headquarters in possession of reclassification papers pertaining to such reported officers will immediately forward these papers.

As D-Day approached, the Army issued orders in relation to the briefing of individual units and the logistics involved within the build up.

Service of Supply Report: Early in May 1944 word was received that all assault, follow-up and part of build-up troops would move from concentration areas for final marshalling in Southern Base Section by Y-15. 'Y' was the designation for 1st June 1944 used as a code.

There was little operational importance to 'Y' – merely a reference.

The transport network became busy with tanks, 2½ ton trucks, and train after train loaded with 'foot' troops. Each convoy had movement instructions from Southern Base Section directing it to an RCRP (Road Convoy Regulating Point), at the entrance to the marshalling area. All approach roads were patrolled by Military Police to prevent convoy commanders from becoming lost on the narrow, confusing roads of Southern England. Upon arrival at the RCRP, the Service of Supply personnel there checked the convoy for proper number of personnel and vehicles, and they were led to the proper camp by a military escort. The camp to be occupied was determined by Transportation Corps personnel, dependent upon the type of vehicle in the unit, the roads over which it must travel and the time schedule.

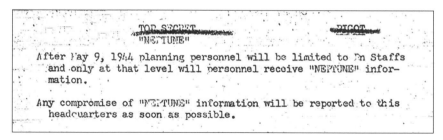

On 9 May the above order was issued stating that only members of the battalion staff would have access to NEPTUNE information. This would restrict any other members of the Ranger group from seeing the full operational plan.

BRIEFING

a. Corps and divisions may brief the necessary personnel for planning purposes at times to be established by their own needs. Discretion will be used in the number briefed and the time of briefing.

First U. S. Army General and Special Staff Sections will prepare appropriate plans for the briefing of army units.

b. All units will be briefed prior to marshalling.

c. Corps are responsible for the briefing of all corps units (assigned and attached). Insofar as possible, corps units of battalion or comparable size will be briefed by officers within the unit.

d. Briefing will be conducted at times fixed by the Assault Division Commanders in accordance with the above schedule and plans for embarking. Times will be prior to marshalling but as near the loading time as possible for security reasons.

e. Briefing facilities will be furnished by SOS in the marshalling areas.

f. Maps for briefing will be furnished as set forth in Annex No. 9f.

ALERTING OF UNITS

a. Army units and each corps headquarters will be alerted by Headquarters First U. S. Army. Each corps will in turn be responsible for alerting all units assigned or attached to it. See Annex No. 22a. for a proposed form for the Alert Order.

b. Upon receipt of the Alert Order, units will comply with the provisions of " European Theater of Operations, Preparation for Overseas Movement.

EMBARKATION

a. The Transportation Corps will call forward units in the order of their priority as established by First U. S. Army, from the Marshalling Areas to the Embarkation Points.

b. For the embarkation of initial shipping, the First U. S. Army is allotted all marshalling and embarkation facilities west of Poole (inclusive).

c. Annex No. 22b. shows the Final Assembly and Loading Points for Assault and Follow-up Forces.

WATERPROOFING

Waterproofing is the responsibility of each unit. SOS will provide supervision and some assistance and will furnish materials, but each unit must accomplish its own waterproofing. A final check and completion of waterproofing will be made at the embarkation area or if necessary on board the vessels. (See Ordnance Annex No. 8 and G-4 Annex No. 5).

POSTPONEMENT

a. Postponement may be for a one (1) to two (2) day period or for up to a twenty-eight (28) day period.

b. In case of a day to day postponement, troops on board LSI, APA and LST will remain on board. Troops on board LCT or LCI that are alongside berths may be disembarked. Personnel in LCT or LCI not secured alongside may be disembarked as determined by conditions at the time.

c. In case of a longer period of postponement all troops will be disembarked and will return to Marshalling Areas. Vehicles will not be taken off the lift.

d. In case of any disembarkation, care and maintenance parties will remain on board vehicle loaded vessels. Such personnel should be rotated.

9 May 1944
A Company 5th Rangers – Swanage, Dorset

James W. Gabaree: *After our intensive training in Scotland we were sent for further training on sheer cliffs near the town of Swanage on the channel coast. Some of us were billeted in a hotel located on the beach. For security reasons we were not allowed to go into town. Our room was located on the third floor. A guard and the first sergeant were located in the lobby. This created a problem for the young GI's who wanted some action and the company of ladies. Our secret weapons were the ropes in our possession to be used in the coming invasion. We secured one end of the rope inside the room, and out of the window we went. We slid down the ropes, landed on the beach, and went on our way to town. The hike to town was a bit scary, as we did not know if the beach was mined. Our escapade came to an abrupt end because our company lieutenant was waiting for us when we came off the beach upon reaching the town.*

B Company 5th Rangers – Swanage, Dorset.
Paragraphs 1a and b of letter, HQ V Corps, subject, 'Desertion' dated 21 April 1944, were read to the members of B Company at 1930 hours, on 9 May 1944.
C Company 5th Rangers – Swanage, Dorset.
Paragraphs 1a and b of letter, HQ V Corps, subject, 'Desertion' dated 21 April 1944, were read to the members of C Company at 1715 hours, on 9 May 1944.
D Company 5th Rangers – Swanage, Dorset.
Paragraphs 1a and b of letter, HQ V Corps, subject, 'Desertion' dated 21 April 1944, were read to the members of D Company at 1515 hours, on 9 May 1944.
E Company 5th Rangers – Swanage, Dorset.
F Company 5th Rangers – Swanage, Dorset.
Medical Detachment 5th Rangers – Swanage, Dorset.
Headquarters Company 5th Rangers – Swanage, Dorset.

2nd Battalion Historical Narrative.

> On 9 May, the 2nd and 5th Ranger Battalions were formed into a Provisional Ranger Group, commanded by Lt Col Rudder. The Battalion planning Staffs were admitted into the Group War Office and preparations for D-Day were increased.
>
> Training was continued with Companies D/E/F perfecting their cliff climing techniques while Companies A/B/C conducted forced marches and firing problems.

Maurice Prince: *The city of Swanage was a typical commercial and prosperous-looking resort town on the south middle coast of England. Its lovely beach and the majestic hills enclosing the town attracted many tourists and visitors to spend his or her vacation here. The cool, clear ocean and the white sandy beaches were delightful parts of the town's features.*

The community itself could boast of several hotels, a couple of movie houses, innumerable pubs, cafes and other such businesses as one would expect to find in such a city.

Swanage being a coastal town and having a bay suitable for harbouring ships, was a natural target for the enemy Luftwaffe. So far, except for our stay in Folkestone, we never had much trouble from the Luftwaffe. Here, though, every night we were to undergo an actual air raid. About 2 or 3 a.m. our sleep was to be surely interrupted by the warning sirens and if that didn't do it, then the thunderous noise caused by the firing of the Ack-Ack and machine gun units on top of our hill certainly would. Most of us never left our beds just pulled the covers over our heads and hoped and prayed that the Jerries wouldn't drop any bombs around our place; and they didn't. We were too lazy and tired to run for the air raid shelters. In fact, no one ran for the shelters, not even the civilians. A lot of trust and faith was had in the English air defences and after having seen some of their work, I can easily see the reason for that.

A Company 2nd Rangers – Swanage, Dorset.
B Company 2nd Rangers – Swanage, Dorset.
Pvt. Richard A. Rogers.
Paragraphs 1a and b of letter, HQ V Corps, subject, 'Desertion' dated 21 April 1944, were read to the above named enlisted man at 0900 hours, on 9 May 1944.

C Company 2nd Rangers – Swanage, Dorset.

D Company 2nd Rangers – Swanage, Dorset.

Captain Slater was relieved of principal Duty as Company Commander and placed on Detached Service with Battalion HQ.

1st Lt. Baugh was relieved from assigned and transferred to C Company 2nd Btn.

1st Lt. McBride assumed principal Duty as Company Commander while Captain Slater was relieved of his duties. Alerted for departure.

E Company 2nd Rangers – Swanage, Dorset.

1st Lt. Theodore E. Lapres was relieved of command.

1st Lt. Gilbert. C. Baugh was assigned and joined from Company D of this Btn. in place of 1st Lt. Lapres. Alerted for departure.

F Company 2nd Rangers – Swanage, Dorset.

No change. Alerted for departure.

[Author: Around this time there are no further F Company reports for approximately three weeks]

Medical Detachment 2nd Rangers – Swanage, Dorset.

No change. Alerted for departure.

Paragraphs 1a and b of letter, HQ V Corps, subject, 'Desertion' dated 21st April 1944, were read to the members of the Medical detachment present at a formation of the detachment at 0800 hours, on 9 May 1944.

Headquarters Company 2nd Rangers – Swanage, Dorset.

Sixteen enlisted men went from Duty to Detached Service with Ranger Group HQ.

Sgt. Russell G. Worman, T/4 James K. Patrick Jr., T/5 Neal B. Berke, T/5 Henry Bungard, T/5 George M. Clark, T/5 Robert J. Cooker, T/5 Takser L. Hooks, T/5 Francis Kolodziejczak, T/5 Howard J. Lefferts, T/5 Ira E. Lick, Pfc. William F. Webber, Pfc. Thomas B. Caudle Jr, Pfc. Joseph R. M. Cournoyer, Pfc. Charles A. Faris Jr, Pfc. Robert G. Hoffman, Pfc. Roland J. Paradis.

The following three officers are placed on Detached Service with the Provisional Ranger Group HQ:

Lt. Colonel James E. Rudder.

Captain Frank H. Corder.

Captain Harvey J. Cook.

1st Lt. James R. McCullers Jr. was relieved of his principal Duty as Battalion Mess Officer and assumes principal Duty as Special Operations Officer.

Captain Harold K. Slater was attached from D Company 2nd Btn and given the principal Duty of Executive Officer and Btn S-3.

1st Lt. Anthony Bazzocchi went from Duty to Detached Service with Provisional Ranger Group Headquarters.

Pfc. Philip G. Robida went from Duty to Detached Service with Provisional Ranger Group Headquarters.

Pvt. Gerald O. Sejba was assigned and joined from HQ 10th Replacement Depot APO 874 US Army as of 15 April 1944.

Alerted for departure.

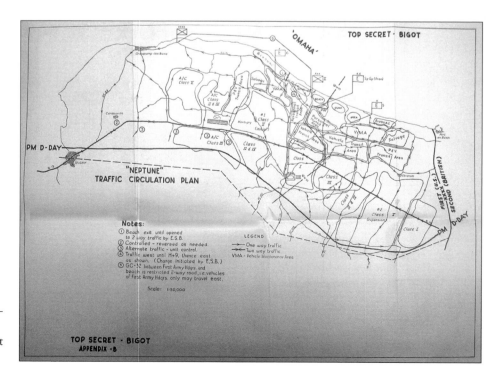

A traffic map released by the Army for the Omaha Sector – clearly marking Omaha beach at the top.

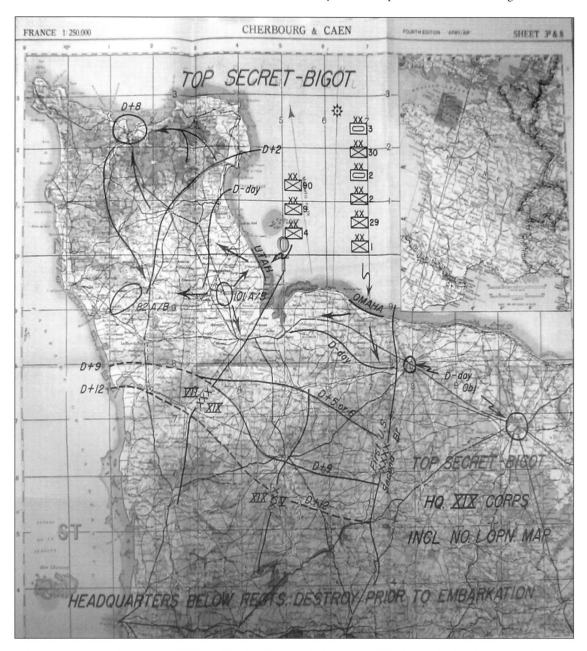

A larger scale map showing the D-Day objective line in relation to the Cherbourg Peninsula – and subsequent objective lines for the days following.

Next page: A corresponding map showing the proposed Beach Maintenance and Assembly Areas. Without the D-Day Objective Line being achieved, the follow-on units would all be out of sync with the rest of the invasion.

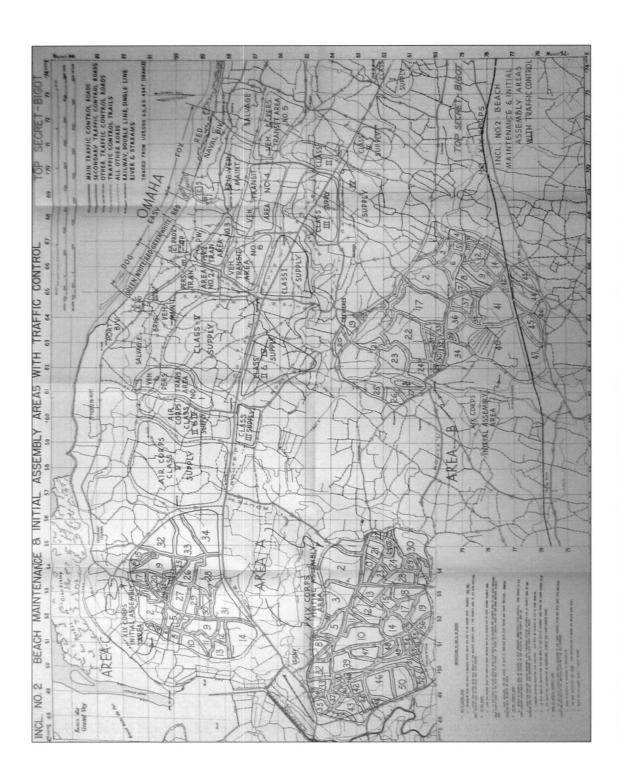

TOP SECRET-BIGOT

MAIN TRAFFIC CONTROL ROADS
SECONDARY TRAFFIC CONTROL ROADS
OTHER TRAFFIC CONTROL ROADS
TRAFFIC CONTROL TRAILS
ALL OTHER ROADS
RAILWAY, DOUBLE LINE, SINGLE LINE
RIVER & STREAMS

TRACED FROM 1/25,000 55,65 4547 (FRANCE)

OMAHA

INCL. NO.2 BEACH
MAINTENANCE & INITIAL
ASSEMBLY AREAS
WITH TRAFFIC CONTROL

TOP SECRET-BIGOT

~~SECRET~~

HEADQUARTERS 1ST U.S. INFANTRY DIVISION
APO 1, U.S. Army

Copy No. **3**

Ref No. K1079

File No. AG 337-5-9

```
:::::::::::::::::::
:                 :
:Auth: CG 1st US  :
:       Inf Div   :
:Date: 9 May 44   :
:Initials:        :
:::::::::::::::::::
```

9 May 1944

SUBJECT: Communications Conference.

TO   :   See Distribution.

    1. A conference for communications officers will be held at the 1st
Signal Company, Bryanstone Camp, near Blandford, at 1000, Thursday, 11 May 1944,
for critique of Exercise FABIUS and discussion of other communications problems.

    2. Communications officers of the following units will attend this
conference:

             1st Signal Company
             16th Infantry
             18th Infantry
             26th Infantry
             116th Infantry
             Headquarters 1st US Infantry Division Artillery
             Headquarters Ranger Group (For 2d and 5th Ranger Battalions)
             Engineer Group Headquarters (Provisional)
             5th Engineer Special Brigade
             348th Engineer Shore Battalion
             37th Engineer Shore Battalion
             149th Engineer Shore Battalion
             3d Armored Group Headquarters
             16th AA Group Headquarters

    3. The number of assistant communications officers and subordinate
unit communications officers attending this conference is left to the discretion
of commanders of units listed in paragraph 2 above.

             By command of Major General HUEBNER:

                                         LEONIDAS GAVALAS
                                         Lt. Col., A.G.D.
                                         Adjutant General

DISTRIBUTION:

CofS	CO 1st Sig Co	CO 116th Inf	CO 348th Engr S Bn
G-2	CO 16th Inf	CG 1st US Inf Div Arty	CO 37th Engr S Bn
G-3	CO 18th Inf	CO Ranger Gp	CO 149th Engr S Bn
Sig O	CO 26th Inf	CG Engr Spec Brig Gp	CO 3d Armd Gp
AG	CO 16th AA Gp	CO 5th ESB	AG File

10 May 1944
5th Rangers – Companies A – F, Medical and HQ – Swanage, Dorset.
2nd Lt. Jay Mehaffey was assigned and joined C Co. from Co. B this Btn and assumed principal Duty as Platoon Leader.

2nd Battalion Historical Narrative.

> *A Battalion beach assault exercise was conducted during this period, employing the until-then secret DUKW's mounting fire-fighting type extension ladders. The troops landed as per schedule and Companies D/E/F scaled the 100 foot cliffs, securing the necessary beachhead but the exercise was handicapped because the overly-inflated tires of the DUKW's would not grip the water-soaked sand. The Battalion returned to Swanage by motor.*

A Company 2nd Rangers – Swanage, Dorset.
No change. Alerted for departure.
B Company 2nd Rangers – Swanage, Dorset.
T/Sgt. Edward A. Andrusz.
Paragraphs 1a and b of letter, HQ V Corps, subject, 'Desertion' dated 21 April 1944, were read to the above named enlisted man at 0900 hours, on 10 May 1944.
C, D, E, F & Medical Companies 2nd Rangers – Swanage, Dorset.
Alerted for departure.
Headquarters Company 2nd Rangers – Swanage, Dorset.
The following three enlisted men were assigned and joined as of 9 May 1944 – they were then immediately sent on Detached Service with Ranger Group HQ: Pvt. Thomas J. Armbruster, T/5 Steve M. Mead, Pfc. Guy C. Shoaf.
Alerted for departure.

Next page: The German 'Order of Battle' for the 'West' area was updated, along with bombing targets and coastal defence/artillery positions in the Operation Neptune area. (Apologies for the quality of the image.)

```
              S E C R E T
```

HEADQUARTERS, ALLIED EXPEDITIONARY AIR FORCE
Kestrel Grove, Hive Road,
Stanmore, Middx.

REF: AEAF/TS.13165/Air.   10th May, 1944.

SUBJECT: Bombing Operations – A.E.A.F.

TO: Air Marshal Commanding, Second Tactical Air Force (Main) (6)
          Commanding General, Ninth Air Force (Advanced) (4)
          Air Marshal Commanding, Air Defence of Great Britain (3)
          Air Officer Commanding, No. 38 Group (3)
          Commanding ――――, Ninth Air Force (Rear) (2)

          1. The following bombing operations of the Ninth Air Force and
Second Tactical Air Force for the period 11 May 1944 to 17 May 1944 inclusive
will be conducted as follows and in the priority shown below:-

Priority 1.   10% of the weekly operational effort on CROSSBOW.

Priority 2.   Coastal Defence Batteries as specified in Appendix 'A' attached.

Priority 3.   Rail road centers as shown in Appendix 'A' to Directive this
              Headquarters. dated 7 May, 1944 and of even reference.

Priority 4.   Airfields according to list shown in Appendix 'B' attached.
              At least 40% of the airfields shown in Appendix 'B' will be
              attacked by the Eighth Air Force during this same period, and
              it is necessary that lateral co-ordination be continuously main-
              tained between the Eighth Air Force at Pinetree and the Combined
              Planning Committee at Uxbridge in reference to the attacks on any
              of the airfields in Appendix B.

Priority 5.   Rail bridges according to the list shown in Appendix 'C' attached.
              The attack on the aforementioned bridges will be accomplished
              simultaneously with the necessary effort to destroy each. In the
              event insufficient damage is accomplished on the bridges a further
              attack will be made within the same operational period. No attacks
              of any kind will be made on bridges on the Seine river until further
              notice from this Headquarters.

Priority 6.   Special targets:-

              (a) The following target will be attacked by Medium altitude
                   bombardment with the period of bombing operations included
                   in this directive.

TARGET	OPERATIONAL NO.	REMARKS
LE HAVRE	Z-532	Illustration S5482/3. East edge of Bassin Du Canada, used as a loading point for minelaying and tank landing craft.

              (b) Radar installations – Chimneys.

                   Attack on radar installations (Chimneys) as shown in Appendix

                                                    "D" will be

                        A 10759

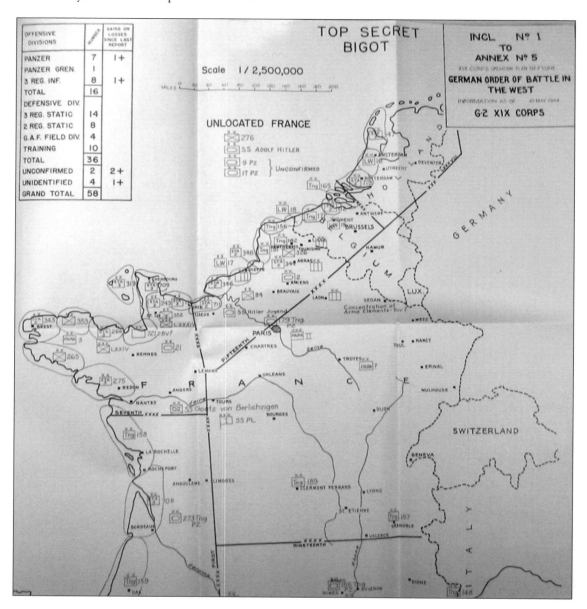

TOP SECRET
BIGOT

Scale   1 / 2,500,000

INCL   N° 1
TO
ANNEX N° 5

GERMAN ORDER OF BATTLE IN
THE WEST

G·2 XIX CORPS

OFFENSIVE DIVISIONS	NUMBER	GAINS OR LOSSES SINCE LAST REPORT
PANZER	7	1+
PANZER GREN.	1	
3 REG. INF.	8	1+
TOTAL	16	
DEFENSIVE DIV.		
3 REG. STATIC	14	
2 REG. STATIC	8	
G.A.F. FIELD DIV.	4	
TRAINING	10	
TOTAL	36	
UNCONFIRMED	2	2+
UNIDENTIFIED	4	1+
GRAND TOTAL	58	

UNLOCATED FRANCE

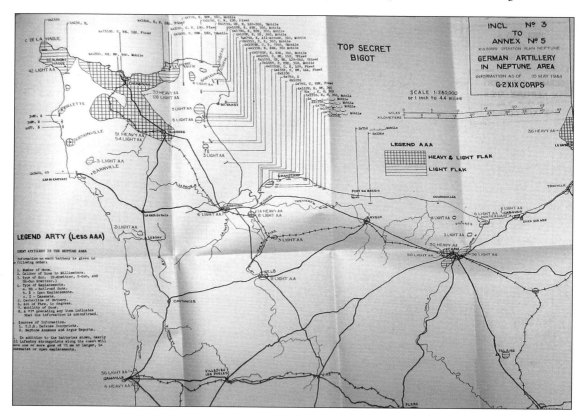

A blow-up of the Rangers' area of assault – showing gun positions and weapon calibres.

On 10 May the major Field Order was issued – this was the definitive order for the Rangers and their objectives. Although in brief, these orders had not changed for the Rangers. *'Capture Pointe du Hoc, seize and secure that portion of D-Day phase line in its zone of action prior to two hours before dark on D-Day.'* Again there was the constant necessity for all units, including the Rangers, to carry out their missions and reach that inland position.

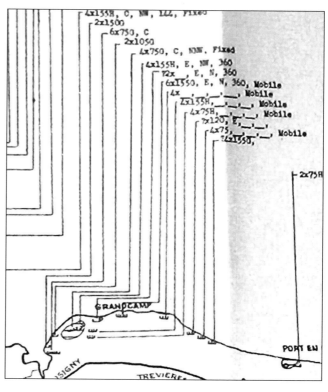

Page 1 of 5 Pages   ~~TOP SECRET~~   Ref No. F-1   ~~PAGE ~~
                                "NEPTUNE"

: ~~TOP SECRET~~ :
:By Authority of CG :   HQ CT 18
:1st US Inf Div   :   APO 1, USA
:10 May 1944   :   10 May 1944
:Initials: :
                                    COPY NO: **31**

Field Order Number 19

MAPS: GSGS 4250, 1/50,000, FRANCE.
      SHEETS: 6E/6; 6F/2; 7E/5; 7F/1

1. a. For information of the enemy see current intelligence plan and S-2
        Annex, Annex #2.

    b. (1) The first US Army, associated US and Allied naval and air forces
             and the British Second Army, will conduct a simultaneous
             assault on the continent of Europe with the mission of establish-
             ing a beachhead from which further offensive operations can be
             developed.

        (2) The 50th British Division will assault the beaches on the left
             of the 1st US Infantry Division and will capture BAYEUX on
             D-Day.

        (3) The US VII Corps will assault the beaches on the right of the
             1st US Infantry Division.

        (4) The 101st Airborne Division will drop on the area behind
             VIERVILLE (4299) - CARENTAN (3894) during the night D - 1,
             D-Day, with the main objective of assisting the seaborne land-
             ing of the VII Corps.

        (5) The 11th Amphibious Force will provide escort and support the
             landing of the 1st US Infantry Division (reinforced), clear
             underwater mine fields and obstacles off-shore, protect the
             transport area ans assist the landing with gunfire, both pre-
             arranged and on call.

        (6) The 9th US Air Force will support the attack of the 1st US Inf-
             antry Division, reinforced, by prearranged bombing missions
             prior to H-Hour and by missions on call after H-Hour.

        (7) The 29th US Infantry Division, (less Regimental Combat Team 116)
             with Regimental Combat Team 26 and other troops attached, will
             land on Beach Omaha behind the initial assault.

        (8) The 1st US Infantry Division, less Regimental Combat Team 26,
             with Regimental Combat Team 116 will make the initial assault
             on Beach Omaha at H-Hour on D-Day with two Regimental Combat
             Teams abreast, reduce the beach defenses in it's zone of action,
             secure the Beachhead Maintenance Line, secure the D-Day phase
             line two hours before dark on D-Day. It will cover the land-
             ing of the remainder of the V Corps and will be prepared to
             participate in the extension of the beachhead to the south and
             the south-west.

             (a) Combat Team 116, reinforced lands at H-Hour, D-Day on
                  Beaches Omaha Easy Green, Dog Red, Dog White, Dog Green,
                  Baker and Charlie; reduce beach defenses in it's zone of
                  action, seize and secure that portion of the Beachhead
                  Maintenance line in it's zone of action, capture POINTE
                  DU HOE. seize and secure that portion of D-Day phase
                  line in it's zone of action.prior to two hours before
                  dark on D-Day

An order dated 10 May directly placed the responsibility for the distribution of Intelligence Planning maps upon individual *'Unit Commanders'*.

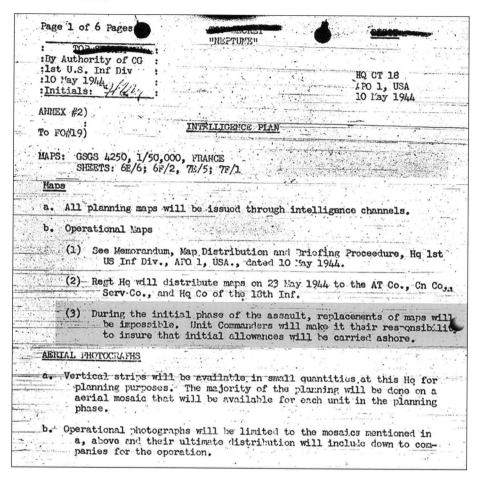

11 May 1944

5th Rangers – Companies A – F, Medical and HQ – Swanage, Dorset.

2nd Rangers – Companies A – F, Medical and HQ – Swanage, Dorset.

Maurice Prince: *We continued on with our training with emphasis being placed on cliff scaling. The nearby cliffs were very adaptable to this type of work so we practised and improved our skill in overcoming this obstacle. A new method was uncovered to surmount this handicap, that was the amphibious duck with automatic ladder attached. We used to make beach landings in this vehicle, press the button and watch as the ladder shot skyward 100 feet, place it against the cliff and then clamber up.*

Stress was also placed on the amount of ammunition we were to carry during our attack. We finally reached a sort of a compromise and it worked out so that each rifleman would carry sixteen clips of M1 ammo, two hand grenades and two anti-tank grenades. The B.A.R. man would have his separate individual load, while each man would have a basic load for the weapon he was armed with.

Invasion was in the air as basic loads were tested and improved. New supplies and equipment were issued and a close check was made to ensure that everything that was to play a part in the coming assault was in good working order.

Yet with all this hustle and bustle we still found time to visit town each evening. The local Red Cross with its inviting cokes, coffee and donuts sort of attracted us more than the other places of town. I can also say that the pubs and cafes also fared well, thanks to our patronage. The local amusement centre also did a thriving business as Rangers took their girlfriends out to have a big time.

Our complete stay in Swanage lasted twelve days, but now as I look back it seems as if we were there for a longer period of time. It doesn't appear reasonable that we crammed so much into so little time.

On 11 May an updated and revised set of Neptune Orders were issued.

```
                                              BIGOT
                                              NEPTUNE

                                    Annex No. 2 to V Corps

                                 OPERATIONS PLAN NEPTUNE

                                        Copy No.      92
```

```
                              ANNEX No. 2
                               (REVISED)

                                   TO

                        V CORPS OPERATIONS PLAN

                               NEPTUNE

                       PRIORITY OF UNITS FOR LANDING
```

```
    NOTE:   Troop List for Operation NEPTUNE is being
            constantly revised due to changes in al-
            location of lift, logistical requirements,
            and limitations on forces that may be
            landed on any one tide.  These revisions
            have in some cases been completed subse-
            quent to approval of other Annexes.  In all
            cases where there is conflict between the
            Annex and the Troop List, the latest re-
            vised Troop List will govern.
```

```
                    Revised as of 11 May  1944
```

```
                                              - BIGOT

                                - 1 -
```

TOP SECRET
"NEPTUNE"   BIGOT

Page 1 of 3 pages

```
:          TOP SECRET          :
:AUTH: CG,ENGR SP BRIG GP:
:INIT:                        :
:DATE: 11 May 1944      :
```

G-2 ESTIMATE OF THE ENEMY SITUATION   Reg No. E 290

Hq Engr Sp Brig Group
APO 230, United States Army
11 May 1944

1. SUMMARY OF THE ENEMY SITUATION

   a. The OMAHA beaches are defended by elements of the 716th Static Division. Entire sector defended by this division extends from OUISTREHAM (U1179), west to the mouth of the River Douve (T4590). This division was formed in April 1941 in France and has never been out of that country. It was composed originally of older reserve personnel (landesschutzen) but has been called upon frequently to furnish replacements for more active units. The equivalent of at least two battalions are Russian and Polish Troops. Division is known to consist of the 726 and 736 Grenadier and 656 Artillery Regiments. A third infantry regiment probably does not exist, but certain divisional units as a reconnaissance and/or an anti-tank battalion are probably present. Division headquarters is located at CAEN (U0368). Defensive dispositions place the 726 Inf Regt in the immediate OMAHA beach area. Regimental headquarters is located at BAYEUX (T7879). One battalion is believed to have its headquarters at GRANDCAMP-LES-BAINS, a second at ISIGNY, and the third at BAYEUX. 726th Infantry is supported by four batteries of field artillery.
      For organization of ground and locations of weapons, see defense overlay. Practically all artillery, close support and anti-tank weapons allotted to the 726th Inf have been integrated into the coastal "crust" defenses.

   b. For location of other static, coastal defense divisions, see OB sketch. Generally, such divisions have similar organization, history and personnel as the 716th Div described above.

   c. The 352 Inf Div, located in the vicinity of ST. LO (T5063), is organized as a field division. It is probably mobile and at full strength. This division, identified in March 1944, is believed to have been made up from battle trained, depleted units from the Russian front.
      The 21 Panzer Division, E of RENNES (Y0053) and the SS Panzer Division "HITLER JUGEND" at LISIEUX (Q1388) are within a 100 mile radius of the assault area. Both of these units are considered to be well equipped and composed of first class troops. 21 Panzer is spread over a wide area; some units are within 50 miles of the beach. "HITLER JUGEND" is 50 - 60 miles from beaches. Large formations of both units can reach the assault area in about ten hours if no delay is imposed by friendly action.

TOP SECRET
"NEPTUNE"

- 1 -

TOP SECRET
"NEPTUNE"
BIGOT

d. German Air Force disposition on Western Front 1 May 1944:

	WESTERN FRANCE	EASTERN FRANCE	HOLLAND	NORTHERN GERMANY	DENMARK NORWAY	TOTALS
Single Engine Fighters	35	75	30	620	55	815
Twin Engine Fighters	45	185	95	400	10	735
Fighter Bombers	–	30	–	–	–	30
Long Range Bombers	115	70	–	250	10	445
Reconn- aissance	75	10	10	5	75	175

e. Only enemy naval forces actually stationed in the OMAHA area are several converted invasion barges (T.L.C. Type III). These mount two 88mm guns, one or two 37mm guns, possibly several machine guns, and are employed for coastal patrol. Light naval forces of destroyers and E boats are avail- able for defense of the area.

f. See Terrain Study for climate and terrain.

g. It is reported that the French population has been evacuated from coastal areas except for those needed by the Germans. Persons residing in this area, like all Frenchmen, are highly individualistic and automatically resent any show of authority. Except for a few individuals, they are Anti-German and Anti-Vichy, but are not especially pro-Allied Nations. However, a hostile attitude of the majority is unlikely, and sabotage of our installations by civilians other than those belonging to collaborat- ionist groups is improbable.

2. ENEMY CAPABILITIES

a. Enemy can:

(1) Defend the coastal crust positions with present garrisons plus rein- forcements from reserve units now stationed in the interior.

(2) Launch counter attacks, especially from the SE, to restore his situation with 352 Field Division, elements of the 243 Static Division, armored formations from 21 Panzer and SS Panzer HITLER JUGEND in addition to garrison troops of 716 Division by evening of D Day. Rapidity of counter attack reaction is dependent upon degree of surprise, if any, inflicted upon enemy.

TOP SECRET
"NEPTUNE"

- 2 -

TOP SECRET
"NEPTUNE"

Page 3 of 3 pages   BIGOT

(3) Withdraw initially to line behind the inundated valley of the River AURE.

b. Conclusions:

Adoption of (3) above is unlikely. It is presumed that enemy will make every effort to withstand the initial assault and wipe out the beachhead, utilizing all available forces and weapons as soon as definite commitment of our forces to the assault area is confirmed. Heavy air attacks will be made against the beaches and shipping. Toxic chemicals may be employed. Air-borne attack is possible with paratroopers now stationed at MELUN, SW of Paris. Hit-and-run tactics by light naval forces are to be expected. Enemy has had years to plan, prepare demolitions, construct obstacles, mine, booby trap, rehearse, and otherwise prepare to resist and impede our operations in this area.

VIVIEN G. CLARK
Lt Colonel, GSC
AC of S,   G-2

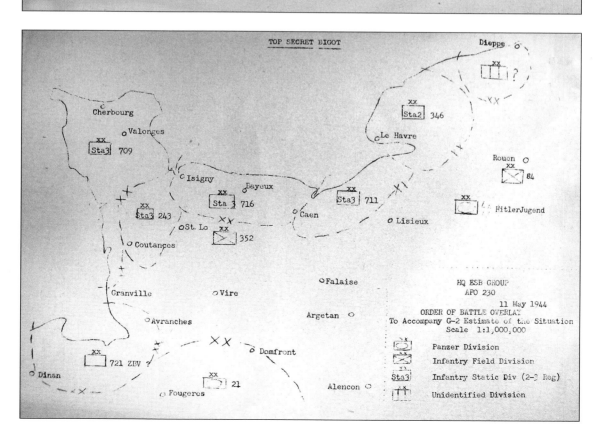

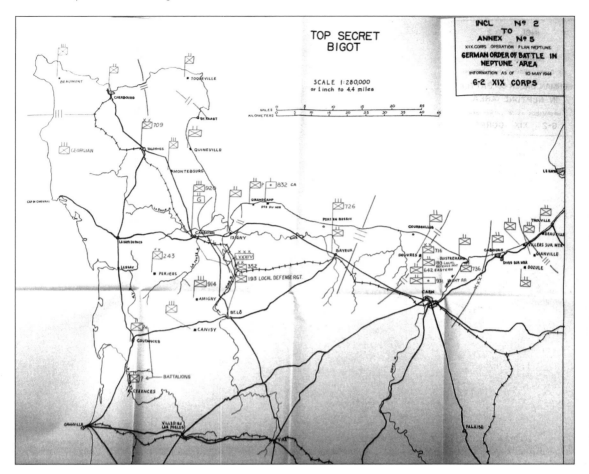

G-2 Intelligence *'estimates of the enemy situation'* for 11 May 1944.

Page 1 of 8 pages TOP-SECRET BIGOT
"NEPTUNE" ZA 215

Hq 1st US Inf Div
APO 1, US Army
11 May 1944

COPY NO. 054

```
: TOP-SECRET :
:Authority:  CG:
:1st US Inf Div:
:11 May 1944  :
:Initials:     :
```

G-2 ESTIMATE OF THE ENEMY SITUATION #4

MAPS: GSGS 4249 (1/100,000) - Sheets 6E, 6F, 7F.
GSGS 2738 (1/250,000) - Sheets 3A & 8.
GSGS 4250 (1/50,000) - Sheets 6E/5, 6E/6, 7E/5, 5F/2 &
6F/1, 6F/2, 7F/1.
GSGS 4347 (1/25,000) - Sheets 34/18 NW, NE, SW, SE.
34/16 NW, NE, SW, SE
37/16 NW, SW.
37/18 SW.

INDEX

NOTE

The intelligence contained in this estimate supplements previous estimates. It should be read in conjunction with these, as it does not repeat those portions which remain unchanged.

- 1 -

TOP-SECRET
"NEPTUNE"

1.   SUMMARY OF THE ENEMY SITUATION.

    a.   Enemy Order of Battle.

        (1)   Forces in the Assault Area.

        No change.

        (2)   Adjacent Units.

        (a)   Divisional headquarters of 243d Infantry Division is located at PERIERS.

        (b)   The infantry regiment at CARENTAN has been identified as the 920th of the 243d Infantry Division. It may include the Tartar Battalion now located southeast of CARENTAN in the area ST. PELLERIN, MONT MARTIN, and ST. JEAN DE DAYE. This Tartar Battalion came from Southern France where it was a portion of the "Ost Legion" (Eastern Legion). The 240 series of infantry divisions have recently been reported as having three regiments each of two battalions with a third battalion of foreign troops added to each regiment.

        (3)   Enemy Reserves.

        (a)   Local Reserves.

        1.   Divisional headquarters of the 352d Infantry Division is at CANISY rather than ST. LO. The division's emblem is ⋈ . Reports indicate at least two artillery battalions in the southern part of the division area in the vicinity of CONDE SUR VIRE and TESSY SUR VIRE.

        2.   Schnelle Brigade 30 has its headquarters at COUTANCES. It controls three battalions, the 517th Mobile Battalion at ST. LO, a battalion at COUTANCES and another at CERENCES.

        3.   In the 352d Infantry Division area a few tanks have been recently observed. This may indicate an attachment of one company of tanks to the Division similar to the reported attachment of a company to the 716th Infantry Division. On 20 April a few tanks were seen in AIRE, 10 miles north of ST. LO, and a few tanks and a company of motorized infantry at VILLERS BOCAGE, east of CAUMONT.

        (b)   Mobile Reserves.

        1.   The 21st Panzer Division, with headquarters at RENNES, is spread over the area ST. MALO - PONTORSON - RENNES - PLOERMEL - JUGON. This area was previously occupied by two panzer training divisions.

TOP-SECRET
                                "NEPTUNE"   BIGOT

        2.   12th SS Panzer Division Hitlerjugend is in
the area BERNAY - EVREUX - DREUX - LE MERLERAULT, somewhat to the
south of the area formerly occupied by 10th SS Panzer Division
FRUNDSBERG.

        3.   The 3d Parachute Division has only two re-
giments at HOULGATE-SIZUN. The third regiment is believed to be
training at BRON.

        4.   The staff of the 721st Infantry Division has
been identified in the COTES DU NORD at ST. MALO. It is an administrative staff zbV (for special employment) to control the
Russian battalions in this sector.

    b.   Enemy Defenses.

    (1)   Beach Defenses.

        (a)   As of 25 April 1944, the rows of hedgehogs on
Beach 46 ran from 64899184 to 69148955. Approximately 1,000 units
have been emplaced.

        (b)   The rows of Element "C" mentioned in Estimate #3
have been slightly extended and a new row has been added opposite
the VIERVILLE entrance. Element "C" now runs from 64969194 to
65389168 (32 units), from 65499160 to 67009060 (101 units), and
from 68768984 to 69378956 (47 units).

        (c)   Cover of 27 April 1944 showed a number of stakes
or posts placed between 66559093 and 66789081, these appear to be
from 12 to 15 feet high and from 15 to 20 feet apart. There are
at least 25 stakes.

        (d)   Cover of 27 April 1944 showed small holes in the
sand visible along several stretches of the hedgehogs. The holes
lie immediately behind or in front of the hedgehogs. There appears
to be one hole opposite each hedgehog. These holes may have been
scoured out by water running through the obstacles, although such
marked scouring has not been observed before. They may be holes
left by hedgehogs which sank into the sand and had to be moved to
new positions. It is possible, however, that they are connected
with mining, which has occurred on some other beaches. During a
recent air attack on a coastal battery at BENERVILLE, east of
DEAUVILLE, a 1,000 pound bomb was dropped some 700 yards offshore
causing sympathetic detonations of mines in a belt of underwater
obstacles near the shore. The pattern of the explosions was
staggered with approximately 100 feet between explosions.

    (2)   Inland Defenses.

        (a)   New enemy installations have been located in or
near the coastal villages in rear of Beach 46:

                        - 3 -
                     TOP-SECRET
                      "NEPTUNE"

1. STE HONORINE Area:

        73138680: Troops in group of houses.

2. COLLEVILLE Area:

        68448979: 2 probable AT guns.
        68538863: 4 probable mortar positions.
        68598838: Probable AT position with field
                    of fire except for laying
                    directly on road from beach.
        68718830: Open pit 10 feet square.

3. ST LAURENT Area:

        67438977 - 67288972 - 67318964 - 67328946:
                    3 row minefield approximately
                    20' wide.
        67328946-67178930-67168922-67368928-
        67448928-and 67698894-67838897-67818890-
        67888892-67908898-67898900-67898898-
        67888901-67918907-67828915: 1 row mine-
                    field.
        66448976: 1 pillbox.
        66428971: 3 MG positions.
        66238920: Troops and trenches in group of
                    houses.

4. VIERVILLE Area:

        64889066: Infantry weapon position.
        64949063: Infantry weapon position.
        65039059: Infantry weapon position.
        64789047: Pillbox.
        65109032: Pillbox.

    (b) Additional installations have been located to the
north of BAYEUX-ISIGNY road.

    1. Underground Installations.

        56908880: Five underground shelters or
                    storage bunkers. Size 25' x
                    25'. Area surrounded by wire.
        59759225: Two shelters under construction.
        60708820: Eight underground shelters or
                    storage bunkers in orchard.
                    Size 25' x 25'.
        62208870: Previously mentioned as emplace-
                    ments but probably shelters or
                    for storage. There are a total
                    of ten measuring 18' x 18' in-
                    side and 35' x 35' overall.

- 4 -

TOP-SECRET   BIGOT
"NEPTUNE"

> 65188792: Approximately 13' x 13'. May
>   be shelter.
> 65208810: Approximately 13' x 13'. May
>   be shelter.
> 657875:   One shelter.

2. Troop Billets In Houses:

> 55609130
> 55609040
> 56059290
> 56609125
> 59609980
> 60209010
> 65708735
> 69558640
> 71708630
> 72158755
> 73058690

3. Trenches:

> 61539273: Trench 60' long.
> 61539293: Trench 60' long.
> 64208950: Shelter trench.
> 64278291: Trench at a crossroads. Length
>   40'.
> 75878780: Trench east of PORT-en-BESSIN.
>   Length 64'.
> 76128775: Trench extending north and south
>   along cliff. Length 155'.
> 78408750: Old trench lengthened in easter-
>   ly direction by 60'.
> Town of TREVIERES has 10 trenches on out-
>   skirts about 80' long and evenly spaced
>   about town.

4. Miscellaneous:

> 56109140: Two mast aerial.
> 56809220: Wireless station.
> 631887:   Small dump.
> 666862:   Small dump.
> 72288660: Supply dump in wooded area.
> 72508640: Supply dump in wooded area.

c. Enemy Artillery.

(1) No additional enemy artillery has been reported in the 726th Infantry sector:

- 5 -

TOP-SECRET
"NEPTUNE"

The comment below: *'Some damage was done to one gun and to the two casements under construction'*

(a)   The battery position at 529915 is still being casemated. No guns are visible.   The four guns 500 yards south-east of this site in open positions can no longer be seen.

(b)   The battery at 533918 remains unchanged.

(c)   The six gun battery on POINTE DU HOE was recently bombed. Some damage was done to one gun and to the two casemates under construction.

(d)   The field battery at VAUX-SUR-AURE (792831) is reported to be unoccupied.

(e)   The battery position at LONGUES (797871) is nearing completion. No guns have been seen as yet but it is reported that a battery of four 105mm or 155mm artillery pieces had target practice in this area in January. The four concrete casemates are 52 x 65 feet.

(2)   The installations at 599934 and 622887 are not new artillery positions as was initially thought but groups of shelters, possibly used as dumps.

(3)   There has been no confirmation of the report of two railway guns at CARENTAN. To date, neither ground reports nor photo interpretation have indicated any activity in the CARENTAN area suggesting the employment of such guns.

d.   Climate and Terrain.

(1)   ETOUSA Engineer reports state that the soil in the assault area consists mainly of a marly limestone and hardpan. Difficulty will be encountered in digging five foot deep foxholes in this soil with entrenching tools normally used. When foxholes are dug, the spoil will be a light color (grey to white), and will contrast sharply with surrounding topsoil unless camouflage precautions are strictly enforced. The stream bottoms have limestone beds covered with gravel.

(2)   The sandbars at the western end of the beach are now completely covered at lowest low water. Continuous shifting of sands on the beach makes it impossible to estimate the depth of water in the vicinity of these sand bars on D-day.

(3)   There is a now flooded area just east of SURRAIN between 682859 and 680850. This area is approximately 2,000 yards wide and follows the AURE River. The flooded area between 695851 and 704847 is also approximately 2,000 yards wide and follows the AURE River. Both of these areas appear to have a maximum depth of 1½ feet but do not average more than 6 to 9 inches.

- 6 -

Below: Lt. Colonel Rudder is marked as having received five copies of this report.

```
Page 8 of 8 pages        TOP-SECRET              BIGOT
                          "NEPTUNE"

DISTRIBUTION:  (Cont'd)
                                      No. Copies    Copy Nos.

CO, CT 16                                10         127 - 136
CO, CT 18                                10         137 - 146
CO, CT 26                                10         147 - 156
CO, Ranger Force                          5         157 - 161
CO, 1st Engr Bn                           1            162
CO, 1st Med Bn                            1            163
CO, 1st Rcn Tp                            1            164
CO, 1st Sig Co                            1            165
CO, 1st QM Co                             1            166
CO, 701st Ord (LM) Co                     1            167
CO, Div Hq Co                             1            168
G-2 Extra                                57         169 - 225

* Incl in V Corps copies.
```

The revised landing diagram for Omaha Beach was released on 11 May and highlighted are the units landing on Omaha Beach from the Rangers. C Company 2nd Battalion were to land in front of A&B Companies 2nd Battalion – followed by the whole of the 5th Battalion at H-Hour +60 minutes – subject to them having not already landed at Pointe du Hoc. The rest of the 5th Battalion to land in five minute delays after that.

LANDING DIAGRAM, OMAHA BEACH
(SECTOR OF 116th RCT)

	EASY GREEN	DOG RED	DOG WHITE	DOG GREEN
H-5			◇◇◇◇ ◇◇◇◇ ◇◇◇◇ ◇◇◇◇ Co C (DD) 743 Tk Bn	◇◇◇◇ ◇◇◇◇ ◇◇◇◇ ◇◇◇◇ Co B (DD) 743 Tk Bn
H HOUR	T T T T Co A 743 Tk Bn	T T T T Co A 743 Tk Bn		
H+01	V V V V V V Co E 116 Inf	V V V V V V Co F 116 Inf	V V V V V V Co G 116 Inf	A A A A A A Co A 116 Inf
H+03	M M M 146 Engr CT	M M M M 146 Engr CT Demolitions Control Boat	M M M 146 Engr CT	M M M 146 Engr CT A A Co C 2d Ranger Bn
H+30	V V V V V CoH ⌐HQ CoE CoH⌐ AAAW Btry └─116 Inf─┘ AAAW Btry	HQ HQ HQ Co V V V V V V V V 2d Bn CoH CoF CoH 2d Bn └─116 Inf─┘ AAAW Btry	V V V V V CoH HQ CoG CoH AAAW Btry └─116 Inf─┘ AAAW Btry	A A A A A A A V Co B HQ CoA Co B └─116 Inf─┘ AAAW Btry
H+40	M 112 Engr Bn	112 Engr V V V V M Co D 81 Cml Wpns Bn 149 Engr Beach Bn	V M 149 Engr 121 Engr Bn Beach Bn	HQ A A A A V V V V V 1st Bn 116 Co D 116 Inf 149 Beach Bn 121 Engr
H+50	V V V V V V Co L 116 Inf	V V V V V V V V Co I 116 Inf	V V V V V V Co K 116 Inf	M V V V V V 121 Engr Co C 116 Inf Bn
H+57		V V V V V V V V V HQ Co 3d Bn └─Co M 116 Inf─┘		V V Co B 81 Cml Wpns Bn
H+60	T 	V T T T T 112 Engr Bn	V HQ a HQ Co 116 Inf	T T T A A A A 121 Engr Bn Co Aa B 2d Ranger Bn
H+65				A A A A A A A 5th Ranger Bn
H+70	I 149 Engr Beach Bn	I 112 Engr Bn	I Alt HQ a HQ Co 116 Inf	M T T A A A A A A A A 121 Engr Bn 5th Ranger Bn
H+90			T T T T T 58 FA Bn Armd	
H+100			I 6th Engr Sp Brig	
H+110	⊟⊟⊟⊟ ⊟⊟⊟⊟ ⊟⊟⊟⊟ III FA Bn (3 Btry's in DUKWS)	⊟ ⊟ ⊟ ⊟ ⊟ AT Plat 2d Bn AT Plat 3d Bn ↑ 29 Sig Bn		⊟ ⊟ ⊟ ⊟ ⊟ ⊟ ⊟ ⊟ AT Plat Cn Co 116 Inf 1st Bn
H+120	T T T 467 AAAW Bn AT Co 116 Inf 467 AAAW Bn	T T T T T AT Co 116 Inf 467 AAAW Bn 149 Engr Beach Bn	T T 467 AAAW Bn	T T 467 AAAW Bn
H+150		└─DD Tanks─┘ T T T	I HQ Co 116 Inf 104 Med Bn	
H+180 to H+215	T T	⊟⊟⊟⊟⊟⊟⊟⊟⊟⊟⊟ 461 Amphibious Truck Co	M T M T M T └─Navy Salvage─┘	T T T T T
H+225	⊟⊟⊟⊟⊟⊟⊟⊟⊟⊟⊟⊟⊟⊟⊟⊟ 461 Amph Trk Co	T	T T	

I LCI	M LCM	A LCA	◇ DD Tank	*Note: Plan as of II May*	
	T LCT	V LCVP	⊟ DUKW		

---

12 May 1944

5th Rangers – Companies A – F, Medical and HQ – Swanage, Dorset.

2nd Rangers – Companies A – F, Medical and HQ – Swanage, Dorset.

A revised Beach map was issued.

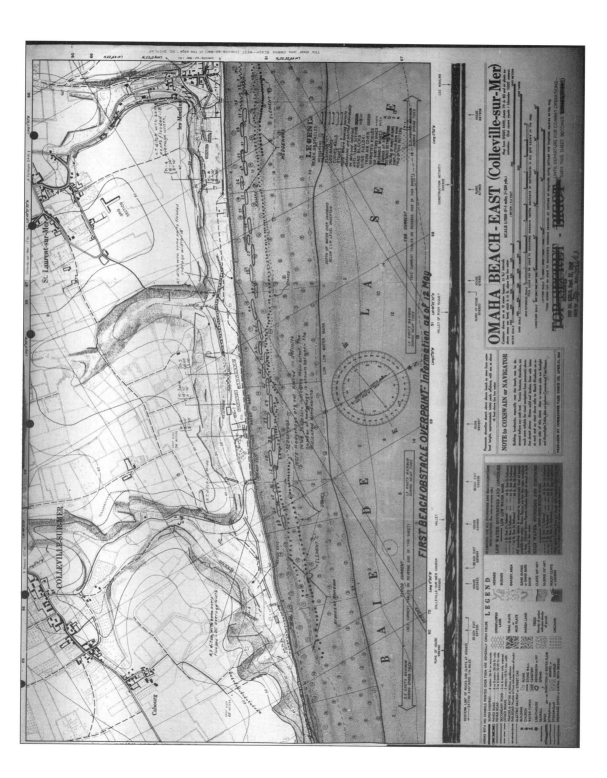

OMAHA BEACH - EAST (Colleville-sur-Mer)

FIRST BEACH OBSTACLE OVERPRINT Information as of 12 May

Naval Orders issued and dated 12 May:

TOP SECRET

OPERATION NEPTUNE—NAVAL ORDERS

(Short Title : ON)

ON 8.—Instructions for Bombarding Forces—*continued*

Appendix II.—The Fire Plan

This appendix includes relevant information and instructions contained in the Joint Fire Plan issued by the Joint Commanders-in-Chief.

2. In general, the methods taken to neutralize or destroy enemy defences will be as follows :—

Coastal and Field Batteries.

(a) Priority being given to those which will interfere most with the approach of the Naval Forces, certain batteries, selected on a joint basis on Army Group level are being bombed pre D day. The air effort which can be allotted to this task is limited by the necessity to bomb batteries in other areas, for cover purposes ; and by the air operations immediately prior to D day designed to distract attention from the assault area.

(b) During the night of D–1/D day the heavy night bomber effort will be concentrated on ten selected batteries, this number being the limit of availability of night bombing aids.

(c) In the early daylight hours of D day, a proportion of the medium bomber effort will be used to bomb six batteries.

(d) On D day, coastal and field batteries which threaten the beaches and sea approaches will be engaged with naval gunfire. Instructions regarding the timing of naval bombardment are contained in ON 8, para. 32.

(e) A proportion of the fighter bomber effort may be used to attack suitable batteries during the touch down period. The selection of batteries is not yet firm, and, therefore, they are not included in this Appendix.

Beach Defences

(f) Commencing at about H–45, the available heavy and medium day bomber effort will be concentrated on the neutralization and destruction of beach defences. The total tonnage of bombs is allocated in the general ratio of 2 to 3, as between the Western and Eastern Task Forces, and will be approximately 4,200 tons.

(g) During the final approach, beach defences will be engaged by assault craft and destroyers.

3. Assault Force Commanders, in association with their Military Commanders, are responsible for selecting beach targets for assault craft and destroyers, and for deciding the times for opening and ceasing fire.

Effect of Pre D day bombing on the D day Fire Plan

4. Batteries in the NEPTUNE area (see Table A) selected for pre D day bombing have all already been attacked once, with a limited degree of success. Although it is intended to bomb them again before D day, it is unlikely that there will be sufficient positive evidence of damage done to justify their withdrawal from the D day fire plan. If, however, certain batteries are known to have been destroyed or very severely damaged, alternative targets for bombers prior to H hour will be selected by the Joint Commanders-in-Chief, and Task and Assault Force Commanders will be kept informed.

5. Similarly, should the effect of pre D day bombing be sufficient to justify amendment to the list of targets for naval bombardment (Table C) the list will be amended after consultation with Task Force Commanders.

Summary of Tables to this Appendix

6. *Table A* .. Battery targets for pre D day bombing.

Table B .. Battery targets for night Heavy and Medium bombers prior to H hour.

Table C .. Battery targets for Naval Bombardment.

Table D .. Spotting Aircraft : programme of Sorties and Pre-arranged Briefing.

Table E .. Beach targets for day Heavy and Medium bombers during the assault.

TOP SECRET   OPERATION NEPTUNE—NAVAL ORDERS
(Short Title : ON)

─────────

ON 8.—Instructions for Bombarding Forces—*continued*

Table B.—Battery Targets for Night, Heavy and Medium Bombers prior to H Hour

Night Heavy Bombers (up till Civil Twilight)

Target	Map Reference
POINTE DU HOE	586937
LA PERNELLE	365200
FONTENAY SUR MER	368044
MORSALINES	354139
ST. MARTIN DE VARREVILLE	405980
SALLENELLES	155776
HOULGATE	256809
BENERVILLE	422107
BARFLEUR	394228
RIVA BELLA	117797

2. Timing will be arranged so that those batteries which are the greatest menace to the Assault Forces are bombed during the period when Assault Forces reach the lowering position, subject to the necessity for bombing certain batteries early in the night in order to avoid endangering airborne troops.

Medium Bombers (between Civil Twilight + ten minutes and H hour)

Target	Map Reference
3. LA PERNELLE	365200
POINTE DU HOE	586937
MAISY	533918
RIVA BELLA	117797
OUISTREHAM	103779
MONT FLEURY	918861

TOP SECRET

OPERATION NEPTUNE—NAVAL ORDERS

(Short Title : ON)

ON 8.—Instructions for Bombarding Forces—*continued*

Table A.—Battery Targets for Pre D day Bombing

The following batteries in the NEPTUNE area have already been bombed once. (See Appendix II, para. 4.)

Target	*Map Reference*
(a) LE GRAND CLOS (LE HAVRE)	467307
(b) FONTENAY SUR MER	368044
(c) BENERVILLE	422107
(d) HOULGATE	256809
(e) POINTE DU HOE	586937
(f) RIVA BELLA	117797
(g) LA PERNELLE	365200
(h) SALLENELLES	155776
(i) MORSALINES	354139
(h) VILLERVILLE	486156

TOP SECRET

OPERATION NEPTUNE—NAVAL ORDERS

(Short Title : ON)

ON 8.—Instructions for Bombarding Forces—*continued*

Table E.—Beach Targets for Day Heavy and Medium Bombers during the Assault

U.S. Sector

(a) Beach OMAHA	(b) Beach UTAH
623935	435992
637927	442982
645918	451969
648915	418017
655912	429000
664907	442972
666906	447975
668903	448958
677900	456953
678896	493904
688895	505916
698890	538934
750880	545932
755878	
758877	

TOP SECRET   OPERATION NEPTUNE—NAVAL ORDERS

(Short Title : ON)

ON 8.—Instructions for Bombarding Forces—*continued*

Table C.—Battery Targets for Naval Bombardment

Instructions regarding the timing of naval bombardment are laid down in ON 8, paragraph 32.

2. The detailing of ships to the targets listed below is the responsibility of Task and Assault Force Commanders.

3. Task and Assault Force Commanders are at liberty to propose amendments or to make last minute adjustments to the list in the light of latest intelligence, but Allied Naval Commander-in-Chief must be kept informed, in order that the re-briefing of spotting aircraft (Table E) can be arranged.

4.

Target Name	Map Reference
BARFLEUR	394228
LA PERNELLE	365200
MORSALINES	354139
OZEVILLE	343057
CHATEAU DE COURCY	362054
FONTENAY SUR MER	368044
EMONDVILLE	359023
MAISY II	531914
MAISY I	533918
POINTE DU HOE	586937
VILLERVILLE	486156
BENERVILLE	422107
HOULGATE	256809
RIVA BELLA	117797
OUISTREHAM	103779
COLLEVILLE SUR ORNE	076782
MOULINEAUX	972808
MONT FLEURY	918861
VER SUR MER	917844
ARROMANCHES I	848853
ARROMANCHES II	846848
LONGUES	797871
VAUX-SUR-AURE	792831

Note.—The batteries at ST. MARTIN DE VARREVILLE (405980) and SALLENELLES (155776) will only be targets for naval bombardment if called for by shore observers in the event of the airborne troops requiring this support.

13 May 1944

5th Rangers – Companies A – F, Medical and HQ – Swanage, Dorset.
S/Sgt. Mongeon D Co. went from sick in quarters to Duty.
2nd Rangers – Companies A – F, Medical and HQ – Swanage, Dorset.

Dated 13 May the Omaha Beach co-ordinates were confirmed and all previous beach divisions and map co-ordinates were rescinded. [Again apologies for the quality of the images.]

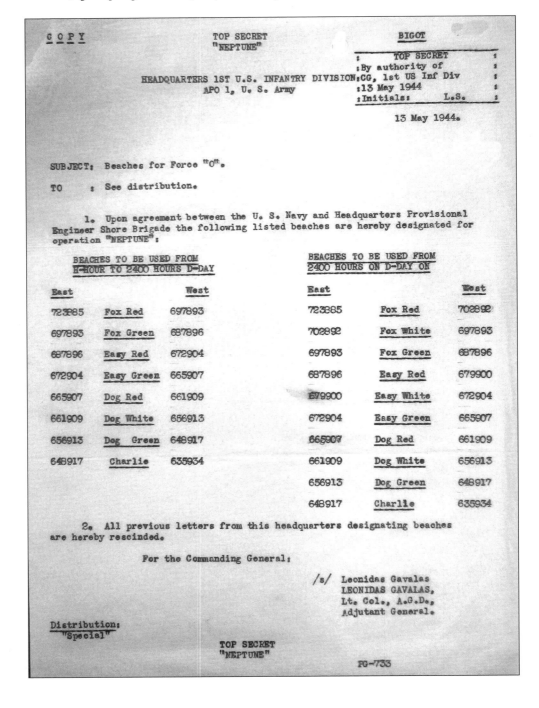

SECRET.

OPERATIONS FOR PERIOD 11-17 MAY, INCLUSIVE

APPENDIX "A" (Continued)

COAST DEFENCE BATTERIES.

Serial	Target	Map Reference	Tac.Dos.No.	Remarks.
7.	☒ BENERVILLE	422107	4900/J/184	6x170 m.m. guns 3 pill boxes.
8.	☒ POINTE DU HOE	586937	4901W/J/1	6x155 m.m. guns, 3 light A.A. 1 pill box.
9.	DUNKIRK	224845	5102E/J/169	280 m.m. Ry. guns, 4 light AA guns.
10.	WIMEREUX	694603 to 700601	5001E/J/151	2x280 m.m. guns at 702607.
11.	GRAVELINES	991805	Refer to annotated photo.	6 open emplace- ments for 150 m.m. guns.
12	FORT MARDICK	188849	5102E/J/1"3	6x150 m.m. guns.

Serial 1 LE HAVRE/DIGUE SUD.

☒ Uncompleted Batteries.

ENEMY COASTAL RADAR STATIONS - CONTINUED.

SECRET.
PAGE THREE

A 10748

Ser. No.	Serial Letter	RHUBARB APPENDIX XII No.	Name.	T.T. DOSSIER. Name.	Ref.	PINPOINT	TARGET. MAP REF:	DESCRIPTION.	REMARKS.
615	S	41	POINTE ET RAZ DE LA PENCEE	ENGLESQUEVILLE LA PERCEE.	4901W/J/4.	00°56'20"W. 49°23'37"N.	4040B/26NE. 623934.	2 Giant Wuerzburgs.	Target area shown in Illus- tn: 4901W/7(a) does not cover the most Easterly Giant Wuerzburg.
616	F	46	(a)CHERBOURG/ FERMANVILLE (LA BRASSERIE)	GARNEVILLE	4902W/K/7.	01°28'09"W. 49°40'05"N.	4040B/17NW. 254257.	Chimney.	
617	T	46	(b)CHERBOURG/ FERMANVILLE (LA BRASSERIE)	GARNEVILLE.	4902W/K/7.	01°28'09"W. 49°40'05"N.	4040B/17NW. 254257.	2 Giant Wuerzburgs.	
618 A	V	48	CAP DE LA HAGUE/AUDERVILLE	AUDERVILLE	4902W/K/1.	01°56'04"W. 49°42'51"N.	4040B/16NE. 922326.	2 Giant Wuerzburgs.	(Illustration 4902W/4(h) and N.E.portion of Illus- trn: 4902W/4(j) cover location of targets.
619 A	W.	49	CAP DE LA HAGUE/JERQUETT	JOBOURG.	4902W/K/15	01°54'28"W. 49°41'07"N.	4040B/16NE. 939292.	Giant Wuerzburg.	

(620 to 699)

APPENDIX "B"

COASTAL DEFENCES

SECRET

A 0733

Serial	Name	Reference	T.T.D. Illustration (If Necessary)	Tac. Dos. No.	Remarks
274	☒ GATTEVILLE	392877		4902W/J/258	6x155 mm guns; 4 casemates
275	☒ ST. MARTIN DU VARREVILLE	405080		4902W/J/102	4x155 mm Hows.; casemates under construction
276	☒ MAISY I	533918		4902W/J/7	4x155 mm Hows.; Open
277	☒ LONGUES	797871		4901W/J/125	4x155 mm guns; casemates under construction

Below: A GSGS Intelligence Map dated 13 May was issued covering Pointe du Hoc to the Pointe et Raz de la Percée.

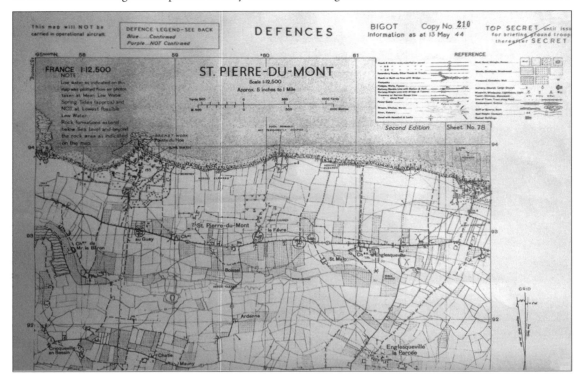

Below: A blow up of the Pointe du Hoc battery area.

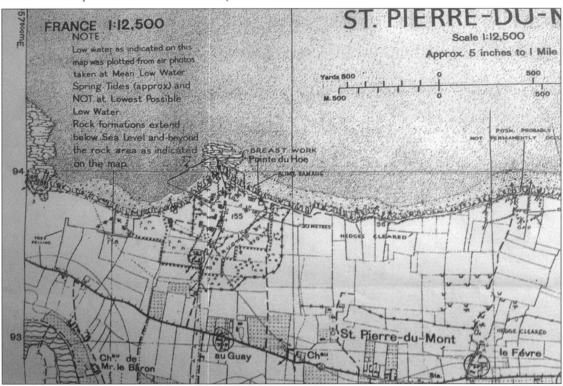

The map indicates that there are now four casements under construction and for the first time it does not say '6' guns are installed. Indicated here in black (for clarification) are the original 6 positions. However, the gun on Pit No.5 is marked with a 'U' next to it. This means that the position is now 'unoccupied'. There was the earlier intelligence reference indicating that one of the guns had been damaged, but it did not say which one. It could have been No.5. This would indicate that there were now four operational guns on pits No.1, 2, 3 & 6 and another one in the open near pit No.4. Equally, the damage could have been done to any of the other five guns, which would mean that there were now four operational guns in total.

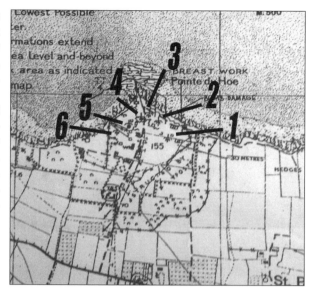

14 May 1944
5th Rangers – Companies A – F, Medical and HQ – Swanage, Dorset.
2nd Rangers – Companies A – F, Medical and HQ – Swanage, Dorset.

Next page: A revised set of sea level diagrams were produced and these could also be used to orientate the troops when landing.

APPENDIX 1 TO ANNEX A,
to OPERATION ORDER BS-44
TOP SECRET - NEPTUNE

NOTE:

HOUSES IN AREA ARE BEING PROGRESSIVELY DESTROYED NOTABLY AT HAMEL AU PRETRE. THEY WILL BE FURTHER DESTROYED BY BOMBARDMENT AND SHOULD NOT BE DEPENDED ON FOR RECOGNITION.

COURSEULLES

ARROMANCHES

SECTOR DOG

DOG WHITE
700 yards

DOG RED
450 yards

DOG WHITE
700 yards

Look for the next valley to the left of the valley at Exit D1. The village of LES MOULINS at the entrance of this valley marks Exit D3, which leads to ST. LAURENT. Sector DOG extends from Exit D1 to the center of LES MOULINS, including Exit D3. This 1 1/4 mile stretch of coast is backed by a grassy bluff 120 feet high. There is a strip of flatland averaging 100 yards wide be-

The right side of DOG WHITE Beach is marked by the left group of houses at HAMEL AU PRETRE. Here the beach is backed by a wave-cut embankment 4-8 feet high with intermittent rough stone wall. This embankment extends to the left to a point slightly beyond the houses, where it reaches a masonry wall 4-8 feet high backing the left side of the beach. This wall is broken by the sea near its right end and for 150 feet. In front of the left end of the embankment and the right 2/3 of the wall, 15 breakwaters project at a 60° angle. All but the farthest breakwater to the left are on DOG WHITE Beach. The left flank of the beach is midway between the left group of houses at HAMEL AU PRETRE and LES MOULINS. A paved road backs the wall and embankment the entire length of the beach.

EXIT F1

NOT VISIBLE

69N80 741

by a masonry wall 4-8 feet high. The remaining beach is backed by a low wave-cut embank. The paved shore road runs directly behind and Exit D3, a paved road, leads inland from through the center of the village.

Look for a cliff topped by steep rugged bluffs 200 feet high and broken by valleys as it extends to the left out of sight. This cliff rises from the beach 1,150 yards to the left of the right flank of Sector FOX. The sector continues for about 3,000 yards along the cliff to the village of

ST. HONORINE-DES-PERTES, where the cliff is broken by a valley. 1 3/4 miles still further to the left the breakwaters of PORT-EN-BESSIN should be visible.

FOX GREEN
1135 yards

FOX RED

The right flank of FOX RED Beach is at the point where the cliff rises from above level. The left flank is at a valley occupied by the few houses of ST. HONORINE-DES-PERTES. Behind the right side of the beach, the bluff forms a flat-topped, semi-circular headland. Exit F1 (which leaves the beach just to the right of the right flank) bears diagonally up the face of the headland. The left side of

62902 785

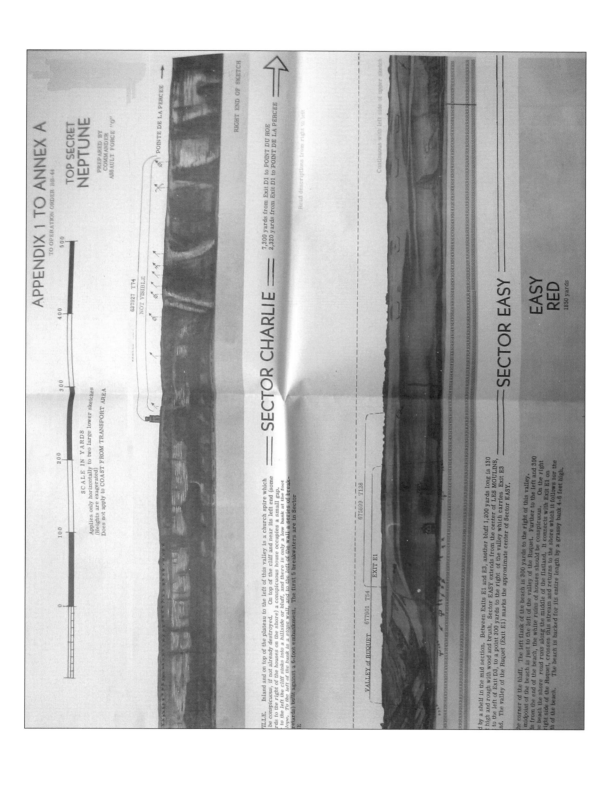

TOP SECRET
NEPTUNE

PREPARED BY
COMMANDER
ASSAULT FORCE "O"

SCALE IN YARDS
Applies only horizontally to two large lower sketches
(Heights are exagerated)
Does not apply to COAST FROM TRANSPORT AREA

0   100   200   300   400   500

POINTE DE LA PERCEE →

RIGHT END OF SKETCH

637927 T74
NOT VISIBLE

═══ SECTOR CHARLIE ═══   7,300 yards from Exit D1 to POINT DU HOE
2,320 yards from Exit D1 to POINT DE LA PERCEE

Read descriptions from right to left

Continues with left side of upper sketch

═══ SECTOR EASY ═══

EASY
RED

1650 yards

VALLEY of RUQUET 677901 T54   EXIT E1   673669 T128

ILLE.   Inland and on top of the plateau to the left of this valley is a church spire which be conspicuous, if not already destroyed.   On top of the cliff and near its left end (some rds to the right of the houses on the shore) a conspicuous house occupies a small gap. to the left the cliff sinks into a hillside or bluff, and there is only a low bank at the foot ... The left of the bank is a right wall, and to the left of the wall a series of break- ...) built against a 6-foot embankment.   The first 5 breakwaters are in Sector E.

d by a shelf in the mid section.   Between Exits E1 and E3, another bluff 1,200 yards long is 130 high and rough with wood and brush.   Sector EASY extends from the center of LES MOULINS, to the left of Exit D3, to a point 300 yards to the right of the valley which carries Exit E3 nd.   The valley of the Ruquet (Exit E1) marks the approximate center of Sector EASY.

he corner of the bluff.   The left flank of the beach is 300 yards to the right of this valley, midpoint of the beach is just to the left of the valley of the Ruquet.   Further to the left and 300 ... from the end of the beach, the white ruins of houses should be conspicuous.   On the right ... each for shore road runs along the middle of the flatland.   It connects with Exit E1 on right side of the Ruquet, crosses this stream and returns to the shore which it follows for the th of the beach.   The beach is backed for its entire length by a grassy bank 4-6 feet high.

DEFENSES AS OF 14 MAY 1944

M.G.	
R.M.G. or A.T.	
PILL BOX	
CASEMATE (gun less than 75mm.)	
BARRED WIRE	
ELEMENT C	cccc
HEDGEHOGS	HHH
RAMPS or RAILS	RRR
STAKES	ssss

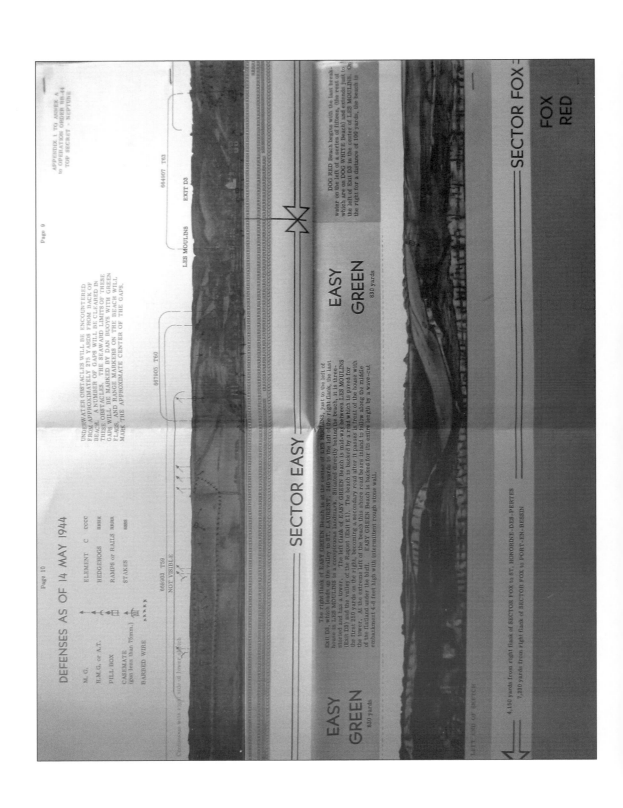

UNDERWATER OBSTACLES WILL BE ENCOUNTERED FROM APPROXIMATELY 275 YARDS FROM BACK OF BEACH. A NUMBER OF GAPS WILL BE CLEARED IN THESE OBSTACLES. THE SEAWARD LIMITS OF THESE GAPS WILL BE MARKED BY DAN BUOYS WITH GREEN FLAGS, AND RANGE MARKERS ON THE BEACH WILL MARK THE APPROXIMATE CENTER OF THE GAPS.

666303 T59

NOT VISIBLE

667005 T60

LES MOULINS

664907 T63

EXIT D3

= SECTOR EASY =

The right flank of EASY GREEN Beach is at the center of LES MOULINS, just to the left of Exit D3 which leads up the valley to ST. LAURENT. 340 yards to the left of the right flank, the last house in LES MOULINS is a conspicuous landmark. Situated directly behind the beach, it is three-storied and has a tower. The left flank of EASY GREEN Beach is mid-way between LES MOULINS (Exit D3) and the valley of the Ruquet (Exit E1). The beach is backed by a road which is paved for the first 150 yards on the right, becoming a secondary road after it passes in front of the house with the tower. At the extreme left of the beach this shore road bears inland to follow along the middle of the flatland under the bluff. EASY GREEN Beach is backed by a wave-cut embankment 4-8 feet high with intermittent rough stone wall.

EASY GREEN
830 yards

EASY GREEN
830 yards

= SECTOR EASY =

DOG RED Beach begins with the last break-water on the left of a series of fifteen, the rest of which are on DOG WHITE Beach and extend up to the left of Exit D3 in the center of LES MOULINS. On the right for a distance of 100 yards, the beach is

= SECTOR FOX =

FOX
RED

= SECTOR FOX =

LEFT END OF SKETCH

4,150 yards from right flank of SECTOR FOX to ST. HONORINE-DES-PERTES
7,230 yards from right flank of SECTOR FOX to PORT-EN-BESSIN

Revised Army report dated 14 May states the personnel numbers in each Ranger Battalion as of 15 May.

```
Page 1 of 8 Pages                "NEPTUNE"                    BIGOT

                                                        :By authority of  :
Hq-1st US Inf Div                                       :CG, 1st US Inf Div:
.APO #1, U.S. Army                                      :    14 May 1944   :
14 May 1944                                             :Initials: F W G   :

ANNEX #3 )                     TROOP LIST
                        BEACH "OMAHA" - FORCE "O"
TO FO #35)                                              Copy No.  053


No. :           Unit                          :Personnel :  Vehicles

    4. :  2d Ranger Bn                             534   :    38
    5. :  5th Ranger Bn                            533   :    30
```

On 15 May a final conference was held at St Paul's School under the supervision of SHAEF. At this meeting every principal member of the British Chiefs of Staff and the War Cabinet attended, as did King George VI and Allied generals, including General Bradley, General Eisenhower, General Ramsay, Field Marshal Smuts, Air Chief Marshal Leigh-Mallory and the Prime Minister. The purpose of the conference was to prove to all attending that everything had been done to solve issues and smooth away any problems with the proposed landings.

---

15 May 1944   15 May Navy Report: *At 21st Army Group Headquarters a meeting took place at which a general outline of the complete 'NEPTUNE' plan was presented by each of the respective Commanders-in-Chief and the Task Force Commanders. Included in the audience were H.M. The King, the Prime Minister and General SMUTS, each of whom also addressed the assembled officers, who were restricted to senior officers of the three services concerned with the planning and execution of the Operation.*

A.N.C.X.F. outlined the Naval plan and N.C.E.T.F. and N.C.W.T.F. added details for their respective forces. Army and Air Force Commanders-in-Chief and Force Commanders also gave their plans and intentions, and the Supreme Commander summed up. Great if sober confidence in the outcome of the operation was evident through the meeting. The need for flexibility to meet events which might not go in accord with plans was emphasised by both Prime Minister and A.N.C.X.F.

5th Rangers – Companies A – F, Medical and HQ – Swanage, Dorset.
Tec 5 Herring returned to Duty from the 316th Station Hospital. Pfc Smith and Pfc Nelson were transferred in grade to the Detachment of Patients 95th General Hospital APO 143 US Army.
2nd Rangers – Companies A – F, Medical and HQ – Swanage, Dorset.

Relevant to the Rangers' defence both in England and then on Omaha Beach were smoke units. During April and May 1944 three smoke generator battalion headquarters were organized provisionally, and later activated. Two of these were to supervise the projected screening operations at ports in the European Theatre of Operations. One of these then drew up and implemented the detailed plans for screening Omaha Beach and its temporary harbour. Another of these battalions co-ordinated screening operations at the Weymouth and Portland harbours during the period when ships were concentrating for the invasion of Normandy.

The Weymouth-Portland area was subjected to enemy air attack on three different occasions between the organisation of the provisional smoke generator battalion and D-Day. The first bombing occurred on 15 May when a large-area screen was erected in time to prevent aimed bombing, and no damage resulted from enemy action. On 28 May, the area was again attacked by enemy bombers. On this occasion the Battalion was prepared to operate – but was not ordered to make smoke. As a result, the area suffered damage from the attack, and one officer and two enlisted men of the Battalion were wounded. The third and last attack occurred on 29 May, but smoke covered the target and no damage was done by enemy aircraft. The 25th Smoke Battalion remained at Weymouth until 28 June, but was not called upon to operate after 29 May.

A Weymouth pub was heavily damaged during the raid.

On 15 May the Utah Beach plans were formalised and the landing plans were given to senior officers. The obvious relevance to the Rangers was that the Utah landings were time critical. The guns at Maisy were able to fire directly over open sights at the landing ships approaching and disembarking men onto that beach. Therefore it was essential that the Rangers achieved their mission to knock out the Maisy Batteries as soon as possible. Any delay in the Rangers completing their mission could result in casualties on Utah Beach during all stages of the landings there.

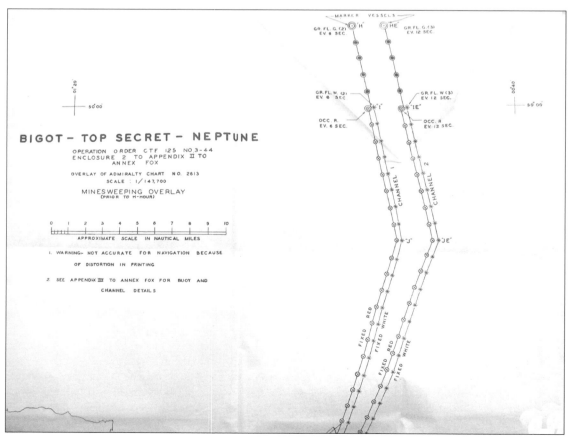

On the plan below – the approaches to the Utah navy sector run right in front of the Maisy guns.

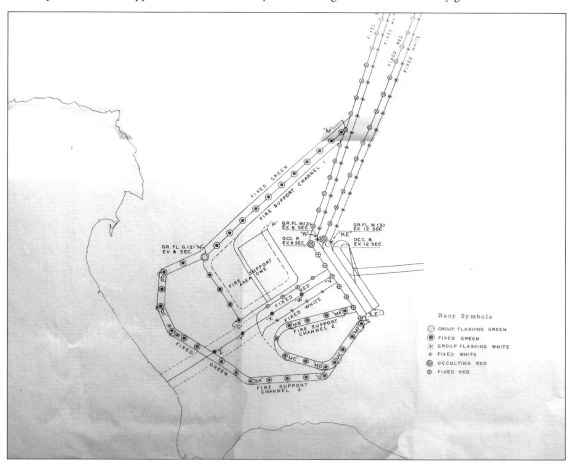

Also released on 15 May were the Utah Beach Naval targets, which include duplicates of the Rangers' targets. Target 1 – Pointe du Hoc, Targets 5, 16 and 16A – Maisy were all clear dangers to the safe landing of troops.

These particular gun positions were unique in that they presented duplicate targets for both landing groups. Although the Utah landing elements were landing some way from the Omaha Sector – they were still in a position to be attacked by these guns. The Navy supporting the Utah landings were given these targets – as well as the Omaha Beach Naval units.

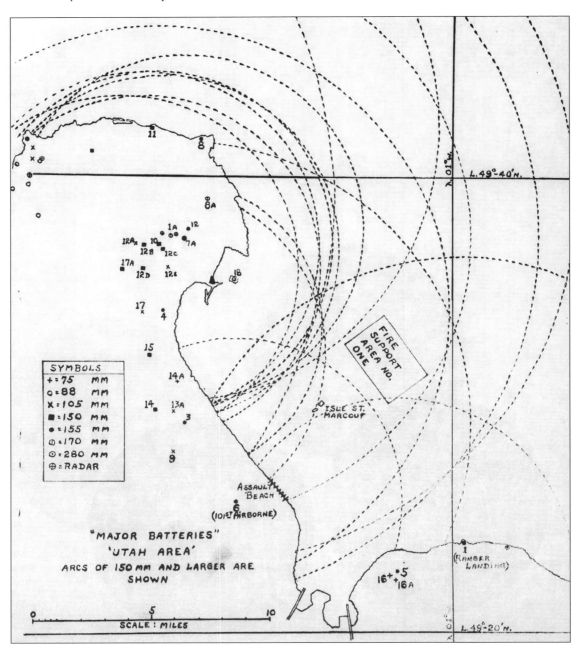

SYMBOLS
+ = 75 MM
○ = 88 MM
X = 105 MM
■ = 150 MM
● = 155 MM
⊕ = 170 MM
⊙ = 280 MM
⊕ = RADAR

"MAJOR BATTERIES"
'UTAH AREA'
ARCS OF 150 MM AND LARGER ARE
SHOWN

FIRE SUPPORT AREA NO. ONE

ISLE ST. MARCOUF

ASSAULT BEACH
6
(101ST AIRBORNE)

1
(RANGER LANDING)

16 + 5
+ 16A

L.49°-40'N.

L.49°-20'N.

SCALE : MILES

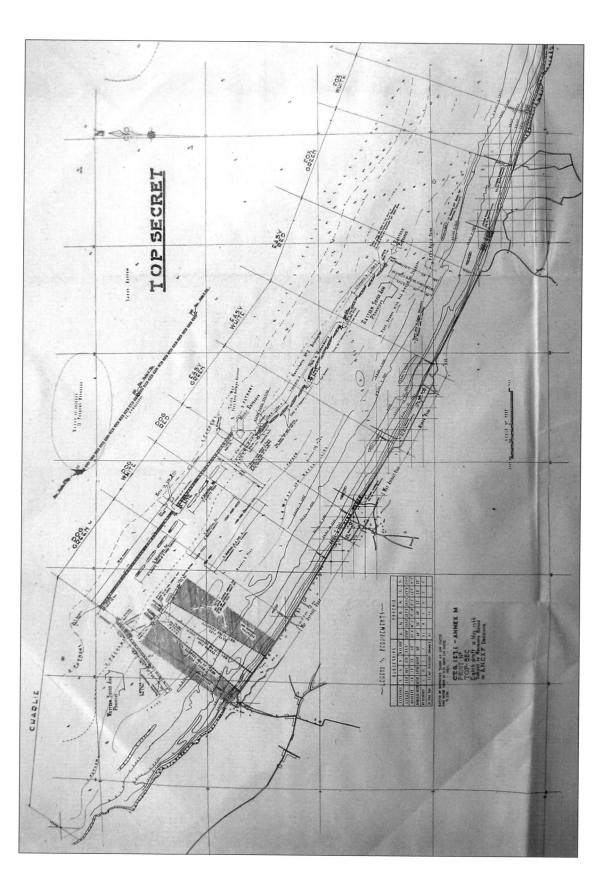

Previous page: Dated 15 May - this is a very detailed map of Omaha Beach which shows the planned positioning of the Mulberry Harbour.

The following paperwork describes the work of the Air Support Parties – some of whom were to land with the Rangers.

TOP SECRET - BIGOT & NEPTUNE

ANNEX "BAKER" to   15 May 1944
OPERATION ORDER
  No. 3-44

Serial: 00010

    (ii). Air Support Parties. Ninth Air Force will attach an Air Support Party to each Regimental Combat team in its initial assault, and to each Division and Corps Headquarters. The Air Support Parties will disembark with the Assault Divisions and Corps to which they are attached. Each party will be equipped with vehicular mounted radio equipment capable of operating on both HF and VHF and will provide the means for procuring direct air support. No Naval personnel are included in those parties. Aircraft on "air alert" status may be directed on missions from Air Support requests through 9th Air Force Operations Representatives in Flagships. The Air Support Parties are designed and equipped to function as Visual Control Posts if required, and will be employed in this role when necessary in accordance with normal practice.
    (iii). Communications. Assault Force Flagship in which the Division Headquarters are embarked will include in their permanent equipment, a wireless station designed to act as an Air Support Party while Divisional HQ remains afloat. When a Division HQ goes ashore, its special assault Air Support Party will go with it. This Air Support Party will take over from the Force Flagship which will continue to maintain a listening watch. At all times, whether Division HQ is afloat or ashore, the Flagship will be prepared to act as a relay station should any Air Support Party on its net be unable to pass its messages to UXBRIDGE.
    (iv). Bombardment.
        (1) Prearranged missions. General priority for the fire support program is given to the neutralization or destruction of batteries that might interfere with the approach of the Naval Forces. Batteries covering the sea approaches and the beaches are regarded as primary targets for the heavy night and medium Oboe bombers, while beach defenses should normally be dealt with by daylight heavy and medium bombers. Because of the prohibitive effort required to achieve destruction, the restricted number of AP bombs available, and the need, for security reasons, to include two batteries outside the NEPTUNE area for each one within it, the number of targets to be engaged prior to D day has had to be restricted. With the exception of the batteries indicated below, which are specifically selected for neutralization in the assault phase, attacks on batteries will be confined to those in open emplacements or under construction, with a view to harassing rather than destructive effect.
        Pre-D day bombing targets have been assigned in the Western Task Force Area as follows:

POINTE DO HOE	586937
CRISBECQ	368044

        The Naval Assault Forces will occupy Transport Area during the middle period of the night bombing, (between Civil Twilight Minus 2 hours and Civil Twilight Minus 1 hour). Therefore, the batteries selected for bombing in this period by the heavy night bombers are those which are the greatest menace to the Transport Area. They include:

                                             ANNEX "BAKER"
                                           AIR PLAN

TOP SECRET - BIGOT - NEPTUNE

ANNEX "BAKER" to   15 May 1944
OPERATION ORDER
   No. 3-44

Serial: 00010

Target Name	Location	Approximate Timings
POINTE DU HOE	586937	Civil Twilight-2 hrs to Civil Twilight-1 hr
LA PERNELLE	365200	" " -1 " " "
~~FONTENAY-SUR~~ ~~MER~~ CRISBECA	368044	" ' " -1 " " "
MORSALINES	354139	" " -1 " " "
ST MARTIN DE VARREVILLE	405980	" " -4½ " " " -3½hrs

The minimum number of batteries have been engaged in the early
period in order to compress the maximum amount of bombing into the
period nearest to H hour.
Medium bombers have been assigned targets to include the
following:

Target Name	Location	Approximate Timings
CATTEVILLE	394227	H hour
POINTE DU HOE	586937	H hour
MAISY	533918	Civil Twilight ≠ 10 minutes

Heavy and Medium bomber missions will attack the beach defenses on UTAH beaches with a total of 860 short tons of bombs, from
H - 30 minutes to H hour. Coordinates and weight of effort are:

451969	120 tons
442982	120 tons
435992	120 tons
456953	60 tons
448958	60 tons
442972	60 tons
429000	60 tons
418017	60 tons
447975	60 tons
493904	35 tons
505916	35 tons
538934	35 tons
545932	35 tons

Between H - 30 minutes and H hour, fighter bombers will
attack battery positions including the following:

POINTE DU HOE	586939	
LA PERNELLE	365201	
MORSALINES	354137	
MAISY	533918	ANNEX "BAKER"
MONTFARVILLE ~~CATTEVILLE~~	394227	AIR PLAN

The following documents dated 15 May are the Utah Beach Naval Taskforce bombardment targets by number, and this is paperwork which would not have been seen by the Rangers. The Utah Naval force also allocated resources to both Pointe du Hoc and Maisy batteries. [Author: Another version of this information also exists for the Army with the exact same wording and date, but in a different format. This has not been included here.]

TOP SECRET - BIGOT - NEPTUNE

APPENDIX TWO TO ANNEX "LOG" to   15 May 1944
OPERATION ORDER
   NO. 3-44

Serial: 00010

BATTERY NEUTRALIZATION PLAN - PLAN ZEBRA

   1. ASSUMPTIONS

      (a) That minesweepers or other friendly craft are taken under fire by
          enemy shore batteries before regular bombardment stations have been
          assumed.

      (b) That own craft are actually being endangered and require assistance.

      (c) That detection of our approach appears certain and therefore that
          the need for witholding fire no longer exists.

      (d) That neither air spot nor Shore Fire Control spot is available.

      (e) That enemy batteries which are firing cannot be identified.

   2. This plan requires ships to fire on targets according to the tables below.
It is based on the times ships will come into range of the longer range guns on
shore.

   3. This plan will be placed into effect by signal.

   4. (a) H minus 300 to H minus 180.

SHIP	TARGET
NEVADA	1A
TUSCALOOSA	8A
QUINCY	8
HAWKINS	1

      (b) H minus 180 to H minus 120.

EREBUS	8
BLACK PRINCE	8A
TUSCALOOSA	1A
QUINCY	4
NEVADA	3
HAWKINS	1
ENTERPRISE	5

      (c) H minus 120 continuing.

EREBUS	8, 8A
BLACK PRINCE	12, 18
TUSCALOOSA	1A, 7A
QUINCY	4, 17
NEVADA	3, 9
HAWKINS	1, 5
FITCH (if in range)	14, 15
CORRY	13A, 14A

   5. If air spot does not materialize after H minus 40, ships continue
firing in accordance with paragraph 4(c) above. No provisions have been made for
the remaining ships of Fire Support Group as they will be engaged in beach neutralization in accordance with Appendix IV this Annex.

                                              -1-

PAGE 1 of 2 PAGES   APPENDIX TWO TO ANNEX "DOG"
                                                BATTERY NEUTRAZIZATION PLAN - PLAN ZEBRA

APPENDIX V TO ANNEX "D" to
OPERATION PLAN
No. 3-44

ENEMY COASTAL BATTERIES - UTAH AREA

(Coordinates Indicate Center of the Position)

NOTE: U/C = Under Construction

First Army Number	Grid Coordinates	No./Cal./Type Guns	Casemates	Max Range (Yards)	Facing	Eleva-tion Yards	Front (Yards)	Probable Area Covered	Comments
1	5809379	6x155mm (6.1") French guns, probably GPF	4 U/C	25,000	N	38	245	Entire Utah Area	Partially damaged by Aerial bombardment 4/25/44.
1A	36602005	4x170mm (6.7") guns	4 U/C	32,371	NE			Entire Utah Area	
2	26502680	4x240mm (9.4" or 280mm (11") guns	4 U/C	35,000 or 40000	NNE	77	1034	Entire Utah Area	
3	36830425	6x155mm (6.1") guns	2 U/C - 2 com-pleted	25,000	NE	22	254	Entire Utah Area, except Trans-port Area	Partially damaged by Aerial bombardment 4/19/44
4	35481379	6x155mm (6.1") guns	No	25,000	E	88	286	Entire Utah Area except Trans-port Area.	Photos show one case ment at 361145 (1 kilometer N.E. of 35481379).
5	53309180	4x155mm (6.1") hows	No	13,000	NW	16	118	Utah Beach: part of boat lanes and gunfire support areas	2 additional em-placements may be U/C.
6	40599802	4x155 (6.1") hows	4 U/C	13,000	NE	25	154	Utah Beach: part of boat lanes and gunfire support area.	2 possible Radar sets at 40329800 and 40369814.

APPENDIX V TO ANNEX "D"
ENEMY COASTAL BATTERIES - UTAH AREA
NAVAL GUNFIRE SUPPORT PLAN

ENEMY COASTAL BATTERIES - UTAH AREA (CONT'D)

(Coordinates Indicate Center of the Position)

NOTE: U/C = Under Construction

First Army Number	Grid Coordinates	No./Cal./Type Guns	Casemates	Max Range (Yards)	Facing	Elevation (Yards)	Front (Yards)	Probable Area Covered	Comments
7	2460 2650	4x170mm(6.7") guns	No	32,371	N	77	436	Part of Gunfire Support Area	Battery questioned 4/9/44 cover reveals there is still no apparent activity
7A	372198	6x105mm Guns or Hows	Yes	19000 or 13,000	ESE E		217	Part of gunfire support areas	New position and 1st gunfire – 6 gun battery entirely casemated in Utah area.
8	39202750	6x155mm (6.1") guns	4 U/C	25,000	N	11	339	Part of gunfire support area	
8A	39402295	4x170mm (6.7") guns	No	32,371	ESE	25	180	Entire Utah Area	New Position
9	35950219	4x105mm (4.14") Fd gun Hows	4 completed	13,000	E	24	176	Utah Beach part of boat lanes & gunfire support areas	Also reported as 155mm(6.1").
11	35342900	3x150mm (5.9)	Yes	24,000	N	-	112	Part gunfire support area.	Also reported as 105 mm Hows.
12	37762038	4x155mm (6.1") Hows	No.	13,000	E	16	209	Part gunfire support area.	
13A	36130563	4x105mm (4.14") Hows or - 75mm (2.95)	U/C	13,000 or 10,300	E	27	193	Utah Beach part of boat lanes & gunfire support areas.	

APPENDIX V TO ANNEX "D"

ENEMY COASTAL BATTERIES - UTAH AREA
NAVAL GUNFIRE SUPPORT PLAN

APPENDIX V TO ANNEX "D" TO OPERATION PLAN NO. 3-44

(Coordinates Indicate Center of the Position)

NOTE: U/C = Under Construction

First Army Number	Grid Coordinates	No./Cal./Type Guns	Casemates	Max Range (Yards)	Facing	Elevation (Yards)	Front (Yards)	Probable Area Covered	Comments
14	34370570	2x150mm (5.9")	No	14,600	ENE	33	52	Utah Beach part of boat lanes & gunfire support area	Unoccupied at last report
14A	36110801	4x105mm (4.14") Hows. or - 75mm (2.95")	Yes	13,000 or 10,300	NE	44	179	Utah Beach Part of boat lanes & gunfire support areas.	
15	34141017	4x150mm (5.9") Hows	No	13,000	E	33	154	Part gunfire support area	
16	52699154	4x75mm (2.95")	U/C	10,300	NNW	11	168	Part of Gunfire support area, boat lanes Utah Beach.	Infantry strong point with 4 small casemates U/C
17	34051390	2x105mm (4.14") Hows. 2x75mm (2.95")	Yes	13,000 10,300	E	91	131	Part of gunfire support area.	
18	41251591	3x75mm (2.95")	Yes	10,300	SSW NNE	-	-	Part of gunfire support area.	
19	599934	-	No	-	-	-	-		4 prepared but unoccupied gun positions at infantry strong-point.
20	353040	Arty Hq.							Chateau at this location probably used as Hq. for all arty in area.)

APPENDIX V TO ANNEX "D"
ENEMY COASTAL BATTERIES - UTAH AREA
NAVAL GUNFIRE SUPPORT PLAN

TOP SECRET - BIGOT - NEPTUNE

APPENDIX FIVE TO ANNEX "DOG" TO   15 May 1944
OPERATION ORDER
   No. 3-44

Serial: 00010

ENEMY BEACH DEFENSES AND STRONG POINTS - UTAH AREA

I

First Army Number.	Coordinates	Description
30	545932	Defended Locality. Infantry position in the built-up area of GRANDCAMP. Two pillboxes. One light gun at the end of the Eastern mole. Three guns, probably field, reported on the coast in this area. Elevation - 12 yards.
32	538934	Defended Locality. X Infantry position on the open coast West of GRANDCAMP. Three pillboxes. One 37mm A/Tk gun. One 47mm A/Tk gun in a light turret. One shelter. 2 x 150mm guns reported in this area. Elevation - 10 yards.
34	527934	Defended locality. X Infantry position on coast in open country NW of MAISY. Three pillboxes. One casemate, three shelters. Position surrounded by wire. Elevation - 10 yards.
36	521931	Wired and mined infantry position approx 770 yds wide and 220 yds deep. Elevation - 10 yards.
38	511922	Defended locality. X Infantry position on the coast in open country North of GEFOSSE-FONTENAY. Two pillboxes. Position surrounded by wire. Belt of mines protecting the rear of the position. Elevation - 8 yards.
40	505916	Defended locality. X Infantry position on the coast in open country NW of GEFOSSE-FONTENAY. 2 x 105mm guns in open emplacements reported here. One pillbox. One shelter. Rear of position protected by belt of mines in between wire. Elevation - 8 yards.
42	493904	Defended locality. Infantry position on the coast in open country covering the PASSE d'ISIGNY. 2 x 150mm guns in open emplacements reported here. Three pillboxes. One searchlight. One casemate. One A/Tk gun. Two shelters. Elevation - 8 yards.
44	445891	Small bridge. Elevation 6 yards.
46	448910	Defended locality. Infantry position on the coast at LE GRAND VEY. One 75mm gun. One A/Tk gun in tank turret with co-axial MG reported. Rear of position protected by wire. Elevation 8 yards.

PAGE 5 of 9   APPENDIX FIVE TO ANNEX "DOG"
                                               NAVAL GUNFIRE SUPPORT PLAN

Below: The Naval Minesweeping chart for both Utah and Omaha approaches. AREA 60 covered the overlap of the two sectors.

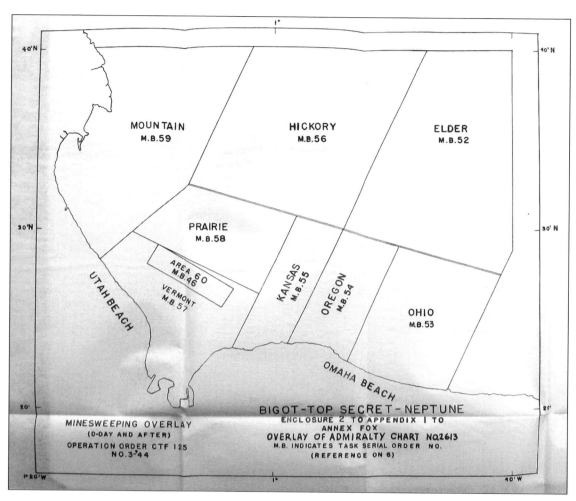

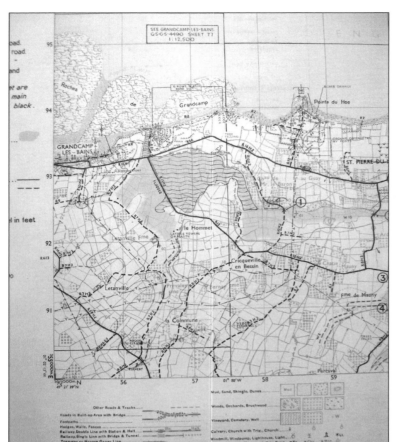

This GSGS Map is marked May 1944. It continues to show the complete removal of one of the guns at Pointe du Hoc. It was the one which had originally been on concrete position No.5.

The map states that there are four guns in pits and one is still in the open. Depending upon interpretation – it could now mean that there are only four guns which are operational and one is still in place, but damaged.

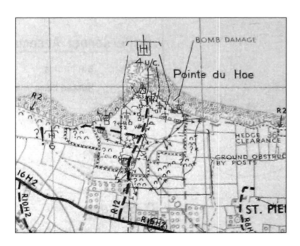

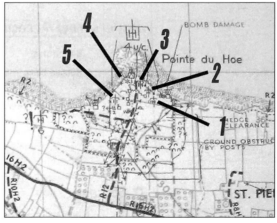

Next page: The same map showing a concentration of German forces to the rear of Pointe du Hoc – marked 'TPS' (Troop Concentration) – this location is approximately 1 mile inland from the Pointe – south of the Grandcamp-les-Bains to Vierville road.

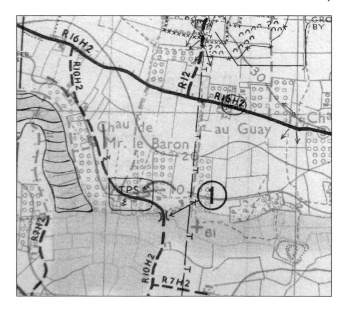

Below: The same map shows a detailed illustration of the Radar Station layout and gun positions at Pointe et Raz de la Percée.

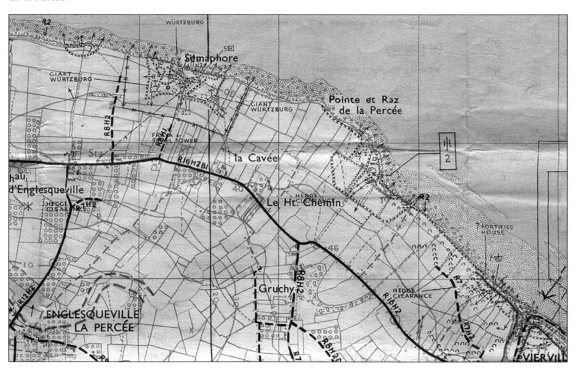

Below: The 15 May S-2 Intelligence report on the *estimation of the enemy situation* – highlighted are the major Ranger targets.

Ref No.
D-4

Hqs 26th RCT
APO #1, US Army
15 May 1944

ANNEX NO. 2)
                    :—S-2 ESTIMATE OF THE ENEMY SITUATION #1
To FO NO. 4)

: By Authority of :
: CG, 1st US Inf Div :
: 15 May 1944 :
: Initials: JKR :

COPY NO.   58

(b) The 726th Infantry Regiment with headquarters at BAYEUX, has three battalions. One battalion, with headquarters at ISIGNY, is thought to be responsible for the defenses around the mouth of the DOUVE, but not including CARENTAN. Its section includes the positions on the VIRE estuary and those along Beach 48 on the eastern approach to ISIGNY. Another battalion is thought to have its headquarters at GRANDCAMP-LES-BAINS and it is believed to be responsible for the defense of the coast from a point 4,000 yards west of GRANDCAMP to LONGUES. (This battalion is holding a 21 mile coastal front or approximately the same frontage as the entire regiment on its east flank.) A third battalion with headquarters at BAYEUX may be holding the coastal sector PORT-EN-BESSIN - LONGUES. It is thought that this is the reserve battalion of the 726th Infantry Regiment.

(c) The 726th Infantry Regiment is supported by 4 batteries of artillery in addition to a considerable number of close support infantry and anti-tank guns in the coastal strongpoints. Three of these are field artillery batteries, two located about 1500 yards southwest of MAISY, and one at VAUX-SUR-AURE north of BAYEUX. The 4th is the second battery, 832nd armored coastal artillery battalion at POINTE-DU HOE. Two new artillery battery positions are now thought to be under construction in the 726th Infantry area, one about a 1,000 yards east of POINTE DU HOE, the other 2,000 yards northeast of LONGUEVILLE. At the present time no guns are reported in these positions.

b. Enemy Defenses.

(1) General.

(a) Known enemy defenses PORT-EN-BESSIN - ISIGNY consists of a series of strongpoints on the coast or slightly inland. Most of them are reinforced infantry positions covering exits from the beaches. Others furnish local protection to enemy coastal batteries and special installations such as the radar station west of POINTE ET RAS DE LA PERCEE.

(d) Aerial photographs taken in March 1944 indicate that considerable work has been accomplished since December 1943 in the beach defense areas. The construction of the anti-tank ditches across the beach exits north of COLLEVILLE and ST LAURENT, and the erection of new pillboxes and shelters in beach strongpoints are examples. From other sources, indications show that the enemy is hastening his defense construction program along the entire channel coast, and that for the first time all-around defenses of larger inland towns, such as CAUMONT and BAYEUX, are being prepared.

(2) Beach Defenses.

(a) For detailed study of enemy defenses see overlay Appendix #3 to Annex #2 "Overlay - Enemy Defenses".

(b) Infantry Positions.

From PORT-EN-BESSIN to GRANDCAMP there are 30 occupied positions including the radar station and the coastal battery. These are manned it is estimated by 5 or 6 companies exclusive of the coastal batteries and specialist personnel of the radar station. From the position northwest of MAISY to that on the dykes overlooking the VIRE estuary at 472880, there are 15 defended areas holding an estimated 2 to 2½ companies. Also there are 2 field artillery batteries southwest of MAISY. Garrisons of the individual strongpoints are listed below; these are estimated on the basis of size and installations of each position:

3.   COLLEVILLE-SUR-MER.

a.   Defended Locality – (598890). Infantry position on the coast in open country northeast of COLLEVILLE-SUR-MER: 2 pillboxes and 4 shelters, 2 rows of wire are on the flanks and rear with mines between on the south and east. There are mines on the beach to the north of this position. Position is garrisoned by about 2 squads.

b.   Defended Locality – (593894). An infantry position on the coast in open country north of COLLEVILLE-SUR-MER: 1 pillbox; houses have been demolished in the area. Garrison – approximately one squad.

c.   Defended Locality – (587895). Infantry position on the coast north of COLLEVILLE-SUR-MER; 3 light infantry guns, probably 75mm; 1 artillery OP; 4 shelters; 1 pillbox; 1 casemate for a light gun; position surrounded by wire and garrisoned by approximately one platoon.

4.   ST LAURENT-SUR-MER.

a.   Defended Post – (578896). A small infantry position inland from the coast: 1 AA machine gun; 1 searchlight; 1 pillbox; 2 shelters, surrounded by wire and garrisoned by approximately one squad.

b.   Defended Locality – (577900). Infantry position on the coast near ST LAURENT-SUR-MER: Position is surrounded by wire, with mines to the southeast; the position contains 1 pillbox, 1 shelter, and 1 AT gun is reported there but this/unconfirmed.

c.   Defended Locality under construction – (574899). 3 pillboxes or gun casemates under construction near the edge of the plateau. 2 shelters under construction on the plateau. 1 small ammunition depot under construction. The future garrison is estimated at about 2 squads.

d.   Defended Locality – (568903). An infantry strongpoint 200 yards inland from the coast near ST LAURENT-SUR-MER; contains 2 pillboxes, 1 concrete OP, 3 shelters completed and 1 large shelter is under construction; 1 AA machine gun; position is surrounded by wire with mines to the front and also probably to the rear. Garrison is approximately 1 platoon.

e.   Defended Locality – (565905). Infantry position on the coast in built-up areas of ST LAURENT-SUR-MER; 1 AA machine gun, 3 pill boxes; 2 shelters; the beach is reported probably mined; the position is surrounded by wire and garrisoned by approximately 2 squads.

f.   Defended Post – (563907). A small infantry position on the coast in built up areas of ST LAURENT-SUR-MER containing 1 pillbox and garrisoned by approximately 1 squad.

5.   VIERVILLE-SUR-MER.

a.   Defended Locality – (555913). Infantry position on the coast near VIERVILLE-SUR-MER: 2 shelters; 1 pillbox; 1 81mm mortar; 1 AA machine gun; possibly 1 75mm infantry gun; position is surrounded by wire and garrisoned by approximately 1 squad.

b.   Defended Locality – (548915). An infantry position on the coast in VIERVILLE-SUR-MER; 2 pillboxes; 1 shelter; an AT gun, possibly 75mm reported; 1 AA machine gun; an AT ditch is reported across the road at 548916, (not confirmed by aerial photographs). The position is surrounded by wire on the flanks and rear with a mine belt to the south and east. Garrison for this position is approximately 1 platoon.

c. Defended Locality - (945918). An infantry
position on the coast immediately west of VIERVILLE-SUR-MER containing 1 pillbox and 1 gun casemate for a light gun. The position is surrounded by wire
and garrisoned by approximately 1 squad.

d. Defended Locality - (635928). An infantry posi-
tion on the coast in open country at POINTE ET RAZ DE LA PERCEE. The position
contains 2 light guns, 3 pillboxes and 1 shelter. Mobile flak is often present in this area. An artillery OP has been reported here. Position is surrounded by wire and garrisoned by approximately 1 platoon.

(c) Pillboxes.

There are approximately 21 concrete pillboxes cover-
ing Beach 46. About 10 of these are located on the flat area between the beach
and the plateau and are sited to provide bands of grazing fire on the beach.
The remainder are on high ground immediately to the rear of the beach. They
are placed to deliver plunging fire on the beach and on approaching craft. They
also cover corridors leading inland from the beach. Many of the houses on the
beach have been reported fortified and converted into pillboxes. There are
about 8 pillboxes in the vicinity of PORT-EN-BESSIN, 4 covering the beach exit
of GRANDCAMP, 3 on the beach at GRANDCAMP and 3 on the strongpoint west of
GRANDCAMP.

(d) Wire.

There are no continuous bands of wire entanglements
covering the length of Beach 46. There is, however, a band on the beach from
the strongpoint at 687895 north of COLLEVILLE to about 200 yards east of the
strongpoint at 677900 north of ST LAURENT, and another band from the corridor
at VIERVILLE-SUR-MER along the escarpment to POINTE ET RAZ DE LA PERCEE. With
the exception of the strongpoints northeast of COLLEVILLE at 698890 and that
at VIERVILLE (648915), all strongpoints in the rear of the beach are completely surrounded by wire, usually single bands. The excepted strongpoints are
protected by a band on the flank and rear. Strongpoints in the vicinity of ST
HONORINE-DES-PERTES, PORT-EN-BESSIN, The radar station, POINTE DU HOE and GRAND-
CAMP are protected by wire to the flanks and rear. Inland strongpoints only
are completely surrounded by wire.

(e) Mines.

No continuous belt of mines has been reported along
Beach 46. Vulnerable areas including main exits have, however, been mined.

2. COLLEVILLE.

a. 701890 - 700892 - Probable mine belt.

b. 6989 - Several four-row mine belts in this
area. Quite possible some may be dummy belts.

13

3. ST LAURENT.

   a. 677899 - Mines between wire.

   b. 668905 - Mines reported in front and possibly in rear of strongpoint.

4. ST LAURENT to VIERVILLE.

   a. 655906 - 652914 - Mines reported every 30 feet along side of road and in gardens of villas. Three rows.

5. VIERVILLE to POINTE ET RAZ DE LA PERCEE.

   a. 647917 - 637925 - Cliffs reported mined.

   b. 648915 - Mines between wire in rear of strong-point.

(f) Obstacles.

1. Information available at the present time indicates that there are no underwater obstacles along the principle part of Beach 46. There is however indication that the enemy is placing underwater obstacles along many beaches in the west. February coverage indicates newly placed underwater obstacles in the beach area about 17 miles east of Beach 46. Recent information indicates that many of these obstacles are breaking up and becoming displaced due to the surf. Underwater obstacles constructed on other beaches in the NEPTUNE area have generally been placed 75 to 150 yards from the high water line. If so placed on Beach 46, they would be exposed until about 3 hours before high water.

2. The two sand bars off the beach northwest of VIERVILLE-SUR-MER are covered by 24 feet of water at high tide, and by 1 to 2 feet of water at lowest tide. There are three runnels extending parallel to the beach for its entire length. At low tide these runnels are exposed and are filled with water varying in depth from 9 inches in the upper runnel to 2 feet 8 inches in the lower.

3. There is a strip of shingle, about 15 yards wide, extending along the entire beach near the high water mark. It is composed of stones about 2 inches in diameter and forms a ridge with a gradient on the lower side of 1/8 to 1/10.

4. A seawall 8 feet in height extends from the exit at 649917 to a point 500 yards to the southeast at 554914. At the latter point there is a break of 200 yards and then a wall 2 feet 6 inches high (reduced to this height by drifting sands) extends 2,000 yards to the southeast to 573902. A series of low wooden groynes extend at right angles to the seawall between 558912 - 561909.

5. Anti-tank ditches have been constructed recently across the beach exits to COLLEVILLE and ST LAURENT. That north of COLLEVILLE runs from 694894 - 590895 - 589895 with a short break at the strongpoint at 692894. Another runs across the low ground near the entrance to ST LAURENT along the RUQUET River from 583897 - 578898. This ditch is still under construction. A third ditch blocks the exit from LES MOULINS at 555906.

6. The ramp to the beach at ST HONORINE has been blown.

7. The following other obstacles have been located:

   a. PORT-EN-BESSIN.

      755859 - 7 fixed road blocks,
                1 movable road block.

753873 - Fixed road block.

755879 - Anti-Tank wall.

723885 - Movable road block.

b. COLLEVILLE.

589893 - Movable road block.

577900 - 576899 - Wall road block, with 12 foot
gap; road block is 8 feet high and 6
feet thick.

594905 - 3 movable wire road blocks, probably
knife rests.

c. VIERVILLE.

648917 - Tank trap reported near road; trench
5 feet 6 inches wide covered with tar-
paulin.

648917 - Round topped wall 5 feet thick and
7 feet high diagonally across road
in 2 staggered 18 foot sections; gap
3 feet wide reported.

(3) Artillery.

(a) In the coastal strongpoints between PORT-EN-BESSIN and
ISIGNY there are 20 light guns or gun howitzers of 75mm or 105mm calibre and
7 anti-tank guns, the largest of which is a 75mm gun.

2. COLLEVILLE.

a. 687895 - 3 light infantry guns, probably 75mm,
in strongpoint on the hill.

3. VIERVILLE.
    a. 655913 – One light infantry gun, possibly
        75mm, in strongpoint on the plateau.
    b. 648915 – One 75mm anti-tank gun guarding
        beach exit road.
    c. 635928 – 2 light infantry guns, 75mm, in
        strongpoint on bluff.
4. GRANDCAMP-LES-BAINS.
    a. 545934 – 3 105mm howitzers in built up area
        with a light gun, 75mm, at the end
        of the eastern mole.
    b. 538934 – One 37mm and one 47mm anti-tank gun
        in beach strongpoint.
5. GEFOSSE-FONTENAY.
    a. 505916 – 2 105mm gun howitzers in beach strong-
        point.
    b. 493904 – One 150mm infantry gun and one light
        anti-tank gun in beach strongpoint.
6. ISIGNY.
    a. 493877 – 2 light anti-tank guns in strong-
        point.

(b) In addition to the artillery in the coastal strongpoints, there are four enemy artillery batteries in the assault area or in
position in adjacent defense sectors from which they could bring fire into
the assault area.

    1. VAUX-SUR-AURE.
        a. 793832 – 4 (?) 105mm field gun-howitzers
            (also have been reported as 150mm).
            Range about 13,000 yards. Emplace-
            ments: Circular pits 30 feet in di-
            ameter. OP: unlocated; believed to
            be on high ground near COMMES. Com-
            mand Post: unlocated; possibly on
            edge of wood in rear of gun position.
            Billeting area: some huts and houses
            in wooded park in rear. Communica-
            tions: telephone (overhead cable).

    2. POINTE-DU-HOE.
        a. 586937 – 6 155mm (6.1 inches). French guns,
            possibly type GPF, range 22,000 to
            25,000 yards. Guns on wheel mount-
            ings, the wheels being secured to
            the central pivot of a concrete
            emplacement about 40 feet in dia-
            meter. Each gun is camouflaged with
            netting; there is no turret or gun
            shield. B.O.P. reinforced concrete
            shelter on headland in front of gun
            position. Location of OPs unknown,
            shelters and magazines are under-
            ground and are constructed with rein-
            forced concrete, and are connected
            with gun emplacements by trenches
            which are partly covered over.

    3. SOUTHWEST MAISY.
        a. 528915 – 4 field guns (thought to be 75mm
            with range of about 10,000 yards).
            Guns are mounted in open circular
            pits about 25 feet in diameter. The
            battery faces the VIRE estuary.
        b. 533198 – 4 155mm (6.1 inches) howitzers.
            Range estimated at 13,000 yards (?).
            Howitzers are mounted in open circu-
            lar pits, 35 feet in diameter and
            the battery faces the VIRE estuary.

> c. New emplacements for artillery have recently been located at MONTIGNY (523887), near ST PIERRE-DU-MONT (598934), and southwest of MAISY at (530913). All appear to be four-gun battery positions; the first two are not reported manned as yet.
> d. Two railway guns, 280mm, range 40,000 yards, are believed to be in the vicinity of CARENTAN; and from 2 to 5 railway guns of the same type and calibre have been reported as recently as January 1944 at TORIGNY (5354).
> e. The only major unit of AA artillery in the assault area is the 12 gun battery of 88mm dual-purpose guns which has been reported but not confirmed in the vicinity of HALT (4882) west of ISIGNY.
> f. No Nebelwerfers have been reported in the assault area of the CT 26.
>
> (5) Radar Stations.
> Only one enemy radar station located about 1500 yards west of POINTE ET RAZ DE LA PERCEE (525934). This is a coast watching station and contains one frame, and two giant Wurzburgs. The range of this station is from 10 to 35 miles.
>
> c. Enemy Morale.
> (1) From intelligence reports, the morale of the coast defense divisions, of which the 709th, 711th and the 716th are typical, is not good. They contain a good 25% of non-Germans and a further 50% of men who, in varying degrees, are elderly, juvenile, tired or unfit. Considering the length of time they have been training for static defense roles, they should be reasonably good. In general, their equipment is second rate, their motor transport is practically nil and supporting elements and services are very inadequate. It is believed that the combat value of these defensive divisions is materially less than that of a first class infantry division.
> (2) The morale of troops in offensive divisions is better than that of troops in static divisions. Their combat efficiency will depend on their strength; the status of their equipment and the percentage of foreigners within the unit.

On 16 May 1944 the Rangers were given a US Army booklet concerning capture by the enemy, written by the Chief of Staff, G.C. Marshall. It reads as follows:

16 May 1944

A Company 5th Rangers – Swanage, Dorset.
Paragraphs 1a and b of letter, HQ V Corps, subject, 'Desertion' dated 21 April 1944, were read to the members of A Company present at a formation of the detachment at 0845 hours, on 16 May 1944.

5th Rangers – Companies B – F, Medical and HQ – Swanage, Dorset.

2nd Rangers – Companies A – F, Medical and HQ – Swanage, Dorset.

PRISONERS OF WAR

Commanders of combat units and other units responsible for the handling of prisoners of war will insure that the personnel of such units have a thorough knowledge of the principles to be observed in relation to prisoners of war, as set forth in 'Rules of Warfare'. Particular emphasis will be placed on the provisions of the Geneva Convention of July 27th 1929, relative to the treatment of prisoners of war.

Attention will be especially directed to the fact that the rights of prisoners of war, as set forth by treaty, are not theoretical, but are binding on all US troops in the same manner as are the laws and constitution of the United States. Violation of such rights by US troops may result in retaliation by the enemy in the form of reprisal.

Questions requiring interpretation of the Geneva Convention of July 27th 1929 relative to the treatment of prisoners of war, will be submitted to this headquarters…

Signed Chief of Staff R.B. Lovett. Brigadier General, USA, Adjutant General.

John Reville Lt. F Company 5th Battalion: *Two weeks before D-Day we were finally told where we were going to land. We were behind barbed wire so we couldn't let the cat out of the bag. It was all about Pointe du Hoc. I remember Schneider – he had been in combat before. I do remember him making a speech… 'don't kill prisoners – for the simple fact that you can't keep that a secret – it will come out and what will happen – it is morally wrong and is going to make your job harder. When that German in there thinks that if he comes out he is going to get shot, he won't – don't kill prisoners.'*

17 May 1944   Navy Report dated 17 May: *A number of reconnaissance landings on the French coast were carried out, under arrangements by Chief of Combined Operations, to investigate the extent of recently reported obstructions on beaches below high water line. On the night of the 17th and 18th two officers failed to return from one of these missions in the PAS DE CALAIS Area.*

Results of these sorties suggested that the obstructions so far inspected, could be adequately dealt with in an assault, particularly when tackled dry-shod.

5th Rangers – Companies A – F, Medical and HQ – Dorchester, Dorset.

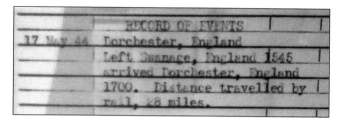

Medical personnel started to be distributed and assigned to individual companies.

A Company 2nd Rangers – Dorchester, Dorset.
Pfcs William K. Doinoff was attached to A Company from Headquarters Company 2nd Btn.
T/5 Donald F. Mentzer and Pfc. Robert C. Lambert joined A Company from the Medical Detachment of the 2nd Btn.
Alerted for departure – then left Swanage, Dorset at 1530 hours by train and arrived in Dorchester at 1800 hours.
B Company 2nd Rangers – Dorchester, Dorset.
Pfc. Frederick A. O'Neal was attached and joined this company for Duty from the Medical Detachment of Headquarters Company 2nd Btn.
B Company departed Swanage, Dorset by train at 1530 hours and arrived in Dorchester, Dorset at 1800 hours. Alerted for departure.
C Company 2nd Rangers – Dorchester, Dorset.
S/Sgt. Priesman was appointed to the rank of T/Sgt.
Pfc. James A. Machan was attached from Headquarters Company 2nd Btn.
T/5 Randall R. Rinker was attached from the Medical Detachment of the 2nd Btn for Duty, rations and quarters.
C Company departed Swanage, Dorset by train at 1530 hours and arrived in Dorchester, Dorset at 1800 hours. Alerted for departure.
D Company 2nd Rangers – Swanage, Dorset. Alerted for departure.
E Company 2nd Rangers – Swanage, Dorset. No change. Alerted for departure.
F Company 2nd Rangers – Swanage, Dorset. No change. Alerted for departure.
Medical Detachment 2nd Rangers – Dorchester, Dorset.
The Medical Detachment departed Swanage, Dorset by train at 1530 hours and arrived in Dorchester, Dorset at 1800 hours.
Headquarters Company 2nd Rangers – Swanage, Dorset. No change. Alerted for departure.

On 17 May the US Army G-2 Intelligence reports on enemy strengths and disposition became available. Copies of these (five in total) were signed out by Colonel Rudder.

Of particular interest here is the location of the nearest German armoured units to the Omaha Sector – which are shown to be some distance way. The estimate is that armoured units would only become involved against the Omaha landings on either D+1 or D+2 at the earliest, thus ensuring that the Rangers have time to complete their allotted missions on D-Day – before the Germans have time to react in force in the days that followed.

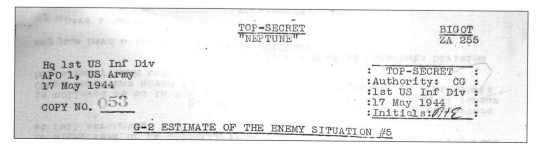

1. SUMMARY OF THE ENEMY SITUATION.

    a. <u>Enemy Order of Battle</u>.

        (1) <u>Forces in the Assault Area</u>.

            (a) Train movements from the CAEN area in late April indicate that the 716th Division may have moved from the assault area to the BREST PENINSULA No new identification from this area, however, has been received.

            (b) The presence of enough flatcars in BAYEUX to transport a battalion may indicate that at least one armored battalion is in the vicinity.

        (2) <u>Adjacent Units</u>.

           No change.

        (3) <u>Enemy Reserves</u>.

            (a) <u>Local Reserves</u>.

                The 21st Panzer Division has moved to the CAEN-ARGENTAN area. (See Estimate #1 for details of organization).

            (b) <u>Mobile Reserves</u>.

                <u>1</u>. 17th SS Panzergrenadier Division GOETZ von BERLICHINGEN has moved to the RENNES area from THOUARS. (See Estimate #1 for details of organization). Three tank battalions have been reported with the division but no definite identification has been received to substantiate this report.

                <u>2</u>. An unidentified panzer division has moved to ORLEANS from the east. This division is at full strength.

                <u>3</u>. 1st SS Panzer Division ADOLPH HITLER recently arrived in BELGIUM is reported possibly moving to BRITTANY.

                <u>4</u>. An unidentified infantry division has moved to NIORT east of LA ROCHELLE from the east. The division is reported at full strength.

                <u>5</u>. An unidentified panzer corps headquarters is believed to be in NORMANDY or BRITTANY. This may be 1st SS Panzer Corps which has moved to FORMERIE northwest of BEAUVAIS. This Corps has a heavy tank battalion attached.

                <u>6</u>. It is believed that 3d Parachute Division may now have a third regiment in BRITTANY.

TOP-SECRET   BIGOT
"NEPTUNE"

b. Enemy Defenses.

(1) Beach Defenses.

(a) As of 12 May 1944 the line of hedgehogs on Beach 46 runs from 64859191 to 69128956. Each segment of the line, previously containing one row of hedgehogs, now contains three or more rows staggered in depth. Gaps between segments have been filled. At 68808965 wiring among the hedgehogs has started. Approximately 3,000 hedgehogs have been emplaced.

(b) Two rows of ramp type obstacles about 55 feet apart have been placed in front of the hedgehogs. One row extends from 64529208 to 68868973 (200 units) and from 68748972 to 69438949 (41 units); the other row runs from 64509205 to 64899191 (21 units) and from 65549147 to 66989062 (72 units). The ramp type obstacles are the single pole type. The ramp member rests on single supports at the end and center.

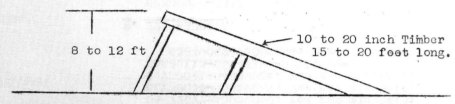

8 to 12 ft   10 to 20 inch Timber
                              15 to 20 feet long.

Steel ramps or the inverted V type ramp have not yet made their appearance on Beach 46.

(c) The single row of stakes first noticed on cover of 25 April 1944 now extends from 64539214 to 68778978 running behind the line of Element "C" and in front of the foremost row of ramp obstacles. The stakes are approximately 60 feet apart except for a short distance opposite LES MOULINS (from 66509095 to 66729082) where they are spaced at 10 foot intervals. From 68888980 to 68958978 and from 69058974 to 69128972 there are short rows of stakes in front of the Element "C". A band of stakes four rows deep and staggered in depth runs from 69128953 to 70178932 closing off the eastern edge of the beach.

(d) The Element "C" runs from 64919197 to 65329171 (32 units), from 65429166 to 67179067 (103 units), and from 68768983 to 69838942 (47 units). Very little increase in Element "C" has occurred since Estimate #4.

(e) No further evidence of the mining of underwater obstacles on Beach 46 has been found. Mines have however been reported attached to stakes on beaches out of the NEPTUNE area. It is thought these are ordinary Teller mines. A report of an experienced tactical reconnaissance pilot states there is a single line of mines some 400 yards offshore and half submerged at low water between VIERVILLE and ST PIERRE DU MONT. These, if they exist, are probably naval mines.

(f) A sketch map showing the placement of these obstacles is attached as Appendix "A".

(2) Inland Defenses.

(a) New mined areas have been located as follows:

1. VIERVILLE.

63959220-64079228: Six row minebelt.
64029220-64109213: Five row minebelt.
64159228-64179213: Six row minebelt.
64909146-65109141: Three row minebelt.
64879077-65059060: Two row minebelt.
65139056-65039037: Two row minebelt.
64739041-64929036: Two row minebelt.
65539113-65549100-65719080-
    65849082-65869086: Three row minebelt.

2. ST. LAURENT.

66308878-66458868-66608872: Two row minebelt.
67538983-67458970-67408970-67358966-
    67338945-67228930-67468916-67648900-
    67648893-67808890-67888898-67988904-
    68009010-67909012-67829010: Three row
                                    minebelt.
67878896-68038896-67978906: Three row mine-
                                    belt.
68128914-68198905: Three row minebelt.

3. COLLEVILLE.

68108980-68288973: Five or six row minebelt.
68238970-68358968: Five or six row minebelt.
68408970-68508968: Five or six row minebelt.
68438960-68558957: Five or six row minebelt.
68598966-68668962: Five or six row minebelt.
68438893-68398883-68408873-68488869-
    68458862-68408862: Three row minebelt.
68398852-68358850: Three row minebelt.
68338891-68498882: Three row minebelt.

TOP-SECRET   BIGOT
"NEPTUNE"

4. GRANDCAMP.

55989323-56079330: Five row minebelt.
56049324-56169327: Five row minebelt.
56049333-56139340: Five row minebelt.

Mines completely cover area bounded by the
GRANDCAMP sluice on the west, the highway on the south, ocean on the
north, and the road on the east from 57259360-57309390. There is a
total of eighteen (18) belts of either five (5) or six (6) rows.

5. MAISY.

51649251-51839274: Five or six row minebelt.
51829288-51969289: Five or six row minebelt.
51909240-52019260: Six row minebelt.

(b) Photographic cover of 9 May 1944 shows several
fields back of Beach 46 broken by a regular pattern of shallow excavations about three (3) feet in diameter and sixty (60) feet apart.
The holes are not deep enough to cast a shadow, but are easily seen
because of the light colored spoil. It is possible mines have been
sown in these areas, although the method used is unusual. It is also
possible these holes are meant for steel rails or some other type of
tank obstacle. The fields in which these holes appear are located
as follows:

636910   678884
640914   697884
645901   697881
649905   723879
653895   726878
657890   727877
662896   728878
664889   730878
667883   731876
671890

TOP-SECRET
"NEPTUNE"   BIGOT

(c) New Pillboxes.

54409280: Possible pillbox.
59899380: Possible pillbox.
66609050: Two possible pillboxes.
67508990: Possible pillbox.
71168875: Possible pillbox.

(d) New Shelters or Bunkers.

50658905: Two shelters.
51109099, 51139130, 51209080,
  51359127, 51539117, 51579116,
  51649137, 51709159, 51829172,
  51969145, 51989152, 52039152,
  52289113, 52319120, 51139115: One shelter at
                                    each point.
624935: Eight new shelters under construction.
75028800: Possible shelter.
75158443: Shelter.
75108440: Shelter under construction.
75208445: Shelter under construction.

(e) A new anti-tank ditch has been dug from 68628944 to 68728947 to protect the strong-point on the western side of the COLLEVILLE exit. An extension to anti-tank ditch at LES MOULINS has been dug from 66209076 to 66279080.

2. CONCLUSION.

(a) Enemy Capabilities.

(1) Capabilities (1) through (3), no change.

(2) Capability (4) changes to include the possibility of the counterattack from BAYEUX including up to a Battalion of tanks. These tanks may be part of the 21st Armored Division.

(3) Capabilities (5), (6) and (7), no change.

(4) Capability (8) changes to support for the 352d Infantry Division counterattacks by elements of SS Division GOETZ von BERLICHINGEN. Two battalions of tanks and other elements might be utilized.

TOP-SECRET   BIGOT
"NEPTUNE"

        (3) Of the seven German armored Divisions in FRANCE, BELGIUM and HOLLAND six are now located within 150 miles of the NEPTUNE Assault area. This is based on the assumption that the move of SS Division ADOLF HITLER into the area is confirmed. Present known dispositions indicate that SS Division HITLER JUGEND and 21st Panzer Division are capable of intervening on D-day, and although it is probable that due to terrain and dispositions they will move against the British, it is possible that elements of 21st Panzer Division may counterattack in the 1st US Infantry Division area on D-day. On D/1 or D/2 it is possible for any one of these six armored Divisions to be engaged on the 1st US Infantry Division front, but it is considered likely that GOETZ von BERLICHINGEN will be the first to make its weight felt in this sector.

                                Robert F Evans
                           ROBERT F. EVANS,
                           Lt. Col., G.S.C.,
                           A. C. of S., G-2.

APPENDIX A – Sketch Map showing Underwater Obstacles Beach 46.

DISTRIBUTION:

	No. Copies	Copy Nos.
CG, V Corps	50	1 - 50
*CG, 21st Army Gp		
*CG, 1st Army		
Div QM, 1st US Inf Div	1	112
CO, CT 116	10	117 - 126
CO, CT 16	10	127 - 136
CO, CT 18	10	137 - 146
CO, CT 26	10	147 - 156
CO, Ranger Force	5	157 - 161
CO, 1st Engr (C) Bn	1	162

18 May 1944

5th Rangers – Companies A – F, Medical and HQ – Dorchester, Dorset.

A, B & C Companies 2nd Rangers – Dorchester, Dorset. No change. Alerted for departure.

D Company 2nd Rangers – Swanage, Dorset.

Pfc. Socha went from Duty to absent (sick) to the 95th General Hospital, Ringwood, Dorset.

T/5 Mendenhall went from sick in quarters to Duty. Alerted for departure.

E Company 2nd Rangers – Swanage, Dorset. Alerted for departure.

Medical Detachment 2nd Rangers – Dorchester, Dorset. Alerted for departure.

Headquarters Company 2nd Rangers – Swanage, Dorset. Alerted for departure.

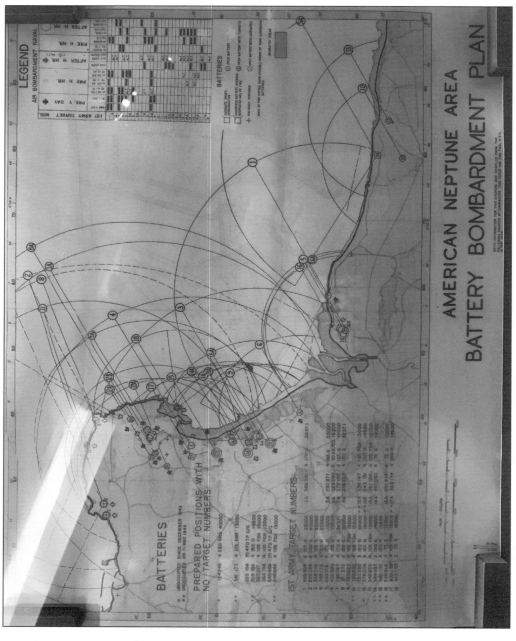

AMERICAN NEPTUNE AREA
BATTERY BOMBARDMENT PLAN

On the 18th May the Army Intelligence issued their regular update on the Neptune Battery Bombardment Plan. It indicates Pointe du Hoc covering a large area of both US landing beaches and the boat approach lanes. The 3 batteries at Maisy are indicated to be able to hit the southern end of Utah and the Western end of Omaha Beaches.

The text shown on the map for each Battery reads:

Target No 1 = 6 x 155 G (Gun)   Range 25,000
Target No 5 = 4 x 155 H (Howitzer) Range 13,000

Target No 16 = 4 x 75 G (Gun)   Range 13,000
Target No 16A = 4 x 75 G (Gun)   Range 13,000

19 May 1944

5th Rangers – Companies A – F, Medical and HQ – Dorchester, Dorset.
A Company 2nd Rangers – Dorchester, Dorset. Alerted for departure.

Frank Kennard: *At Swanage along with Wilkin I was billeted in the gardener's cottage (on a large estate). A British signals company occupied the estate mansion. My host family was Mr & Mrs Reese-Reynolds and their two young daughters (under 10). I frequently baby-sat for them, but otherwise I was pretty much a 'flunky' for Wilkin. I paid a guinea a week for room and board. The line companies were scattered. I never got over to the Isle of Wight.*

Lt. Kennard did not undertake much of the standard Ranger training because of his speciality with the half-tracks. He did not, for example, have to undergo the intensive and varied weapons training the other men did in the surrounding area.

Frank Kennard: *In Swanage we had multiple numbers of climbing ropes hung from tall trees. But I didn't practise on them. The men had extensive practice on them, but not me, as I was going to ride off the beach in a half-track!*

Despite the daily training, the men would visit the town every evening and many girls became regular dates for the men. This blissful existence lasted for twelve days and on 19 May they left Swanage for the marshalling area at Camp D5 in Broadmayne, near Dorchester.

Maurice Prince: *On May 19 we departed from Swanage to reach our new area. We were in trim fighting condition and ready to tackle the German Supermen. We couldn't help but feel that it was now just a small matter of time before we made the Channel crossing that was to bring us into mortal conflict with our sworn enemy. And we were right in that assumption, for the next stop in our journey brought us to the marshalling area just outside of Dorchester from where we made our final preparations to take up the challenge of the fanatic Nazis, who sat so smugly and contently in fortified positions on the high ground, covering the entrances of the beaches. Just daring us to come over.*

B Company 2nd Rangers – Swanage, Dorset. Alerted for departure.
C Company 2nd Rangers – Dorchester, Dorset. Alerted for departure.
D Company 2nd Rangers – Swanage, Dorset. Alerted for departure.
E Company 2nd Rangers – Swanage, Dorset. Alerted for departure.
F Company 2nd Rangers – Swanage, Dorset. Alerted for departure.
Medical Detachment 2nd Rangers – Dorchester, Dorset. Alerted for departure.
Headquarters Company 2nd Rangers – Swanage, Dorset.

On 19 May Major General Huebner started to visit each and every unit within his command, that would be landing on D-Day.

HEADQUARTERS 1ST INFANTRY DIVISION
APO #1, U. S. Army

O-3 (JOURNAL*

Time : (From 0001
(To 2400

Date 19 May 1944   CP Location LANGTON HOUSE, BLANDFORD
ENGLAND

TIME	NO.	FROM	SYNOPSIS	REC'D VIA	DISPOSITION#
0001	1		Journal opened		
1100	2		Maj Gen HUEBNER, CG 1st Inf Div visited all Inf and Arty Bns that will participate in forthcoming operations.		
2400	3		Journal closed		

NOTES:
*Delete one.
"Rec'd Via" column will indicate how message was transmitted, i.e., Tp - telephone; Rad - radio; Tgp - telegraph; Tpe - teletype.
#Following abbreviations only will be used in this column, other information will be written out: M - Noted on situation map; J - Appended to journal (applies to Overlays, Msg blanks, written orders, etc.); CG, C/S, etc. - indicates information passed on to Officer indicated; T- indicates information disseminated to units or troops, as indicated in text of message.
(Revised 3 Jan.'44)

- 1 -

The regular statement of Ranger personnel and vehicle figures were issued.

<u>Page 3 Revised as
of 19 May 1944</u>

TROOP LIST

BEACH OMAHA - FORCE "O"

BIGOT
NEPTUNE
Annex No. 2 to
V CORPS OPERATIONS
PLAN NEPTUNE
(REVISED)

UNIT	VEHICLES	PERSONNEL
2nd Ranger Bn	38	554
5th Ranger Bn	30	533

BIGOT
NEPTUNE
Annex No 2 to
V CORPS OPERATIONS
PLAN NEPTUNE
(REVISED)

TROOP LIST

BEACH OMAHA

BUILD-UP PRIORITY

(Shuttle Service Beginning D -/- 2)

ITME	FIRST ARMY NUMBER	UNIT	ASSIGNMENT OR ATTACHMENT	VEHICLES	PERSONNEL
124	A2721-2722	2nd and 5th Ranger Bns	Atchd V	26	38

Below: 19 May. An aerial reconnaissance photograph of Omaha Beach. It is captioned 'Element "C" partially buried. It is believed that here the obstacles have sunk into the sand.' The next photograph is captioned 'Hedgehogs partially buried. It is believed that in this case the sand built up around the obstacles'.

Below: Naval planning documents showing the flow of landing craft towards the beach – and the flanking positions of the battleships, cruisers and destroyers alongside them. Followed by the breakdown of the Naval Fire Plan including the Naval personnel attached to the Rangers.

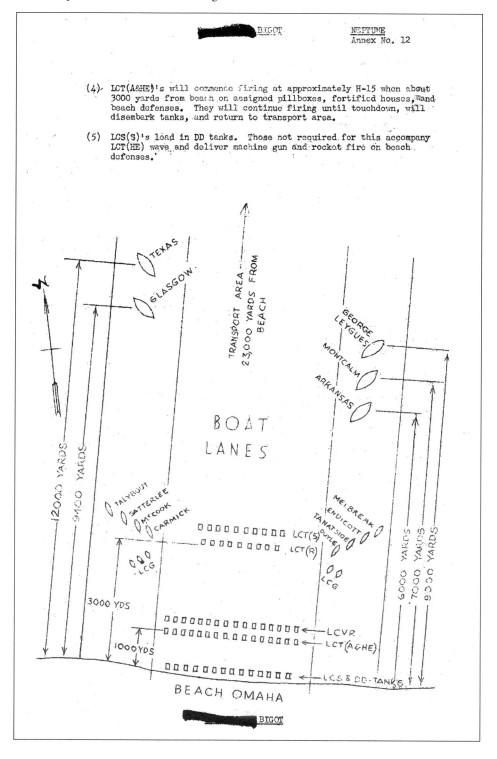

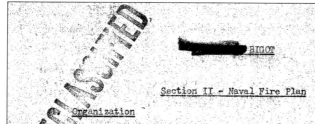

BIGOT

Section II - Naval Fire Plan

1. Organization

a. Fire Support Ships   12 Destroyers

2 Battleships   USS Endicott   USS Baldwin
  USS Texas   USS Doyle   USS Thompson
  USS Arkansas   USS Satterlee   USS Harding
                       USS McCook   HMS Talybont
3 Cruisers   USS Carmick   HMS Tanatside
  HMS Glasgow   USS Frankford   HMS Melbreak
  FS Montcalm
  FS Georges Leygues

b. Fire Support Craft

5 Landing Craft, Gun - LCG(L)   10 Landing Craft, Tank - LCT(5)
9 Landing Craft, Rocket - LCT(R)   with 36 M7 105mm SPMT's fir-
16 Landing Craft, Tank - LCT(A&HE)   ing afloat.
   with 32 M4 tanks firing afloat.   24 Landing Craft, Support-LCS(S)

2. Missions

a. Fire Support Ships: To protect shipping from attack and to support the initial assault and subsequent advance inland.

b. Fire Support Craft: Prior to touchdown to furnish area fire on and in rear of beaches and point fire on beach defenses.

3. Employment and Coordination of Fire Support.

a. As soon as visibility permits, battleships and cruisers will fire on designated batteries and strongpoints. Ships completing tasks before H hour will fire on beach targets. Destroyers will furnish close support fires on designated strongpoints on and in rear of beaches. After H hour, ships will deliver fires called for by Shore Fire Control Parties.

b. Fire Support Craft: Prior to touchdown to furnish area fire on and in rear of beaches and point fire on beach defenses.

(1) LCG(L)'s will accompany leading wave on flanks and in boat lanes, neutralizing assigned beach targets and targets of opportunity by direct fire. Fire will be shifted to flank targets before it endangers advancing troops.

(2) LCT(R)'s will take position in line abreast about 3000 yards off-shore of specified target areas in time to fire on assigned targets when leading wave is about 300 yards offshore. They will then clear boat lanes and return to transport area. Six will re-load with HE rockets and when directed will fire on flank targets. Three will reload with smoke and HE rockets and be prepared to fire when directed. Reloading will be completed by H / 210.

(3) LCT(5)'s will take position in line abreast in boat lanes and will commence firing at approximately H-30 when about 8000 yards from beach on assigned area targets behind beaches. At H-5 they will clear boat lanes and return to rendezvous area.

- 3 -

BIGOT

BIGOT

NEPTUNE
Annex No. 12

4. Target Designation:

a. The Lambert grid will be used for Naval target designation. Supporting ships and shore fire control parties will be furnished 1/50,000 scale map charts and 1/25,000 vertical mosaics gridded with the Lambert grid.

b. Gridded obliques will be furnished naval gunfire spotters to facilita target identification, but Merton coordinates will not be used for target designation.

c. Beach sketches marked to show locations of targets will be furnished to all craft participating in the prearranged fire plan.

5. Naval Shore Fire Control Parties.

a. Attached to 1st Division: Nine parties, 294th Joint Assault Signal Company.

b. Attached to 29th Division: Nine parties, 293d Joint Assault Signal Company, two of which will be allotted to Ranger Units.

c. Artillery Air OP's used to adjust naval gun fire will operate through battalion fire direction centers and attached naval liaison officers.

6. Liaison

a. One Naval liaison officer will accompany each FA battalion and each division artillery and corps artillery headquarters.

b. One corps artillery liaison officer will accompany each division artillery headquarters.

7. Ammunition: Commanding Officers, 58th and 62d Armored Field Artillery Battalions (SP) and 745th Tank Battalion (Med), will requisition and load on craft ammunition to be expended during firing afloat. This will be in addition to basic load.

SP Battalion   - 100 Rounds per Howitzer
Tank Battalion - 150 Rounds per Tank firing

BIGOT

Orders for Co-ordination of Intelligence Activities were issued. *In order to further co-ordinate British and United States Intelligence activities, the following policy is enunciated. United States units, while under 21st Army Group, will continue to follow Unites States procedure. All headquarters should be sufficiently familiar with both United States and British intelligence terminology and procedures to have complete understanding of intelligence documents written in either style, and to understand readily all normal intelligence activities.*

Direct daily liaison between corps and divisions and the photographic and reconnaissance units flying missions in support of them is highly desirable.

In addition to the written counter-intelligence plans prepared by corps and division headquarters, written counter-intelligence plans for the concentration and embarkation period will be prepared by regimental and battalion headquarters with a written check list furnished to company commanders. Special attention will be given to attached and supporting units. These counter-intelligence plans will be co-ordinated with appropriate SOS, Navy and Air Force units and with British Commands and Regional Security Liaison Officers.

Topographic Data: All officers should be reminded of the necessity for collecting topographic data for the correction and revision of existing maps and air charts.

Aerial Photography: Photographs provided for Planning Staff prior to D-Day.

The following photography will be provided for staffs operation 'Neptune' for planning and for use during the operation on the scale of one set for First United States Army Planning Group and one set covering the appropriate area for each corps and assault division.

(1)   *Basic coverage. 1/20,000 to 1/30,000 vertical photography, without overlap, of the Cherbourg Penninsula.*
(2)   *Beach Coverage.*
    a)   *1/10,000 or larger vertical coverage of the coastline in the First United States Army sector to a depth of 4,000 yards inland, with sufficient overlap for stereoscopic study.*
    b)   *Oblique coverage of the coast for topography and hydrography.*
    c)   *Oblique coverage of the coast from sea-level altitude to provide panoramas of the landing beaches.*
(3)   *Inland Coverage of the Assault Area. 1/15,000 to 1/20,000 vertical photography of a strip ten miles deep from the coast, excluding the 1/10,000 vertical coverage mentioned above, with sufficient overlap for stereoscopic study.*
(4)   *Special Coverage of Critical Areas. 1/10,000 or larger, vertical coverage with sufficient overlap for stereoscopic study will be provided.*

In the period immediately preceding D-Day, last minute aerial reconnaissance will be required of 21st Army Group to secure visual observation and photography covering the following items: last minute changes in enemy beach defences, especially underwater obstacles, new wire, minefields or evidence of reinforcements, such as increase in flak, constructional activity, evidence of new installations or bivouacs, movement of railroad artillery, additional artillery emplacements, etc.

'Security prior to D-Day' – Special attention will be directed toward:

1)   *The safeguarding of all information relating to the objective area and the known or surmised date of the operation together with the strength of forces and methods to be employed. The security discipline of troop movements.*

The denial to unauthorised pressmen and photographers of access to troops.

The discouraging of speculation about any special devices or methods to be used.

The publicising of punishments for security violations.

No one oriented in target area, date, force or means to be employed in operation 'Neptune' will fly over or go into enemy held territory or otherwise expose himself to capture by the enemy prior to Y-Day.

Any compromise of information or of documents concerning 'Neptune' will be reported immediately to the AC of S. G-2. First US Army.

Commanders conducting training exercises involving regiments or larger units, will take special steps to bar civilians from the training area whenever possible. Security measures applied to all exercises involving embarkation will be in all possible respects as complete and as stringently enforced as for operation 'Neptune'.

Map supply sources will roll and code maps (quantities of 50 to 20) using the Siminel (sic) Code System and will properly safeguard rolled and coded map stocks until distribution to tactical units.

Personnel engaged in the preparation and reproduction of special maps and photographs which disclose the target area will be classified as Bigot-Neptune. Special maps and photographs will be packaged and coded by reproduction personnel as directed by First United States Army and will be delivered by classified personnel to advance map depots in marshalling areas not sooner than D minus 18.

Advance map depots in marshalling areas will be stocked with packaged and coded stocks immediately prior to date of issue and, in any case, not sooner than D minus 18. Packaged and coded maps only will be issued by advance map depots in sealed marshalling areas.

Issue of packaged operation maps to tactical units will be:- To units scheduled for briefing prior to H-Hour, not sooner than twenty-four hours immediately prior to briefing, and, in any case, not previously to the sealing of troops in marshalling areas.

To troops not scheduled for briefing prior to H-Hour – at the latest practical time after H-Hour.

Map depots will be situated in, or near, marshalling areas. Huts, tents, or requisitioned buildings within marshalling area camps will be used for briefing. Briefing buildings or tents will be guarded when in use, and when they contain classified information. Briefing will take place at the latest practical moment. Only official telephone calls and telegrams approved by camp Commander, will go out after briefing starts.

Maps covering the proposed area of operations are available at the following scales.

GSGS No	Scale
2957	1/4,000,000
2758	1/1,000,000
4042 & 2738	1/250,000 (Army Air)
4336 & 4249	1/1,000,000 (Layered and Unlayered)
4250	1/50,000
4347	1/25,000 (two maps)
4238	1/200,000 (road map)

Special large scale assault and beach maps carrying defence overprints will be issued as required under Army Group arrangements. Certain town plans are also being prepared. Particulars can be obtained from Director of Survey 21st Army Group.

All maps for the assault, follow up and early build-up will be issued to units and formations from depots in or near the Marshalling Areas under static Command arrangements, but Armies will be responsible for issuing detailed instructions to their units and formations as to which maps will be drawn and from which depots. They will also prepare detailed timetables for guidance of issue groups.

Security arrangements connected with map issuing for planning and operations will be covered in the Security Instructions issued separately.

All map depots in the United Kingdom organised for the overseas operation will be under the general control of 21st Army Group who will, in consultation with Army Staff, ensure that sufficient map stocks are available to meet requirements. The siting of all such depots will be an integral part of the mounting plan.

CONFIDENTIAL

UNIT	EACH OF (5)	STRATEGICAL EUROPE (TOPO) 1/4,000,000 GSGS 2957	EUROPE (TOPO) 1/1,000,000 GSGS 2758	EUROPE (AIR) 1/500,000 GSGS 4072	TACTICAL ROAD MAPS 1/200,000 & OTHER	TOPO MAPS 1/250,000	TOPO MAPS 1/100,000	TOPO MAPS 1/50,000	TOPO MAPS 1/25,000	PHOTO MAPS (1) 1/25,000	TOWN MAPS (2) 1/10,000	DEFENSE OVERPRINTS 1/50,000	DEFENSE OVERPRINTS 1/25,000	TRIG STATION DATA MAPS	MAP INDICES
RANGER BATTALION	I	0	I	0	35	10	10	50	50	5	5	0	50	0	I

Above: The map list recording quantities of maps issued for use by the Rangers. 'TACTICAL – DEFENCE OVERPRINTS 1/25,000' covers Vierville to St. Marie du Mont and Pointe du Hoc – and then to the east of Grandcamp, and the second map in the same series covers Grandcamp and Maisy and it also shows the southern end of Utah Beach. The Rangers were allocated fifty copies of each of these maps which cover their missions.

The army also issued details on the availability of scale models for use as aids during the briefing stages in the Marshalling areas:

MODELS (Army): In view of the limited resources for making accurate relief models, the following are being provided by 21st Army Group to cover the area of operations.

a) Scale 1/25,000 – The Eastern area is covered by a series with a vertical scale exaggeration of 4/1. The Western area is covered by a series at an exaggerated vertical scale of 2/1. No further production of these series is contemplated, but existing models may be procured through HQ 21st Army Group. It may be possible after completing first priority tasks to undertake further work on models of this scale for First United States Army.

Scale 1/5,000 (horizontal and vertical) – This series covers the coastal belt to a depth of about 3 miles only. Four copies of each model will be available. Distribution will be to Armies from 21st Army Group. It may be possible to take on an extension of this series inland at a later date. Armies will submit their requirements for such extensions.

Scale 1/5,000 Horizontal 1/1,000 Vertical – The question of the provision of these models for United States sector either here or in Washington is now under discussion.

Model making facilities. In order that formations and units may make up accurate and reliable models for briefing purposes at a larger scale, a team of model makers is being organised by 21st Army Group. This team will undertake the training of unit model makers who will then build their own models in the areas allotted for briefing after these have been set up under security arrangements. All materials required will be supplied by 21st Army Group. Unit model makers will be trained at a central installation being organised by 21st Army Group where models can also be made under full security arrangements by unit teams.

---

20 May 1944

5th Rangers – Companies A – F, Medical and HQ – Dorchester, Dorset.

A, B & C Companies 2nd Rangers – Dorchester, Dorset. Alerted for departure.

Maurice Prince: *Our final base of operation in 'Merrie Ole England' was to be the marshalling area outside the city limits of Dorchester. This campsite was in the immediate vicinity of the staging area we had previously visited, so that we had a fair idea of the situation and setting we were to become a part of. Nothing had changed the status of calm serenity that shrouded this place with peacefulness.*

The ordinary hum-drum, easy way life that had existed in days before was unaffected by the modern busy, stepped-up pace of life. Although the war was strangely present here, it didn't interfere with the works of nature. It was rapturous to sit back and to admire the scenery that confronted us. It was to this setting that the final curtain in the play of death was beginning to rise.

If England seemed peaceful and calm at this time of year, it had nothing on us Rangers. We relaxed and took life easy. No signs of tenseness and alertness could be seen in our actions, or manners. We went about our functions in the same routine style as we did when back in the States; we were untroubled and unperturbed by the vastness of the coming events.

We had come a long way since our first day overseas. Bude, Titchfield, Folkestone, etc. They were milestones in the road we had travelled. We had trained, worked, drilled, and played hard, and now these days were ended, as far as we were concerned we were no longer administrative soldiers. We were combat men. We were only a stone's throw away from our enemy and we were anxiously waiting to bridge this gap.

We did very little training in this area as we were like fighters on the night before ring-time. We were in the pink of condition and in the best of physical and mental stature, resting as it were like the fatted Thanksgiving turkey before the kill. Our morale and spirit were excellent. We never forgot to joke and kid one another. Singing and whistling was heard all the time. We were the same bunch of Rangers here as we were in any other place we had been. Just because we were to undertake the greatest mission in our lives, we didn't let a thing like that affect us in the least.

D, E & F Companies 2nd Rangers – Swanage, Dorset. Alerted for departure.

Medical Detachment 2nd Rangers – Dorchester, Dorset. Alerted for departure.

Headquarters Company 2nd Rangers – Swanage, Dorset. Alerted for departure.

On 20 May US Army Instructions were issued for vacating camp, billets and installations: *It is the desire of the Theatre Commander that US troops vacating accommodations in the UK leave the British people impressed with the high standard of discipline and training in the US Army. It is essential that camps, billets and installations be released in the best possible condition.*

Unit commanders will ensure that all personnel understand that the condition and manner in which a unit leaves its quarters are the best measure of its morale and unit pride.

When a unit vacates its accommodations, a Marching-Out Inspection will be held, attended by a base section representative, a British QC representative, and the unit commander. The local British Quartering Commandant will be notified prior to the vacating of billets. When facilities are not returned to the British, it is desirable, although not obligatory, for the local British Quartering Commandant to be present at the marching-out. As this inspection requires an inventory and an agreed statement of the condition of buildings and equipment, it is essential that maintenance be kept up-to-date, inventories be kept current, and a general state of preparation for departure be observed.

A certificate will be executed and forwarded to the appropriate base section commander by each company and similar commander whose unit is vacating its accommodations, certifying that all indebtedness has been settled, including that of the officers under his command.

A complete final tour of buildings and area will be made immediately prior to the departure of the troops and the commanders of all echelons will be held responsible that their subordinate units leave the camps which they vacate, in proper condition.

By command of General Eisenhower
R.B. Lord, Brigadier General, GSC, Deputy Chief of Staff.

20 May saw Major General Huebner continue with his visits to all of the units under his command.

HEADQUARTERS 1ST INFANTRY DIVISION
APO #1, U. S. Army

G-3 (JOURNAL*
**(DIARY*

Time (From   0001
(To   2400

Date   20 May 1944   CP Location   LANGTON HOUSE, BLANDFORD
                                              ENGLAND

TIME	NO.	FROM	SYNOPSIS	REC'D VIA	DISPOSITION#
0001	1		Journal opened		
1400	2		Maj Gen Huebner, CG 1st Inf Div visited remainder of Inf and Arty bns in the Div that will participate in forthcoming operations.		
2400	3		Journal closed		

NOTES:
     *Delete one.
     "Rec'd Via" column will indicate how message was transmitted, i.e., Tp – telephone; Rad – radio; Tgp – telegraph; Tpe – teletype.
     #Following abbreviations only will be used in this column, other information will be written out: M – Noted on situation map; J – Appended to journal (applies to Overlays, Msg blanks, written orders, etc.); CG, C/S, etc. – indicates information passed on to Officer indicated; T – indicates information disseminated to units or troops, as indicated in text of message.
(Revised 3 Jan. '44)

– 1 –

Also on 20 May instructions were issued to Landing Craft Coxwains on where to go once they had disembarked their passengers.

```
11thPHIB/A4-3(1)(a)                      WESTERN NAVAL TASK FORCE
Serial: 00681                            ASSAULT FORCE "O"
                                         (TASK FORCE ONE TWO FOUR)
TOP SECRET - NEPTUNE                     U.S.S. ANCON, Flagship
                                         PORTLAND, DORSET
                                         20 May 1944: 1200
```

ANNEX D TO OPERATION ORDER BB-44
ATTACK LANDING PLAN SECTION 3
MASTER BOAT AND CRAFT EMPLOYMENT PLAN
(b) FOR SECOND TRIP

    After initial trip, all boats return to parent ship except as hereafter provided. All boats ordered to report to other ships for second trip will report immediately upon return from initial trip or after rendezvous as ordered by Assault Group Commanders.

No. and Types	From	Report to
6 LCA	PRINCESS MAUD	ARUNDEL
8 LCA	PRINCE CHARLES	ARUNDEL
7 LCA	PRINCE LEOPOLD	DIX
6 LCA	BEN MY CHREE	DIX
7 LCA	PRINCE BAUDOUIN	THURSTON
6 LCA	AMSTERDAM	THURSTON
16 LCVP	ASSAULT GROUP O-1	ARUNDEL
8 LCVP	ASSAULT GROUP O-1	DIX
8 LCVP	ASSAULT GROUP O-2	DIX
16 LCVP	ASSAULT GROUP O-2	THURSTON
3 LCT	O-1, LCTs 2339,2425,2049	DIX
3 LCT	O-1, LCTs 2008,2228,2043	ARUNDEL
4 LCT	O-1, LCTs 540, 542, 276, 209	LST 375
3 LCT	O-1, LCTs 293, 2287, 2037	THURSTON
1 LCI	O-2, 1 LCI from Survivors	ARUNDEL
	of H / 70 and H / 100	
	waves.	
1 LCM	ASSAULT GROUP O-1	DIX
1 LCM	ASSAULT GROUP O-1	THURSTON

    After second trip all boats and craft lent to other ships will return to parent ship unless released by Assault Group Commander of the assault group to which they are regularly assigned.

```
                                         J. L. HALL, Jr.,
                                         Rear Admiral, U. S. Navy,
                                         Commander TASK FORCE ONE TWO FOUR.
D. MacQUEEN,
Flag Secretary.
```

ANNEX D TO OPERATION ORDER BB-44
ATTACK LANDING PLAN SECTION 3
MASTER BOAT AND CRAFT EMPLOYMENT
PLAN (b) FOR SECOND TRIP

On 20 May 1944 a report landed on the desk of the Chief of Combined Operations, Director of Experiments for Operational Requirements in Whitehall. It referred to the recent trials of Rangers' specialist equipment (automatic ladders) at Burton Bradstock (to be covered in more detail in a future book) and stated:

> *From this report it appears that the ladder equipment functions satisfactorily, but that the users need to know more about its capabilities and limitations particularly in regard to choice of landing places and position on cliff for erection.*
>
> *This is merely a matter of training and will presumably be attended to.*
>
> *The rocket projected ladder is not one of our projects, but the same criticism as above seems to apply. Angle of elevation in relation to the foot and head of the cliff, windage and different weights of ladder or rope must be taken into account.*

Following these trials, four models were constructed for the operation and more training was undertaken.

For the protection of the guns, special waterproof covers were made to shield them, and these were designed to be quickly removable after the approach to the beach and when the craft had landed. The covers were also put over the ends to disguise them and they also provided shelter for the microphone and guns during bad weather. It is interesting to note the three guns on the end of the ladders. There is some debate as to the exact weapons used for this purpose, as period papers suggest 'Aerial Browning Machine Guns', 'BAR' rifles, Lewis guns and even 'Vickers K Guns'. This photograph appears to show three Browning Automatic Rifles.

Provision was also made for six spare pans or magazines of ammunition to be stored at the ladder top. It was a guideline and it was decided that the total weight of guns, ammunition and man should not exceed more than 450lbs and that the arrangement of guns and ammunition should be balanced accordingly. It was important that these figures were monitored, as if not, there was a danger that the ladder could be strained when fully extended.

A later report stated:

The advantages of this method of scaling are:

a) It needs no special training except for the operator.
b) It provides covering fire from the first.
c) It is very rapid.
d) It is relatively silent.
e) It is at its best on over-hanging cliffs.
f) It carries up with it beach to cliff top telephone.

The disadvantages are:

a) It is limited to 100ft in theory and probably 80 ft in practice.
b) It needs a suitable beach free from obstructions and solid enough to take the vehicle.
c) Its ceiling drops rapidly as the slope of the cliff decreases.
d) It is not readily available.

Another method of climbing was by the use of projected grapnels.

The principle of projecting a rope by means of a rocket consisted of a 2in rocket fitted with a grapnel head fired from a modified projector.

The tail of the rocket was connected by an 8ft wire strap to 90 fathoms of 2½in rope packed in two boxes. The rocket was fired electrically by a 4-volt battery through a firing lead 20ft long.

Alternatives to plain ropes were also produced. Rope ladders and 2½in ropes fitted with wooden toggle bars were tried. The rope ladders were for use when the cliff was vertical or had an overhang and the toggle ropes on sloping cliffs, in place of plain rope. It was found that often on a sloping cliff there would be a short vertical face to climb and the toggle ropes were easier to climb than the plain.

The rope ladders were packed in rectangular boxes and the toggle ropes in the same size box as the plain ropes.

Rocket projectors were also fitted to the sides of the British Landing Craft Assault boats belonging to the 2nd Battalion companies, who would be the first to scale Pointe du Hoc. Six rocket projectors were fitted onto each LCA, three per side and they were designed to be detachable, so that they could be taken ashore if necessary.

The configuration for each LCA meant that it would be in a position to fire two rope ladders, two toggle ropes and two plain ropes. It was noted at the time that this method was suitable only when the beach was narrow enough and the angle of fire and range could be carefully judged.

Here the whole process is described in the 'Small Unit Actions' report:

Ten LCAs would be sufficient to boat the three small Ranger companies and headquarters party, including signal and medical personnel, with an average of 21-22 men on a craft. Each LCA was fitted with three pairs of rocket mounts, at bow, amid-ship, and stern, wired so that they could be fired in series of pairs from one control point at the stern. Plain half-inch ropes were carried by one pair of rockets, affixed to the rocket's base by a connecting wire. A second pair was rigged for rope of the same size fitted with toggles, small wooden crossbars a few inches long inserted at about one-foot intervals, the third pair of rockets was attached to light rope ladders with rungs every two feet. The rockets were headed by grapnels. The rope or ladder for each rocket was coiled in a box directly behind the rocket mount. Each craft carried, in addition to the six mounted rockets, a pair of small, hand-projector-type rockets attached to plain ropes. These could be easily carried ashore if necessary.

Extension ladders were of two types. One, carried by each LCA, consisted of 112 feet of tubular-steel, 4-foot sections weighing 4 pounds each; these ladders were partly assembled in advance in 16-foot lengths. For mounting the whole ladder in escalade work, a man would climb to the top of a length, haul up and attach the next 16-foot section, and repeat this process until the necessary height was reached. As a final auxiliary for climbing, four DUKWs would come in close behind the first wave, each carrying a 100-foot extension ladder, fire-department type, with three folding sections. Two Lewis machine guns were mounted at the top of each of these ladders, which would be particularly useful for getting up supplies.

Speed was essential for this operation, and the small assault force was equipped for shock action of limited duration, with a minimum load of supplies and weapons. Dressed in fatigue uniform, each Ranger carried a D-bar for rations, two grenades, and his weapon, normally the M-1 rifle. A few of the men selected for going first up the ropes carried pistols or carbines. Heavier weapons were limited to four BARs and two light mortars per company. Ten thermite grenades, for demolition, were distributed within each company. Two supply boats (LCAs) would come in a few minutes after the assault wave, with packs, extra rations and ammunition, two 81mm mortars, demolitions, and equipment for hauling supplies up the cliff.

Close up of the rocket propelled grapnels fixed to the LCAs.

For signaling, each LCA carried the following:

(e) L.C.A.   1 pair binoculars for flotilla leaders (Pattern 343).
1 tricoloured torch (not for sub-divisional leaders) (Pattern X.2151).
1 signalling torch (Pattern 16001).
1 pair of hand flags (Pattern 019).
1 set of special flags.
1 aldis lamp for flotilla leaders (Pattern 5110D).
1 megaphone.
1 Pattern 1038 lantern for sub-divisional leaders (1 in 3 craft).

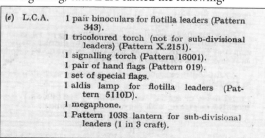

Below: The correct pattern for group landings and timed approaches to a beach.

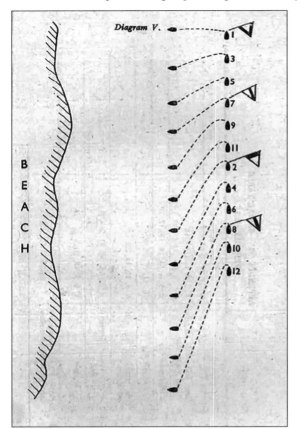

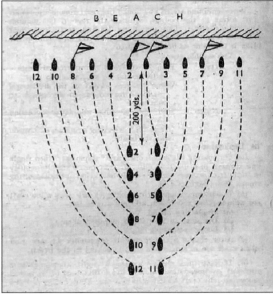

LCAs of the 2nd Battalion approaching the Burton Bradstock cliffs in southern England.

All of the 2nd Battalion LCAs are shown here during practice. From left to right – LCAs numbered 858, 668, 860 & 861 launching their rockets at the cliffs. Note the six rockets mounted to the exterior of each LCA – three per side. Additionally to the fixed rockets, the men onboard have portable launchers, which could be taken onto the beach and fired by hand.

The flash and smoke as the rocket-propelled grapnel is fired from the beach.

Below: The empty rocket tubes can be seen on the decks of LCA 884.

A British officer walks away as the Rangers storm the shore during the practice.

The ladders are prepared after the grapnels have attached to the top of the cliff. To the left of the photograph are the ladders with conventional rungs. To the right a rope with wooden grips spaced at regular intervals. In the centre there are lengths of ladders – which are being joined together to make a vertical ladder. It was from one of these that a Ranger fell 50 feet.

A rocket and 'hot boxes' of ropes dismounted from an LCA and placed on the ground.

These rockets worked well, but the Rangers required a much lighter projector – so a specialist Schermuly Mortar (shown below) was produced. The requirement was that it could be carried by one man – and the grapnel was to carry a one-inch line to a height of 100ft.

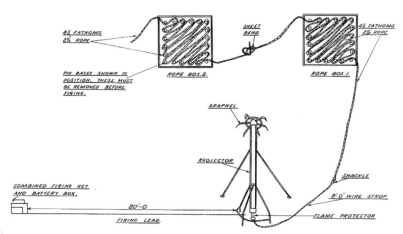

DIAGRAMMATIC LAYOUT OF PROJECTED GRAPNEL.

As a final scaling method, the Rangers were given specially designed and manufactured ladders which were produced in 4ft sections.

Each man was supposed to carry a single section of ladder which was then assembled at the bottom of the cliff. In the photograph on the next page, one man is seen struggling with a group of ladder sections. As the ladder is built up, it is then pulled to the top of the cliff by men who have already reached the top. Each length is then added below as the others go up. On the

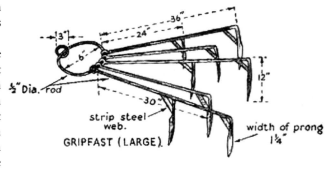

top section of each ladder there were additional hooks added to give the ladder a grip against the cliff and a line with a small set of grapnels – known as a gripfast – was used to anchor the weight of the ladders to the cliff top.

During the trials, the ladders proved easy to erect, however, they had a tendency to come apart halfway up – and this was blamed on faulty assembly from the bottom. A rope around the climber was also recommended as a safety precaution.

Below: Rangers carry the ladder pieces in bundles across the beach and then put them together in sections.

Once completed, the sections are hauled upwards using a rope.

On top of the cliff, a pulley system quickly lifts ladders, equipment and stretchers to and from the top. Note the Rangers diamond on the back of the helmet.

Captain John Raaen, 5th Battalion explains why the Rangers decided to use the diamond on their helmets:

> *After Operation Fabius we found some of our Rangers ended up following 29th Division leaders because there was, as always, confusion after a landing. The solution that came out was to place the orange diamond on the back of our helmets. Rangers followed only Ranger non-coms and officers after that.*

Below: Dated 20 May 1944 – the following photographs come from a revised version of the earlier May intelligence map.

The map covers the radar station at Pointe de la Percée and Point du Hoc in some detail. It now indicates a further downgrading of the weaponry at Pointe du Hoc. There are still four casements 'Under Construction' (4 x U/C), and now the map specifically says to 'DELETE' two of the open emplacements (originally numbered 4 & 5). Delete the one gun on original Pit 6 – and also to delete the gun in the open field position close to the Pointe (previously gun from Pit 4). On the original, colour version of the map, it shows the amendments in red so that they stand out. The gun on original position 6 is clearly to be removed, and then it appears to be replaced by a very similar-looking gun symbol – which does not make a lot of sense. This now leaves: four casements under construction, four gun pits (numbered here 1, 2, 3 & 4) – but Pit No.4 may be occupied or not – it is very unclear. Pits No.1, 2 & 3 are shown to be occupied and there is a possibility that one of them could still be damaged. The number six and the '!' mark indicates a dummy position.

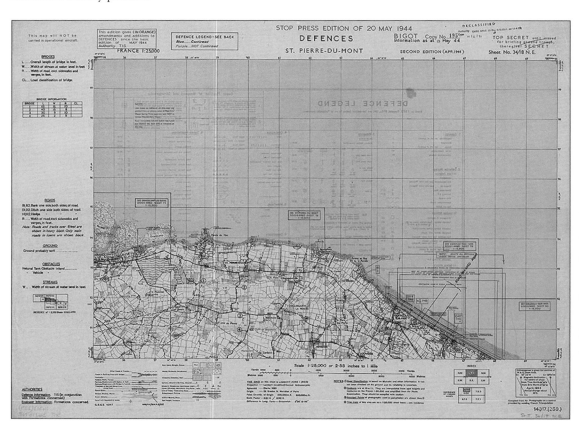

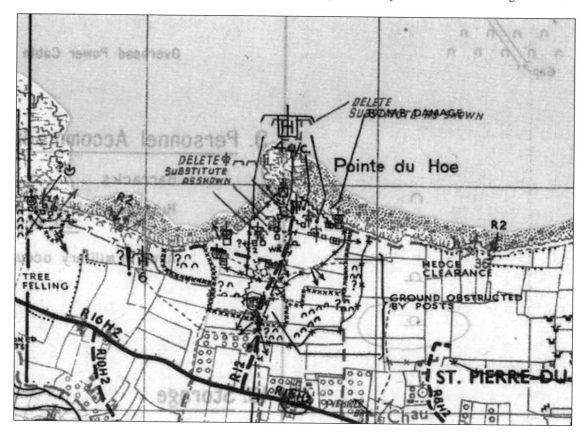

By way of clarification. The map shows four guns on open emplacements – marked 1 to 4. The map specifically says to now delete the following : *1x gun in open emplacement, 2 emplacements and one gun in a field emplacement.* By adding these amendments to an existing map, it was much cheaper and quicker than reprinting more new maps.

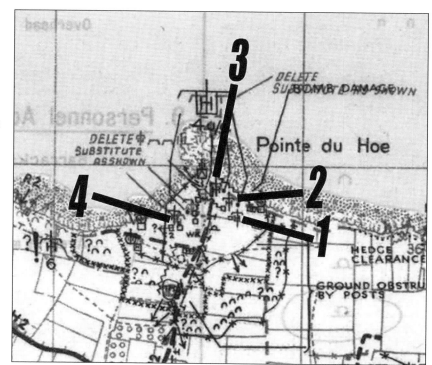

Below, the details of the amended areas of the GSGS map showing Pointe et Raz de la Percée radar station area.

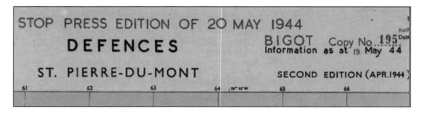

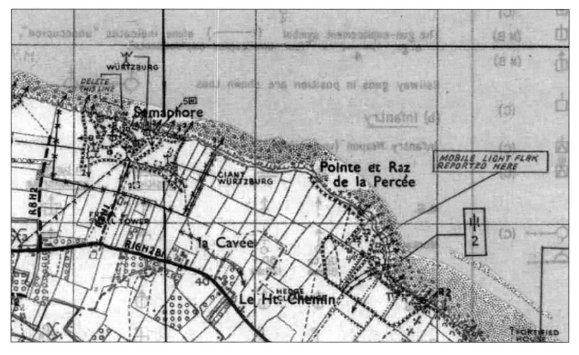

Whilst the intelligence maps are based on up to date reconnaissance photographs showing Pointe du Hoc as being under construction with four guns, the written intelligence reports continue to list Pointe du Hoc as being a six-gun battery of 155mm guns. The various disciplines of intelligence took a while to marry up. But all maps are now starting to contain the same detailed information that was provided to the Rangers in the Neptune Monograph.

The regular updated targeting information printed on 20 May shows Targets 1, 5 and 16. This document now shows the Les Perruques (Maisy I) battery as having 4 x 155mm howitzers which is a change to the earlier reports which stated six guns.

11thPHIB/A4-3(1)(a)
Serial: 00681

T0P SECRET - NEPTUNE

WESTERN NAVAL TASK FORCE
ASSAULT FORCE "O"
(TASK FORCE ONE TWO FOUR)
U.S.S. ANCON, Flagship,
PORTLAND, DORSET.
20 May 1944; 1200.

APPENDIX 2
TO ANNEX F
GUNFIRE SUPPORT PLAN
LIST OF TARGETS

TARGET NO.	COORDINATES	DESCRIPTION
T 1	58609390	6 Guns, 155 mm
T 5	53309180	4 Guns, 155 mm, 5 concrete shelters, 3 MGs, 1 Hut
T10	79268316	4 Guns, 105 mm
T16	52159150	4 Guns, 75 mm, 2 MGs, 1 Pillbox, 3 Shelters
T20	77008600	Strongpoint with possible 75 Cal Guns
T21	76708775	7 MGs, 1 Pillbox
T22	76008780	2 MGs, 1 Hut, 1 Shelter
T23	75808785	4 MGs, 1 AT Gun
T24	75508790	1 Pillbox
T25	75308795	1 Pillbox, 1 MG
T26	75308838	1 Pillbox
T27	75008805	1 4.7 Gun, 3 AA Guns, 6 Pillboxes
T28	75008790	5 MGs, 3 Shelters
T29	74908710	9 MGs, Road block, Troops in houses
T30	74508815	Strongpoint, 2 Arty Guns, 2 Shelters
T31	73238843	Pillbox
T32	72698850	3 MGs
T33	72208860	2 Concrete shelters, 16 MGs, Road blocks
T34	72108780	Houses
T35	72098740	Houses
T36	71808800	Houses
T37	71198810	Houses
T38	71218880	C/D Gun in concrete
T39	70498820	Houses
T40	69908910	5 Pillboxes, 2 MGs, 2 Concrete shelters
T41	69558930	3 Pillboxes
T42	69508830	Houses
T43	69308940	3 Pillboxes, 1 Concrete shelter, 4 MGs, AT Ditch
T44	69408910	Beach Exit
T45	69308883	Beach Exit, 1 Camouflaged position
T46	69108820	Troops in Houses
T47	68808950)	(4 Casemates, 3 Concrete Shelters, 5 MGs, 1 AT Gun,
T50	68708943)	(3 Pillboxes, 1 Med Gun, 1 Casemate u/c
T48	68808910	Beach Exit
T49	68608870	Beach Exit
T51	68368970	Construction Activity
T52	68128978	AT Ditch
T53	67808970	AA Gun, 4 Concrete Shelters, 2 Pillboxes, 5 MGs
T54	67609010	4 Guns in concrete, 6 MGs, 4 Inf weapons
T55	67558930	Beach Exit
T56	67458780	Troops
T57	67109010	4 Emplacements unoccupied

APPENDIX 2 to ANNEX F
GUNFIRE SUPPORT PLAN
LIST OF TARGETS

11thPHIB/A4-3(1)(a)
Serial: 00681

TOP SECRET - NEPTUNE

WESTERN NAVAL TASK FORCE
ASSAULT FORCE "O"
(TASK FORCE ONE TWO FOUR)
U.S.S. ANCON, Flagship,
PORTLAND, DORSET.
20 May 1944; 1200.

APPENDIX 2
TO ANNEX E
GUNFIRE SUPPORT PLAN
LIST OF TARGETS

TARGET NO.	COORDINATES	DESCRIPTION
T58	67148932	Troops
T59	66809030	1 AA/MG, 8 Concrete Shelters, Concrete OP, 3 Pill-boxes, 2 Concrete Shelters under construction
T60	66739060	Fortified house, 1 Pillbox, 2 Concrete Shelters
T61	66609030	11 MGs, 3 weapon emplacements, 3 Pillboxes
T62	66258960	2 MGs, possible CP
T63	66459073	6 MGs, 1 Pillbox
T64	66309020	Beach Exit
T65	66149075	Radar Station
T66	65689100	1 Pillbox, 3 MGs
T67	65509120	Fortified House
T68	65389120	5 Concrete Shelters, 1 Pillbox, 10 MGs, 1 AA Gun, Infantry weapons unspecified
T69	65109150	3 MGs, 1 AT Gun
T70	64809120	Possible AT Gun, possible fortified houses
T71	64809170	4 Pillboxes, 6 MGs, 3 Concrete Shelters, 1 AA/MG, 1 AT Gun
T72	64509190	2 Pillboxes, 4 Mortars, 2 Emplacements, 11 MGs
T73	64808660	Cross Roads
T74	63709273)	(4 Concrete Shelters, 1 OP, 4 Pillboxes, 14 MGs
T75	63629302)	(AT weapons, Hutted Camp
T76	62479350)	(13 MGs, 2 Pillboxes, 10 Concrete Shelters, 6 Concrete
T77	62229350)	(Shelters u/c, Wurzburg, Radar Station, Battery of 4 AA Guns, 1 Searchlight, 1 Hutted Camp
T78	62209060	Troops
T79	62208870	2 MGs, Supply Depot
T80	61179165	2 MGs, Houses
T81	61229270	Strongpoint
T82	60609380	1 MG
T83	60209380	10 MGs, 2 Concrete Shelters
T84	59409288	Road Junction, Houses
T85	58609307	Troops in houses
T86	58509345	1 AT Gun
T87	58409155	Possible CP, Cable trench junction
T88	57609390	3 MGs, 2 Pillboxes, 2 Shelters
T89	57409390	1 MG
T90	57359335	2 Gun positions, Troops
T91	56559365	12 MGs, 1 Pillbox, 2 Shelters
T92	56208926	Strongpoint, Troops in Houses, 7 MGs
T93	55809330	29 MGs, 3 Pillboxes, 4 Shelters, 2 Flak Guns
T94	55409260	Houses with Troops
T95	55279327	Houses, 1 MG, 1 Pillbox
T96	54609100	Cable trench junction, Possible CP

APPENDIX 2 to ANNEX E
GUNFIRE SUPPORT PLAN
LIST OF TARGETS

```
11thPHIB/A4-3(1)(a)                          WESTERN NAVAL TASK FORCE
Serial: 00681                                ASSAULT FORCE "O"
                                             (TASK FORCE ONE TWO FOUR)
TOP SECRET - NEPTUNE                         U.S.S. ANCON, Flagship,
                                             PORTLAND, DORSET,
                        APPENDIX 2           20 May 1944; 1200.
                       TO ANNEX E
                  GUNFIRE SUPPORT PLAN
                    LIST OF TARGETS
```

TARGET NO.	COORDINATES	DESCRIPTION
T97	54459335	7 MGs, 1 Pillbox, 1 Flak Gun, 4 Road Blocks
T98	54459290	Strongpoint with 9 MGs, possible CP
T99	54309353	1 Light Gun
T100	54159235	Houses with Troops
T101	54309190	Houses with Troops
T102	54009205	Strongpoint
T103	53909230	4 Possible Gun Positions, Troops in Houses
T104	53809340	Road Block, Houses, 14 MGs, 3 Pillboxes
T105	53609240	Houses
T106	53309350	2 MGs
T107	53159050	Possible CP, Cable trench junction
T108	53029130	Houses with Troops
T109	52709350	4 Pillboxes, 4 MGs, 4 Concrete Shelters
T110	52609070	Troops in Houses
T111	52159330	13 MGs, 2 Concrete Shelters
T112	51708670	Troops in Houses, 1 MG
T113	51109240	11 MGs, 2 Pillboxes
T114	51109120	Strongpoint, 7 MGs
T115	50909215	2 MGs
T116	50728824	2 MGs, 1 Shelter under construction
T117	50509160	2 MGs, 1 Pillbox
T118	50359080	Strongpoint, 4 Pillboxes, 1 MG
T119	50208570	Strongpoint, 1 Concrete Shelter
T120	49709060	4 AT Gun, 1 Pillbox, 1 MG
T121	49708840	4 MGs
T122	49309040	5 Pillboxes, 1 AT Gun, 3 MGs
T123	49208780	Bridge, 4 Pillboxes, 3 AT Guns, 2 Flak Guns, 2 MGs
T124	59909340	Ammunition Depot
T125	57959370	6 Flak Guns
T126	62208370	Ammunition Depot
T127	61609370	4 MGs, 1 Pillbox
T128	67508995	2 Pillboxes, C/D casemate, 3 MGs, 1 Concrete Shelter
T129	79708710	Casemating under construction
T130	66309058	4 MGs, 2 Pillboxes, 1 AT Gun
T150	76218090	Road junctions in town
T151	76108210	Houses with Troops
T152	75917876	Bridge and Road Junction
T153	75178457	Troops, 5 MGs, CP, Cable trench junction
T154	75107765	Road and Railroad Crossing
T155	74488066	4 MGs, Houses

```
                              APPENDIX 2 to ANNEX E
                              GUNFIRE SUPPORT PLAN
                                LIST OF TARGETS
```

11thPHIB/A4-3(1)(a)
Serial: 00681

TOP SECRET - NEPTUNE

WESTERN NAVAL TASK FORCE
ASSAULT FORCE "O"
(TASK FORCE ONE TWO FOUR)
U.S.S. ANCON, Flagship,
PORTLAND, DORSET.
20 May 1944.

APPENDIX 2
TO ANNEX E
GUNFIRE SUPPORT PLAN
LIST OF TARGETS

TARGET NO.	COORDINATES	DESCRIPTION
T156	73708320	Bridge over Canal, Road Junction
T157	73708320	Bridge over Canal, Road Junction
	73348213	Road Junction in Town
T158	72417800	Road and Railroad Crossing
T159	71908283	Road Crossing
T160	71408490	Troops
T161	71318280	4 Possible Arty Emplacements
T162	69768393	Road Junction
T163	69267752	Bridge and Road Junction
T164	65788134	Road Junction
T165	64667700	Railroad Underpass
T166	64308390	Troops in Town
T167	64308441	Bridge
T168	61508360	Road Junction
T169	60308158	2 Road Crossings
T170	55218424	Road Junction
T180	58408240	6 MGs

NOTE: Coordinates shown represent center of strong point or position.
More detailed information on target is given in 1/25,000 TIS
maps furnished.

D. MacQUEEN,
Flag Secretary.

Below: The Naval assignments for USS *Texas*. Target No 1 – to be attacked first.

11thPHIB/A4-3(1)(a)
Serial: 00681

TOP SECRET - NEPTUNE
OPERATION ORDER
No. BB-44

WESTERN NAVAL TASK FORCE
ASSAULT FORCE "O"
TASK FORCE ONE TWO FOUR
U.S.S. ANCON, Flagship,
PORTLAND, DORSET,
20 MAY 1944; 1200

APPENDIX 3 TO ANNEX E
TO OPERATION ORDER BB-44
SCHEDULE OF FIRES

1.   Target assignments and schedule of fires for major units,
destroyers and LCG(L)s are as follows:

FS No.	SHIP	TARGET	TIME	ROUNDS	REMARKS
11	TEXAS	T1, T86	H-40 to H-5	Up to 250	14" air spot 65% AP 35% HC
11	TEXAS	T88, T89	H-25 to H-10	100	5"
11	TEXAS	T88, T89	H-4 to H	12	14" Air Spot HC

11thPHIB/A4-3(1)(a)
Serial: 00681

TOP SECRET – NEPTUNE
OPERATION ORDER
No. BB-44

WESTERN NAVAL TASK FORCE
ASSAULT FORCE "O"
(TASK FORCE ONE TWO FOUR)
U.S.S. ANCON, Flagship,
PORTLAND, DORSET,
20 MAY 1944; 1200

APPENDIX 3 TO ANNEX E
TO OPERATION ORDER BB-44
SCHEDULE OF FIRES

5. Control vessels take under fire with 3"/50 guns following pillboxes:

PRIMARY CONTROL VESSEL FOR BEACH	TARGET	PILLBOX	TIME	ROUNDS
FOX GREEN	T41	69848908	H-25 to H-5	50 AP
EASY RED	T53	67709008	H-25 to H-5	50 AP
EASY GREEN	T60	66709060	H-25 to H-5	50 AP
DOG RED	T63	66499074	H-25 to H-5	50 AP
DOG WHITE	T67	65459126	H-25 to H-5	50 AP
DOG GREEN	T71	64829177	H-25 to H-5	50 AP

6. LCS(S) commence firing at range of 1100 yards. Proceed toward beach delivering machine gun and rocket fire on machine gun emplacements, pillboxes and other targets of opportunity on and behind beaches. LCS(S) carry 48 HE rockets, 6 smoke rockets. Do not fire smoke rockets on beach in close support.

D. MacQueen

D. MacQUEEN,
Flag Secretary.

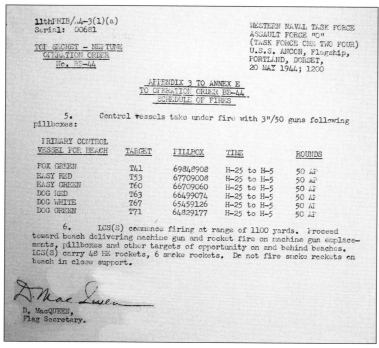

Below is an assignment table for targets to enable the Air Force to co-ordinate with the Navy on target positions and timings for bombardment.

Target with grid reference 528915 is the rear of La Martinière.
Target with grid reference 533918 is Les Perruques (Maisy I).

11thPHIB/A4-3(1)(a)
Serial: 00681

TOP SECRET NEPTUNE

WESTERN NAVAL TASK FORCE
ASSAULT FORCE "O"
(TASK FORCE ONE TWO FOUR)
U.S.S. ANCON, Flagship
PORTLAND, DORSET
20 May 1944: 1200

ASSIGNMENT OF TARGETS FOR AIR SPOTTING

		Sunrise -40 to Sunrise +5	Sunrise +5 to Sunrise +50	+50 to +95	+95 to +140	+140 to +185	+185 to +230	+230 to +275	+275 to +320	+320 to +365	
GROUP	SHIP	1	2	3	4	5	6	7	8	9	REM. PERIODS ASSIGNED
9	TEXAS and after Period 8 GLASGOW	586939 & -------- 576938 --------		*612916 -------------- *533918 --------------					*528915 --------- *533918 ---------		
10	ARKANSAS	664907 & 666906	643839 & ----- *797871 -----		*643839 ----------------- *797871 -----------------						
12	GLASGOW BELLONA	668903 *649906	*649906 ----- *622905 -----		X	*622905 ------- *557847 -------			X	X	X
14	MONTCALM (Per. 1-2) GEORGES LEYGUES (Per. 5-6)	750879 --------- 755878 ---------		X	X	*752855 & --- *714849 ---		X	X	X	X

APPENDIX 5 TO ANNEX E
TO OPERATION ORDER BB-44
ASSIGNMENT OF TARGETS FOR
AIR SPOTTING

11thPHIB/A4-3(1)(~)
Serial: 00681

SECRET — NEPTUNE
OPERATION ORDER
No. BB-44

WESTERN NAVAL TASK FORCE
ASSAULT FORCE "O"
(TASK FORCE ONE TWO FOUR)
U.S.S. ANCON, Flagship.
PORTLAND, DORSET,
20 May 1944: 1200.

1.   Information.   Essential information is contained in NAVAL COMMANDER
WESTERN TASK FORCE NEPTUNE Monograph and in the Intelligence Plan,
Annex A to NAVAL COMMANDER WESTERN TASK FORCE Operation Plan No. 2-44.
Both sources of information are to be distributed down to and including
LCTs.   Shore line sketches are to be distributed down to and including
LCVPs.

Additional information for those who need to know, and not repeated here,
is contained in operation plans and orders issued by higher authority
and distributed only to Major Task Force Commanders of the WESTERN NAVAL
TASK FORCE.

NEPTUNE is a joint British—United States Operation, the object of which
is to secure a lodgement on the Continent from which further offensive
operations can be developed.   It is a part of a large strategic plan
designed to bring about total defeat of GERMANY by means of heavy and
concentrated assaults upon GERMAN-occupied EUROPE from the UNITED KINGDOM,
the MEDITERRANEAN, and RUSSIA.   OVERLORD is the name used for this
operation when target date, target or target area is not expressed.

The operation is commanded by Supreme Commander, Allied Expeditionary
Force, General Eisenhower, under whom, exercising command jointly are:

     NAVAL — Allied Naval Commander-in-Chief, Expeditionary Force —
          Admiral Sir Bertram H. Ramsay.

     ARMY — Commander-in-Chief, 21 Army Group —
          General Sir Bernard L. Montgomery.

     AIR — Commander-in-Chief, Allied Expeditionary Air Force —
          Air Marshall Sir Trafford L. Leigh-Mallory.

The attack will be launched in two adjacent sectors in the BAY OF THE
SEINE.   Simultaneous assaults will be made by the EASTERN NAVAL TASK
FORCE composed of ASSAULT FORCES "S", "J", and "G" and by the WESTERN
NAVAL TASK FORCE composed of ASSAULT FORCES "O" and "U".   The dividing
boundary between the NAVAL TASK FORCES starts at the root of PORT-EN-
BESSIN Western Breakwater, thence 025° true to Meridian 0° 40' West,
thence northward along this meridian to latitude 49° 40' North.

The WESTERN NAVAL TASK FORCE is commanded by Rear Admiral Kirk, USN, and
Assault Force "U" by Rear Admiral Moon, USN.   A follow-up force, Force
"B", under Commodore Edgar, USN, will arrive in the OMAHA area commenc-
ing on the second tide on D day and will land under the direction of the
Commander Force "O".   The Army component of the WESTERN TASK FORCE is
the 1st U.S. Army Commanded by Lieutenant-General Bradley, USA.   Subor-
dinate Army Commanders are Major General Gerow, V Corps (Force "O"),
Major General Collins, VII Corps (Force "U"), Major General Huebner, 1st
Infantry Division (Force "O"), Major General Gearhardt, 29th Infantry
Division (Force "B"), and Major General Barton, 4th Infantry Division
(Force "U").

11thIHIB/A4-3(1)(a)   WESTERN NAVAL TASK FORCE
Serial: 00681   ASSAULT FORCE "O"
                            (TASK FORCE ONE TWO FOUR)
TOP SECRET - NEPTUNE   U.S.S. ANCON, Flagship,
OPERATION ORDER   PORTLAND, DORSET,
   No. BB-44   20 MAY 1944; 1200.

                APPENDIX 5 TO ANNEX E
            TO OPERATION ORDER NO. BB-44
          ARRANGEMENTS FOR SPOTTING AIRCRAFT

   (2) Spotters will be particularly alert on D day to seek out
       rocket guns and mortars along the communication line
       688860, 650877, 620890.

   (3) Spotters in period 1 will inform firing ships when leading
       waves (LCT(A) - LCT(HE) -LCA) beach. They will check fire
       when leading waves come within 800 yards of target areas.

   (4) Spotters of Group NINE will inform TEXAS at H plus one hour
       fifty-five minutes whether batteries at MAISY (528915 and
       533918) are still in operation. TEXAS will immediately
       inform Commander Force "O".

   (5) Ships will where possible after period SEVEN release
       spotting aircraft when at mid-period it appears there
       will be no requirement for their services.

6. Arrangements for Artillery Observation Plan Spotting. As soon as it is
possible for artillery observation planes to be operated from the far shore,
these planes will be utilized to augment the spotting provided by the Shore
Fire Control Parties. These planes will be operated by artillery Battalion
CIs. Pilots will be briefed on desired targets and will spot through Fire
Direction Centers.

D. MacQUEEN,
Flag Secretary.

To avoid confusion between British Royal Navy crews and those of the US ships, a chart of 'comparative terminology' was produced and issued on 20 May.

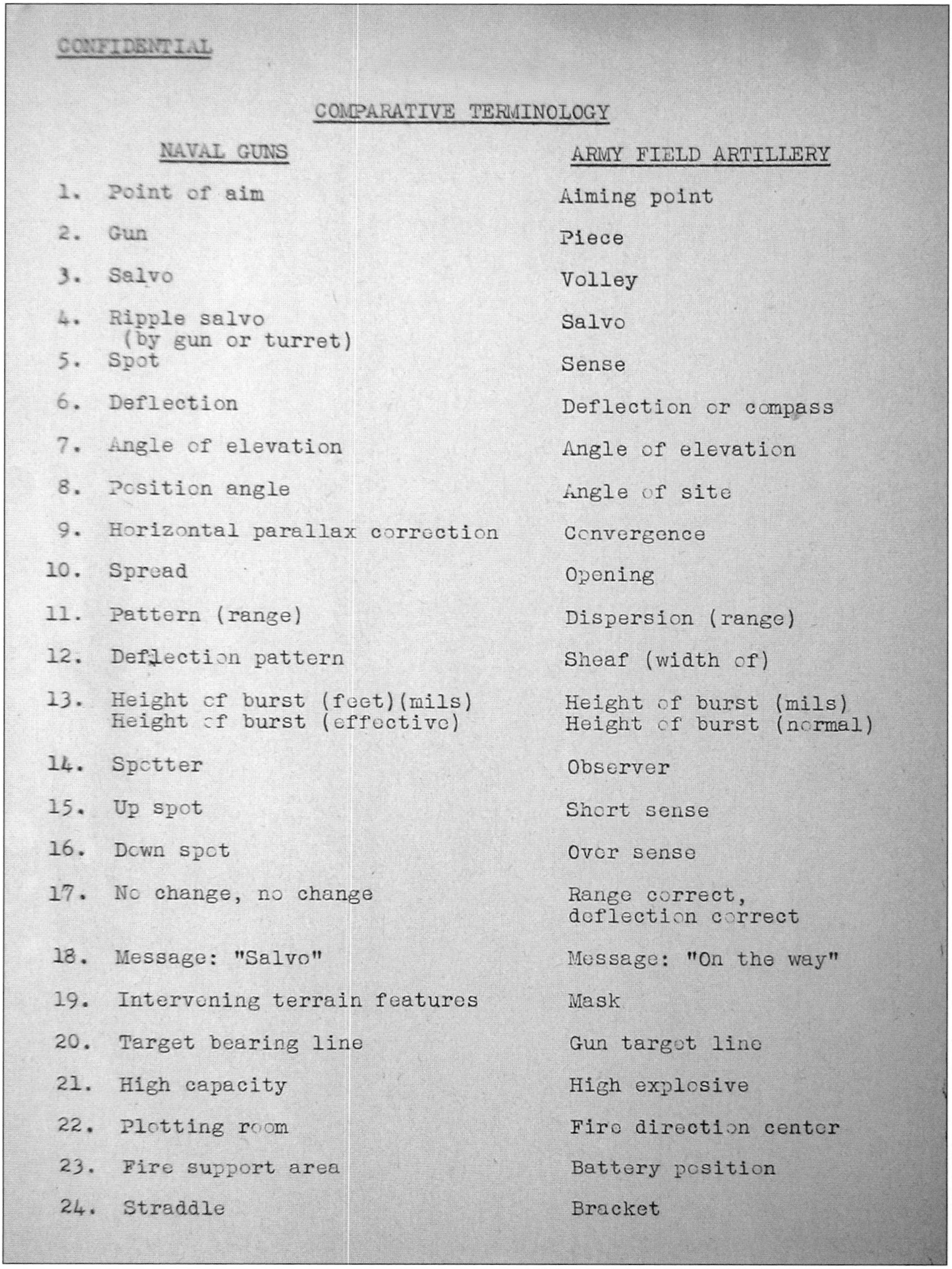

CONFIDENTIAL

COMPARATIVE TERMINOLOGY

NAVAL GUNS	ARMY FIELD ARTILLERY
1. Point of aim	Aiming point
2. Gun	Piece
3. Salvo	Volley
4. Ripple salvo (by gun or turret)	Salvo
5. Spot	Sense
6. Deflection	Deflection or compass
7. Angle of elevation	Angle of elevation
8. Position angle	Angle of site
9. Horizontal parallax correction	Convergence
10. Spread	Opening
11. Pattern (range)	Dispersion (range)
12. Deflection pattern	Sheaf (width of)
13. Height of burst (feet)(mils) Height of burst (effective)	Height of burst (mils) Height of burst (normal)
14. Spotter	Observer
15. Up spot	Short sense
16. Down spot	Over sense
17. No change, no change	Range correct, deflection correct
18. Message: "Salvo"	Message: "On the way"
19. Intervening terrain features	Mask
20. Target bearing line	Gun target line
21. High capacity	High explosive
22. Plotting room	Fire direction center
23. Fire support area	Battery position
24. Straddle	Bracket

20 May landing orders.

```
11thPHIB/A4-3(1)(a)                    WESTERN NAVAL TASK FORCE
Serial: 00681                          ASSAULT FORCE "O"
                                       (TASK FORCE ONE TWO FOUR)
DECLASSIFIED         EPTUNE            U.S.S. ANCON, Flagship,
                                       PORTLAND, DORSET,
OPERATION ORDER                        20 MAY 1944; 1200.
  No. BB-44

TASK ORGANIZATION                                         851
```

(a)   __Landing Force__ - Major General Huebner, USA.
(124.1)

        1st U.S. Infantry Division (less 26th R.C.T., plus 115th & 116th
            R.C.T.s of the 29th Infantry Division, plus 2nd & 5th
            Ranger Battalions), Reinforced.

(b)   __Shore Party__ - Brigadier General Hoge, USA.
(124.2)

2/3ds	5th Engineer Special Brigade.
2/3ds	6th U.S. Naval Beach Battalion.
1/3d	6th Engineer Special Brigade.
1/3d	7th U.S. Naval Beach Battalion.

(c)   __Assault Group O-1__ - Captain Fritzsche, USCG.
(124.3)   Captain Imlay, USCG, Deputy.

APAs	CHASE(F), HENRICO	2 APAs
LCH	LCI(L)-87 (RF)	1 LCH
LSI(L)	EMPIRE ANVIL	1 LSI(L)
LSTs	309, 314, 357, 373, 374, 376	6 LSTs
LCI(L)s	83, 85, 88, 89, 493	5 LCI(L)s
LCTs	, 13, 20, 25, 195, 199, 200, 201, 206, 209, 213, 271, 276, 293, 335, 537, 538, 539, 540, 541, 542, 543, 544, 545, 546, 547, 548, 549, 550, 598, 599, 600, 601, 602, 603, 623, 624, 625, 626, 637, 638, 769, 814, 815, 856, 2008, 2037, 2043, 2049, 2228, 2287, 2339, 2425, 2437.	53 LCTs
LCM(3)s, as assigned.		18 LCM(3)s
PCs	552, 553	2 PCs
SCs	1291, 1307	2 SCs
MLs	113, 187	2 MLs
LCCs	10, 20	2 LCCs

(d)   __Assault Group O-2__ - Captain Bailey, USN.
(124.4)   Captain Wright, USN, Deputy.

APAs	CARROLL(F), JEFFERSON	2 APAs
LCH	LCI(L)-86 (RF)	1 LCH
LSI(L)	EMPIRE JAVELIN	1 LSI(L)
LSTs	310, 315, 316, 317, 332, 372.	6 LSTs
LCI(L)s	84, 90, 91, 92, 94, 408, 409, 410, 411, 412, 413, 540, 541, 553, 554, 555, 557.	17 LCI(L)s

- 1 -

Below: 2nd Rangers vehicle loading information.

11thPHIB/A4-3(1)(
Serial: CC681

TOP SECRET — NEPTUNE

WESTERN NAVAL TASK FORCE
ASSAULT FORCE "O"
(TASK FORCE ONE TWO FOUR)
U.S.S. ANCON, Flagship.
PORTLAND, DORSET.
20 May 1944 ; 1200

ANNEX D
TO OPERATION ORDER BB-44
ATTACK LANDING PLAN
SECTION 2(b)(4)
LOT ASSIGNMENT TABLE
FOR 116th RCT

Army Serial No.	Navy No.	Units Loaded	Personnel	Vehicles	LOT Wave No.	Beach	Landing Time
LOT(6) 102	704	Co's B&C,147th Engr Bn; 3rd Bn,116th Inf 3565th Ord. Co.S	51	3	A52 DG	DOG GREEN	H/60
LOT(6) 100	614	3rd Bn,116th Inf Co's A&C, 149th Engr Bn; 3565th Ord.Co	65	14	85 DR	DOG RED	H/60
LOT(6) 106	612	3rd Bn. 116th Inf. 743rd Tank Bn,112th Engr. Bn.	65	15	83 DR	DOG RED	H/60
LOT(6) 103	536	Co's A&C 149th Engr Bn, 1st Bn,116th Inf	55	11	81 DR	DOG RED	H/60
LOT(6) 104	613	2nd Bn, 116th Inf. Co's A&C,149th Engr Bn 293rd JASCO, 3565th Ord Co.	63	14	82DR	DOG RED	H/60
LOT(6) 98	569	112th Engr Bn, 2nd, Bn.-Cannon Co,Service Co, 116th Inf	69	13	71 EG	EASY GREEN	H/60
LOT(6) 114	775	A&P Pl,1st Bn.116th Inf; 2nd Engr Bn; 743rd Tank Bn.	62	12	A10-3DG	DOG GREEN	H/70
LOT(6) 105	705	2nd & 3rd, 116th Inf 743rd Tank Bn, 121st Engr(C) Bn.	67	15	A10-1DG	DOG GREEN	H/70
LOT(5) 74	197	58th(Armd) FA Bn	57	11	95 DW	DOG WHITE	H/90
LOT(5) 42	364	58th (Armd) FA Bn	57	11	93 DW	DOG WHITE	H/90
LOT(5) 43	332	58th (Armd) FA Bn 111th FA Ln Party	62	11	91 DW	DOG WHITE	H/90
LOT(5) 44	207	58th (Armd) FA Bn	57	11	92 DW	DOG WHITE	H/90
LOT(5) 45	29	58th Armd FA Bn;743rd Tk Bn; Co B&C,147th Engr Bn; 121st Engr Bn; 500th Coll.Co.	66	11	94 DW	DOG WHITE	H/90

- 19 -

ANNEX D TO OPERATION ORDER BB-44
ATTACK LANDING PLAN
SECTION 2(b)(4)
LOT ASSIGNMENT TABLE
FOR 116th RCT

Below: The vehicle loading for the 5th Battalion.

```
11thPHIB/A4-3(1)(                                    .ESTERN NAVAL TASK FORCE
Serial: CC681                                        ASSAULT FORCE "O"
                                                     (TASK FORCE ONE TWO FOUR)
TOP SECRET - NEPTUNE                                 U.S.S. ANCON, Flagship.
                                                     PORTLAND, DORSET.
                                                     20 May 1944 ; 1200
                        ANNEX D
                 TO OPERATION ORDER BB-44
                   ATTACK LANDING PLAN
                     SECTION 2(b)(4)
                   LCT ASSIGNMENT TABLE
                     FOR 116th RCT
```

Army Serial No.	Navy No.	Units Loaded	Personnel.	Vehicles	LCT Wave No.	Beach	Landing Time
LCT(6) 105	617	Co A 149th Eng.Bn NSFCP, 58 Armd FA Bn Air Support Party,320 Bar Bln Bn	43	12	12-3DR	DOG RED	H/130
LCT(6) 110	571	121st Eng. (C) Bn.5th Rngr.Bn. 320th Bar Bln Bn	27	14	14-1DW	DOG WHITE	H/225
LCT(6) 107	572	Co.C,149th Eng. Bn. 58th Armd FA Bn.Recon Plat,3565th Ord Co 320 Bar Bln Bn	45	7	14-2DW	DOG WHITE	H/225
LCT(6) 109	573	Co.C, 149th Eng.Bn 293rd JASCO,58th Armd FA Bn.743rd Tk Bn 320th Bar Bln Bn	54	10	14-1DR	DOG RED	H/225
LCT(6) 87	313	H&S Co.149th Eng Bn 967th QM Serv Co; 320th Bar Bln Bn	44	2	14-3EG	EASY GREEN	H/330
LCT(6) 85	665	H&S Co. 149th Eng.Bn 967th QM Serv;320th Bar Bln Bn	44	2	14-2EG	EASY GREEN	H/330
LCT(6) 86	666	H&S Co,149th Eng Bn; 967th QM Serv.Co: 320th Bar Bln Bn	44	2	14-1EG	EASY GREEN	H/330

```
                              ANNEX D TO OPERATION ORDER BB-44
                              ATTACK LANDING PLAN
                              SECTION 2(b)(4)
                              LCT ASSIGNMENT TABLE
                              FOR 116th RCT
```

DECLASSIFIED 100

Below: The Ranger landing ships' allocation of LCAs for the assault.

11thPHIB/A4-3(1)(a)   WESTERN NAVAL TASK FORCE
Serial: 00681   ASSAULT FORCE "O"
                                             (TASK FORCE ONE TWO FOUR)
TOP SECRET - NEPTUNE   U.S.S. ANCON, Flagship
                                             PORTLAND, DORSET
                                             20 May 1944: 1200

ANNEX D TO OPERATION ORDER BB-44
ATTACK LANDING PLAN SECTION 2(d)(1)
LSI ASSIGNMENT TABLE FOR ASSAULT GROUP O-4

Note: Assault Group O-4 lifts the 2nd and 5th Ranger Battalions.
Note: Be prepared to divert Ranger companies scheduled for Beach DOG GREEN
       to Beach CHARLIE if initial landing on CHARLIE meets with unexpectedly
       quick success.

Army Ser. No.	Navy Name	Units Loaded	Personnel	Vehicles	Beach	Landing Time
LSI(H) No. 1	BEN MY CHREE	Co F, Dets, Co E & Bn Hq, 2nd Rngr Bn, 58th FA Bn Dt	112	None	CHARLIE	H hour
LSI(H) No. 2	AMSTERDAM	Dets Co D, E & Bn Hq 2nd Rngr Bn, NSFCP	105	None	CHARLIE	H hour
LSI(H) No. 3	PRINCESS MAUD	Spec Engr Navy Unit *	385	- -	EASY GREEN DOG RED DOG WHITE DOG GREEN	H ≠ 03
LSI(S) No. 1	PRINCE CHARLES	Det. 29th Recon, Rg Staff, Co's A,B,C, Hq 2nd Rngr Batt. NFSP, 58th FA Bn	262	None	DOG GREEN	H ≠ 03 to H ≠ 60
LSI(S) No. 2	PRINCE LEOPOLD	Co A,B,E, Hq Det 5th Rngr Bn	244	None	DOG GREEN	H ≠ 65
LSI(S) No. 3	PRINCE BAUDOUIN	Co's C,D,F, Hq Det 5th Ranger Bn	246	None	DOG GREEN	H ≠ 70

*: Special Engineer - Navy Unit boated in LCMs Nos. 17-27 (inclusive) of
    US LCM Flot. One, which report alongside PRINCESS MAUD upon arrival in
    Transport Area. Spares (LCMs 28-36) also rendezvous at PRINCESS MAUD.

ANNEX D TO OPERATION ORDER BB-44
ATTACK LANDING PLAN SECTION 2(d)(1)
LSI ASSIGNMENT TABLE FOR
ASSAULT GROUP O-4

11thPHIB/A4-3(1)(
Serial: CC681

TOP SECRET – NEPTUNE

WESTERN NAVAL TASK FORCE
ASSAULT FORCE "O"
(TASK FORCE ONE TWO FOUR)
U.S.S. ANCON, Flagship.
PORTLAND, DORSET.
20 May 1944 : 1200

ANNEX D
TO OPERATION ORDER BB-44
ATTACK LANDING PLAN
SECTION 2(b)(4)
LCT ASSIGNMENT TABLE
FOR 116th RCT

Army Serial No.	Navy No.	Units Loaded	Personnel	Vehicles	LCT Wave No.	Beach	Landing time
LCT(5) 33	27	467th AA(AW)Bn,H&S Co.149th Engr Bn	60	12	12-1DG	DOG GREEN	H/120
LCT(5) 38	214	467th AA(AW) Bn.	62	11	12-2DG	DOG GREEN	H/120
LCT(5) 35	147	Hq Co 116th Inf. 467th AA(AW) Bn	59	13	11-1DW	DOG WHITE	H/120
LCT(5) 39	155	467th AA(AW) Bn	61	11	11-2DW	DOG WHITE	H/120
LCT(6) 115	776	Co C,147th Engr.Bn. Co A&B 149th Eng.Bn 500th Coll.Co;Cannon Co, 116th Inf.	55	3	11-5DR	DOG RED	H/120
LCT(5) 36	149	467th AA(AW) Bn,Co A 149th Eng.Bn	60	12	11-3DR	DOG RED	H/120
LCT(6) 88	616	2nd Rangr.Bn; Hq Co.116th Inf.467th AA(AW) Bn.	48	11	11-1DR	DOG RED	H/120
LCT(5) 40	85	467th AA(AW) Bn	61	11	11-2DR	DOG RED	H/120
LCT(6) 56	615	112th Eng.Bn.Hq.Co. AT Co. 116th Inf.	50	12	11-4DR	DOG RED	H/120
LCT(5) 37	30	H&S Co. 149th Eng. Bn; 467th AA(AW) Bn.	60	12	10-3EG	EASY GREEN	H/120
LCT(5) 32	294	AT Co. 116th Inf.	63	15	10-1EG	EASY GREEN	H/120
LCT(5) 41	214	467th AA(AW) Bn.	61	11	10-2EG	EASY GREEN	H/120
LCT(6) 112	714	743rd Tk.Bn. 2nd Rngr.Bn. 5th Armd FA Bn	36	16	13-5DG	DOG GREEN	H/130
LCT(6) 113	757	2nd Rngr.Bn.5th Rngr Bn. USPOP	45	19	13-3DG	DOG GREEN	H/130
LCT(5) 47	2297	467th AA(AW) Bn 2nd & 5th Rngr.Bn.Rngr air Support.	34	16	13-1DG	DOG GREEN	H/130
LCT(5) 111	570	743rd Tank Bn.58th Armd FA Bn	43	9	13-5DW	DOG WHITE	H/130

ANNEX D TO OPERATION ORDER BB-44
ATTACK LANDING PLAN
SECTION 2(b)(4)
LCT ASSIGNMENT TABLE
FOR 116th RCT

11thPHIB/A4-3(1)(a)   WESTERN NAVAL TASK FORCE
Serial: 00681   ASSAULT FORCE "O"
                                             (TASK FORCE ONE TWO FOUR)
TOP SECRET - NEPTUNE   U.S.S. ANCON, Flagship
                                             PORTLAND, DORSET
                                             20 May 1944: 1200

                 ANNEX D TO OPERATION ORDER BB-44
                 ATTACK LANDING PLAN SECTION 2(d)(2)
                 LCT ASSIGNMENT TABLE FOR ASSAULT GROUP O-4

    Note: Assault Group O-4 lifts 2nd and 5th Ranger Battalions.

    Note: LCT 413 releases DUKWs in time for them to land at H hour
          immediately behind LCA wave on CHARLIE beach.

Army Ser. No.	Navy No.	Units Loaded	Person- nel	Vehi- cles	LCT Wave No.	Beach	Landing Time
LCT(5) 46	413	2nd Rngr Bn	33	4 DUKWs	31C	CHARLIE	H hour for DUKWs

```
11thPHIB/A4-3(1)(a)                    WESTERN NAVAL TASK FORCE
Serial: 00681                          ASSAULT FORCE "O"
                                       (TASK FORCE ONE TWO FOUR)
TOP SECRET - NEPTUNE                   U.S.S. ANCON, Flagship
                                       PORTLAND, DORSET
                                       20 May 1944:  1200
```

ANNEX D TO OPERATION ORDER BB-44
ATTACK LANDING PLAN
MASTER BOAT EMPLOYMENT PLAN   ASSAULT GROUP O-1

ARMY SER. NO. : SHIP	CRAFT REQUIRED IN ASSAULT	CRAFT CARRIED BY SHIP	EXTRA CRAFT NEEDED BY SHIP	SOURCE AND NO. OF EXTRA CRAFT	TIME EXTRA CRAFT REPORT TO THIS SHIP
LSI(H) No. 1 BEN MY CHREE	6 LCA	6 LCA	None	None	
LSI(H) No. 2 MESTER DAM	6 LCA	6 LCA	None	None	
LSI(H) No 3 PRINCESS MAUD	0	6 LCA	None	None	
LSI(S) No. 1 PRINCE CHARLES	8 LCA	8 LCA	None	None	
LSI(S) No. 2 PRINCE LEOPOLD	7 LCA	7 LCA	None	None	
LSI(S) No. 3 PRINCE BAUDOUIN	7 LCA	7 LCA	None	None	

The laying of smoke screens across Omaha Beach was revisited again, as it was seen as vital to the success of the landings. A comprehensive series of screens was to be laid by aircraft and these planes could provide smoke to allow the Rangers to get in closer to their objectives before being spotted by the defenders. The details of these suggested flights were outlined in a document released on 20 May.

PLAN ONE: 'All units make smoke with all available means.'

Pointe du Hoc is now described as a *'4 gun battery'* of 155mm guns.

11th HIB/A4-3(1)(a)
Serial: 00681

TOP SECRET – NEPTUNE

WESTERN NAVAL TASK FORCE
ASSAULT FORCE "O"
(TASK FORCE ONE TWO FOUR)
U.S.S. ANCON, Flagship,
PORTLAND, DORSET,
20 MAY 1944; 1200

APPENDIX 2 TO ANNEX F TO
OPERATION ORDER BB-44
CONTINGENT PLAN FOR USE OF SMOKE AIRCRAFT

1. Information
(a) Enemy batteries capable of inflicting grave damage on ships of Assault
Force "O" exist at Point du Hoe and Port En Bessin. Enemy machine guns
and light artillery are situated all along high ground in back of OMAHA
beaches.
(b) A total of sixteen (16) A-20 (Boston) aircraft are available to Naval
Commander Western Task Force for smoke tasks.

2. Assumptions:
(a) That smoke tasks by aircraft on ground alert will be provided on
request to NCWTF. Requests must be timed so that they can reach
UXBRIDGE (air headquarters) at least six hours before task is required.
(b) Once planes are in the air smoke tasks cannot be changed except to
cancel the mission or to delay it within the limited endurance of the
planes.
(c) That although batteries have radar control available, the efficacy
of the radar will be seriously impaired by radar countermeasures, bombardment or bombing.

3. This plan provides for the screening of Force "O" against enemy batteries
at Point due Hoe and Port En Bessin and along OMAHA beaches by smoke
aircraft in order to protect own ships and craft.

4. Smoke planes will proceed on order of NCWTF in accordance with one of
the following plans:

(a) Screening against battery of 4 155 mm guns at Point due Hoe:
    (1) Wind on shore   Diagram 1   Plan 13.
    (2) Wind flanking easterly   Diagram 2   Plan 14.
    (3) Wind flanking westerly   Diagram 3   Plan 15.
    (4) Wind off-shore   Diagram 4   Plan 16.
(b) Screening against battery of 5 75mm guns at Port En Bessin:
    (1) Wind on shore   Diagram 5   Plan 17.
    (2) Wind flanking easterly   Diagram 6   Plan 18.
    (3) Wind flanking westerly   Diagram 7   Plan 19.
    (4) Wind off-shore   Diagram 8   Plan 20.
(c) Screening against machine guns and light artillery on OMAHA beaches:
    (1) Wind light off-shore   Diagram 9   Plan 11.

D. MacQUEEN
Flag Secretary.

J.L. HALL, Jr.,
Rear Admiral, U. S. Navy,
Commander TASK FORCE ONE TWO FOUR

APPENDIX 2 TO ANNEX F TO
OPERATION ORDER BB-44

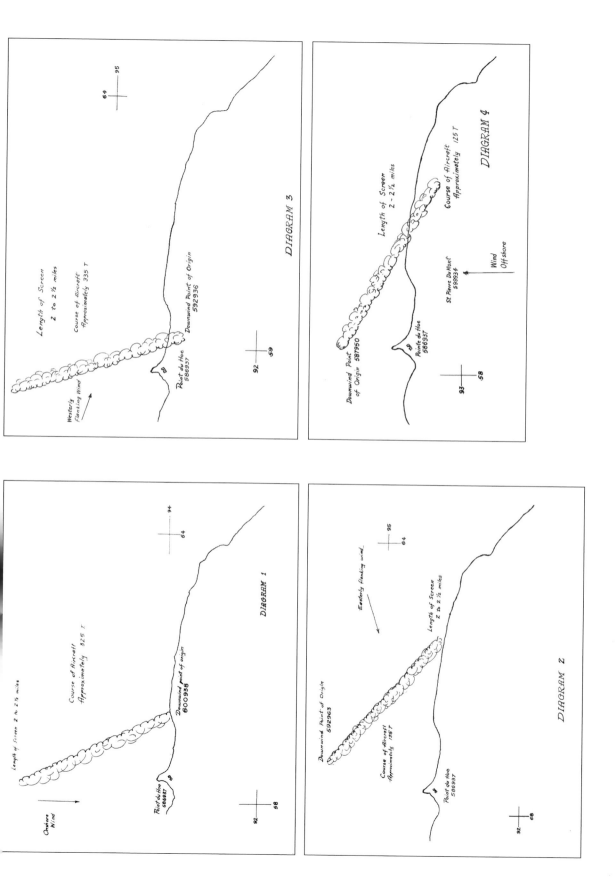

DIAGRAM 1

Length of Screen 2 to 2½ miles

Course of Aircraft Approximately 325 T

Onshore Wind

Downwind point of origin 600958

Point du Hoe 586937

94
64
92
58

DIAGRAM 2

Downwind Point of Origin 592963

Easterly flanking wind.

Length of Screen 2 to 2½ miles

Course of Aircraft Approximately 136 T

Point du Hoe 586937

95
64
92
66

DIAGRAM 3

Length of Screen 2 to 2½ miles

Course of Aircraft Approximately 335 T

Westerly Flanking Wind

Downwind Point of Origin 592936

Point du Hoe 586937

64
95
92
59

DIAGRAM 4

Length of Screen 2 - 2½ miles

Course of Aircraft Approximately 125 T

Downwind Point of Origin 587950

St Pierre DuMont 599934

Wind Offshore

Pointe du Hoe 586937

93
58

The last one, the plan for laying smoke all along Omaha Beach.

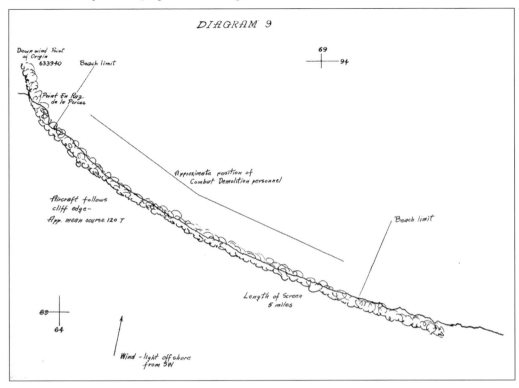

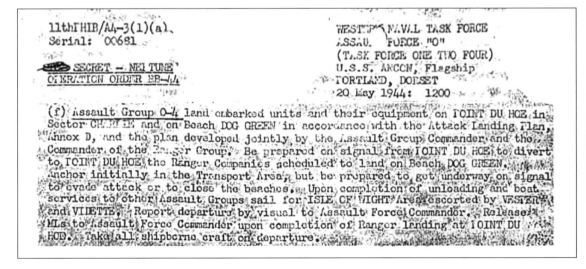

Operational orders of 20 May. A detailed set of orders were released which included a general outline of the invasion plans, supporting Naval, Air Force and group troops information and a detailed section of Enemy and Topographical information. Not to mention the individual unit missions for D-Day.

Shown here is the information from those orders, which directly relate to the Rangers' activities.

HEADQUARTERS
FIRST UNITED STATES ARMY
APO 230

381 (c)   20 May 1944

Subject : Operation " Neptune ".
To   : Commanding General, V Corps.
          Commanding General, VII Corps.
          Commanding General, XIX Corps.
          Commanding General, 1st Engineer Special Brigade.
          Commanding General, 5th Engineer Special Brigade.
          Commanding General, 6th Engineer Special Brigade.

1. At a time and date to be indicated later, you will put in effect Operation " Neptune " as outlined in First U. S. Army Operations Plan " Neptune ", 25 February 1944, as amended.

2. Administrative instructions are being issued to you separately in First Army Administrative Order No. 1.

3. Commanding General, V Corps, and Commanding General, VII Corps, will command all units ashore within their respective areas until Headquarters First U. S. Army is established.   At this time, Corps Commanders will be informed as to which Army units revert to Army control.

4. Should it prove necessary as the operation develops, to change the order of arrival of units as now scheduled in build-up tables, List A and List B, request for such changes will be submitted to First U. S. Army for approval and necessary action.

By command of the Army Commander :

S. E. SENIOR,
Lt. Colonel, AGD,
Asst. Adjutant General.

DISTRIBUTION :
     Cy 1- 2-CG, V Corps.
          3- 4-CG, VII Corps.
          5- 6-CG, XIX Corps.
          7- 8-CG, 1st ESB.
          9-10-CG, 5th ESB.
        11-12-CG, 6th ESB.
          13-AG/TSC.
     14-20-G-3 (Plans & Ops.).

c. *Naval Gunfire Support Plan.*

(1) The following forces will be available to support the Western Task Force :

1 " R " class battleship (Ramillies) (4-15″ Guns)
1 Monitor (2-15′ guns)
7 Cruisers
16 Destroyers
9 LCG(L)
14 LCT(R)
16 LCT(A)   (carry minimum two (2) tanks each which
6 LCT (slightly armored)   (will fire during approach.
54 LCP(L) Smoke
36 LCS(S)

(2) Shore Fire Control Parties will be provided for each infantry battalion of the three assault divisions and in addition three (3) Shore Fire Control Parties and nine (9) artillery observers will be attached to airborne forces.

(3) When mixed forces are operating together, i.e., British warships supporting U. S. troops, the communication code and method of control of gunfire used will be that normally used by the naval gunfire spotter or air spotter concerned. Bombardment Liaison Officers (British) will be provided for all supporting ships both British and U. S., and U. S. Naval Gunfire Liaison will be provided for British ships (cruisers and above) which support U. S. Forces. These officers will perform the necessary liaison and interpretation duties.

(4) The heavier gunfire support ships, 1 BB, 1 Monitor, and 7 cruisers, will commence firing upon coast defense batteries from H–40 minutes or earlier, if necessary, and continue until the battery has been silenced or captured.

(5) The destroyers will be assigned to deliver close support fire on the landing beaches from about H–20 minutes until fire must be lifted for safety to troops. The targets for these destroyers will be strong points and defenses on the beaches and on the flanks of the beaches. If any coastal batteries are silenced prior to H Hour, cruiser fire will be directed on the beach defenses.

(6) In addition the major task of support craft will be to take part in the beach drenching.

(7) Close support fire will be delivered on call from Shore Fire Control Parties with assault battalions from battleships, cruisers and destroyers. No indirect fire from LCG(L) will be employed.

b. *Preliminary Air Bombardment.*

(1) The over-riding commitment in the assault phase will be the gaining and maintaining of air superiority. Subject to this, the maximum possible effort will be made available during the period night of D–1/D Day and D Day, and subsequently as necessary for the vital tasks of assisting the Navy to neutralize the coast defenses, help the land forces in their initial occupation of the bridgehead, and delay the arrival of the enemy's immediate reserves and reinforcements. These roles will call for night and day bombing.

(2) Attacks on enemy reinforcements will require prearranged bombing of special key points, and in addition a proportion of the bomber effort will be held in readiness to engage opportunity targets.

(3) Coast artillery and field batteries will be engaged by Naval and Air bombardment of selected points in beach defenses.

(4) The assault will be immediately preceded by prearranged Naval and Air bombardment of selected points in beach defenses.

(5) The *final* list of beach defense targets for prearranged Naval and Air Fire support will be forwarded by Armies, after consultation with associated Naval and Air Forces, to Headquarters, 21 Army Group not later than 15 March.

c. *Air Support Subsequent to the Assault.*

(1) On and from D Day some proportion of our available air effort will have to be held in reserve for attacks of opportunity, such as concentrations, rail and road movements, and to meet unforeseen contingencies.

(2) A proportion of the bomber effort will be held in readiness to engage targets of opportunity.

II. MISSION

6. *MISSION OF FIRST U. S. ARMY*

a. *Scheme of Attack.*

The First U. S. Army will launch a simultaneous assault on Beaches Utah and Omaha on D Day and H Hour; it will capture on D Day objectives as shown in Assault Plan (Annex No. 19), and thereafter will advance as rapidly as the situation permits, capturing Cherbourg with the minimum of delay and developing Vierville-sur-Mer, Colleville-sur-Mer beachhead southwards towards St. Lo in conformity with the advance of the Second British Army. The attack on Utah Beach will be made by the VII Corps with the 4th Division (Force "U") in the initial assault, and the attack on Omaha Beach will be made by the V Corps with a composite division of the 1st and 29th Infantry Divisions (Force "O") and the 2nd and 5th Ranger Battalions in the initial assault, and the remainder of the divisions in the immediate follow-up (Force "B"). For organization of assault and follow-up forces, see Annex No. 2. For number and type of landing ships and craft which may be unloaded on each of the first three tides, see Annex No. 19.

III. OPERATIONS

8. *V CORPS*

a. *Troops.*
2nd and 5th Ranger Battalions.
Force " O " - See Annex No. 2.
Force " B " - See Annex No. 2.
Build-up Units - See Annex No. 2a.

b. *Mission.*
Assault Omaha Beach with 2nd and 5th Ranger Battalions and Force " O " on D Day at H Hour ; capture objectives as shown in Annex No. 19, on D Day and thereafter advance in accordance with instructions to be issued by Headquarters First U. S. Army.

c. *Enemy Dispositions.* (See Sketch Map Annex 1 c (3).

(1) In Omaha Beach (Bayeux-Isigny) sector, the defenses consist of beach strong-points and company and battalion headquarters strong-points further inland. Strong-points extend along the beaches throughout the 716th Divisional section and vary in strength from half a platoon to one platoon, reinforced in most cases with heavier weapons, usually two infantry and/or anti-tank guns per strong-point. They are not regularly spaced but are sited to cover vulnerable beaches and approaches. Interspersed between infantry strong-points are a number of AA. CA. Navy and FA artillery strong-points. Elaborate fire plans exist with bands of fire of the weapons within each strong-point interlocking, and weapons in adjacent strong-points mutually supporting. Alternative positions are prepared for all infantry weapons. At night, or in bad visibility, continuous patrolling is carried out between strong-points with a stationary sentry at each strong-point.

a. *Artillery.* (See Sketch Map - Annex 1c (6).

(1) *Coastal Artillery.* (See Sketch Map - Annex 1 c (6).

(2) *Field Artillery.* There is known to be one battalion of field artillery behind the defenses of Utah beach (49-ISIS) and another battalion behind the defenses of Omaha beach DEF (46-ISIS) and B (47-ISIS). These may be in addition to the organic field artillery battalions of the divisions concerned. The 709th Infantry Division is believed to have a field artillery regiment, with two battalions and the 716th Infantry Division is also believed to have two battalions of field artillery.

The following document lists the array of other units who were informed of the Rangers' activities on D-Day. The reason for this was to ensure that friendly fire could be avoided. If everyone knew where the Rangers would be and when, the risk would be minimised.

DISTRIBUTION

	COPY Nos
Commander-in-Chief, 21 Army Group	1
Naval Commander, Western Task Force	2
Commanding General, 9th USAAF	3
General Officer Commanding, 2nd British Army	4
Commanding General, First U. S. Army	5
21 Army Group (for internal and onward distribution)	6 - 35
SHAEF	
ANXF	
AEAF	
Second British Army	36 - 39
Western Naval Task Force (for internal and onward distribution)	40 - 60
COMNAVEU	
Naval Commander, Western Task Force	
Naval Commander, Force " O "	
Naval Commander, Force " U "	
Naval Commander, Force " B "	
Com Lan Crab 11th Phib	
9th U. S. Air Force (for internal and onward distribution)	61 - 122
USSTAF	
TAF (incl. 83 and 84 Group)	
85 Group	
38 Group	
IX Troop Carrier Command	
IX Bomber Command	
IX Fighter Command	
XIX Air Support Command	
IX Air Support Command	
IX Air Defense Command	
C.O., 10th Rcn Wing	
ETOUSA (to include SOS)	123 - 157
FUSAG	158 - 172
First U. S. Army	173 - 197
V Corps (for internal and onward distribution)	198 - 212
VII Corps (for internal and onward distribution)	213 - 227
XIX Corps (for internal and onward distribution)	228 - 242
VIII Corps (for internal and onward distribution)	243 - 247
Third U. S. Army	248 - 257
101st Airborne Division	258 - 262
82nd Airborne Division	263 - 267
1st Engr Spec Brig	268 - 272
5th Engr Spec Brig	273 - 277
6th Engr Spec Brig	278 - 282
47th AAA Brigade	283 - 284
SO/SOE	285 - 286
Spares	287 - 324

Each ship was allocated a call sign to allow accurate communication of gunfire support to be delivered by the Navy. This information was disseminated by USS *Ancon* – the Omaha Assault Force command ship – to other vessels and units on land.

11th.HIB/AA-3(1)(a)
Serial: 00681

TO. SECRET - NEPTUNE

WESTERN NAVAL TASK FORCE
ASSAULT FORCE "O"
(TASK FORCE ONE TWO FOUR)
U.S.S. ANCON, Flagship
PORTLAND, DORSET
20 MAY 1944; 1200.

APPENDIX 8 TO ANNEX H
TO OPERATION ORDER BB-44
SHORE FIRE CONTROL FREQUENCIES

1.   This Appendix duplicates to some extent instructions and and information contained in Annex F, Gunfire Support Plan. Its primary purpose is to consolidate Gunfire Support information which pertains to communications.

2.   Assault Force "O" Auxiliary Frequency - 2716 kcs.

3.   Force "O" Common Bombardment Calling Frequency - 4300 kcs.

4.   Shore Fire Control Frequencies, Force "O".

Shore Fire Control Party	Call Signs	Ship	Call Signs	AM Freq.	"A" Channel FM Radio	"B" Channel FM Radio
1	DJX	USS SATTERLEE	TAS	5595	27.0 mcs	32.0 mcs
2	FGH	HMS GLASGOW	SLG	5638	34.4	32.0
3	KRD	USS McCOOK	CMC	4825	27.4	32.0
4	MKR	USS CARMICK	MRC	4440	34.0	32.0
5	SJT	USS TEXAS	SXT	3840	30.0	32.0
6	NAD	111 FDC		4300	----	32.0
7	ZAI	USS DOYLE	LYD	5445	33.6	32.4
8	FAT	USS ENDICOTT	CDN	5615	29.8	32.4
9	KMA	FS MONTCALM	TNM	4125	30.4	32.4
10	HOF	7 FDC		4300	----	32.4
11	CWR	USS BALDWIN	DLB	4620	33.2	32.4
12	LSG	USS BALDWIN	DLB	4620	33.2	32.4
13	DBR	USS ARKANSAS	NKR	3900	30.7	32.4
14	PBR	32 FDC		4300	----	32.4
15	AVA	1st Artillery		4300	----	32.4
16	TBN	USS THOMPSON	MHT	4335	31.0	32.0
17	BGK	USS FRANKFORD	ARF	4673	32.8	32.0
18	PAD	USS THOMPSON	MHT	4335	31.0	32.0
19	FRX	11th FDC		4300	----	32.0
20	JBA	USS HARDING	RAH	4025	31.4	32.4
21	SDA	FS GEORGES LEYGUES	GRG	5387	29.4	32.4
22	NSR	USS HARDING	RAH	4025	31.4	32.4
23	PLS	33 FDC		4300	----	32.4
24	QFJ	HMS GLASGOW	SLG	5638	31.6	32.0
25	RGA					

APPENDIX 8 TO ANNEX H
TO OPERATION ORDER BB-44
SHORE FIRE CONTROL FREQUENCIES

11thΓΗΙΒ/Λ4-3(1)(a)
Serial: 00681

TOP SECRET – NEPTUNE
OPERATION ORDER
No. BB-44

WESTERN NAVAL TASK FORCE
ASSAULT FORCE "O"
(TASK FORCE ONE TWO FOUR)
U.S.S. ANCON, Flagship,
PORTLAND, DORSET,
20 MAY 1944; 1200

APPENDIX 4 TO ANNEX E
TO OPERATION ORDER NO. BB-44
CALL SIGNS AND FREQUENCIES

1. The Shore fire control communication net is designed to permit quick and positive communications with a maximum of security. As far as possible one FM and one AM frequency will be assigned to each ship-shore fire control party circuit. In addition, there will be a common FM channel for each division and a common fire support frequency (bombardment calling wave, 4300 kcs.) for all parties.

2. Shore fire control parties will guard assigned frequencies on the "A" channel of their SCR 609 sets and will set the "B" channels on the Division common channel (32.4 mcs for the 1st Division, 32.0 mcs for the 29th Division). They will normally guard their assigned frequencies on their SCR 284 sets. Artillery battalion headquarters and division artillery NGLOs will guard the common channels, both AM and FM.

3. Gunfire Support Ships will ship in their SCR 608 sets crystals for the FM frequencies assigned the division they normally support (Fire Support Group ONE supports 29th Division, Fire Support Group TWO supports 1st Division) plus the common frequency of the other division. They will normally guard the assigned FM frequency and the division common FM frequency. If temporarily unassigned to a specific shore fire control party they will guard both division common frequencies. They will guard their assigned SFCP frequency (AM) and maintain a receiver watch on the bombardment calling wave. If unassigned to a specific shore fire control party they will guard the bombardment calling wave.

4. The initial assignment of call signs and frequencies to ships and shore fire control parties is as follows: (In all cases call sign for NGLO is generated by adding "1" to that for the F.O. Example: NGLO for SFCP 1 has call DJX1.)

Force "O"

SFCP No.	Unit	Call Sign	FM Frequency	AM Frequency	Ship	Call Sign
1	2ndR	DJX	27.0	016 – 5595	SATTERLEE	TAS
2	5thR	FGH	34.4	017 – 5638	GLASGOW	SLG
3	(1)116	KRD	27.4	013 – 4825	McCOOK	CMC
4	(2)116	MKR	34.0	02 – 4440	CARMICK	MRC
5	(3)116	SJT	30.0	07 – 3840	TEXAS	SXT
6	111FDC	NAD	32.0	BCW – 4300	—	—
7	(1)16	ZIW	33.6	015 – 5445	DOYLE	LYD
8	(2)16	FAT	29.8	U7 – 5615	ENDICOTT	CDN
9	(3)16	KMA	30.4	09 – 4125	MONTCALM	TNM
10	7FDC	HOF	32.4	BCW – 4300	—	—

APPENDIX 4 TO ANNEX E TO OPERATION
ORDER NO. BB-44 CALL SIGNS AND
FREQUENCIES.

21 May 1944
5th Rangers – Companies A – F, Medical and HQ – Dorchester, Dorset.
A, B & C Companies 2nd Rangers – Dorchester, Dorset. Alerted for departure.
D, E & F Companies 2nd Rangers – Swanage, Dorset. Alerted for departure.
Medical Detachment 2nd Rangers – Dorchester, Dorset. Alerted for departure.
Headquarters Company 2nd Rangers – Dorchester, Dorset. Alerted for departure.

On the next page is an aircraft allocation to target plan. It shows the time period in which any given target would be attacked from the air or with the help of aircraft spotting for the Navy. [Apologies for the quality – the original is in poor shape.]

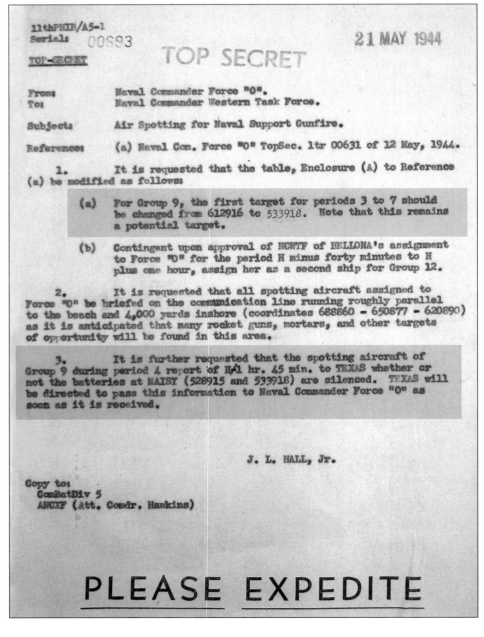

11thPHIB/A5-1
Serial: 00693

TOP SECRET   **TOP SECRET**   21 MAY 1944

From: Naval Commander Force "O".
To: Naval Commander Western Task Force.

Subject: Air Spotting for Naval Support Gunfire.

Reference: (a) Naval Com. Force "O" TopSec. 1tr 00631 of 12 May, 1944.

      1.   It is requested that the table, Enclosure (A) to Reference
(a) be modified as follows:

      (a)   For Group 9, the first target for periods 3 to 7 should
             be changed from 612916 to 533918. Note that this remains
             a potential target.

      (b)   Contingent upon approval of NCWTF of BELLONA's assignment
             to Force "O" for the period H minus forty minutes to H
             plus one hour, assign her as a second ship for Group 12.

      2.   It is requested that all spotting aircraft assigned to
Force "O" be briefed on the communication line running roughly parallel
to the beach and 4,000 yards inshore (coordinates 688860 – 650877 – 620890)
as it is anticipated that many rocket guns, mortars, and other targets
of opportunity will be found in this area.

      3.   It is further requested that the spotting aircraft of
Group 9 during period 4 report of H-1 hr. 45 min. to TEXAS whether or
not the batteries at MAISY (528915 and 533918) are silenced. TEXAS will
be directed to pass this information to Naval Commander Force "O" as
soon as it is received.

                         J. L. HALL, Jr.

Copy to:
   ComBatDiv 5
   ANCXF (Att. Comdr. Hawkins)

PLEASE EXPEDITE

A change in target numbers now includes the Les Perruques battery in their targeting for Naval Group 9. There is also a direct request that confirmation of Maisy being silenced is passed to the Naval Commander *'as soon as it is received'.*

SIG.4 - TOP SECRET

SHIPPING AIRCRAFT - FRAMEWORK OF SCHEDULES AND SEARCH ANGLE PATTERNS.

As a guide, here are some of the grid references for the Rangers' area of operations.

523932 Maisy Beach defences and observation post
527923 Unoccupied dummy battery
528915 La Martinière Battery
531914 Foucher's Farm Battery
533918 Les Perruques Battery
586935 Pointe du Hoc
586932 Au Guay
582926 Field to the back of PdH
598935 St. Pierre du Mont battery (presumed to be guns)
625935 Radar Station area
623934 Radar Station area

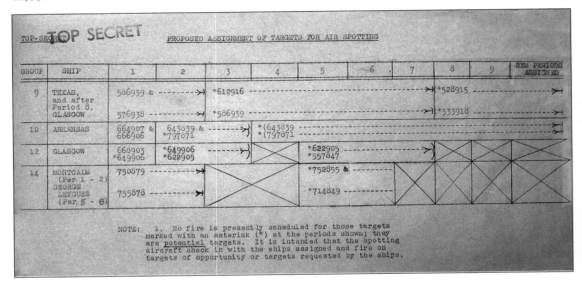

TOP SECRET   PROPOSED ASSIGNMENT OF TARGETS FOR AIR SPOTTING

GROUP	SHIP	1	2	3	4	5	6	7	8	9	REM PERIODS ASSIGNED
9	TEXAS, and after Period 8, GLASGOW	586939 & ----→	*612916 --------------						*528915 --------		----→
		576938 ----→	*586939 --------------						*533918 --------		----→
10	ARKANSAS	664907 & 666906	643839 & *797871 ----→	*(643839 *(797871 --------------							----→
12	GLASGOW	668903 *649906	*649906 *622905	----→		*622905 *557847 --------		----→			
14	MONTCALM (Per. 1 - 2)	750879 ----→				*752855 & --------					
	GEORGE LEYGUES (Per. 5 - 6)	755878 ----→				*714849 --------					

NOTE: 1. No fire is presently scheduled for those targets marked with an asterisk (*) at the periods shown; they are potential targets. It is intended that the spotting aircraft check in with the ships assigned and fire on targets of opportunity or targets requested by the ships.

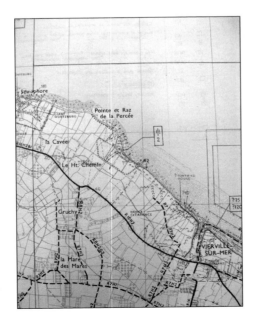

Dated 21 May – a GSGS map for Pointe et Raz de la Percée and an assault map of the same area.

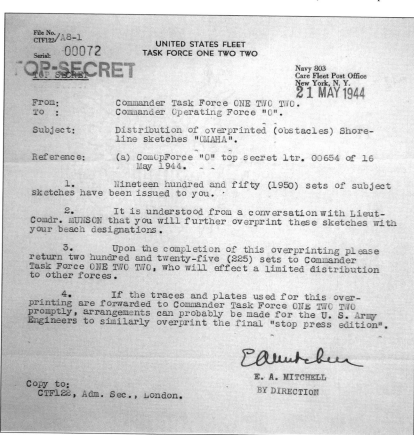

An order to overprint already existing maps of the beach obstacles was issued. This will have been suggested because the obstacles would have been developing and increasing – and also it was important that all those landing in the first waves had as up-to-date an information as possible. As mentioned before, the reuse of existing maps also saved both time and money. An example of an overprinted map is shown below the order.

Below: Further updates to the beach obstacle maps for Vierville-sur-Mer and Colleville-sur-Mer were also released recording changes earlier in the month along that beach front.

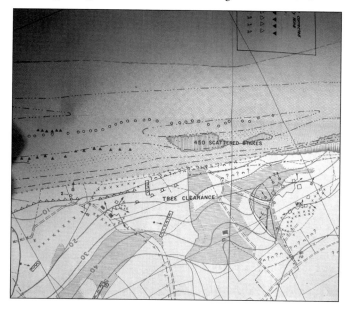
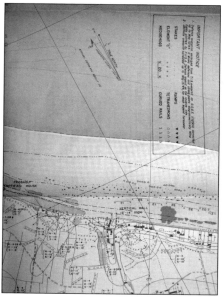

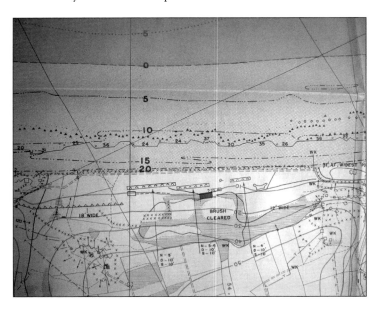

---

22 May 1944   Navy Report dated 22 May: *To obviate the danger to security that might arise when a large number of Press correspondents would be mobilised and disappear from their usual haunts shortly before D-Day, a practice mobilisation took place. Approximately 80 Press correspondents, to be attached to the Task Forces, were called to the Admiralty and dispatched by road to their respective ships for 24 hours. They were given brief instructions on the need for this cover move and the security angle involved. Several useful lessons were learned which proved that this item of cover deception had been highly successful.*

5th Rangers –   Paragraphs 1a and b of letter, HQ V Corps, subject, 'Desertion' dated 21 April 1944, were read to a number of men
Companies A – F,   from D Company who had been absent during previous readings.
Medical and HQ –   This took place at 0900hrs.
Dorchester, Dorset.

Below: Confirmation in writing that this warning was also given to an additional man from the 5th Battalion.

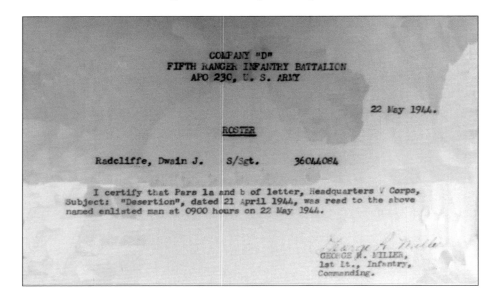

2nd Battlion Historical Narrative.

> On 22 May, the Battalion moved by rail to Staging Area D-5 near Dorchester and the Battalion commenced briefing in preparation for the assigned mission. Rubber models procured thru Army channels and plaster models, constructed by Intelligence personnel, assisted in this instruction. Companies D/E/F continued to work out on ropes attached to trees in the camp.

A, B & C Companies 2nd Rangers – Dorchester, Dorset. Alerted for departure.

D Company 2nd Rangers – Dorchester, Dorset.
Pfc. Gertz was attached to D Company from the 2nd Btn Medical Detachment for Duty.
D Company left Swanage at 1300 hours and arrived in Dorchester, Dorset at 1500 hours.

E Company 2nd Rangers – Dorchester, Dorset.
Pfc. Robert K. Ros was attached to E Company from Headquarters Company 2nd Btn.
Pfc. Michael McDonough was attached to E Company from the 2nd Btn Medical Detachment for Duty.
E Company left Swanage at 1300 hours and arrived in Dorchester, Dorset at 1500 hours.

F Company 2nd Rangers – Dorchester, Dorset.
T/5 Emmet P. Gillespie was attached to F Company from Headquarters Company 2nd Btn.
T/5 Charles W. Korb was attached to F Company from the Medical Detachment 2nd Btn.
F Company left Swanage at 1300 hours and arrived in Dorchester, Dorset at 1500 hours.

Medical Detachment 2nd Rangers – Dorchester, Dorset.
Pfc. McDonough went from Duty to Detached Service with E Company 2nd Btn.
Pfc. Geitz went from Duty to Detached Service with D Company 2nd Btn.
T/5 Korb went from Duty to Detached Service with F Company 2nd Btn.

Headquarters Company 2nd Rangers – Dorchester, Dorset.
Pvt. Granville Harrison was assigned and joined from HQ XIX Corps per auth 5th Ind, HQ FUSA 220.33, dated 15 May 1944.
The following officer and four enlisted men were attached for Duty, rations and quarters from the 165th Signal Photo Company per SO#73 par 1, HQ 30th Inf. Division, APO 30, dated 16 May 1944. As of 18 May 1944.
1st Lt. Amos P. Potts.
Sgt. Worden P. Lovell.
T/4 Irving Lomasky.
Pfc. Keghan Nigohosian.
Pvt. Herbert J. Stark.
T/5 Emmet P. Gillespie went from Duty to Detached Service with F Company 2nd Btn.
Pfc. Robert K. Roe went from Duty to Detached Service with E Company 2nd Btn.
The following thirty enlisted men returned from Detached Service to Duty.
T/5 Paul Galloway, Cpl. Harley R. Sampson, T/5 John Casino, Pvt. James W. Willis, T/5 Budford L. Riddle, T/Sgt. Joseph J. Zimkus, Pfc. Robert G. Schmitt, T/5 Gilbert N. Gleckl, Pfc. William Bass, Pfc. Raymond N. Hubert, Pfc. Ledford L. Carpenter, Pfc. Walter O. Akridge, Pfc. Alfred F. Elsie, Pfc. William A. McKitrick, Pfc. Eugene J. Zielke, M/Sgt. Robert N. Lemin, 1 Sgt. John Erderly, T/5 John Keating, T/5 Alvin S. Rustebakke, Pfc. Henry S. Farrar, T/Sgt. Edward Gurney, T/5 Paul W. French, Pfc. Ivor R. Jones, Pfc. Hellmuth M. Strassburger, Pfc. Leo D. Yates, T/Sgt. John V. Koepfer, Sgt. Charles S. Tolias, T/4 Ramsey A. Turner, Cpl. Henry J. Findish, T/5 Mack C. Styles Jr.
The following three men returned from Detached Service with the Ranger Group HQ to Duty.
Pvt. Thomas J. Armbruster, T/5 Steve M. Mead, Pfc. Guy C. Shoaf.
Record of events. Entrucked for new station 1300hrs. Arrived in Dorchester, Dorset 1500hrs.

22 May – The US Army issued a report on activities during this period of time:

<u>SERVICE OF SUPPLY, EUROPEAN THEATRE OF OPERATIONS REPORT</u>

The next week was spent in completing the supply of every unit. If a man lost his carbine, it was replaced at once by the camp supply officer.

Extra personal items, that proved inconvenient to carry were left behind and cared for by the camp personnel – ensuring its eventual return to the owner. Every man was then issued free cigarettes, candy and gum. In addition, he was given sea-sick pills, water purifying tablets, rations for two days and a lifebelt.

Ordnance patrols roamed about each marshalling area – fixing a carburettor here, checking waterproofing there. When necessary, a whole vehicle, already waterproofed was provided.

The men were encouraged to send all extra money home. Then a partial payment was made to all troops – in 'spearhead' currency, special 'invasion' money, resembling the French currency, but stamped and backed by the Allied Governments. Every man was paid 200 Francs, and given the opportunity to change American or English money into Francs at the rate of two (2 cents) per franc.

Unknown to all, over three billion Francs necessary for this payment had been hauled to Headquarters, Southern Base Section in 19 trucks and stored there, under guard, and sent to the marshalling areas as required.

Below: Dated 22 May. Three Aerial Reconnaissance photographs of the Maisy Batteries. The first shows all three batteries. Les Perruques, La Martinière and Foucher's Farm. These were taken prior to a bombing mission scheduled for 24 May. Of note are the white dots in the surrounding fields. These are anti-landing posts placed vertically into the fields at regular intervals.

The second photograph shows the dummy gun batteries in front of the real ones (centre left side of photo).

Lastly, a blow-up of La Martinière (left) and Les Perruques (right). The guns at Foucher's Farm are just off the picture in the centre bottom.

Below is an undated photograph of Maisy - La Martinière Battery. It is difficult to know exactly when this was taken. Note the Maisy church tower in the background and the unfinished casement with wood surrounding it. The large lattice tower noted on the GSGS maps can clearly be seen as a water tower and it was perhaps used for observation. The site and surrounding landscape show very little sign of having suffered from bombing up to this point. There could be two bomb craters to the lower left of the photograph. There seems to be little other damage – and in fact these marks could be spoil from the land clearance.

Circled in white is a Czech 100mm cannon painted in camouflage colours. It was probably being moved towards the unfinished casement and then it was hastily left when the Allied reconnaissance plane flew over. Notice also the lack of personnel on the ground. Most likely they would have all run to shelter when the air alarms sounded.

The wooden water tower is used to create the cement for the structure of the remaining casement. Once a wooden frame was finished in the shape of a casement, the concrete could be poured very quickly into the frame, acting like a mould. The same field gun is just in shot to the right centre of the next photograph – in the open (indicated by the white circle). The photograph confirms that three of the casements are complete and that work was only being done to the last casement. Also of note is the fact that there were queries being raised suggesting that the guns at La Martinière had already all been moved to Target 16A. These photographs go some way to prove that Target No.16 was armed and Target 16A was in fact a battery of additional guns. [In 2008 a set of wheels for a 150mm cannon were found at Target 16A]. There is a small light railway also visible in these photographs. This was used for moving ammunition from a row of small storage bunkers and up to the casements.

A close-up of the cannon in the open – of note is the camouflage paintwork. It was presumably waiting for the completion of the last casement to give it a permanent shelter.

```
                    HEADQUARTERS 1ST INFANTRY DIVISION
                         APO #1, U. S. Army
                              G-3 (JOURNAL*
                                 (DIARY*
                                                  (From  0001
                                           Time                    
                                                  (To    2400
      Date     22 May 1944         GP Location    LANGTON HOUSE,BLANDFORD
                                                       ENGLAND
    TIME  | NO. | FROM |           SYNOPSIS            | REC'D | DISPOSITION#
          |     |      |                               |  VIA  |
    0001  |  1  |      | Journal opened                |       |
    1400  |  2  |      | Conf at 1st Inf Div Hq attended by all |   |
          |     |      | Regt, Bn, Bde Gp Comdrs and Brig Gen Cota, | |
          |     |      | ACG 29th Inf Div               |      |
    2400  |  3  |      | Journal closed                 |      |

 NOTES:
       *Delete one.
       "Rec'd Via" column will indicate how message was transmitted, i.e., Tp - tele-
 phone; Rad - radio; Tgp - telegraph; Tpe - teletype.
       #Following abbreviations only will be used in this column, other information will
 be written out:  M - Noted on situation map;  J - Appended to journal (applies to Over-
 lays, Msg blanks, written orders, etc.);  CG, C/S, etc. - indicates information passed
 on to Officer indicated;  T- indicates information disseminated to units or troops, as
 indicated in text of message.
 (Revised 3 Jan. '44)
                                     - 1 -
```

Back on the South Coast of England on 22 May Major General Huebner organised a conference at 1st Infantry Division Headquarters which was to be attended by all unit commanders.

23 May 1944   Navy Report 23 May: *'Supreme Commander signaled in special code his decision that D-Day was provisionally fixed to be the 5th of June.'*

5th Rangers – Companies A – F, Medical and HQ – Dorchester, Dorset.

A, B, C, D & E Companies 2nd Rangers – Dorchester, Dorset. No change. Alerted for departure.

F Company 2nd Rangers – Dorchester, Dorset.
Officers 1st Lt. Jonathan H. Harwood and Lt. (Navy) Kenneth S. Norton were relieved of attached for Duty, rations and quarters.
As were the following twelve enlisted men.
Pvt. Ramon G. Rolande, Pvt. Paul Rascon, Pvt. Pete P. Simundich, T/5 Edward G. Heineck, Pvt. Harold F. Plank, Pvt. Mitchell Goldenstein, Pfc. Albert Kamente, Pvt. Howard J. Erickson, Pvt. Carlos C. Arvizu, Pvt. Paul E. Kimbrough, Pvt. John Gallagher, Pvt. Aurhur E. Gable.

Medical Detachment 2nd Rangers – Dorchester, Dorset. No change.

Headquarters Company 2nd Rangers – Dorchester, Dorset.
The following two officers were attached for Duty, rations and quarters. 1st Lt. Jonathan Harwood, Lt. Kenneth S. Norton.
The following twelve enlisted men were attached for Duty, rations and quarters.
Pvt. Peter P. Simundich, T/5 Edward G. Heineck, Pvt. Howard J. Erickson, Pvt. Ramon G. Rolande, Pfc. Albert Kamente, Pvt. Harold F. Plank, Pvt. Mitchell H. Goldenstein, Pvt. Paul Rascon, Pvt. John Gallagher, Pvt. Charles C. Arvizu, Pvt. Arthur E. Gable, Pvt. Paul Kimbrough.

Next page: Dated 23 May, this is a Fighter Bombing Targets list. Interestingly it states *'Serials 2 & 5 are being casemated. The question of whether they are to be attacked is now under joint consideration.'* Indicating, one assumes, that both positions – La Pernelle Battery and Pointe du Hoc – were possibly now being considered as non-targets.

Tuesday, 23 May 1944 the US 386th Bomb Group undertook Mission Number 177 to bomb Maisy. Details of the mission are as follows:

One of the sand tables produced to show the assault troops the layout of the beaches and rear defences.

At take off time 1655 hours; four to six-tenths cumulus with a base of 2,500 feet, tops to 4,000 feet. Altostratus clouds from six to eight-tenths with a base of 6,500 feet with tops of 8,000 feet. Visibility will be five miles in haze. The route out will have no low clouds, eight-tenths altostratus over south England. Nine to ten-tenths over the channel with tops to 8,000 feet – visibility above the clouds is eight to ten miles. Target area at 1830 hours, ten-tenths altocumulus tops to 8,000 feet – no low clouds, visibility above clouds will be good. The return route to base will remain unchanged.

The route out from base to Brighton to 49 Degrees 43 Minutes North – 00 Degrees 17 Minutes West to target. Turn Right off target to Brighton to base. Bomb load in all ships will be 2 x 2,000 pound general purpose demolition bombs. Fusing to be one-tenth nose and one-fortieth tail. Both Path Finder planes will each carry 4 x 600 pound general purpose demolition type bombs. Intervalometer setting is one hundred feet. Bomb run altitude will be 11,900 feet. Radio call sign for the first box is, Animal, second box will be, Bouncefoot. Briefing was concluded with a ten second count down to synchronize all watches at 1605 hours.

Bombs hit in the target area straddling a road running in front of the battery, and extending southwest down the road toward Maisy 2. The 386th Bomb Group sustained no casualties, no losses, and no battle damage during the mission. In the target area at 12,000 feet the temperature was minus one degree Centigrade, the wind was from 350 degrees at 23 miles per hour.

SCHEDULE "H" – ASSAULT PROGRAMME

SECTION D – FIGHTER BOMBERS

Serial	Timing	Targets	Type of Aircraft Employed	Effort Allotted	Remarks
		TARGETS IN US SECTOR			(a) Serials 7 – 13 are also in Schedule D. If surprise is NOT considered lost these serials will be taken on in this schedule. If surprise is lost they will be engaged on D-1.
1	HU – 30 min to HU hour	BARFLEURS Bty 394228	Fighter Bombers		
2	"	LA PERNELLE Bty 365200	"		
3	"	MORSALINES Bty 355136	"		
4	"	MAISY Bty 533918	"		(b) Timings of serials 1 – 6 will be arranged between NCETF, Commander First United States Army and Commander Advanced AEAF.
5	"	POINTE DU HOE Bty 586938	"		
6	"	MAISY II Bty 531914	"		(c) This section will be confirmed on D – 3.
		TARGETS FOR 82 AIRBORNE DIVISION			(d) Alternate targets if any of serials 1 – 6 are badly damaged before D day :-
7		Bridge 096894	"		GIBRAINE Bty 37820,
8		Bridge 104889	"		MAISY 11a Bty 528916)
9		Bridge 121881	"		
10	As early as possible after CT	Bridge 147895	"		(e) Serials 2 and 5 are being consumed. The question of whether they are to be attacked is now under joint consideration.
11	"	Bridge NORTH or LESSAY 1876	"		
12	"	Embankment 190905	"		
13		Embankment 268925	"		
		TARGETS IN BRITISH SECTOR 30 CORPS FRONT			
14	HG + 5 mins to HG + 20 mins	Locality 876752	"		
15	"	VAUX SUR AURE Bty 792831	"		
16	"	Rocket Gun emplacements 869033	"		
		1 CORPS FRONT			
17	HJ + 5 mins to HJ + 20 mins	MERVILLEAUX Bty 972808	"		
18	"	Bty 994818	"		
19	"	PERIERS-SUR-LE-DAN 047772	"		

SCHEDULE 'D'–NEPTUNE D-1 BOMBING

SECTION A – SURPRISE NOT CONSIDERED LOST

(This programme will be carried out unless otherwise ordered)

NIGHT
TOP SECRET

Page_____

Timing	Targets	Type of Aircraft Employed	Effort Allotted	Remarks
D - 1 afternoon and evening	Headquarters	Day Heavy		(a) Serials 1 - 3 will be chosen later. Annotated air photographs of these serials will be sent by 21 Army Group GSI to AEAF by D - 6 at the latest.
"	Headquarters	"		
"	Headquarters	"		(b) Final selection of targets as follows will be made on D - 3 :
D - 1 afternoon and evening	GATTEVILLE Bty 392277	"		Two Headquarters
"	BARFLEUR Bty 394228	"		Five Batteries
"	CHATEAU DE COURCY Bty 361054	"		Four Fighter Control/Telephone Exchanges
"	LA PERNELLE Bty 365200	"		Two Telephone Exchanges.
"	FONTENAY SUR MER Bty 348044	"	25% of Day Heavy Bomber Force.	
"	AZEVILLE Bty 360022	"		
"	ST MARTIN DE VAR EVILLE Bty 405980	"		
"	MAISY I Bty 533918	"		
"	POINTE DU HOE Bty 586937	"		
"	VAUX SUR AURE Bty 792331	"		
"	MOULINEAUX Bty 972808	"		
"	OUISTREHAM I Bty 117797	"		
"	SALLENELLES Bty 155776	"		
"	HOULGATE Bty 256809	"		
"	BENERVILLE Bty 422107	"		
"	LE HAVRE Bty 468311	"		
D - 1 afternoon and evening	TELEPHONE EXCHANGES			
	ST LO 408632	Light		
	PORT L'EVEQUE 525040	"		
D - 1 afternoon and evening	FIGHTER CONTROL/TELEPHONE EXCHANGES			
	RENNES X 980502	Medium		
"	CHANTILLY S 150792	"		
"	JOUY-EN-JOSAS R 94735	"		
"	BERNAY Q 197143	"		

SCHEDULE 'H'–ASSAULT PROGRAMME

SECTION B – MEDIUM BOMBING (EARLY SCHEDULE)

SECRET
TOP SECRET

Page_____

Serial	Timing	Targets	Type of Aircraft Employed	Effort Allotted	Remarks
1	HU Hour	BARFLEUR Bty 394228	Medium		(a) Alternative target if serial 3 badly damaged before D Day.
2	HU Hour	MAISY I Bty 533918	"		MONT COQUEREL Bty 361080
3	HU Hour	POINTE DU HOE Bty 586938	"		CHATEAU DE COURSY Bty 361054
4	GT - 15 mins to GT + 10 mins	MONT FLEURY Bty 918861	"		AZEVILLE Bty 360022
5	GT - 15 mins to GT + 10 mins	OUISTREHAM II Bty 103779	"		MAISY II Bty 528916
6	GT - 15 mins to GT + 10 mins	OUISTREHAM I Bty 117797	"		(b) Alternative targets to serials 4 - 6 if MONT FLEURY Bty is in section A.
					OUISTREHAM II Bty 103779
					(two attacks)
					LONGUES Bty 797874
					(c) Alternative targets to serials 4 - 6 if MONT FLEURY and LONGUES Btys in section A.
					OUISTREHAM II Bty 103779
					ARROMANCHES III Bty 860863
					(d) This section will be confirmed on D - 2.

SCHEDULE 'B' PRE D DAY BOMBIN

SECTION A – DAY

Serial	Timing	Targets		Type of Aircraft Employed		Efor Allot
1		LA PERNELLE Bty 365200	(NEPTUNE)	Day Medium		
2		FONTENAY SUR MER Bty 368044	(NEPTUNE)	"	"	
3		POINT DU HOE Bty 586938	(NEPTUNE)	"	"	
4		OUISTREHAM I Bty 117797	(NEPTUNE)	"	"	
5		HOULGATE Bty 256809	(NEPTUNE)	"	"	
6		BENERVILLE Bty 422107	(NEPTUNE)	"	"	
7		LE HAVRE/LE GRAND CLOS Bty 467307	(NEPTUNE)	"	"	
8		ETRETAT/ST MARIE AU BOSC Bty 565452		"	"	
9		FECAMP I Bty 687529		"	"	
10		FECAMP II Bty 713556		"	"	
11	Any day before D-3	DIEPPE Bty 152673		"	"	
12		LE TREPORT/AULT Bty 521856		"	"	
13		ETAPLES Bty 676317		"	"	
14		ETAPLES/ST CECILY Bty 644371		"	"	
15		HARDELOT Bty 651436		"	"	
16		WIMEREUX Bty 694603		"	"	
17		BASINGHAM/MARQUISE Bty 733660		"	"	
18		CALAIS/SANGATTE Bty 815763		"	"	
19		GRAVELINES Bty 991805		"	"	
20		FORT HARDICK Bty 188849		"	"	
21		DUNKIRK Bty 281846		"	"	

In order to support the cover plan for every targe bombed inside the NEPTUNE area two targets are bombed outside the area.

Below: Revised late May GSGS Intelligence Map covering the Maisy area.

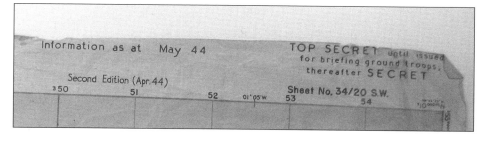

Information as at   May 44   TOP SECRET until issued
                                              for briefing ground troops,
                                                   thereafter SECRET
       Second Edition (Apr.44)
   350   51   52   01°05'W Sheet No. 34/20 S.W.
                                               53   54

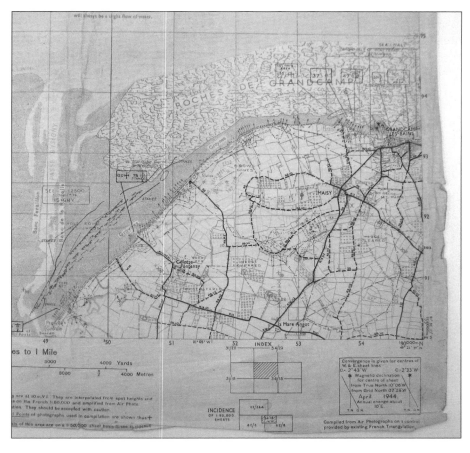

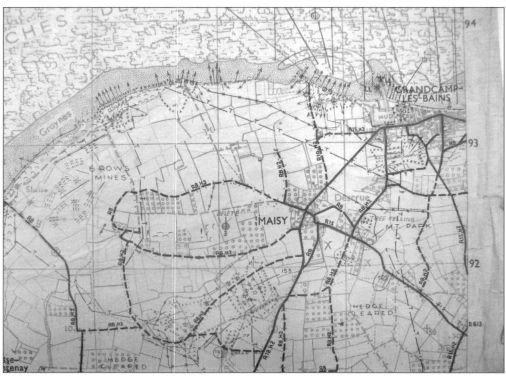

24 May 1944

5th Rangers – Companies A – F, Medical and HQ – Dorchester, Dorset.

A Co. Sgt. Stanley Bojara went from absent sick in the 228th Station Hospital to transferred in grade to Detachment of Patients 228th Station Hospital.

2nd Rangers – Companies A – F, Medical and HQ – Dorchester, Dorset

<u>SERVICE OF SUPPLY EUROPEAN THEATRE OF OPERATIONS REPORT</u>: *Briefing began. And the all-important problem of preventing leakage of information was tackled. All troops were literally 'sealed in' the camps, by over 2,000 security personnel. Wire had been strung around the perimeter, and patrols beat back and forth to prevent some stray getting in as well as out, with the vital word that 'this is it'.*

Anyone entering the camp was accompanied by a guard to prevent him from talking of unauthorised matters.

All deliveries and collections were made at the entrance to camp. Every single man was given the general picture. Every soldier knew his particular job. Maps, air photos in complete detail eased the problem. Why, it was just like the exercises – so similar was the enemy coast to the areas used in training. The practice beach had been copied to the last pill box and machine gun nest.

Below is a US Air Force reconnaissance photograph taken after the evening bombing mission on the Maisy positions.

Below: Blow-up of the La Martinière Battery. Note the bomb that has landed amongst the minefield to the front of the battery. It has set off bands of mines – represented here by a series of small dots in a curving line in front of the position. There is also another large crater to the rear of the site. It fell in an area of field close by. But there is not one shown falling in an area where it could have caused any substantial damage.

Below: An enlargement of the Les Perruques (Maisy I) Battery. Both positions sustained little of no direct damage to their gun emplacements – thus leaving them both fully operational.

---

25 May 1944   A Navy Report was produced dated 25 May: *Supreme Commander ordered that from 0001hrs all mail, including parcels, of personnel taking part in 'NEPTUNE' was to be impounded until further notice. Telephone and cable facilities were also to be forbidden and private telegrams only to be sent in cases of emergency by special permission of the Commanding Officer. These measures were taken in conjunction with, and prior to, the order to open Operation Orders.*

ORDER FOR NEPTUNE TO BE EXECUTED
a)   *At 2330, on request from A.N.C.X.F. Admiralty general message was promulgated to all holders of Operation Orders that they were now to be opened and Operation NEPTUNE carried out.*
b)   *Nomination of D-Day and H-Hour were not included as had been the original intention.*

Weather problems on D-Day.
The main problem of the definite fixing of D-Day was now suitable weather conditions. The special organisation set up to provide weather forecasts consisted of three Meteorological Officers on the staffs of Supreme Commander A.N.C.X.F. and Air Commander-in-Chief. A.E.A.F., respectively. In their meetings to produce two forecasts daily these officers had the assistance of direct telephone contact with the meteorological departments of Admiralty, Air Ministry and U.S. Weather Service.

The trend of weather could be forecast for three days ahead, but it was found in practice that due to the abnormally unsettled state of the weather, these trend forecasts did not give reliable results, and that a sufficiently accurate forecast to justify embarking on the invasion could only be made one day ahead. Yet the first convoys had to sail a day and a half prior to H-Hour. It therefore followed that the sailings had to be ordered on the trend forecast, but the final decision by the Supreme Commander could only be reached 24 hours prior to H-Hour.

5th Rangers – Companies A – F, Medical and HQ – Dorchester, Dorset.

2nd Rangers – Companies A – F, Medical and HQ – Dorchester, Dorset

Below: The regular V Corps updated target list issued on 25 May 1944.

Page 1 of 4 pages.

TOP SECRET
"NEPTUNE"

BIGOT

Hq 1st US Inf Div
APO #1, U.S. Army
25 May 1944

```
:     TOP SECRET     :
:By authority of    :
:CG, 1st US Inf Div:
:25 May 1944        :
:Initials:          :
```

Appendix 2)
            :
TO ANNEX 6)   V CORPS TARGET LIST
            :
TO FO   35)

TARGET NO.	COORDINATES	DESCRIPTION
T1	58609390	6 Guns, 155mm
T5	53309180	4 Guns, 155mm, 5 concrete shelters, 3 MGs, 1 Hut
T10	79268316	4 Guns, 105mm
T16	52159150	4 Guns, 75mm, 2 MGs, 1 Pillbox, 3 Shelters
T20	77008600	Strongpoint with possible 75 Cal Guns
T21	76708775	7 MGs, 1 Pillbox
T22	76008780	2 MGs, 1 Hut, 1 Shelter
T23	75808785	4 MGs, 1 AT Gun
T24	75508790	1 Pillbox
T25	75308795	1 Pillbox, 1 MG
T26	75308838	1 Pillbox
T27	75008805	1 4.7 Gun, 3 AA Guns, 6 Pillboxes
T28	75008790	5 MGs, 3 Shelters
T29	74908710	9 MGs, Road block, Troops in houses
T30	74508815	Strongpoint, 2 Arty Guns, 2 Shelters
T31	73238843	Pillbox
T32	72698850	3 MGs
T33	72208860	2 Concrete shelters, 16 MGs, Road blocks
T34	72108780	Houses
T35	72098740	Houses
T36	71808800	Houses
T37	71198810	Houses
T38	71218880	C/D Gun in concrete
T39	70498820	Houses
T40	69908910	5 Pillboxes, 2 MGs, 2 Concrete shelters
T41	69558930	3 Pillboxes
T42	69508830	Houses
T43	69308940	3 Pillboxes, 1 Concrete shelter, 4 MGs, AT Ditch
T44	69408910	Beach Exit
T45	69308883	Beach Exit, 1 Camouflaged position
T46	69108820	Troops in Houses
T47	68808950)	(4 Casemates, 3 Concrete Shelters, 5 MGs, 1
T50	68708943) - - - - (AT Gun, 3 Pillboxes, 1 Med Gun, 1 Casemate u/c
T48	68808910	Beach Exit
T49	68608870	Beach Exit
T51	68368970	Construction activity
T52	68128978	AT Ditch
T53	67808970	AA Gun, 4 Concrete Shelters, 2 Pillboxes, 5 MGs

- 1 -

TOP SECRET
"NEPTUNE"

Page _2_ of _4_ pages.   TOP SECRET   BIGOT
                            "NEPTUNE"

                                                DESCRIPTION
   TARGET NO.   COORDINATES

      T54   67609010   4 Guns in concrete, 6 MGs, 4 Inf weapons
      T55   67558930   Beach Exit
      T56   67458780   Troops
      T57   67109010   4 Emplacements unoccupied
      T58   67148932   Troops
      T59   66809030   1 AA/MG, 8 Concrete Shelters, Concrete OP, 3
                                 Pillboxes, 2 Concrete Shelters under construc-
                                 tion
      T60   66739060   Fortified house, 1 Pillbox, 2 Concrete Shelters
      T61   66609030   11 MGs, 3 weapon emplacements, 3 Pillboxes
      T62   66258960   2 MGs, possible CP
      T63   66459073   6 MGs, 1 Pillbox
      T64   65309020   Beach Exit
      T65   66149075   Radar Station
      T66   65689100   1 Pillbox, 3 MGs
      T67   65509120   Fortified House
      T68   65389120   5 Concrete Shelters, 1 Pillbox, 10 MGs, 1 AA
                                 Gun, Infantry weapons unspecified
      T69   65109150   3 MGs, 1 AT Gun
      T70   64809120   Possible AT Gun, possible fortified houses
      T71   64809170   4 Pillboxes, 6 MGs, 3 Concrete Shelters, 1 AA/
                                 MG, 1 AT Gun
      T72   64509190   2 Pillboxes, 4 Mortars, 2 Emplacements, 11 MGs,
                                 1 Casemate
      T73   64808660   Cross Roads
      T74   63709273) — —(4 Concrete Shelters, 1 OP, 4 Pillboxes, 14 MGs
      T75   63629302)   (AT weapons, Hutted Camp
      T76   62479350,   (13 MGs, 2 Pillboxes, 10 Concrete Shelters, 6
      T77   62229350) — —(Concrete Shelters u/c, Wurzburg, Radar Station,
                                 (Battery of 4 AA Guns, 1 Searchlight, 1 Hutted
                                 (Camp
      T78   62209060   Troops
      T79   62208870   2 MGs, Supply Depot
      T80   61179165   2 MGs, houses
      T81   61229270   Strongpoint
      T82   60609380   1 MG
      T83   60209380   10 MGs, 2 Concrete Shelters
      T84   59409288   Road Junction, Houses
      T85   58609307   Troops in houses
      T86   58509345   1 AT Gun
      T87   58409155   Possible CP, Cable trench junction
      T88   57609390   3 MGs, 2 Pillboxes, 2 Shelters
      T89   57409390   1 MG
      T90   57359335   2 Gun positions, Troops
      T91   56559365   12 MGs, 1 Pillbox, 2 Shelters
      T92   56208926   Strongpoint, Troops in houses, 7 MGs
      T93   55809330   29 MGs, 3 Pillboxes, 4 Shelters, 2 Flak Guns
      T94   55409260   Houses with troops
      T95   55279327   Houses, 1 MG, 1 Pillbox
      T96   54609100   Cable trench junction, Possible CP
      T97   54459335   7 MGs, 1 Pillbox, 1 Flak Gun, 4 Road Blocks
      T98   54459290   Strongpoint with 9 MGs, possible CP

                         - 2 -

                     TOP   SECRET
                     "NEPTUNE"

TOP   SECRET
"NEPTUNE"   BIGOT

TARGET NO.	COORDINATES	DESCRIPTION
T99	54309353	1 Light Gun
T100	54159235	Houses with Troops
T101	54309190	Houses with Troops
T102	54009205	Strongpoint
T103	53909230	4 Possible Gun Positions, Troops in Houses
T104	53809340	Road Block, Houses, 14 MGs, 3 Pillboxes
T105	53609240	Houses
T106	53309350	2 MGs
T107	53159050	Possible CP, Cable trench junction
T108	53029130	Houses with Troops
T109	52709350	4 Pillboxes, 4 MGs, 4 Concrete Shelters
T110	52609070	Troops in Houses
T111	52159330	13 MGs, 2 Concrete Shelters
T112	51708670	Troops in Houses, 1 MG
T113	51109240	11 MGs, 2 Pillboxes
T114	51109120	Strongpoint, 7 MGs
T115	50909215	2 MGs
T116	50728824	2 MGs, 1 Shelter under construction
T117	50509160	2 MGs, 1 Pillbox
T118	50359080	Strongpoint, 4 Pillboxes, 1 MG
T119	50208570	Strongpoint, 1 Concrete Shelter
T120	49709060	1 AT Gun, 1 Pillbox, 1 MG
T121	49708840	4 MGs
T122	49309040	5 Pillboxes, 1 AT Gun, 3 MGs
T123	49208780	Bridge, 4 Pillboxes, 3 AT Guns, 2 Flak Guns, 2 MGs
T124	59909340	Ammunition Depot
T125	57959370	6 Flak Guns
T127	61609370	4 MGs, 1 Pillbox
T128	67508995	2 Pillboxes, C/D casemate, 3 MGs, 1 Concrete Shelter
T129	79708710	Casemating under construction
T130	66309058	4 MGs, 2 Pillboxes, 1 AT Gun
T150	76218090	Road junctions in town
T151	76108210	Houses with Troops
T152	75917876	Bridge and Road junction
T153	75178457	Troops, 5 MGs, CP, Cable trench junction
T154	75107765	Road and Railroad Crossing
T155	74488066	4 MGs, Houses
T156	73708320	Bridge over Canal, Road junction
T157	73348213	Road junction in town
T158	72417800	Road and Railroad Crossing
T159	71908283	Road Crossing
T160	71408490	Troops
T161	71318280	4 Possible Arty Emplacements
T162	69768393	Road junction
T163	69267752	Bridge and Road junction
T164	65788134	Road junction
T165	64667700	Railroad underpass
T166	64308390	Troops in town
T167	64308441	Bridge

- 3 -

Dated 25 May 1944 – Air Bombardment and pre-arranged naval bombardment plan. It covers all of the Omaha Sector targets which would be subject to air bombardment. Target B is Pointe du Hoc and Target A is Maisy.

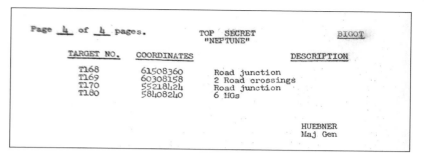

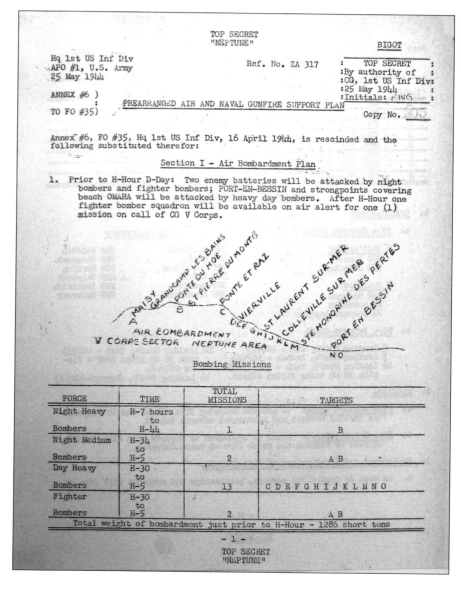

T5 is Maisy – Les Perruques and T1 is Pointe du Hoc.

TOP SECRET
"NEPTUNE"

BIGOT

TARGET	TARGET LIST REFERENCE	TARGET	TARGET LIST REFERENCE
A	- T5	I	- T54
B	- T1	J	- T53
C	- T74, T75	K	- T47, T50
D	- T71, T72	L	- T43
E	- T69, T70	M	- T40
F	- T66, T67, T68	N	- T27, T28, T30
G	- T60, T63, T65, T130	O	- T22, T23, T24
H	- T57, T59, T61		

Section II – Naval Fire Plan

1. Organization

   a. Fire Support Ships

   2 Battleships
     USS Texas
     USS Arkansas

   3 Cruisers
     HMS Glasgow
     FS Montcalm
     FS Georges Leygues

   12 Destroyers

USS Endicott	USS Baldwin
USS Doyle	USS Thompson
USS Satterlee	USS Harding
USS McCook	HMS Talybont
USS Carmick	HMS Tanatside
USS Frankford	HMS Melbreak

   b. Fire Support Craft

   5 Landing Craft, Gun – LCG(L)
   9 Landing Craft, Rocket – LCT(R)
   16 Landing Craft, Tank – LCT(A&HE)
     with 32 M4 tanks firing afloat.

   10 Landing Craft, Tank – LCT(5)
     with 36 M7 105mm SPMT's firing afloat.
   24 Landing Craft, Support–LCS(S)

2. Missions

   a. Fire Support Ships: To protect shipping from attack and to support the initial assault and subsequent advance inland.

   b. Fire Support Craft: Prior to touchdown to furnish area fire on and in rear of beaches and point fire on beach defenses.

3. Employment and Coordination of Fire Support.

   a. As soon as visibility permits, battleships and cruisers will fire on

- 2 -

TOP SECRET
"NEPTUNE"

designated batteries and strongpoints. Ships completing tasks before H-Hour will fire on beach targets. Destroyers will furnish
close support fires on designated strongpoints on and in rear of
beaches. After H-Hour, ships will deliver fires called for by Shore
Fire Control Parties.

b. Fire Support Craft: Prior to touchdown to furnish area fire on and
   in rear of beaches and point fire on beach defenses.

   (1) LCG(L)'s will accompany leading wave on flanks and in boat lanes,
       neutralizing assigned beach targets and targets of opportunity
       by direct fire. Fire will be shifted to flank targets before
       it endangers advancing troops.

   (2) LCT(R)'s will take position in line abreast about 3000 yards off-
       shore of specified target areas in time to fire on assigned
       targets when leading wave is about 3000 yards offshore. They
       will then clear boat lanes and return to transport area. Six
       will reload with HE rockets and when directed will fire on flank
       targets. Three will reload with smoke and HE rockets and be
       prepared to fire when directed. Reloading will be completed
       by H ≠ 210.

   (3) LCT(5)'s will take position in line abreast in boat lanes and
       will commence firing at approximately H-30 when about 8000
       yards from beach on assigned area targets behind beaches. At
       H-5 they will clear boat lanes and return to rendezvous area.

   (4) LCT(A&HE)'s will commence firing at approximately H-15 when about
       3000 yards from beach on assigned pillboxes, fortified houses,
       and beach defenses. They will continue firing until touchdown,
       will disembark tanks, and return to transport area.

   (5) LCS(S)'s lead in DD tanks. Those not required for this accompany
       LCT(HE) wave and deliver machine gun and rocket fire on beach
       defenses.

```
                              TOP SECRET
                               "NEPTUNE"                              BIGOT
```

4. Target Designation:

    a. The Lambert grid will be used for Naval target designation. Support-
        ing ships and shore fire control parties will be furnished 1/50,000
        scale map charts and 1/25,000 vertical mosaics gridded with the Lam-
        bert grid.

    b. Gridded obliques will be furnished naval gunfire spotters to facili-
        tate target identification, but Merton coordinates will not be used
        for target designation.

    c. Beach sketches marked to show locations of targets will be furnished
        to all craft participating in the prearranged fire plan.

5. Naval Shore Fire Control Parties.

    a. Attached to 1st Division: Nine parties, 294th Joint Assault Signal
        Company.

    b. Attached to 29th Division: Nine parties, 293d Joint Assault Signal
        Company, two of which will be allotted to Ranger Units.

    c. Artillery Air OP's used to adjust naval gun fire will operate through
        battalion fire direction centers and attached naval liaison officers.

6. Liaison

    a. One Naval liaison officer will accompany each FA battalion and each
        division artillery and corps artillery headquarters.

    b. One corps artillery liaison officer will accompany each division
        artillery headquarters.

7. Ammunition: Commanding Officers, 58th and 62d Armored Field Artillery Bat-
        talions (SP) and 745th Tank Battalion (Med), will requisition and load
        on craft ammunition to be expended during firing afloat. This will be
        in addition to basic load.

                    SP Battalion - 100 rounds per howitzer
                    Tank Battalion - 150 rounds per tank firing

                                        HUEBNER
                                        Maj Gen

OFFICIAL: *Gibb*
               GIBB
               G-3

APPENDICES:
    Appendix 1 - Naval Fire Plan
    Appendix 2 - V Corps Target List
DISTRIBUTION:
Same as FO 35

                              - 5 -

                        TOP SECRET
                         "NEPTUNE"

Next page: 25 May Naval Fire Plan with target numbers.

Hq 1st US Inf Div
APO #1, U.S. Army
25 May 1944

APPENDIX #1)
TO ANNEX #6)
TO FO #35)

TOP SECRET
"NEPTUNE"

BIGOT

: TOP SECRET :
:By authority of :
:CG, 1st US Inf Div:
:25 May 1944 :
:Initials: FW/G :

NAVAL FIRE PLAN

SHIP	ARMAMENT	TOTAL ROUNDS	RANGE IN THOUSANDS OF YARDS	FIRE SUPT AREA	TARGET	TIME	NO. OF ROUNDS	REMARKS	BALANCE OF AMMUNITION
1	2	3	4	5	6	7	8	9	10
1. Battleships									
USS Texas (BB)	10x14"	1000	18	3 Anchored Position	T1,T86	H-40 to H-5	up to 250	14" Air Spot 65% AP, 35% HC	738x14"
					T88,T89	H-25 to H-10	100	5"	1700x5"
	6x5"	1800	18	Anchored Position	T88,T89	H-4 to H hour	12	14" Air Spot HC	
USS Arkansas (BB)	12x12"	1356	18	4 Anchored Position	T60,T63,T65	H-40 to H-5	385	12" Air Spot Rock Salvos 30% AP 70% HC	921x12"
	6x5"	1800	18	Anchored Position	T166	H to H/1 Hr	50	12" Air Spot Harassing	1550x5"
					T43	H-40 to H-7	250	5"	
2. Cruisers									
HMS Glasgow (CL)	12x6"	2400	24	3 Anchored Position	T59,T61	H-36 to H-3	400	Rock Salvos Air Spot	2000
FS Montcalm (CL)	6x152mm	1020	28	4 Anchored Position	Port-En-Bessin T22,T23,T24,T25 T27,T28,T29	H-40 to H/30	300	Cover Area Air Spot	720

25 May G-2 Intelligence, 1st Infantry Division report: *'G-2 estimate of the enemy situation.'*

```
                              TOP-SECRET                    BIGOT
                              "NEPTUNE"                     ZA 314

   Hq 1st US Inf Div                            :   TOP-SECRET   :
   APO 1, US Army                               : Authority:  CG :
   25 May 1944                                  : 1st US Inf Div :
                                                : 25 May 1944    :
   COPY NO.  31                                 : Initials:  AC  :


                                  NOTE

           The intelligence contained in this estimate supplements
     previous estimates.  It should be read in conjunction with these,
     as it does not repeat those portions which remain unchanged.
```

```
       b.   Enemy Defenses.

       (1)   Beach Defenses.

              (a)  Underwater obstacles on Beach 46 have been mined.
     Ordinary Teller mines (42) have been wired to the tops of nearly
     all ramp type obstacles.  About one stake in five has been similar-
     ly mined.  A few Elements "C" have mines fixed to the top of the
     centerpost.  The mines have been waterproofed and are believed to
     have only pressure igniters.  Apparently mines have not been placed
     in the sand among the obstacles.

              (b)  The anti-tank wall across the exit at VIERVILLE
     now runs from 64829176 to 64899170  with a gap at 64849174.

       (2)   Inland Defenses.

              (a)  Additional minefields not listed in previous
     estimates are as follows:

                       500911
                       506917-510922
                       517925-518926    (6 rows)
                       518925-518926    (6 rows)
                       520929-520930    (6 rows)
                       557932-558932
                       560932-562932
                       560932-560935
                       561933-562934
                       574937-574939
                       582936-583936
                       584935-584936
                       585933-586933
                       587933-588935
                       588935-589937
                       659907-660907
                       658906-659905
                       657905-657906
                       658903-658905
                       660903-662903
                       661904-661903
                       660907-662904
                       684896-685896
                       697893-698893
                       700886-702886
                       703887-704887
                       705889-706890



                              TOP-SECRET
                              "NEPTUNE"
```

```
TOP-SECRET                    BIGOT
"NEPTUNE"


      706889-707889
      708887-710887-710889
      710888-711888
      712887-712888
      713887-713888
      715886-716887
      714888-715888
      728884-729885
      737883-744883
```

(b) The regular pattern of shallow excavations in the fields back of OMAHA Beach mentioned in Par. (2) (b), Estimate #5, is now thought to be caused by the emplacement of posts to hinder airborne landings.

2. CONCLUSIONS.

a. Enemy Capabilities.

(1) The enemy may defend Beach OMAHA using approximately four companies from 726th Infantry Regiment to man the defenses and up to five artillery batteries for support.

(2) The enemy defense of the beach may be strengthened by up to a battalion of armor and supporting armored infantry from 21st Panzer Division prior to or during the assault.

(3) The enemy may use counter-attacking elements of approximately company size to attempt to retake strong points immediately following their loss.

(4) The enemy may support the beach defense with rocket and mortar fire, and air attacks.

(5) Anytime after the beach crust of defenses has been breached the enemy may counter-attack with battalion size forces; a battalion from ISIGNY northeast against elements of the 116th RCT, a battalion from TREVIERS north against the 16th and 18th RCTs, and a battalion from BAYEUX west against the 16th and 18th RCTs. The latter may be supported by up to a battalion of tanks.

(6) Anytime after noon of D-day the enemy may counter-attack northeast from the ISIGNY area with up to an RCT of 91st or 243d Division, north from the BALLEROY area with an RCT of the 352d Division and west from BAYEUX with minor elements of 21st Panzer Division.

(7) During the night of D-day - D ≠ 1 the enemy may drop parachute troops anywhere within the beachhead to disorganize the area preparatory to a dawn counter-attack.

```
TOP-SECRET
"NEPTUNE"
```

---

26 May 1944

5th Rangers – Companies A – F, Medical and HQ – Dorchester, Dorset.
2nd Rangers – Companies A – F, Medical and HQ – Dorchester, Dorset.

---

27 May 1944

5th Rangers – Companies A – F, Medical and HQ – Dorchester, Dorset.
2nd Rangers – Companies A – F, Medical and HQ – Dorchester, Dorset.

SECOND REVISION
ANNEX 12
TO
OPERATIONS PLAN
NEPTUNE

27 May 1944

PREARRANGED AIR AND NAVAL BOMBARDMENT PLAN

1. Air Bombardment Plan — The air support for Operations Plan
NEPTUNE, is based upon the attack of battery positions, beach defense
localities, bridges, road embankments, cable junctions — command posts,
and communication centers. First Army target numbers of battery positions, defense localities, and terrain features are listed in Appendix
1. Nine phases of the prearranged air support plan are outlined below:

    a. Pre-Y day Bombardment. (Prior to D-3/D-2 night).

    (1) Air effort has been allocated for five battery posi-
tions in the First Army sector. Two battery positions outside the
NEPTUNE Area are bombed for each battery position bombed within the
area to maintain security. First Army battery positions included in
this phase are indicated below:

Day Medium Bombers	Night Heavy Bombers
1 (POINTE DU HOE — 586938)	8A (BARFLEUR — 396229)
3 (FONTENAY SUR MER — 368042)	4 (MORSALINES — 355138)
1A (LA PERNELLE — 365199)	

    (2) Additional bombing during this period will include the
cutting of rail communications which will directly hinder the rail movement of enemy reserves to the NEPTUNE Area. Targets are railway centers
converging from Northeast FRANCE and BELGIUM, routes through ORLEANS,
and more distant rail centers in FRANCE and BELGIUM with primary object
of "cover" and secondary object of long term effect on rail movements.
This bombing will not commence before Y-15 day and terminates on D-4 day.

    (3) A cover plan called FORTITUDE will require the bombing
of battery positions, communication centers, strong points, and beach defences in the DIEPPE and PAS DE CALAIS areas by day and night heavy bombers and day medium bombers. Allotment of air effort is as follows:
D-3 day — 40% day heavy bombers; D-2 day — 30% of day heavy bombers; D-1
day — 25% of day heavy bombers and a proportion of medium bombers; D-3/D-2
night — 30% of night heavy bombers; D-2/D-1 night — 30% of night heavy
bombers. In case D day is postponed, two additional D-2 day and D-2/D-1
night schedules have been planned.

    b. D-1 Day Bombardment.

    Bombing missions on this day are based on two plans: First,
where surprise for the assault on D day is NOT considered lost; second,
where surprise for the attack on D-day is considered lost.

    (1) Case I - Surprise is NOT lost. (Late afternoon and
evening prior to midnight D-1/D day).

    Twenty-five percent of the day heavy bombers and a
proportion of the medium and light bombers are available. Final selection
of NEPTUNE Area targets as follows will be made on D-3 day: Five battery
positions, two headquarters, four fighter-control telephone exchanges, and
two telephone exchanges.

- 1 -

T O P   S E C R E T   B I G O T

Page 2 of 8 pages.

(a) Battery positions to be considered for bombing
by day heavy bombers are listed in the following order of priority:

6 (ST.MARTIN DE VARREVILLE - 405980)   3 (FONTENAY SUR MER - 368042)
9 (AZEVILLE - 360022)   1 (POINTE DU HOE - 586938)
9A (CHATEAU DU COURCY - 361054)   1A (LA PERNELLE - 365199)

(b) Headquarters to be bombed by day heavy bombers
will be selected on D-3 day.

SCHEDULE H-ASSAULT PROGRAMME

Revised 27 May 1944
BIGOT
TOP SECRET
Page

SECTION D - FIGHTER BOMBERS

Timing	Targets	Type of Aircraft Employed	Effort Allotted	Remarks
HU - Hour to HU + 10 min	TARGETS IN US SECTOR BARFLEURS Bty 394228	TAF		(a) Serials 7 - 13 are also in Schedule D. If surprise is NOT considered lost these serials will be taken on in this schedule. If surprise is lost they will be engaged on D - 1.
" "	LA PERNELLE Bty 365200	"		
" "	MORSALINES Bty 355438	"		(b) Timings of serials 4 - 6 will be arranged between NCWTF, Commander First United States Army and Commander Advanced AEAF.
" "	MAISY Bty 533918	"		
" "	POINTE DU HOE Bty 586938	"		(c) This section will be confirmed on D - 5.
" "	MAISY II Bty 531914	"		(d) Alternative targets if any of serials 4 - 6 are badly damaged before D day:-
	TARGETS FOR 82 AIRBORNE DIVISION Bridge 096898			AIGREMONT Bty 578204
	Bridge 104899			MAISY IIa Bty 528916
As early as possible after CT	Bridge 124881			(e) Serials 2 and 5 are being casemated. The question of whether they are to be attacked is now under joint consideration.
	Bridge 147899			
	Bridge NORTH of LESSAY 1876	"		
	Embankment 190905	"		

Repeated again on 27 May – it states the following: *the Serials 2 and 5 are being casemated. The question of whether they are to be attacked is now under joint consideration.* There is no indication what *joint consideration* actually means, but one must suspect that this was a debate between the Army and the Air Force and/or Navy as to the continued relevance of La Pernelle Battery and Pointe du Hoc as operational targets. In which case the Rangers' mission to Pointe du Hoc would be cancelled and perhaps a direct beach front assault on Maisy would be proposed instead.

Below: A blow-up of the relevant text. [Author: The targets called Serials do not have the same target numbers as the Army ones for the sector. i.e. part (e) Pointe du Hoc is Target No 1 – but in this case Serial No 5.]

(d) Alternative targets if any of serials 4 - 6 are badly
damaged before D day:-

AIGREMONT Bty 578204

MAISY IIa Bty 528916

(e) Serials 2 and 5 are being casemated. The
question of whether they are to be attacked is
now under joint consideration.

T O P   S E C R E T   B I G O T

Page 3 of 8 pages.

(2) Battery positions to be bombed by heavy bombers. (prior to midnight D-1/D day to Civil Twilight, D day).

100% of the night heavy bombers will attack targets in this phase.

1 (POINTE DU HOE - 586938)   4 (MORSALINES - 355138)
1A (LA PERNELLE - 365199)   6 (ST.MARTIN DE VARREVILLE-405980)
3 (FONTENAY SUR MER - 368042)   8A (BARFLEUR - 396229)

Battery positions 3 and 6 will be bombed prior to mid-night D-1/D day since airborne troops will be near these targets at that time.

Alternate targets, in order of priority, if battery positions 1, 1A, 3, 4, and 8A are destroyed in pre-Y day bombing, are:

5 (MAISY - 533918)
7A (LA PERNELLE II - 372198)
5A (LONGUES - 797871)

(3) Battery positions to be bombed by medium bombers. (H-30 minutes to H-15 minutes, D day).

1 (POINTE DU HOE - 586938)
8A (BARFLEUR - 396229)
5 (MAISY I - 533918)

Alternate targets, in order of priority, if battery positions 1 and 8A are destroyed in pre-Y day bombing, are:

16 (MAISY II - 528916)
14A (MONT COQUEREL - 351080)

d. D Day Bombardment.

(1) Beach defense localities. (Prior to H hour).

(a) Beach OMAHA:

The following listed localities will be attacked from H-30 minutes to H-5 minutes by heavy bombers:

Coordinates	Effort	Coordinates	Effort
637928	129 tons	678896	88.2 tons
646919	88.2 "	688894	88.2 "
649916	88.2 "	693893	88.2 "
655912	129 "	699890	129 "
666905	88.2 "	748880	86 "
668902	88.2 "	756878	107.5 "
677900	88.2 "		

Planes late for time over target may bomb up to H-2 minutes. After H-2 minutes, planes will bomb alternate target listed in paragraph 1 d (1)(c) 1.

(b) Beach UTAH:

The following listed localities will be attacked from H-10 minutes to H-2 minutes by medium bombers:

Coordinates	Effort	Coordinates	Effort
442972	108 tons	429000	72 tons
442982	108 tons	448958	72 tons
451969	108 tons	456953	72 tons
435992	108 tons		

Planes late for time over target may bomb up to H hour. After H hour, planes will bomb alternate targets listed in paragraph 1 d (1)(c) 2.

-3-

T O P   S E C R E T   B I G O T

(c) Alternate targets, to be bombed in case planes arrive late for time over target are:

   1. - Main roads and intersections through FORET DE CERISY (6570).

   2. Battery Positions   Beach defense localities
       5 (MAISY I - 533918)   493904   545932
       16 (MAISY II - 528916)   505916   512924
       16A (MAISY IIa - 531914)   538934   527934

   (2) Battery positions to be bombed by day heavy bombers. (H-15 minutes to H-5 minutes).

       1 (POINTE DU HOE - 586938)   1A (LA PERNELLE - 365199)

   (3) The communication center of CARENTAN (3984) will be bombed by one day heavy bomber mission during the same time as listed in the paragraph next above.

   (4) Battery positions to be bombed by fighter bombers. (H hour to H/10 minutes, D day).

       4 (MORSALINES - 355138)   8A (BARFLEUR - 396229)
       5 (MAISY I - 533918)   16A (MAISY IIa - 531914)

       If battery position 4 is destroyed in pre-Y day bombing, alternate target is 16 (MAISY II - 528916).

   (5) Cable junctions - command posts at 584915 and 686861 will be bombed by one fighter bomber squadron each at the same time as listed in paragraph 1 d (4) above.

   (6) Bridges, road embankment, and cable junctions - command posts listed in paragraph 1 b (2)(f), (g), and (h) above will be bombed by fighter bombers at first light D day, providing they have not been bombed during the D-1 day schedule when surprise is lost. Fuze time on bombs will be the minimum consistant with safety for planes making skip bombing missions on these targets.

   (7) Each corps will have one squadron of fighter bombers on air alert in their sector as soon as desired after first light. Possible request missions, as well as planned missions in the event communication failures, will be arranged between corps and an air force representative who will be available for this coordination prior to D-3 day.

       (a) Air alert mission - V Corps.

           From H/120 minutes to H/150 minutes, D day. To bomb battery position 5 (MAISY I - 533918) or 16 (MAISY II - 528916) or defense locality at 792832. In case of a communications failure or for any other reason, and the aircraft are unable to contact the command ship for definite orders prior to the expiration of the 30 minute airborne period, then one of the three targets listed above, in order of priority, will be bombed.

       (b) Air alert mission - VII Corps

           As soon as practicable after dawn. To attack battery position 6 (ST. MARTIN DE VARREVILLE - 405980) on call of the 101st Airborne Division. If the mission on battery position 6 is not desired due to the situation at the time, then the squadron will attack any other target requested. If communication fails, the town of CARENTAN (3984) will be bombed as an alternate target.

   (7) First and second turn around bombing effort, at about H/6 and H/15 hours respectively, will attack targets in order of priority as follows: Road centers, battery positions on the flanks, LOIRE road and railroad bridges. Final selection will be made on D-2 day from the following targets:

- 4 -

2. Naval Bombardment Plan - The naval gunfire support for Operations Plan NEPTUNE will assist the landing and subsequent advance inland and along the coast, initially by fire on prearranged targets and later on call. Allocation of fire support ships is as follows:

Force "O" - 2 Battleships, 3 Light Cruisers, 9 Destroyers, 3 Hunt Destroyers.

Force "U" - 1 Battleship, 1 Monitor, 3 Heavy Cruisers, 2 Light Cruisers, 1 Gun Boat, 8 Destroyers.

Reserve fire support group - 1 Heavy Cruiser, 1 Light Cruiser, and 17 Destroyers. Tentative future assignment of reserve Destroyers is 10 to Force "O" and 7 to Force "U".

Three phases of naval gunfire support are outlined below:

a. Counterbattery:

Time: H-30 minutes until silenced.

Battery positions to be attacked are listed as follows:

8A (BARFLEUR - 396229)	15 (LESTRE - 342102)
8 (GATTEVILLE - 391275)	14 (OZEVILLE - 344057)
12 (AIGREMONT - 378204)	9 (AZEVILLE - 360022)
1A (LA PERNELLE - 365199)	5 (MAISY I - 533918)
4 (MORSALINES - 355138)	16 (MAISY II - 528916)
3 (FONTENAY SUR MER - 368042)	1 (POINTE DU HOE - 586938)
7A (LA PERNELLE - 372198)	17 (LA FOSSE - 339138)

Battery positions 3, 9, and 14 will be attacked only upon coordination with Airborne Naval Shore Fire Control Parties since these targets are in the airborne divisions' areas.

b. Attack of Beach Defenses:

(1) Time: H-20 minutes to H hour.

This drenching fire will be delivered by close support destroyers and support craft. Details concerning allotment and use of support craft are included in Annex 2, Organization of Assault and Follow

- 7 -

TOP SECRET BIGOT

Next page: Target No.16 is marked as 4 – 75mm G ? (gun) with a question mark as to the calibre of weapon in situ. It is estimated on many allied plans as having 75mm guns. [post-battle they were found to be modified Czech 100mm cannons.]

Maisy – Les Perruques is now marked as having 6 – 155mm howitzers and Pointe du Hoc as having 6 – 155mm cannons.

T O P _ S E C R E T _ B I G O T

APPENDIX 1
TO
SECOND REVISION ANNEX 12

Enemy Installations and Terrain Features in First Army Sector of
Neptune Area

Enemy Battery Positions

First Army Number	Coordinates	Description	Location
1	586938	6-155 G	Pointe Du Hoe
1A	365199	4-170 G	La Pernelle
2	266268	4-280 G?	Fermanville
3	368042	4-155 G	Fontenay Sur-Mer
4	355138	6-155 G	Morsalines
5	533018	6-155 H	Maisy I
5A	797171	4-105 u/c	Longues
6	405680	4-155 H	St. Martin De Varreville
6A	369040	6-88 G?	
7	246264	4-170 G	Les Landes
7A	372198	6-105 G?	La Pernelle II
8	591175	6-155 G	Gatteville
8A	396229	4-170 G	Barfleur
9	360022	4-105 GH	Azeville
9A	361154	4-105 GH	Chateau De Courcy
10	792632	3-150 G?	Vaux-Sur-Aure
11	353290	4-155 H?	Pte De Neville
12	378204	4-105 GH	Aigremont
12A	336197	4-105 GH	Hameau Valette
12B	346191	4-150 H?	La Pisseterie
12C	358186	4-150 H?	
12D	341174	4-150 H?	
12E	362174	4-105 GH?	
13	848853	4-105 GH	Arromanches
13A	341056	4-105 GH	Fontenay
14	344057	2-150 H	Ozeville
14A	361080	4-75 G?	Mont Coquerel
15	342102	4-150 H	Lestre
16	528916	4-75 G?	Maisy II
16A	531914	4-75 G?	Maisy IIa
17	339138	4-105 GH	La Fosse
17A	323174	4-150 H?	Coimbot
18	413159	?	Tatihou
19	304273	4-75?	Les Sens
19A	258279	4-105 GH	Val Bourcin
19B	259267	4-105 GH u/c?	Carneville
20	262265	6-88	
20A	259222	6-88	
20B	241243	6-88?	Maupertus

Enemy Installations and Terrain Features in First Army Sector of
Neptune Area (cont'd)

V Corps Sector

First Army Number	Coordinates	Description	Location
27	770860	St Pt (75's?)	Chau du Bosq
29	767877	MG St Pt	Port-en-Bessin
31	760878	MG St Pt	Port-en-Bessin
33	758878	MG St Pt	Port-en-Bessin
35	755879	Pillbox	Port-en-Bessin
37	753879	Pillbox	Port-en-Bessin
39	753883	Pillbox	Port-en-Bessin
41	750880	Pillbox	Port-en-Bessin
43	750879	MG St Pt	Port-en-Bessin
45	749871	MG St Pt	Huppain
47	745881	St Pt Guns	Port-en-Bessin
49	732884	Pillbox	Ste. Honorine-des Pertes
51	727885	MG St Pt	Le Val des Moulins
53	727886	MG St Pt	Le Val des Moulins
55	721878	Houses	Cabourg
57	721874	Houses	Chau de Grandval
59	718880	Houses	Ste. Honorine-des Pertes
61	712881	Houses	La Vallee
63	712888	C/D Gun	Ste. Honorine-des Pertes
65	705882	Houses	Le Grand Hameau
67	699891	Pillboxes	Cabourg
69	695893	Pillboxes	Cabourg
71	695885	Houses	Cabourg
73	693894	Pillboxes MGs	Colleville-sur-Mer
75	694891	Beach Exit	Colleville-sur-Mer
77	693888	Beach Exit	Colleville-sur-Mer

VII Corps Sector

First Army Number	Coordinates	Description	Location
28	545932	105's	Grandcamp les Dunes
30	536934	MG & 37's	Grandcamp les Dunes
32			
34			
36	521931	MG St Pt	N.W. Maisy
38	511922	MG St Pt	N. Getosse Fontenay
40	505916	105 H St Pt	N.W. Getosse Fontenay
42	493904	Large casement Flak Tower	Pte du Gruin
44	445891	MG St Pt	Pt de Brevands
46	443910	MG St Pt	S Pouppeville
48	446916	MG St Pt	S Pouppeville
50	447927	MG St Pt	S Pouppeville
52	443928	MG St Pt	S Pouppeville
54	451940	MG St Pt	N.E. Pouppeville
56	456953	MG St Pt	Beau Juillot
58	443958	MG St Pt	N. Beau Guillot
60	451969	MG St Pt	Grande Dune
62	442972	MG St Pt	La Madeleine
?64	447975	Mines ?	N. of La Madeleine
66	442982	MG Fort 105s?	N.W. La Madeleine
68	443982	MG Fort	N.W. La Madeleine
70	435992	MG St Pt	Les Dunes de Varreville
72	438993	MG St Pt	Les Dunes de Varreville
74	429000	MG St Pt	Les Dunes de Varreville
76	423009	MG St Pt	Hotel de Cruttes
78	418017	MG St Pt	Hotel de Cruttes

- 2 -

Enemy Installations and Terrain Features in First Army Sector of
Neptune Area (cont'd)

V Corps Sector

First Army Number	Coordinates	Description	Location
79	691882	Trpsin Houses	Colleville-sur-Mer
81	688895	St Pts - MG	Colleville-sur-Mer
83	687894	Pillboxes	Colleville-sur-Mer
85	688891	Beach Exit	Colleville-sur-Mer
87	686887	Beach Exit	Colleville-sur-Mer
89	683897	Construction	Colleville-sur-Mer
91	681898	AT Ditch	Colleville-sur-Mer
93	678897	MG Pillboxes	St. Laurent-sur-Mer
95	676901	St Pt Guns & MGs	St. Laurent-sur-Mer
97	675893	Beach Exit	St. Laurent-sur-Mer
99	674878	Troops	Colleville-sur-Mer
101	671901	Unoccupied Emplacements	St. Laurent-sur-Mer
103	671893	Troops	St. Laurent-sur-Mer
105	666903	Shelters-Pillboxes	St. Laurent-sur-Mer
107	667906	Port St Pt	Les Moulins
109	666903	St Pt MGs	Les Moulins
111	662896	MGs	St. Laurent-sur-Mer
113	664907	Pillbox - MGs	Les Moulins
115	663902	Beach Exit	St. Laurent-sur-Mer
117	661907	Radar Sta	Hamel au Pretre
119	? 656910	MGs Pillbox	Hamel au Pretre
121	655912	Fort House	Hamel au Pretre
123	653912	MG Pillbox-Shelters	Hamel au Pretre
125	651915	MG St Pt	Hamel au Pretre
127	648912	Fort Houses (?)	Vierville-sur-Mer
129	648917	Pillboxes & MGs Shelters	Vierville-sur-Mer

VII Corps Sector

First Army Number	Coordinates	Description	Location
80	413020	MG St Pt	Fort de Foucarville
82	411024	MG St Pt	Pte Hav des Dunes
84	407035	MG St Pt	Gd Hau des Dunes
86	397046	MG St Pt	Gd Hau des Dunes
88	392057	MG St Pt	Taret de St Marcouf
90	388064	MG St Pt	Pt St Marcouf
92	385069	MG St Pt	de Fontenay
94	376070	MG St Pt	N.W. Taret de Fontenay
96	349077	MG St Pt	W. Michauderie
98	376082	MG St Pt	Bains
100	374086	MG St Pt	Red te Simon
102	370095	MG St Pt	La Maison Rouge
104	362100	MG St Pt	W. Fort d'Anneville
106	364108	MG St Pt	N.W. Fort d'Anneville
108	364115	MG St Pt	La Belle Croix
110	362125	MG St Pt	Eglise de Crenneville
112	357143	MG St Pt	Beauvais
114	366146	MG St Pt	Morsalines
116	364168	MG St Pt	Quettehou
118	370169	MG St Pt	Quetteheu
120	380162	MG St Pt	St Vaast la Houque
122	388145	MG St Pt	La Houque
124	394155	MG St Pt	St Vaast la Houque
126	396166	MG St Pt	St Vaast la Houque
128	404186	MG St Pt	Point de Saire
130	412187	MG St Pt	Jonville

Enemy Installations and Terrain Features in First Army Sector of Neptune Area (cont'd)

V Corps Sector

First Army Number	Coordinates	Description	Location
131	641919	MGs Pillboxes	Vierville-sur-Mer
133	648866	Cross Roads	Fornigny
135	637927	MGs - Pillboxes - Shelters	le Ht Chemin
137	636930	AT Guns	Pt et Raz de la Percee
139	624935	St Pt	La Guay
141	622935	Radar - AA Guns	La Guay
143	622906	Troops	Asnieres
145	622887	MGs - Depot	Montigny
147	611916	MGs - Houses	Englesqueville la Percee
149	612927	St Pt	Chau d' Englesqueville
151	606933	1 MG	St. Pierre-du-Mont
153	602838	St Pt MGs	St. Pierre-du-Mont
155	594929	RJ	Boisse
157	586931	Troops	Au Guay
159	585934	1 AT Gun	Au Guay
161	584915	Cable Jct-CP?	Criqueville on Bessin
163	576939	St Pt	Grandcamp-les Bains
165	574939	1 MG	Grandcamp-les Bains
167	573933	Gun Psns-Trps	Grandcamp-les Bains
169	565936	St Pt	Grandcamp-les Bains
171	562893	St Pt - Trps	Chau de Jucoville
173	558933	St Pt	Grandcamp-les Bains
175	554926	Troops	Grandcamp-les Bains
177	552932	Pillbox	Grandcamp-les Bains
179	546910	Cable Jct - CP ?	Grandcamp-les Bains
181	544933	St Pt	Grandcamp-les Bains
183	544929	St Pt - CP ?	Grandcamp-les Bains
185	543935	1 Lt Gun	Grandcamp-les Bains
187	541923	Troops	Grandcamp-les Bains

VII Corps Sector

First Army Number	Coordinates	Description	Location
132	423182	MG St Pt	Point de Saire
134	425198	MG St Pt	Point de Fouty
136	395846	Town	Carentan
138	399869	Bridge	La Barquette
140	419873	Bridge	Penemo
142	382865	Bridge	Pont de Douve
144	365872	Bridge	S. St Come du fort
146	413928	Town	St Marie du Mont
148	414968	MG St Pt	L'Audeville
150	410988	Road	St Martin de Varreville
152	402999	Road	Veauquobert
154	348964	Town	St Mere Eglise
156	362932	Road Crossing	Le Bout de LaVille
158	339937	Town	Chef du Pont
160	321929	Bridge	Les Merieux
162	309911	Bridge	Beauzeville la Bastille
164	314956	Bridge	la Fiere
166	269928	Bridge	Pont l'Abbe (Etienville)
168	242080	Town	Valognes
170	195945	Town	St Sauveur la Vicomte
172	189909	Bridge	La Val Pepin
174	196877	Hill	West of Les Rouland
176	177842	Town	La Haye Du Puits
178	183760	Town	Lessay
180	167879	Hill	W. of St. Nicolas de Pierre Pont
182	146890	Town	St Sauveur de Pierre Pont
184	095894	Town	St Lo d'Ourville
186	103902	Cross road	N.E. of St. Lo d'Ourville
188	123929	Town	Boseville

- 4 -

TOP SECRET BIGOT

Enemy Installations and Terrain Features in First Army Sector of   Page 5 of 7 pages
Neptune Area (cont'd)

V Corps Sector

First Army Number	Coordinates	Description	Location
189	563919	Troops	Grandcamp-les Bains
191	560920	St Pt	Grandcamp-les Bains
193	569923	Gun Psns - ? Troops	Sta. Maisy
195	568934	St Pt	Sta. Maisy
197	566924	Houses	Sta. Maisy
199	563935	2 MGs	Sta. Maisy
201	561905	Calbe Jct - CP ?	Sta. Maisy
203	560913	Troops	Sta. Maisy
205	567935	St Pt	Sta. Maisy
207	566907	Troops	Sta. Maisy
209	562933	St Pt	Sta. Maisy
211	567867	Troops	Osmanville
213	561924	St Pt	Lock
215	561912	St Pt	Lock
217	560921	2 MG	St. Clement
219	567882	St.Pt	St. Clement
221	565916	St Pt	Gefosse-Fontenay
223	564908	St Pt	Fontenay
225	562857	St Pt	Isigny
227	457906	St Pt	Fontenay
229	457884	4 MGs	St. Clement
231	453904	Pillboxes	Isigny
233	452878	Bridge - Pillboxes	Isigny
235	459934	Ammo Depot	St. Pierre-du-Mont
237	579937	Flak Guns	Grandcamp-les Bains
239	616937	St Pt	St. Piere-du-Mont
241	675899	St Pt	St. Laurent-sur-Mer
243	767871	Constructions	Longues
245	663906	St Pt	St. Laurent-sur-Mer
247	762809	RJ	Vaucelles
249	761821	Troops	Sully

VII Corps Sector

First Army Number	Coordinates	Description	Location
190	135942	Hill	N. of Bellee
192	093957	Town	Fierville
194	032949	Town	Barneville-Sur-Mer
196	136985	Town	St. Jacques-de-Nehou
198	103982	Hill	North of Le Boulle
200	067989	Hill	North of Langeterie
202	124043	Town	Bricquebec
220	421211	Inf Strong Point	Maltot
222	417222	Inf Strong Point	La Mer
224	411227	Inf Strong Point	La Mer
226	417233	Inf Strong Point	Montfarville
228	407244	Inf Strong Point	Les Ruches
230	402252	Inf Strong Point	Barfleur
232	405255	Inf Strong Point	Barfleur
234	405216	Inf Strong Point	Crasville
236	407237	Inf Strong Point	Montfarville
238	385245	Inf Strong Point	La Moignero
240	382247	Inf Strong Point	La Moignero
242	382243	Inf Strong Point	La Moignero
244	383254	Inf Strong Point	Denneville
246	386278	Inf Strong Point	Gattoville
248	321257	Inf Strong Point	Varouville
250	361206	Inf Strong Point	La Pernelle

TOP SECRET BIGOT

An Air Force bombing evaluation of the mission to Maisy – Les Perruques was released on 27 May 1944, Neptune Argus 30, Appendix A: '*This medium howitzer battery was bombed on 23 May 1944. No damage was caused to the emplacements, all four of which are occupied. The road in front of the battery is cratered and one bomb hit in the wire perimeter. (5008-10 of sortie US17/75, 24 May 1944)*

The Eleventh Amphibious Force Intelligence Report shown here confirms that the Pointe du Hoc battery is 'Concrete under construction' – and Maisy Les Perruques is stated as having 6 x 155mm cannons. It lists the La Martinière battery (No. 16) being in Fontenay. In reality, it is within metres of the Fontenay town boundary – but it is still physically in Maisy village.

TOP SECRET
B-I-G-O-T

COAST DEFENSE BATTERIES

NO. BATT	GRID	LOCATION	EMPLACEMENT	RANGE	AREA	PROPOSED AIR BOMBARDMENT
1 6-155G	586938	Pointe du Hoc	Concrete under construction	25,000	OMAHA	(a) Pre Y-day (b) Night Heavy (c) Night Medium
1A 4-170G	365201	La Pernelle	Open	30,000	UTAH	(a) Pre Y-day (b) Night Heavy (c) Night Medium (d) Fighter Bomb. ers
2 4-240G	265267	Carneville	Turrets and casemates U/C	40,000	PEN-INSULA	(a) Pre Y-day
3 6-155G	368044	Fontenay	Casemates under construction. (Open)	25,000	UTAH	(a) Night Heavy (b) Fighter Bomb-ers
4 6-155G	354139	Morsalines	Open concrete	25,000	UTAH	(a) Night Heavy (b) Fighter Bomb-ers
5 6-155H	533918	Maisy	Open	13,000	OMAHA	(a) Night Medium (b) Fighter Bomb-ers
6 4-155H	405980	Varreville	Casemates U/C	13,000	UTAH	Night Heavy
7 4-170G	246264	Les Movlins	Turrets	32,000	PEN-INSULA	(Existance doubtful)
8 6-155G	392277	Gatteville	Report Casements U/C	25,000	PEN-INSULA	
8A 4-170?	394228	Gatteville	Open	30,000	UTAH	
9 4-105GH	360022	Emondeville	Casemate	13,000	UTAH	
10 4-105GH	792831	Beauvis	Open	13,000	OMAHA	
11 4-150GH	354291	Pte de Neville	1 Casemate	25,000	UTAH	
12 4-150H	378204	Vicel	Open	14,600	UTAH	
13 4-105GH	848853	Ryes	Open	13,000	OMAHA	
14 4-105GH	343057	Ozeville	Open	13,000	UTAH	Day Fighter Bomber
15 4-105GH	342102	Versailles	Open	13,000	UTAH	

B-I-G-O-T-

COAST DEFENSE BATTERIES

No. BATT	GRID	LOCATION	EMPLACEMENT	RANGE	AREA	PROPOSED AIR BOMBARDMENT
16 4-77	528915	Fontenay	Open	10,300	UTAH	Fighter Bombers
17 3-105GH	339138	La Fosse	2 Casemates ?	13,000	UTAH	
18 3-75	413160	Tatihou	Casemate ?	13,000	UTAH	

28 May 1944   Navy Report dated 28 May states that: *D-Day and H-Hour has been named.*

At 1800 A.N.C.X.F. signalled that D-Day was fixed as 5th June and H-Hour for respective Assault Force was to be:

Forces S & G	*0645*
Force J (right sector)	*0655*
Force J (left sector)	*0705*
Force O	*0610*
Force U	*0600*

The naming of D-Day with the previous order to '*carry out Operation NEPTUNE*' was the executive signal which started all the intricate movement and actions detailed in Operation Orders. It was the intention that no further signal would be made, unless weather conditions forced a postponement of D-Day. Personnel became 'sealed' in ships in accordance with their orders.

5th Rangers – Companies A – F, Medical and HQ – Dorchester, Dorset.

2nd Rangers – Companies A – F, Medical and HQ – Dorchester, Dorset.

On 28 May, German bombs and mines were dropped in and around Portland Harbour, where the ships of Force O were lying; movement in the harbour and its approaches had to be stopped until 2200.

---

29 May 1944
5th Rangers – Companies A – F, Medical and HQ – Dorchester, Dorset.

2nd Rangers – Companies A – F, Medical and HQ – Dorchester, Dorset.

Maurice Prince: *What little training we did do was to retain ourselves physically and to keep us in the best of condition. We did some close order drill and body exercises. Small hikes and some double timing around the area would conclude our training. Generally, the entire afternoon was given to sports with softball leading all the other games.*

Our pleasant stay in this area was quite often interfered with by the Jerry Luftwaffe that came over nightly to visit us and also the P-38 air base which was situated to the rear of us. I guess the Nazis were making a last desperate but futile attempt to do as much damage and destruction as was possible to hamper our efforts in the coming invasion. It was during one of these air raids that we came closest to being bombed out in our entire stay in the E.T.O. and that included our combat days.

It was sometime during the dark hours of early morning. We had all retired and were sleeping soundly, when out of the clear skies came the throbbing and deafening roar of aeroplane engines over our bivouac area. Being asleep and senses dulled, our first reaction was that the plane was out of control and was heading earthward in our vicinity. No time was lost in seeking cover. The noises had aroused the entire area and everyone was making wild and mad dashes for the trenches we had dug for cases such as this. The whistling of bombs as they hurtled through space made us realize that we were in the midst of an air raid. The thunderous crash of the bombs as they hit the ground proved the proximity of the danger to us. The ground about just shook and quivered for a moment. Stoves, cots, equipment, and loose material that hung on the sides of the tents and huts fell down or were turned over. Loose gravel and dirt plus shrapnel literally filled the air. It was a big bomb and to say that we weren't scared would be telling an untruth. The enemy plane continued to circle our area. The bursts of ack-ack and machine gun fire that were sent after it did our hearts good. The drone of friendly aircraft coming to the rescue didn't hurt our feelings and when the Jerry plane took off never to return again for that evening, we all gave a sigh of relief and went back to sleep.

The bombs had landed in our motor pool across the road from us. There had been one dud of two that actually fell. This dud had buried itself about ten feet into the earth in about the same place as where the first bomb had gone off. We were lucky that we didn't sustain any casualties that caused hospitalisation, as some of the boys did receive minor cuts and wounds. An M.P. outfit which was billeted in the motor pool – did have a few of their men killed and some seriously wounded. We also lost a couple of vehicles, but on the whole, damage to equipment was slight. I hate to think what would have happened had that missile of death landed about a hundred yards to the left and had gone off in our immediate area. I'm afraid that there wouldn't have been much of Able Co. or Baker Co. for that matter as they were billeted next to us – to make the initial assault on D-Day.

The 29 May Police report of that specific incident was duly sent to the Chief Constable's office in Dorchester.

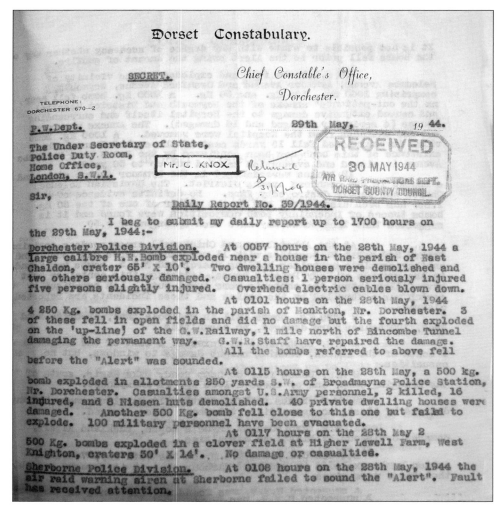

Dorset Constabulary.

SECRET.

Chief Constable's Office,
Dorchester.

TELEPHONE:
DORCHESTER 670—2

P.W.Dept.

The Under Secretary of State,
Police Duty Room,
Home Office,
London, S.W.1.

29th May,   19 44.

Mr. C. KNOX

RECEIVED
30 MAY 1944
AIR RAID ... DEPT.
DORSET COUNTY COUNCIL.

Sir,

Daily Report No. 39/1944.

I beg to submit my daily report up to 1700 hours on
the 29th May, 1944:-

Dorchester Police Division.   At 0057 hours on the 28th May, 1944 a
large calibre H.E.Bomb exploded near a house in the parish of East
Chaldon, crater 65' X 10'.   Two dwelling houses were demolished and
two others seriously damaged. Casualties: 1 person seriously injured
five persons slightly injured.   Overhead electric cables blown down.
At 0101 hours on the 28th May, 1944
4 250 Kg. bombs exploded in the parish of Monkton, Nr. Dorchester. 3
of these fell in open fields and did no damage but the fourth exploded
on the 'up-line) of the G.W.Railway, 1 mile north of Bincombe Tunnel
damaging the permanent way.   G.W.R.Staff have repaired the damage.
All the bombs referred to above fell
before the "Alert" was sounded.
At 0115 hours on the 28th May, a 500 kg.
bomb exploded in allotments 250 yards S.W. of Broadmayne Police Station,
Nr. Dorchester. Casualties amongst U.S.Army personnel, 2 killed, 16
injured, and 8 Nissen huts demolished.   40 private dwelling houses were
damaged.   Another 500 Kg. bomb fell close to this one but failed to
explode. 100 military personnel have been evacuated.
At 0117 hours on the 28th May 2
500 Kg. bombs exploded in a clover field at Higher Lewell Farm, West
Knighton, craters 50' X 14'.   No damage or casualties.
Sherborne Police Division.   At 0108 hours on the 28th May, 1944 the
air raid warning siren at Sherborne failed to sound the "Alert". Fault
has received attention.

In a follow-up Air Force reconnaissance report dated 29 May 1944 – No: WO 205/172, '*Pre D-Day bombing of batteries – Neptune area*' – consolidated report on results of bombing to 28 May 1944: [Maisy – Les Perruques]. '*No damage to the battery. All emplacements occupied.*'

---

30 May 1944
5th Rangers – Companies A – F, Medical and HQ –
Dorchester, Dorset.

2nd Rangers – Companies A – F, Medical and HQ
– Dorchester, Dorset.

Maurice Prince: *Before we were oriented and briefed on our mission, we were allowed to visit the cities of Weymouth and Dorchester. Both these places are fairly large and therefore have many recreational facilities to entertain the GIs, so we found out. Although these places were crowded with Army and Naval personnel, we always managed to do alright for ourselves. Our main trouble lay in getting transportation.*
Since these cities were four or five miles away from our camp site, and being most of our vehicles were either red-lined or being prepared and waterproofed for the coming invasion, this was a task in itself. Many was the road march we were forced to take because of the lack of motorized conveyances.
It was at this place that we made our final preparations for the invasion. We stripped down our equipment and supplies to the barest of essentials. We put all our belongings, plus that of four other men into one duffle bag, while the rest of our possessions had to be either given away, turned in or carried on our backs. We were issued our basic loads of ammo plus

an extra first aid kit, which had a morphine syrette and tourniquet in it. Two life preservers were also handed to us for emergency use in the channel.

We moved from our original field to another area a bit farther down the road. What had been the cause for this exodus I'll never know, except maybe the bomb dud which had as yet not been removed, marked our former area as a danger zone.

It was in this new area that we received a fighting talk by the commanding general of the famous 1st Inf. Div. He didn't speak long and didn't say anything new. He did heap his praises on us for our fine reputation and splendid showing. He called us the finest bunch of soldiers in the entire Army and that he was proud that we were going to operate together in the same area when we crossed the Channel. The speech was most flattering and heartening. I'll never forget that day in the last week of May when our platoon leader (then Lt. White) gathered us together in one of the pyramidal tents and simply said 'Well, men, this is it.' Then he calmly proceeded to unroll the maps and charts he had been carrying under his arm and began to orient and brief us on the coming invasion.

(Note-due to the high secrets of these documents and maps, plus the danger and hazardness of our mission, these papers had to be destroyed lest perchance they fell into enemy hands, so that now my records are very incomplete concerning the plans which were handed down to us about the part our Battalion was to enact in the coming invasion. Please bear with me and forgive me if any discrepencies appear in the following paragraph.)

Well, it seems like the Battalion mission was to occupy the high coastal ground at Pointe du Hoe, France – vicinity of Isigny. This vital piece of terrain commanded all approaches to the beaches in this area and was heavily fortified and able to meet out destruction to our crafts in the nearby waters. In order to insure our assault landing, this piece of heavily fortified ground had to be captured. Pointe Du Hoe became the target for the Rangers, there and then.

The Heinies had built up a formidable and practical defence here and had considered it impossible to attack. There was a battery of six huge 155s long range guns which menaced the sea entrances and shipping in the surrounding waters. These huge guns were casemented in large concrete pillboxes, whose thickness exceeded six to eight feet in depth. These structures were further protected and covered by anti-aircraft defences, a series of tunnel-like communications trenches, and open emplacements for both their automatic weapons and riflemen. To supplement this, there were light artillery pieces and mortars, plus an intricate arrangement of minefields and deceptively placed booby traps. Encircling the entire position were large bands of barbed wire, both of the concertina and double-apron fenced mines.

The Pointe itself was a massive fortress which lay on top of a cliff. This cliff was surrounded on three sides by water and was a sheer drop of over 100 feet from the top to the rocky beach below, so that now as we studied the enemy's situation, we could well realize why cliff scaling had been of such importance in our training. No wonder Hitler, himself, had boasted of the impunity of this position and of the foolishness of the allies to ever think, less try, to break thru this impregnable fortress.

The exact number of enemy personnel operating all the guns and batteries here were unknown to our G-2, but it was estimated that a good guess would place the enemy's troops at 150 to 200 men. The morale of the enemy was known to be good, while the calibre of the Jerries only fair (because, I suppose, of the exertion the Russians placed on the eastern front, which needed the best troops of the Nazis to meet that threat.)

Now that we had a complete picture of the enemy's situation, we could visualise the problems and tasks which would confront us in our attack. We saw that we'd have to overcome a position which was defended in a manner which the military genius of the Nazi had so strongly erected. While to top this off, they had selected the most inaccessible piece of terrain to construct this defence on, so that not only had we to fight our way forward once we touched shore, but we first had to overcome the obstacle of a sheer cliff that mother nature had so fortunately provided for the Germans in order to get into the fight.

On the other side of the ledger, or our side of the fence, we were to have the following support: an aerial bombardment on the Pointe a few minutes before touchdown or H-Hour, which was to be the greatest concentration of bombs ever rained down on one area at one time in the history of aviation. (Now that I look back on this and after seeing all the damage done by this attack, I know that an exaggeration was made in that statement.) The direct fire support of the navy in our zone of action with the disposal of the great battleship Texas, plus a couple of destroyers and cruisers to be at our beck and call. Then we were to have and we did get, our air force to give us fighter cover support all the time and all the while we were attacking. Secret and new fighting tanks were also to hit the beaches at the same time we were, and they were to aid us so that we weren't to be out there by ourselves. Meanwhile paratroopers and glider troops were to have chuted and glided to earth somewhere in the rear of the enemy, cut off his communications, cause disorder, chaos, do damage, inflict casualties and tie up the enemy's reserves.

Taking our situation into hand, our task didn't seem too bad. We were cocky and arrogant and felt that we could pull off this job and do it in a typical Ranger manner. Our egotism and faith in ourselves never faltered. We just knew we could swing the deal.

Now that the enemy and our own situation was known, all we needed was a plan to carry out our mission. So the Battalion drew up the blueprints and each company followed suit, using this master-plan for a pattern.

The Battalion blueprint for this operation ran along these lines. The actual assault of the Pointe was to be made by D-E-F Co.'s. They were to come in from the seaward side, overcome the cliff obstacle and continue to take the Pointe. They were to have the use of two amphibious ladder-carrying Dukws to help them in scaling the cliffs. Ropes and rope ladders were also to be carried, in case the vehicles couldn't make a desired landing. They were to touchdown on shore, H-Hour minus thirty minutes. This was to give them thirty minutes in which to accomplish their mission. This was so, because the other three companies were to be awaiting the outcome of these companies. If the attackers on the Pointe were to be successful in their assault, in the allotted time, then A-B-C Co.'s were to follow in the footsteps of D-E-F Co.'s, push thru them and continue the line of advance till the town of Grandcamps-les-Bains was taken. If the men on the Pointe didn't radio in or signal the mission completed in their given time, then A-B-C Co.'s were to take it for granted that D-E-F Co.'s had been unsuccessful. A-B-C Co.'s were then to hit the beach ('Omaha-dog-green') which was about four miles due south of the Pointe, push up the coastal road and attack the Pointe frontally and try to contact their brother companies who were to be in that vicinity.

Besides the battle plan which was drawn up for us, there had to be certain administrative arrangements to be taken care of. Communications and signal systems had to be arranged, not only between the attacking forces, but also between us and the Navy.

Aid stations and supply bases had to be found and made accessible to us. C.P.'s and O.P.'s had to be picked out and a million and one other minor and important details had to be planned out, so that each man would know exactly the minutest of details and know precisely how every thing fitted together in this giant jig-saw puzzle.

We were endlessly briefed and oriented on our roles in this coming drama. We intensely scrutinized maps and remembered all the terrain features, which were to be in our zone of action. Special aerial photos were handed us to study, and a rubber model map was specially constructed so that each and every terrain feature was sharply imbued in our minds.

We got so that every man could have manoeuvered over this land blindfolded although we never had seen that piece of ground in our lives before. Each man got to know, not only his own part, but that of his buddies, so that in case of casualties, one man if necessity required, would have carried out two men's work, if not he would know which link of the chain was missing and know how to cope with the situation then.

Not only did we know our own individual jobs and knew our companies and Battalion's mission, but we also learned the jobs of units which we were to be operating alongside with. We got so that we knew every angle of the big picture and there wasn't a thing in the entire Army's plan of battle that we weren't familiar with.

Victor Miller, 5th Battalion: *We were put into a camp with armed guards patrolling outside with orders to shoot anyone leaving. Our D-Day assignment was then given to us. Scale models of the French coast showed every house and tree. Through some strange lack of intelligence, it was never mentioned that the hedgerows there were much different than the hedgerows we hiked among in England. Our assignment was to knock out six 155mm guns on Pointe du Hoc.*

Shown is a Beach map plan of obstacles for the Utah Beach area directly opposite the Maisy Battery – La Martinière. This area would be under direct fire from that battery if the Rangers did not reach it, or the combined attacks by the Navy and Air Force were ineffective.

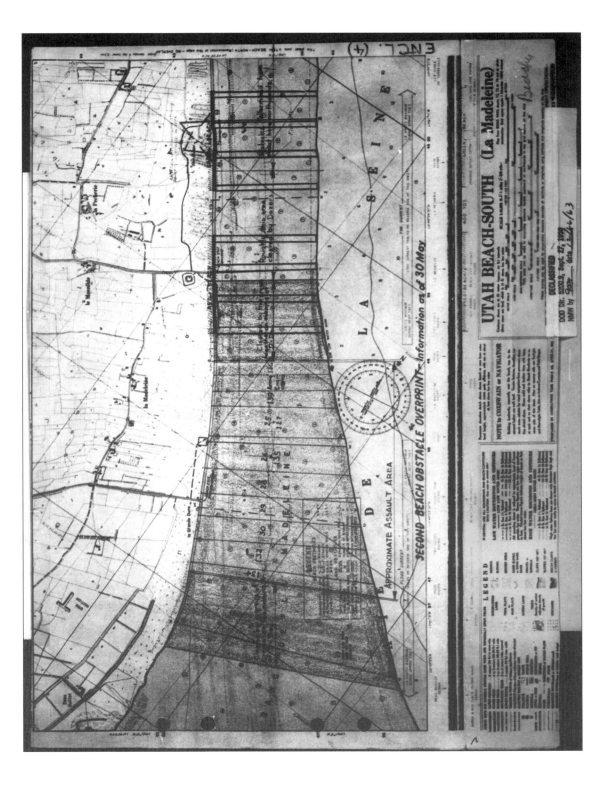

ENCL. (4)

UTAH BEACH-SOUTH (La Madeleine)

SECOND BEACH OBSTACLE OVERPRINT - Information as of 30 May

APPROXIMATE ASSAULT AREA

LA DE LA MADELEINE

LA SEINE

LEGEND

DECLASSIFIED
DOD Dir. 5200.9, Sept. 27, 1958
NMW by _____ date 8-14-63

31 May 1944   On 31 May the Royal Navy issued a report based on the following:

The Daily Telegraph
A curious point in security had arisen since 22nd May, in the Daily Telegraph crossword puzzle. A remarkable number of the codewords used in NEPTUNE formed the correct answers to clues. Not only the word 'NEPTUNE' itself was a solution, but also 'OVERLORD, OMAHA, UTAH, MULBERRY, WHALE' etc. The matter was under investigation by the Naval Intelligence Section.

A Special Order of the Day was issued by A.N.C.X.F. for distribution, after briefing, to each officer and many of the Allied Naval Expeditionary Force, worded as follows: *It is to be our privilege to take part in the greatest amphibious operation in history – a necessary preliminary to the opening of the Western Front in Europe which, in conjunction with the great Russian advance, will crush the fighting power of GERMANY.*

This is the opportunity which we have long awaited and which must be seized and pursued with relentless determination: the hopes and prayers of the free world and of the enslaved peoples of Europe will be with us and we cannot fail them.

Our task, in conjunction with the Merchant Navies of the United Nations, and supported by the Allied Air Forces, is to carry the Allied Expeditionary Force to the Continent, to establish it there in a secure bridgehead and to build it up and maintain it at a rate which will outmatch that of the enemy.

Let no one underestimate the magnitude of this task.

The Germans are desperate and will resist fiercely until we out-manoeuver and out-fight them, which we can and will do. To every one of you will be given the opportunity to show by his determination and resource that dauntless spirit of resolution which individually strengthens and inspires and which, collectively, is irresistible.

I count on every man to do his utmost to ensure the success of this enterprise, which is the climax of the European war.
Good luck to you all and God speed.
B.H. Ramsay
Admiral, Allied Naval Commander-in-Chief – Expeditionary force.

5th Rangers – Companies A – F, Medical and HQ –
Dorchester, Dorset
2nd Rangers – Companies A – F, Medical and HQ –
Dorchester, Dorset

A series of US Air Force reconnaissance photographs were taken after a bombing mission, covering the Omaha coastline, with particular interest shown to the Ranger objectives.

The Radar Station at Pointe et Raz de la Percée.

The area of Pointe du Hoc.

Below: A lower-level aerial photograph of the Radar Station. Shows cratering from bombs.

Looking from the sea over Grandcamp harbour and inland.

Three photographs looking to the east of Grandcamp-les-Bains – Pointe du Hoc is just beyond the right of this image.

Photograph of Grandcamp-les-Bains.

A lower-level photograph of Maisy village and the Batteries after bombing.

A wider view of the Maisy Battery and down to the coastline.

The batteries at Maisy – post bombing.

The coastline in front of Maisy.

The batteries at Maisy in context with Grandcamp-les-Bains harbour.

Form SOSTC - 10

HEADQUARTERS
SERVICES OF SUPPLY, ETOUSA
OFFICE OF THE CHIEF OF TRANSPORTATION
TRAFFIC DIVISION, APO 887

UNIT VEHICLE DATA

Before executing this form unit commanders are cautioned to read carefully the instructions contained in paragraph 42, "Preparation for Overseas Movement - ETOUSA", dated 21 July 1943. This form will be completed in duplicate and forwarded by officer courier in time to reach the above address by the date specified in warning order.

(a) Unit Serial No._____ (b) Unit Designation_____

FINAL LOCATION OF UNIT PRIOR TO MOVEMENT TO PORT

(c) Town_____ (d) County_____ (e) Base Section_____ (f) Map Coordinates_____

(g) Location of Unit Vehicle Park_____ (h) Telephone No. of C.O._____

	QUAN-TITY	TYPE	MAKE	MODEL	MEASUREMENT				WEIGHT			
					LENGTH Ft. Ins.	WIDTH Ft. Ins.	AREA IN SQ. FT. (e x f)	HEIGHT CUT DOWN Ft. Ins.	EMPTY		LOADED OR EQUIPPED	
1									Tons 2240 lbs	Cwt. 112 lbs	Tons 2240 lbs	Cwt. 112 lbs
2	(a)	(b)	(c)	(d)	(e)	(f)	(g)	(h)	(i)		(j)	
3												
4												
5												
6												
7												
8												
9												
10												
11												
12												
13												
14												
15												

TO BE CLASSIFIED

UNIT BREAKDOWN SHEET

APPENDIX "A"

FROM CONCENTRATION AREA_____

UNIT PRIORITY NO._____   UNIT NAME_____

CRAFT LOAD & NO.	PERSONNEL		VEHICLES		DEP. FROM CONC. AREA			ROUTE C/A TO S/A	ARR.STAGING AREA RP OR DETRAINING STATION		S/A ACCOM.		REMARKS
	OFF.	E.M.	NO.	TYPE	DATE	TIME	INITIAL POINT OR ENTRAINING STA		LOCATION	DATE TIME	PERS. BILLET	VEH PARK	
a	b	c	d	e	f	g	h	i	j	k	l	m n	o

IMPORTANT: The front left side of each vehicle will be marked:_____

Every unit was responsible for completing paperwork for each vehicle under its control and then recording that each vehicle had been placed onto the relevant ship. The following form was created and issued for this purpose.

FORM SOSTC – 8

HEADQUARTERS
SERVICES OF SUPPLY ETOUSA
OFFICE OF THE CHIEF OF TRANSPORTATION
TRAFFIC DIVISION APO 887

UNIT PERSONNEL DATA

Information required for movement of troops to port for embarkation overseas. To be executed in duplicate by unit commander for each Company, Battery, Detachment and/or similar unit based upon FINAL INFORMATION and forwarded by officer courier to reach the above address by the date specified in the warning order. For full information refer to paragraph 35, "Preparation for Overseas Movement-ETOUSA", dated 21 July 1943.

(a) Unit Serial No._____ (b) Unit Designation_____

FINAL LOCATION OF UNIT PRIOR TO MOVEMENT TO PORT

(c) Town_____ (d) County_____ (e) Base Section_____

(f) Map Coordinates_____ (g) Entraining Point_____

(h) Telephone No. of C.O._____

ACTUAL STRENGTH AUTHORIZED FOR EMBARKATION

(i) Officers_____ (j) Nurses_____ (k) WO_____ (l) EM_____ (m) Total_____

DATE AND HEADQUARTERS OF WARNING ORDER_____

REMARKS_____

_____

Signature_____
(PRINT AND SIGN)

Commanding_____
(UNIT DESIGNATION)

Hq SOS USAPP 8-43/20M/13486

TO BE CLASSIFIED
SECRET

SHIP SHEET

SHIP/CRAFT NO. _____

APPENDIX "B"

FROM STAGING AREA CAMP_____ I.P._____ PORT DISTRICT_____ PACP_____

PRIORITY NO.	UNIT NAME	PERSONNEL OFF.	PERSONNEL E.M.	VEHICLES NO.	VEHICLES TYPE	STAGING AREA ACCOMMODATION PERS. BILLET	STAGING AREA ACCOMMODATION VEH. PARK	DEP I.P. DATE	DEP I.P. TIME	ROUTE TO PORT AREA	PORT DISTRICT ARRIVE PACP DATE	PORT DISTRICT ARRIVE PACP TIME	PORT DISTRICT BERTH OR HARD NO.	FORECAST SAILING DATE	FORECAST SAILING TIME	REMARKS
a	b	c	d	e	f	g	h	i	j	k	l	m	n	o	p	q

Chapter 9

June 1944 – Rangers Lead the Way

This letter, written by Allied Supreme Commander Dwight D. Eisenhower, was to be read to the men as they left for Normandy.

SUPREME HEADQUARTERS

ALLIED EXPEDITIONARY FORCE

Soldiers, Sailors and Airmen of the Allied Expeditionary Force!
You are about to embark upon the Great Crusade, toward which we have striven these many months. The eyes of the World are upon you. The hopes and prayers of liberty-loving people everywhere march with you. In company with our brave Allies and brother-in-arms on other Fronts, you will bring about the destruction of the German war machine, the elimination of Nazi tyranny over the oppressed peoples of Europe, and security for ourselves in a free world.

Your task will not be an easy one. Your enemy is well trained, well equipped and battle-hardened. He will fight savagely.

But this is the year 1944! Much has happened since the Nazi triumphs of 1940-41. The United Nations have inflicted upon the Germans great defeats, in open battle, man-to-man. Our air offensive has seriously reduced their strength in the air and their capacity to wage war on the ground. Our Home Fronts have given us an overwhelming superiority in weapons and munitions of war, and placed at our disposal great reserves of trained fighting men. The tide has turned! The free men of the world are marching together to Victory!

I have full confidence in your courage, devotion to duty and skill in battle. We will accept nothing less than full Victory!

Good Luck! And let us all beseech the blessing of Almighty God upon this great noble undertaking.

Dwight D. Eisenhower.

1 June 1944

Below: An update of beach obstacles on Omaha Beach.

11thPHIB/A8

Serial:

TOP SECRET **TOP SECRET**

According to recent information the following underwater obstacles were found on OMAHA Beach: element "C", stakes, ramps and hedgehogs with wire stretched between the stakes on FOX RED Beach.

Some of the element "C" have been knocked over on its face and many of the hedgehogs are half buried in the sand.

In general, alternate elements "C" have teller-mines fitted to the top of the central forward upright member, although in some cases mines are fitted to successive elements "C".

Approximately fifty percent of the ramp-type obstacles, particularly those in the forward row, have teller-mines fitted to the top end of the ramp. No instances of mines lower down the ramps have been seen in this area to date, but they have appeared in other areas.

Many of the stakes have mines attached to their tops.

No hedgehogs on this beach have mines attached but some hedgehogs on other beaches have a teller-mine fastened to the top of the landward arm.

Although none appeared on OMAHA Beach as late as 19 May, 1944, it is interesting to note that on some other beaches shells 6" or less are attached to some stakes and ramps instead of teller-mines. It is thought that these shells are being used for mines.

Enclosure (A) to 11th Phib
serial CO 251 dated 1 June 1944

0	
01	
N1	
N2	
N3	
N4	
20	
70	
75	
05	
5/29/44	
DATE	
C.B.MUNSON	
ORIG.	
fox	
YEO	

PLEASE EXPEDITE

Navy Report 1 June: At 1200 A.N.C.S.F. assumed operational command of NEPTUNE forces, and general control of operations in the CHANNEL.

Wireless silence. At 0001 wireless silence by ships and craft of the assault forces was imposed for the ensuing 24 hours. During the silence a bogus wireless training exercise was carried out as the first move in a cover plan (code-name FORTITUDE SOUTH) designed to delay the enemy in making an advance appreciation of H-Hour.

'Exercise AIRSHOW' was carried out, in which aircraft with the special distinctive markings adopted for NEPTUNE, flew over as many assault ships and units as possible to assist in future recognition.

The information given to each ship on identification of Allied planes was brief.

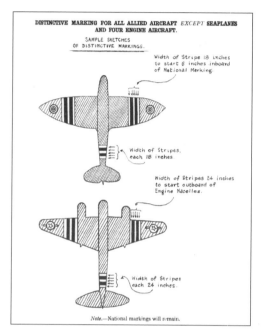

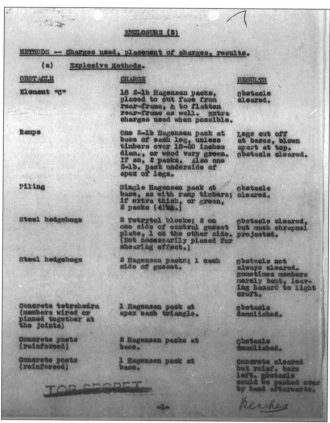

The results of tests on the destruction of German obstacles were widely circulated – primarily to aid assault troops when it came to making decisions on how to destroy them.

OBSTACLE	CHARGE	RESULTS
Tellermines 35, 42, 43	1 Hagensen pack, or 1 Tetrytol Block, or 1 ½-lb. block TNT	Tellermine countermined.
Tellermines 35, 42, 43	1 Number Eight cap placed in detonator	Tellermine detonated.

(b) Non-Explosive Methods.

All the above obstacles were successfully removed with caterpillars, dozers, tank dozers, or tanks, if the tellermines had been removed first. Tellermines can be removed by hand after unscrewing detonator, if it is desired to avoid the shrapnel caused by blowing them.

Hedgehogs were eliminated by undoing bolts from central gusset plates, allowing obstacle to collapse.

(c) Fixed Flamethrowers.

From Lt. Smith's description, these were the same as those seen by the writer at Grandcamp, a specimen of which was recovered for forwarding to the U.S.A. These flamethrowers are a simple tank, filled with a petroleum creosota mixture, which is ejected through a goose-neck nozzle by gas pressure from a burning pyrotechnic cartridge. The mixture is ignited by another similar cartridge wired and fired electrically in parallel with the first one. The flame lasts about 1½ minutes and has a range of 50-75 feet depending on the wind. It has a general terror value, and a specific value against vehicles or concentrations of men approaching the seawall within its range.

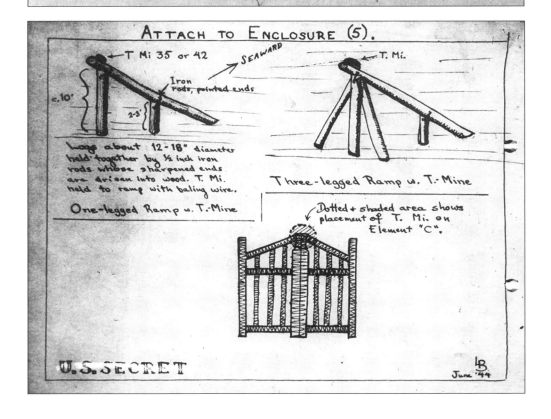

5th Battalion Incidents, Messages and Orders Report:

> 1 June - VOCG First Inf Div; left Dorchester England
> by vehicle 0700. Arrived Weymouth, England
> 0939, went aboard LCA's, left Weymouth
> Harbor arrived at and boarded HMS Leopold,
> Boudouin, and Prince Charles at 1045.

A Company 5th Rangers – Onboard HMS *Leopold*, Weymouth, England.
B Company 5th Rangers – Onboard HMS *Leopold*, Weymouth, England.

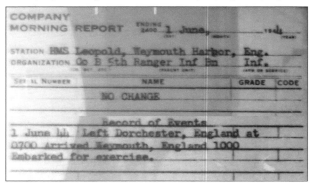

C Company 5th Rangers – Onboard HMS *Boudin* (sic) [Author: HMS Prince Baudouin], Weymouth Harbour, England.
D Company 5th Rangers – Onboard HMS *Boudin*, Weymouth Harbour, England.
E Company 5th Rangers – Onboard HMS *Leopold*, Weymouth Harbour, England.
F Company 5th Rangers – Onboard HMS *Boudin*, Weymouth Harbour, England.

Medical Detachment 5th Rangers – Onboard HMS *Leopold*, Weymouth, England.
Headquarters Company 5th Rangers – Onboard HMS *Leopold*, Weymouth, England.

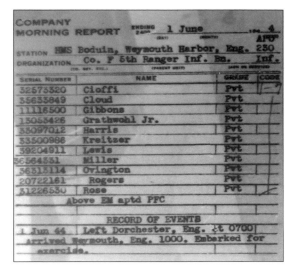

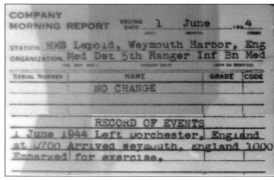

2nd Battalion After Action Report.

On 1 June, the Battalion moved by motor to Weymouth for embarkation as follows:

Companies A/B/C with Battalion Headquarters and Communication personnel - HMS Prince Charles.

Company D and the 2nd Platoon/Company E - HMS Amsterdam.

Company F plus the 1st Platoon/Company E and the Battalion Command Post Detachment - HMS Ben My Chree.

The Battalion as part of the Provisional Ranger Group was attached to the 116th Infantry for operations. The mission assigned to the Battalion was to destroy the battery on Pointe du Hoe and to establish an initial beachhead on the coast of France. The plans by which the Battalion would attempt to carry out this mission are included in the various Force Histories.

A Company 2nd Rangers – Aboard Ship.
A Company left Dorchester at 0815 hours in trucks and arrived at Weymouth, Dorset at 0900 hours. They boarded ship at 1100 hours.

B Company 2nd Rangers – Aboard Ship.
B Company left Dorchester at 0815 hours in trucks and arrived at Weymouth, Dorset at 0900 hours. They boarded ship at 1100 hours.

C Company 2nd Rangers – Aboard Ship.
C Company left Dorchester at 0815 hours in trucks and arrived at Weymouth, Dorset at 0900 hours. They boarded ship at 1100 hours.

D Company 2nd Rangers – Aboard Ship.
D Company left Dorchester at 1000 hours in trucks and arrived at Weymouth, Dorset at 1115 hours. They boarded ship at 1230 hours.

E Company 2nd Rangers – Aboard Ship.
E Company left Dorchester at 1000 hours in trucks and arrived at Weymouth, Dorset at 1115 hours. They boarded ship at 1230 hours.

F Company 2nd Rangers – Aboard Ship. F Company boarded SS Ben-my-Chree.

i) Embarkation

Maurice Prince: *Came the day of June 1 and we found ourselves aboard the same Belgian ship which had carried us thru on our previous manoeuvers. It was like old home week. We made ourselves as comfortable as was possible and settled down to enjoy our coming trip across the channel.*

We had left the marshalling area fully prepared for the invasion. We were loaded down with our equipment and basic loads. We had come down to our jumping off place, (port of Weymouth) in enclosed trucks. Our morale and spirits had never been better.

We sang all the way down. One would never realize that we characters were embarking on an assault that was to bring us so much loss, while gaining for us the esteem of the entire world. We de-trucked at a point outside the pier.

Orders for moving into the port area as they were issued.

MOVEMENT INTO THE PORT AREA

         Units arriving at the Port Area CP in complete Craft Loads will be dispatched or guided to parking areas along the roads leading to the Embarkation Point. A representative of Port District Administrative HQ will collect all maps and other documents before the Craft Load proceeds to the Embarkation Point. At the Port Area CP located just behind the Embarkation Point, the Craft Load's papers, i.e. AF W-5169 and SHIP SHEET will be checked for discrepancies, casualties etc. (these documents will be collected by the TCEO just prior to actual embarkation).

         US Personnel embarking on Assault and Follow-Up convoys will be issued life preservers by TC personnel at hards (or where Task Force Commander designates.

Rangers disembarked from their trucks on the main road into Weymouth town. They then walked down through 'the gardens' via a passageway to the beach and seafront walkway.

Maurice Prince: *We then entered the pier and proceeded to march along till we reached the Red Cross coffee and donut stands which were doing business here, gratis, of course. We partook in our last coffee and donuts on the shores of England with hearty gusto and great gulps. Our stomachs were well appeased by the Java and sinkers.*

The tea and coffee tent provided by the Red Cross with a sign that reads 'from the folks back home'. Weymouth Pavilion can be seen in the background.

Each man carried his own kit and the men have their gas masks strapped to their chests. Others are wearing their life preservers and some are still carrying them in their cardboard box of issue.

Maurice Prince: *We continued our march, burdened down by our heavy loads until we reached the docks where our LCAs awaited to take us to our mother ship.*

Both British and US Troops were stationed along the seafront to keep out unwanted attention from the public. There were only military vehicles parked and no civilians were allowed along the whole of the esplanade for security reasons. There were no locals around to wave goodbye to the Rangers – there were only the official military photographers and approved reporters.

Next page: A photographer's patch appears to be worn on the right shoulder by a man in the column – the Rangers' diamond badge being worn beneath it. The Photographers Badge could only be worn under certain regulations – but it appears this one was not being worn correctly. On 13 May 1944 ETOUSA had issued a circular No 51 which ordered that *'While on official photographic assignments in the theatre, each Signal Corps photographer will wear an identifying patch, measuring 3" x 3" on the left sleeve of his outer garment (other than the raincoat), 4 inches above the cuff. Brassard will not be worn. The patch will be green*

and orange in colour and will bear the Signal Corps device and the words 'Cameraman, Official'. The patch will be procured and issued by the Chief Signal Officer, from his headquarters.'

Maurice Prince: *Cameras and photographers were having a field day. Moving picture machines were busily engaged at preserving our features for posterity. Inquiring reporters were shooting questions and interviewing us, as we moved along. Wise cracks and humorous jokes were flung about as though we hadn't a worry in the world. Gaity was quite in evidence as the boys broke out in vocal refrains, such songs as, 'Roll Me Over', 'I've Been Working on the Railroad', 'Tennessee is a Hell of a Place to be In' and others filled the air. A good time and a good showing was had by all. More spirit was displayed here than in a haunted house.*

This photograph was taken from the Pavilion looking towards the Rangers as they approach and then load down onto their LCAs.

A US Army Report stated: *On 1st June 1944 the loading started. 'L' day, or loading day, had been a closely guarded secret, and the men were moved swiftly aboard their respective craft. Marshalling into craft load had been done after briefing so that troops would learn their job as a unit. Food and water had been placed aboard by Service of Supply from sea dumps, near the hards. Static personnel stood by to carry out the processing of troops in the event weather, or other circumstances forced a postponement of the invasion.*

LCA 883 approaches the jetty. It does not yet have its rockets fitted on the deck.

The men were being helped by the Royal Navy onto pontoons and then onto each individual landing craft. Their heavy loads made it difficult to negotiate the steep gap between the harbour edge and the boats. Also visible are the extra life vests wrapped around vital equipment such as radios.

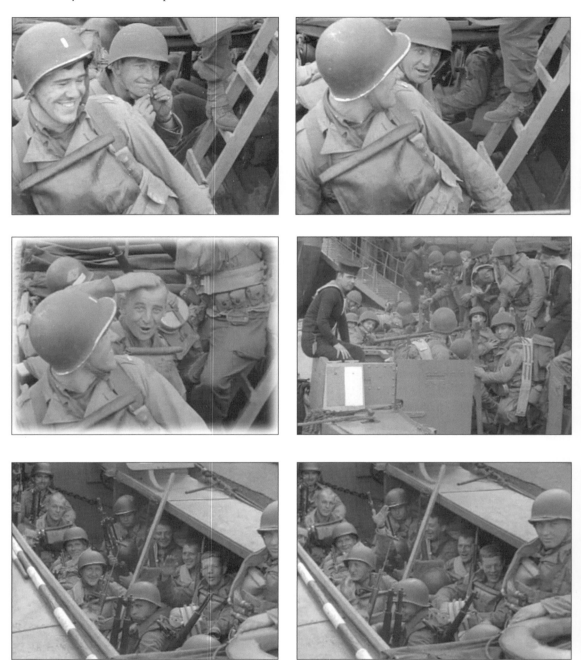

The men are packed together with one row on each side and another down the centre.

Tall items such as bazookas, rifles and Bangalore torpedoes are pointed vertically.

Above: Men from A Company 5th Battalion are loading. Lt. Charles Parker is the last man to board – he is on the right with his back to the camera.

Once each group of men were loaded, they waited for the signal to leave in convoy.

Jack Burke A Co. 5th: *I attached a gas mask to my chest along with a life preserver that could be inflated in an emergency.*

James W. Gabaree A Co. 5th: *We discovered while in training, that if the life preserver was worn around the waist and you were wounded and became unconscious, you tipped upside down due to the heavy load we carried on our backs. When we boarded the LCAs I wore mine diagonally, across my left shoulder down to the belt line on my right side.*

Dick Hathaway A Co. 5th: *All soldiers carried a heavy load of equipment into combat, although different soldiers carried slightly different equipment, depending on their mission. The same was true in the Rangers. I wore a steel helmet and a liner. Underneath that, I wore a wool-knit cap. The battle dress was an impregnated, olive drab, fatigue-type uniform that was designed to reduce casualties should the Germans use toxic chemicals. We used stripped-down field packs and carried some 'K' and a 'D' ration (fortified chocolate bar), a mess kit with knife, fork and spoon. And a rain-coat. Attached to the pack was a bayonet and an entrenching shovel. I had an eighty-one millimeter white phosphorous mortar round tied on the top of my pack, which I was to drop once I was on the beach. This was to provide extra ammunition. Everyone carried extra explosives.*

I wore my trousers bloused over my jump boots. I carried an M-1 rifle and wore a cartridge belt, which was held up by a pair of suspenders that also held my pack. On my cartridge belt, I carried a pair of wire cutters, a lensatic compass, a canteen full of water, a fighting knife, with a stiletto-type knife strapped to my lower left leg. I also carried two concussion grenades, two anti-tank rifle grenades, and a grenade launcher. I wore a first-aid packet on my cartridge belt with another, with a morphine syringe tied on my left shoulder. On my wrist I wore an issued twenty-one jeweled Hamilton wristwatch. I wore a life preserver around my waist, that could be inflated by squeezing two CO cylinders built into the belt. It could also be inflated by blowing into a mouthpiece. Strapped to my left leg was an assault gas mask in a rubber waterproof container.

Next page: The top picture shows non-Rangers boarding LCAs belonging to the mother ship *Princess Maud*. These landing craft from the 'PM' were to be used as back-up vessels for the Rangers in the event of any problems with their own boats.

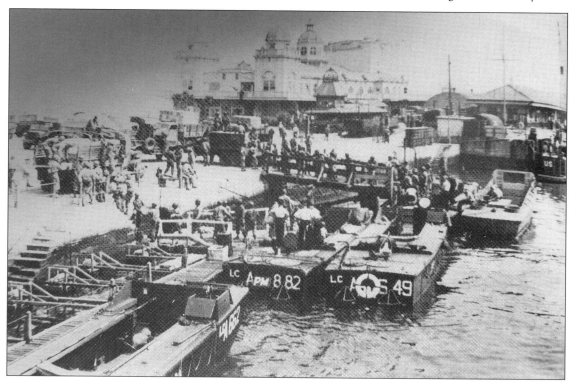

Maurice Prince: *We said our last farewells to some Navy personnel and to the reporters who were allowed on the dock. We then boarded our cramped LCAs and prepared to ride out to our awaiting mother boat. We were sixty-four men and three officers, plus the added headquarters personnel of two first aid men and one '300' radio operator.*

Our ship lay anchored off the coastline in the bay of Weymouth. All about us and as far as the eye could see were other vessels of all shapes and sizes. Some bore the proud, majestic insignias of the Royal Navy, while others had the painting and bore the gallant flag of our own Navy. It was an inspiring sight to view this immense flotilla.

Out on the far horizon was the line of the ever watchful and ever alerted battle ships of our combined Navies. Enemy E boat alerts had been received and these cruisers and destroyers were making sure that no harm came to our small, vulnerable crafts. The huge, friendly-looking anti-aircraft balloons that protected the city of Weymouth presented a pretty picture as they lazily floated about the upper stratosphere. The friendly aircraft that continually roved overhead gave us the assured feeling that we were being well being taken care of – such as a mother bird protecting her little ones. There were so many ships all around us that I couldn't help but think what a splendid opportunity

Other assault units boarding LCVP (Higgins Boats). These units were to land alongside the Rangers on Omaha Beach.

this would be for an enemy air raid, but I suppose the Luftwaffe didn't think that way, or have the gumption or the planes to stage a raid. Whatever the reason was, they didn't attack.

Medical Detachment 2nd Rangers – Aboard Ship.
The Medical Detachment left Dorchester at 0815 hours in trucks and arrived at Weymouth, Dorset at 0900 hours. They boarded ship at 1100 hours.
Headquarters Company 2nd Rangers – Aboard Ship.
Headquarters Company left Dorchester at 0815 hours in trucks and arrived at Weymouth, Dorset at 0900 hours. They boarded ship at 1100 hours.

USS *Satterlee* – ship's report recorded the following detail.

<u>Naval Gunfire Support.</u>

Many lessons were learned in the gunfire support mission.

Our Shore Fire Control Party came aboard before the Fabius I exercise. We worked with them in a later shore bombardment exercise. We had several communication drills. They came aboard again in Portland just before D-day. There was a complete and intimate understanding between the ship and the Ranger Shore Fire Control Party. As a result, during the close support firing, communications were uniformly excellent. It was as if the Shore Fire Control Party was in our C.I.C.

Incidently, these fine young men were a great source of inspiration to the SATTERLEE. Everyone who had contact with them was greatly impressed by their enthusiasm, determination, and courage. They knew they had a tough assignment and were ready for it. And they had the ship ready to back them. To this one factor can be attributed the success of our mission.

There could be no better method of authentication than to send "Hello, Rocky", and then to hear the familiar voice come back "Hello, Joe, this is Rocky". This should provide a valuable lesson for future operations.

2 June 1944   Navy Weather Report 2 June: *Weather: Fair to cloudy. Wind N.N.W. force 4, backing slowly. Sea slight. Weather forecast indicated less favourable conditions for 5th June.*
   Commanders meeting. At 1030 the Supreme Commander held a meeting at Battle Headquarters attended by Commanders-in-Chief and their Chiefs of Staff to consider the weather forecast. Less favourable conditions were predicted for D-Day, particularly as regards cloud, and cloud base, which was of particular concern to the Air Force authorities since it would adversely affect the passage of the Airborne Divisions.

A Company 5th Rangers – Onboard HMS *Leopold*, Weymouth, England.
B Company 5th Rangers – Onboard HMS *Leopold*, Weymouth, England.
C Company 5th Rangers – Onboard HMS *Baudouin*, Weymouth Harbour, England.
D Company 5th Rangers – Onboard HMS *Baudouin*, Weymouth Harbour, England.
E Company 5th Rangers – Onboard HMS *Leopold*, Weymouth, England.
F Company 5th Rangers – Onboard HMS *Baudouin*, Weymouth Harbour, England.
Medical Detachment 5th Rangers – Onboard HMS *Leopold*, Weymouth, England.
Headquarters Company 5th Rangers – Onboard HMS *Leopold*, Weymouth, England.

Below: The SS *Ben-my-Chree* ready for D-Day with its camouflaged finish.

2nd Btn – F Company boarded the SS *Ben-my-Chree*.
2nd Battalion After Action Report. (written one month after D-Day).

```
         On 2-3 June, the Battalion vehicles, including the four
    "ladder-DUKW's", loaded from the Hard at Portland.

         The period 2-5 June was spent in final briefing and the
    perfecting of small unit plans. At 040400, a portion of the
    LST convoy sailed but was later recalled due to heavy seas
    which necessitated a 24-hour postponement.

         The LST convoy moved out again on the afternoon of June
    5, and at 051630, the troopships weighed anchor. The voyage
    was uneventful except for an "Air Alert" at 060200, with the
    "all Clear" sounding soon afterward. The transport area was
    reached at 0300.

         The following narratives of the D-Day actions of the
    three Forces were compiled from memory-histories written by
    eye-witnesses one month following the action. The actions of
    Force A on Pointe du Hoe and Forces B and C on Omaha Beach,
    being composed of a multitude of individual and small unit
    actions, cannot be completely portrayed in these narratives
    which are necessarily based on eye-witness accounts of but a
    portion of the men taking part in the action. To cover this
    need and to provide a thorough, factual history of the D-Day
    actions on Pointe du Hoe and Omaha Dog Green Beach, Lt Col
    Taylor of the War Department Historical Section conducted a
    series of personal interviews with the D-Day veterans during
    October, 1944; the sum of which is at present in the process
    of publication. The following narrative-histories have been
    checked with the draft copy of this report and were found to
    be correct.

         Each Force History is divided into three phases; these
    are as follows:

    The Plan of Attack    The Beach Assault    The Subsequent Act-
    ion.
```

2nd Rangers Companies A – F, Medical and HQ – Aboard ship.
1st Lt. Rafferty was appointed Captain as of 1 June 1944.

Maurice Prince: *Once more we were to find ourselves aboard the same mother ship which had been our home in our previous manoeuvres. We were so familiar with this craft that it felt like old home week. We already had our private nooks and crannies selected so that no time was lost, or confusion resulted, when we unpacked and settled down.*

For five days our boat lay anchored off the coast of Weymouth. It was during these days that we got the splendid opportunities to go on deck, inhale the exhilarating sea air, and imbibe freely the salty sea-water.

It was great sport to encircle the deck and to view the coastline with its sheer cliffs and level beaches; to see the city of Weymouth with its modern buildings; to note the ever present barrage balloons so playfully being tossed about by the winds and to watch the various amphibious birds that were continually flying about and ever so often diving in graceful swoops to catch fish in the sea. The weather the first couple of days we were at sea was cool and moderate. At times heavy rain clouds would come out and darken the skies, but rain never fell. The channel water was rough. We could feel our ship rocking each time the waves rushed against our ship. We knew then that the channel would be a strong barrier we would have to overcome before we could successfully launch our success.

There was nothing unusual or extraordinary about our activities while on ship. We went about our duties in the same routine manner as though we were still dry running. No signs of nervousness or undo fidgeting could be observed as we went about our businesses. We all knew what was expected of us and we didn't want to disappoint anyone.

Although we were playing a game against death and destruction, we had a strong faith that the final score would end in our favour.

Our quarters were fairly crowded, as we were crammed into the first tow-hold below deck. Our sleeping arrangements consisted of hammocks that were hung from the ceiling and held in place by large hooks, that were screwed into the posts that ran from the floor to the ceiling. This was a new way and an experience of doing bunk fatigue. I'll never forget my first attempt to enter one of these contraptions and tried to get some shuteye. Since these hammocks were close to five feet off the deck floor it entailed a certain amount of athletic agility to enter one of these things. If you were too active, you'd find yourself out of these hammocks, but on the other side, if you weren't much of an athlete like myself, you'd find yourself with one leg in and one leg out, swinging to and fro, like some comedian doing acrobatics, at first I thought I'd never make it, but with a tenacity born from a desperation to get some sleep, I finally made it. Now that I had gotten in, all I had to do was curl my body into a question mark and try to get some forty winks, well to make a long story short, I conquered this fangled Navy booby trap and went off to dreamland on the double time.

So far, we hadn't the slightest idea of when the actual day of invasion would be. We all had our surmises, but nothing official. We continued to rehearse our battle plans, discussing and debating all the possibilities that might arise in such a great undertaking. The minutest of details were taken into consideration and alternate plans made for every contingency. Everything concerning our doings and activities were learned by heart, every spot of land was imprinted in our minds and even today we can easily recall the familiar names of Pointe Du Hoe, Grandcamp-le-Bains, Vierville-sur-Mer, Omaha dog green beach, etc. Everything which was humanly possible to insure the success of the huge mission – was undertaken; nothing, not even the most incredible incident was left to chance. The big brass and big dealers had spent many hours arranging and planning. They had outdone themselves in their preparations. Our fates laid in their hands, now, and in those of our Maker above us.

Our ammunition, weapons and equipment were continually being checked to make certain that they were in the best of working order. Our life belts were tested to make sure that they wouldn't fail us if the emergency arose to use them. Administrative and other details were looked into so that nothing escaped our vigilance. We had a job to do and we did want to show the world the way a Ranger could do his task. And we did.

While on board ship, we had one change made in our company. This change was decided on for the better as our company Lt., Lt. Rafferty got himself promoted to Captain. He had finally made his rating, which he had so righteously worked for and earned for himself. Congratulations were extended and hands were shaken.

There were other promotions made by other officers in the Battalion, so that to celebrate this occasion, a party was thrown for them. There were lots of drinks present. It was only natural that some of this liquor be handed down to the enlisted men so that they too could share in the merriment. That evening everyone went to bed happy with all worries drowned and forgotten. So we went back to our hammocks and got ourselves that extra-day's rest.

Jack Burke, 5th Rangers: *Onboard HMS Leopold we went over our D-Day objectives after we were briefed, we cleaned our weapons, did physical exercises, played cards and read books. We all did a lot of yacking about what to expect on the invasion. I was briefed along with all of A Company on Pointe du Hoc as our secondary mission by Lt. Parker.*

The G-3 Journal for the HQ 1st Inf. Division reported at 1400hrs that the Divisional Command Post was preparing for movement overseas.

HEADQUARTERS 1ST INFANTRY DIVISION
APO #1, U. S. Army

G-3 (JOURNAL*
(CHART*

Time : (From 0001
      (To   2400

Date 2 June 1944   CP Location LANGTON HOUSE, BLANDFORD
                                                   ENGLAND

TIME	NO.	FROM	SYNOPSIS	REC'D VIA	DISPOSITION#
0001	1		Journal opened		
1400	2		Div CP started preparations for movement overseas.		
2400	3		Journal closed		

NOTES:
*Delete one.
"Rec'd Via" column will indicate how message was transmitted; i.e., Tp – telephone; Rad – radio; Tgp – telegraph; Tpe – teletype.
#Following abbreviations only will be used in this column, other information will be written out: M – Noted on situation map; J – Appended to journal (applies to Overlays, Msg blanks, written orders, etc.); CG, G/S, etc. – indicates information passed on to Officer indicated; T – indicates information disseminated to units or troops, as indicated in text of message.
(Revised 3 Jan.'44)
- 1 -

ii) Omaha Beach

---

3 June 1944   On 3 June Major General Huebner held a top-level meeting with his Intelligence personnel – as well as unit and battalion commanders – at his main headquarters, which by 1155am moved from Langton House in Blandford Forum to aboard USS *Ancon* in Portland Harbour. As is highlighted, Lt. Colonel Rudder attended that meeting. Also highlighted is the order for the Combat Teams to try and get to Isigny on D-Day – and also to *'push inland rapidly. Work at night under cover of darkness as much as possible.'* And the interesting order, that patrols should consist of *'rinf companies'*.

[Author: I am unsure if the 'r' stands for 'rifle' – or 'Ranger' companies – but the order is clear. Small patrols were not to be the order of the day. The men were to advance and patrol by using whole companies and on foot – without waiting for the beach exits to clear for vehicles. In the case of the Ranger units, whose job it was to clear the flank, this order would involve around 65 men per company – creating a very powerful and much larger group than a conventional combat 'patrol'.] Overwhelming force and rapid advancement were to be the methods used.

Langton House was situated in the small town of Blandford Forum and was occupied by the Divisional HQ of the 1st US Infantry Division.

The G-3 Journal for the HQ 1st Inf. Division confirms the movement of the Advanced Forward Command Post to USS *Samuel Chase*.

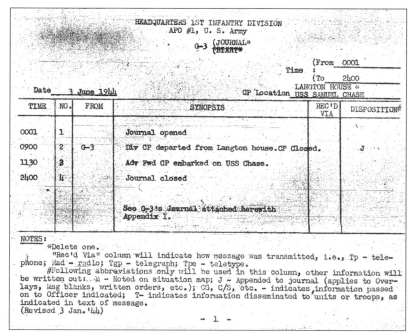

Below: The weather forecast for 3-7 June was issued as well as a 'prearranged bombardment plan' confirmed.

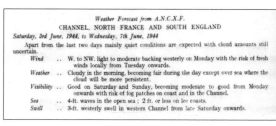

Weather Forecast from A.N.C.X.F.

CHANNEL, NORTH FRANCE AND SOUTH ENGLAND

Saturday, 3rd June, 1944, to Wednesday, 7th June, 1944

Apart from the last two days mainly quiet conditions are expected with cloud amounts still uncertain.

Wind	..	W. to NW. light to moderate backing westerly on Monday with the risk of fresh winds locally more persistent.
Weather	..	Cloudy in the morning, becoming fair during the day except over sea where the cloud will be more persistent.
Visibility	..	Good on Saturday and Sunday, becoming moderate to good from Monday onwards with risk of fog patches on coast and in the Channel.
Sea	..	4-ft. waves in the open sea ; 2 ft. or less on lee coasts.
Swell	..	3-ft. westerly swell in western Channel from late Saturday onwards.

Twenty-five percent of the day heavy bombers and a proportion of the medium and light bombers are available. Final selection of " Neptune " area targets as follows will be made on D-3 day : Five battery positions, two head-quarters, four fighter-control telephone exchanges and two telephone exchanges.

(a) Battery positions to be considered for bombing by day heavy bombers are listed in the following order of priority :

6 (St. Martin-de-Varreville – 405980)	3 (Fontenay-sur-Mer – 368042)	
9 (Azeville – 360022)	1 (Pointe-du-Hoe – 586938)	
9A (Chateau-du-Courcy – 361054)	1A (La Pernelle – 365199)	

PREARRANGED AIR AND NAVAL BOMBARDMENT PLAN

1. AIR BOMBARDMENT PLAN

The air support for Operations Plan " Neptune ", is based upon the attack of battery positions, beach defense localities, bridges, road embankments, cable junctions – command posts and communication centers. First Army target numbers of battery positions, defense localities and terrain features are listed in Appendix 1. Nine phases of the prearranged air support plan are outlined below :
a. Pre-Y day Bombardment. (Prior to D-3/D-2 night).

(1) Air effort has been allocated for five battery positions in the First Army sector. Two battery positions outside the " Neptune " area are bombed for each battery position bombed within the area to maintain security. First Army battery positions included in this phase are indicated below :

Day Medium Bombers	Night Heavy Bombers
1 (Pointe-du-Hoe – 586938)	8A (Barfleur – 396229)
3 (Fontenay-sur-Mer – 368042)	4 (Mor-alines – 355138)
1A (La Pernelle – 365199)	

HEADQUARTERS 1ST INFANTRY DIVISION
APO #1, U. S. Army

G-3 (JOURNAL*
(XXXXXX

Time : (From 0001B
(To 2400B

Date 3 June 1944

CP Location Langton House, Blandford Dorset, England and USS ANCON, Portland Harbor

TIME	NO.	FROM	SYNOPSIS	REC'D VIA	DISPOSITION
0001	1		Journal opened.		
0920	2		Div CP departed Langton House for Portland		
1110	3		Div CP arrived Portland and split for loading on APA #1 & LSH.		
1155	4		Following Officers, Div Hq boarded USS ANCON in Portland Harbor: Maj Gen HUEBNER, CG; Cols Mason, C/S; VanValin, Div Surg; Lt Cols Gibb, G-3; Eymer, G-4; Ware, G-1; Evans, G-2; Pickett, Div Sig; Wright, Div QM; and enlisted personnel.		
1800	5		Command conference held in senior ward-room attended by Maj Gens HEROW, GC V Corps; HUEBNER, CG 1st Div; Brig Gens WYMAN, ACG Div; ANDRUS, CG DA; COTA, ACG 29 Div; HELMICK, CG V Corps Arty; C/S & DC/S V Corps, CO CT 16, CO CT 18, CO CT 116, CO CT 115, CO Rngr Gp, CO 3d Armd Gp, CO 16 AAA Gp, Div Sig O, Div C/S, G-3, G-4, and Bn Cmdrs CTs. Gen Huenber commended officers on loading and waterproofing of vehs, stated good weather for next 3 days, warned of German rocket launchers and difficulty of determining loc by angle or timing. Asst G-2 gave intelligence changes, which were few. Gen Huebner emphasised need of taking high grd quickly and ogn for ctr-atk as soon as possible. Directed 115 CT to try to get ISIGNY on D-day if conditions were favorable as it can be more easily held than taken from a holding force. Be agressive but not foolhardy. Patrol consist of		

NOTES:
*Delete one.
"Rec'd Via" column will indicate how message was transmitted, i.e., Tp - telephone; Rad - radio; Tgp - telegraph; Tpe - teletype.
#Following abbreviations only will be used in this column, other information will be written out: M - Noted on situation map; J - Appended to journal (applies to Overlays, Msg blanks, written orders, etc.); CG, C/S, etc. - indicates information passed on to Officer indicated; T- indicates information disseminated to units or troops, as indicated in text of message.
(Revised 3 Jan. '44)

- 1 -

G-3 Journal* XXXXXX for 3 June 1944 Cont'd.

TIME	NO.	FROM	SYNOPSIS	REC'D VIA	DISPOSITION#
	5	Cont'd	rinf companies. May be necessary to take tks of 3d Bn 16 Inf to cover assbly of CT 26. Hope to send CT 115 to vic 5482 if conditions are favorable D-day. Regardless of opening of veh beach exits the foot-trs must push inland rapidly. Work at night under cover of darkness as much as possible as the enemy is least effective at that time. Be on lookout for infiltration to our rear lines.		
2400	6		Journal closed.		

USS *Ancon* war diary entry for the 3 June recorded the arrival of Major General Huebner and his staff onboard.

```
3 June 1944 - Major General HUEBNER, U.S.A., Commanding General
              FIRST Infantry Division and Staff came aboard for
              the impending operation.
```

US Navy situation report 3 June: *Weather: Cloudy, with cloud base lowering. Wind W. Force 3-4 backing to S.W. increasing to force 5, Sea slight, increasing to moderate.*

Commanders meeting was held at 0430 and again at 2130 to consider the weather forecast. Less favourable weather conditions were again forecast for 5th June with a westerly wind expected to reach force 5 on the evening of 4th June. The forecast also indicated the likelihood of low cloud unfavourable to parachute troops, spotting aircraft and the passage of the airborne divisions.

It was predicted that there was no prospect of the moonlight and cloud base at 2,000 ft., which were requirements for the glider operations. This involved serious implications for the assault forces on the flanks at U and S beaches, whose operations were considered to be largely dependent for their success on the support of the airborne divisions.

The problems arising during the meeting at 2130 were still of more particular concern to the Army and Air Force than to the Navy. A.N.C.X.F. held the view that the conditions predicted for the 5th June would not prevent the Navy undertaking its task if reasonable protection from the air was available.

The Supreme Commander decided to await a possible change in forecast in the next six hours.

5th Battalion Incidents, Messages and Orders Reported D-Day as 5 June:

```
3 June - VOCG First Inf Div; D-Day announced, 5 June
         1944, H-Hour 0610.
```

A Company 5th Rangers – Onboard HMS *Leopold*, Weymouth, England.
B Company 5th Rangers – Onboard HMS *Leopold*, Weymouth, England.
C Company 5th Rangers – Onboard HMS *Prince Baudouin*, Weymouth Harbour, England.
D Company 5th Rangers – Onboard HMS *Prince Baudouin*, Weymouth Harbour, England.
E Company 5th Rangers – Onboard HMS *Leopold*, Weymouth Harbour, England.
F Company 5th Rangers – Onboard HMS *Prince Baudouin*, Weymouth Harbour, England.
Medical Detachment 5th Rangers – Onboard HMS *Leopold*, Weymouth, England.
Headquarters Company 5th Rangers – Onboard HMS *Leopold*, Weymouth, England.

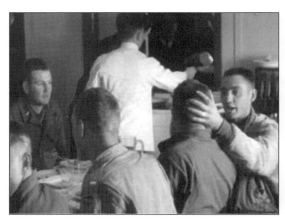

Ranger officers enjoying a meal served onboard ship, courtesy of the Royal Navy.

2nd Rangers Companies A – F, Medical – Aboard ship.
Headquarters Company 2nd Rangers – Aboard Ship.
Captain Cleveland Lytle was appointed to the rank of Major.

1st Lt. Frank Kennard: *On leaving the Hard Standing we motored (in an endless column) to the port and parked in long columns at a very large flat area where there were hundreds of vehicles immediately adjacent to a quay on which there were permanent loading ramp(s). Over a long time each vehicle was directed to the quay where it turned around and backed down the permanent ramp and onto its LC. The weather was Okay (no rain) and at no time was the procedure interrupted by enemy action (there was zero).*

I had 2 half-tracks with 75mm guns (referred to as a cannon platoon) and our invasion vessel was small LC which also carried a couple of half-tracks with quad 50 calibre machine guns and one or two jeeps from the 741st AA/AW Bn. Lt Conway Epperson with another 2-gun platoon was aboard a different landing craft. Our vehicles were parked on the roadside in 'loading order' in 'notches' that had been carved on the shoulder of the road. They were all numbered with numerals corresponding to the number of the landing craft.

At the appropriate time on June 3rd all of the units pulled out onto the road, thus forming an endless column. Traveling to the Port and, all along the way we had civilians cheering us on! We proceeded to a large flat area – a hard standing at Portland and in a highly controlled order went down a ramp onto our LC. We then sailed into the outer harbor and waited to form up with other LC's, in our landing wave (8 or 10 LC's).

Weather conditions were not bad and we pulled out into the 'outer' harbor. The landing date was pushed forward from June 5 to 6 so we slept on board (I slept on a bunch of 10-in-1 ration boxes).

4 June 1944   US Navy Weather Report 4 June: *Weather: Overcast, low cloud, wind S.W. force 6, sea moderate, rainfall at night. Forecast wind veering, cloud conditions expected to deteriorate with little improvement before 7th June. At 1100 Admiralty promulgated a warning that a S.W. gale, force 8 was imminent in IRISH SEA.*

Weather Forecast from A.N.C.X.F.
CHANNEL AREA, NORTH FRANCE, AND SOUTH ENGLAND

Sunday, 4th June to Thursday, 8th June, 1944

Cloud conditions are now expected to deteriorate as from Sunday with little prospect of improvement before late Wednesday.

Wind	W.S.W. force 5 in Northern Channel areas, Force 3 to 4 on lee coasts of France veering W.N.W. late Wednesday or early Thursday and then decreasing by one force on English coasts.
Weather	Overcast in the early morning with cloud base at 500 ft. to 1,000 ft. becoming fair inland during the day but only partial clearances at sea. Cloud decreasing generally with veer of wind on Wednesday or Thursday. Some slight drizzle locally on Sunday and a period of light rain with the veer of wind.
Visibility	Moderate with risk of fog in all sea areas on Sunday, risk decreasing thereafter. Good visibility after veer of wind.
Sea	5 ft. waves in the open sea, 2 to 3 ft. waves on the lee coast of France.
Swell	3 ft. westerly swell in the Western Channel.

The Supreme Commander and the Commanders-in-Chief were informed of this forecast, and the unsettled nature of the weather was stressed. It was, however, decided to continue with the operation as planned.

COMMANDERS MEETING REPORT – POSTPONEMENT OF D-DAY
The Supreme Commander held a meeting of Commanders-in-Chief at 0415 when the weather forecast submitted by Meteorological Officers was pessimistic. It was decided that launching of the operation must be postponed by one day.

Commanders-in-Chief of Home Commanders and Admiralty were advised by telephone between 0440 and 0450. A general signal ordering the postponement was promulgated from A.N.C.X.F. Headquarters at 0515, and the signal included the alterations necessary in timing of H-Hour on the new D-Day.

At 2115 the Supreme Commander held a meeting of Commanders-in-Chief. The existing weather conditions were still bad, with weather charts typical of December rather than June. The Meteorological Officers, however, considered there seemed a good chance of suitable conditions existing on the morning of the 6th. They also considered that no reliable opinion could be formed of the weather to be expected on the 8th June, which was the next acceptable date after the 6th June.

It was decided therefore to order the operation to proceed and confirmation of D-Day as 6th June was signaled.

1930   4th June
. The following forecast was issued :—

Weather Forecast from A.N.C.X.F.

CHANNEL AREA, NORTH FRANCE AND SOUTH ENGLAND

Weather conditions are now very unsettled and quiet periods are likely to be of short duration.

Monday and Tuesday, 5th and 6th June

Wind	W.N.W. force 5 slowly backing and decreasing force 3 to 4 on Monday. Continuing to back S.W. on Tuesday and freshening later in the day.
Weather	Fair, with a few scattered showers at first, becoming overcast on Tuesday.
Visibility	Mainly good.
Sea and Swell	Waves six feet in open sea decreasing slowly.
Outlook	Unsettled, westerly weather continuing.

The Supreme Commander and his Commanders-in-Chief were now informed that there was a chance of suitable conditions on 6th June, but that the weather remained extremely unsettled, and that it was quite impossible at present to forecast the weather to be expected on Thursday, 8th June.

USS *Ancon* war diary:

```
4 June 1944 - Upon receipt of orders from Naval Commander Western
              Task Force, Commander Task Force ONE TWO FOUR issued
              orders to all ships of his force that the operation
              was postponed twenty-four hours.
```

5th Battalion Incidents, Messages and Orders Report:

```
4 June - CO talked to Bn re-D-Day, what to expect
         etc. VOCG, D-Day postponed to 6 June 1944
         H-Hour 0630.
```

A Company 5th Rangers – Onboard HMS *Leopold*, Weymouth, England.

B Company 5th Rangers – Onboard HMS *Leopold*, Weymouth, England.

C Company 5th Rangers – Onboard HMS *Prince Baudouin*, Weymouth Harbour, England.

D Company 5th Rangers – Onboard HMS *Prince Baudouin*, Weymouth Harbour, England.

E Company 5th Rangers –Onboard HMS *Leopold*, Weymouth Harbour, England.

F Company 5th Rangers – Onboard HMS *Prince Baudouin*, Weymouth Harbour, England.

Medical Detachment 5th Rangers – Onboard HMS *Leopold*, Weymouth, England.

Headquarters Company 5th Rangers – Onboard HMS *Leopold*, Weymouth, England.

2nd Rangers Companies A – F, Medical – Aboard ship.

Headquarters Company 2nd Rangers – Aboard Ship.
Major Cleveland Lytle went from Duty to Hospital.

Maurice Prince: *We finally received the word that 0700 a.m., Monday June 5th would be H-Hour. So on the evening prior it found us in full and completed preparedness. The weather was cool and cloudy while the channel water was rough and turbulent. A last minute's cancellation gave us a new lease on life for twenty-four hours longer, not that we wanted or needed it. In fact, this was a bad break as we felt like condemned men, who had received a reprieve for a day. We had been anxious to get it over with and now we were to be delayed. Oh well, maybe it was all for the better, as after all even though we knew we could beat the Heinies, the channel was too much even for us Rangers to buck. So we went back to our hammocks and got ourselves that extra-day's rest.*

Frank Kennard: *D-Day was delayed but we did not debark. We cruised around in circles. It was rainy and there was no shelter. Some time on June 5 the landing was set for June 6 and all landing craft (except troop transports but not LST's) formed up into 3 enormously long columns maintaining a 'headway' of 300 yards between each craft. Overhead there was an endless number of fighter planes all with special markings on the wings and fuselage (three white stripes) which we had never seen before. I thought it was an entirely new airforce (not the 8th or RAF).*

General Eisenhower's diary entry for 4 June: *We met with the Meteorologic Committee twice daily, once at 9.30pm in the evening and once at 4am in the morning. The committee, comprising both British and American personnel was headed by a dour but canny Scot, Group Captain J. M. Stagg. At these meetings every bit of evidence was carefully presented, carefully analysed by the experts, and carefully studied by the assembled commanders.*

The final conference for determining the feasibility of attacking on the tentatively selected day, June 5, was scheduled for 4am on June 4th.

Weighing all factors, I decided that the attack would have to be postponed. This decision necessitated the immediate dispatch of orders to the vessels and troops already at sea and created some doubt as to whether they could be ready twenty-four hours later in case the next day should prove favourable for the assault.

Aerial reconnaissance photograph showing Pointe du Hoc heavily bombed. Note the clear outline of the fake gun battery in the fields some way over to the left of the Pointe.

At 3.30am the next morning our little camp was shaking and shuddering under a wind of almost hurricane proportions and the accompanying rain seemed to be travelling in horizontal streaks. The mile-long trip through muddy roads to the naval headquarters *was anything but a cheerful one, since it seems impossible that in such conditions there was any reason for even discussing the situation.*

Their next astonishing declaration was that by the following morning a period of relatively good weather, heretofore completely unexpected, would ensue, lasting probably thirty-six hours. The long-term prediction was not good, but they did give us assurance that this short period of good weather would intervene between the exhaustion of the storm we were then experiencing and the beginning of the next spell of really bad weather.

(Eisenhower Presidential Library and Museum – Kansas).

A close up of the fake gun battery to the west of Pointe du Hoc.

5 June 1944

June 5 weather report.

0730   5th June

The following forecast was issued :—

Weather Forecast from A.N.C.X.F.

Developments over night show slight improvement in the general situation which at the moment appears more favourable.

Monday and Tuesday, 5th and 6th June

Wind	West to north-west moderate, decreasing slightly, and backing south-west light to moderate during Tuesday.
Weather	Fair to cloudy with local showers and bright periods today, becoming fair or fine overnight with low cloud increasing from the west late Tuesday, and becoming overcast with base of cloud about 1,000 ft.
Visibility	Mainly good.
Sea	5-ft. waves decreasing slowly to 3 to 4 ft. in open sea ; less than 2 ft. on lee-shores on French coast.
Swell	Nil.

Wednesday, Thursday and Friday, 7th to 9th June

Wind	Mainly westerly moderate, with risk of local freshening at times.
Weather	Cloudy but with clear intervals.
Visibility	Good.
Sea	3 to 4 ft. in open sea ; less than 2 ft. on lee-shores.
Swell	Nil.

5th Battalion Incidents, Messages and Orders Report:

```
5 June - 1000 VOCO;  get packs and all equipment set.
         1300 VOCO; prime all charges. Load all crew
         served wpns and individual equipment on
         LCA's.
         1630 ships hoisted anchor. Joined Convoy
         in Channel.
```

A Company 5th Rangers – Onboard HMS *Leopold*, Weymouth Harbour, England.

B Company 5th Rangers – HMS *Leopold*, Weymouth Harbour, England.

C Company 5th Rangers – HMS *Prince Baudouin* – English Channel.

D Company 5th Rangers – Onboard HMS *Prince Baudouin* – English Channel.

E Company 5th Rangers – Onboard HMS *Leopold*, Weymouth Harbour, England.

F Company 5th Rangers – Onboard HMS *Prince Baudouin* – English Channel.

Medical Detachment 5th Rangers – Onboard HMS *Leopold* – English Channel.

Headquarters Company 5th Rangers – Onboard HMS *Leopold* – English Channel.

2nd Rangers Companies A – F, Medical and HQ – Aboard ship.

COMPANY
MORNING REPORT   ENDING 2400 5 June   1944
                        (MONTH)   (YEAR)
STATION HMS Leopold, Weymouth, Harbor, Eng.
ORGANIZATION Co B 5th Ranger Inf Bn   Inf.
            (CO. DET. ETC.)   (PARENT UNIT)   (ARM OR SERVICE)
SERIAL NUMBER   NAME   GRADE   CODE
            NO CHANGE

RECORD OF EVENTS
5 June 44 Left Weymouth Harbor, Eng. at
1600 enroute to transport area.

COMPANY
MORNING REPORT   ENDING 2400 5 June   4
                        (MONTH)   APO 230 (YEAR)
STATION HMS Boduin, Somewhere in Eng. Channel
ORGANIZATION 5th Ranger Inf Bn   Inf
            (CO. DET. ETC.)   (PARENT UNIT)   (ARM OR SERVICE)
SERIAL NUMBER   NAME   GRADE   CODE
            NO CHANGE

RECORD OF EVENTS
5 June 44 Left Weymouth Harbor, Eng.
at 1600 enroute to transport area.

COMPANY
MORNING REPORT   ENDING 2400 5 June   4
                        (DAY)   (MONTH)   194 (YEAR)
STATION HMS Boduin, Somewhere in Eng.Channel
ORGANIZATION Co D, 5th Ranger Inf Bn   Inf 1
            (CO. DET. ETC.)   (PARENT UNIT)   (ARM OR SERVICE)
SERIAL NUMBER   NAME   GRADE   CODE

RECORD OF EVENTS
5 Jun 44 Left Weymouth Harbor, England at 1600 enroute to transport area.

COMPANY
MORNING REPORT   ENDING 2400 5 June   194 4
                        (YEAR)
STATION HMS Leopold Weymouth Harbor Eng
ORGANIZATION Co E 5th Ranger Inf Bn Inf
            (ARM OR SERVICE)
SERIAL NUMBER   NAME   GRADE   CODE
            NO CHANGE

RECORD OF EVENTS
5 June 1944 Left Weymouth England
1600 enroute to transport area

COMPANY
MORNING REPORT   ENDING 2400 5 June   4
                        (DAY)   (MONTH)   194 (YEAR)
STATION HMS Boduin, Somewhere in Eng. Channel
ORGANIZATION Co. F 5th Ranger Inf. Bn.   Inf.
            (CO. DET. ETC.)   (PARENT UNIT)   (ARM OR SERVICE)
SERIAL NUMBER   NAME   GRADE   CODE

RECORD OF EVENTS
5 Jun 44   Left Weymouth Harbor, England at
1600 enroute to transport area

HEADQUARTERS
MORNING REPORT   ENDING 2400 5 June   194 4
                        (DAY)   (MONTH)   (YEAR)
STATION HMS Leopold, Weymouth Harbor, Eng.
ORGANIZATION Hq 5th Ranger Inf Bn   Inf.
            (HEADQUARTERS)   (PARENT UNIT)   (ARM OR SERVICE)
SERIAL NUMBER   NAME   GRADE   CODE
            NO CHANGE

RECORD OF EVENTS
5 June 44 Left Weymouth Harbor, Eng. at
1600 enroute to transport area.

COMPANY
MORNING REPORT   ENDING 2400 5 June   4
                        (DAY)   (MONTH)   194 (YEAR)
STATION HMS Leopold, Weymouth Harbor, Eng
ORGANIZATION Med Det 5th Ranger Inf Bn   Med
            (CO. DET. ETC.)   (PARENT UNIT)   (ARM OR SERVICE)
SERIAL NUMBER   NAME   GRADE   CODE
            NO CHANGE

RECORD OF EVENTS
5 June 1944 Left Weymouth Harbor, Eng
at 1600 enroute to transport area.

HMS *Prince Charles* which carried eight LCAs – four
on each side.

1st Infantry Division unit history:

        Force "O" sailed from PORTLAND HARBOR, WEYMOUTH, DORSET, approx-
imately 0530 hours 5 June 1944; USS ANCON (headquarters ship Force "O")
passed the harbor breakwater at 1630 hours; the USS CHASE (first alternate
headquarters Force "O") sailed at 1725 hours and the entire convoy began
to sail east along the south English coast.

> Messages from the Commander, Supreme Headquarters Allied Expeditionary Forces, Commanding General, 21st Army Group, and Commanding General, 1st US Army were read on 5 June 1944 to the Army officers and men "On the eve of their departure for the invasion".

SUPREME HEADQUARTERS ALLIED EXPEDITIONARY FORCE

Soldiers, Sailors and Airmen of the Allied Expeditionary Force!

You are about to embark upon the Great Crusade, toward which we have striven these many months. The eyes of the world are upon you. The hopes and prayers of liberty-loving people everywhere march with you. In company with our brave Allies and brothers-in-arms on other Fronts, you will bring about the destruction of the German war machine, the elimination of Nazi tyranny over the oppressed peoples of Europe, and security for ourselves in a free world.

Your task will not be an easy one. Your enemy is well trained, well equipped and battle-hardened. He will fight savagely.

But this is the year 1944! Much has happened since the Nazi triumphs of 1940-41. The United Nations have inflicted upon the Germans great defeats, in open battle, man-to-man. Our air offensive has seriously reduced their strength in the air and their capacity to wage war on the ground. Our Home Fronts have given us an overwhelming superiority in weapons and munitions of war, and placed at our disposal great reserves of trained fighting men. The tide has turned! The free men of the world are marching together to Victory!

I have full confidence in your courage, devotion to duty and skill in battle. We will accept nothing less than full Victory!

Good Luck! And let us all beseech the blessing of Almighty God upon this great and noble undertaking.

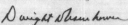

Maurice Prince: The day of June 5th found no difference in the atmosphere in the boat. It was spent in the same uneventful manner as any other day previously spent aboard. The same men who generally did the debating and arguing on the merits and demerits of certain parts of the invasion were heatedly going strong in their discussions, while the men who always were lazy, lounged and slept in their rat-holes (as we nicknamed our hammocks). Then the same bunch of card players were having their usual games and from the interested and concentrated looks upon their features, one would never know that these men, too, were to be a part in the coming assault of tomorrow. Invasion or no invasion, that card game had to go on. What a group of men, everyone as unperturbed by the coming historical event as a thick-skinned rhinoceros with a fly on its back.

Then there was a section of men who were more conscious of the facilitation of carrying and hauling of equipment during the attack. Original and novel methods were demonstrated such as extra pockets sewed on the pants leg, which made a good carrying place for grenades, another was the taking off the meat can carrier and placing it behind the cartridge belt for a similar purpose. Other minor details were brought to our attention, which would make the individual soldier's burden much lighter and much easier to carry and handle. Nothing great or inventive, but surprisingly helpful to the GI in the coming assault.

That evening our ship hauled anchor and sailed out, keeping its rightful place in the vast fleet. Our new D-Day was June 6th which 0700 was H-Hour. The waters that separated us from the enemy was finally being gapped. In our minds we reviewed our parts and chat of our mission, which would it be? Would it be to follow D-E-F Co.'s up the cliff or land at Omaha dog green. Whatever it would be, history was now in the offing.

The evening of June 5 found no changes in the morale or spirit of us Rangers. Appetites hadn't lost one iota of their fullness. There was the same quibbling and quarrelling over the chow as there always had been. We Rangers were just as hungry on this evening as on any other evening. Sometimes I wonder if these brave men fully recognized and realized the dangers in the parts and roles they were to be playing.

I honestly and truthfully believe they knew, but were too manly to let it get the better of them and to show it. I also believe that in every task they had previously handled, they had made such a good showing of the job, that they had acquired a confidence in themselves and in each other, so as not to let a thing like the invasion get them downhearted. It is small wonder that a Ranger will cockily walk along the streets of life with two Ranger patches boldly emblazoned, one on each shoulder and in fancy embroidery and challenge any one or all that dares cross his path.

Our ship was making slow progress as it steadily cleaved its way thru the choppy waters of the channel. The ship was lurching vehemently as the rough waves swooshed against it. We held our course though and kept our place in the armada.

We had retired early that night as we were to load into our LCAs at 3 a.m. This was because they wanted us off our mother ship as she presented too large and compact a target to the enemy. Where as in our small LCAs we were a smaller target and better deployed.

I suppose all our thoughts that night were of the invasion. We couldn't hold off any pretences to ourselves any longer. So far our only hint of such an operation had been our realistic, but simulated exercises off the English coast. Naturally, these problems were hard physically, but we had no casualties and were always able to keep together and retain our control. What would happen if casualties would arise and control became lax? This and a million other problems haunted our dreams that last night aboard ship.

6 June 1944

Omaha Beach

Navy weather report:

> **1930 6th June**
>
> The following forecast was issued :—
>
> ### CHANNEL AREA, NORTH FRANCE AND SOUTH ENGLAND.
>
> Quieter conditions are now setting in but weather is expected to be rather cloudy.
>
> **Tuesday and Wednesday, 6th and 7th June**
>
> | | |
> |---|---|
> | *Wind* | West-north-west force 4 at first backing west force 3 to 4. |
> | *Weather* | Cloudy with occasional fair periods on Tuesday. |
> | *Visibility* | Mainly good with risk of coastal and sea-fog patches on Wednesday. |
> | *Sea* | 3 ft. in open sea decreasing to less than 2 ft. on lee coast. |
>
> **Further Outlook for Thursday to Saturday**
>
> Quiet conditions with westerly winds, mainly force 4. Mainly cloudy but with clear intervals, and some risk of fog patches until early Friday. Visibility otherwise good.

From HMS *Prince Charles* AAR. 0353 Lt. Col. Rudder had gone over to the *Ben-my-Chree* to prepare for landing.

> **0353**   No. 2 craft lowered to embarkation level. Craft took Colonel RUDDER to BEN MY CHREE.

The Commanding officer USS *Slatterlee* produced this report:

> <u>Weather. The Approach to the Assault Area.</u>
>
> The weather was terrible. Station keeping during the approach with the mine-sweepers was difficult. During the 360° turn, ships and small craft in channels 3 and 4 became mixed and confused. During this time and again later near the transport area, the position of the ships supporting the mine-sweepers was such that they could have offered very little protection against enemy surface craft. It was fortunate that no opposition or mines were encountered.
>
> After H-hour, we watched the Ranger units approaching the beach and saw that the bad weather made it very difficult and caused heavy loss. The weather delayed the landing past the scheduled time and caused the element of surprise to be lost and caused a great reduction in the effectiveness of the preparation firing. When it became obvious (about 0200) that weather would delay the landings, H-hour should have been delayed. Ammunition available would not permit continuing preparation firing from the scheduled commencement until the delayed time of arrival of the first waves on the beach.

Frank Kennard Cannon Company Commander 2nd Btn: *There was terrific planning and almost perfect execution of marshalling, loading and traveling in an absolutely AWESOME armada to the off-shore rendezvous-area. Massive aerial and naval bombardment of the entire beachhead, along with no opposition, produced a feeling the landing forces could not and would not be stopped.*

Jack Burke A Co. Medic 5th Battalion: *When we started loading into the landing crafts from the HMS Leopold, the spirits of the Rangers were jovial, but we were disciplined in taking our positions as we were trained.*

When we started our ride to the rendezvous positions, the seas got very fraught and sea-sickness took its toll on many guys in our boat. Fortunately I was not one of them. I was in the rear of the craft so I got up on the back next to the coxswain to see what was going on and to my amasement, and I didn't know it at the time, but I was watching a historic moment. It was approaching daylight, the sky was absolutely loaded with planes, and then to my right the battleship USS Texas fired broadside and the flashes from those 15-inch guns were frightening as the battleship heaved over from the blast – and then righted itself. You could see the huge smoke rings go out and also see the shell in flight on its way to the beach. I said to myself that no one could survive this shelling and we were going for 'a cake walk' when we hit the beach...

As we got closer to the beach, I got down in the landing craft and we began to get in range of the German artillery and small arms firing. At times you could hear the pinging of bullets and the loud explosions from the shells.

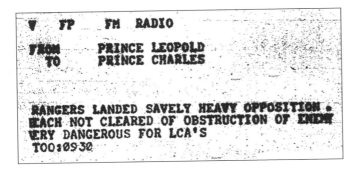

```
▼  FP    FM  RADIO

FROM       PRINCE LEOPOLD
  TO       PRINCE CHARLES


RANGERS LANDED SAVELY HEAVY OPPOSITION .
BEACH NOT CLEARED OF OBSTRUCTION OF ENEMY
VERY DANGEROUS FOR LCA'S
TOO:0930
```

5th Battalion After Action Report:

SUBJECT: Action Against Enemy, Reports After/After Action Reports

TO   : The Adjutant General, Washington, D. C.

1. The following is the story of the Fifth Ranger Infantry Battalion from the landing on the coast of France on D-Day, 6 June 1944, to 10 June 1944 which was the unit's last day of combat during the month of June:

D-Day 6 June 1944

At 0530 hours the Fifth Ranger Battalion loaded into L. C. A.'s from the mother ships, H. M. S. Prince Leopold and Prince Boudouin, and started the ten mile run to the coast of France. The morale of the men was excellent, the weather cloudy, and the sea very choppy.

About five miles from shore, one (1) L. C. A. containing the First Platoon and a part of company headquarters of Company F had shipped so much water that it was forced to drop out of the formation. This platoon did not make the assault landing with the battalion but did land near the St. Laurent-sur-Mer Beach exit at 0900 after transferring to a passing L. C. T.

The beach was protected by a large number of under-water obstacles consisting of elements "C", hedgehogs and tetrahedra, many of which had Teller-Mines attached. Mortar and artillery shells were bursting in the area of these obstacles and a heavy concentration of small-arms fire swept the beach. A four foot sea-wall ran laterally along the beach about 75 yards from the waters edge. Friendly troops were observed utilizing the protective cover afforded by this wall. A pall of smoke obscured the sharply rising ground immediately in the rear of and overlooking the beach. Our naval bombardment evidently had set fire to the vegetation covering the hill.

The L. C. A.'s slowly threaded their way through gaps in the lines of obstacles and at H/75, 0745, the first wave consisting of one half Battalion Headquarters, Companies A, B, and E, landed on Omaha Dog White Beach at a point approximately 800 yards East of Exit D-1-. The Battalion Commander, Lieutenant Colonel Max F. Schneider, had ordered the flotilla commander to touch down his craft east of the intended landing point, Dog Green, because the tremendous volume of fire which covered that portion of the beach was inflicting a large number of casualties on the preceeding wave.

The first wave crossed the beach in good order with few casualties, halted temporarily in rear of the sea wall, and immediately reorganized.

The second wave, consisting of one half Battalion Headquarters, Companies C, D, and one (1) Platoon of Company F, duplicated the feat of the first wave.

At a signal from the Battalion Commander the leading echelon scrambled over the wall, blew gaps in the protective wire, and protected from enemy observation by the curtain of rising smoke advanced unhesitatingly to a point near the top of the hill. Here the smoke had cleared and the topographical crest was being swept by effective automatic weapons fire. First Lieutenant Francis W. Dawson, Company D, led his platoon over the top and wiped out a strongpoint thereby enabling the battalion to advance.

Because of numerous mine fields the battalion now changed into a column formation and, after winding through their intricate pattern, the leading unit, Company B, reached the St. Laurent-sur-Mer—Vierville-sur-Mer road at a point approximately one (1) Kilometre east of Vierville-sur-Mer. During the advance numerous Germans, well concealed in weapons pits constructed in hedgerows, were killed.

-2-   UNCLASSIFIED

Company B advanced toward Vierville-sur-Mer receiving heavy sniper and machine gun fire. Several direct hits from enemy artillery on the rear of the battalion column caused numerous casualties. Company E attempted a penetration to the South but was halted by intense machine gun fire. An 81 mm mortar concentration fired by Company C knocked out several of these positions but they were rapidly replaced and the advance remained halted.

The weight of the attack was shifted toward Vierville-sur-Mer and, after overcoming considerable sniper resistance, the battalion advanced through the village to its western outskirts where it was again held up by a large volume of concerted machine gun and sniper fire. At this point contact was established with the Commanding Officer First Battalion 116th Infantry and approximately 150 men of his unit. Dusk was falling and the battalion was ordered to dig-in a perimeter defense for the night. Companies A, B, and C of the Second Ranger Battalion, numbering approximately 80 men, also assumed a portion of the defense area. Tanks of the 743rd Tank Battalion moved within the defense area where they remained for the night. Except for occasional exchanges with enemy snipers and machine guns the night was one of little activity.

One (1) platoon of Company A which became separated from the battalion after crossing the sea-wall proceeded through Vierville-sur-Mer to the rallying point southwest of the town, arriving there at 1600 hours. In accomplishing this feat they captured 12 Germans and killed at least an equal number. Leaving the rallying point shortly thereafter this unit fought its way through to rointe du Hoe (the Battalion objective) and contacted the Second Ranger Battalion, arriving there at about 2200 hours.

The platoon from F Company which landed near St. Laurent-sur-Mer received a large amount of artillery and machine gun fire on the beach. Patrols were sent out to locate the remainder of the Fifth Battalion but were unable to gain contact. Attempting to move along the beach toward Vierville-sur-Mer this platoon was subjected to artillery fire receiving 8 casualties. After advancing 600 yards to the West the unit was engaged by a superior force and pinned down. When darkness fell the platoon retained this position.

The results for the first day were about 100 prisoners taken, 150 enemy dead, and approximately 60 Rangers killed and wounded.

5th Battalion Incidents, Messages and Orders Report:

6 June - 0530 embarking from HMS ships in transport area.
0545 lowered to channel and shoved off.
0700 we are approximately 5 kilometers from the coast of France. VOC
0750 landing on Omaha Beach, Vierville-sur-Mer approximately 1/2 kilometer S D-1 exit. This is the initial assault on German occupied coast of France. Enemy fire was heavy as we struggled across the the beach. Casualties seem to be heavy but this is no time for check-awaiting orders-hugging beach wall.
0753 VOCG 29th Inf Div: "lead the way Rangers" VOCO "Co B lead way cleared path thru barbed entanglements.
Co's A & F take the flanks knock out the pillboxes to our left and right.
Co's C, D, E, & CP groups "lets go" get those MG's and snipers to out front" (2 hours later near Vierville-sur-Mer) and we went over the wall and on over the burning hill at the beaches edge and pushed inward toward Vierville, under constant enemy fire machine guns, automatic pistols, snipers rifles, mortars and self propelled 88's.
1043 reaching outskirts village Vierville-sur-Mer. Sniper fire is heavy. Two MG nests located in a building, knocked out. Infiltrating thru town, snipers are thinning out rapidly. Several patrols are searching building to building while the battalion is moving on cautiously.
1400 CO can't contact anyone by radio.
1935 have reached westerly outskirts of town. VOCO all around defense. No perimeter defense of the town can be established. 116th Inf has not moved up to our left.

No contact can be made. CP set up in shed at towns edge. 2300 twenty three U.S. tanks are moving up thru the town and into their prearranged transport area, which is inside our defense. Known casualties to now, 2400 6 June 1944; Hq Co T/Sgt Walter J Zack (KIA), T/5 Vincent Walters, T/5 Theadore Wells, Pfc Arthur McCullough, T/Sgt Wilfred McGuire, T/4 James V Fitzgerald, T/5 Thomas Lanham, (SWA & LWA); Med Det Cpl John Amador (LWA); Co A, 1st Lt OSCAR SUCHIER (LWA), T/5 William Fox, Pfc Chester A Tarlano, Pfc Bernard V Spring, (KIA), Sgt James O'Hare, Pfc Earl R Moynihan, Pfc Bernard Berkowitz, Pfc Stephen J Beck, Pfc Daniel D Farley, Pfc Anthony A Vullo, Pvt James W Gabaree, Cpl Michael G Zifcak, Pfc John P Bellows (SWA & LWA); Co B, S/Sgt William E Reilly, T/5 Elmo E Banning, T/5 Clinton O Read, Pfc Nickolas (NMI) Wassil, Pvt Raymond F Wilhelm (KIA), S/Sgt James R Copeland, S/Sgt Walter N McIlwain, Sgt Dalton Boudreaux, T/5 Lawrence Antrim, T/5 Ashley R Kimball, Cpl Clayton E Gardner (SWA & LWA); Co C, T/5 Robert M Goldacker (SWA); Co D, T/5 Stephen (NMI) Szerscz, Pfc Harry I Bolton (KIA), T/Sgt Louis (NMI) Rock, S/Sgt Dwain J Radcliffe, Sgt Richard E Bendix, T/5 Aldus P Krieder, Pfc Denman E Wolfe, Pvt Ray E Olcott, T/5 Andrew J Rose, Pfc Elmer L Lunsford Pvt Russell F Vossen (SWA & LWA); Co E, 1st Lt DEE C ANDERSON, Pfc Matthew E Morse, Pfc Robert C Steinen (KIA), 1st Lt WOODFORD L MOORE, 1st Sgt Sandy Martin Jr, Sgt Lloyd Posey, T/5 John W Manifold (SWA), S/Sgt Robert S Stucker, Pfc James E Mercer, Pfc Elmer F Shilling (LWA) ; Co F, Pfc Boward J Gardner, Pfc Bernard J Laboda, Pfc Robert T Miller, (KIA), 1st Sgt Howard A MacDonald (SWA), S/Sgt Orville Rosenblad, T/5 Roy F Nard, Pfc Clark L Baker, Pfc Stephen W Minor, Pfc Louis (NMI) Smolich, Pfc Richard T Sorenson (LWA).

A Company 5th Rangers – Vierville-sur-Mer, France.
B Company 5th Rangers – Vierville-sur-Mer, France.
C Company 5th Rangers – Vierville-sur-Mer, France.
D Company 5th Rangers – Vierville-sur-Mer, France.
E Company 5th Rangers – Vierville-sur-Mer, France.
F Company 5th Rangers – Vierville-sur-Mer, France.

COMPANY MORNING REPORT ENDING 2400 6 June 194 4

STATION Vierville, Ser Mur, France
ORGANIZATION Co "A" 5th Ranger Inf Bn Inf

Serial Number	Name	Grade
O-1287617	Suchier, Oscar A	1st Lt
	Above Off dy to LWA	
32171456	Fox, William J.	Tec 5
12159974	Tarlano, Chester A.	Pfc
25627617	Spring, Bernard V.	Pfc
	Above Em dy to KIA	
20101734	O'Hare, James J.	Sgt
37144495	Moynihan, Earl R	Pfc
	Above Em dy to SWA	
12159238	Berkowitz, Bernard	Pfc
32069536	Beck, Stephen J.	Pfc
35656387	Farley, Daniel D.Jr	Pfc
32531611	Vullo, Anthony A.	Pfc
36071305	Gabaree, James W.	Pvt
	Above Em dy to LWA	
31056508	Zifcak, Michael G	Cpl
11085468	Bellows, John P.	Pfc
	Above Em LWA	

COMPANY MORNING REPORT ENDING 2400 6 June 194 4

STATION Vierville Ser Mur, France APO 230
ORGANIZATION Co B 5th Ranger Inf Bn Inf

Serial Number	Name	Grade	Code
32147081	Reilly, William F.	S/Sgt	
32516256	Banning, Elmo E.	Tec 5	
15104074	Read, Clinton O.	Tec 5	
31196645	Wessil, Nickolas NMI	Pfc	
33431735	Wilhelm, Raymond F.	Pvt	
	Above EM dy to KIA		
15086742	Copeland, James R.	S/Sgt	
31060771	McIlwain, Walter N.	S/Sgt	
38484092	Boudreaux, Dalton L.	Sgt	
33491453	Antrim, Lawrence S.	Tec 5	
37152511	Kimball, Ashley R.	Tec 5	
	Above EM dy to SWA		
31226449	Gardner, Clayton E.	Cpl	
	Prom dy to SIA		

RECORD OF EVENTS
6 June 44 Embarked into LCA fr HMS Leopold
in transport area at 0530 Landed at beach
at Vierville Ser Mur at 0730 for participation in initial assault on coast of
France Smashed beach defenses and captured
Vierville Ser Mur.

OFFICER	FLD O & CAPT	1ST LT	2D LT	WO	FLT O

COMPANY MORNING REPORT ENDING 2400 6 June 4

STATION Vierville Ser Mur. France APO 23
ORGANIZATION Co C 5th Ranger Inf Bn Inf

Serial Number	Name	Grade	Code
36459619	Goldacker, Robert M.Tec 5		
	Fr Dy to SWA		

RECORD OF EVENTS
6 June 44 Embarked into LCA fr HMS
Boudin in transport area at 0530
Landed at beach at Vierville Ser
Mur at 0730 for participation in
initial assault on coast of France.
Smashed defenses and captd Vierville

OFFICER STRENGTH	FLD O & CAPT	1ST LT	2D LT	WO	FLT O
	PRES ABS'T	PRES ABS'T	PRES ABS'T	PRES ABS'T	PRES ABS'T

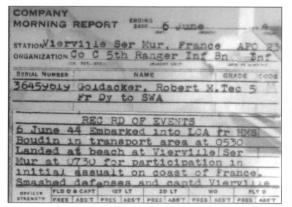

RECORD OF EVENTS
6 June 1944 mbarked into LCA fr HMS
Leopold in transport area at 0530
anded on beach at Vierville Sur Mer
at 0730 for participation in initial
assault on the coast of France
Smashed beach defenses and captured
Vierville Sur Mer

COMPANY MORNING REPORT ENDING 2400 6 June 4

STATION Vierville Ser Mur, France
ORGANIZATION Co D, 5th Ranger Inf Bn Inf

Serial Number	Name	Grade	Code
35605996	Szerecz, Stephen NMI	Tec 5	
37242999	Bolton, Harry I.	Pfc	
	Above EM dy to KIA		
20724725	Rock, Louis (NMI)	Tech/Sgt	
36044084	Radcliffe, Dwain J.	S/Sgt	
39463606	Bendix, Richard E.	Sgt	
33501061	Kreider, Aldus F.	Tec 5	
15060573	Wolfe, Denman E.	Pfc	
32577202	Olcott, Ray E.	Pvt	
	Above EM dy to SWA		
39697192	Rose, Andrew J.	Tec 5	
20721747	Lunsford, Elmer L.	Pfc	
35743126	Vossen, Russell F.	Pvt	
	Above EM dy to LWA		

6 Jun 44   RECORD OF EVENTS
Embarked into LCA fr HMS Boduin
in transport area at 0530 Landed at
beach at Vierville Ser Mur at 0730 for
Participation in initial assault on
coast of France.Smashed beach defenses
and captured Vierville Ser Mur.

OFFICER	FLD O & CAPT	1ST LT	2D LT	WO	FLT O

COMPANY MORNING REPORT ENDING 2400 6 June 194 4

STATION Vierville Ser Mur, France APO 230
ORGANIZATION Co. F 5th Ranger Inf. Bn. Inf.

Serial Number	Name	Grade	Code
52587514	Gardner, Howard, J.	PFC	M
33359431	Laboda, Bernard, J.	PFC	
36564331	Miller, Robert, T.	PFC	
	Above EM dy to KIA		
11117444	MacDonald, Howard, A.	1st/Sgt.	
	Dy to SWA		
20722145	Rosenblad, Orvylle, A.	S/Sgt.	
35608613	Rand, Roy, F.	Tec 5	
35573107	Baker, Clark, L.	PFC	
34153831	Minor, Stephen, W.	PFC	
39464061	Smolich, Louis, NMI	PFC	
31154675	Sorenson, Richard, T.	PFC	
	Above EM dy to LWA		

RECORD OF EVENTS
6 Jun 44 Embarked in LCA fr HMS Boduin in transport area at 0530 Landed at beach at Vierville Ser Mur at 0750 for Part in initial assault on coast of France. Smashed beach defences and captured Vierville Ser Mur.

32762678	Spier, Andrew, L.	Tec 5	
13053426	Grathwohl Jr., Henry, L	PFC	
	Above EM LWA		

OFFICER | FLO O & CAPT | 1ST LT | 2D LT | WO | FLT O

COMPANY MORNING REPORT ENDING 2400 6 June 194 4

STATION Vierville Sur Mer, France APO 230
ORGANIZATION Hq Co 5th Ranger Inf Bn

Serial Number	Name	Grade	Code
37466056	Zach Walter J.	T/Sgt	
	Fr dy to KIA		
12099357	Walters Vincent W.	Tec 5	
	Fr DS Provisional Ranger Group Headquarters		
	APO 230 U S Army to SWA		
35717397	Wells Theodore H.	Tec 5	
	Fr DS Provisional Ranger Group Headquarters		
	APO 230 U S Army to LWA		
36439191	McCullough Arthur J.	Pfc	
	Fr dy to LWA		
20721430	McGuire Wilfred F.	T/Sgt	
31035200	Fitzgerald James V.	Tec 4	
69474705	Lanham Thomas E.	Tec 5	
	Above 3 EM LWA		

RECORD OF EVENTS
6 June 1944 Embarked into LCA fr HMS Leopold in transport area at 0530 Landed at beach at Vierville Sur Mer at 0730 for participation in initial assault on coast of France. Smashed beach defenses and captured Vierville Sur Mer.

OFFICER | FLO O & CAPT | 1ST LT | 2D LT | WO | FLT O

COMPANY MORNING REPORT ENDING 2400 6 June 194 4

STATION Vierville Sur Mer, France APO 230
ORGANIZATION Med Det 5th Ranger Inf Bn Med

Serial Number	Name	Grade	Code
36811568	Amador, John P	Cpl	
	Fr dy to LWA		

RECORD OF EVENTS
6 June 1944 Embarked into LCA fr HMS Leopold in transport area at 0530 Landed at beach at Vierville Sur Mer at 0730 for participation in initial assault on coast of France. Smashed beach defenses and captured Vierville Sur Mer.

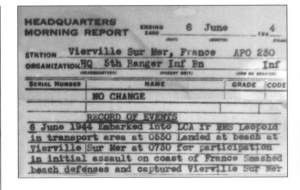

HEADQUARTERS MORNING REPORT ENDING 2400 6 June 194 4

STATION Vierville Sur Mer, France APO 230
ORGANIZATION HQ 5th Ranger Inf Bn Inf

Serial Number	Name	Grade	Code
	NO CHANGE		

RECORD OF EVENTS
6 June 1944 Embarked into LCA fr HMS Leopold in transport area at 0530 Landed at beach at Vierville Sur Mer at 0730 for participation in initial assault on coast of France. Smashed beach defenses and captured Vierville Sur Mer.

Sgt. John Hodgson (F Company 5th Btn) kept a daily log of F Company casualties and those Killed in Action in a small pocket book. For D-Day his notes read as follows:

Killed in Action:
Pfc Robert T. Miller 36564311 killed in Vierville-sur-Mer.
Pfc Howard J. Gardner 32587514 killed in Vierville-sur-Mer.
Pfc Bernard J. Laboda 33359431 killed in Vierville-sur-Mer.

Wounded in Action:
1st Sgt Howard A. MacDonald 11117444.
Sgt Cinton L. Fogel 39308984.
S/Sgt Orvylle A. Rosenblad 20722145.
Pfc Stephen W. Minor 34153831.
Pfc Louis Smolich 39464061.
T/5 Roy Rand 35608613.

Pfc Clark Baker 33573107.
Pfc Robert Ovington 36313114.
Pfc Richard T. Sorenson 31154675.

Medical Detachment 5th Rangers – Vierville-sur-Mer, France.
Headquarters Company 5th Rangers – Vierville-sur-Mer, France.

At 8am on 6 June General Eisenhower wrote the following letter.

TOP SECRET   TOP SECRET

SHAEF
STAFF MESSAGE CONTROL
INCOMING MESSAGE

EYES ONLY

SHAEF CP   SHAEF 83/06

Filed 060800B June   TOR 060930B June

U R G E N T

FROM   : SHAEF COMMAND POST, PERSONAL FROM GENERAL EISENHOWER

TO   : AGWAR-TO GENERAL MARSHALL FOR HIS EYES ONLY; SHAEF FOR INFORMATION

REF NO : 90016, 6 June 1944

Local time is now 8 in the morning.

I have as yet no information concerning the actual landings nor of our progress through beach obstacles. Communique will not be issued until we have word that leading ground troops are actually ashore.

All preliminary reports are satisfactory. Airborne formations apparently landed in good order with losses out of approximately 1250 airplanes participating about 30. Preliminary bombings by air went off as scheduled. Navy reports sweeping some mines, but so far as is known channels are clear and operation proceeding as planned. In early morning hours reaction from shore batteries was sufficiently light that some of the naval spotting planes have returned awaiting call.

The weather yesterday which was original date selected was impossible all along the target coast. Today conditions are vastly improved both by sea and air and we have the prospect of at least reasonably favorable weather for the next several days.

Yesterday, I visited British troops about to embark and last night saw a great portion of a United States airborne division just prior to its takeoff. The enthusiasm, toughness and obvious fitness of every single man were high and the light of battle was in their eyes.

I will keep you informed.

DISTRIBUTION:

1. SUPREME COMMANDER ✔

2. CHIEF OF STAFF

3. SGS

4. Gen. Strong (G-2)

5. Gen. Bull (G-3)   TOP SECRET

COPY NO 1
SUPREME COMMANDER

466

174

One of a small number of photographs taken during the landings show the bluffs behind Omaha Beach on fire.

iii) Pointe du Hoc

Prior to the Rangers landing at Pointe du Hoc, the German 352nd Infantry Division's radio log noted the following:
[Au Guay is the village directly behind Pointe du Hoc.]

```
                              4.35 Hours

Report from Gren Regt 916:
An American 1/Lt taken prisoner near St. P le Guay testified that along
with the parachute troops also dummy dolls are being dropped, which explode
when contacting the ground.                                          .
```

From early in the morning the Germans had been made aware of an operation against Pointe du Hoc and also of the use of dummy paratroopers by the Allies.

RAF bombing records for the night of the 5th and the morning of 6 June show that they were using the Oboe marker system to attack Coastal Gun Batteries; included in this group is a mission to bomb Maisy I. (Oboe was a radio based location system devised in 1941 and used by the RAF to improve bombing missions. Oboe operators in England sent signals to aircraft whilst in flight, to help them pinpoint a particular target on the ground).

OBOE DAILY REPORT.
FOR OPERATIONS NIGHT 5/6. JUNE, 1944 (CONT.)

SECRET

TARGET.	CHANNEL.	MARK.	NO. OF AIRCRAFT USED.	FAILURES.		REMARKS.
				AIRBORNE.	GROUND.	
LA PERNELLE	3	I	1	NIL	NIL	5/5
	11	II	1			
	12	II	1			
	13	II	1			
MAISY I.	3	I	1	NIL	NIL	5/5.
	11	II	1			
	12	II	1			
	13	II	1			1 a/c failure (bomb release gear)
HOULGATE.	3	I	1	NIL	NIL	4/5
	11	II	1	NIL	NIL	
	12	II	1	NIL	1	
	13	II	1	NIL	NIL	
	1	II	1	NIL	NIL	
OUISTREHAM.	3	I	1	NIL	NIL	5/5.
	11	II	1			
	12	II	1			1 a/c failure – release not given due to bad flying
	13	II	1			

NOTES.

① 41 out of 50 a/c serviceable OBOE.   41/50

② There were two a/c failures not attributable to OBOE and therefore the marking success was   39/50

③ Serviceability exceptionally high standard for these operations.

6/6/44.

2nd Battalion – Small Unit Action Report:

A Naval Shore Fire Control Party (12 men) and a forward observer of the 58th Armored Field Artillery Battalion were attached to Lt. Col. Rudder's headquarters, and then distributed among the four LCAs carrying Company E.

The Landing

D-Day weather was unfavorable for a landing assault – with rough seas that imperiled small landing craft during their approach to the beaches. Early visibility along the coast was poor, and an eastward-setting tidal current helped to produce errors in navigation. The results, on the Omaha Beach sectors, were delays in reaching shore and enough mis-landing of assault craft to interfere seriously with the early schedule for the attack. The Ranger force did not escape these difficulties.

Shortly after leaving their transports (the LSI's Ben My Chree and Amsterdam), the craft began to suffer from the results of the heavy going. Eight miles from shore LCA 860, carrying Capt. Harold K. Slater and 20 men of Company D, swamped in the 4-foot choppy waves. The personnel were picked up by rescue craft and carried to England. Ten minutes later one of the supply craft sank, with only one survivor. The other supply craft were soon in trouble and had to jettison all the packs of Companies D and E in order to stay afloat. The other craft survived, with varying degrees of trouble; several shipped so much water that the men had to bail with their helmets to help the pumps. From the start, all the Rangers were soaked with spray. In one respect they enjoyed exceptional luck: there were very few cases of seasickness, in contrast to the general record at Omaha. Despite being wet, cold, and cramped by the three-hour trip, personnel of the three Ranger companies reached the shore in good shape for immediate and strenuous action. The most serious effect of the wetting was to soak the climbing ropes and rope ladders, making them heavier.

The leading group of nine surviving LCAs kept good formation, in a double column ready to fan out as they neared shore. Unfortunately, the guide craft lost its bearings as the coast line came in sight, and headed straight for Pointe de la Percée, three miles east of the target. When Colonel Rudder, in the lead LCA, realized the error he intervened and turned the column westward. But the damage had been done. The mistake cost more than 30 minutes in reaching Pointe du Hoe; instead of landing at H-Hour, the first Ranger craft touched down about H+38, a delay that determined the whole course of action at the Pointe for the next two days. The main Ranger flotilla, eight companies strong, was following in from the transports, watching anxiously for the signal of success at Pointe du Hoe (two successive flares shot by 60-mm mortars). By 0700, if no message or signal had come, Colonel Schneider's force was scheduled to adopt the alternate plan of action and land at the Vierville beach.

They waited ten minutes beyond the time limit and then received by radio the code word TILT, prearranged signal to follow the alternative plan. So Colonel Schneider turned in toward Vierville, where the 5th Rangers and A and B of the 2nd landed at 0745. Pending the outcome at Omaha Beach, and the success of Colonel Schneider's force in fighting cross-country to the Pointe, Colonel Rudder's three companies would fight alone.

The error in direction had further consequences. The correction headed Colonel Rudder's column of LCAs back toward Pointe du Hoe, but now on a westerly course, roughly paralleling the cliffs and only a few hundred yards offshore. The flotilla thus had to run the gauntlet of fire from German strongpoints along three miles of coast. Fortunately these were few, and their fire was wild and intermittent. The only serious casualty was a DUKW, hit by 20-mm fire as it neared the target area. Five of the nine men aboard were killed or wounded.

The Commanding officer's report from USS *Satterlee*:

> From daylight until the Rangers approached the beach there was no sign of life or activity around POINTE DU HOE. It looked as if the bombardment had knocked them out completely. There were no visible targets. Fire was reduced to conserve ammunition because we did not know for how long the weather would delay the landing. This was a mistake. We should have continued neutralization fire at the scheduled rate against the face of the cliff and we should have called on the TEXAS, who was available, to support us in this mission. As the Rangers hit the beach, the Germans came out of their holes and opened up with their machine guns. From then on we were firing on the Germans directly and on the points where machine-gun fire could be detected. We should never have eased up enough to allow the enemy time enough to get out of their hiding places. This mistake can be attributed to two causes: lack of experience of the Commanding Officer in actual shore bombardment and over-confidence in the effectiveness of the air bombardment. There were no failures of material.

2nd Battalion – Small Unit Action Report continued:

The plan for landings had to be changed as a result of the misdirected approach. Since the column of LCAs was now coming at the Pointe from east instead of north, Company D's craft would not be able to swing out of column and reach the west side of the promontory in time to assault with the other units. Therefore, to effect synchronized attack, the nine assault craft deployed and came in on line together at the east side.

A final result of the delay was apparent as they reached the goal. Naval fire had halted just before H-Hour, and the enemy on Pointe du Hoe had 40 minutes to recover from the effects of the bombardment. As the LCAs neared the Pointe, they received scattered small-arms and automatic fire, and enemy troops were observed moving near the edge of the cliff. There was, however, no indication of artillery in action from the enemy positions.

At 0710, as the first craft were grounding under the cliffs, radio silence was broken to send Colonel Schneider the order for landing at Vierville. The message was acknowledged. The small assault force was now entirely alone as it came in to a hostile shore.

The British destroyer Talybont, *which had taken part in the early bombardment of Pointe du Hoe at a range of 2.7 miles, saw the flotilla heading in on a wrong course, and found it difficult to understand, 'as* Texas' *fall of shot on Pointe du Hoe was obvious.' As the Rangers corrected course and came under fire from the cliff positions, the* Talybont *closed range and for 15 minutes (0645-0700) raked enemy firing positions with 4-inch and 2-pounder shells. Meantime, the U.S. destroyer* Satterlee, *2,500 yards from Pointe du Hoe, could see enemy troops assembling on the cliff, and opened with main battery and machine-gun fire.*

At 0540 HMS Talybont, *a Type III escort destroyer, moved down the fire support channel to take up position to bombard land targets. It was situated midway between USS* Satterlee *and USS* Thompson. *At 0550 it opened fire at a range of less than half a mile on pillboxes or machine gun emplacements which could not be seen – it was decided to cover the top of the cliff in the target area as thoroughly as possible prior to the Ranger landings. At 0600 the Rangers aboard a landing craft passed the ship. It was not realised at the time that they were heading for the wrong point and instead of Pointe du Hoc they were going east towards Pointe Raz de la Percée. At 0615 the* Talybont *ceased fire – yet less than one minute later it opened fire on other targets again. 0630 The Rangers in ML204, whose mistake in navigation had obviously been realized, were making for the correct destination of Pointe du Hoc.*

HMS Talybont*: 0630* Talybont *fired on targets 81 and 82. 0640 noted that fire was opened on the Rangers from the Germans onshore with two light machine guns. Three rear DUWKs were being fired on and taking casualties. 0640 Gunfire was shifted to the cliff face and top in the area where the guns were thought to be firing from.* Talybont *opened fire with its 2 pounder pompoms and the return fire from the shores was spasmodic. Two of the Rangers' DUKWs were hit – one badly. Shortly thereafter a further 2 light machine guns opened fire from the shore and another DUKW was put out of action.*

At 0646 Gunfire was maintained on the vicinity of targets 81, 82 and the Rangers sustained no more casualties from these areas. 0700 Talybont *ceased firing on targets 81 and 82. However, the Rangers were still under small arms fire from Pointe du Hoc.*

USS Satterlee *was already giving gunfire support against these positions so by 0703* Talybont *engaged other targets and by 0710 it withdrew from Fire Support Area.*

HMS Talybont *After Action Report: 'Targets 67, 77 were evidently completely neutralised or destroyed. Targets 81, 82 though engaged for 25 minutes prior to 'H' hour were only 60% neutralised. It is considered that up to four LMG's were in action against the Rangers.*

In the opinion of the Lt Commander of the HMS Talybont*: 'The mistake in identification of the target by ML 204 is difficult to understand as* Texas *fall of shot was obvious. Their course from Raz de le Percée along the shore to Pointe du Hoc was suicidal.'*

The Cliff Assault

The nine LCAs touched down on a front of about 500 yards, the right-hand craft just under the tip of Pointe du Hoe, and the others spaced fairly evenly. No great distance separated some of the boat teams, but according to plan they went into action as separate units, each facing its particular problems of escalade and opposition.

In certain general respects, their problems were similar. The 30-yard strip of beach between water and cliff had been completely cratered by bombs. The craters were to handicap the unloading of men and supplies and were to render the DUKWs useless after landing, for these craft were nowhere able to cross the sand and get close enough to the cliff to reach it with their extension ladders. The cliff face showed extensive marks of the naval and air bombardment; huge chunks of the top had been torn out, forming talus mounds at the base. A few grenades were thrown down or rolled over the edge as the first Rangers crossed the sand, and enemy small-arms fire came from scattered points along the cliff edge. Particularly dangerous was enfilade fire, including automatic weapons, from the German position on the left flank of the beach. Once at the foot of the cliff, the Rangers were better off, for the piles of debris gave partial defilade from the flanking fires, and the enemy directly above would have to expose themselves in order to place observed fire or to aim their grenades.

Naval support came to the aid of the Rangers at this critical moment. The destroyer Satterlee *watched the craft reach shore, and saw the enemy firing from the cliff above. The* Satterlee *immediately took the cliff tops under fire from its 5-inch guns and 40-mm machine guns. Fire control was excellent, despite attempts of enemy machine guns and a heavier gun to counter the destroyer's effort. Comdr. J. W. Marshall, commanding the* Satterlee*, believed this fire was decisive in enabling the Rangers to get up the cliff. However, his impression that the assault force 'was pinned under the cliff and being rapidly cut to pieces by enemy fire' is not confirmed by the speed with which the escalade got under way, or by other details of the landing. Curiously enough, only three or four men out of 120 survivors interviewed remembered noticing naval fire after touchdown. One of these was Colonel Rudder, who 'had the living hell scared out of him' by explosions which brought down a section of cliff just over his head, and which came from an unknown source. Both impressions – the Rangers, that there was no fire support worth mentioning, and the* Satterlee's*, that the Rangers were pinned down are easily understandable under the circumstances of battle and the difficulties of observation. The probability is that the destroyer's fire on the cliff top, at the moment when the Rangers were starting their assault, did a great deal to prevent effective enemy opposition at the decisive moment.*

In any event, the assault went forward without check. Ranger casualties on the beach totalled about 15, most of them from the raking fire to their left. In something less than ten minutes from landing, the first Ranger parties were getting over the cratered edges of the cliff top. The story of the boat teams will be given in order from right to left, roughly the order of landing.

LCA 861. Carrying a boat team of Company E, commanded by 1st Lt. Theodore E. Lapres, Jr., this craft grounded about 25 yards from the bottom of the cliff. Three or four Germans were standing on the cliff edge, shooting down at the craft. Rangers near the stern took these enemy under fire and drove them out of sight. At the instant of touchdown the rear pair of rockets was fired, then the other two pairs in succession. All the ropes fell short of the cliff edge, as a result of being thoroughly soaked. In some cases not more than half the length of rope or ladder was lifted from the containing box.

As the Rangers crossed the strip of cratered sand, grenades were thrown down from above them, or rolled over the cliff edge. These were of the 'potato-masher' type, with heavy concussion effects but small fragmentation. They caused two casualties. The hand-rockets were carried ashore, and the first one was fired at 15 yards from the cliff. It went over the top and caught. Pfc. Harry W. Roberts started up the hand-line, bracing his feet against the 80-degree slope. He made about 25 feet; the rope slipped or was cut, and Roberts slithered down. The second rocket was fired and the grapnel caught. Roberts went up again, made the top (he estimated his climbing time at 40 seconds), and pulled into a small cratered niche just under the edge. As he arrived, the rope was cut. Roberts tied it to a picket. This pulled out under the weight of the next man, and the rope fell off the cliff, marooning Roberts. However, a 20-foot mound of clay knocked off the cliff enabled Roberts' team to get far enough up the side to throw him a rope. This time he lay across it, and five men, including Lieutenant Lapres, came up. Roberts had not yet seen an enemy and had not been under fire. Without waiting for further arrivals, the six Rangers started for their objective, the heavily constructed OP at the north tip of the fortified area. About ten minutes had elapsed since touchdown.

Just after Lapres' group got up, a heavy explosion occurred above the rest of 861's team, waiting their turn on the rope. Pfc. Paul L. Medeiros was half buried under debris from the cliff. None of the men knew what caused the explosion, whether a naval shell, or the detonation of a German mine of a peculiar type found later at one or two places along the cliff edge. The enemy had hung naval shells (200-mm or larger) over the edge, attached by wire to a pull-type firing device and fitted with a short-delay time fuze. The explosion had no effect on the escalade. Medeiros and four more Rangers came up quickly, found Roberts' party already gone and out of sight, and followed from the cliff edge toward the same objective.

LCA 862. This craft, carrying 15 Rangers and NSFC personnel, landed about 100 yards left of the flank LCA. The men had no trouble in disembarking, but once on the sand they found themselves exposed to machine-gun fire from eastward of the landing area. One man was killed and one wounded by this fire; two more injured by grenade fragments.

The forward pair of rockets had been fired immediately on touchdown, followed by all four others together. One plain and two toggle ropes reached the top, but one toggle rope pulled out. Tech. 5 Victor J. Aguzzi, 1st Lt. Joseph E. Leagans (commanding the team), and S/Sgt. Joseph J. Cleaves went up the two remaining ropes, arrived at the top almost together, and fell into a convenient shell hole just beyond the edge. There they paused only long enough for two more men to join; then, following standard Ranger tactics, the five moved off without waiting for the rest of the team, who came up a few minutes later.

LCA 888. Colonel Rudder's craft, first to hit the beach, had 15 men of Company E and 6 headquarters personnel, including Lt. J. W. Eikner, communications officer. A few enemy troops were seen on the cliff edge as the LCA neared shore, but, when Sgt. Dominick B. Boggetto shot one German off the edge with a BAR, the others disappeared. The Rangers had trouble in getting through the beach craters; neck deep in water, they found it hard to climb out because of the slick clay bottom. A few grenades came over the cliff without causing casualties.

The rockets were fired in series, at 35 yards from the cliff base. None of the waterlogged ropes reached the top. When two Rangers, best of the group at free-climbing, tried to work up the smashed cliff face without ropes, they were balked by the slippery clay surface, which gave way too easily to permit knife-holds. Bombs or shells had brought down a mass of wet clay from the cliff top, forming a mound 35 to 40 feet high against the cliff. A 16-foot section of the extension ladder, with a toggle rope attached, was carried to the top of the mound and set up. A Ranger climbed the ladder, cut a foothold in the cliff, and stood in this to hold the ladder while a second man climbed it for another 16 feet. The top man repeated the process, and this time Tech. 5 George J. Putzek reached the edge. Lying flat, with the ladder on his arms, he held on while a man below climbed the toggle rope, then the ladder.

From there on it was easy. As the first men up moved a few yards from the cliff edge to protect the climbers, they found plenty of cover in bomb craters, and no sign of an enemy. In 15 minutes from landing, all the Company E men from LCA 888 were up and ready to move on. Colonel Rudder and headquarters personnel remained for the moment below, finding shelter from enfilade fire in a shallow cave at the bottom of the cliff. By 0725, 1st Lt. James W. Eikner had his equipment set up and flashed word by SCR 300 that Colonel Rudder's force had landed. Five minutes later he sent out the code word indicating 'men up the cliff'; the 'Roger' that receipted for this message, again on SCR 300, was Eikner's last communication of D-Day on the Ranger command net. When he sent the message PRAISE THE LORD ('all men up cliff') at 0745, no response was forthcoming.

LCA 722. Twenty yards left of Colonel Rudder's craft, LCA 722 hit shore with 15 Company E Rangers, 5 headquarters men, a Stars and Stripes photographer, and a Commando officer who had assisted the Rangers in training. Touchdown was made at the edge of a crater, and the men could not avoid it in debarking. Enemy grenades were ineffectual, and the craters and debris on the beach gave sufficient cover from enfilading fire from the left. The only casualty was Pfc. John J. Sillman, wounded three times as the craft came in, hit twice on the beach, and destined to survive. A good deal of assorted equipment came on this craft, including the SCR 284, two pigeons, a 60-mm mortar with ammunition, and some demolitions. All were got ashore without loss, though it took manoeuvering to avoid the deep water in the crater. Tech. 4 C. S. Parker and two other communications men hefted the big radio set on a pack board, and managed to get it in and working before the first climbers from 722 reached the top.

The rockets had been fired just before landing. One ladder and one plain rope got up and held (LCA 722 had experienced no trouble with water, and the ropes were comparatively dry). The single rope lay in a slight crevice, but the ladder came down on an overhang where it seemed exposed to the flanking fire and would be hard to climb. Tech. 5 Edward P. Smith tried the plain rope and found he could easily 'walk it up'. On top three or four minutes after landing, he saw a group of Germans to his right throwing grenades over the cliff. Sgt. Hayward A. Robey joined Smith with a BAR. Robey lay in a shallow niche at the cliff edge and sprayed the grenadiers with 40 or 50 rounds, fast fire. Three of the enemy dropped and the rest disappeared into shelters. Pfc. Frank H. Peterson, lightly wounded on the beach by a grenade, joined up and the three Rangers went off on their mission without waiting for the next climbers.

The mortar section in this boat team remained below, according to plan, with the purpose of setting up their 60-mm on the beach to deliver supporting fires. But the beach was too exposed to make this practicable, and time was consumed in getting ammunition from the one surviving supply craft. About 0745 the mortar team went on top without having yet fired.

LCA 668. Company D's craft had been scheduled to land on the west side of the Pointe. As a result of the change in angle of approach, the two surviving LCAs came in to the left of Company E, and in the center of the Ranger line.

LCA 668 grounded short of the beach strip, as a result of boulders knocked from the cliff by bombardment. The men had to swim in about 20 feet. While 1st Sgt. Leonard G. Lomell was bringing in a box of rope and a hand-projector rocket, he was wounded in the side by a machine-gun bullet but reached shore and kept going. Despite the unusual distance from the cliff, and the very wet ropes, three rockets had carried the cliff edge with a toggle rope and the two rope ladders. However, the grapnels on the ladders just made the top; since the lead rope connecting grapnels with the top of the ladders was 40 feet long, the Rangers had, in effect, two plain ropes and a toggle. Sergeant Lomell put his best climber on the toggle while he tried one of the ladders. All ropes were on an overhang, and only the toggle line proved practicable. Even on it, climbing would be slow, so Lomell called for the extension ladders. Picking a spot high on the talus, his men found that one 16-foot section added to a 20-foot section reached the top of the vertical stretch, beyond which a slide of debris had reduced the slope enough to make it negotiable without ropes. Two men had got up by the toggle rope; the rest used the ladder and made the top quickly. Grenades caused some annoyance until the first men up could cover the rest of the party. Twelve men moved off from the edge with Sergeant Lomell and 1st Lt. George F. Kerchner.

LCA 858. Shipping enough water all the way in to keep the Rangers busy, this craft nevertheless kept up fairly well and was only a minute or two behind the others at the beach. The men were put out into a crater and went over their heads in muddy water. Despite the wetting, a bazooka was the only piece of equipment put out of action. Three men were hit by machine-gun fire from the east flank.

The rockets were fired in series, the plain ropes first. All the ropes were wet, and only one hand-line got over the cliff. It lay in a crevice that would give some protection from enemy flanking fire, but the direct approach to the foot of the rope was exposed. The Company D Rangers worked their way to the rope through the piles of debris at the cliff base. While one man helped the wounded get to Colonel Rudder's CP, where the medics had set up, all the party went up this one rope and found it not too hard going. They could get footholds in the cliff face, and a big crater reduced the steepness of the climb near the top. The group was up within 15 minutes. As in most other cases, the first few men on top had moved off together, and the boat team did not operate as a unit after the escalade.

LCA 887. As a result of Company D's unscheduled landing in the center of the line of craft, the three carrying Company F were crowded eastward, all of them touching down beyond the area originally assigned them. Few of the Rangers realized this at the time.

LCA 887 had not been much bothered by either water or enemy action on the trip in. The craft grounded five yards out from dry beach, and the shorter men got a ducking in the inevitable crater. No equipment trouble resulted; even Sgt. William L. Petty's BAR, wet here and muddied later when he slipped on the cliff, fired perfectly when first needed. Some enemy fire, including automatic weapons, came from either flank. Two Rangers were wounded.

Just before hitting the beach the two forward rockets were fired. Only one of the plain lines carried, and 1st Lt. Robert C. Arman, commanding the team, figured the heavier ropes had no chance. So, all four of the mounted rockets, together with the boxes carrying toggle ropes and ladders, were taken out on the sand – a matter of ten minutes' heavy work, while the coxswain of the LCA did a notable job of holding the craft in at the beach edge. When the rockets were set up for firing, the lead wire for making the firing connection was missing. Tech/Sgt. John I. Cripps fired all four in turn by touching the short connection, three feet from the rocket base, with his 'hot-box'. Each time, the flashback blinded Cripps and blew sand and mud all over him. The other Rangers saw him clean his eyes, shake his head, and go after the next rocket: 'he was a hell-of-a-looking mess.' But all the ropes went up, and made it possible for the party to make the top. Sergeant Petty and some other expert climbers had already tried the plain rope and failed; it was on a straight fall, requiring hand-over-hand work with no footholds possible, and the men had trouble with their muddy hands and clothes on the wet rope.

Sergeant Petty started up one of the ladders, got 30 feet up, and then slid all the way back on the cliff face when the grapnel pulled out. Tech. 5 Carl Winsch was going up the other ladder when fire from somewhere on the flanks began to chip the cliff all around him. Petty went up after Winsch, and found him, unwounded, in a shell hole at the top. Here Petty waited for two more Rangers and then they set out for their objective.

LCA 884. This craft, the target for considerable enemy fire from cliff positions on the way to the Point, had replied with its Lewis guns and the BARs of the Rangers. Touchdown was made on the edge of a shell hole, in water shoulder-high. Three Rangers were hit by fire coming from the left flank. When rockets were fired in series, front to rear, four got over the cliff, but every rope lay in such position as to be fully exposed to the continuing enemy small-arms fire. Moreover, the Rangers were so muddled in getting through the craters on the beach that the plain ropes would have been unusable after the first climber went up. The only rope ladder that reached the top was caught below on beach boulders and hung at an awkward angle. Several men tried the other ropes without success, and Pvt. William E. Anderson got only part way up in his attempt at free-climbing. 1st Lt. Jacob J. Hill finally took the group over to the left, where they used the ladders of 883's boat team.

LCA 883. Last in the column of approach, this craft was last to reach shore, nearly 300 yards left of its planned position and considerably beyond the edge of the main fortified area on Pointe du Hoe. Just to their left, a jut in the cliff protected the boat team from the flanking fire that caused so much trouble for the other landing parties. They made a dry landing, and had a perfect score with the six rockets. This gave an opportunity to use the climbing assignments on a full schedule, using every rope. Nevertheless the going was hard, even on the ladders. 1st Lt. Richard A. Wintz, on a plain rope, found it impossible to get any footholds on the slippery cliff. The wet and muddy rope made it difficult for hand-over-hand pulling, and at the top Wintz was 'never so tired in his life.' He found six men together and started them out immediately.

Summary. The first great difficulty, landing and getting up the cliff, had been surmounted. Enemy resistance, despite the delayed landing, had been weak and ineffective except for the enfilade fire from the machine gun position just east of Pointe du Hoe. The equipment and training for escalade had met the test. On only two craft had the mounted rockets failed to get at least one rope over the cliff top. The hand-projectors and extension ladders had been useful as supplementary equipment where the ropes failed, and only one boat team found it necessary to use the ropes of another party. The three DUKWs, stopped at the water's edge by craters, could not bring their mechanically operated extension ladders into play. One of them made the trial, only to have the ladder rest on the cliff side at a considerable angle, short of the top and unbalanced by the motion of the surf.

The assault met unforeseen circumstances, but their effects were not always to the disadvantage of the enterprise. Craters in the beach had made the landings slower and wetter than expected, had neutralized the DUKWs, and had impeded unloading of ammunition and supplies; on the other hand, they gave some cover from enemy fire. Damage done to the cliff face by bombardment seems, on the whole, to have helped the escalade work, for the piles of debris not only gave cover from the enfilade fire but reduced the height of the climb, particularly for use of extension ladders. The top of the cliff was much cut back by craters, further reducing the areas of sheer slope and providing cover for the first arrivals at the top.

The climbing parties had gone ahead with speed, determination, and resourcefulness, ready to improvise when necessary. This was the main reason for their success, and for the fact that within 30 minutes from touchdown all the attacking force was on top except for casualties, headquarters personnel, and some mortar men (30 to 40 Rangers out of about 190).

Capture of the Pointe

Troops landing at Omaha Beach on D-Day have frequently registered, in records and interviews, their disappointment at finding little visible evidence of the preliminary bombardment, which was expected to 'make the beach a shambles'. No such complaint could be made by the 2nd Rangers at Pointe du Hoe. As they came up from the ropes they found themselves in a bewildering wasteland of ground literally torn to pieces by bombs and heavy naval shells. Expected landmarks were gone; craters and mounds of wreckage were everywhere, obscuring remnants of paths and trenches. The Rangers had studied these few acres for months, using excellent photographs and large-scale maps that showed every slight feature of terrain and fortifications. Now, they found themselves in danger of losing their way as soon as they made a few steps from the ragged cliff edge into the chaos of holes and debris. Obtaining cover was no problem, but maintaining contact within groups as large as a squad would be almost impossible during movement.

There were other causes for the 'confused' nature of the action that took place on the Pointe, characterized as it was by infiltration of many and separate groups of Rangers through all parts of the enemy defenses. The prearranged tactics of the Ranger force emphasized movement with the greatest speed and by small groups. As the first few men on a rope reached the top at any point, they moved off at once for their objectives, without waiting for the rest of their boat group, and without taking time to form an organized section or platoon, or attempting to make contact with neighboring parties. In the climbing phase, so intent were the men on their own work that only in exceptional cases was any Ranger party aware of what other boat groups were doing, or even that other boat teams were on the beach. As the later climbers gained the cliff top, they too went off in small groups; over a period of 15 to 30 minutes a series of these parties was forming at the cliff edge and fanning out in all directions. At least 20 of them could be distinguished, but it is as impossible to trace their movements in exact order or timing as it must have been difficult for the Germans to spot the lines of the attack and organize to meet it.

Yet in essence the attack followed a definite plan and order. As first objectives, each platoon (whatever number of groups it split into) had a limited part of the enemy defensive system to reach and deal with. Every man knew what this mission was, and where to go. The outcome was an action without clear pattern in detail, but with very clearly defined results.

The first and chief objectives were the gun emplacements and the OP near the end of the Point. Company E had the OP and No.3 position as its assignment; Company D, the western gun emplacements (4, 5, and 6); Company F, guns 1 and 2 and the machine-gun position at the edge of the cliff, just east of the main fortified area. Once these objectives were taken, the plan had been to assemble at a phase line near the south edge of the fortified area. From here, D, F, and most of E would strike inland for the coastal highway about 1,000 yards south, cross it, and establish a road block against enemy movement from the west. A platoon of Company E was to remain on the Pointe with the headquarters group and arrange for perimeter defence of the captured fortifications.

There were, inevitably, deviations from this plan. Some Rangers of Companies D and E failed to reach the assembly area in time for the next phase of movement, or were kept on the Pointe to meet unexpected developments. On the eastern flank, two boat teams of Company F became involved in an action that lasted most of the day. But, by and large, movement went very nearly according to plan, a plan based on confidence in the ability of small, pick-up groups to work independently toward main objectives. This confidence was rewarded by success.

As the first Ranger elements left the cliff and started for their objectives, they met no opposition except near the OP. Most of the Rangers saw no enemy, and were hardly aware of sporadic fire coming from along the cliff to the west of the Pointe. Their main trouble was in finding and identifying the gun positions in the wreckage of the fortified area. One party after another reached its allotted emplacement, to make the same discovery: the open gun positions were pulverized, the casemates were heavily damaged, but there was no sign of the guns or of artillery equipment. Evidently, the 155's had been removed from the Pointe before the period of major bombardments. The advance groups moved on inland toward the assembly area.

The only fighting took place at the tip of the Pointe. Here, the first men up from LCA 861 found themselves about 20 feet to seaward of the massive and undamaged concrete OP. As S/Sgt. Charles H. Denbo and Private Roberts crawled five feet toward a trench, small-arms fire, including machine guns, started up from slits in the OP. The Rangers threw four grenades at the slits, and three went in. The machine gun stopped firing, but Denbo was wounded by a rifle bullet. Lieutenant Lapres, Sgt. Andrew J. Yardley, Pfc. William D. Bell, and Tech/Sgt.

Photograph of men from the 2nd Battalion reported to have been taken from inside a crater at Pointe du Hoc. The white crop marks were added later to prepare the photograph for publication.

Harold W. Gunther joined up in the trench. Yardley had a bazooka, and his first round hit the edge of the firing slit; the second went through. Taking advantage of this, the group left Yardley to watch the embrasure and dashed around the OP without drawing enemy fire. On the other side of the structure they found Corporal Aguzzi, watching the main entrance from the landward side.

Lapres' party pushed on toward gun position No.4 and points inland.

Aguzzi had come up from LCA 862, southeast of the OP, with Lieutenant Leagans and Sergeant Cleaves. As they started away from the edge, joined by Tech. 5 LeRoy J. Thompson and Pfc. Charles H. Bellows, Jr., they saw a German close to the OP, throwing grenades over the cliff from shelter of a trench. The OP was not their job, but the party decided to go after the grenadier. Bellows crawled over to No.3 gun position to cover the advance of the party. They threw grenades at the German and moved into the trench when he ducked under the entrance to the OP. Aguzzi found a shell hole from which he could watch the main entrance, while three Rangers tried to skirt the OP on the east and get at it from the rear. Cleaves was wounded by a mine the only casualty from this cause during the day. Thompson got close enough to hear a radio working inside the OP, looked for the aerial on top, and shot it off. After throwing a grenade through the entrance Lieutenant Leagans and Thompson decided to let the OP wait for demolitions, and went off on their original mission farther inland. Aguzzi, staying to watch the entrance, was surprised a few minutes later by the appearance of Lieutenant Lapres' party, coming from the rear of the OP. Two small groups of Rangers had been attacking the OP from opposite sides, neither aware of the other's presence.

This was not the last group to pass Aguzzi from the tip of the Pointe. After Lapres' men had moved past the OP, four more Rangers from LCA 861 came up the single rope. As they joined Yardley in the trench facing the embrasure, enemy small-arms fire opened up again. The five Rangers talked it over. They had further missions on the other side of the OP, but there were still enemy in the structure, who could not be left free to bring fire on the men still down on the beach. Medeiros and Yardley considered going down to get demolitions, but decided they couldn't give enough covering fire to get a Ranger close to the embrasure with the explosive. Finally, it was decided to leave Yardley and Medeiros in position to 'button-up' the seaward side of the OP while the others went past. With Yardley and Medeiros watching to cover their movement with fire, the three Rangers went along the trench to pass the OP on the west side. Near the end of the trench, small-arms fire came at them from some position on the top of the OP which Medeiros could not spot, and Pfc. George W. Mackey was killed; the two others made it safely to the inland side.

For the rest of D-Day and through the following night, Yardley and Medeiros stayed in their trench on one side of the OP while Aguzzi watched the main entrance. Neither guard knew the other was there. Demolitions could have been used on Aguzzi's side, but nobody bothered to bring them up for use; there was no sign of action from the enemy in the OP. (On the afternoon of D+1 the nest was finally cleaned out. Two satchel charges of C-2 were thrown in the entrance, and Aguzzi, still on guard, figured the enemy must be wiped out. But eight unwounded Germans swarmed out with their hands up, and only one body was found inside. The Rangers were never sure how many enemy had been in the post, for the OP, like most positions in the fortified area, was connected with underground passages which the Rangers had neither numbers nor time to investigate fully. These underground routes, connecting shelters with each other and with a maze of ruined trenches, probably contributed to troubles on the Pointe during D-Day.)

Except at the OP, the first Ranger groups had crossed through the fortified area without seeing an enemy. The last parties to arrive from the beach began to get some evidence that there were still Germans close by. The anti-aircraft position just west of the Pointe put bursts of automatic fire on any Rangers who exposed themselves, and sniping started from the area near gun position No.6. A group from Company D (LCA 858) was working through that vicinity; their story is known only from the one survivor of the action.

Pfc. William Cruz, slightly wounded on the beach, came up just after Colonel Rudder had moved his CP to the cliff top (about 0745), and Cruz was assigned to guard the CP. He and Ranger Eberle went after a sniper near gun position No.4, and in doing so drew machine-gun fire from the anti-aircraft position to the west. Somebody ordered them to 'go after it'. When they started out, sliding from cover of one crater to another, they came up with Tech/Sgt. Richard J. Spleen, Tech/Sgt. Clifton E. Mains, and a group of eight or ten Rangers, in cover just west of No.6 position. This party was considering an attack on the anti-aircraft position, but hesitated to open fire for fear of drawing German artillery shells, which were beginning to hit near the fortified area from positions somewhere inland. After a time the Rangers started to crawl through shell holes toward the anti-aircraft position, slowed by fear of mines. A German helmet came up out of a crater ahead; the Rangers near Cruz saw the stick under it and knew enough to avoid fire, but somebody just behind them took the bait. Almost immediately, artillery and mortar shells began to search the area. Bunched too closely in a row of shell holes, the Company D party took off in all directions to spread out.

Private Cruz moved back toward No.6 emplacement, and found himself completely alone in the maze of craters. Yelling to locate the others, he heard Sergeant Mains call 'OK'. After a 15-minute wait, with enemy fire diminishing, Cruz began to crawl back toward the Pointe. Just as he reached a ruined trench near No. 6 position, he saw Sergeant Spleen and two other Rangers disappear around the corner of a connecting trench. Without warning, intense small-arms fire started up, not only from the anti-aircraft position to the west but from German machine pistols close by. As he hugged the bottom of the trench, Cruz could hear men moving. A few Germans passed by on his limited horizon, but without noticing him. Then, only a few yards from his hole, guns were thrown into the air; Cruz thought they came up from the trench where Spleen's party had been. Cruz kept quiet, the burst of firing died away quickly, and no one else came in sight. After a considerable wait, Cruz crawled back toward the CP, only 200 yards away. Near the wrecked No. 6 emplacement, he passed a pile of American weapons lying on the ground, 8 or 9 rifles and some revolvers and Tommy guns. He figured these were left there when the Rangers surrendered.

Observation on the Pointe was so limited that no one else had seen the action or any part of it. Ten Rangers had simply disappeared, with Cruz's report and the abandoned weapons as the only indication of their fate. The best guess was that the Germans had attacked by filtering into the area through wrecked trenches connecting the fortified zone with the anti-aircraft gun; as another possibility, they may have emerged from underground shelters on the Pointe.

Cruz's report served notice at Colonel Rudder's CP that trouble could be expected from the west flank of the Pointe. In fact, enemy opposition based on the anti-aircraft position was to be a source of serious difficulty for the next two days.

Advance to the Highway

The revival of German resistance at the Pointe was unknown to the Ranger parties which had been first to cross it, drawing only scattered fire from the western flank. As they passed beyond the fortified area, some artillery and mortar shells began to drop near them, and they were aware of light small-arms fire from ahead (south). This slowed down the leaders, and the original parties of two and three men began to merge in larger groups. The Rangers from Companies E and D (less elements detained on the Pointe) tended to come together on an axis of advance along the north-south exit road from the Pointe to the highway. Somewhat to their east, the one boat team of Company F that left the Pointe area struck south on a course through fields. The early advance inland can best be followed in terms of these two main groups.

The bulk of the group that started down the exit road was made up of Rangers from LCAs 888 (Company E) and 858 (Company D). The party from 888 had come up, after some delay, on extension ladders and started out with 15 men under 1st Sgt. Robert W. Lang. After finding No.3 casemate, a junk-pile of broken steel and concrete, Lang's group moved south. They began to meet artillery fire, coming in salvos of three, and shifting toward the Pointe with each salvo. Lang stopped for a moment to try for a contact on his 536 radio, with the idea of warning the fire-support party that his men were moving out of the fortified area. He could not make his connection. When he started forward again, artillery fire was falling between him and his men ahead, so Lang turned left into the torn-up fields, where he picked up three stray Rangers of Company E, and then joined a group under Lieutenant Arman of Company F.

The Company E Rangers meanwhile were reaching the assembly area, near the start of the exit road. Here they met up with a dozen men of Company D, who had checked gun positions Nos.4 and 5 and had left Sergeant Spleen with a few men near No. 6 to deal with enemy who were firing from the anti-aircraft position.

2nd Battalion – Small Unit Action Report continues:

The D and E group now amounted to about 30 men. Without waiting for others to arrive, they started along the exit road, taking as much cover as possible in a communications trench along its edge, and keeping in a single file. German artillery, estimated as light guns (75s or 88s), were searching the area with timed fire, and from the assembly area onward, the Rangers began to meet machine-gun fire from the right flank, and small-arms fire to their left front. They suffered serious casualties in the next few hundred yards: seven killed and eight wounded. Despite these losses, the total size of the force was increasing as it caught up with small advance parties who had left the Pointe earlier, or as latecomers tagged on to the rear of the file.

The first objective was a group of ruined farm buildings, almost halfway to the highway. German snipers who had been using the building pulled out before the Rangers got there. Fire from destroyers' guns as well as enemy shells was hitting around the farm, and the Rangers made no pause. Ahead, the ground was open, and the trench used thus far in the advance came to an end at the buildings. The next cover, 35 to 40 yards south, was a communications trench that crossed the exit road. To reach it, men were sent out one or two at a time, moving fast and taking different routes across an area exposed to machine-gun fire. The only casualty was a Ranger who fell on a comrade's bayonet as he jumped into the trench. Beyond the trench a pair of concrete pillars flanked the exit road, with a crude roadblock between the pillars. Three Germans came straight down the road toward the Pointe, spotted the Rangers, and ducked behind the block. BAR fire failed to flush them out, but after one round (a dud) from a bazooka, the Germans fled. The Rangers resumed their advance down the exit road. Some machine-gun fire had been coming from the next farm; Lapres reached it with his four men to find the enemy had left. For a few minutes Lapres was isolated there, as machine-gun fire from the flanks pinned down the main Ranger party. Some friendly support fire, which the Rangers could not trace, apparently silenced the machine guns.

This was the last of German resistance and Lapres' advance party made the final stretch to the blacktop without any trouble. As they came to it, they saw Tech. 5 Davis of Company F coming through the fields on their left, and a few minutes later a larger party of Company F men came along the highway from the east. At 0815, barely an hour since the landing, the Rangers had reached their final objective – good time, even though enemy opposition had clearly suffered from disorganization. As the survivors of the group put it later, the reason for the speed of their advance was simple: enemy artillery fire seemed to be 'tailing them all the way', and this discouraged any delay.

Most of Company F's parties had stayed near the Pointe, drawn successively into a fight on the eastern flank. The party that reached the highway was from LCA 887, led by Lieutenant Arman and Sergeant Petty. Petty and three men had left the cliff edge first, found No.2 gun position destroyed and empty, and then started south on a course about 200 yards east of the exit road. When they reached the outskirts of the fortified area, Lieutenant Arman joined them with five more Rangers, and decided to push toward the blacktop without waiting for the rest of his platoon.

Their course led through what had been marked on their maps as a mined area, wired and dotted with posts set against air landings. The bombardment, which had churned up the ground even this far from the Pointe, may have detonated the mines or buried them in debris, for they gave the Rangers no trouble. Lieutenant Arman's men could see shells hit along the exit road to their right; for their own part, they saw no enemy. Enemy mortars somewhere to the south put down pattern fire in fields near them, but the fire was apparently unobserved and caused no casualties. The group of a dozen men worked forward in squad column, covering the distance from crater to crater in short bounds. As they came to the ruins of a farm lane, running north-south between hedgerows, Sergeant Lang and three Company E men came over from the east and joined the advance.

Lieutenant Arman led the party straight down the lane, while Petty went left across fields to scout toward the Chateau. There was no sign of enemy on this flank and Petty rejoined at the intersection of the lane with the blacktop highway, where the Rangers turned west, moving along the edges. As they reached the cluster of houses forming the hamlet of Au Guay, a machine gun opened up about 100 yards ahead, somewhere near the road. The enemy had delivered his fire too soon; the Rangers scattered without suffering casualties and began to work around the south edge of the hamlet to reach the enemy gun. Sergeant Petty, with two men, was startled by the sudden appearance of two Germans apparently rising out of the ground, not ten feet away. Petty dropped flat and fired his BAR as he fell. The burst missed, but the Germans were already shouting 'Kamerad'. They had come out of a deep shelter hole which Petty's men had not spotted. The Rangers found no other enemy at Au Guay, and the machine gun had disappeared when they reached the west side of the hamlet. Within a few minutes Arman's party met the Rangers who had come out to the highway along the exit road.

Beside the two main groups whose course has been followed to the highway, several smaller parties reached the same objective on their own. One of these can be followed in detail; this is worthwhile as illustrating other aspects of a 'confused' action. The continuity in this story is furnished by Private Anderson. Landing in LCA 884, he went up on the ladders of the next craft to his left, at the extreme left of the landing zone. On top, he and two other 884 men decided on their own to go after the German emplacement, somewhere near the cliff edge to their east, which was still raking the landing beach with automatic weapons. (They were unaware that some of 883's men had already started on the same mission, nor did they see them during their own effort.) Moving fast along a hedgerow that skirted the cliff, they got to within a hundred yards of the enemy emplacement, could not locate the position of the guns, and decided these must be out of reach below the cliff top.

Reversing course back to the ladders, Anderson left the other two Rangers and joined Pfc. John Bacho and S/Sgt. James E. Fulton, who were just starting south through the fields to make the blacktop. The three men followed along hedgerow lines, using the 'Buddy' system, one man covering as two moved, in a leap-frogging advance. Within a hundred yards they caught up with Lieutenant Hill and two other Rangers from 884, going in the same direction. The only sign of enemy was occasional sniper fire. At the first lateral hedgerow they turned west; Bacho and Fulton went through the hedgerow to guard the flanks and lost touch with the others, eventually joining Lieutenant Arman's group near the highway.

Hill's party, now four men, worked west to reach the double-hedgerowed lane, picking up a willing prisoner from the field on their right. Machine-gun fire to the west, near the exit road, drew their attention, and the four Rangers started angling in that direction. As they were passing through a field of stubble wheat, automatic fire came at them from the direction of Pointe du Hoe, and forced them to crawl. So far the gun they were after had not spotted them and was not firing in their direction. About 25 feet from the exit road, Lieutenant Hill and Anderson reached the cover of a low embankment. The machine gun was just beyond the road ahead of them. Hill stood up to look at the position and to Anderson's amazement shouted, 'You ... . you couldn't hit a bull in the ass with a bass fiddle!' This drew enemy fire; as Hill dropped back into cover, Anderson tossed him a grenade, Hill threw it, and the machine-gun fire stopped. A few minutes later, Lieutenant Lapres came down the exit road with the advance group of Company E, and Hill's action may have saved this party from surprise fire. The four Company F men now served as flank patrol for the further advance along the exit road, moving one hedgerow to the left of Lapres. Anderson, as he neared the blacktop, fired at somebody to the west near the road intersection, but was not sure (later) whether it was a German or Sergeant Lang.

The Rangers at the highway numbered about 50 men, with all three companies represented. Their mission was to block movement along the coastal highway; expecting to see the 116th Infantry and the 5th Rangers arrive at any moment on the Vierville road, their main concern was the highway west, toward Grandcamp. Such enemy resistance as had been met seemed to come from west and south, so they made their dispositions accordingly. Bordering the south side of the highway near its junction with the exit road, a series of narrow fields ended in a hedgerow that ran east-west, overlooked orchards sloping down to a creek, and gave some observation across the small valley of the creek. Along the hedgerow they found enemy dugouts and fox holes conveniently prepared on the north side of the hedge. The contingents from Company E and Company F occupied this line for a distance of four fields, two to each side of a lane that ran from the highway down to the creek. An outpost of Company F men went down the gentle slope toward the creek and took position where they could watch the farther side of the little valley. A German dugout near the lane was picked for a CP, used by Lieutenant Arman (Company F) and Lieutenants Lapres and Leagans of Company E. Except for two stragglers picked up in the fields, there was no sign of enemy in the neighborhood.

The 20 men of Company D were given the assignment of covering the west flank toward Grandcamp. Sergeant Lomell placed his men along both edges of the highway, with a combat outpost at the western end of his line consisting of a BAR man and six riflemen with a grenade launcher. This outpost could cover the road and had good observation toward the valley between the Rangers and Grandcamp. The rest of the Company D men could watch the fields north and south of the highway. Toward the sea, the fields were believed to be mined, and this would simplify defense on that side.

Active patrolling was started at once on all sides of the thinly-held positions. About 0900, a two-man patrol from D went down the double-hedgerowed lane that ran south from the highway near Company D's outpost. About 250 yards along the lane, Sergeant Lomell and S/Sgt. Jack E. Kuhn walked into a camouflaged gun position; there, set up in battery, were five of the enemy 155's missing from the Pointe. They were in position to fire toward Utah Beach, but could easily have been switched for use against Omaha. Piles of ammunition were at hand, points on the shells and charges ready, but there was no indication of recent firing. Not a German was in sight, and occasional sniper fire from a distance could hardly be intended *as a defense of the battery. So effective was the camouflage that Lomell and Kuhn, though they could later spot the guns from the highway, had seen nothing until they were right in the position.*

With Kuhn covering him against possible defenders, Sergeant Lomell went into the battery and set off thermite grenades in the recoil mechanism of two guns, effectively disabling them. After bashing in the sights, of a third gun, he went back for more grenades. Before he could return, another patrol from Company E had finished the job. This patrol, led by S/Sgt. Frank A. Rupinski, had come through the fields and (like Lomell and Kuhn) were in the gun position before they saw it. Failing to notice the fact that some disabling work had already been done, Rupinski's patrol dropped a thermite grenade down each barrel, and removed some of the sights. After throwing grenades into the powder charges and starting a fire, the patrol decided the guns were out of action and withdrew.

Just why the German guns were thus left completely undefended and unused is still a mystery. One theory, based on the fact that some artillerymen were captured that day on the Pointe, was that bombardment caught them there in quarters, and they were unable to get back to their position. All that can be stated with assurance is that the Germans were put off balance and disorganized by the combined effects of bombardment and assault, to such an extent that they never used the most dangerous battery near the assault beaches, but left it in condition to be destroyed by weak patrols.

---

6 June

Small Unit Action Report continued:

Ranger landings at Omaha Beach

Eighteen LCAs, carrying the 5th Ranger Battalion and Companies A and B of the 2nd Rangers, had been waiting in the assembly area for word of the assault on Pointe du Hoe. One LCA had already been swamped further out, its men transferring to a passing LCT. After delaying 15 minutes beyond the time limit (0700), the Rangers still had no word and were forced to conclude that the assault had not succeeded. According to plan, they started in toward Dog Green to land behind the 1st Battalion of the 116th and go inland through the Vierville exit.

Approaching shore, Lt. Col. Max F. Schneider got a clear impression of the conditions on Dog Green and ordered the flotilla to swing east. Even so, Companies A and B of the 2nd Rangers, on the right flank, came in on the edge of Dog Green and experienced what the 1st BLT of the 116th had already been through. One of their 5 craft was sunk by a mine in the outer obstacles, and the 34 men had to swim in under fire. Small-arms and mortar fire caught the other craft as they touched down. The small Ranger companies numbered about 65 officers and men each; some 35 in Company A and 27 in Company B got to the sea wall. Only a few hundred yards further east, on the favoured section of Dog White, 13 out of the 14 craft carrying the 5th Battalion touched down close together, in two waves. LCI 91 was struck and set afire while the Rangers were passing through the obstacles beside it, but none of their craft was hit. The 450 men of the battalion got across the beach and up to the sea wall with a loss of only 5 or 6 men to scattered small-arms fire. They found the sea-wall shelter already fully occupied by 116th troops, and crowded in behind them.

By and large, the later waves of assault infantry on the western beaches had fared much better than in the first landings. Five of the eight companies of the 116th RCT had landed with sections well together and losses relatively light. Some had been shielded by the smoke of burning grass, but the better fortune was probably due also to the fact that, as landings increased in volume, enemy positions still in action were not able to concentrate on the many targets offered. By 0730, in contrast to the earlier situation, assault units were lined along the whole beach-front in the 116th's zone. The weakest area was in front of Exit D-1; Dog Green, the zone of the 1st BTL, had almost no assault elements on it capable of further action.

Beginning at 0730, regimental command parties began to arrive. The main command group of the 116th RCT included Col. Charles D. W. Canham and General Cota. LCVP 71 came in on Dog White, bumping an obstacle and nudging the Teller mine until it dropped off, without exploding. Landing in three feet of water, the party lost one officer in getting across the exposed area. From the standpoint of influencing further operations, they could not have hit a better point in the 116th zone. To their right and left, Company C and some 2nd Battalion elements were crowded against the embankment on a front of a few hundred yards, the main Ranger force was about to come into the same area, and enemy fire from the bluffs just ahead was masked by smoke and ineffective. The command group was well located to play a major role in the next phase of action.

The following message was received by the Naval Commander Western Task Force, "First wave landed Dog Green 0635B, second wave 0636B, first wave assault group O-1 landed 0635B, one LCA capsized, one LCT (A) sinking with engine room flooded. Success signal for capture of PONTE DU HOE was reported by V Corps". A report was received at 0807B that "Returning boats reported floating mines near the beach endangering landing; many boats swamped and many personnel in the water".

The most important penetration on the western beaches was made by Company C, 116th Infantry and by the 5th Ranger Battalion, which had landed partly on top of Company C. Both units were in relatively good condition after the landings and had suffered only minor losses, but the men were crowded shoulder to shoulder, sometimes several rows deep, along the shingle at the base of the timber sea wall.

The 5th Ranger Battalion joined the advance very soon after it started and some of the Rangers were intermingled with Company C as they went forward. The battalion had reached the sea wall just before 0800, in platoon formations. Hasty preparations were made for assault, and Colonel Schneider passed the word 'Tallyho' to his officers, this being the order for each platoon to make its own way beyond the bluffs to the assembly area south of Vierville. About 0810 the Rangers began to cross the road; what with the confusion at the beach and the smoke ahead, few of them realized that Company C was already on the move in the same zone. Four gaps were blown in the wire with bangalores and the men went across the beach flat at the double, then slowed to a crawl on the steep hillside. Heavy smoke covered them on the climb, forcing some men to put on gas masks. By the time the crest was reached, platoon formations were disorganized and contacts lost. Just over the bluff top, German warning signs enabled the Rangers to avoid a minefield from which engineers later took 150 mines. The first groups up, a platoon of Company A and some men of Company E, went straight on inland and disappeared. The other platoons were on top by 0830 and stopped to reorganize. On the left flank of the battalion, Company D's platoons had to clean out a few Germans from a trench system along the bluff edge, knocking out a machine gun sited just below the crest and firing along the beach. The battalion had lost only eight men, to small-arms fire that became more ineffective as the movement progressed across the beach flat.

The advance from Dog White Beach had taken place on a narrow front of less than 300 yards. By 0830 the last groups were leaving the sea wall, and the command party established itself temporarily halfway up the bluff. Unsuccessful efforts were made to reach 1st Division units by SCR 300. Fire from enemy mortars began to range in on the slope for the first time, killing two men standing near General Cota and knocking down the General and his aide. The headquarters party moved on up to the top, joined by some elements of Company G and a machine-gun platoon of Company H, which had reached Dog White after moving laterally along the sea wall from D-3 draw. The command party found work to do on the high ground. Company C, the 5th Ranger Battalion, and small elements of other units were intermingled in the fields just beyond the bluff, disordered by the advance and not sure of the next move. Scattered small- arms fire was keeping men down, and some shells began to hit in the vicinity.

Just east of Dog White, the penetration area was widened before 0900 by the action of small parties from Companies F and B. Remnants of three boat sections of Company F crossed the beach flat and got up the bluff; a short distance behind them came an isolated section of B. Neither group had to contend with enemy resistance at the crest. The Company F sections drifted right and eventually joined the 5th Rangers. The Company B party of a dozen men started left, toward Les Moulins, and was stopped by a machine gun. 1st Lt. William B. Williams assaulted it single-handed, was wounded, and ordered his men to move to Vierville.

The penetrations described thus far opened the way for progress inland on an important scale, but they do not tell the whole story of the assault. At several parts of the beach lesser groups fought their way off the flat in isolated battles, often without knowing what was happening elsewhere. Stray boat sections of assault infantry, scratch parties of engineers, advance elements of artillery units, stranded Navy men, and other personnel took part in small actions which helped in weakening and disorganizing enemy resistance along the beaches. Few of these actions got into the records, and some cannot be located accurately in place and time. Two, involving Ranger units, can be taken as examples.

Company C, 2nd Ranger Battalion, was probably the first assault unit to reach the high ground (beach sector Charlie) and did so in an area where cliffs begin to border the western beach. Landing in the opening assault wave, about 30 men survived the ordeal of crossing the sands and found shelter at the base of a 90-foot cliff, impossible to climb except at a few points. Three men went off immediately to the west, looking for a spot to go up. Three hundred yards away they tried a crevice in the slope and made it by using bayonets for successive hand holds, pulling each other along. 1st Lt. William D. Moody, in charge of the party, brought along 4 toggle ropes and attached them to stakes in a minefield 15 feet below the crest. Enemy small-arms fire opened up from the left, near a supposedly fortified house. Moody and one Ranger went along the cliff edge toward the house, reached a point above Company C, and shouted down directions. The unit displaced to the ropes and monkey-walked them to the top; all men were up by 0730. While the movement was in progress, Capt. Ralph E. Goranson saw an LCVP landing troops (a section of Company B, 116th RCT) just below on the beach and sent a man back to guide them to the ropes.

Captain Goranson decided to go left toward the fortified house and knock out any enemy positions there which would cause trouble on Dog Beach; then, to proceed on his mission toward Pointe et Raz de la Percée. When the house was reached, the Rangers found that just beyond it lay a German strongpoint consisting of a maze of dugouts and trenches, including machine-gun emplacements and a mortar position. Captain Goranson put men in an abandoned trench just west of the house and started to feel out the enemy positions on the other side. This began a series of small attacks which continued for hours without any decisive result. The boat section of Company B, 116th RCT, came up early and joined in, but even with this reinforcement Captain Goranson's party was too small to knock out the enemy position. Three or four times, attacking parties got around the house and into the German positions, destroying the mortar post and inflicting heavy losses. Enemy reinforcements kept coming up along communication trenches from the Vierville draw, and the Ranger parties were not quite able to clean out the system of trenches and dugouts. Finally, toward the end of the afternoon, the Rangers and the Company B section succeeded in occupying the strongpoint and ending resistance. They had suffered only 2 casualties; (a Quartermaster burial party later reported 69 enemy dead in the position). This action had tied up one of the main German firing positions protecting the Vierville draw.

Small elements of the 2nd Ranger Battalion also fought their own way off Dog White, just west of the main penetration area. Less than half of Companies A and B had reached the shelter of the sea wall, about 0740. Some tanks, firing at enemy emplacements, were scattered along the beach, but the Rangers saw no other troops and had the impression of being alone on the beach; less than a quarter mile to their left, the 5th Ranger Battalion was touching down on a beach already crowded with assault infantry. Within a few minutes of reaching the wall, the survivors of Companies A and B dashed over the promenade road beyond the sea wall and got into the cover of shrubbery surrounding the wrecked villas that line this stretch of the beach flat. Eighteen Rangers of Company B turned right and, hugging the foot of the slope, went several hundred yards toward the Vierville draw, intending to go up that exit in accordance with original plans. Nearing the draw and facing heavy fire on an open stretch of the flat, the group re-traced its steps.

Meantime, Company A's men and a few from B, after crossing the road in several scattered groups led by non-commissioned officers, had worked through the villas and were trying the bluff at different points. They were joined by a machinegun section of Company D, 116th RCT, and three DD tanks helped by silencing enemy positions on the flanks which had been giving trouble. Two Rangers of Company A reached the top above and found enemy trenches, containing two or three machine gun emplacements, in plain sight just beyond the military crest. In a few minutes another group of six Rangers joined up, and they started out to investigate the apparently empty trenches. Machine-gun fire opened from two points as Germans came out of dugouts and manned their positions. They had waited too long. The leading Rangers were within 20 yards, and more small parties were coming up behind them. Working in twos and threes, they mopped up the enemy emplacements, taking six prisoners and killing as many more. Only three of the attacking force were casualties. Company B now came up, having got back from its try toward the Vierville exit, and the 5th Ranger Battalion was in sight on the bluff top to the left. The 2nd Battalion men joined them for the move inland. This action took place between 0800 and 0830, widened the area of penetration on Dog White, and probably aided in the success of the larger advance to the east by covering its right flank.

In the period 0800-0900, upwards of 600 men went off Dog White Beach. Besides Company C, which led the way, the advance included most of the main Ranger force (eight companies), 116th Headquarters, some engineer troops of the 121st Engineer Combat Battalion, and fragments of Companies B, F, G, and H. Reaching the top in small groups, the troops tended to stop and bunch in the first fields near the edge of the bluff. What little order they had was lost as they became intermingled with units arriving later, and reorganization was a slow process. Though there were no enemy positions in action near by, snipers, harassing long-range fire from a few machine guns, and a brief period of shelling from 88-mm guns contributed to the confusion, and it was two hours before much progress was made. One small group had long since gone *inland by itself. A platoon of 5th Battalion Rangers, 1st Lt. Charles H. Parker, Jr., commanding, on reaching the bluff crest had seen no other troops, and immediately started southwest to get around Vierville and reach the battalion assembly area. After making a half-mile without meeting opposition, the platoon was stopped by enemy fire from hedgerows near the Chateau de Vaumicel, just south of Vierville.*

They spent the rest of the morning working past this fire toward the chateau grounds.

When the CP group of the 116th RCT came over the bluff after 0900 they found Rangers and 116th elements scattered all through the fields ahead, with leading elements near the coastal highway. The communications section of headquarters had landed on another beach; the only working radio belonged to the liaison officer of the 743rd Tank Battalion. Completely out of touch with division, Colonel Canham had no contacts with any of his battalion headquarters, did not know what was happening at the exits in the 116th area, and could only assume that the rest of the assault battalions were on their way to assembly areas.

Below: 1st Infantry Division After Action Report: The report states that Maisy Battery has been destroyed. [Author: Yet the battery continued to fire throughout the day and beyond. It is likely again that the battery simply ceased fire during this attack. Interesting also, that no communication was made from the 1st Inf. Div. to tell Lt. Col. Rudder that this had happened, one assumes because it did not change his orders and he would still be required to reach his D-Day assault line (beyond Maisy) two hours before midnight.]

> The Division Commander notified Commanding General, 50th Division that progress was slow, with fighting on the beaches.
>
> Word was received at 0930B that the Rangers had landed safely with heavy opposition; the beach was not clear of obstacles and dangerous for LCA's. At this time, the Division was told that one Allied squadron armed with 2000 pound bombs was attacking MAISY battery, which was reported by 0945B as being completely destroyed.
>
> The Division notified the Navy that enemy fire on beach Easy Red was keeping LCI's from landing. At 0950B, the Assistant Division Commander notified the Division Commander aboard the USS ANCON, "There are too many vehicles on the beach; send combat troops." Special Situation Report 1 to the Naval Commander, WTF, stated, "The first wave landed Easy Red at 0635, Dog Green 0635 second wave Dog Green 0636 and second through seventh wave landed Easy Red by 0735. 3d Battalion 16th Infantry Regimental CP exit E-3 Easy Red and moved to the right. Unconfirmed reports from V Corps report capture of POINTE DU HOE. Landing

Other Maisy-related radio reports were issued and received in the morning of D-Day – here are some examples.

> V SC
> FROM   CTF 124
> ACTION   DIV BAT 5
>
> FIGHTER BOMBERS REPOTEEEEEE REPORT MAISY BATTERIES DESTROYED BT 061006B
>
> PLAIN LANGUAGE   ROUTINE

> SB   VISUAL
>
> FROM DIV BAT 5
> ACTION CTF 124
>
> LAST REPORT FROM PLANE WAS THAT BATTERIES AT MAISY WERE COMPLETLY DESTROYED HAVE BEEN UNABLE TO VERIFY FROM SFCP NUMBER   L ONE BATTERIES HAVE NOT FIRED AT ANYTIME DURING NIGHT X BT 060945

> V SC   OP   SECRET
> FROM   HQ V CORPS (NR 2)
> ACTION   HQ 1ST ARMY, ACHERNAR
> INFO   30 BRIT CORPS
>   OBSTACLES MINED, PROGRESS SLOW, 1ST BN
> 116TH INF REPORTED 0748 BEING HELD UP BY
> M 6 FIRE.   BATTERY MAISY REPORTED FIRING YET
>
> 0624 AIR ALERT MISSION REPORTED NOT FIRING
> FROM MAISY AT PEEEEEEO917.   TWO LCT'S
> KNOCKED OUT OF EEEE BY ARTILLERY FIRE, DO
> TANKS FOR FOX GREEN SWAMPED BETWEEN DISEMBARK-
> ATION POINT AND LINE OF DEPARTURE.(SIGNED
> GEROW) BT 0945B
> CC WA FIRE, DD

> V CIC
> AIR TO GROUND RADIO
>
> ONE SQUADRON ARMED WITH 2000 LB BOMBS ATTACKING MAISY BATTERY

Below: 'Maisy reported firing at 0824hrs.' Later: 'Mission reported no firing from Maisy at 0917hrs.'

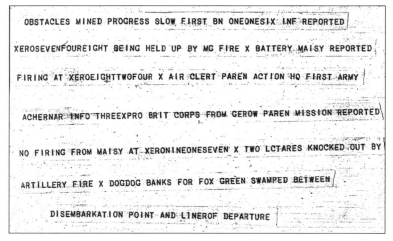

OBSTACLES MINED PROGRESS SLOW FIRST BN ONEONESIX INF REPORTED

XEROSEVENFOUREIGHT BEING HELD UP BY MG FIRE X BATTERY MAISY REPORTED

FIRING AT XEROEIGHTTWOFOUR X AIR CLERT PAREN ACTION HQ FIRST ARMY

ACHERNAR INFO THREEXPRO BRIT CORPS FROM GEROW PAREN MISSION REPORTED

NO FIRING FROM MAISY AT XERONINEONESEVEN X TWO LCTARES KNOCKED OUT BY

ARTILLERY FIRE X DOGDOG BANKS FOR FOX GREEN SWAMPED BETWEEN

DISEMBARKATION POINT AND LINEROF DEPARTURE

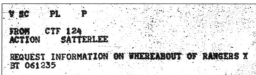

V SC   PL   P

FROM   CTF 124
ACTION   SATTERLEE

REQUEST INFORMATION ON WHEREABOUT OF RANGERS X
BT 061235

1006hrs Maisy is reported destroyed – again.

1006	65	CTF 124	Fighter bombers report MAISY btrys destroyed at 061006B.	Rad	Div Bat 5 & J

The Historical Division report:

Movement finally began between 1000-1100, with General Cota assisting in getting units started. The 5th Ranger Battalion planned to push across the coastal highway and go around Vierville to the south, while the 116th elements went toward the village. The Rangers' advance in column was stopped when the first elements reached the highway and an enemy machine gun opened up from the hedgerow one field to the south. The column halted while a platoon went after the machine gun by working down an axial hedgerow. In the course of this action, another enemy machine gun opened up to the left of the first. Another Ranger platoon attacked this gun, and once again uncovered new enemy fire positions along the hedgerows still farther east. A third outflanking attack was started, ran into additional machine-gun fire, and was called back pending an attempt to get artillery support. The 58th Armored Field Artillery Battalion had just put some guns ashore, but the forward observer reported that their fire at this range was impossible because of the mask presented by the bluff. About four hours had been consumed in these efforts.

At 1400 the Rangers gave up the attempt to move south from the highway and instead, followed the coastal highway into Vierville. That route had already been taken several hours before. Company C and small elements of other 116th Companies, some of them moving in isolated groups, had gone that way; so had Company B of the 5th Rangers, which headed down the Vierville highway under the mistaken impression that the Ranger Battalion column was following just behind. With General Cota close behind the leading elements, Vierville was entered before 1100. Except for scattered fire from the outskirts when the advance was starting, no enemy resistance was encountered. A platoon of Company B, 116th Infantry, went through Vierville out of contact with the rest and turned south toward the chateau. On the way, they encountered a German resistance nest, assaulted it, and took 14 prisoners. A little beyond the chateau, the platoon was attacked by Germans who had just deployed from three trucks coming up from the south. The Company B unit, reduced to 25 men and lacking automatic weapons, withdrew to the chateau and stopped the enemy attack with well-aimed rifle fire. Here they were joined about noon by Parker's platoon from Company A, 5th Rangers, which had been coming toward the chateau across country. Neither party knew there were any other friendly forces near Vierville.

Company B of the 5th Rangers and Company C, 116th Infantry, passed through Vierville before noon and started west on the coastal highway toward Pointe du Hoe. About 500 yards out of Vierville they were stopped by fire from prepared emplacements along hedgerows which ran at right angles to the highway. During the next few hours, the Rangers and Company C worked together in efforts to outflank or neutralize this position. Enemy machine-gun positions were well camouflaged and hard to locate; every time a move was started across open fields, it was checked by fire from German rifles and automatic weapons at ranges of two to three hundred yards. At 1700 the main Ranger force came up and plans for an attack were started, then called off later in the evening. Colonel Canham decided not to press the effort along the coastal highway toward Pointe du Hoe, since the 5th Rangers constituted the larger part of his forces for defense of Vierville.

The command group of the 116th RCT had come through Vierville about noon on its way to the prearranged CP location, a little southwest of the village. When the small party reached that spot, sniped at all the way, they found themselves out of contact with any friendly units and uncomfortably isolated. A platoon of Company B, 5th Rangers, came by on a flanking maneuver and was impressed as a guard for the CP. Patrols sent towards Louvieres to find the 2nd Battalion fought their way for a thousand yards south through scattered opposition and returned without having seen any friendly forces. Small skirmishes took place near the CP all afternoon, and 15 Germans were killed in the immediate vicinity. At 1830, the commander of the 1st Battalion reported in, having got up from Charlie Beach, and Colonel Canham found out for the first time what had happened on the beaches in front of Vierville exit. Toward midnight, he learned that the 2nd and 3rd Battalions were near St-Laurent.

At nightfall the Vierville area was the weakest part of the beachhead. The 5th Ranger Battalion, remnants of the 1st Battalion, 116th, and a few small elements of engineer units and of the 2nd and 3rd Battalions (a group from Company K arrived in the evening and was used for headquarters security) were holding defensive positions west and southwest of the village. Separated during the day, these units were finally brought into contact, but no other friendly forces in any strength were nearer than St-Laurent. No reinforcements had landed in the Vierville sector, and the exit from the beach was only beginning to open for traffic by dark.

Yet, had there been any force on hand to use for the purpose, the Vierville draw could have been cleaned up any time during the afternoon. Between 1200 and 1300, heavy naval fire, directed by shore observers with the 116th and including the main batteries of the Texas, was put on the strongpoint guarding D-1 draw. After the first four salvos of four rounds each, the destroyer McCook radioed shore that Germans were leaving concrete emplacements to surrender, 30 prisoners being taken by engineers on the beach. Further fire completed the neutralization of the heavily fortified area. Shortly after the naval guns stopped firing, General Cota went down the exit road to the beach to find out why no traffic had yet come through. Accompanied by four or five men, he got all the way down, past the strongpoints and the anti-tank wall and out onto the beach flat, without drawing more than scattered small-arms fire. Five Germans, taken prisoner from holes in the cliff-side along the way, led the party through a minefield at the entrance. The general saw little activity on the beach flat at D-1. The only infantry nearby were the exhausted remnants of Company A, 116th, and the tanks were further east along the flat.

General Cota walked along the promenade road to investigate conditions at Les Moulins, after finding that engineer troops were about to start work on the obstacles in the Vierville draw.

One 5th Ranger platoon (Company A) managed to get all the way to Pointe du Hoe, four miles through enemy-infested country. At 1430, Lieutenant Parker left the chateau south of Vierville and started for the 5th Rangers' assembly area. On the way, they encountered a small enemy strongpoint and overwhelmed it, killing 2 Germans and capturing 12. The 24 Rangers reached their assembly area, found no one there, concluded the 5th Battalion had gone on toward Pointe du Hoe, and decided to follow. Taking the prisoners with them and moving on secondary roads south of the coastal highway, the platoon got through Englesqueville and on to a point almost south of their goal before they were stopped by fire from prepared enemy positions. Trying again to 'bull through' the opposition, the Rangers found themselves out-flanked and nearly surrounded; they had to fight their way out and make a short withdrawal. They then left the roads, struck north across country, and about 2100 joined the inland group of 2nd Battalion Rangers, in their defensive positions just south of the Grandcamp-Vierville highway. The Company A platoon had not seen the 5th Battalion since leaving the beach, but still believed it must be close behind and so informed Colonel Rudder at the Pointe.

Small Unit Actions Report at Pointe du Hoc continues:

Morning at the Pointe: Action on the Left Flank

The D-Day fighting at Pointe du Hoe can be followed in terms of two main groups: the force that reached the highway and took positions there, and the Rangers who stayed in or near the fortified area at the Pointe itself. Some stayed according to plan; others were diverted from going inland by circumstance and, above all, by the revival of German resistance near or in the fortified area. Two of the three boat teams of Company F were stopped by this resistance in carrying out their first assignments, becoming involved in a series of actions that held them all day near the cliffs just east of the fortified zone.

LCAs 883 and 884 had beached on this flank, several hundred yards to the left of their planned touchdown. Lieutenant Wintz, in command of 883, failed at first to realize that he was facing the cliffs outside the fortified area, and thought bomb damage must be the reason for the unfamiliar look of the terrain. When the first half-dozen men were up the ropes, Wintz sent them out to occupy hedgerows meeting at the southeast corner of the first field inland. Ducking in and out of craters, the men reached the ruined hedgerows without drawing fire; Wintz sent out the rest of the boat team as they came up, except for the mortar men. Men from LCA 884 were beginning to come up on 883's ladders, as Wintz went along the cliffs to the west looking for the company commander, Capt. Otto Masny. But Masny had gone over to the Pointe, and Wintz was not to see him until the end of the day.

Lieutenant Wintz had now oriented himself. His men, plus some from 884 (a few others from 884 went off on their own, inland), were just east of the base of the Pointe. South of them were shell-ploughed fields stretching toward St-Pierre-du-Mont and crossed by only a few hedgerows. Occasional artillery fire and some sniping began from this direction, forcing the Rangers into cover and costing them one rifleman. To the east, about 200 yards along the cliffs from the Company F position, the German automatic weapon (variously described as a machine gun or a light anti-aircraft gun) which had caused so much trouble during the landing was now firing toward the Pointe over the heads of Wintz's men. Except that the gun was somewhere close to the cliff, its position could not be located.

This enemy emplacement, sited to cause trouble for the Rangers still along the beach, was included in the original Company F objectives, and Lieutenant Wintz decided to 'go after it' with five men. Sgt. Charles F. Weilage had set up his mortar in a crater near the cliff, ready to fire once the enemy's position was fixed. A hedgerow skirted the cliff edge eastward; using a drainage ditch on the inland side of this hedgerow, the party worked slowly along, making every effort to stay under cover.

As far as Wintz knew, this was the first attempt to get at the troublesome gun west of the Pointe. Actually, it was the third, a fact that brings out again the scattered and impromptu nature of the early fighting near the Pointe, and the difficulties of maintaining control or observation in the cut-up terrain.

By the time Wintz started (somewhere between 0800 and 0830), two other groups had gone east to reach the German gun position. Almost immediately after getting up, Private Anderson and two other Company F Rangers had started out, failed to locate the gun, and returned. Captain Masny, before he went over to the Pointe, had sent out a three-man patrol consisting of 1st Sgt. Charles E. Frederick, S/Sgt. Robert G. Youso, and Pfc. Herman W. Kiihnl. They started along an east-west hedgerow one field inland, with Frederick covering the other two for the first move. Someone brought up an order for Frederick to report back to Captain Masny; the other two went on, thinking Frederick was following. They got to within 20 yards of where they thought the gun position must be, and as Youso half rose to throw a grenade, he was shot by a German rifleman. Kiihnl went back to find Frederick, while Youso crawled toward safety on the seaward side of the cliff-skirting hedgerow. The two leading Rangers of Wintz's party met him there after he had made about 75 yards.

Wintz's small attacking force was strung out along 200 yards of the cliff hedgerow, with Wintz near the rear, bringing up four more riflemen and an observer for the mortar. The enemy had spotted their movement, and small-arms fire was covering an open space along the route, wounding one man and slowing progress. Nevertheless, the advance was still continuing when an order came from the rear to pull back.

The order had come from some distance and was based on a misapprehension. Sergeant Frederick, called back earlier to report to Captain Masny, had gone as far as No.1 gun position without locating him. Here, Frederick received the order by word of mouth for bringing Wintz back. Frederick relayed the message, but was worried by it and went further into the fortified area to find Masny and verify the order. When Frederick located his captain, Masny explained that he thought Wintz's party was starting south toward the highway, and the purpose of his order had been to keep them near the Pointe. Captain Masny did want the German machine gun neutralized, so Sergeant

Frederick sent a messenger at once, revoking the recall order and telling Wintz to push the attack. It was too late; Wintz and his party were back in their starting positions, having brought their two wounded in.

Lieutenant Wintz reorganized for another effort, again along the cliff edge. It was the fourth attempt at flanking the gun position. Just after movement started, orders came to halt the attack. The message came on SCR 300, one of the few times that a radio order got through from the CP on the Pointe to any of the scattered Ranger parties. Colonel Rudder had decided to try naval fire on the cliff strongpoint. Wintz's men were well situated to observe (and enjoy) the results. A destroyer pulled close in, and, according to the Rangers' recollection, seven salvos were used: they blew the top of the cliff into the sea, and that ended the Rangers' troubles with automatic fire from the eastern cliff position, though German snipers continued to operate from that sector.

It was now well along in the morning (time estimates vary from 1100 to 1200). Before naval fire solved the worst difficulty on the east flank, several hours had been spent in action, which illustrated the difficulties of coordinating action among the scattered Ranger parties. Most of the troops from LCAs 883 and 884, originally scheduled to move on to the highway, had become thoroughly involved near the Pointe and were now kept in the right-angle hedgerow position selected by Lieutenant Wintz at the start of his action. It was suitable for protecting the east side of the Rangers' position from attack.

Morning at the Pointe: The CP Group

Colonel Rudder had gone on top at 0745, and established his CP in a crater between the cliff and a destroyed anti-aircraft gun emplacement. Most of the assault parties had left the fortified area on their several missions, and Colonel Rudder could only wait for reports. Observation in the churned-up wasteland left by the bombardment was very limited, and for the moment there was little that he could do to exercise control. However, there was some work to do near at hand, as the enemy gave disturbing signs of reviving his resistance close to the Pointe. According to testimony by the communications section, this was a British destroyer, with spotting done by Lieutenant Johnson, observer of the 58th Armored Field Artillery Battalion.

Enemy snipers were active, some of them operating inside the fortified area, and steps were immediately taken to eradicate them. Some of the last parties up the cliff, together with headquarters personnel, were sent out to hunt them down. These efforts, repeated many times, were never entirely successful. Through the rest of D-Day, the CP and the whole Pointe area were harassed by snipers who came out of tunnels and trenches, to find plenty of cover in the cratered debris. Patrols combed over the maze of underground positions, but it seemed impossible to clean them out with the small force available. At no time were the snipers numerous, and there were periods when the Rangers could move in the open with impunity, anywhere on the Pointe. But these intervals of calm would be broken at any time by scattered small-arms fire from every direction, or by bursts of automatic fire from the German anti-aircraft position, 300 yards west on the edge of the cliff. Colonel Rudder sustained a thigh wound from this fire during the morning.

Within a half hour after Colonel Rudder's arrival on top, a first attempt to knock out this western strongpoint had ended with the destruction of Sergeant Spleen's small attacking force. This made it clear that the anti-aircraft position was the main center of enemy resistance near the Pointe, and the most dangerous because it afforded a base either for attack into the Rangers' foothold on the Pointe or for efforts to cut off the parties that had gone inland.

Captain Masny, after helping to set up Company F's positions on the left flank, had come over to find Colonel Rudder and was impressed into service at headquarters. He was given the mission of forming a perimeter defense for the CP, using headquarters personnel and any Rangers who had not gone inland. As he was organizing this defense, fire opened up again from the anti-aircraft position. Like Sergeant Spleen earlier, Masny collected the nearest men at hand and went out to attack. Starting with eight men, the group picked up a few more Rangers as it went through the fortified area toward the exit road, planning to swing west. Among the additions was a mortar section from LCA 722. Much earlier, this mortar had been set up to deliver supporting fire for the Company E group moving inland under Lieutenant Lapres. S/Sgt. Millard W. Hayden had accompanied the group, taking with him a sound power phone and half a mile of wire. No calls for fire had come, and communication had been broken off, so the mortar section decided to move inland and join Hayden. Before they had gone far, they were recalled for support of Masny's group, which also had a 30-cal. machine gun, taken off a DUKW.

Masny's force turned west where the exit road met the remains of a lane that led toward the enemy strongpoint. They had made only a hundred yards progress when rifle, machine-gun, and mortar fire opened up, from their left flank as well as from the strongpoint. Scattered among craters, the Rangers started a fire fight, the mortar set up in a hole about 50 yards to the rear of the riflemen where Masny directed its fire. When a white flag showed over the

German emplacement, the men with Masny were wary and stayed under cover. But two Rangers on the right of the skirmish line, near gun position No.6, stood up in the open. Masny's yell of warning was too late to save them from a burst of machine-gun bullets, and the fire fight resumed. German artillery came into action, from somewhere inland. The first rounds were over; the next rounds began to 'creep' back until they bracketed the hedgerow-marked lane which was the axis of the Rangers' attack. There the fire held, right on the lane, 'the prettiest fire I ever saw' (Captain Masny). His attack was smashed in short order; four men were killed and nearly every Ranger in the group was hit. Masny, wounded in the arm, shouted 'Withdraw! Every man for himself!' after the second burst, and the remnants crawled back to the exit road and over to the CP, with snipers killing two more on the way. All its ammunition shot away, the mortar was abandoned at its firing position.

That was the last effort of the day to assault the anti-aircraft emplacement; the two ill-fated attempts had cost 15 to 20 casualties. Several attempts were made to knock out the anti-aircraft position by naval fire, with the Satterlee expending many rounds in futile bombardment. The position was just too far from the edge of the cliff to be blasted off by undercutting fire (such as destroyed the emplacement on the other side of the Pointe), and yet was too close to the cliff to be reached directly by the flat trajectory of the destroyer's guns, from their lower firing level.

A wild shell from British ship HMS *Glasgow* landed next Lt. Col. Rudder's command post killing Captain Harwood and wounding Lieutenant Norton. The blast knocked Colonel Rudder to the ground. Lieutenant Vermeer commented later that it must have been a coloured marker shell, because it covered all the men completely in yellow die.

Naval supporting fires nevertheless gave the Rangers inestimable aid, and from very early in the assault. At 0728, the Satterlee made its first contact with the Naval Shore Fire Control Party, and was immediately given target requests followed by spotting reports from the shore observers. However, radio transmission was uncertain (SCR 284), and a new difficulty arose when the signals party moved to the CP on top of the cliff. Attempts to communicate by radio drew enemy artillery fire immediately, suggesting that the Germans were picking up the transmission and using it to register on the CP. Lieutenant Eikner then turned to other means, and made successful contact by signal lamps. These were used with good results during the rest of the day, though radio transmission for fire control was resumed in the afternoon. Personnel of the Fire Control Party observed results not merely from the Pointe but from positions inland, sending spotting data back to the Pointe by SCR 536 for relay to the ships. Targets given the Satterlee included inland assembly areas at St-Pierre and Au Guay road junctions, strongpoints toward Grandcamp, and, especially, the anti-aircraft position west of the Pointe. By 1723 the Satterlee had expended 70 per cent (the prescribed maximum) of her ammunition, having fired 164 salvos, plus six minutes of fire for effect, in support of the Rangers since H-Hour. The Barton and Thompson moved in near the Pointe to relieve the Satterlee, and before dark the NSFCP transmitted data for night fire on road junctions and other targets.

US Signal Corps photograph with caption: 'Chateau behind Pointe du Hoc. Damaged to two salvos fired by U.S.S. *Satterlee*'. Machine guns in this house were holding up Rangers. Germans ran out as shelling began and were killed by Rangers who were only 75 yards away. Seaward view.'

USS *Barton* After Action Report:

> On some targets, such as the chateaux, hitting was delayed in the interests of safety. As our own forces were immediately in front of the buildings, it was necessary to apply arbitrary out spots on the initial salvos. The spot was then reduced until the second story of the building was hit.

US Signal Corps caption: 'Behind Pointe du Hoc. Group of farm buildings fired on by USS Harding on call from Shore Fire Control Party. Fire very effective. These houses contained machine guns and observation posts.'

Small Unit Actions Report Pointe du Hoc continues:

Little success was had in communicating with friendly ground forces, either the 5th Rangers or 29th Division units. Apparently the SOI (signal operating instructions) had been changed just before D-Day without notification to Colonel Rudder's communications section; though Lieutenant Eikner more than once contacted friendly units ashore at the main landing beaches, he was unable to get any answers or to stay in touch. He attributed this to his inability to give proper authentication to his messages. Colonel Rudder thus was in complete ignorance of the progress of the great assault at Omaha Beach, for the naval vessels, if they had any information, did not send it to the Pointe. Between noon and 1300 Colonel Rudder sent out a message by all available means, SCR 300, SCR 284 (through the Satterlee), and pigeon: 'Located Pointe du Hoe mission accomplished need ammunition and reinforcements many casualties' By 1500 the 116th Infantry replied, stating its inability to decipher the message, which was repeated. About the same time, the destroyer relayed in reply a brief message from the 1st Division commander, General Huebner: 'No reinforcements available.' The Rangers' noon message was the only word received from Pointe du Hoe on D-Day by higher headquarters (V Corps had it by mid-afternoon), and was the cause for considerable anxiety as to the Rangers' situation.

The medical section with the Ranger assault force passed a busy morning. Capt. Walter E. Block and two of his enlisted personnel came in on LCA 722; three aid men were distributed in other craft. The aid men had pack carriers with 50 feet of rope coiled on top, so that if enemy fire made necessary a quick crossing of the beach, the packs could be left behind and pulled over later. The two men with Captain Block carried aid kits, and Block himself lugged an 81-mm mortar shell case, waterproofed to serve as a container for medical supplies. All the equipment got to the cliff base in good condition. When the CP moved to the top, Block left one man to care for some seriously wounded Rangers who could not be moved from the beach. Later in the morning one of the aid men and Lt. Col. Trevor, British Commando officer who had accompanied the assault, assembled sections of an extension ladder on the beach and got it mounted conveniently for service in moving wounded and getting supplies up the cliff.

Colonel Rudder and Captain Block were concerned over the problem of caring for the considerable number of wounded, many of whom needed to be evacuated. At 1350, by signal light communication, the destroyer Barton *was asked to send in a boat to take off the casualties. At 1430, a small motorboat from the* Barton *made the attempt, towing a rubber boat astern. Enemy machine-gun fire from along the cliffs east of Pointe du Hoe harassed the* Barton's *motorboat, wounding one of the crew and preventing a landing. Block had to leave several of the seriously wounded Rangers overnight on the beach, in a cave at the base of the cliff.*

[Author: Navy ship the USS *Barton* After Action Report covers these events in a little more detail and indicates that it was indeed in contact with the Rangers.]

```
     3.      On 6 June, BARTON relieved U.S.S. HERNDON (DD
638) on station #4, off Point Du Hoe.  As her shore fire
control party could not be contacted, BARTON patrolled sta-
tion, awaiting targets of opportunity.  Shortly thereafter,
a party of the 2nd Ranger Battalion was observed, taking
shelter from German fire beneath the lip of the cliff.  A
number of German prisoners had been taken, and were under
guard on the beach.  Communications were established by
flashing light, and in response to a request for a boat to
evacuate several wounded, the motor whaleboat was sent in.
This boat, under the command of the First Lieutenant,
reached a point twenty yards from the beach before being
forced to retire by heavy and accurate machine gun fire
from nearby enemy positions.  The boat was holed several
times, EACON, Garnet Lee, 620 31 84, PhM2c, V6, USNR, was
wounded in the hip, and a soldier (previously recovered
from an unseaworthy LCT) was struck squarely on the helmet
while returning the fire.  He was stunned but uninjured.
```

```
BARTON thereupon opened fire on these enemy positions, spots
being received by light from the Shore Fire Control Parties
of Lieutenant NORTON, USN, and Lieutenant JOHNSON, USA, oper-
ating with the 2nd Rangers.  Several positions were neutrali-
zed or destroyed, and the enfilading fire which had harassed
the group ceased.

     4.      Following the destruction of these targets, radio
communication was established on a common frequency, and BAR-
TON continued to fire on targets designated by this party.
An enemy counterattack on the road west of Grandcamp Les Bains
(556912) was engaged, after which fire was shifted to a con-
centration southest of this town (567924).  The SFCP reported
to the BARTON "Good shooting!  BARTON was ordered to return to
her night station off Port En Bessin at 1930.
```

```
          Chronological order of events pertinent to shore
bombardment:

     6 June 1944.

     1230  Relieved U.S.S. HERNDON on station #4, off
           Pointe Du Hoe.
     1300  Personnel observed on cliff, taking cover from
           enemy fire.  Communications established, party
           identified as 2nd Ranger Battalion.
     1435  Motor whaleboat left ship to pick up casualties.
     1519  Motor whaleboat returned to ship holed by machine
           gun fire, one casualty.  Unable to reach beach.
     1522  Opened fire on enemy machine gun positions, as
           directed by 2nd Rangers.
     1625  Ceased fire, having expended 130 rounds 5"/38 AA
           Common.
     1645  Opened fire on road east of Grandcamp Les Bains.
     1700  Ceased fire, having expended 43 rounds 5"/38 AA
           Common.
     1902  Opened fire on enemy concentration southeast of
           Grandcamp Les Bains.
     1925  Ceased fire, having expended 44 rounds 5"/38 AA
           Common.
     1930  Proceeded to night station #4, off Port En Bessin.
```

6 June 1944

0000B   Proceeding via channel number two to Transport Area.

0515B   Sighted KE buoy marking beginning of Transport Area.

0650B   Released Convoy U2A2 in Transport Area and proceeded to patrol to north and northwest of Transport Area.

1145B   BARTON proceeding to relieve HERNDON in Fire Support Station Number Four in accordance with orders from Commander Task Force 125.

1215B   Relieved HERNDON on station. HERNDON reported she was unable to pick up here shore fire control party (SFCP 29). BARTON unable to contact party. Ordered to patrol station and fire at targets of opportunity.

1300B   Observed personnel on cliff just to eastward of Target Number One apparently under enemy fire. Established communication by flashing light. Identified party as 2nd Ranger Battalion.

1325B   2nd Ranger Battalion requested reinforcements and a boat to remove wounded and German prisoners. Message was relayed to Commander Assault Force "U", (Commander Task Force 125) in ANCON.

1435B   Sent motor whaleboat to beach to pick up casualties.

1452B   Motor whaleboat taken under heavy fire by enemy machine guns. Boat was forced to withdraw.

1519B   Motor whaleboat returned to ship with one personnel casualty and hull holed by machine gun.

1522B   Opened fire on enemy machine gun position between 2000 and 5000 yards to eastward of Target Number One along edge of cliff as directed by 2nd Ranger Battalion. Ceased fire at 1625B having expended 130 rounds of 5"/38 cal. AA common ammunition.

1630B   Established voice communications with 2nd Ranger Battalion on their frequency.

1645B   Opened fire on road to eastward of Grand Camp Les Bains (556912) where enemy was counter-attacking against 2nd Ranger Battalion. Ceased fire at 1700B having expended 43 rounds of 5"/38 cal. AA common ammunition.

1902B   Opened fire on enemy concentration at 567924. Ceased fire at 1925B, having expended 44 rounds of 5"/38 cal. AA common ammunition.

The 6 June USS *Texas* War Diary records the following ammunition expenditure on Pointe du Hoc and Maisy – Les Perruques.

TABLE OF GUNFIRE SUPPORT, U.S.S. TEXAS								
TARGET	Map Grid Ref	Date	ComFire	Cease	AP	HC	Total	Airspot
1. Pt. Du Hoe	586939	6/6	0550	0624	155	100	255	"
2. T88, 89 Fortified Pos.	575939	6/6	0626	0630	11	0	11	"
3. T85 Fortified Pos.	586932	6/6	0742	0747	0	17	17	"
4. T5 Fortified Pos.	533918	6/6	0810	0824	0	26	26	"
5. Mobile Field Batt.	568893	6/6	1033	1056	0	40	40	"
6. Gun Pos in trees	618925	6/6	1117	1128	0	26	26	"
7. Exit D-1	648917	6/6	1223	1250	0	6	6	Foretop Spot

Narrative of that ammunition expenditure.

6 June   USS *Texas*: *Heavy AA fire was observed over the beach areas. By 0300* Texas *and* Glasgow *were manoeuvered into Western Fire support lane clear of the transport area and* Texas *anchored for short stay in position 092 degrees 11.8 miles from Isles St. Marcouf to await dawn for scheduled pre H-Hour bombardment of assigned targets. Observed heavy air bombardment of 155mm battery (Target T-1) on Pointe du Hoc and on batteries in Utah beach.*

At 0550 (H-40) commenced main battery bombardment of German Coastal defence battery of 6 x 155mm guns on Pointe du Hoc.

At 0625 lifted fire from Pointe du Hoc and shifted to strongpoint on cliff 1000 yards west of Pointe du Hoc.

At 0742 opened fire with main battery expending 17 rounds of HE ammunition and at 0810 opened fire on howitzer battery expending 20 rounds of HE ammunition. At 1035 opened fire with main battery expending 40 rounds of HE ammunition and again at 1117 opened fire on new target expending 26 rounds of HE. All fire was delivered by air spot and the air spotter reported all targets completely destroyed.

The initial landing was accomplished but apparently became stalled by snipers, unreduced pillboxes and strongpoints particularly in area of beach near Exit D-1 at Vierville-sur-Mer. The exit was impossible due to machine guns in houses lining the exit and concealed howitzer battery was delivering devastating fire on the adjacent beach. At 1207 the Texas *got underway and moved into position 5,000 yards off Exit D-1 to clear out the snipers and machine guns with main battery fire opening fire at 1223. This fire plus that of several destroyers completely demolished all structures in the exit reducing them to rubble. The steeple of the church in Vierville-sur-Mer was neatly sawn off by destroyer fire apparently destroying the German observation post as the howitzer fire slackened and became erratic.*

At 1315 Texas *anchored in position bearing 356 degrees distant 2.8 miles from church spire in Vierville-sur-Mer. Increased activity was observed on the beach as the army units previously pinned down by the howitzer fire began to free up and clear the beach. At 1400 delivered main battery fire on AA battery west of Vierville. Delivered 5" fire on suspected observation post in Vierville at 1941. Most of the fire during the afternoon was direct fire on the beach employing top spotters.*

Arriving in her designated position HMS *Glasgow* opened fire on prearranged targets with the help of air spotters. She was in touch by radio with her SFCP and was off station 3.1 miles north of Vierville Church.

HMS *Glasgow*: *At 1420* HMS *Glasgow shifted berth to engage targets to her westward at Maisy.*

USS *Herndon* proceeded towards the French coast ahead of the assault waves. Her mission was to bombard and destroy coastal targets, primarily situated between Grandcamp and the Carentan Estuary. All the targets were classified as being defended localities and either contained field guns, AA guns, troop concentrations and/or command and control structures for the German defenders. One of these beach front positions was the forward observation position in front of the batteries at Maisy called La Casino.

To this end it was most successful, and the positions it bombarded were not able or capable of engaging the first assault waves as they landed. In this mission alone they expended 212 rounds of 5" shells during a forty-minute bombardment.

At 0655 it was reported that one of the Maisy defensive Anti-Aircraft batteries was firing. It was observed and taken under fire. The *Herndon*'s Action Report reads: '*At 0655 an active AA shore battery in the town of Maisy (Target 103) was observed and taken under fire. Ceased firing at 0703 having expended 42 rounds of 5" AA common ammunition. Battery was silenced.*'

Small Unit Actions Report – Pointe du Hoc continues:

Afternoon Counter-attacks

The Germans made two efforts against the Pointe during the afternoon, both of them hitting Lieutenant Wintz's force from south and west. The first attack came over the fields that stretched toward St-Pierre-du-Mont, where Lieutenant Wintz's Rangers spotted riflemen coming through the craters, with at least one machine-gun section. When the enemy reached the hedgerow one field south of Wintz's line, they set up the machine gun and started a fire fight that went on for an hour. Some artillery and mortar fire supported the effort, but most of the enemy shells went over into the

Pointe area. Company F had a mortar in position, but it was short of ammunition and held its fire. They had no BAR's on the flank facing the attack, and naval fire could not be called in against the Germans so close to the Ranger lines. The attack was met and stopped by well-sustained rifle fire; after a time the German fire weakened and men could be seen drifting back. Wintz's force sustained no casualties.

The next German effort came shortly after 1600 and was much more dangerous. It hit the right end of Company F's thin line. Two BAR's as well as the mortar section were on this wing, but only a few riflemen, and the right flank (toward the anti-aircraft position) was 'in the air'. Moving near the exit road, the Germans were close in on this flank before they were observed. S/Sgt. Herman E. Stein and Pfc. Cloise A. Manning were near gun position No.1, changing craters after a close burst of enemy shells, when they saw a dozen Germans, with a machine gun, almost due west and moving fast toward the Pointe. About the same time S/Sgt. Eugene E. Elder, at the mortar, spotted some enemy to the south, close by and crawling through craters. Sergeant Stein opened with surprise fire from his BAR at 40 yards, hit a couple of men in the group to the west, and scared the others into a short withdrawal.

This check disorganized the attack for a few valuable moments; when the Germans rallied, their firing line extended well beyond Company F's flank, but their fire was high and wild. The few Rangers on that wing took hurried measures to meet the danger. Stein sent a message over to the mortar position, warning of the enemy's location, and eight riflemen came over from the left to help defend against any thrust behind Company F and onto the Pointe. With Sgt. Murrell F. Stinette observing and relaying corrections by call to Sergeant Elder, the Rangers' mortar opened at 60-yards range. The first shells burst right on the advance group of enemy, driving them out of their holes into a hasty withdrawal. Shifting its fire a little south, the mortar flushed another German party, who suffered casualties from the BAR's as they ran for cover.

That was the end of an attack that had got in very close to the Pointe and threatened to cut off Wintz's group. Quick reaction by the Rangers, and very rapid and accurate mortaring, had knocked the enemy off balance and given them no time to recover. A mortar in the attacking force was never used; their two machine guns were set up a few times, only to be chased into new cover by Sergeant Elder's mortar. Elder fired about 75 rounds during the action, all without increments, which had been wetted in landing. He found that the mortars could be used effectively at the short range, making the range changes accurately enough by calling for turns on the elevation and traversing handles.

Until darkness fell, there were occasional light skirmishes with German riflemen still in the fields beyond Lieutenant Wintz's position. The enemy seemed to be trying to feel out the Ranger strength on the east flank, but no more attacks developed. Toward nightfall, Lieutenant Wintz drew in his forces toward the Pointe to form a closer perimeter defense. The men were scattered through convenient shell holes, close enough to call to each other. Wintz took a patrol through the whole Pointe area, including the gun positions, to search out the snipers who were still appearing behind the perimeter. He failed to locate a single enemy.

The Company F men from LCAs 883 and 884, numbering originally about 40, had suffered casualties of 5 killed and 10 wounded during the day's fighting on and near the Pointe. Among the killed were Lieutenant Hill, who had gone out beyond the highway in the morning with the advance parties. Toward afternoon, Hill started back to the Pointe, to report to the CP. On the way in, Lieutenant Hill and Private Bacho heard machine-gun fire in the fields east of the exit road and went over to investigate. About 300 yards away from the Company F line, they started across a hedgerow to get at a machine gun which Hill had spotted two fields over to the east. Bacho looked over the hedgerow and saw a dozen Germans lying on the open ground in a field corner, talking. Hill decided to grenade them. He and Bacho threw their first two over the hedge, then lumped into a ditch. The grenades misfired and stirred up a hornet's nest. The startled Germans began to throw their 'potato-mashers'; one exploded harmlessly right between Hill and Bacho, but in the next instant Hill was shot through the chest by a machine-pistol bullet. Bacho threw over his remaining grenades, including one with thermite charge which 'seemed to confuse the enemy', and inflicted some casualties. When a rifle bullet went through the top of Bacho's helmet he decided to play dead. The Germans came up to the hedgerow and looked over, but concluded the Rangers were finished. Some time later Bacho was able to crawl away to a crater. He spent the afternoon in the general area through which the first German attacks were coming, but, though he heard shots fired around him, Bacho saw no Germans and had no idea that an enemy counterattack was under way. At dark, he was able to get back to the Pointe.

The Advance Group During D-Day

For some time after the highway was reached, small parties of Rangers drifted in to join their platoons, so that by noon there were over 60 men to hold the forward position, a half mile inland from the Pointe. Among the arrivals were three paratroopers of the 101st Airborne Division, scheduled to drop early that morning north of Carentan, 15 miles away, but dropped instead near Pointe du Hoe.

The main action of the day was vigorous and continued patrolling, undertaken by combat patrols of six or seven men who went out on the flanks of the highway position, and particularly to the south into the small valley. The patrols found no organized enemy positions and encountered no strong forces. A number of Germans, who had evidently been bypassed near the Pointe and were trying to work south, straggled into the Rangers' positions from the seaward side and were killed or captured. Patrols rounded up other scattered enemy groups.

Typical of the way men on both sides were cut off and isolated during the first two days was a capture within the Ranger lines. About noon Sergeant Petty came back to the CP to get a rifle for one of his men. Just as he arrived, Sgt. James R. Alexander fired his BAR back toward the highway at two Germans who appeared by a gate, halfway down the lane. One German fell, and Petty and Alexander went over to examine the body, three other Rangers tagging along for no particular reason. Petty was sitting astride the gate, looking at the dead German, when somebody yelled 'Kamerad' from the ditch bordering the lane. Three Germans were coming out of the ditch. Sgt. Walter J. Borowski fired some shots into the hedgerow on the chance that there might be more men hiding. Two more Germans came out. Then the hedgerow was searched in earnest, but without further results. Two of the prisoners, a captain and a noncom, said they had had a machine gun, which the Rangers were unable to find. Altogether, about 40 prisoners were taken in by Ranger patrols and outposts, to be grouped under guard in the field near the CP.

Sergeant Petty also figured in a good deal of shooting that took place at the outpost south of the CP and near the creek. He and his nine men were well situated to watch movement across the valley. At intervals during the day, small groups of enemy came into easy range, moving west along the country road toward Grandcamp. Perhaps fleeing from the Omaha area, these parties seemed to be disorganized, and put up no fight when Petty opened fire with his BAR. Using surprise fire, Petty inflicted some 30 casualties during the afternoon, including 2 of a party of 7 Poles, shot at before the Rangers realized they were coming forward to surrender.

Patrols found evidence late in the day that the Germans were present in some strength south and southwest of the Rangers' highway positions, but there was no sign of preparation for counter-attack. The nearest approach to trouble came north of the highway, near Company D's roadblock. About 1600 Sergeant Lomell, near his CP hole where the highway was joined by the lane containing the German battery, happened to glance over the 5-foot stone wall edging the highway and saw a German force of about 50 men coming through an orchard from the direction of the Pointe. The enemy was moving in well-organized fashion, with scouts out ahead, and Lomell could see two machine-gun sections and a mortar. There was no time to make any preparation, or even to pass word down the Ranger line. Lomell could only hope that the enemy would pass by and that his own men would have the sense to hold their fire, for the 20 Rangers of Company D, scattered along 150 yards of highway, would have had little chance against a force this size. But the Germans were not attacking, nor, as their course soon made clear, were they aware of the Rangers' position. About 30 feet from the wall, the column turned westward and moved parallel to the highway beyond the roadblock position, then south across the blacktop and out of sight. Showing excellent control, the Rangers had made no move that would betray their location.

Intermittent harassing fire fell near the Rangers during the day, but the air and tree bursts caused only one casualty, a paratrooper who got tired of ducking into his fox hole and was hit by the next shell. From the sea, friendly destroyer fire was being directed from the Pointe at inland targets. Occasionally rounds fell short or uncomfortably close; little could be done about this as communication from the forward group to the Pointe depended on runners and patrols, and no member of the Naval Shore Fire Control Party was available for the highway group. Men going back to the Pointe were nearly always engaged by snipers, and sometimes had to fight their way on both trips as German resistance revived near the Pointe. Lieutenant Lapres twice went back to Colonel Rudder's CP, getting ammunition and, on one trip, a radio which failed to work. On his morning passage, Lapres drew heavy fire from west of the exit road; his attempts in the afternoon were entirely blocked off by Germans who had infiltrated between the two Ranger Groups.

About 2100, still two hours before dark, a party of 23 men from Company A, 5th Ranger Battalion came into the Ranger lines from the east. Led by 1st Lt. Charles H. Parker, Jr., this force was the 1st Platoon of Company A. The record of its fight from Omaha Beach to the Pointe is one of the sagas of D-Day. Parker's platoon became separated from the 5th Ranger Battalion during the first penetration of the German beach defenses between Vierville and St-Laurent, about 0815. Unaware that the battalion had become involved in a fire fight just inland from the beach, the platoon had made its way south of Vierville to the battalion assembly area. Finding no friendly troops there, Parker concluded they must have preceded him and set out west. After fighting two hot actions, one of which netted a score of prisoners, while the other nearly trapped his platoon, Parker got cross country all the way to St-Pierre-du-Mont and walked into the 2nd Ranger position at the highway. He was surprised to learn that the 5th Rangers had not arrived, but was sure they must be close behind him on another route. A patrol was sent in at once to Colonel Rudder with this heartening news. Parker's men stayed with the forward group at the highway as they prepared their night defenses.

Pfc James Gabaree was with the men from A Company 5th Battalion who arrived that evening at the Pointe:

'Sniping, as far as I know, is recognized as a legitimate means of warfare. And yet there is something sneaking about it that outrages the American sense of fairness.

Here in Normandy the Germans have gone in for sniping in a wholesale manner. There are snipers everywhere. There are snipers in trees, in buildings, in piles of wreckage, in the grass. But mainly they are in the high, bushy hedgerows that form the fences of all the Normandy fields and line every roadside and lane.

It is perfect sniping country. A man can hide himself in the thick fence-row shrubbery with several days' rations, and it's like hunting a needle in a haystack to find him. Every mile we advance, there are dozens of snipers left behind us. They pick off our soldiers one by one as they walk down the roads or across the fields.

It is a country of little fields, every one bordered by a thick hedge and a high fence of trees. There is hardly any place where you can see beyond the field ahead of you. Most of the time a soldier doesn't see more than a hundred yards in any direction. In other places the ground is flooded and swampy with a growth of high, jungle like grass. In this kind of stuff it is almost man-to-man warfare.

Our men were deployed with the 2nd band to secure the Pointe and block the German advance. Night fell, and enemy attacked with a vengeance and enormous firepower, shouting and blowing whistles. At one point they were within fifty yards of us. To our men in the foxholes it was practically hand-to-hand combat, we were in a survival mode.'

Small Unit Action Report: The German Night Attack: First Phase
Twilight in early June, on reckoning by British War Time, lasted until 2300. As night approached, and still no word came from Omaha Beach, Colonel Rudder faced a difficult command decision with regard to disposition of his limited forces. Of his original 200 men over a third were casualties, though many of the lightly wounded (including Colonel Rudder) were staying in action. Ammunition was low, especially in grenades and mortar shells. The Germans were still holding the anti-aircraft position close to the Pointe on the west, and had shown themselves in some force on the eastern flank as well. Communications between the Pointe and the highway group had always been precarious, and the latter force, numbering more than half of the Rangers, would be particularly exposed to counterattack that might cut it off from the shore. Either of the two Ranger positions was in danger; Colonel Trevor, the Commando officer, remarked casually in the CP that 'never have I been so convinced of anything as that I will be either a prisoner of war or a casualty by morning.'

Colonel Rudder decided to leave the highway force in place. He was still expecting the arrival of the 5th Rangers and 116th Infantry units along the Vierville road, carrying out the D-Day program, and this expectation had been strengthened when Colonel Rudder heard that Parker's platoon had actually arrived, reporting (erroneously) that the rest of the 5th Rangers were probably just behind them. It was important, Colonel Rudder thought, to maintain the block on the Grandcamp highway and so deny that vital road to the enemy. Even though German resistance had stiffened during the day, their counterattacks against the weaker force on the Pointe had been ineffective, and they had made no efforts against the highway position. As a final consideration, Colonel Rudder and his staff had very strong fears (proved by the next day's experience to be unfounded) of the danger from German artillery if his force were concentrated in a restricted area at the Pointe. Lieutenant Lapres, who had reached the Pointe with a patrol just before dark, went back inland with orders to hold the position.

Out beyond the highway, the Rangers made a few alterations in their positions to get ready for night defense.

The main indications of enemy strength were to the south and west, and the greater number of the 85 men at hand (including Lieutenant Parker's platoon of 5th Rangers) were disposed to guard against attacks from those quarters.

The day positions of Company D were obviously too extended for safety, and its 20 men were drawn in to form the right flank of the main Ranger position, on a hedgerow that ran south from the highway to Company E's fox holes. Lieutenant Kerchner and a BAR man were at the angle formed by intersecting hedgerows where E and D joined; Sergeant Lomell was near the center of D's line. Two men were put out west of Kerchner's post, about half way to the lane bordering the next field. Another outpost of two Rangers, one with a BAR, was in the angle where that lane met the blacktop. The rest of Kerchner's men were strung out at wide intervals along the 300 yards of hedgerow, in a ditch running along the embankment.

Company E's 30 men held their day positions on the hedge-line running east toward the main CP. Some half dozen of the 5th Ranger men were distributed along their front. A few yards south of the angle where E and D connected, two riflemen were posted in the orchard that sloped away gently toward the creek; two more Rangers, one a BAR man, were 75 yards further out. The post of Lieutenant Leagans (2nd Platoon) was in a German-prepared dugout near the middle of E's hedgerow, with a BAR man and a rifleman in the corner of the orchard on the other side of the hedgerow, and another rifleman 50 yards south on the boundary between the orchard and a wheatfield. A third BAR man was 20 yards west of Leagans' station. Between Leagans and the angle where Company D's line began, about 10 riflemen occupied fox holes north of the hedge, one group fairly close to the angle and the rest bunched near Leagans, an arrangement thought better for purposes of communication. From east of Leagans' post over to the main CP on the lane, the 1st Platoon of Company E and some 5th Rangers continued the hedgerow line, with main strength near the CP, where the Rangers were placed two to a fox hole for greater safety in night fighting. Sergeant Robey with a BAR was in the corner of the wheat field just south of the CP, with a good field of fire to the southwest. In addition to their own four BAR's, Company E platoons had found and set up three German machine guns (two model '34's and one '42'), for which ammunition was available.

East from the CP, the line that Company F had held in daylight was shortened to 100 yards. Near the lane that ran back from CP to highway, three Rangers with a BAR were placed in a trench that gave them a field of fire through a gateway into the orchard southeast of the CP. Beyond them were two men of Company F and some 5th Battalion Rangers. Sergeant Petty and seven men, including some 5th Rangers, still held an outpost along the stone wall at the foot of the wheat field. Their advantages of observation from this position would be sharply reduced at night, and Petty was under orders to withdraw if an attack developed in his vicinity.

The main Ranger position thus formed a right angle, facing southwest, with equal sides about 300 yards long on two fields that ran back to the highway. The 30 or 40 German prisoners were put in fox holes in these fields, not far from the CP, and two Rangers were regarded as sufficient guard. Little concern was felt for the open flank to the east, protected by three men with a BAR near the highway, and by a half dozen of Parker's 5th Rangers along the lane between the CP and the road.

Certain features of the night arrangements are worth noting, in view of later developments. The 5th Ranger platoon of 23 men had been scattered in small batches at various points and did not operate as a tactical unit under Lieutenant Parker. He and his assistant, 1st Lt. Stanley D. Zelepsky, were at the main CP with Arman and Lapres. Command functions in the Ranger force, made up of elements of four companies, were not centralized. During the day, the D, E, and F parties had co-operated on a more or less informal basis, with co-ordination secured by consultation of the four officers, Lieutenants Kerchner (D), Leagans and Lapres (E), and Arman (F). When plans had to be made in the morning as to positions for the day, Lieutenant Arman was the senior officer at hand and seems to have made the decisions. After that he did not consider himself in command in any formal sense. The decision to shorten up and tighten the defenses for the night was taken when Lieutenant Kerchner came over to Arman's post and reported seeing Germans in some strength to the southwest. Arman, Lapres, and Kerchner talked it over and agreed as to readjustment of positions.

As they settled in for night defense, the main worry of the Rangers was their ammunition supply, now running short, especially for the BAR's. Very few U.S. grenades were left; although a plentiful supply of German 'potato-mashers' were found in prepared positions around the CP, the Rangers had a poor opinion of their effectiveness. A few Rangers had lost their rifles and were using German weapons, for which ammunition was in good supply. Companies D and E had three Tommy guns each, and E had three German machine guns. The Rangers had had nothing to eat since leaving ship except the individual D-bars, but in the excitement and activity of the day few men had felt the need for food.

Even before Lieutenant Kerchner's report, the officers had felt particularly apprehensive about the area southwest of their angle position. At the bottom of the little valley to the south, a country road ran more or less parallel to the Ranger lines, west from a bridge close by Sergeant Petty's outpost and then northwest toward the highway. From their higher ground, the Rangers could watch this road during daylight, but at night it was too far away for good observation. Houses, hedgerows, and orchards along it would give cover for assembly of troops. It was in this area, a few hundred yards southwest of the angle in the Rangers' right position, that Lieutenant Kerchner had observed German activity at dusk.

Despite a moon nearly full and only partly obscured by clouds, the Rangers found visibility poor in front of their angle, particularly into the orchards on the south. Here the ground sloped off 30 feet in 300 yards, and the fields of fire had been good for a daylight action.

About 2330 the Rangers posted in front of the D-E corner were startled by a general outburst of whistles and shouts, close by on the orchard slope. Enemy fire opened immediately and in considerable volume. Sgt. Michael J. Branley and Pfc. Robert D. Carty, in position west of the corner, saw tracer fire from a machine gun to their right and only 25 yards from Company D's side of the angle. South of the corner, in Company E's outpost, the men spotted another machine gun to the west, about 50 yards from Company E's defensive line. Neither outpost had seen or heard the enemy approach through the orchard. At the angle, and along E's front, the Rangers returned the enemy fire at once, the BAR's firing in full bursts. Carty and Branley started back toward the corner to get better firing positions; Carty was killed by a grenade, and his companion, hit in the shoulder by a bullet, managed to crawl to the hedgerow.

In the Company E outpost, Corporal Thompson and Hornhardt were almost walked over by a group of Germans who came suddenly around a hump in the north-south hedgerow dividing the orchard. Thompson saw their silhouettes against the sky, so the Rangers got in their fire first at point-blank range and knocked down three of the enemy. The others went flat and threw grenades, one of them exploding in Thompson's face and cutting him badly. He gave his BAR to Hornhardt and they started back for the corner.

Only a few minutes after the firing began, an immense sheet of flame shot up over to the west, near the position of the abandoned German guns. (The Rangers' guess was that, somehow, more powder charges had been set off in the ammunition dump.) The orchard slopes were fully lit up, and many Germans could be seen outlined against the glare. The flare died almost at once, and the firing ended at the same time. It is possible that the powder explosion had disconcerted the Germans and ended their effort, but more probably the attack was only a preliminary probe by combat patrols, trying to locate Ranger positions by drawing their fire. This brief action brought about a few changes in the Ranger positions, affecting the outposts and the west side of the angle (Company D). Certain things that happened began to show some of the difficulties of night fighting. Thompson and Hornhardt got back to the corner and found nobody at that position; when they called for Sergeant Rupinski, there was no answer. (He was 20 yards away, to the east, but did not hear them; there were two Company D men close by with a BAR, but Thompson missed seeing them too.) The outpost pair decided everybody must have pulled back across the field, so they started north along Company D's hedgerow and finally encountered Rangers in position near the highway end of the hedgerow. (They had passed others on the way without spotting them in their holes under the hedgerow.)

Lieutenant Kerchner and Sgt. Harry J. Fate were now at this end of the Company D line. When the firing began, with greatest concentration near Kerchner's post at the angle, he had the impression that the attack was going to roll right over them. So he and Fate went north along the hedgerow; as they started, Kerchner told Fate his plan. He would collect the D platoon near the highway, circle west and then south, and hit the German attack in the flank. Kerchner called to his men to follow as he ran along the hedgerow, but in the general uproar of the fire they failed to hear him. On reaching the highway he found only two men had joined up; the fire fight was already dying out, and the plan for a counterattack was given up. Lieutenant Kerchner decided to stay near the highway.

The net result of these shifts was to weaken the angle position toward which the German attack had come. Both outposts to south of it had come in, the two 5th Ranger men appearing at the main CP and telling Lieutenant Arman that they had been ordered to withdraw. (There is no way of tracing whether, why, or by whom such an order was given.) Two Rangers who had been near the angle were casualties; six others, including a BAR man and the only officer at that sector (Kerchner), had gone to other parts of the line. No information on these changes in strength at the angle seems to have reached Lieutenant Arman's CP. Neither Lieutenant Kerchner on D's thinly held front, nor (apparently) Lieutenant Leagans in Company E made any move to strengthen the corner position. So far as can be determined no one visited the corner to see what the situation was.

On the east wing of the Rangers' position there had been no firing. Neither the first platoon of E (Lieutenant Lapres) nor the Company F men had been involved so far. Down near the creek, in Sergeant Petty's exposed outpost, the men were alarmed by the fire but couldn't locate it; they thought it was back near the highway, and some even believed it was the 116th pushing along the blacktop to relieve the Rangers at the Pointe. Petty, a little after the skirmish ended and quiet had settled down again, heard 'clinking' sounds over toward the farm buildings west of his post. He put it down to noise made by farm animals. But after another short spell of quiet, a machine gun opened up from that flank, some of the shots ricocheting off a farm roller which Petty had placed against the stone wall for cover to his right. Petty's men stayed quiet, and after two short bursts the enemy fire stopped. Petty decided, in accordance with earlier instructions, that he should pull back up the slope to the CP. His group made the trip without drawing enemy fire. Petty with his BAR and Dix with a machine gun reinforced the CP position, while the rest of his men were put on the Company F line farther east.

At the CP, where Lieutenant Arman was stationed and to which other officers came occasionally, everything was quiet. After the fire fight ended, one or two Rangers from E's line reported in, and Lieutenant Lapres went over to the west to see what had happened. Two noncoms went along the E front to see if there were any casualties and if weapons were working properly. They passed word to expect more attacks. Lieutenant Arman was not informed in any detail of Company E's situation, and knew nothing about D. As far as Company F was concerned, he thought for a time of moving it south toward the creek, to bring flanking fire on any further German attack toward the angle, but decided against this idea because of the danger of firing on friendly positions. The group of German prisoners near the CP was moved farther out, into the middle of the field, and ordered to dig in for their own protection.

Night Attack: Second Phase

About 0100 the Germans came in with a stronger effort, hitting again from the south and southwest against the right of Company E's line. Once again the Germans had got through the fields and orchard to within 50 yards of the Rangers without being spotted. The attack opened with whistles, followed by what seemed to be shouting of names up and down the front a sort of 'roll call'. (Some Rangers believed the Germans were locating their men in relation to each other for beginning the assault, but the general view was that the enemy was trying to scare the defence). The shouting was followed immediately by heavy firing, including machine guns and machine pistols. Much of the fire was tracer, somewhat high and inaccurate, designed for morale effect, but ball ammunition was spraying the *hedgerow eastward from the angle. Wild mortar fire was put into the field behind the hedgerow, and some Rangers reported the enemy threw in a few mortar shells by hand. The Germans also used grenades.*

Beyond this general characterization of the attack, the survivors' recollections of this action are confused and hard to fit into any clear pattern. Lieutenant Arman, at the CP to the east of the main fighting, had the impression of two distinct stages in the attack: first, a period of intense but wild fire; then, after a short pause, another burst of whistles and shouts followed by an assault. The main weight of the attack certainly came near the angle in the Rangers' lines, but – and this is a measure of the lack of communications during this night action – nobody knew then, or was sure later, what happened at the corner position. Of the survivors interviewed, Tech. 5 John S. Burnett was about 25 yards east of the angle and Branley (wounded) had crawled about 30 yards north of it, along Company D's hedgerow. Branley reports hearing Tech. 5 Henry S. Stecki's BAR open up from the corner (other Rangers, farther away, confirm this) and fire almost continuously for about two minutes. Then grenades exploded near the corner. After a short lull the BAR fired again, there were some more grenades, and then Germans could be heard talking near the position.

Burnett at first made the same report, pointing to the conclusion that the Germans had occupied the corner. Later, he changed his story and insisted that the Ranger's BAR (Stecki) was still in action after the second German attack. Lieutenant Zelepsky (5th Ranger officer at Arman's CP) remembers being told that the enemy had broken into the Ranger lines, and recalls the impression of men at the CP that the angle was lost and the Germans were in the field. Lieutenant Arman has the same recollection, and thinks the BAR fire at the corner was not heard after the opening of the second attack. The weight of the evidence, pending information from Rangers who were later taken prisoner, suggests that the enemy had captured the angle, held only by a BAR man and one rifleman.

It is much more clear that, whatever happened at the angle, nobody at any distance north or east of that position knew, after the attack, just what the situation was. North of the corner, Company D's men (who had so far not taken part in the fire fight) lay quiet and did not investigate. Twenty-five yards eastward, Burnett and Sergeant Rupinski made no move to find out what had taken place. Over at the main CP, Lieutenant Lapres and Lieutenant Arman had agreed that Company D's hedgerow was overrun; they were discussing plans for withdrawal if the Germans made another attack. They had no communication with Company D, and did not try to send it word of their plan. The officers of the 5th Ranger platoon (Parker and Zelepsky) were supposedly told of the plan, but they do not recall hearing about it before it was carried out.

Near the middle of Company E's line, a Ranger remembers that word was passed down the line to avoid wild firing. Ammunition was running low.

Night Attack: Finale

The third German attack came at some time near 0300. In general character, this one developed like the second: the same whistles and roll calling to start with, then heavy and inaccurate fire, involving several machine guns and burp guns which sprayed the hedgerow and the fields beyond. Mortar fire, somewhat increased in volume, was falling in the area where the prisoners were grouped.

This time the enemy pressure extended farther east, reaching into the wheat field south of the CP. From different accounts, machine guns were spotted in the orchard below the 2d Platoon of E and also directly south of the CP. An officer at the CP had the impression that machine-gun fire also came from the field inside the Rangers' positions, near the angle. This observation fits the theory that the Germans had captured the angle earlier, but the report might be based on high fire from a gun west of the angle, in the orchard where one was spotted in the first attack. The only certainty is that there was a great deal of fire, much of it indirect, and that it had the result of confusing the defence; some Rangers even believed that the enemy were in the rear of their position, near the blacktop.

Lieutenant Arman reports that (as in the second attack) the preliminary burst of shooting was followed by a brief pause, preceding the real assault. Whatever the sequence, the western half of Company E's line was overrun in a short time after the attack began. Only a few incidents of the action can be recovered from survivors who were in or near that area. There is enough evidence to suggest that, even if the angle had been taken earlier, the main penetration now came near the middle of E's hedgerow and rolled up the Ranger positions west from there to the angle.

One fox hole east of Lieutenant Leagans' post at the junction of the two platoons, Pfc. Harold D. Main (who had been wounded by a grenade) heard the Germans coming up close in the wheat just beyond the hedgerow. After a pause following the heavy opening fire, they rushed the hedgerow to Main's right, and Crook's BAR went silent. Minutes later, Main could hear Germans talking on his side of the hedge and knew what had happened. He crawled under the thick tangle of vines and briars into the middle of the hedgerow. Hidden there, he heard S/Sgt. Curtis A. Simmons surrender, only 15 feet away, but the Germans came no farther east.

Burnett, still in his fox hole 25 yards east of the corner, confirms the impression that the decisive action was not on his right, toward the angle, but left, toward Lieutenant Leagans' post. Near Burnett the Germans had worked through the orchard close to the Rangers, and their automatic fire ripped through the hedgerow, keeping the defenders down. The Rangers had plenty of German grenades and used them freely in a close-range exchange. To Burnett, the fight seemed to go on an hour (it can only have been minutes). He became aware that Sergeant Boggetto's BAR, to the left, had stopped firing; then a burst of German fire began to sweep along the Ranger side of the hedge, coming from the east and enfilading the 2nd Platoon's fox holes. Burnett and the man next to him were wounded. The enemy had evidently broken into the field to their left. Burnett could also spot them to his right in the angle. He heard Sergeant Rupinski arguing with a few Rangers, trying to decide whether they could fight it out. The talk ended by Rupinski shouting 'Kamerad'. The Germans moved in and rounded up the survivors, many of them wounded, including Burnett. Lieutenant Leagans was dead. About 20 Rangers were taken off the field, nearly all from Leagans' platoon of E, and moved to a German CP a mile to the south. Here, Burnett saw a force, estimated at a company, coming by the CP from the south, and judged the post was a battalion CP because of the presence nearby of an aid station.

From the varied and sometimes irreconcilable stories of the Rangers who were near Lieutenant Arman's CP, one gets a fair reflection of the confusion that existed under the difficulties of this last phase in a night battle. Arman reports that after the opening fire he, Lapres, and the 5th Ranger officers went ahead with the plan to withdraw, already agreed on. Arman had no idea whether Leagans of Company D knew the plan. According to Lieutenant Zelepsky (5th Rangers), there was little or no prearranged plan: men began to come in from E's line to the west, reporting the Germans had broken the position, and the report was confirmed by enemy fire that seemed to come from the field inside the angle. This led to a hasty decision to withdraw. Sgt. Lawrence Lare remembers a man running across the field from the west to report that Company D was wiped out. Smith and Tech. 5 Charles H. Dunlap, who had been near Main's fox hole, came in to the CP (because their guns had jammed) to report that there were no Rangers left between their former position and the CP. Some of the 5th Ranger men who had been in the Company E line later said that the 2nd Rangers 'pulled out and left them there'.

According to plan or not, a withdrawal took place from the CP area just before it started, that wing of the Ranger line saw some action for the first time that night. Following the first burst of German fire, which indicated the enemy were now south of the CP in the wheatfield, some more Rangers were put into the northeast corner of that field to strengthen the group already there. The reinforcements included Sergeant Petty with his BAR, S/Sgt. Frederick A. Dix with a German machine gun, and some Company F riflemen. A German party came eastward crossing the upper end of the wheatfield; they were starting through the hedgerow embankment into the lane when Dix saw them only a few feet away from his post in the lane. He turned around to use the captured machine gun. It jammed on the first round, and a rifle bullet from some Ranger firing down the lane behind Dix hit a glancing blow on his helmet, stunning him. Recovering, and starting to crawl along the hedgerow ditch back to the CP, Dix heard Petty yell 'Down!' just before opening with his BAR on Germans coming up the lane. Sergeant Robey's BAR joined in, and this fire broke up the only attack that came close to the CP. One German was caught crawling along the hedgerow into the CP area, and was killed by a grenade that landed directly under his chest. Plenty of fire was coming across the wheat field from the west, but no assault was tried from that quarter.

As the volume of enemy fire built up again from south and west, indicating a new rush was at hand, hasty and informal measures were taken to pass the word around for withdrawal back to the highway and the Pointe. Some Rangers failed to get the notice and were temporarily left behind. Petty and Robey were told to bring up the rear and cover the withdrawal with their BARs. Non-commissioned officers tried hurriedly to round up their men. Once started, movement was fast. S/Sgt. Richard N. Hathaway of the 5th Rangers had been posted halfway back to the highway, along the lane. His first notice of what was happening came when men ran by toward the north. Hathaway stuck his head through the hedgerow and shouted 'Hey! What's up? Where you going?' The nearest man stopped running, put his rifle in Hathaway's face, and demanded the password. Hathaway was so rattled that he could just remember the word in time. Told 'the Germans are right behind us – get out quick to the Pointe!' He collected part of his group (he couldn't find some, but they came in later), and went north. There could be no question of bringing back the prisoners.

As the parties arrived at the blacktop, there was no sign of any pursuit, and an effort was made to reorganize those Rangers at hand and to see that none were left. A hasty check-up showed that the Company F men were nearly all there, but only a scattering of E and none from D. Lieutenant Arman figured that the Germans might have infiltrated between the highway and the Pointe, so he sent one party over to the east and then into the Pointe across fields. Lieutenant Arman and a second party, including some of Company E, went back by the exit road. The 5th Ranger men made their way through the completely unfamiliar terrain in scattered parties (and were afterward resentful of their having been cast adrift, though what happened was probably inevitable under the circumstances of night withdrawal). All told, about 50 men got back to the Pointe, shortly after 0400, and were put at once into an improvised defensive line from gun position No.5 to gun position No.3. Very little could be done to organize the position before daylight.

Colonel Rudder was told that the rest of the force had been destroyed. 'Neutralized' would have been a more exact word. All Company E Rangers from Main's fox hole to the angle had been killed or captured, and a few men of D near the corner had been included in the disaster. But from about 30 yards north of the angle and on to the highway, the rest of D's contingent (some dozen men) were still in their original positions, scattered along 250 yards of hedgerow. They had no notice of a withdrawal. When they realized it was under way, they had no chance to move, with Germans in the fields to their rear and flanks. Daylight was near, and the 12 men stayed in the deep drainage ditch, overhung with the heavy vegetation of the hedgerow. They had delivered no fire during the attacks and could only hope the Germans had not spotted their positions.

On the east-west hedgerow, between the breakthrough area and the CP, three more Rangers had been left behind in the confusion of withdrawal. Main was one. Another was Tech. 5 Earl Theobold, who had been in the field guarding prisoners. During the final attack he came over to the hedgerow near Main 'to help out'. He could find no Ranger, and soon heard German voices near the CP, so he hid in the ditch. Pfc. Loring L. Wadsworth, in the same sector and about 75 yards from Main, had missed the word of withdrawal. When he finally called to his nearest neighbor, who had been only a few yards off, Wadsworth got no answer, and stayed put under a tangle of briars.

The German 352nd Infantry Division Telephone Log for 6 June records the following mentions of the action at Pointe du Hoc.

8.05 Hours

Report from the Gren Regt 916:
Weak enemy forces have penetrated into Point du Hoc. One platoon of the 9/Gren Regt 726 will be committed to launch a counterattack.

8.19 Hours

Report from the Gren Regt 916:
Enemy troops have landed near DW No 62. Details are still lacking. A battalion of the Task Force Meyer has been committed against the enemy landed north of Colleville. Some tanks have been landed north of Vierville. The enemy ahead of the DW No 66 and 68 is being attacked by our forces. Near Point du Hoc the enemy has climbed up the steep coast line (by means of rope ladders fall from the shells) the strongpoint has started fighting.

9.15 Hours

Report from the Gren Regt 916:
Ahead of the Defense Work No 65, northeast of St Laurent, sixty to seventy landing boats are debarking at present. No reports have been received from St P Point du Hoc. Situation ahead of Grandcamp is unaltered. Defense Works 65-68 and 70 are occupied by the enemy. Further considerable debarkments near the Defense Works No 65 and 66 have been ascertained.

<u>11.10 Hours</u>

Report from the 3 Battalion/Gren Regt 726:
The Defense Works No 66 and 68 north of St Laurent, contrary to previous
reports are still firmly in our hands. On the other hand, the enemy with
the strength of two companies has penetrated into St P Point du Hoc.
Reserves, which were available, have been committed against Point du Hoc
with the object of restoring the previous situation. From the men-of-war
on the high sea the enemy is firing the steep coast line with special
shells from which a rope ladder is falling out, with the help of which the
steep slopes can be climbed.

352 Inf Div   <u>12.25 Hours</u>

Ia reports to the Chief-of-Staff of LXXXIV AK:
New reports one enemy activities is submitted, see report at 12.20 hrs.
The occupation troops at St P Point du Hoc are encircled by two enemy
companies. A counterattack with portions of the 3 Battalion/Gren Regt 726
has been launched. The Corps HQ will have the Mobile Brigade 30 to be
brought up and subordinated to the Division assuming probably the defense
of the right wing.

<u>18.25 Hours</u>

The Commander of the Div from the command post of Gren Regt 916 to Ia:
The 1 Battalion/Gren Regt 914 has the order to clear up the situation at
the strongpoint Point du Hoc by a counterattack. A counterattack from the
East with detachments from the strongpoint le Guy has also been started.

<u>19.40 Hours</u>

Divisional Commander to the Ia:
The defensive line on the sector of the Gren Regt 916 extends from the
eastern suburbs of Colleville over 69c, 69 to 71cc Beginning with the
Defense Work No 74 to the West everything is in order . The enemy at St P
Point du Hoc is contained from east and south by the 9 Company/Gren Regt 726.

[Author: The following report is the strangest one of them all. To my knowledge no paratroopers were landing near Au Guay at 7.45pm on the evening of 6 June. It is however, possible that the Germans had captured one of the paratroopers who landed early in the morning before the Rangers arrived at Pointe du Hoc – and thus they made an assumption that other paratroopers had also landed at this position.]

<u>1945 Hours</u>

Report from the Gren Regt 916:
Parachute troops landing near St P le Guay.

The last radio report from the German 352nd Inf. Div. which concerned the Rangers' area of attack was this one.

```
                      22.10 Hours

In of the Div to Chelf-of-Staff of the Corps HQ.:
One battalion of the Mobile Brigade 30 in the middle sector is to be subor-
dinated to the Oren Regt 916 as the situation near Grandcamp is uncertain.
The parachutists there have joined with the terrorists (French Underground
Movement).
```

6 June
2nd Ranger Battalion After Action Report

Force "A"   Companies D/E/F

The Plan of Attack:

    Force "A", comprising Companies D/E/F and the Bn Hq Det
with attached Naval Shore Fire Party and Photographic Party,
accompanied by two British Official Observers, commanded by
Lt Col James E. Rudder, was to land at H-Hour on Beach Charlie (Pointe du Hoe) with the mission of destroying the six
gun coastal battery located thereon and establishing a perimeter 1000 yards inland so as to protect the landing of the
Force "C". In support were the battleship "Texas", a number
of destroyers, and several flights of attack-bombers available on call as long as the Ranger Force remained within the
limiting range.

The Beach Assault:

    Companies D/E/F plus attached parties lowered away at
0445. Heavy seas imperiled the heavily-laden craft, each of
which carried a large amount of cliff-scaling apparatus in
addition to the normal complement of men. The LCA's shipped
water so badly that the pumps could not cope with the amount
received and the men, some of whom were sea-sick, assisted
in keeping the craft afloat by bailing water with their helmets.

    About 0530, the LCA containing Captain Harold K. Slater
and twenty men, including the Company Commander, of Company
D, radioed that it was sinking. These men were picked up by
a British Gun-boat after several hours in the water and were
evacuated to England, suffering from exposure. Another Supply craft never reached shore and its' two Ranger occupants
have been reported as KIA.

    Radio contact was gained with the "ladder-DUKW's" at
0545; they reported that all was well. Later, as the DUKW's
neared the shore, they were subjected to intense long-range
MG and artillery fire which wounded several men seriously
and sank one of these craft. Altho every effort was made,
the DUKW's could not gain a footing on the beach due to the
large craters caused by the preliminary bombardment and were
all lost thru enemy action. The surviving personnel assisted in action on the Pointe.

    "Touch-down" was at 0705, thirty-five minutes late due
to an error in direction by the guide-craft. The flotilla of
LCA's came in almost at Pointe El Raz de la Percee and, in
moving parallel to the cliff-line to Pointe du Hoe, had to
run a gauntlet of plunging MG and rifle fire which caused a
number of casualties. It was during this parallel movement
that the first DUKW was knocked out.

    The preparatory fire from the 14-inch guns of the Texas
ceased as planned at H-5. The plans of Force "A" called for

- 2 -

The Naval Shore Fire Control Parties acted as liaison for the Ranger units on the ground and were able to call upon the Navy to deliver shells where needed. One such unit – Naval Shore Fire Control Party No.3 was composed of 2 officers and 12 enlisted men and were tasked with providing support for the 1st Battalion 116th Infantry Regimental Combat Team on D-Day and the 5th Rangers.

60-mm mortar fire from the LCA's during the five minutes before H-Hour. The lapse in landing time caused by the error in navigation allowed the enemy forty minutes in which to recover from the effects of the bombardment and man their positions in readiness to repel the assault.

As the LCA's neared the beach, they were met by a hail of MG and rifle fire. The climbing-ropes were so water-soaked that the rockets could not carry the extra weight to the desired height. Only one craft succeeded in placing all six of it's ropes on top of the 100-foot cliff. Others fired their rocket-mortars from the beach, some assembled steel ladders, while those first up scaled the cliff free-hand, aided by the rubble which the softening-up bombardment caused on the beach. The enemy shifted his fire to the men on the ropes and added a constant rain of grenades. Lt Col Trevor, one of the British Observers, proved invaluable in calming the men in their initial action. His extreme coolness and showmanship tactics caused the men to forget themselves and within one half-hour after landing, all the men, including the walking wounded, were on top of the cliff. The Force CP and Aid Station were set up in a cave on the beach directly under the enemy OP. Pre-arranged messages were sent to Group Headquarters and were "Rogered" for. The Medics, destined to receive no evacuation until H+36-hours, cared for the wounded under cover of the over-hanging cliffs.

The Subsequent Action:

To show the completeness of the small-unit planning, the following Company Plan of Attack is submitted as an example:

Company E was divided into four assault teams, based on principles taught by the A.T.C. The first team, which was to ascend the cliff not more than 25-yards from the Number 3 gun, was to destroy that gun and its' casemate. (Note: The enemy was then in the process of casemating all guns and a study of aerial cover flown D-5 showed that four guns were still in open emplacements, pending completion of their individual casemates.) The second team was to ascend the cliff, push rapidly thru the position to the Vierville-Grandcamp Road and, in conjunction with elements from Companies D/F, organize a perimeter to stop any enemy reinforcement threat. The third team had the mission of destroying the concrete OP, aided by the fourth team, if necessary. All teams were then to proceed to take up positions on the perimeter as soon as they had completed their initial mission.

The scene that greeted the Rangers as they reached "topside" was one of utter destruction. The preliminary bombing and naval shelling had pitted the terrain with deep craters, leaving not an inch of topsoil unturned. Investigation showed only one gun remaining on the Pointe; this had been knocked from its' mountings by the guns of the Texas. The remaining five guns were later discovered about 1000-yards in-land

- 3 -

and were destroyed by patrols. Only a few installations a-
bove ground had survived the terrific shelling prior to the
landing operation.

The enemy, having been permitted to reorganize his defenses due to the unforeseen time lapse, provided stiff opposition from concealed MG and sniper posts. The first men
up the cliff engaged the defenders at short-range, and as
more and more men came up the ropes, their determined drive
forced the enemy back from his cliff-edge positions. Company E personnel, led by their Company Commander, Captain
Gilbert C. Baugh, successfully assaulted a still-active
pillbox, taking a number of prisoners in the action at the
cost of having their Captain seriously wounded. The third
and fourth sections of Company E, after a short but fierce
battle, succeeded in neutralizing the OP but were unable
to destroy it as planned due to a landslide burying the demolitions on the beach. It being unable to force the steel
doors, a guard was placed on the position, pending the obtaining of additional explosive and the remaining men pushed out for the perimeter as planned.

Company D, ascending the cliff to the left of the OP,
discovered that the guns assigned them had been withdrawn.
Moving according to plan, this force pushed out to the perimeter, overcoming scattered opposition, and going into position on the right with twenty men.

Company F, having been fortunate with its' rocket-mortars, ascended the cliff in good order altho s/a fire and
grenades were directed at the men on the ropes. Clearing
the ground to the left of Company E, as planned, Company F
moved 300-yards inland before being pinned down by heavy
artillery and sniper fire. About twenty men by-passed the
sniper resistance and, moving thru a zone of mortar fire,
reached the main road and established contact with the second section of Company E, already in position. That portion of Company F remaining near the beach repulsed two enemy counterattacks during the afternoon, without casualty.
The accurate fire of the 60-mm mortar proved extremely effective in forcing the enemy to disclose his position and,
when he attempted to escape this fire, the riflemen would
cut him down.

By noon, sufficient men had made their way thru to the
road so that a perimeter was definitely established with
Company F on the left, Company E in the center, and Company
D on the right. Patrols were immediately dispatched to the
front, capturing several enemy and killing many more. A
patrol from Company D located the five remaining guns in a
partially wooded area about 1000-yards to the right rear of
the road. Destroying two guns by placing thermite grenades
on the breechblocks, the patrol then returned to the perimeter for more grenades. Returning to the area, they found
that the remaining three guns had been destroyed by a patrol from Company E during their absence.

- 4 -

Lt. Coit Coker USNR was in SFCP 3: *We landed with Capt. Hawks of Company C at about 0740, approximately one mile east of the scheduled landing place. (opposite D1 Exit). The ramp of the LCVP went down a foot and then stuck. Some Company C men were stuck in it and I do not know if they were ever extricated. Another man had his leg crushed between our craft and an adjacent one. Capt. Hawks jumped over the side and was nearly crushed between our craft and one on the other side – but finally was pulled back in without injury.*

His craft was sinking and the ramp was stuck. The only way off it was jumping over the side, but that was not without problems. To their right only 30 yards away a boat received a direct hit and burst into flames. Struggling with all their equipment, his unit swam to the shallow water and eventually made it to the seawall without further injuries.

We set up on the beach (about 0830) and contacted the destroyer McCook, telling her to stand by. I then took Kelly with me on a scouting party up the beach towards D1 in an effort to locate the 1st Battalion, but we were unsuccessful. On this trip an 88 burst nearby and a small piece of shrapnel struck my right knee cap causing a

        Infiltration via concealed routes by the enemy behind
    the outpost line and extremely accurate 88-mm fire severed
    communications between the perimeter and the Force CP. In
    hedgerow fighting during the afternoon, the men on the per-
    imeter totaled forty enemy captured and fifty killed, with
    Sgt Petty accounting for three-fifths of this total with
    his BAR marksmanship.

        Back on the Pointe, the Command Group moved top-side
    at 0830 into a large, cliff-edge crater. The Aid Station
    remained on the beach until all the wounded were cared for;
    at about 1300, it was set up in a pillbox just forward of
    the CP. Many of those wounded elected to remain at their
    posts after treatment and were highly instrumental in the
    success of the operation.

        Communication was limited to Naval units only. Means
    employed were the SCR-284 and the Signal Lamp EE-84, with
    the Lamp proving the more effective of the two during day-
    light only. At 1130, a Pgn Msg was sent to CG 1st Div; Msg
    as follows: "Enemy battery on Pointe du Hoe destroyed"
    This Msg was never receipted for. Messages to the Navy re-
    questing aid in evacuating casualties resulted in a small
    dory being sent in, only to be destroyed by enemy fire.
    The SCR-284 and the Signal Lamp also provided Shore Fire
    Control, with the Lamp again affording the best results.
    At 1400, SCR-300 contact was made with the 116th Infantry;
    Msg sent was as follows: "Many casualties, need reinforce-
    ments, my position is Pointe du Hoe (In code)". Expecting
    an immediate reply, the radio was kept open thru-out the
    night but it wasn't until 070615 that a reply was received
    stating that the message had been received and acted upon.
    Another Pgn Msg was sent to CG 1st Div during the afternoon
    of D-Day; Msg as follows: "Many casualties, ammunition al-
    most gone, need reinforcements". This Msg was also never
    receipted for. Altho efforts were continually made to con-
    tact the remainder of the Ranger Force, none were success-
    ful. The only enemy action directed at the CP during day-
    light consisted of mid-range auto-weapon and sniper fire.

        An enemy strongpoint several hundred yards to the West
    of the position was troublesome thru-out the day and tho
    three different attempts were made to knock it out, lack of
    cover and extremely accurate artillery fire made this po-
    sition impregnable. During late afternoon, a destroyer ap-
    proached to within point-blank range of the position and
    completely destroyed it.

        A check made of the perimeter in the late afternoon
    totaled sixty-five men; the casualties reported were:

        Company D, being split up, could make no assessment.

        Company E suffered 5 EM KIA, one officer and 15 EM SWA,
    and 8 EM MIA.

        Company F suffered one officer and 4 EM KIA, one offi-
    cer and 8 EM SWA, and 2 EM MIA

                        - 5 -

superficial wound. About 0930 all of us crossed over the remainder of the beach and worked up the slope, under enemy observation and fire, to the edge of the plateau on top.

Here we joined by Captain Vavruska (NGFO of 5th Ranger Battalion) and all of us joined with Lt. Vandervoort (1st Battalion) and his platoon and commenced working toward the D1 Exit.

On the plateau was a field of grass (650903) with numerous fox-holes containing Germans. It was decided about noon to bring naval fire on this field by spotting in deflection from well to the right (to avoid hitting ourselves) crossing D1 exit.

2nd Battalion After Action Report – Force C – A & B Companies and 5th Btn.

Force "C"   Companies A/B

The Plan of Attack:

Force "C", consisting of Companies A/B, plus the bulk of the Bn Hq Det, was to land under control of the CO 5th Ranger Battalion, by either of two plans, as follows:

Plan I – Upon the receipt of a pre-arranged signal from Force "A", prior to H+45-minutes, stating their mission had been successful, the Force would proceed to Pointe du Hoe, ascend the cliffs by means of the DUKW-ladders, and Companies A/B would revert to the control of the CO 2nd Ranger Battalion.

Plan II – If the "Success" signal was not received from Force "A" by the appointed time, Force "C" was to land at Omaha Dog Green Beach at H+60-minutes and, with Company B acting as point and Company A as flank protection, would precede the 5th Ranger Battalion to Pointe du Hoe, as swiftly as possible, along a prearranged cross-country route. When the Pointe was reached, Companies A/B would form a defense line to protect the rear of the 5th Ranger Battalion which would make a frontal attack on the Pointe du Hoe defenses.

The Beach Assault:

Companies A/B plus the Bn Hq Det lowered away at 0615 and made rendevous with the 5th Ranger Battalion according to plan. The heavy seas caused many men to become seasick on the run-in. The majority of the men stood up to gain relief from the sea-breeze and to watch the bombardment of the beach. "Listening Watch" was maintained in the Headquarters craft for signals from Force "A". At approximately 0700, the flotilla of LCA's lay-to for five minutes awaiting word from Force "A". An unintelligible message was received at 0715; the only recognizable word being "Charlie". The SCR-284 was set up but failed to contact either Force "A" or the Force Headquarters Ship, the Prince Charles. The radio communications on the Guide-craft also failed, when it was desired to use that means of transmission. Precious minutes were also spent when the loudhailer on the Guide-LCA also failed to function properly.

By this time, the line of LCA's was so near to shore that a landing on Omaha Dog Green Beach was mandatory. As the craft throttled down to thread the mined under-water obstacle area, artillery shells began to straddle the boats. At 0735, a craft containing the 2nd Platoon/Company B either struck a mine or received a direct hit. The resulting explosion severely wounded one officer and several men. Sinking quickly, the LCA threw its' occupants

A Company 2nd Rangers – Vierville-sur-Mer, France.   Maurice Prince: *It was pitch dark when the time came for us to load into LCAs. Our mother ship was now anchored about thirteen miles off the French coast. The water was beating furiously against our boat.*

We had to come out into this inky void from our lightened quarters below, we were momentarily blinded. With all our crowding and milling about, we loaded onto our LCAs without the slightest of confusion, thanks to our previous dry run practices. We were literally jammed into our assault boats, a section at a time. Generally these crafts were supposed to hold thirty to thirty-five men, but we were close to forty men and fully loaded down with heavy packs and equipment. We were packed together as tightly as the proverbial sardines in the can.

```
into deep water. Losing most of their equipment in the
process, these men were forced to swim until they could
get a footing for the dash across the beach.

    "Ramps Down" was at 0740. The 2nd Ranger portion of
Force "C" was landed directly into the face of withering
sniper, MG, mortar, and artillery fire - none of which had
been cleared prior to their arrival. This first wave came
in about one thousand yards to the left of the Beach Exit,
the planned "Touch-down" area.   The 5th Ranger Battalion
was caused in to be brought in still further to the left
on order of its' Battalion Commander, when he observed the
plight of the first wave. The entire 5th Ranger Battalion
came across the beach with but a minimum of casualties.

    Six craft were in the first wave to hit the beach at
H+70-minutes. From left to right, they were as follows:

2 Co A LCA's  -  Gp Hq LCA  -  Bn HQ LCA  -  2 Co B LCA's

    Machine gun fire directly into the open ramps of the
LCA's caused a number of casualties, forcing the survivors
to dive thru a hail of lead into the sea. Some men pro-
ceeded ashore as they had done in countless training man-
euvers; others, dropped in chest-deep water, swam ashore
under-water, then, dashed across the 100-yards of beach to
the cover of the sea-wall. T/5 Ray of Company A had a me-
thod all his own; standing upright to better guage the
pattern of the constantly shifting MG cross-fire, he would
lightly step out of the way of the sand-spurts as they
reached for him. During subsequent action, this indivi-
dual, again standing up and firing his BAR from the hip,
accounted for a number of the enemy.

    The greater part of the enemy's fire was enfilad-
ing the beach from the right with a strongpoint consisting
of one MG protected by a number of riflemen located on the
bluff 200-yards to Company A's front. This gun killed the
Commander of Company A when he neglected his own safety to
direct his men across the fire-swept beach. By 0805, all
the men surviving the beach holocaust were reorganizing un-
der cover of the fortified-house line.

The Subsequent Action:

    Advancing first as individuals and later as teams, as
more and more of the men made their way across the beach,
the Rangers of Company A stormed the bluff to their front
to knock out the machine gun which was, literally, firing
down their throats. The bluff-line being finally cleared
the Company was then reorganized under leadership of their
NCO's, all the officers having become casualties on the
beach. (The Company was to be without officers until D+2)
```

The 1st Platoon/Company B, led by their Company Commander, crossed the beach in good order. Attempting to continue according to plan, Captain Edgar L. Arnold led his men along the beach road toward Exit D-t. Contacting and working with a platoon of Amphibious tanks, this force searched a number of the fortified houses under severe sniper fire. The strength of the enemy defenses added to the small number of men remaining in fighting condition forced the Captain to undertake the alternate plan, that of returning to the landing site and moving inland over the bluff. This platoon joined the remaining elements of Company A at the top of the bluff and, moving off with Company A, soon made contact with the 5th Ranger Battalion.

The six survivors of the 2nd Platoon/Company B, after obtaining weapons and ammunition, ascended the bluff under cover of smoke from the smouldering vegetation. Joining up with seven men of Company A who were now in possesion of the enemy MG, this group pushed on inland to be the first to contact the 5th Ranger Battalion. These men volunteered to continue according to plan, that of leading the 5th Battalion to the Pointe but the CO 5th Ranger Battalion denied their request.

The Bn Hq Det also suffered heavy casualties, commencing with the first officer off the LCA being hit by mortar fragments. Those of the survivors who did not contact the Companies for the move to the 5th Ranger Battalion aided the Battalion Medical Detachment, which performed heroic measures in aiding the wounded on the beach. The loss of the greater part of their CP equipment in the bullet-churned waters caused these men to revert to riflemen, assisting in the clearing out of snipers still operating in the beach area. The detachment went into position on the bluff for the first night.

Having been released, due to their depleted state, from the mission of preceding the 5th Battalion to Pointe du Hoe, Companies A/B were palced in Force "C" Reserve. Captain Arnold then reorganized the remnants into one understrength company. This composite Company, moving in reserve, followed the 5th Ranger Battalion to, and thru, Vierville, without further incident. Bivouac was set up for the night just East of Vierville and a perimeter defense was established. A patrol which returned to the beach for ammunition, contacted Company C at 2130 and directed the Company to the location of Force "C". This patrol returned safely at 2230. A mixed unit of approximately ten Medium and Light tanks of the 743rd Tank Battalion closed into the bivouac area that evening. Strong security posts were maintained thru-out the night.

Our two boats (one assault boat for each platoon, plus the extra headquarters company personnel assigned to the company) were gently lowered to the waters below. Our boats bobbled about like a tiny cork caught in a riptide. The channel on this side was much rougher and choppier than on the English side. The incoming spray dampened and soaked us through and through. The night was terribly cold and the water colder so that besides being uncomfortable, we were miserable to boot.

Dawn was beginning to break. We were as yet drifting about. So far we hadn't been fired on by the enemy and neither had our naval guns opened up. I was sadly mistaken in the concept that I was a good sailor, as the effects of the up and down, to and fro motion of our frail craft made me and a good many other boys horribly sick. Puke bags which had been issued to us prior to our embarking the LCAs came into play. A few boys were leaning over the rails trying to revive themselves by having the onrushing waters wet their faces.

Expert handling was needed to keep our LCAs on their courses. It was most fortunate that we received this skilful manipulation. Zero hour for the other companies to land on the Pointe was now approaching. A rending and thunderous ovation of shells whizzing overhead signalled the beginning and the breaking loose of all hell.

Our supporting Navy was starting its softening up process of the enemy's beach defences. As yet, we were still out of accurate fire range of the enemy guns, although some return shells did land to our rear. The distant and distinct hum of friendly aircraft became audible and soon the planes and bombers became visible. I personally couldn't appreciate or take notice of the greatness of our attack, as my face at this time was deeply buried in the puke bag. Our lieutenant who was watching the proceedings gave us a fairly descriptive resume, anyway, as much as his advantageous position allowed him of the raging battle.

Robert Gary – A Company 2nd Rangers: *Going in, everyone was a bit nervous – some seasick and that was a mess. We were on a British LCA – I remember specifically our training being so realistic. It seemed just like another training mission. The weather was so bad that it attracted your attention. Approaching the beach we had trained and been rehearsed so thoroughly that we knew exactly what to do and how to do it. The only thing that changed was that originally we were going to follow in with D and F companies and attack the Pointe, but it took them so long to get in and up that we then had to cancel that and land on Dog Green beach.*

They lowered the ramp and we went out in water up to our necks. The first thing we got rid of was our gas masks. We were wearing impregnated clothing and it was awful. We also had the inflatable life vests. We got rid of those in a hurry.

Maurice Prince: *By this time, we could picture our brother companies scaling the cliffs and assaulting the Pointe. We could actually see the returning bombers as they flew back to their bases. They had completed their part in the neutralization of the Pointe. More enemy shells began to land in our vicinity. Our own Navy guns were still firing away. The great belches of flame that shot forward after each round left the giant muzzles, gave promise that the enemy was 'hurting'.*

We were anxiously awaiting word from our companies on the Pointe. Our features were tense and alert; everyone was straining forward as if trying to snap an imaginary leash that held him back. Our CO. who was in our boat nervously scanned his timepiece. No word from the companies on the Pointe as yet and the deadline fastly approaching. Other LCAs were beginning to make the run to shore. Some of these boats were equipped with rocket firing equipment and they were using them. No one was standing up in our boat now except the coxswain and the gunner. Things were beginning to get hot. The enemy was bringing up his larger artillery pieces. Artillery shells were landing nearby and even machine gun and small arms fire were hitting the water about us, but on the whole this shelling and firing was inaccurate.

Time was running out for the companies on the Pointe. Our CO. signalled that we'd make the run to the beach. (We couldn't wait any longer.) Excitement was mounting, enemy shelling increased; the water was terribly rough and choppy and many a wave engulfed our craft and threatened to overturn it. The artful handling of the vessel by the veteran English sailor saved the day. He cleaved and dodged his way forward, we were coming in fast as so were many other similar crafts. Enemy accuracy increased, small arms and machine gun bullets began to bounce off our bullet-proofed sides.

The shore began to take on new and larger aspects. We could clearly view the beach and surrounding terrain. The bursting of shells upon the shore wasn't exactly tonic for our morale, we seemed to be on top of the beach, when a scraping and searing sound rended thru the air. Our crafts came to an abrupt stop that marked the finish to our ride. Ramps were quickly lowered. Men hastily jumped and dived into the icy, waist-deep water. We were about seventy-five yards from the shore. Bullets were really flying about now. Cleverly concealed and smartly defended enemy positions gave the Jerry a decided advantage over us. Casualties were being received by us. Men were being hit while in the water. It was a struggle to maintain balance in the surf and to dodge the withering hail of enemy fire. We were helpless, like ducks in a shooting gallery.

Our Navy and planes hadn't completely neutralized these positions at all and now our landings were masking the fire of our Navy. It was up to us, the footslogger alone now. The cold water, the excitement and confusion gave me and the others who were sick a quick cure. I looked back and saw what had caused our craft to stop. It wasn't a sandbar as I had originally surmised, but underwater obstacles that had been placed by the enemy. Thank God they weren't mined. On the left, a beached LCI stood smouldering and burning. On all sides of us dead bodies of Americans. GI's were floating around. We had no feeling for them, but now we had a score to settle with those dirty Nazi bastards.

Robert Edlin – A Company 2nd Ranger Battalion: *Our LCA hit a sandbar. We were seventy-five yards from the shore, and the ramp went down. We went off the sides in case the craft was swept onto us by a wave. A boat carrying B Company took a direct hit on the ramp from a mortar or mine and I saw men sinking all around me. I tried to grab a couple of them. There were bodies from the 116th floating everywhere. They were face down in the water with packs still on their backs. They had inflated their life jackets and turned upside down and drowned. I went across the beach to get to the sea wall.*

Maurice Prince: *Our men began to spread out, to deploy and to reorganize into their squads and sections, upon reaching the shoreline. Our return covering fire was inadequate and inaccurate. Our only hope and salvage lay in reaching cover on land and storming the enemy in a frontal attack.*

Our fighter planes, meanwhile, were dealing out death and destruction to German artillery positions in the rear, but enemy mortar and small arms fire were causing us many deaths and other casualties. We gained shore and found momentary respite on a pile of rocks that ran parallel to the waters edge, about one hundred yards across the beach. But before we had reached this cover, we had to go through a curtain of lead and chance a continual artillery barrage – which covered this entire section of open beach.

Men were stripping themselves of their packs and excess ammunition. They had become too waterlogged and were too much of a hindrance to carry. Lifebelts were also shed as we dashed to the precarious safety afforded us by the rock-pile. All those that reached this cover did so, by sheer luck, rather than skill. Murderous enemy close range automatic fire was sweeping everything in sight and mowing down soldier after soldier.

We were exhausted and tired on reaching the rock-pile. There seemed to be no end to the enemy resistance. Another hasty re-organization of the squads present was made. We were fighting mad, we dished into the fray in headlong flight, shooting up everything that looked like the enemy.

Other soldiers plus Rangers were now running and dashing about, with us Rangers out in front. We were getting closer to the enemy and already some of our boys were assaulting their positions. The popping of hand grenades and the flashing of bayonets put an end to many a Heinie's activity. Tanks which had floated in on the beach began to give us covering fire and neutralised a strongly-encased enemy machine gun position that was covering the beach.

You couldn't help but admire the cleverness and the strategism of the Jerry defences. They had built their lines well, taking advantage of the commanding terrain, and using a skillful system of camouflage to conceal their defences. We had been under their observation at all times, while we had difficulties in locating from where they were shooting at us.

Rangers were beginning to assault the hilly defences of the enemy using automatic weapons, rifles, hand grenades and other arms that they had been equipped with. There was no stopping us though enemy fire was taking its toll. Teamwork plus individual Ranger initiative was driving the enemy from his covered position. Prisoners were being taken, but not for long. We didn't have the time and men for them. Anyway, we couldn't bother with them.

Once we gained a foothold on the hill, we were in a position to flank the enemy's strongpoints. Another hasty reorganisation was effected. We relentlessly drove and forged ahead. One emplacement after another was wiped out. Enemy artillery wasn't as heavy on the hill as it was being poured down on the beaches, so that we were not harassed too much by shelling. Sniper small arms were about all the enemy resistance being put up now. A few of our combat patrols quickly took care of that.

We were in a 'giving' position now. Our true and accurate firing was putting the final touches to the lives of the fanatical Germans. We had seen our buddies fall, below, now we were avenging them with a fury that knew no bounds.

We were unmerciful and cruel, but he who lives by the sword, must die by the sword. That morning brought many a Jerry face to face with his Maker.

Individual heroism was being displayed on all parts of the battlefield. Medics were doing yeomen service, wounded men were dragging wounded men to safety, brave men went gallantly to their graves storming impregnable positions, every one was doing his share and more. I could easily write a volume on individual accounts of bravery. I would like, though, to recount one story of heroism which should set an example, not that more was done, but it is much a story of human sacrifice that I would like to relate it. It's about our CO. Captain Rafferty who was killed in action in the line of duty.

German soldiers surrendering to an American officer.

Our CO. was the first man off the assault boat. He had just waded through the water and had reached the beach, when a spray of machine gun fire had wounded him in the leg. It hadn't taken him long to size up the fighting situation. He realised to stay on the open sandy beach was suicide. He repeatedly shouted, hollered, cajoled, and urged his men to keep on going ahead, refusing to budge from his own uncovered place, so that he could be in a better position to control his men. He was masterful and inspiring as he yelled and directed his men forward. When the last man passed him, he made a vain attempt to seek personal safety, but a direct hit of an enemy 88 put a climax to his career as an officer and Ranger. A quick ending to a most courageous leader.

We were now in full control of the hill. The enemy had been subdued. Soldiers from other units were now following our lead. These men who had been stunned by the unexpectedness of the enemy counter-attacks were now being brought out of their lethargy. We had shown them what could be done and how it could be done. Our undaunted and fighting spirit had manifested itself. Those troops took on new life and new courage from us, and valiantly aided us in our drive.

We had now established a small beachhead. Assault crafts from other units were continuously landing. They were still being subjected to artillery fire – but they had no small arms fire to contend with. We had taken care of that part. Our fighter planes were still hammering away at rear enemy installations and giving us the protective cover we had been promised. Engineers were clearing mine fields and blowing obstacles on the beach. Tanks were landing and going forth to battle. Everyone was taking his place in this global drama. But, yet, it was us Rangers, who were out in front, leading and showing the way.

Information began to pour in from individuals who still remained in our company about the other members who were absent. The combined stories presented a tale of woe. Our CO. had been killed, both of our platoon leaders had been wounded, and were put out of action, the First Sgt. was reported as missing, and probably dead (later on his dog tags were found hanging on a cross, in the Army cemetery at Verville-sur-Mer) and the names of the men killed and wounded sounded like someone calling off the company roster. We had landed on the shores of Normandy with sixty-seven enlisted men and three officers. When we counted noses on top of the hill that morning, we had no officers, and only twenty-two enlisted men. There wasn't a throat that didn't have a lump in it and there wasn't an eye that tears didn't stream from. I know, I was there. These fearless men were human, they had lost their buddies and comrades, who only last night joked and played. Now they were gone. They had given their all for their country.

We were without leaders, fatigued from our arduous and gruelling fighting, disheartened by the sad news of our fallen comrades, but yet we never stopped in our pushing forward. We had paid a heavy price for our gains, but we had taken a good total in return. How many krauts we left dead that morning I'll never know, but I'm sure for every man we lost, we got four or five in his place. We had established a decent size beachhead where every moment saw new troops and new supplies arriving and disembarking.

We had captured and destroyed innumerable Heinie weapons and equipment and we had lifted the morale of other fighting men who had seen us in action and had come forward to aid us. We conclusively disproved the myth of the German super race that day. We had shown the world what could be done if the right action was taken at the right time.

We proved that the Heinies could be beaten if a little teamwork and brainwork were co-ordinated with the guts and stamina needed. We displayed the might and tenacity that makes the democratic way of life stronger than the Nazi way, and actually showed it.

Although we had done our share of the fighting, we had as yet to complete our mission. We still had to take the Pointe and contact our Brother companies there. A complete reorganisation of A.B.C. companies was effected on top of the hill that overlooked the beach at Vierville-sur-Mer, so as to remedy that situation. Captain Arnold (then Co of Baker Co.) was put in command of our task force. Our three companies combined hardly made one full Ranger company. We had sustained heavy casualties, which had depleted our ranks.

We formed on the coastal road, which led to the Pointe. We took up the approach march formation and continued our line of advance. Our plan for taking the Pointe was a simple one. We were to follow up this coastal road until the road junction which led to the Pointe was reached. Here we were to do a flanking movement and assault the enemy in a frontal attack. Our order of march was: Able Co. to lead off as point, With Baker and Charley companies in support, while elements of the 116th Regiment was to compose the main body. To this we had the direct support of four tanks, which were to be directly under our control.

It was now getting on in the afternoon. The weather was moderate and rather cool for this time of the year. I hate to think how much more miserable we would have been had that day been one of those hot June days. What with all our running and fighting we had done, we would have all been worn out to a frazzle and we would never have been able to keep up our attack.

1st Infantry Division Radio messages were sent to Commanding General 1st Inf. Div. stating that from information received (via prisoners), the Command Post for the 12th Company 726th Regiment was located in Grandcamp-les-Bains.

> 1245 - Msg. to CG 1st Div-Prisoners stated tnat the CP 10th Co., 726th at St. Laurent- sur-Mer. CP 12th Co., 726th at Grandcamp-les-Bains. That is in the 116th Sector. 916th in sector of 16th Inf. CP, 5th Co., 916th at Surrain. The 916th relieved the 915th two weeks ago.

The 1st Infantry Division Radio log at 4.35pm makes the following report.

> At 1635B, two Ranger Battalions reported that there was no opposition in their sector and other battalions were "OK".

[Author: It is difficult to see why any Ranger on or around Omaha Beach or Vierville would have suggested there was 'no opposition in their sector' – in reality quite the opposite was the case.]

Maurice Prince: *We started out cautiously, feeling our way forward. Enemy artillery was now falling intermittently into our positions, causing casualties here and there. Our company escaped unscathed. We ran into sniper small arms fire as we approached the coastal town of Vierville-sur-Mer. Our point and combat patrols took that situation into hand. A house to house search of the town was inaugurated by these fighting teams, which cleared out all enemy elements and cleared the town of snipers.*

Our procedure was steady but tedious, so that darkness was beginning to envelope us before we could advance further outside the town. A halt was declared, while a conference by our leaders was held. Combat patrols were sent back to contact friendly units to our rear and flanks. It was decided that we set up bivouac for the night at a road junction down the road a couple of hundred yards away. We holed up there for the night and took up defensive positions. We were all tired and fatigued. We hadn't rested once during the day. And had been up since 3 a.m., continuously fighting and forging ahead.

We dug in for the night and set up a hasty perimeter, or all-around defence of our area, which consisted of strongpoints and outposts. Our patrols, meanwhile, had returned with negative information, concerning the enemy. G-2 reports that were handed down to us weren't exactly what the doctor ordered. We were told to hold ourselves ready for an enemy counter-attack of tanks and foot troops, which was imminent to come that night.

There we were, just a handful of men plus a few tanks – which had established a bivouac in a field across the road from us. Now, tired and weary as we were, we couldn't get to sleep as that night a million and one things plagued our minds. Chiefly, what happened to our companies at the Pointe? How were we going to repel the enemy when he counter-attacked? What about the enemy shelling, etc.? These and other questions ran thru our minds that first night on French soil.

We had been most fortunate in that all day not one enemy airplane had been sighted. We did have one alert, but I never saw the Jerry planes and didn't see any counter actions taken. But now, under the cover of night, the Luftwaffe began to sally forth to administer death, destruction and damage. Their target being the dormant Navy, that still lay vengeful and protecting off the French coast. Also they were out to destroy all our gains and installations on the beach itself.

From our vantage point we could clearly view the scene as our beach and naval defences put up a brilliant barrage that turned the night into day. We could ascertain distinctly the bursting of flak, and we could follow the flight of the parabolic machine gun tracers as they made their way skyward. The huge search-light beams as they criss-crossed in search of the enemy menace formed weird designs in the skies. Bombs were being dropped upon our vessels at sea. We could clearly view the great splashes formed each time the bombs struck the water. Thanks to the strength and effectiveness of our anti-aircraft defences, the enemy lacked the correct precision to score a direct hit. I didn't see a bomb come close.

The raid ended as quickly as it had started. All then became quiet and dark. Ghostly silence hung over the land with eerie unnaturalness. We were now alone on guard by ourselves at our small outposts waiting and expecting. We strained our eyes to the utmost, to pierce the inky veil of night. The slightest noise or movement was a certainty to bring us to stark attention and alertness. Our nerves were on edge, we were entertaining the report of an enemy attack: and we were making sure that we wouldn't be caught off guard and off balance.

2nd Battalion After Action Report – Force B.

```
Force "B"                                              Company C

The Plan of Attack:

     Force B, consisting of Company C,  commanded by Cap-
tain Ralph E. Goranson,  was to land with Company A/116th
Infantry at H+3-minutes  on Omaha Dog Green Beach,  Vier-
ville-sur-Mer,  and destroy the installations  located on
Pointe El Raz de la Percee.  Upon the completion  of this
initial mission, Company C was to proceed along the cliff
line, destroying all installations along the route taken,
to  Pointe du Hoe.  One Amphibious Tank Platoon,  two if
necessary, was to be "On call" to the Company for the in-
itial mission.  Company C/116th Infantry  was to provide
flanking protection during the movement to Pointe du Hoe.

The Beach Assault:

     Company C,  consisting of three officers and 65 men,
lowered away at 0430  and proceeded to the rendevous area
where contact was made with Company A/116th Infantry. The
run-in to the beach  was hampered by heavy seas,  causing
the majority of the men  to become seasick.  Near shore,
AT fire  scored several direct hits  on one of the LCA's,
smashing the ramp and causing severe casualties.  The men
disembarked  into the face  of intense rifle, MG, mortar,
and artillery fire.  Moving individually,  slowed down to
a walk by their illness  and the soft,  water-soaked sand,
the survivors  had to cross almost  300 yards  of exposed
beach before coming  under the cover of the cliffs to the
East  of Exit D-1.  The casualties  suffered in crossing
the beach were:

     19 KIA; 13 SWA; 5 LWA, who elected to remain duty.

The Subsequent Action:

     The intensive  enemy fire  making movement  thru the
Beach Exit impossible,  Plan 2 was put into effect.   One
officer and two men moved along the cliff to the East un-
til a spot was found  where free-hand climbing was possi-
ble.  Ascending the cliff  and  making fast several ropes
which had been brought along for that purpose, this party
then guided the remainder of the Company "top-side".   One
LCA containing 116th Infantry troops touched-down at this
position  and twenty men of Company B/116th Infantry were
also brought up the ropes.

     Reconnaissance patrols  brought back the information
that  enemy troops  located in the house  and surrounding
entrenchments  to the West of the Company's position were
placing  enfilade fire  on the beach.   The area had been
subjected to forty-five minutes of Naval bombardment but,
even tho the house was partially destroyed. the enemy had
reoccupied  the positions.   Captain Goranson decided to
```

```
clear out this position  before proceeding on East to the
initial objective.  Small  combat patrols  cleaned out a
number of mortar and MG emplacements, but the enemy  con-
tinued to reinforce the garrison with troops who made en-
try into the position from Vierville by means of conceal-
ed passages.  The Company was forced to remain in the lo-
cality to wipe out these new arrivals as fast as they ap-
peared.  By mid-afternoon,  when this flow of reinforce-
ments ceased, sixty-nine enemy had been killed at a price
of two casualties to the Company.

     At about 1430, Captain Goranson led a patrol East to
reconnoiter Pointe Percee.  The party arrived in position
from where they could observe the Pointe, just in time to
watch the close-in destroyer  knock out the position with
direct hits.  Satisfied  that the mission  of destroying
Pointe El Raz de la Percee was completed.  Captain Goran-
son then returned to his Company.  A destroyer started to
open fire on Company C's position  about this time but an
alert Observer on the beach soon caused this fire to stop.

     Contact was later established  with the 116th Infan-
try and Company C moved down to the Beach Exit.  A patrol
from Force "C" was contacted here and, upon receiving the
location of that Force, Company C proceeded thereto with-
out incident, arriving at the Force bivouac  area at about
2200-hours.

     From this point on, Company C worked with Force "C".
```

iv) Casualties

B Company 2nd Rangers – Vierville-sur-Mer, France.

Captain Rafferty was Killed in Action.

1st Lt. Edlin from Duty to Wounded in Action.

1st Lt. White from Duty to hospital (slightly injured in Action).

The following 12 enlisted men were Killed in Action.

1st Sgt. Sowa	Sgt. Charles Rich	Pfc. Joseph V. Daniels
S/Sgt. John C. Biddle	T/5 Charles Bollia	Pfc. John C. Shanahan
S/Sgt. Davis	T/5 George Selepec	Pfc. Earl W. Shireman
S/Sgt. Smith	Pfc. Robert Dailey	Pfc. Joseph R. Trainor

The following 20 men were sent from Duty to hospital with wounds.

S/Sgt. Ralph W. Hoyt	T/4 Donald F. Mentzer	Pfc. Bakalar
S/Sgt. William V. Klaus	T/5 Kenneth K. Bladorn	Pfc. Carl C. Cerwin
S/Sgt. Leonard L. Lavandoski	T/5 Harry E. Brewster	Pfc. Robert P. Gary
Sgt. John F. Donovan	T/5 William H. Kwasnicki	Pfc. Garland V. Hart
Sgt. Donald E. Fendley	T/5 George F. Lawrence	Pfc. Roy L. Latham
Sgt. George H. Hellers	T/5 James W. Slagle	Pfc. Robert C. Lambert
Sgt. Theodore A. James	T/5 Orville E. Wright	

The following two men were Wounded in Action and transferred from Duty to hospital.

Pfc. Raymond Tollefson

Pfc. Clyde S. Pattison

T/5 Percy C. Hower suffered a minor leg wound and remained on Duty.

Pfc. Donald L. Ashline suffered a minor wound to his left arm and remained on Duty.

Pfc. Elmer Davidson suffered a minor wound to his right calf and remained on Duty.

Pfc. Gerald H. Schroeder suffered a minor wound to his left arm and remained on Duty.

Pfc. Raymond K. Ferguson suffered a minor wound to his left knee, but remained on Duty.

Record of events: Map being used was a GSGS4250. Scale 1:50,000.

Made landing on operational beach Omaha – Dog Green and advanced through Vierville-sur-Mer.

B Company 2nd Rangers – Vierville-sur-Mer, France.

1st Lt. Robert M. Brice was Killed in Action.

2nd Lt. Fitzsimmons went from Duty to Wounded in Action at 0730 hours.

The following 11 men were Killed in Action:

S/Sgt. Michael C. Vetovich	T/5 Elmer P. Olander	Pfc. Robert R. Whitehead
Sgt. Joseph W. Shedaker	Pfc. Carl F. Davis	
Sgt. John R. Henwood	Pfc. John Dolinsky	
T/5 Bramkamp	Pfc. George Paniaha	
T/5 Dominick F. Gallo	Pfc. Ollie D. Richardson	

The following 2 enlisted men are Missing in Action:
Pfc. V. White
Pfc Robert E. Wilde

The following 15 enlisted men went from Duty to Hospital as of 0730 hours.

1st Sgt. Manning I. Rubenstein	T/5 Keith Bragg	Pfc. Robert D. Herlihy
S/Sgt. Joseph J. Dorchak	T/5 Charles E. Gould	Pfc. George Lengyel Jr.
S/Sgt. Eugene T. Ferguson	T/5 James E. Jones	Pfc. Simon Smith
Sgt. Eugene B. Baker	T/5. R. Williamson	Pfc. Floyd D. Whicker
Sgt. Paul R. Filzen	Pfc. K. Davis	Pfc. Wilbur L. Eason

Pfc. Earl O'Neal was attached for Duty to Hospital – Lightly Wounded in Action 0730 hours.
T/5 Leonard P. Kassmeir suffered a minor ear wound and remained on Duty.
Sgt. Donald D. DeCapp suffered a minor arm wound and remained on Duty.
Pvt. Wilbur L. Eason received a minor neck wound and remained on Duty.

Record of events: Map being used was a GSGS4250. Scale 1:50,000.
Made landing on operational beach Omaha – Dog Green and advanced through Vierville-sur-Mer.

C Company 2nd Rangers – Vierville-sur-Mer, France.
1st Lt. William D. Moody was Killed in Action.
The following 19 men were Killed in Action:

1st Sgt. Henry S. Golas	T/5 Vayle Miller	Pfc. David L. Goudey
S/Sgt. James A. Kane	T/5 Marvin A. Simko	Pfc. John S. Gourley
Sgt. Walter B. Geldon	Pfc. Harold E. Clendenin	Pfc. Leslie M. Irvin
Sgt. Kenneth A. Hendrickson	Pfc. Sammie Adkins	Pfc. William D. Myers
Sgt. Robert J. Raymond	Pfc. Volney E. Beekler	Pfc. Fred W. Plumlee
T/5 Willis C. Caperton	Pfc. James. E. Donahue	
T/5 William Lynch	Pfc. Wayne D. Goad	

T/5 James A. Machan was attached to C from Headquarters and Killed in Action.
1st Lt. Sidney A. Saloman was Wounded in Action.

The following 13 men were Seriously Wounded in Action and sent to hospital.

S/Sgt. Oliver Reed	Pfc. Jack W. Hasting	Pfc. Elmer P. Watkins
S/Sgt. Harry Wilder	Pfc. Eddie W. Harding	Pfc. Clarence A. Wilson
T/5 Jesse J. Runyan	Pfc. Nelson W. Noyes	Pfc. John Yadlosky
T/5 Steve Stepancevich	Pfc. Morris. D. Poynter	
Pfc. Delmas O Duncan	Pfc. Winfred P. Smith	

S/Sgt. Richard C. Garret suffered a shrapnel wound to the chest.

The following 3 men were Slightly Wounded in Action and were present for Duty.
T/5 Matthew J. Wyder suffered a shrapnel wound to the left shoulder.
Pfc. Brownie L. Bolin suffered a shrapnel wound to his right buttock.
Pfc. Otto K. Stephens suffered a head wound.

Record of events: Map being used was a GSGS4250. Scale 1:50,000.
Made landing on operational beach Omaha – Dog Green and advanced through Vierville-sur-Mer.

D Company 2nd Rangers – Pointe du Hoc, France.
2nd Lt. George F. Kerchner assumes Duty as Company Commander.
The following 5 enlisted men were Killed in Action:

Pfc. Melvin C. Heffelbower	Sgt. Bernard Szewczuk	S/Sgt. Benjamin H. Wirtz
T/5 Clarence J. Long	T/5 William D. Vaughan	

The following 9 men went from Duty to hospital (Seriously Wounded in Action):

Pfc. Leroy G. Adams	Pfc. Robert A. Fruhling	S/Sgt. Fransis J. Pacyga
Pfc. Sheldon Bare	Pfc. Lester W. Harris	T/5 George O. Schneller
Pfc. John F. Conaboy	S/Sgt. Koenig	Sgt. Morris N. Webb

Pfc. William Cruz went from Duty to hospital. Lighty Wounded in Action.

1st Sgt. Leonard G. Lomell suffered a minor wound on his right side, but remained on Duty.

E Company 2nd Rangers – Pointe du Hoc, France.

Pfc. John J. Sillmon went from Duty to Hospital, Seriously Wounded in Action.

The following 2 men were Lightly Wounded in Action and remained on Duty.

Pfc. George T. Roberts, Pfc. Henry A. Wood.

1st Lt. Theodore E. Lapres assumed command of Company.

Record of events: Map being used was a GSGS4250. Scale 1:50,000.

Made landing at 0705 hours on operational beach Omaha – Charlie and advanced to Pointe du Hoc, France.

F Company 2nd Rangers – Pointe du Hoc, France.

1st Lt. Jacob J. Hill was Killed in Action.

The following 4 enlisted men were Killed in Action.

Sgt. Richards	Pfc. Kimble
Pfc. Cole	Pfc. Wieburg

Captain Masny suffered a minor arm wound and remained on Duty.

The following 7 enlisted men went from Duty to Hospital – Wounded in Action:

T/5 John W. Franklin	Pfc. John Bacho	Pfc. John W. White
S/Sgt. William H. Simons	Pfc. Gerald A. Bouchard	
S/Sgt. Robert G. Youso	Pfc. William D. Walsh	

T/5 Charles W. Korb went from attached Headquarters Company to Hospital – Lightly Wounded in Action.

S/Sgt. Otto was Seriously Wounded in Action and evacuated to the battleship *Texas*.

Record of events: Map being used was a GSGS4250. Scale 1:50,000.

Made landing at 0705 hours on operational beach Omaha – Charlie and advanced to Pointe du Hoc, France.

Medical Detachment 2nd Rangers – Vierville-sur-Mer, France.

Record of events: Map being used was a GSGS4250. Scale 1:50,000.

Made landing at 0720 hours on operational beach Omaha – Dog Green.

Headquarters Company 2nd Rangers – Vierville-sur-Mer, France.

Captain Frederick G. Wilkin went from Duty to Hospital Slightly Wounded in Action.

1st Lt. Jonathan H. Harwood from attached from 293rd Joint Assault Signal Co to Killed in Action.

Lt Kenneth S. Norton (USN) from attached from 293rd Joint Assault Signal Co to lightly wounded at Duty.

The following 5 men were Killed in Action:

M/Sgt Robert N. Lemin	Pfc. Henry S. Farrar	Pvt. Rolland F. Revels
Pvt. Frank J. Kosina	Pfc. William H. McWhirter	

Pfc. James A. Machan went from Detached Service with C Company 2nd Btn to Killed in Action.

Pvt. Henry W. Genther from attached from 293rd Joint Assault Signal Co to Killed in Action.

The following 2 men went from Duty to slightly wounded in hospital.

T/5 Edward A. Johnson	T/5 Gerard C. Rotthoff

1st Lt. James R. McCullers went from Duty to Hospital – Wounded in Action.

The following 4 men went from Duty to slightly wounded in hospital.

T/5 Alvin S. Rustebakke	Pfc. Clifton F. Whaley
T/5 Earl W. Sorger	Pfc. Eugene J. Zielke

1st Lt. James W. Eikner assumed principal duty as Company Commander.

The following 2 men went from being attached from 165th Signal Photographic Company for Duty, rations and quarters to Killed in Action.

T/4 Irving Lomasky.   Pfc. Keghan Nigohosian.

Record of events: Map being used was a GSGS4250. Scale 1:50,000.
Made landing on operational beach Omaha – Dog Green.

On Omaha Beach 2nd Battalion cannon company commander Frank Kennard lost his two halftracks: '*We blew a gap in the concertina wire alongside the gravel road between the low beach wall and the anti-tank ditch. In attempting to get over the beach wall to the roadway with the halftracks, we burned out the clutch on one vehicle and the other was hit by some kind of explosive and burned up. I lost two Rangers to intermittent enemy fire.*'

Above: photographs of a destroyed half-track left on the beach (taken after 6 June).

This recollection of the evening of D-Day from 5th Ranger Captain John Raaen shows that often de-waterproofing was not done when the jeep landed. Many were just dumped in order to get off the beach and away from the shelling.

Raaen: '*I reported in to General Gerherdt of our situation. He was very interested in our position and he asked me if there was anything we needed. I told him that we needed ammo and food. Gerherdt turned to Lieutenant Shay and he told him to take us down to the beach and load us up a truck with ammunition. With the help of an engineering sergeant, we de-waterproofed a jeep – took it over to the ammo and loaded it up with mortar and machine-gun ammunition.*'

In addition to the Omaha Beach Naval operations in support of the Rangers – the Naval Taskforce for Utah Beach was also engaging targets on the eastern coastline of the Vire Estuary. These would be the positions expected to be cleared by the Rangers later on 6 June. These targets were also engaged because they were firing directly onto the Utah Beach shipping, or the aircraft flying overhead.

U. S. S. HERNDON (638)

SECRET

S E C R E T

Via :   Commander Task Group 125.8 (Commander Bombardment Group UTAH).
           Commander Task Force 125(Commander Assault Force UTAH).
           Commander Task Force 122 (N.C.W.T.F.).

Subject: Action Report.

1.   In accordance with Annex "Dog" to Commander Task Force 125 Operation Order 3-44, this vessel, part of Task Unit 125.8.4 (Fire Support Unit Four) proceeded down the boat lane ahead of the first Assault Wave to Fire Support Area Four on D Day. At 0550 (H minus 40), June 6, 1944, this vessel carried out shore bombardment to destroy or neutralize the following prearranged enemy shore batteries and defences: Targets 34, 36, 38, 40 and 42. All targets were situated on the eastern bank of the mouth of the River Vire between Grandcamp Le Bains and the Carentan Estuary. All targets were classified as defended, localities. Target #40 consisted of two 105mm guns in open emplacements with one pill box and shelter. Target #42 consisted of an infantry position with three pill boxes, one casement, one anti-tank gun, two shelters and two 150mm guns in open emplacements.

2.   Neutralization fire at the rate of eight (8) rounds per minute was commenced at 0550 (H minus 40). Ceased prearranged fire at 0630 (H hour). Since preselected targets could not be identified indirect fire was employed using data supplied by C.I.C. Results of fire could not be positively determined. However, mission was considered satisfactorily accomplished since batteries taken under fire were temporarily neutralized and did not endanger leading assault waves approaching assault beach within their range and arc of fire.

3.   212 rounds of 5"/38 cal. AA common ammunition were expended during forty minutes of prearranged fire with no casualties.

4.   At 0655 an active AA shore battery in the town of Maisy (T103) was observed and taken under fire. Ceased firing at 0703 having expended 42 rounds of 5"/38 cal. AA common ammunition. Battery was silenced.

5.   At 0735 T40 and again at 0819 T42 active shore batteries were observed to be firing at the boat lanes. Each target was taken under fire with neutralization fire. Expended 53 rounds of 5"/38 Cal. AA common ammunition at

HNLMS *Soemba* 6 June After Action Report states that the *Soemba* was also attacking coastal defence positions along the eastern side of the Vire Estuary and in Grandcamp-les-Bains, including the harbour defences.

Below: The Utah Beach Bombardment Force target numbers for the Vire Estuary 5 and 16 are numbered the same as the Omaha Sector maps.

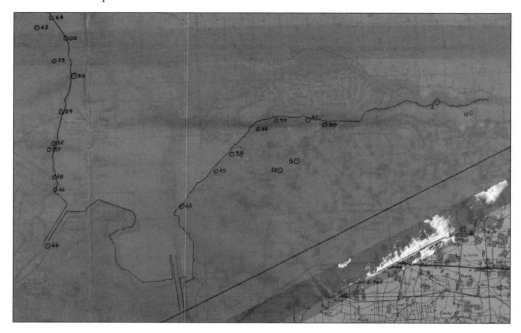

Below: At 2040 hrs the following radio messages were sent by Colonel Talley to the 'Commanding General' 1st Inf. Division on the USS *Ancon*. The text is written out to make it more understandable – but it is clear and unquestionable. The Utah Beach landings were coming under fire from the guns of Maisy and the signal very specifically states Targets 5, 16 and also 16A were doing that firing. The HQ of the Utah landings were requesting permission to take the Maisy positions under fire, and one assumes they were checking that the Rangers had not already arrived at Maisy or they could be in danger from friendly fire.

2040hrs 6 June
To: Commanding General 1st Division.
Message says: *Batteries Number 5, 16 and 16A are firing on Utah Beach, request clearance that it is safe for Uncle Force fire support vessels to fire on these targets.....OVER.*
(Secret: from HQ Fifth Corp – Action Colonel Talley – info HQ First Division).

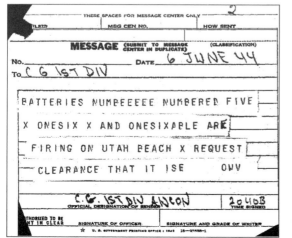
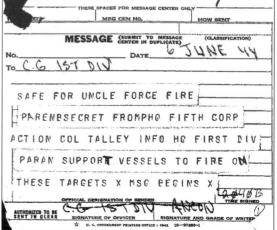

3rd message. Dated 0410 on 7 June .
29th Div. Request actual targets be marked by red smoke shell if possible. Confirm this arrangement.' (From the archives of the 1st Inf. Division).

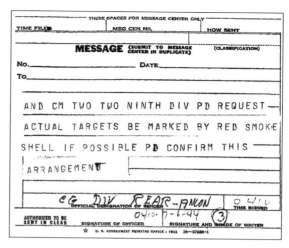

The following is the 352nd Inf. Division's map of German positions at 9pm on 6 June. Of note is the area of coast on the right of the estuary. It shows the Allied penetration into the coastal area away from Omaha Beach.

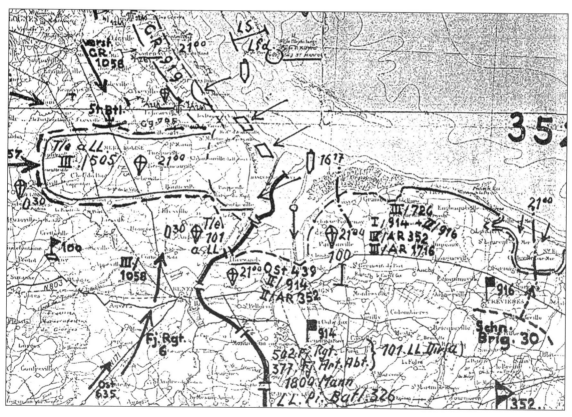

USS *Ellyson* Narrative 7 June:

At 0535 USS *Ellyson* was ordered to relieve USS *Harding* in the bombarding force. She did so and at 0700 established visual communications with Ranger SFCP and at 0800 they established voice radio communications.

At 0918 *Ellyson* was anchored 2¼ miles north of Pointe du Hoc to await orders from fire control party and at 0929 those orders came from a Ranger observation post. The *Ellyson* was to bombard German light gun positions in trees on the edge of the cliff about 800 yards west of Pointe du Hoc. (co-ordinates 579938).

By 0952 after expending 100 rounds, the SFCP reported 'mission successful'.

At 0953 a German shore battery in vicinity of the target commenced firing at USS *Ellyson*. The shells were landing short and the *Ellyson* returned the fire and by 0959 the enemy position had been straddled with shells.

At 1022 fired 16 rounds and then ceased fire on orders from SFCP to allow army infantry and tanks to move in. The total ammunition expended was 124 rounds 5" AA Common.

At 1130 the American Flag was raised over captured position.

5th Battalion Incidents, Messages and Orders Report:

```
0630 reinforced Bn assembled on road to move
to Pointe Du Hoe. 0635 heavy MG and sniper
fire on col rec from left flank. Co's "E &
B" and elements of "A & F with four tanks
left to clear Vierville and area south; re-
mainder of Bn proceeds toward Pointe Du Hoe.
Known casualties to know; Co A, Pfc Paul H
Pavey (KIA), S/Sgt Ted M Walters, T/5 Edward
L Podkowka, Pfc Abbott S Wittels (SWA), Sgt
William R Kalar (SWA); Co D, Pfc Carl F
Charboneau (LWA); Co E, 1st lt WOODFORD
MOORE (DOW). T/5 Floyd A Bursch (KIA), Sgt
William P Fennhahn (LWA).
```

Below, the 5th Battalion After Action Report:

```
                        D/1   7 June 1944

        Plans were made for enlarging the beach-head and for relieving the
three companies of the Second Ranger Battalion at Pointe du Hoe.

        At 0600 a force composed of 80 men from the Second Ranger Battalion
(Cos. A, B and C), Companies C and D of our battalion, 150 men from the
First Battalion 116th Infantry, and 6 tanks of the 743rd Tank Battalion,
advanced toward Pointe du Hoe. Encountering harassing sniper fire this force
advanced to a point approximately one (1) kilometer west of St. Pierre Du Mont
where it received a large concentration of artillery fire. This fire continued
falling from 1000 hours until 1800. The force withdrew to St. Pierre du Mont
and set up a defense in the town. Under cover of darkness a two man patrol
moved through the enemy lines to Pointe du Hoe, contacted the Commanding
Officer Second Ranger Battalion, and returned laying wire to establish
communication between the two forces.

        The remainder of the battalion was given the mission of improving the
beach-head.

        Company B resumed the attack to the southwest from the western edge of
Vierville-sur-Mer at 0630. This unit was not able to advance far but did
knock out several machine gun nests and numerous snipers.

        The remaining platoon of Company A and the remaining platoon of Company F
supported by four tanks of the 743rd Tank Battalion attacked South from the
town wiping out snipers, machine gun nests, and several enemy combat patrols.
Approximately 25 of the enemy were killed and 85 were captured.

        During the night snipers had infiltrated back into the town so Company E
cleaned out the town again.
                        UNCLASSIFIED
```

-3-

UNCLASSIFIED

At approximately 1100 these units were ordered to set up a defense around the town. At 1400 hours, Company E, which was defending the eastern portion of the town beat off a determined counter-attack of about company strength.

At 1900 hours elements of the 116th Infantry moved into the eastern half of the sector and the units of this battalion shifted to the right to defend only the remaining half of the sector.

The A Company platoon on Pointe du Hoe assisted in repulsing three counter-attacks early this morning. A seven man patrol from this platoon made an unsuccessful attempt to infiltrate through the enemy positions to contact the Fifth Ranger Battalion. The remainder of the day was spent manning a portion of the defense area.

The first platoon of Company F attacked inland from the beach at 0800 and by 1400 hours secured their objective, destroying three pillboxes and several weapons emplacements. 8 Germans were killed and 36 captured. At this time the platoon was contacted by Major Street of Admiral Hall's staff, loaded into a L.C.V.P. with food, water, and ammunition; and transported to Pointe du Hoe contacting the Commanding Officer Second Ranger Battalion at 1700 Hours. An eight man patrol from this platoon infiltrated through the enemy positions and by 0800 of D/2 had contacted the force at St. Pierre-du-Mont.

Results for the second day were approximately 150 prisoners taken, 80 killed, and 40 Ranger casualties.

Lt. Coit Coker USNR: *In the morning the battalion, joined by the 5th Rangers, proceeded in column down the highway to St. Pierre du Mont, encountering minor resistance from snipers and machine guns. It was not definitely known whether the 2nd Rangers had been successful in capturing Pointe du Hoc and our mission was to effect or help effect the capture. At St. Pierre enemy fire was directed several hundred yards ahead of us successfully interdicting the way to Pointe du Hoc. Intelligence from friendly natives indicated that the prearranged targets No 5 (Les Perruques) and No 16 (La Martinière) and target No 87 might be delivering this fire.*

I got the battleship Texas *to fire on any observed enemy gun emplacements in the Maisy area using air spot. This fire was delivered about 1300-1400 and the interdicting enemy fire ceased. I do not know how many rounds* Texas *fired, but I do know that on this occasion and on all subsequent occasions when we called on the* Texas *to fire for us with air spot, enemy fire was silenced.*

As he and the Rangers advanced towards Pointe du Hoc, they encountered small enemy actions and it was deemed that perhaps these would develop into counter-attacks on the column. *'We withdrew and formed defensive positions for the night in two hedgerow-bound fields in St. Pierre. The counter-attack never developed further, but about 2000hrs the enemy began inaccurate intermittent artillery fire on the battalion position.'*

USS *Glennon* After Action Report 7 June. *'At about 0900 SFCP 34 commenced designating targets, firing on target No 5 (4 gun 155mm battery).'* SFCP 34 claimed all targets were demolished, approximately 200 rounds of AA common expended.

About 1600 hrs, splashes were noted falling close to the USS *Butler* (CDD34). The source could not be found. The *Butler* backed down as splashes approached, finally turning away when she was straddled. *'No hits were observed.'*

At 1058 a machine gun on the beach opened fire on USS *Harding* as it approached Pointe du Hoc. Eleven minutes later the *Harding* despatched ammunition and food to the Rangers. At 1131 the *Harding* opened fire with its 40mm guns at targets behind Pointe du Hoc – those positions being radioed by the SFCP with the Rangers. They fired 100 rounds and then ceased firing at 1310. However, they were back, firing again at a position behind target 90 at the request of the Rangers.

USS *Barton* After Action Report:

```
             On 7 June, BARTON was again assigned station #4.
As no word had yet been received from her own SFCP, she con-
tinued to work with Lieutenant JOHNSON'S party, still isolated
near the beach.  Lieutenant NORTON'S SFCP had managed to work
its way inland during the night, and was directing the fire of
the TEXAS, as originally scheduled.  During this period BARTON
took various targets under fire.  The first mission was a
strong machine gun position, which was also being bombed and
strafed by a strong flight of Thunderbolts.  Following its
neutralization, fire was shifted to a chateau, occupied by the
enemy.  As friendly troops were in the foreground, the shells
were placed above the second floor.  This target was observed
severely damaged, and the salvos were then walked right through
a grove of trees harboring snipers.  The proximity of friendly
units forbade the use of air bursts, but a shell was seen to
strike a branch and detonate, with evident shrapnel effect.
Several unidentified strongpoints were next engaged, with ex-
cellent results, and a second chateau was heavily hit and ren-
dered useless to the enemy.  The Rangers then moved inland.
BARTON was ordered to return to station off Port En Bessin.
```

```
0600B   2nd Ranger Battalion repeated their request for reen-
        forcement and relief for casualties.  German prisoners
        still seen on beach.

0700B   2nd Ranger Battalion requested fire on machine guns
        at 592938.

0745B   Opened fire on target 592938.

0756B   Shifted to target 492931, chateau in grove of trees.
        The chateau was hit repeatedly and machine gun con-
        centration in grove nearby bombarded.  2nd Ranger
        Battalion observers reported excellent results.
        Ceased fire at 0900B having expended 185 rounds of
        5"/38 cal. AA common ammunition.

0907B   Established communication with assigned Shore Fire
        Control Party 29 and received fire mission.  Unable
        to carry out fire mission because Destroyer Squadron
        SIXTY was ordered to report to Ohio Area.
```

81st Chemical Weapons Btn. After Action Report: *On the morning of June 7, D Company fired its second mission near St. Laurent-sur-Mer at a machine gun nest only 800 yards from the gun position. A concentration of HE completely neutralized the installation. The company then moved northwest, cross-country over difficult terrain, subject to intermittent sniper and machine gun fire, and arrived at Vierville-sur-Mer at 1600 hours, where the commanding officer of the 116th Infantry, 29th Division, assigned it the task of providing security fire.*

It was here that the company was subjected to one of the heaviest shellings it ever experienced. Several batteries of enemy 150mm artillery, firing from the vicinity of Pointe du Hoc, pounded the center of town and the road leading to the beach. Heavy casualties were inflicted on the regimental OP group and on a field artillery battalion coming from the beach. An ammunition dump was blown up, scattering small arms ammunition in all directions. This action caused a withdrawal for the time along the highway. [Author: 'From the vicinity of Pointe du Hoc' – this could well have been fire from the batteries at Maisy].

At 1429 USS *Harding* hit an underwater obstacle about 1500 yards from the beach, but the ship managed to clear the obstruction three minutes later – in the process it had damaged its propellers and sound gear.

According to the After Action Report at 1525: '*Enemy shore battery opened fire at* Harding.' No splashes came close enough to worry them. It is highly likely that Maisy was firing at the *Harding* as it would have been visible to the observers in Grandcamp and Maisy churches. The peninsula sticks out, so the *Harding* would have been in full view approaching the shoreline at that point, and a large target of opportunity within site of observers and the range of the guns.

At 1727 the landing party returned from Pointe du Hoc to the *Harding* and she was soon back in action in support of the Rangers. Again, targets were designated around German positions 90 – 91 at 2200 – they reported that after 48 rounds expended, the *'fire mission was successful.'*

James W. Gabaree: *Our ammunition supplies were very low. The situation was becoming desperate. Seven of us led by Lt. Parker volunteered to try to make contact with the main force on the beach. The patrol advanced, only to discover we were in the middle of a land mine field in open ground with 20 yards to go before we could reach the shelter of a small mound on the cliff's edge.*

German machine gun fire opened up on us before we could reach the berm, killing one man, my best friend, Paul Pavey. While trying to make the run for shelter, I was shot. My comrades pulled me into a crevice in the cliff – but had to leave me to continue on with their mission. I realized that my chance of coming out of this alive was practically nil. The primeval will to live kicked in.

The German foxhole looked like a pretty safe place to be, so I crawled in. I lay next to a dead German, ate his black bread and promptly threw up. I then started to hallucinate. I decided to wait four hours, then kill myself, as I did not relish a slow death. Luck was on my side – a US patrol picked me up.

A Company 5th Rangers – Vierville-sur-Mer, France.
B Company 5th Rangers – Vierville-sur-Mer, France.
C Company 5th Rangers – St. Pierre du Mont, France.
D Company 5th Rangers – Pointe du Hoc, France.
E Company 5th Rangers – Vierville-sur-Mer, France.
F Company 5th Rangers – Pointe du Hoc, France.
Medical Detachment 5th Rangers – Vierville-sur-Mer, France.
Headquarters Company 5th Rangers – Vierville-sur-Mer, France.

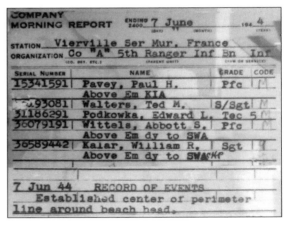

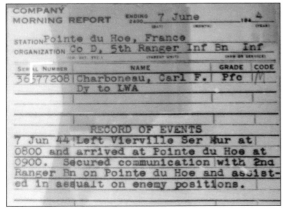

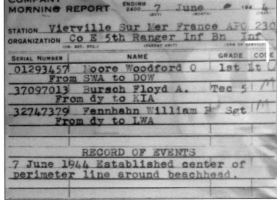

COMPANY
MORNING REPORT ENDING 7 June 194 4

STATION Vierville Sur Mer, France APO 230

ORGANIZATION Med Det 5th Ranger Inf Bn Med

SERIAL NUMBER	NAME	GRADE	CODE
	NO CHANGE		

RECORD OF EVENTS
7 June 1944 Established center of perimeter line around beach head.

COMPANY
MORNING REPORT ENDING 7 June 194 4

STATION Pointe du Hoe, France APO 230

ORGANIZATION Co. F, 5th Ranger Inf. Bn. Inf.

SERIAL NUMBER	NAME	GRADE	CODE
33313114	Ovington, Robert, NMI Dy to LWA	Pfc	

RECORD OF EVENTS
7 Jun 44 Left Vierville Ser Mer at 0800 and arrived at Pointe du Hoe at 0900. Secured communication with 2nd Ranger Bn. on Pointe du Hoe and assisted in assault on enemy positions.

Maurice Prince: *Dawn came and still no attack. We were beginning to feel the relief that only light can bring, after spending miserable moments in the gloom. I don't know why it is, but the fact is ever present, that the soldier doesn't mind dying in the daytime, but come the night with its mist and darkness, there comes along with it man's natural fear and dread of this unknown dimness and causes him uneasiness and terror.*

Artillery shelling had been fairly negligible that night, so that no casualties were sustained by us. That morning when we formed to move out, our fighting strength was unchanged. We advanced forward using the same approach march formation as of yesterday. We advanced cautiously, making use of all the natural cover that the terrain afforded us. We encountered some sniper fire, but once more our combat patrols took care of that danger. Every house which was in our zone of action was thoroughly searched and made

COMPANY
MORNING REPORT ENDING 7 June 194 4

STATION Vierville Sur Mer, France APO 230

ORGANIZATION Hq Co 5th Ranger Inf Bn Inf

SERIAL NUMBER	NAME	GRADE	CODE
34711076	Ootten James E. Fr dy to abs Sk (LD) to 28th Gen Hosp APO 511 U S Army as of 6th June 1944.	Pvt	

RECORD OF EVENTS
7 June 1944 Established center of perimeter line around beach head.

certain that NO enemy lay hidden therein. Information was gathered by the friendly French civilians, but most of the information gained thru this source was of small use to us, as it was too unreliable.

During our march, we received the opportunity to study and to reconnoiter the terrain we were fighting over. Although we had some knowledge beforehand from our aerial and ground map studies, what the ground would look like, this gave us a chance to ascertain for ourselves what it really was. We could notice the level fields, which were all hemmed in by the hedgerows of Normandy fame. The many apple orchards and grassy fields where cows were grazing on. Nothing escaped our vigilance, especially those areas where 'achtung minen' signs stood posted and were surrounded by barbed wire.

2nd Battalion After Action Report – Force A.

> The first counterattack hit the right of the perimeter at 070005 but was driven off by Company D. A much stronger attack directed at Company D at 0030 cost this force eight casualties and drove it into a smaller area. A survivor of these two actions reports the following particulars regarding the enemy form of attack:
>
> > Following heavy but inaccurate mortar and MG fire, the enemy would initiate his assault with loud yelling. His riflemen moved forward at a walk, standing upright and keeping up a continuous flow of talking. Following the second futile attack, the enemy contented himself with using s/a fire to draw our answering fire, then, would lay down a mortar and artillery concentration on the thusly located targets.
>
> At 0130, the enemy shifted his forces to the center of the perimeter. The first attack on a stratigic corner position wiped out the defenders here but the rest of the men held, repulsing the enemy forces. Due to the divided nature of the defense and the darkness of the night, the gact that the enemy had broken the line was not generally known. Information was being sent out to prepare to fall back when the second enemy attack came, smashing thru the shattered corner. The platoon of Company E which bore the brunt of this attack fought on until they were completely enveloped. Fighting their way back to the Point, the survivors of this action joined Company F which had withdrawn when informed to do so as a result of the first attack. A series of strongpoints was then set up around the CP for a last-ditch stand. Company E lost one officer KIA and 19 EM MIA when their position was overrun in the second attack on the center of the perimeter.
>
> With the advent of daylight, the enemy commenced to harrass our position, employing snipers, MG's, mortars, and artillery. Secret passages permitted the enemy to advance snipers to within close-range of the CP but extremely accurate rifle and mortar fire kept these activities to a minimum. Naval fire from the supporting destroyers, assisted by mortar and rifle fire, broke up all enemy attempts to organize for an attack. Two Volunter

We were barely crawling along, moving at a snail's pace, patrols were out seeking snipers, and other members were left to search out buildings and areas. We were very cautious as many signs pointed that the enemy had been very recently in this vicinity. We wanted to make sure that we didn't fall into any of his traps. Intermittent artillery fire also limited our speed. We had to seek cover several times. We never held up in any place for any length of time, we knew speed was essential if we were to aid our brother Rangers on the Pointe. We tried our best to expedite matters and to speed things along.

patrols **blew** up the enemy ammunition dump, his source of supply and his rallying point, and the concrete OP. Forty pounds of C-2 set the interior of the OP on fire, driving out eight enemy who had entered by means of an underground passageway, one of many connecting up the empalcements.

Personnel also assisting in the defense of the Pointe were British sailors from beached LCA's, the surviving men from the sunken DUKW's, and several paratroopers who had been dropped into the sea and had made their way to the Pointe. Lewis machine guns taken from their mountings on top of the DUKW-ladders and the beached LCA's supplanted the worn-out, thru over-use, weapons of the Force. Due to the severe lack of ammunition, captured enemy weapons were also used to a great extent.

Patrols were dispatched during darkness, to determine the intentions of the enemy. Due to the advance of Force "C" this day, the greater part of the enemy strength in the area was deployed to meet this new threat. The only casualties suffered this day were those hit on out-guard.

Communications, supply, and evacuation were much better this day. The fire of several destroyers was controlled by the radio and lamp signals. Requests for supplies and reinforcements sent to the USS Ancon resulted in Major Street, a Staff Officer of the 11th Amphib Force, bringing in an LCI-load of ammunition, medical supplies, and food. This craft also evacuated the casualties, many of whom had been awaiting expert care for thirty-six hours. Later, Major Street brought in a group of 5th Rangers who had become separated from their Battalion on the beach, plus one officer and twelve men of the Cannon Platoon who brought their vehicles safely to the beach, only to have them destroyed thru enemy action. This group had been instrumental in the clearing of Exit D-3 where, acting as infantrymen, they had assisted in the mopping up of several enemy positions still holding out in that area.

From this point on, supplies were brought in upon request and the situation on the Pointe became more hopeful. At 1700, SCR-300 contact was finally established with Company C/5th Ranger Battalion/Force "C", then only 1000-yds away. Lt Col Rudder sent them the following message: "Try and fight thru to us". This message was acknowledged but, being under orders of Higher Headquarters, Force "C" could not comply with the message without the consent of the CO, 116th Infantry.

It was quite paradoxical, as we went along the road, tactically, snooping and pooping. We saw the French civilians boldly walking along the centre of the road, going about their chores and business as if nothing new or different were going on. Most of them hadn't realised what had actually happened and were astonished and surprised to learn that we were real Americans. Once they learned and gained our identities, there wasn't anything they wouldn't do for us. Milk and cider bottles were brought forth and flowers were thrown at us. That was one day we didn't go thirsty or hungry.

We had finally managed to push forward to a place about three hundred yards from the road junction that led to the Pointe, when all hell broke loose in full fury. Our forward elements who had advanced farther than the supporting group

2nd Battalion After Action Report – Force C – A & B Companies and 5th Battalion.

Moving out as infantry-tank teams with the twenty remaining men of Company A as the point, the Force advanced straight down the Grandcamp road toward Pointe du Hoe on the morning of 8 June. Four miles of the road were speedily cleared and the point, investigating all buildings along the route, flushed and killed a number of snipers. Communication with the tanks was difficult, being limited to physical contact only. However, the tanks gave excellent support in placing fire on stubborn resistance. (Note: Prisoners later taken in this area by other friendly forces were amazed by this "crazy advance" which swept right thru several defense lines prepared on both sides of the road)

Just beyond St. Pierre du Mont, 88-mm fire straddled the road but the point led the rest of the column to, and thru it. Slightly later, the column was held up by a huge road crater which the tanks could not negotiate until the tank-dozer could be brought forward to partially fill it in. The first of the tanks then made their way thru the crater when 88-mm fire again hit the column, cutting the point off from the main body. Acting on orders from Higher Headquarters, the Force then fell back but the point, now down to seven men, continued to advance. Reaching the limits of au Guay, the point struck an ambush of four mutually supporting machine guns. The point succeeded in the destroying of one gun and the taking of twelve prisoners at the cost of having two men killed and three injured, T/5 Ray, the "standing" BAR man of Company A again performed notable action in this encounter, altho slightly wounded. The five members of the point then rejoined the Force with their prisoners.

Acting again under orders from Higher Headquarters, the Force withdrew to St Marie du Mont to construct defensive positions to withstand the expected counterattack. It was later discovered that the point had advanced to within but a few hundred yards of the RJ leading to Pointe du Hoe. Ammunition and rations were brought up this evening by the two half-tracks of the Cannon Platoon which had successfully crossed the beach.

had made contact with an organized defence line, which was protecting this vital junction, covering this approach to the Pointe.

So far, in our progress during the day, we had come under some small arms fire and some shelling, but here we were being subjected to both frontal and flanking automatic fire plus artillery. Our point was fighting heroically and had knocked out one enemy machine gun plus the crew and some riflemen, but they had in return sustained a couple of casualties themselves.

We called up our tanks – which had been halted by a huge bomb crater in the road – to come to aid us. Thanks to the skilful manuoeuvering on the tankers' part, they were able to bring up their armour to the very front. Up front it was just a firefight with only small arms being used, as enemy artillery wasn't landing there. We got the tanks to open up on a fortified house that stood at the road junction. Excellent results were obtained as a direct hit blew the house to smithereens.

All we had to contend with now was machine gun fire from our right flank. We tried to get the armour-protected tanks to do this job for us, but could not get any communications through to them, as they were completely buttoned up. I distinctly remember Captain Arnold, who had been up with the front vanguard hammering away at the turret of the tank with his faithful and trusted carbine trying to get them to open up so he could speak to them. He finally made himself heard and got the tankers to unbutton for a short while. He gave them the situation and what he wanted them to do. Bullets were whistling all about. Twigs were being snapped off from bushes behind us and lead was plowing into the tanks themselves. How Captain Arnold remained unharmed is beyond me. He did get a souvenir hole in the end of his carbine to carry about though.

The tanks finally took up the desired position and emptied several boxes of fifty calibre machine-gun slugs into the enemy defences. Our own automatic weapons, plus our expert rifle shooting were adding to the enemy toll. Another boy from our company was wounded in the exchanges of lead and had to go to the rear. The Heinies were now beaten, when out of the clear skies we were subjected to the most intensive and concentrated barrages from an 88 battery we've ever undergone. A direct hit killed one of our men and miraculously missed two others, who were in the same place practically as the one who was killed. There was only one choice for us then, and that was to get out of that spot quickly. We took off down the road, but had to hole up in the ditches alongside the road, as small arms fire from enemy positions further down caused us to halt our movement. We sweated out this terrific bombardment in these natural slit trenches. Another one of our boys was killed when a direct hit struck the ditch he was lying in.

We were out in the middle of no man's land, all by our lonesome. The troops of the main body had stopped when we had started the fight at the road junction and our tanks had been forced to retreat to the rear due to the seriousness of the situation. There we were out in the middle of nowhere, sweating it out with shell after shell landing nearby. I don't know how many shells were thrown at us in the short period we were in those ditches, but I do know that when the barrage lifted, I couldn't recognize the immediate countryside, as it was so cratered and beaten up.

When the barrage ended, we retreated back to our main body for reorganisation. Once more, darkness began to steal over us so that we had to hold off at a position about 800 yards from the Pointe. We dug in here and prepared to bivouac there for the night.

Once again we had to lick our wounds, we were getting weaker and weaker, but still we were pushing, driving, and battling the enemy, causing him to go backwards inch by inch. As yet we hadn't accomplished our mission. We were afraid to even think of the fate that befell our heroic brother Ranger companies on the Pointe. All we could do was hope and pray for the best, for their sake.

We set up our usual perimeter defensive position, setting up a series of outposts and strongpoints. Combat and visiting patrols were sent out to contact both the enemy and friendly troops. We were all weary and fagged out. Another tough day of combat had worn us out physically. We had come through this day's action and although we hadn't done what we had set out to do, we did accomplish the clearing of a town and of the main coastal road. We had closed with the enemy and had forced him to retreat. As yet, we were still out in front, leading and showing the way, forward.

Information which reached us about our rapidly expanding beachhead and of the continual disembarking of troops, supplies, and vehicles, buoyed up our spirits. We knew we weren't fighting by ourselves now, and that we were being backed by the greatest fighting machine this world has ever seen.

That night we ate our 'K' rations, dug our slit trenches deeper, and prepared to pull our guard. We tried to get a little rest while on post. We were set for another imminent enemy counter-attack.

The second night spent on French soil was passed in pain and misery. We were all under great strains. Our arduous fighting of the past couple days were beginning to tell on our tired and worn features. We were anticipating an enemy attack and we thought surely one was in the coming. None did come though.

It was cold that night, colder than we had expected it to be. We weren't equipped against this frost, so besides having to sweat out the Jerries, we had to endure a night of coldness.

Once more, under the cover of darkness, the Luftwaffe came forth to bomb our beach and Naval installations. Once more, we had a front row seat to scan the spectacle of this battle, to watch as anti-aircraft defence put up a brilliant display of fireworks. No bombs landed in our immediate area. We hoped that once more our boys had warded off this danger without too great a harm done to them. No artillery or small arms fire bothered us that night.

Small Unit Actions Report at Pointe du Hoc continues:

Both Theobold and Wadsworth were caught during the next two days. Wadsworth was spotted early in the morning. Theobald lay quiet for most of the day, then thought he was seen by a passing German and bolted out toward the highway, without drawing fire. He hid again in a ditch near the highway, for the night.

Main spent D+1 watching German patrols go by, and a machine gun being set up in the field near his hedgerow. That night he crawled out, threw a grenade in the general direction of the machine gun, and 'lit out for the Point' without drawing enemy fire.

The Company D men lay hidden all the next day under their hedgerow. No enemy search of the area was made, and they saw only a few Germans during the period. Their main cause of worry was fire from naval guns supporting the beleaguered Pointe; from time to time friendly shells came close enough to 'bounce the men around' in their holes, but there were no losses. Late in the day their hopes were raised and then dashed. Four Sherman tanks rolled down the highway toward Grandcamp within sight of the Rangers. But no infantry followed, and in a short while the tanks came back and went off eastward. Germans reappeared in the field at dusk and set up machine-gun positions; the isolated Ranger group settled in for another night. They were freed next morning by the 116th Infantry.

On D+1 Colonel Rudder's force at Pointe du Hoc consisted of about 90 men able to bear arms. Restricted to a few acres, including only a part of the fortified area, they expected to be the target for heavy concentrations of artillery and for assault by enemy ground forces. With the support of strong naval fire, the Rangers held out during the day, and that afternoon their situation was improved by the landing of a craft with food, ammunition, and a platoon of reinforcements. By night they were in touch with patrols of a relief force that had reached St-Pierre-du-Mont, only 1,000 yards away.

A Company 2nd Rangers – Vierville-sur-Mer, France.

The following three men were Wounded in Action:
S/Sgt. Gail H. Belmont
T/5 Richard E. Rankin
T/5 Joseph C. Ray
T/5 Percy C. Hower was Killed in Action.
Pfc. Donald L. Ashline was sent to hospital from Duty.

Record of events: Map being used was a GSGS4250. Scale 1:50,000.
Advanced to St. Pierre du Mont.

B Company 2nd Rangers – Vierville sur Mer, France.

T/5 Leonard P. Kassmeir and Pfc. Christian J. Mohr both went from Duty to being Lightly Wounded in Action.

Record of events: Map being used was a GSGS4250. Scale 1:50,000.
Advanced to St. Pierre du Mont.

C Company 2nd Rangers – Vierville sur Mer, France.

The following three men were sent to Hospital from Duty.
Pfc. Otto K. Stephens
S/Sgt. Paul B. Byzon
S/Sgt. Joseph A. Wetzel

Record of events: Map being used was a GSGS4250. Scale 1:50,000.
Advanced to St. Pierre du Mont.

D Company 2nd Rangers – Pointe du Hoc.

Pfc. Robert C. Carty and S/Sgt. Lawrence M. Johnson Killed in Action Pointe du Hoc.
Sgt. Michael J. Branley from duty to Hospital (LD) Slightly Wounded in Action.

E Company 2nd Rangers – Pointe du Hoc.

1st Lt. Joseph E. Leagans was Killed in Action.

The following three men went from Duty to hospital, Seriously Wounded in Action:
T/5 Leroy J. Thompson
Pfc. Harold D. Main
Pfc. Woodrow Talkington

Record of events: Map being used was a GSGS4250. Scale 1:50,000.

F Company 2nd Rangers – Pointe du Hoc.
S/Sgt. Leon H. Otto went from Seriously Wounded in Action to Died of Wounds.
Pfc. Frederick A. Dix went from Duty to Hospital, Lightly Wounded in Action.

Record of events: Map being used was a GSGS4250. Scale 1:50,000.

Medical Detachment 2nd Rangers – Vierville sur Mer, France.
Record of events: Map being used was a GSGS4250. Scale 1:50,000.
Advanced to St. Pierre du Mont, France.

Headquarters Company 2nd Rangers – Vierville sur Mer, France.
No change. Record of events: Map being used was a GSGS4250. Scale 1:50,000.

After Action Report B Company 743rd Tank Battalion:

> 7 June 1944   Moved out at 0530 in support of 116th Inf. towards.
> Maisy. Machine gun and sniper fire was very heavy. At 0900
> encountered heavy artillery fire (155mm probable). Two tanks hit
> but no injuries sustained. One 57mm AT gun destroyed, 4 pri-
> soners taken, several MG nests destroyed. Withdrew due to added
> enemy heavy fire, returned to bivouac Vierville sur Mer for fuel
> and ammunition.

Below: 1st Infantry Division HQ Artillery Map marked 'Situation overlay as of 1200 – 7th June.'

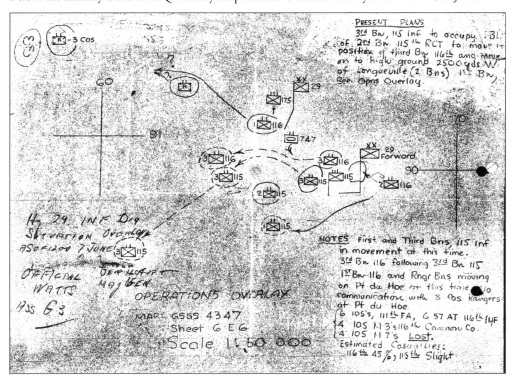

[Author: To aid the reader, I have placed the same overlay onto the correct GSGS map. The two points with the square marked 'R' indicate the Rangers' positions at that time. The one to the upper left indicates the Rangers at Pointe du Hoc, and the one with the arrow leading from the beach is the Ranger force heading towards Pointe du Hoc.]

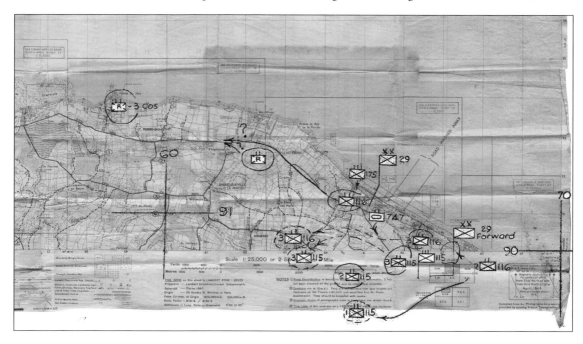

USS *Barton* After Action Reports 7 June:

> 1522B   Opened fire on enemy machine gun position between
>   2000 and 5000 yards to eastward of Target Number One
>   along edge of cliff as directed by 2nd Ranger Bat-
>   talion. Ceased fire at 1625B having expended 130
>   rounds of 5"/38 cal. AA common ammunition.

> 1630B   Established voice communications with 2nd Ranger Bat-
>   talion on their frequency.

> 1645B   Opened fire on road to eastward of Grand Camp Les
>   Bains (556912) where enemy was counter-attacking
>   against 2nd Ranger Battalion. Ceased fire at 1700B
>   having expended 43 rounds of 5"/38 cal. AA common
>   ammunition.

> 1902B   Opened fire on enemy concentration at 567924.
>   Ceased fire at 1925B, having expended 44 rounds of
>   5"/38 cal. AA common ammunition.

USS *O'Brien* After Action Report 7 June.

Bombardment, Coast of France, by U.S.S. O'BRIEN, June 7,
1944; Report of.
- -

II Chronological Narrative

0640   Anchored as before. Underway, proceeding to area off
Chateau de la Barren to report to Commander Destroyer
Division 36 in U.S.S. HARDING for shore bombardment.

1013   Commenced firing on German Pill Box (coordinates
585934), Chateau de la Barren, Normandy, France, as
directed by U. S. Army Ranger Fire Control Party # 1.
Opened fire at range 2850; fired only one salvo.

1014   Ceased firing as directed by Shore Fire Control Group,
having expended six rounds 5"/38 caliber AA Common
ammunition. Observed enemy soldiers running from
location. "Rangers" continued their advance in this
area. Standing by for more targets.

2026   Commenced firing on 2nd German Pill Box (coordinates
586931), Chateau de la Barren, Point de Hoe, Normandy,
France, as directed by U. S. Army Rangers. Opened
fire at range 3250 yards. Fired three ranging salvos,
then, shifted to rapid continuous fire for thirty
seconds, as directed by Shore Fire Control Party.

2033   Ceased firing on target, as directed by Shore Fire
Control Party, having expended 54 rounds of 5"/38
caliber AA Common ammunition. Results not observed
by this ship, but Shore Fire Control Party reported
"target destroyed".

2035   Commenced firing on German Road Block (coordinates
579937,), holding up advance of our troops. Target
designated by U. S. Army Ranger fire control group,
at Chateau de la Barren, Normandy, France. Opened
fire at range 3650 yards. Fired three ranging salvos,
then, as directed by Shore Fire Control Party, shifted
to rapid continuous fire for one minute.

2048   Ceased firing on target, as directed by Shore Fire Control party, having expended 86 rounds 5"/38 caliber AA
Common ammunition. Results of bombardment not observed
but Shore Fire Control Party reported "mission successful".

2128   Commenced firing as directed by U. S. Army Rangers on
German Machine Gun Nest (coordinates 579937) at top of
100 foot cliff, which was blocking advance of Ranger
patrols along beach toward locks, located near Grande
Camp - Les Boins, Normandy, France. Opened fire at range
2550 yards. Fired one ranging salvo which straddled
target, then, shifted to rapid continous fire for thirty
seconds, as directed by shore fire control party.

2133   Ceased firing as directed by Shore Fire Control Party,
having expended 60 rounds 5"/38 caliber AA Common
ammunition. Results of bombardment were not available
for observation, but Shore Fire Control Party reported
"mission sucessful - nice job".

Although the *Glendon* was with the Utah taskforce – she undertook bombardment of Target No.5 – Les Perruques at the request of SFCP 34. USS *Glendon* After Action Report:

> Shore bombardment on the 7th of June was much more satisfying than the previous day, as several targets were designated by SFCP on which excellent results were obtained. As our own troops were advancing toward Quienville from the eastward, we were in a good position to support them and were most anxious to do so.
>
> About 0900, SFCP 34 commenced designating targets, firing on target #5 (4 gun, 155mm battery),

USS *Harding* After Action Report 7th June. [Author: NGLO = Naval Gunnery Liaison Officer]

SYNOPSIS OF EVENTS   7 June 1944

1058B	Machine gun on beach opened fire on HARDING.
1059B	Machine gun ceased fire.
1109B	Sent ammunition replacements and food rations to Rangers in LCT 580.
1131B	Opened fire with 40mm guns at target behind Point Du Hoe.
1132B	Ceased firing.
1249B	Opened fire at various installations in vicinity of target 91. Destroyed target. 100 rounds. This fire requested by Rangers.
1310B	Ceased firing.
1420B	Commenced firing on road behind target 90W on request of Rangers. 44 rounds, **mission reported successful.**
1429B	Ship hit an underwater obstruction, 1500 yards from beach.
1432B	Ship clear of obstruction. Sound gear and both propellers damaged.
1525B	Enemy shore battery opened fire at HARDING. No splashes close.
1558B	Put diver over side to inspect screws. Reported screws badly damaged.
1727B	HARDING landing party returned aboard in LCVP. Reported that MWB wrecked on beach.
2200B	Commenced firing in area behind Point Du Hoe at request of Rangers in vicinity of targets 90-91. Mission successful. 48 rounds.

Ammunition expended – 307 rounds of 5"38 caliber.
Total ammunition expended to date – 764 rounds of 5"38 caliber.

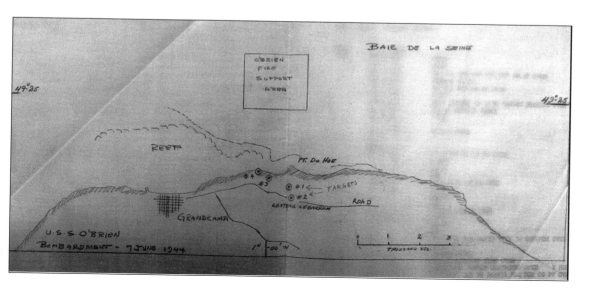

U.S.S. O'BRIEN Bombardment – 7 June 1944

The previous page shows a map drawn by a member of the crew of USS *O'Brien* to illustrate the positions it attacked. There were four targets designated by the Army Ranger Shore Fire Control Party:

Target No.1 – German Pillbox (co-ordinates 585934).
Target No.2 – German Pillbox (co-ordinates 586931).
Target No.3 – German Road Block (co-ordinates 579937).
Target No.4 – German Machine Gun Nest (co-ordinates 576939).

Effectiveness as reported to the ship by the Rangers:
Target No.1 – no report. (it was an empty emplacement).
Target No.2 – Target destroyed. (This was the road block).
Target No.3 – Mission successful. (This was the machine gun on the cliff edge).
Target No.4 – Mission successful. (This was another machine gun position on the cliff edge).

Timed at 0920 – A copy of the radio report to Commanding General 1st Inf. Div. from HQ V Corps states that the Rangers had reported being almost out of ammunition.

Narrative of Actions – USS *Texas* 7 June:

Word was received from destroyers close inshore at Pointe du Hoc that the Ranger Battalion which had landed there at H-Hour on D-Day was still isolated from our own troops. They were running low on provisions and ammunition and had a number of prisoners and casualties to be evacuated. Two LCVPs were obtained and loaded with provisions and ammunition from the destroyers and the Texas *and set in to relieve the Rangers. At 1730 the LCVPs returned with 28 German prisoners (including one officer and several Italians from a labor battalion) and 34 wounded Rangers. The wounded Rangers were given medical attention and for the most part were suffering from minor wounds. One Ranger died during the night from very severe abdominal wounds.*

The view of Pointe du Hoc cliffs from a Landing Craft (probably taken on 7 or 8 June). Fortunately for the Rangers, the 50ft collapse of the cliff face prior to their landing gave many of them a head start on their climb – almost halving the original 90ft height.

Below: A Utah Beach Naval Taskforce Summary 7 June showing Utah forces were also engaging Maisy with gunfire on 7 June. In particular, HMS *Hawkins* for the second day was again firing at Maisy – Les Perruques and reporting it silenced.

7 June, 1944

Bombarding ships resumed original fire support stations. H.M.S. HAWKINS and H.M.S. ENTERPRISE set Force " O " common frequency channel on S.C.R.608s to assist Ranger Shore Fire Control Party in vicinity of Point du Hoe. Heavy shelling of Red and Green Beach continued throughout day.

Air reconnaissance and air spotting available. Great improvements in results.

Reports received from air spotting planes :—

Target.	Ship.	Spotter Comment.
5	HAWKINS	18 hits.
16	HAWKINS	24 hits.
13A	QUINCY	Hits in area.
	TUSCALOOSA	Effective.
	NEVADA	No further activity.
	BLACK PRINCE	Effective.
14	BLACK PRINCE	Neutralized.
3	BLACK PRINCE	Effective.
	NEVADA	Neutralized.
	QUINCY	Neutralized.
	GLENNON	Results effective.
5	HAWKINS	Silenced.
	ENTERPRISE	Shoot effective.
7A	QUINCY	Numerous hits.
	NEVADA	Hits.
7B	QUINCY	Done for.
3	NEVADA	Silenced.
9	NEVADA	Silenced, six casemates destroyed.
15	BLACK PRINCE	Effective.
8A	BLACK PRINCE	Effective.
20	NEVADA	Neutralized.
17	NEVADA	Destroyed.
26	QUINCY	Direct hit.
18	TUSCALOOSA	Effective.
14	TUSCALOOSA	Effective.
14A	TUSCALOOSA	Effective.
1A	EREBUS	Several hits.

Shore Fire Control **Party fire control was particularly effective.**

Below: 7 June HQ 1st Inf. Div. Artillery map overlay. Some of the timings noted in the bottom centre indicate that these notes were written on or after 1345. The two positions indicated to the left are the Batteries at Maisy.

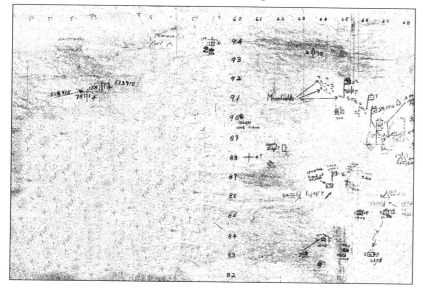

Below: The same overlay but now shown with the correct GSGS intelligence map underneath it. To make the coverage of the width of the map, I have used two GSGS maps and therefore it now makes two images. The original coverage was done over one large map.

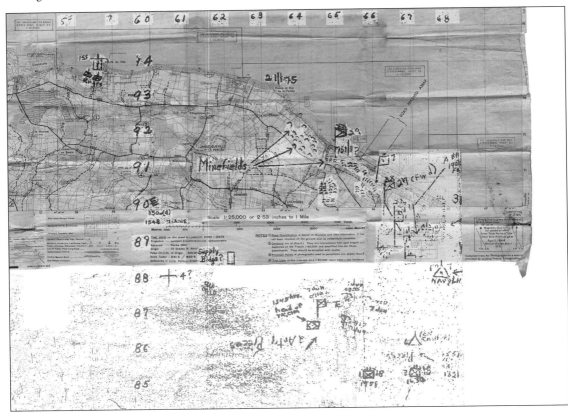

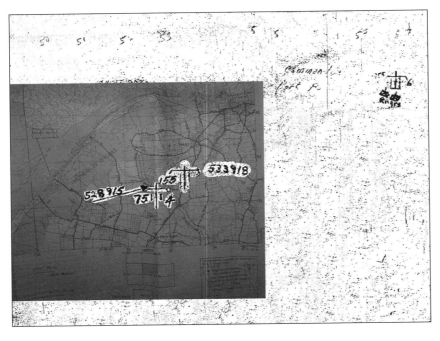

8 June 1944   1st Infantry Division Radio message 0900 7 June.

HQ 1ST US INF DIV APO 1, U. S. Army		G-2 JOURNAL		Time :	(From: 0900 (TO :
Date 8 June 1944				CP: 677881	
TIME	NO.	FROM	SYNOPSIS	REC'D VIA	DISPOSITION #
0900			Col Evans: Anyone relieved the Rangers yet? Col Gaynor: Report last night, they're still there.		

5th Battalion Incidents, Messages and Orders Report:

```
0700 Maj RICHARD P SULLIVAN with Co's C, D,
reached Pointe Du Hoe to assist 2nd Rangers.
0800 VOCG 29th Inf Div; 5th Rangers to proceed
to and take Grande Camp Les Bains.
1000 Rdio to VOCG: met heavy resistance, 1
Kil south of Grande Camp, being held up by heavy
mortar barrage, request support.
Radio VOCG 29th; hold present location till re-
lieved by 116th Regt.
1730 Relieved by 116th Regt.
1920 VOCG; Grande Camp cleared of all resistance.
1930 VOCG; Co'E set up defense around Sleuce
Gate bridge. Remainder Bn, set up all around
defense.
2400 - Enemy planes bombed area light 1/4 Kil
south Grande Camp. CP set up i abandoned German
tunnel.
Casualties; Maj RICHARD P SULLIVAN,Hq (LWA)
Hq Co, S/Sgt LeRoy T Button (SWA), Med Det T/4
David Clawson (LWA), Co B, S/Sgt Vern Detlefsen,
T/5 Joseph W Levesque, Pfc Carl W Morgan Jr (SWA)
Pfc Carl W Morgan Jr (DOW), Co D Pfc Robert F Stein,
(KIA), S/Sgt Stanley T Jakubowski, T/5 Victor I
Wilson (SWA), T/5 John C Smolarek, Pfc Clarence A
Styles (LWA); Co F, Pfc Edward I Mapes (LWA).
```

The destroyer *Shubrick* located the battery at Maisy – La Martinière firing from the eastern side of the Carentan Estuary at 0740. After opening fire, the battery was duly silenced, only to recommence firing at 0820, and it landed a pair of shells close to the hull of the *Shubrick*. USS *Shubrick* then bombarded Maisy again for a further 25 minutes and it again went silent. It was common for the gunners to take cover during such bombardments (just as Werner von Kistowski, a German officer who was sent to guard the Maisy Batteries with his Flak unit on 5 June, describes in his report in Chapter 13). They would then return to their weapons when it was safe to do so. It is likely that once the gunners were inside their shelters, they were well-protected from everything other than a direct hit.

HMS *Hawkins* had the same problem with the Maisy Batteries. It was designated as one of its primary targets on the morning of D-Day, and in the Royal Naval History of WWII it states clearly that Maisy was *'completely destroyed'* on 6 June by HMS *Hawkins*. However, when one examines the gunnery report for HMS *Hawkins* it shows the ship again firing at Maisy on 7 June.

Reports received from spotter planes reported HMS *Hawkins* landing 18 hits on target 5 and 24 hits on target 16 on 7 June. *Hawkins* again fired at Maisy target 5 and spotters again reported it 'silenced'.

The heavily damaged sluice gates referred to by Major Sullivan in his radio message. They are located at the coastline halfway between Pointe du Hoc and Grandcamp-les-Bains.

5th Battalion After Action Report:

D/2   8 June 1944

At 0100 hours orders were received to prepare to move to Pointe du Hoe at 0600. At 0630 hours a force composed of two battalions of the 116th Infantry and three companies of the Fifth Ranger Battalion advanced from Vierville-sur-Mer down the road west toward Pointe du Hoe. No resistnace was encountered and the force at St. Pierre-du-Mont was contacted at 0815.

Companies B and E were given the mission of taking and holding the high ground west of the Sluice Gate at Grandcamp-les-Bains. These companies in column, Company B leading, advanced through the low ground south of the East-West road leading into Grandcamp at 1000. Initially no fire was received and the town appeared to have been deserted by the enemy. The leading elements of the two companies approached to within 25 yards of the bridge where the force was pinned down by a heavy concentration of mortar and machine gun fire. The two companies withdrew to positions on the high ground east of the Sluice-Gate Bridge where they were joined by Company D which had just returned from Pointe-du-Hoe. They were passeed through by the Second and Third Battalions of the 116th Infantry, which, supported by tanks, artillery fire, and naval gun fire, successfully captured the town of Grandcamp-les-Bains. D Company and E Company went into defensive positions protecting the Sluice-gate Bridge and mopped up positions along the coast toward Point du Hoe. B Company occupied a portion of the all round defense set up by the Second Ranger Battalion on the high ground east of the Sluice Gate Bridge.

At 0900 Companies C, D, one platoon F Company, the remainder of A, B, C, of the Second Ranger Battalion, and one Platoon Company A advanced toward Pointe du Ho to assist the three companies of the Second Ranger Battalion. Meeting no resistance they contacted that unit. Companies A and F were now complete organizations.

Shortly thereafter the Rangers were brought under fire by the Third Battalion 116th Infantry and tanks of the 743rd Tank Battalion.. This force was attacking Pointe du Hoe from the south west and inflicted six casualties on our force, two of which were killed.

D Company advanced toward Grandcamp-les-Bains and joined Companies B and E.

Companies A, C, and F advanced east and south of the inundated area toward Maisy as part of a force consisting of the First Battalion 116th Infantry. Two half-tracks of the Second Ranger Battalion were attached to the Rangers. This force halted one-half mile northeast of Maisy for the night, meeting no resistance enroute.

Results for the third day were approximately 20 Germans killed and 35 captured. The battalion had 10 casualties.

USS *Elyson* After Action Report:

1.   From 0500, June 8, 1944, to 0800, June 15, 1944, this vessel was a unit of the Bombardment Force, Assault Force "O", off the Normandy Beachhead in France, and, while thus assigned, conducted three shore bombardments.

2.   At 0927, June 8, 1944, while this vessel was anchored about 2¼ miles north of Pointe du Hoe, a U.S. RANGERS observation post requested fire on German light gun positions in clumps of trees on edge of cliff about 800 yards west of Pointe du Hoe (British LAMBERT grid coordinates 579938). Fire was opened a few minutes later using indirect control from C.I.C., full salvos and 5"/38 A.A. common projectiles set on safe. Communication with the RANGERS was by voice on medium frequency using the AEF Assault Code. Fire was checked after each salvo to await spots from observation post. Shore fire control party was having difficulty spotting. As soon as enemy returned fire his location was observed by Gunnery Officer and a shift was made to direct fire. At 0952 the observation post ordered "cease fire" and reported "mission successful". At 0953 a German shore battery in the vicinity of the target commenced firing at the ELLYSON, shells landing short. Returned the fire using director control. Stated heaving in. At 0959 the enemy straddled. At 1000 got underway and opened range about 2000 yards. At 1022 fired 16 rounds at enemy shore battery. Ceased firing on orders from observation post to allow Army infantry and tanks to move in. Total ammunition expended 124 rounds 5"/38 A.A. common. At 1130 the American flag was hoisted over the captured position.

USS *Enterprise* After Action Report – 7 June – aerial reconnaissance reported shots on target 5 '*Shoot effective.*'

USS *Shubrick* engaged target 16A – the 4 x guns at Maisy – Foucher's Farm. Jim Snakenberg was in the *Shubrick*'s combat information centre:

> *We were stationed right off the beach 7th June. In the afternoon we got a call to fire on an ammo dump. The figures they gave us made us hit the top of a hill, if we depressed we went over the dump. The Ex O (Executive officer) was an old fire control man. He drew a hill and put in the hit we made. He gave me some figures that turned the guns almost straight up. This time we got the call back 'on target, walk and talk'. After firing many times they said target destroyed. A big black smoke came up from the other side of the hill. We knew we had him.'*

That was the end of target No. 16A.

The 1st Battalion plus the 5th Rangers moved from St. Pierre du Mont to Pointe du Hoc to relieve the Rangers who had been cut off.

Lt. Coit Coker: '*There was no opposition until we actually got out on the Pointe and were dispersed in bomb crater positions. Then quite a bit of hell broke loose in the way of mixed enemy and friendly mortar, small arms and tank (friendly) gunfire; shrapnel was flying freely. The remnants of the 2nd Ranger SFCP were still firing. Captain Harwood (FO) had been killed and Lt. Norton (NGLO) injured and evacuated.*

I volunteered our fire power to the 2nd Rangers, but they had no need for us.'

American troops inspecting the damaged Pointe du Hoc casements after the battle.

The 20mm anti-aircraft position which caused the Rangers so much trouble.

Photographs taken at Pointe du Hoc by the US Signal Corps and also from Lt. Brandel's papers.

One of the Pointe du Hoc 'mock' gun positions covered in debris. These did not fool anyone in US Intelligence before D-Day as the pits were marked as being unoccupied on the planning maps.

[Author: The remains of the range-finding position are shown above and it is worth noting that the mount for the rangefinder is intact but empty – the rangefinder had been removed at some time prior to D-Day, and this presents a significant piece of evidence to suggest that the Germans had ceased to use the Pointe du Hoc position for operational guns. In the second, clearer photograph you can see the empty rangefinder mount – which means the observation position on the cliff-top would only have been able to report that there were ships in the Channel – but not anything useful about their range for accurate artillery targeting.]

Many of the German reserve units were equipped with bicycles – they were often used later by American servicemen.

On the next page is a photograph of Pointe du Hoc taken after the battle. Note most of the Rangers' LCAs are still on the beach and also the piles of displaced earth from the cliffs, which very much aided and reduced the Rangers' climb.

A photograph showing Lt. Colonel Rudder and other Rangers greeting the party as it arrived from Omaha Beach. There was no apparent rush for Lt. Colonel Rudder's force to press on to other objectives.

Caption marked on the above photograph reads: *'U.S. Army Rangers resting in the vicinity of Pointe du Hoc, which they assaulted in support of 'Omaha' Beach landings on D-Day, 6 June 1944. Note Ranger in right center, apparently using his middle finger to push cartridges into a M-1 carbine magazine. The carbine and a backpack frame are nearby. This file is the work of a sailor or employee of the US Navy, taken or made as part of that person's official duties.'*

Coit Coker closed up his communications and maintained limited contact with the ship and then *'we proceeded to a point on the road about 1000 yards NW of Au Guay where all three 116th Battalions assembled in preparation for an advance toward Isigny, the Rangers and 2nd and 3rd Battalions planning to advance to the right and the 1st Battalion via Maisy to the left.'*

Suspecting a German observation point in Grandcamp church, Coker suggested to Colonel Canham that they fire on the church at the east end of town. Canham agreed, so Coker proceeded on a Sherman tank to a point several hundred yards up the road. *'From here we delivered observed fire on the church (about 16 rounds) and two 1-minute rapid fire barrages (about 64 rounds) traversing the waterfront. I then requested two minutes of unobserved rapid fire on the town of Maisy, SW of Grandcamp (64 rounds).'*

On his return to the main group he found that Captain Vavruska of the 5th Rangers had organised firing against the church for a second time. *'Both of our fire missions were undertaken by a ship with the call sign RAH.'*

Lee Brown HQ Co. 5th Rangers remembered the same incident: *'We approached the open land in front of Grandcamp and came under sniper fire from Grandcamp church. I watched a lieutenant nearby calling it in and then him saying, 'It's on its way'... and then I saw the steeple blowing in one shot.'*

Just over an hour later HMS *Glasgow* was in action again. Its spotters had seen a water tower in Grandcamp being used as an observation point. Grid ref: 555932. They engaged it with 45 rounds, but only registered several near misses. They also fired at the main road behind it using different co-ordinates (555930) in an attempt to destroy it. It was later discovered that the water tower had tripod legs and due to surrounding woods and buildings, it was a difficult target to hit. The Germans maintained this as an observation position a little longer.

HMS *Glasgow* After Action Report: 1315: *opened fire on Maisy battery (target No 5 – Les Perruques and fired 63 rounds with aerial observation. Aircraft reported 'Fire effective – several direct hits. Many within 50 yards.'*

At 1455 HMS *Glasgow* fired 58 rounds from direct observation from its own deck at German troops crossing the land from Grandcamp towards Pointe du Hoc. This was a position which was open ground, so the Germans stood little chance against the *Glasgow's* guns. This German counter-attack would have been directed squarely at the Rangers and the 116th Infantry waiting to cross the small road bridge over the flooded area.

Below is a 1st Inf. Div. HQ operational map overlay (with map underneath) indicating the position of the US forces within its command at 1040hrs. Whilst units advanced to Pointe du Hoc, other forces continued on past it. The line reached by US forces at that time is the heavy black one.

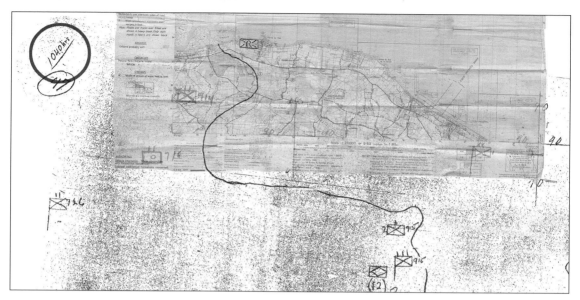

At 1527 HMS *Glasgow*: Opened fire at Maisy Battery and expended 48 rounds. Aircraft reported '*Hits obtained. Fire effective.*'

At 2110 HMS *Glasgow* opened fire on 'suspected gun battery' at grid reference 578918 – this was south of the Rangers' position and could have been responsible for some of the incoming fire they were receiving. After expending 18 rounds, the aircraft reported '*No guns seen but direct hits on farm house. Men ran out. Net results not known.*'

Information from Coit Coker states that by now the 1st Battalion was on the way to Maisy and encountering stiff resistance. Colonel Canham agreed that '*one hour's intermittent fire be placed on Maisy and he said that he would notify the 1st Battalion of this fire. I called for RAH to deliver unobserved intermittent fire of 12 rounds every five minutes on the Maisy area for a period of one hour, which they did from 1500-1600 (144 rounds). Our party caught up with the 1st Battalion outside of Maisy after hitching a ride with cannon company's vehicles.*'

Maisy village had been pretty well destroyed by the intermittent fire and had been evacuated with the exception of one machine gun emplaced in the church steeple; this nest was knocked out by Browning automatic rifles and rifle grenades. However, when the forward part of the Battalion passed the church and reached the main crossroads of the town, the Germans fired a two-gun artillery salvo onto this position.

'*I happened to be with the forward element at the time and was cut off with 40 men and a 2nd Lieutenant.*' He quickly ran along a dirt road lined with evacuated trenches and emplacements. The aim was to get away from the Germans, who obviously had him under observation. Wherever the small group ran, the artillery followed them until the track ended in a meadow.

They were fortunate because none of the shelling produced any casualties. A German emerged from a camouflaged position hoping to lure them into the open and most probably a trap:

'*We motioned him toward us but just at the edge of the field he decided to dive behind a hedgerow, immediately receiving a burst from the Lieutenant's tommy-gun. The Lieutenant and I had a record-quick joint Army-Navy conference and decided that we were in too small a force to continue further and that the only procedure open was to retrace our steps back to Maisy and attempt to find and re-join the rest of the battalion. This we did, finding them on the road just south of the town. Enemy artillery shifted onto us again here, one heavy calibre probably firing from Isigny and the other light calibre short range (horse drawn?) probably from vicinity of targets No 16 [La Martinière] and No 108 [near Foucher's Farm] about 1500 S and SW of Maisy. Under this artillery fire the battalion dispersed to cover again.*'

Setting up his radio set again, he was unable to find ship call sign RAH or the *Texas* – call sign SXT. He did however get in touch with a ship and asked that they relay messages to LBL which he later discovered to be the British cruiser *Bellona* – then via LBL to the *Texas*. This complicated method did however prove successful and he called for aerial reconnaissance to fire on any artillery seen firing near Osmanville and Isigny.

> *We were working under combined difficulties at this point – exasperatingly bad radio communications; shrapnel from enemy fire falling about us, and isolated from the remainder of the battalion. Private Henson is to be commended for his courageous spirit and devotion to duty in sticking by me in a trying situation where nearly all others had taken cover. Finally we were forced to close down and return to the battalion which had re-formed and taken defensive shelter in abandoned enemy entrenchment on the southern outskirts of town.*
>
> *When we reopened, the USS* Bellona *was calling us direct and said they were now assigned to us, also that the USS* Texas *was going to fire a barrage on Isigny for us.*
>
> *In regard to the naval gunfire which we placed on Maisy, I believe that without it the 1st Battalion would either have had extreme difficulty in taking the town and at worst might have fallen into a trap. This belief is based on several facts. The battalion encountered heavy opposition in its approach to Maisy, and there were many entrenchments in the vicinity of the town which had been evacuated, evidently very recently. The town itself had been completely evacuated with the exception of the one machine gun nest. Artillery pieces which had probably been in the area, were no longer present, evidently moved to the south toward Isigny.'*

[Author: This may be a reference to the Les Perruques – Maisy 1 battery's guns having been moved that afternoon towards Osmanville. German reports suggest that this was ordered. It is unclear if and at what time they were moved before the actual assault took place].

On the morning of 8 June the USS *Harding* was laying off Pointe du Hoc with its crew at battle-stations. Enemy planes were reported in the area and the ship patrolled at a slow speed. It was searching for targets of opportunity which might be spotted by its watch officers.

At 1433 NGLO 3 (Naval Gunnery Liaison Officer 3 – the Rangers' SFCP) requested fire on the waterfront of Grandcamp. They fired 160 rounds into the normally sleepy seafront and did so for one hour. It is unlikely that this fire was particularly effective, although some of the small machine-gun positions may have been hit. It is more likely that the shelling had a psychological effect on the defenders more than anything else.

At 1440 NGLO 3 requested that *Harding* opened fire on the town of Maisy using intermittent fire for one hour. It was a move to try and stem the flow of reinforcements moving in from Maisy through Cricqueville towards Pointe du Hoc. It will have also been aimed at the AA position and the battery in the village. Accurate as it was, the naval gunfire would not have guaranteed destruction of either group of positions, so it was probably used as a 'softening up' of the Maisy positions prior to the Rangers' advance.

They ceased fire at 1900 and by 1920 NGLO 3 reported fire on Maisy had been highly effective and that US troops were entering the town.

A Company 5th Rangers – Maisy, France.
Jack Burke, A Co. 5th Rangers: *'On June 8th we were told we were leaving Pointe du Hoc, moving in the direction of Grandcamp-les-Bains – where we encountered heavy German resistance. It must have been in the late afternoon when we came to a hill and it was impossible for us to move forward because we did not have the firepower to attack. We ended up there that night, after taking control of some sluice gates outside of Grandcamp.'*

B Company 5th Rangers – Grandcamp-les-Bains.
C Company 5th Rangers – Maisy, France.
D Company 5th Rangers – Grandcamp-les-Bains, France.
E Company 5th Rangers – Grandcamp-les-Bains.
F Company 5th Rangers – Maisy, France.
Medical Detachment 5th Rangers – Grandcamp-les-Bains, France.
Headquarters Company 5th Rangers – Grandcamp-les-Bains, France.

81st Chemical Weapons Btn. ARR: *At 0530 hours, on June 8, D Company aided in the bloody attack on Grand Champs les Bains and was credited with another enemy machine gun nest.*

COMPANY MORNING REPORT ENDING 2400 8 June 1944

STATION Maisie, France
ORGANIZATION Co "A" 5th Ranger Inf Bn Inf

SERIAL NUMBER	NAME	GRADE	CODE
36589442	Kalar, William R.	Sgt	✓
	Above Em SWA to dy		

RECORD OF EVENTS

8 Jun 44   Left Verville Ser Mur at 0600
arrived at Point de Hoe at 0800.
Enemy strong point captured by
other elements of Ranger Battalions
Left Point de Hoe at 1200 and arrived
at Maisie, France , at 1600.

COMPANY MORNING REPORT ENDING 2400 8 June

STATION Maisie, France   APO
ORGANIZATION Co C 5th Ranger Inf Bn

SERIAL NUMBER	NAME	GRADE	CODE
	NO CHANG.		

RECORD OF EVENTS

8 June 44 Left St. Pierre du Mont at
0600 arrived at Pointe du Hoe at 0800.
Enemy strong point captd by other elements
of Ranger B. Left Pointe du Hoe at 1200
and arrived at Maisie, France at 1600.

COMPANY MORNING REPORT ENDING 2400 8 June 1944

STATION Grandcamp les Bains France APO 230
ORGANIZATION Co E 5th Ranger Inf Bn Inf

SERIAL NUMBER	NAME	GRADE	CODE
	NO CHANGE		

RECORD OF EVENTS

8 June 1944 Left Vierville Sur Mer
at 0600 Arrived at Point du Hoe at
0800 Enemy strongpoint captured by
other elements of Ranger Battalions
Left Point du Hoe at 1200 Arrived
at sluice gates outside Grandcamp
les Bains at 1330 Assisted in assult
on Grandcamp les Bains

COMPANY MORNING REPORT ENDING 2400 8 June 1944

STATION Grandcamp les Bains, France APO 230
ORGANIZATION Hq Co 5th Ranger Inf Bn Inf

SERIAL NUMBER	NAME	GRADE	CODE
33196231	Button LeRoy T.	S/Sgt	
Fr DS Provisional Ranger Group Headquarters			
APO 230 U S Army to SWA			

RECORD OF EVENTS

8 June 1944 Left Vierville Sur Mer at 0600
Arrived at Point De Hoe at 0800 Enemy
strongpoint captured by other elements of
Ranger Battalions Left Point De Hoe at 1200
Arrived at sluice gates outside Grandcamp
les Bains at 1330 Assisted in assault on Grandc
les Bains.

COMPANY MORNING REPORT ENDING 2400 8 June 1944

STATION Grandcamp les Bains, France APO 230
ORGANIZATION Co B 5th Ranger Inf Bn Inf.

SERIAL NUMBER	NAME	GRADE	CODE
37450732	Detlefsen, Vern L.	S/Sgt	
31154656	Levesque, Joseph W.	Tec 5	
35667924	Morgan, Carl W. Jr.	Pfc	
	Above EM fr dy to SWA		
35667924	Morgan, Carl W. Jr.	Pfc	
	From SWA to DOW		

RECORD OF EVENTS

8 June 44 | Left Vierville Ser Mur at 0600
Arrived at Point de Hoe at 0800 Enemy
strongpoint captured by other elements of
Ranger Battalions Left Point de Hoe at
1200 Arrived at sluice gates outside
Grandcamp les Bains at 1330 Assisted in
assault on Grandcamp les Bains.

COMPANY MORNING REPORT ENDING 2400 8 June 4

STATION Grandcamp les Bain, France
ORGANIZATION Co D, 5th Ranger Inf Bn Inf

SERIAL NUMBER	NAME	GRADE	CODE
20101434	Stein, Robert F.	Pfc	
	Dy to KIA		
32573291	Jakubowski, Stanley T.	S/Sgt	
39329532	Wilson, Victor I.	Tec 5	
	Above EM dy to SWA		
32567515	Smolarek, John C.	Tec 5	
17013776	Styles, Clarence A.	Pfc	
	Above EM dy to LWA		

RECORD OF EVENTS

8 Jun 44 Left Pointe du Hoe at 1200
and arrived at sluice gates outside
of Grandcamp les Bain at 1300. Assisted in assault on Grandcamp les Bain.

COMPANY MORNING REPORT ENDING 2400 8 June 4

STATION Maisie, France   APO 230
ORGANIZATION Co. F 5th Ranger Inf. Bn. Inf.

SERIAL NUMBER	NAME	GRADE	CODE
37467459	Mapes, Edward, I.	PFC	
	Dy to LWA		

RECORD OF EVENTS

8 Jun 44   Left Verville Ser Mur at 0600 arr
at Pointe du Hoe at 0800. Enemy strongpoint
captured by other elements of Ranger Bns.
Left Pointe du Hoe at 1200 and arrived at
Maisie, France at 1800.

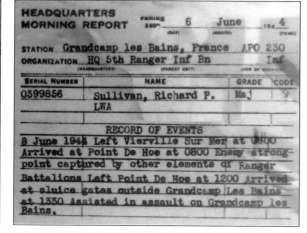

743rd Tank Battalion After Action Report:

8 June 1944   Moved toward West in assault on Pointe Du Hoe at
0600. Were not fired on until in vicinity of Pointe Du Hoe
where Mortar fire started dropping. Were in support of 3rd
Battalion 116th Infantry in assault. Took objective at 1200.
Lt. Ondre injured by Mortar fire and evacuated. Moved on towards
Maisy and because of mines on bridge reversed column and moved
to Grand Camp Les Bains (5593) moved to Maisy via Cricqueville
En Bessin. Entered Maisy under rifle and machine gun fire, passed
south out of Maisy on Isigny road. Enemy arty. and Mortar fire
was falling on the town and only one platoon was taken through.
Two enemy pill boxes in strong point at (532915) were knocked out.
Company returned to (562924) to bivouac. Were attached to 115th
Infantry during this period.   Strength 78 E.M., 5 O.

C Company 743rd Tank Battalion After Action Report:

8 June 1944   Moved out 0600 hrs., Co. "A" in lead. Attacked towards
Pointe Du Hoe (586937) at 1015 hrs. Five tanks dropped out here.
3 tanks hit mines and developed engine trouble. Four tanks were
repairable. Advanced on Grand Camp Les Bains (545931) at 1230 hrs.
One more tank disabled due to mines. Position was taken at 1800 hrs.
and 116th Inf. made crossing. Company was unable to continue on
account of mines. Bivouaced at (567931) until 1130 following day,
reorganized. Knocked out pill box near road. Strength: 86 E.M.,
4 O.

HQ Company 743rd Tank Battalion After Action Report:

8 June 1944   Moved from Transit Area No. 1 at 1000 to bivouac
Area 200 yds west of Vierville Sur Mer where met "B" Company in
bivouac. Major Duncan moved with the Bn. Command H/T and staff
tank at 1230 to join "A" and "C" Companies on the assault on
Pointe Du Hoe. Contacted 116th Inf. and Contacted 116th Inf. Col.
Canham with tanks one mile east of Grandcamps Les Bains. Joined 2nd Bn.
of 116th. Hiked with infantry point to assault Maisy via Cricqueville en Bessin and Vucoville.
to "A" Company.

2nd Ranger Battalion After Action Report 8 June – Force A.

> Sniper fire which commenced at dawn on 8 June, died out as the relieving Force drew near. Becoming aware of the 116th Infantry in attack formation to their front, the Commander of Company F dispatched a patrol to contact them but before the attacking troops could be made aware of the identity of the Force on the Pointe, friendly MG and tank-gun fire caused a number of casualties. Even tho a yellow

> recognition flare was fired and the American flag flown o-ver the CP, tank shells scored several near-misses in that vicinity. Following the cessation of this action, Company E was rejoined by three of its' missing men, two of whom were severely wounded. These men had laid hidden in enemy territory for two days. The portion of Company D, cut-off by the attack which over-ran Company E on D-Day night, re-duced to one officer and twelve men, succeeded in breaking thru on the right to make contact with the 116th Infantry. Force "A" was then joined by the remainder of the Battali-on which had held up near St. Pierre du Monte during the 116th Infantry action.   (See Force "C" account)

2nd Battalion After Action Report – Force C – A & B Companies and 5th Btn.

> The Bn Hq Det assisted in clearing a portion of the hill-top during the morning. Contact was then made with the 5th Ranger Battalion in Vierville and, moving thru the Beach Exit, the detachment joined the 5th Ranger Battalion during the evening of 7 June. The men remained in Vier-ville during the night under sporadic bombing.
>
> While standing by on the morning of 8 June to permit the III/116th Infantry to pass thru their position, Force "C" was rejoined by the men that had become separated on the beach. Moving out at 0900, Company B as the point, the 2nd Ranger elements of Force "C" turned right at the RJ in St Marie du Mont for a new route of approach to the Pointe. Following a short halt during the attack on the

> Pointe by the 116th Infantry, the Companies pushed rapidly on and, passing thru a minefield without casualty, joined Force "A" on Pointe du Hoe at approximately 1200-hours.
>
> During the four-hour period of reorganization, Compa-ny B was dispatched to clear out the remaining installa-tions between Pointe du Hoe and Pointe El Raz de la Percee. This force took a number of prisoners without casualty in the process, returning at the completion of this action to Pointe du Hoe.
>
> Lt Robert Arman of Company F was then placed in com-mand of Company A and Companies A/B reverted to Battalion control.

Small Unit Actions Report PdH: *On the morning of D+2, firing came close to his hideout along the road. It was the 116th Infantry, attacking to relieve the Pointe, but S/Sgt. Theobald could not know that. Leaving the highway and cutting south, he was captured by a machine-gun post near the creek.*

Maurice Prince: When morning came, we again took up the approach march formation to contact our Ranger Companies and take the Pointe. This time our advance wasn't to be halted. We overran the enemy's defence line and broke into the positions on the Pointe.

We finally contacted our brother Ranger Companies, who it seemed were in full possession of this strongpoint. There weren't many of them about, as they had had their share of casualties. It was a happy reunion. Personally, I had doubted if I would ever see any of them again.

It seems from the stories we gathered from them, that they had accomplished their mission, but only after they had had some hectic battles. They had lost all communications contact with us, so that they couldn't let us know of their victory. They had held the Pointe for three days, fighting off one counter attack after another. Although they had lost heavily in men and equipment, they had still retained possession of the Pointe repelling the enemy time after time, again, and again.

This time our Battalion underwent a complete reorganisation. There had been men who had been listed as missing in action, but somehow or other these men turned up.

Our company regained five such men. These Rangers had got themselves separated from us, but had attached themselves to other units in our zone of action and had fought side by side with the soldiers from these other outfits. Now they were back, back to the organisation they were an integral part of. It was good seeing them, as up till now, all men that were listed as missing in action were presumed to be lost to us forever.

Our company finally got itself an officer. Up till now our sprite first platoon Sgt. (Tech. Sgt. White) had been in command of the company. He had done an excellent job. The way he handled his assignment bore credit to him. We got Lt. Salomon (now Captain) from Charley Co., a fine officer and a good leader.

Our reorganisation being completed, we had the task of taking the fortified sea-coast town of Grandcamp-les-Bains, which lay a couple of miles from the Pointe. Due to our strenuous fighting and heavy losses, a last minute's change decided to put us into a reserve position and to let our brethren Ranger Btn., the 5th, do this job for us. And do it they did, in a grand Ranger fashion, overcoming and routing the Heinies in a decisive victory. The Fifth had sustained a few casualties but they made up for it in ground gained, Krauts killed and wounded, plus innumerable stores of weapons, equipment and prisoners taken.

We meanwhile, took up reserve positions in a field halfway between the Pointe and Grandcamp, off the main road. It wasn't much of an area, as it was swampy and damp, but after what we had gone through, it was like Paradise to us. We were now in the rear. That meant we could relax our vigilance and take thing easy, we sat down, lit up cigarettes and contentedly whiled away the moments.

Our supply trucks, which had already landed, caught up to us here. We retrieved our earthly army possessions which were in our duffle bags, we immediately went into a change of clothes, as the ones we were wearing showed the signs and symptoms of being in battle. We got out our wash kits and went to work on our features and bodies. No one used a razor, anyway most of us didn't, as we were going to make our appearance equal the toughness of our esteemed name.

Instead of our usual 'K' rations, we were issued 10-1 rations. That day we were able to partake in our first decent and balanced meal since we had disembarked from our boat. It was appetizing to eat a hot meal, and the hot coffee we drank put new life into us. We almost felt human again, instead of the savage animals we had turned into during our battling.

That night we slept peacefully. There had been the usual air raid upon our beach and naval installations, but our position had been untouched. We felt like new men the next morning; that night's beauty rest had erased the lines of worry from our features.

A Company 2nd Rangers – Grandcamp-les-Bains.

1st Lt. Sidney A. Salomon was assigned to A Company from C Company and assumed principal duty as Company Commander.

Pfc. Seymour Goldman and Roy J. Ebben were attached to A Company from Headquarters Company 2nd Btn for duty and rations.

Record of events: Map being used was a GSGS4250. Scale 1:50,000.

Contacted Companies D, E & F from the 2nd Btn at Pointe du Hoc and advanced to Grandcamp-les-Bains.

B Company 2nd Rangers – Grandcamp-les-Bains.

Contacted Companies D, E & F from the 2nd Btn at Pointe du Hoc and advanced to Grandcamp-les-Bains.

C Company 2nd Rangers – Grandcamp-les-Bains.
S/Sgt. Richard G. Garret went from Duty to Hospital.
1st Lt. Sidney A. Saloman transferred from C Company to A Company 2nd Btn.
Record of events: Map being used was a GSGS4250. Scale 1:50,000.
Contacted Companies D, E & F from the 2nd Btn at Pointe du Hoc and advanced to Grandcamp-les-Bains.

D Company 2nd Rangers – Grandcamp-les-Bains, France.
Pfc. Andrew P. McCorckle was Killed in Action.
1st Lt. Morton L. McBride was Missing in Action as of 6 June 1944.

The following 26 men were listed as Missing in Action as of 6 June 1944:

T/5 Louis J. Bisek	S/Sgt. Patrick F. McCrone	Pfc. Steven J. Sczepanski
T/5 John M. Clifton	T/5 Thomas D. Mendenhall	T/5 Edwin J. Secor
T/Sgt. John J. Corona	S/Sgt. Norman G. Miller	Pfc. Dominick J. Sparaco
Sgt. Joseph R. Devoli	Pfc. John J. Miljavac	T/Sgt. Richard J. Spleen
T/5 Clinton M. Hensley	Pfc. Alvin H. Nance	S/Sgt. Joseph L. Stevens
Pfc. James H. Hudnell	Pfc. John D. Oehlberg	T/5 William A. Walker
S/Sgt. Charles E. Kettering	T/5 Raymond J. Riendeau	T/5 Robert M. Wells
Pfc. Peter Korpalo	Pfc. John J. Riley	Pfc. Newton R. Williams Jr.
Pfc. Harold E. Lester	Pfc. Antonio J. Ruggiero	

Record of events: Map being used was a GSGS4250. Scale 1:50,000.
Contacted Companies A, B & C from the 2nd Btn at Pointe du Hoc and advanced to Grandcamp-les-Bains.

E Company 2nd Rangers – Pointe du Hoc.

The following 7 men were Missing in Action:

T/Sgt. Clifton E. Mains	T/5 Paul P. Knor	Pfc. Richard Hubbard
Sgt. Theodore M. Pilalas	Pfc. Francis J. Connolly	
T/5 John. S. Burnett	Pfc. Duncan N. Daugherty	

Pfc. Harry W. Roberts went from Duty to seriously wounded in hospital.

Record of events: Map being used was a GSGS4250. Scale 1:50,000.
Contacted Companies A, B & C from the 2nd Btn at Pointe du Hoc and advanced to Grandcamp-les-Bains.

F Company 2nd Rangers – Grandcamp-les-Bains.
S/Sgt. James E. Fulton went from Duty to Hospital, Lightly Wounded in Action.
Sgt. McCloskey and Pfc. Madison B. Cobb both went from Duty to Missing in Action.
Record of events: Map being used was a GSGS4250. Scale 1:50,000.
Contacted Companies A, B & C from the 2nd Btn at Pointe du Hoc and advanced to Grandcamp-les-Bains.

Medical Detachment 2nd Rangers – Grandcamp-les-Bains.
Record of events: Map being used was a GSGS4250. Scale 1:50,000.
Contacted Companies D, E & F from the 2nd Btn and advanced to Grandcamp-les-Bains.

Headquarters Company 2nd Rangers – Grandcamp-les-Bains.
Major Cleveland Lytle went from sick in hospital to relieved of assignment and Duty and assigned to 10th Replacement Depot APO874 as of 7 June 1944 – per SO#159, HQ Southern Base Section, SOS ETOUSA.
Captain Harold K. Slater went from Duty to Missing in Action as of 6 June 1944.

The following 6 enlisted men went from Duty to Missing in Action as of 6 June 1944.

Sgt. William L. Mollohan	Pfc. Theodore A. Malburg Jr.	Pfc. Eugene C. Doughty
Pfc. Kenneth L. Wharff	Pfc. John R. Ahart	T/5 Steve M. Mead

T/5 Philip G. Robida went from Detached Service with Group Headquarters to Seriously Wounded in Action, in Hospital. Record of events:-Map being used was a GSGS4250. Scale 1:50,000.
Contacted Companies D, E & F from the 2nd Btn and advanced to Grandcamp-les-Bains.

Reorganization   8 June

During the four-hour period of Battalion reorganization, Intelligence personnel made a search of the still-
burning OP. A considerable amount of material, including
the German Naval Pennant Code, was gathered, and was transmitted to the USS Ancon. A small patrol was then sent out
to locate the 5th Ranger Battalion which was then preparing
to attack Grandcamp. This patrol safely rejoined the Battalion which was standing by on the coastal road.

Just prior to the Battalion departure from the Pointe
at 1600, a Company F patrol located and destroyed a still-
active enemy MG firing from a tree-top. Moving out without
incident to the Vierville-Grandcamp Road, the Battalion was
held up awaiting the return of the contact patrol. Upon
the receipt of the patrol information, Lt Col Rudder moved
the Battalion into bivouac near au Guay to await the clearing of Grandcamp. Moving out by foot at 1700, the Battalion proceeded to another bivouac area in the Sluice Gate
vicinity. Shortly thereafter, the Battalion Supply vehicles
were closed into the area and rations, water, ammunition,
and bed rolls were distributed. The troops rested during
this period with security provided by the "buddy-system",
each unit providing its' own rotating sentry. Altho this
area was bombed during the night, no casualties occurred.

Grandcamp seafront on 8 June was a desolate place with significant bomb and shell damage.

Looking the other way along the harbour wall. The remains of a damaged Renault Tank Turret used by the Germans for harbour defence sits with its top knocked to one side. Note also the anti-boat net still down over the harbour entrance.

Looking into the harbour entrance – now blocked by sunken barges.

After Action Report 58th Armoured Field Artillery – 8 June.

<u>8 June 1944</u>

The Battalion moved in the forenoon to positions north of Longueville, from which fire could be delivered on both Isigny and Maisy.

USS *Harding* After Action Report 8 June.

```
                        8 June 1944

        Lying off Point Du Hoe, crew at Battle Stations standing easy.
0000B   Enemy Air Raid on beach defenses.
0200B   Air Raid over.
0510B   Commenced jamming.  Enemy planes reported in area.
0600B   Commenced patrolling area #3 at slow speeds searching for targets of
        opportunity.
1433B   Opened fire on waterfront of Grandcamp Les Bains at request of NGLO #3.
        160 rounds, firing unobserved by SFCP #3.
1440B   Opened fire on town of Maisy by request of NGLO #3.  73 rounds.
1815B   On request of NGLO #3 opened fire on Maisy using intermittent fire for
        one hour.
1900B   Ceased firing.
1920B   NGLO #3 reported fire on Maisy had been highly effective and that our
        troops were entering the town.
1930B   Closed Texas.
1947B   CDD 36 left ship for Texas.
2010B   Received aboard survivors of Susan B. Anthony.
2043B   CDD 36 returned aboard from Texas.
2100B   Returned to Fire Support Area #3 and lay to.
2332B   Anchored in Fire Support Area #3, Point Du Hoe bearing 240°(T) distant
        4500 yards.

        347 rounds of 5"38 caliber ammunition expended.
```

9 June 1944   Lt. Coit Coker: *'At 0100 we called on the* Bellona *to fire on target No 16 (Maisy II) about 1500 yards SW of our position where mobile artillery was suspected. This fire was spotted by sound and comprised about 26 rounds. To avoid placing the GT (Gun Target) line over our position, the* Bellona *was requested to move to a position NE of the target before opening fire.*

5th Battalion Incidents, Messages and Orders Report:

```
0500 VOCG; Co E patrols to town and along beach to
get stranded snipers and to previous unlocated
enemy mortar positions.
1400 Co E mission completed.
1620 VOCG; 29th Div; move thru Grande Camp along
road and proceed to Osmannville.
2000 arrived 1/2 Kil Osmanville - Set up all
around defense.
2100 VOCG - Co E sent night patrol to river vire
check foot bridge leading to Cherbourg Peninsula.
2400 mission completed. Area Bombed by enemy.
Casualties; Hq Co, Pfc Harry R. Dunham (LWA)
S/Sgt William Scott (NMI), Pfc Henry Santos (NMI)
Pfc George F Chiatello, T/5 Dana W Wallace (MIA)
1st Sgt Jerome V Bugnacki, T/5 James L Sullivan Jr
T/5 Robert D Battice, Pfc Hubert A Putney, Pfc
John H Tucker (SWA); Co D, S/Sgt Charles W Bolmer
(SWA); Co E, T/5 Steven Oboryshko MIA, Pfc Robert
H McCoubrey (SWA), Pfc George J Petersohn (LWA)
Co F Sgt Clinton L Fogel, Sgt Anthony F Muscatello
Tec 5 Nickolas (NMI) Pasuk, T/5 Burton E Ranney.
(LWA)
```

Jack Burke, A Co. 5th Rangers:

The morning of the 9th we were told we would attack an artillery battery. I remember leaving for Maisy and the area was flooded and marsh land across a small bridge and later moving into a wooded area on a dirt road.

A Co. 5th Btn was to attack thru a flood land up the hill. C Co. from the flank and F Co. on their right. A Co. had to avoid the flooded area by moving down about 25 to 50 yards. It must have been around 9 or 10am in the morning when we moved out. We had to change our formation because of the abundance of landmines, while encountering heavy firing from rapid fire machine guns, mortars, etc.

It was a tough scene, but we finally got to the top of the hill and started clearing out the trenches and at this point the Germans started to surrender. There was more to taking this battery because it was much larger than we thought. What surprised me was that we never heard of Maisy Battery in our briefings. I remember they told us on board the ship when we were in Weymouth Harbor that after we accomplished our initial objective on D-Day, we would be going to hook up with the Airborne in and around Isigny.

5th Battalion After Action Report:

```
                        D/3    9 June 1944

        Company E continued to mop-up positions along the coast toward Pointe-du-Hoe
    killing several Germans and capturing about 40.

        At 1300 hours Companies B, D, and E marched directly south from Grandcamp
    on a secondary road, changed direction to the west at Le Manoir, again
    changed direction to the south on the Isigny road, and went into bivouac about
    400 yards west of Osmanville.

        A, C, and F Companies, detached from the First Battalion 116th Infantry
    which had by-passed the battery position southwest of Maisy, were given the
    mission of cleaning out that strong point. They were supported on this mission
    by the two half-tracks Second Ranger Battalion, Company B, 81st Chemical Weapons
    Battalion, and the four 81 mm mortars carried by Company C. A concentration by
    the 58th Field Artillery Battalion preceded the attack. Attacking with two
    companies in column the position was successfully carried. The strong-point
    contained three 105 mm howitzers, numerous small-arms, large stocks of
    ammunition and food, and ejected approximately 90 prisoners. Shortly thereafter
    this force marched to the bivouac area west of Osmanville where it joined
    the remainder of the battalion at 2000 hours.

        At 2100 a three man patrol from Company E was dispatched to reconnoiter the
    Light Engineer Bridge across the Vire River. This patrol accomplished its
    mission and returned at 2400 hours.

        Results for the fourth day were approximately 20 Germans killed, 130
    prisoners, and 18 Ranger casualties.
```

Another A Company man, John Perry recounts the same action: *We went into a flooded area and their mortars opened up on us. They were heavy and there was plenty of machine-gun fire. There were woods to our right as we went uphill and I remember Sullivan and Battice getting hit. Lieutenant Parker gave the order to fix bayonets as we left the swampy ground. The order to fix bayonets was an indication of what was to come. We had to go from bunker to bunker and fight the Germans face to face.*

John Bellows, also with A Company, had stepped onto the swampy ground and was advancing up the hill towards La Martinière when he came under machine-gun fire: 'I remember stepping on the prong of an S-mine and watching with horror as it launched up in the air... fortunately it didn't go off – which is something I will never forget. However, it did set off a chain reaction of some other mines, which wounded some of the other men around me.'

[Author: As this shows, the mines were everywhere, but the men could not stand around to find them. They were coming under fire and had to make a decision to assault the battery or die in the minefield. Another problem was that the mines had been 'chained' together. So once one was detonated, a series of up to ten would go off in a line. The German logic being that advancing troops would spread out and march at a similar pace. As the first man – in this case John Bellows – found, once he tripped one mine a series of others continued to detonate across the line of advancing Rangers. There was nothing that could be done to avoid them.]

Jack Burke: *I was sent down to get the wounded. Jim Sullivan and Bob Battice from A Company had been wounded as the advance started and they were still down in the swampy area. I was standing at the top of the hill with some wounded guys, a couple of wounded Germans and a bunch of prisoners, and Parker said, 'I've got two guys that are badly hurt. They are down at the base down there in that flooded area and we've got to get them out.' The Germans had flooded the lower area and it was all marshy. It was where Battice and Sullivan and a lot of other guys got hit.*

Captain Petrick, who was a medical officer, said to me, 'Go down there and get them.' I kept saying to myself, 'How in the hell can one guy get two guys out of there?' Anyway, being the dumb GI, I went down there. They gave me support with a guy named Joe Vires – he was a BAR man. Looking left back down the hill, there was a wooded area and they were shooting at us from there. He gave me cover from his BAR and I started to run down the hill – then all hell broke loose with machine-gun and rifle fire shooting at me from the left. I could hear the bullets hitting all around me and smashing into the swamp. Sullivan and Battice were together. I mean they were right together, side by side. I guess they got hit at the same time. Battice got hit in the head and Sullivan got hit in the arm, the shoulder and the back. They were both badly wounded and still under fire, but slightly hidden at the base of the hill behind a small mound or hedgerow.'

[Author: Joe Viers was awarded the Silver Star for this action – see awards section].

A Company 5th Rangers – Osmanville, France.
B Company 5th Rangers – Grandcamp-les-Bains, France.
C Company 5th Rangers – Osmanville, France.
D Company 5th Rangers – Osmanville, France.
D Company were involved in clearing out the coastal positions in front of the Maisy Batteries.
E Company 5th Rangers – Osmanville, France.
F Company 5th Rangers – Osmanville, France.

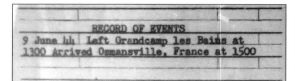

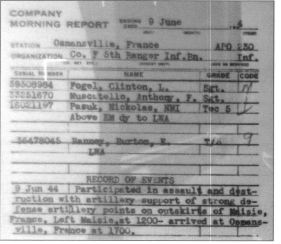

The following 2 pages come from John. C. Hodgson's wartime diary. It shows the F Company 5th Btn losses for D-Day and Maisy.

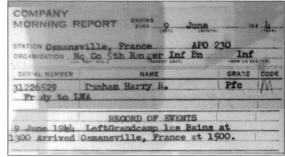

Sgt. Anthony F. Muscatello		
MAISY	6-9-44	33251670
P.F.C. Clark L. Baker		
D-DAY	6-6-44	33573107
P.F.C. Robert (NMI) Ovington		
D-DAY	6-6-44	36313114
P.F.C. Richard G. Sorenson		
D-DAY	6-6-44	31154675
P.F.C. Edward J. Mapes		
MAISY	6-8-44	37467459
T/5 Nicholas (NNI) Pasuk		
MAISY	6-9-44	16021197
S/Sgt. Lysle L. Rogers		
FLAMINGVILLE	7-15-44	20722161

Wounded in Action
Evac. or transferred

1st/Sgt. Howard A. MacDonald		
D-DAY	6-6-44	11117444
Sgt. Clinton L. Fogel		
D-DAY	6-9-44	39308984
S/Sgt. Orvylle A. Rosenblad		
D-DAY	6-6-44	20722145
P.F.C. Stephen W. Minion		
D-DAY	6-6-44	34153831
P.F.C. Louis (NMI) Smolicks		
D-DAY	6-6-44	39464061
T/5 Ray F. Nard		
D-DAY	6-6-44	35608613

Hodgson's pocket diary confirms the same names of F Company Wounded in Action at Maisy:
Sgt. Antony Muscatello 33251670.
Sgt. Clinton L. Fogel 39308984.
T/5 Nicholas Pasuk 16021197.

Medical Detachment 5th Rangers – Osmanville, France.   *Headquarters Company 5th Rangers* – Osmanville, France.

```
COMPANY
MORNING REPORT   ENDING  9  June      194 4
STATION Osmansville, France       APO 230
ORGANIZATION Med Det 5th Ranger Inf Bn   Med
SERIAL NUMBER     NAME        GRADE CODE
              NO CHANGE
              RECORD OF EVENTS
9 June 1944 Left Grandcamp les Bains
at 1300 Arrived Osmansville, France
at 1500.
```

```
COMPANY
MORNING REPORT   ENDING  9  June      194 4
STATION Osmansville, France       APO 230
ORGANIZATION Hq Co 5th Ranger Inf Bn     Inf
SERIAL NUMBER     NAME        GRADE CODE
31226529  Dunham Harry R.     Pfc   M
Fr dy to LWA
              RECORD OF EVENTS
9 June 1944   LeftGrandcamp les Bains at
1300 Arrived Osmansville, France at 1500.
```

743rd Tank Battalion After Action Report:

```
9 June 1944   Stayed in bivouac area all day for maintenance.
Captured 40 prisoners that evening near strong point near Maisy (532915
```

[Author: The grid reference 532915 is the centre of the Maisy I – Les Perruques battery.]

Enemy forces, consisting of remnants of the 726th Infantry
Regiment and 914th, 915th and 916th Infantry Regiments of the 352nd
Infantry Division, were encountered during this period. The artillery
personnel of the 716th Infantry Division were fighting as infantry.

The exact number of enemy casualties is undetermined, but a
conservative estimate lists: Three (3) officers captured and two (2)
killed, two hundred and ninety-eight (298) men captured and one hundred and
forty-six (146) killed. All captured personnel were turned over to infantry
units.

B Company 743rd Tank Battalion After Action Report:

9 June 1944 Moved to Maisy (537923) where received orders to
move South of Maisy. Encountered several pill boxes South of
Maisy which were destroyed. 5th Rangers asked for support on
these pill boxes, 125 prisoners taken. No casualties sustained
by our unit. Ordered back to Maisy to bivouac at 1800.

58th Armoured Field Artillery After Action Report:

9 June 1944

1145	Bn received orders to give direct support to 175th Infantry with two batteries. One Battery in support of 116th Infantry and 5th Ranger Bn.
1445	Received orders to revert full support back to 116th Infantry and 5th Rangers, and remain in general support of 175th Infantry.

58th Armoured Field Artillery Report for ammunition expended on 9 June in support of the Rangers.

AMMUNITION EXPENDITURE FOR JUNE 1944

DATE	NO. MISSIONS	NO. REG.	M48	M54	M60	M84	TOTAL ROUNDS
June 9	2	0	143	72	9		224

2nd Battalion After Action Report.

Moving out on foot in mid-afternoon of 9 June, the
Battalion proceeded thru Grandcamp to a bivouac near Os-
mansville; no incidents were reported enroute. Eight miles
were covered in a misty rain which ceased as the Battalion
closed into the bivouac area. A patrol dispatched to make
contact with the 116th Infantry on the left, was unsuccessful. Normal security measures were taken this night.

81st Chemical Weapons Btn. ARR: *On June 9, B Company, seriously handicapped by the loss of its vehicles, acquired two 6 x 6 trucks from the field artillery. The acquisition of these vehicles solved the immediate transportation difficulties. At the time, B Company was supporting the 5th Ranger Battalion in an attack to clear out the coast fortifications.*

A Company 2nd Rangers – Osmanville, France.
No change. Record of events: Advanced to Osmanville. Map being used was a GSGS4250. Scale 1:50,000.
Maurice Prince: '*The next morning, or D+3, saw us shuttling by foot and by trucks to a new bivouac area just outside the small town of Osmanville (which lies south of Isigny). Our move had been administrative. We weren't bothered by enemy activity. We patrolled our area extensively, but no Germans were found. One uneventful day and night was spent there.*'

B Company 2nd Rangers – Osmanville, France.
No change. Record of events: Map being used was a GSGS4250. Scale 1:50,000. Advanced to Osmanville.

C Company 2nd Rangers – Osmanville, France.
Pfc. Brownie L. Bolin went from Duty to Hospital – Seriously Wounded in Action.
Pfc. Herbert A. King was attached to C Company from Headquarters.

Record of events: Map being used was a GSGS4250. Scale 1:50,000. Advanced to Osmanville.

D Company 2nd Rangers – Osmanville, France.
The following 5 enlisted men went from Duty to Missing in Action as of 7 June 1944:
Pfc. James L. Blum   Sgt. Richard E. McLaughlin   Pfc. Leonard Rubin
Sgt. Emory B. Jones   T/5 Henry S. Stecki

1st Sgt. Lennard Lomell went from Duty to Hospital.
Record of events: Map being used was a GSGS4250. Scale 1:50,000. Advanced to Osmanville.

E Company 2nd Rangers – Osmanville, France.
The following 16 men are Missing in Action:
S/Sgt. Frank A. Rupinski   T/5 Kenneth H. Bargmann   Pfc. Loring L. Wadsworth
S/Sgt. Curtis A. Simmons   T/5 L.A. Brandt   Pvt. Frank B. Robinson
Sgt. Bogetto   Pfc. George H. Crook   Pvt. Harold W. Sehorn
Sgt. Anthony P. Catelani   Pfc. Joseph J. Lock   Pfc. Henry A. Wood
Sgt. Harry G. Fritchman Jr.   Pfc. Salva P. Maimone
Sgt. Aloysius A. Nosal   Pfc. Roy L. Palmer

Record of events: Map being used was a GSGS4250. Scale 1:50,000. Advanced to Osmanvile, France.

F Company 2nd Rangers – Osmanville, France.
Captain Otto Masny went from Duty to Hospital and was relieved of his principal Duty as Company Commander.
1st Lt. Arman assumed temporary Duty as Company Commander.
S/Sgt. James R. Alexander and T/5 Floyd H. Simkins were both recorded as Missing in Action as of 7 June 1944.

Record of events: Map being used was a GSGS4250. Scale 1:50,000. Advanced to Osmanville, France.

Medical Detachment 2nd Rangers – Osmanville, France.
Record of events: Map being used was a GSGS4250. Scale 1:50,000. Advanced to Osmanville, France.

Headquarters Company 2nd Rangers – Osmanville, France.
Pfc. Herbert A. King was attached to C Company 2nd Btn.
Record of events: Map being used was a GSGS4250. Scale 1:50,000. Advanced to Osmanville, France.

Low level reconnaissance photograph of the beach in front of Maisy 9 June.

The centre of Maisy was heavily damaged by naval and aerial bombardment.

Jack Burke A Co 5th: *'The night of the 9th we went down dirt roads and stayed in the woods and were bombed by the Luftwaffe and took some casualties.'*

 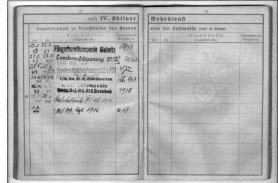

A German soldier's paybook belonging to a German Artilleryman after he was captured at Maisy. His unit is marked as being the 8th battery 1716th Artillery. They were the men manning the battery at La Martinière.

10 June 1944
5th Battalion Incidents, Messages and Orders Report:

```
0600 VOCO; Capt Hefflefinger take Co's C, D, &
F commenceing at Gefusse-Fontenay, proceed north
to coast. Clearing all left resistence and taking
all remaining German prisoners. Mission completed
1530. Total prisoners then 235. Casualties; Hq Co
Sgt Andrew J Caraber, Cpl Harold A Lewis, Pfc
Francis T Coughlin (SWA); Co A T/5 Henry R Seaman,
Pfc Richard L Foley (SWA); Co D Pfc Carmen W
Montello (MIA), Co E S/Sgt Perry D Osborne, Sgt
John B Spurlock, Pfc George W Boles (LWA).
0900 Ranger Bn reverted to V Corps control.
2330 VOCG;V Corps; move by truck to Bois Du Molan
627785 Casualties; Co A Pfc William M Gardner (LWA)
T/5 Dana W Wallace, PfcGeorge F Chiatello (KIA)
0200 arrived VOCO outpost and interior guard set
up. 1000 - Re-equipment nd shortage lists were
made and submitted.
```

5th Battalion After Action Report:

D+4   10 June 1944

At approximately 0430 hours the battalion bivouac area was bombed and the unit suffered three casualties.

Companies C, D, and F were given the mission of mopping up the coastal fortifications from Grandcamp-les-Bains to Isigny. They moved out at 0830 and meeting little resistance, returned at 1530 with approximately 200 prisoners. Mine fields inflicted three casualties on the force.

Patrols in the vicinity of the battalion area captured approximately 35 Germans.

Results for the fifth day were 235 Germans captured and 6 Ranger Casualties.

2.   In five days of fighting this battalion had 23 men killed, 89 wounded, and 2 missing.

Approximately 850 prisoners were taken and 350 Germans killed.

For the Commanding Officer:

Hugo W. Heffelfinger
HUGO W. HEFFELFINGER
Capt.
X-0, S-3

One of the 75mm gun emplacements on the beach at La Casino, along with an observation bunker – they were part of the coastal defences in front of the Maisy Batteries. The area was cleared by companies from the 5th Battalion on 10 June.

A Company 5th Rangers – Osmanville, France.
B Company 5th Rangers – Osmanville, France.
C Company 5th Rangers – Osmanville, France.
D Company 5th Rangers – Osmanville, France.
E Company 5th Rangers – Osmanville, France.
F Company 5th Rangers – Osmanville, France.
Medical Detachment 5th Rangers – Osmanville, France.
Headquarters Company 5th Rangers – Osmanville, France.

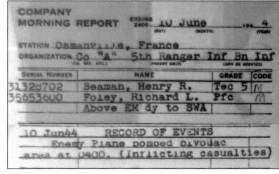

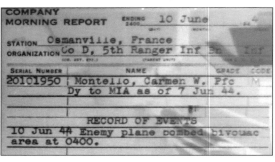

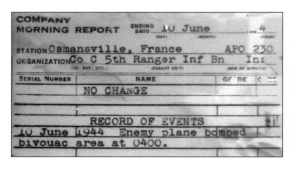

Pfc Francis Coughlin was listed on the Morning Reports as being seriously wounded at Osmanville. Here is the account of what happened to him in his own words: '*I was sent to do a job and 3 other guys came with me – we were blowing up gun emplacements – putting them out of action altogether and one happened to be booby trapped. It was a 75 or 105mm cannon and once you melt the metal you would never get it out. We were putting thermite grenades down the barrels and one guy says, 'hey that's booby trapped... that's about as far as we got and that thing went up. They had shoved a live shell up the breech with just a stick to hold the shell there. They burn at 12,000 degrees but the first one didn't go off and the second one did... and of course it melts almost anything and that's when the shell went off. I ended up in hospital for 6 months. One guy was hit in the head and sent back to the States. I heard the church bells of Osmanville ring – I didn't see them, but I remember laying on the ground and hearing them when I got hit. By June 10th – Saturday they carried me on a stretcher and into an ambulance.*'

The gun emplacements shown on a GSGS map for Osmanville.

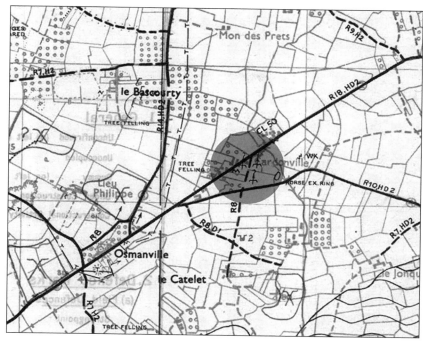

2nd Battalion After Action Report.

> Commencing at 0800, 10 June, patrols from Companies A/B/C searched assigned zones of the area seaward from Osmansville to the coastal road. No contact was made, but evidence showed that the enemy had but recently departed. Captured intelligence material was transmitted to the 29th Division. All searching parties returned safely.

A Company 2nd Rangers – Osmanville, France.
Map being used was a GSGS4250. Scale 1:50,000.
B Company 2nd Rangers – Osmanville, France.
Capt. Arnold was relieved of command and transferred to Headquarters of the 2nd Battalion.
1st Lt. Richard A. Wintz was attached for Duty from F Company from the 2nd Battalion and assumed command.
Record of events: Advanced to Osmanville, France. Map being used was a GSGS4250. Scale 1:50,000.
C Company 2nd Rangers – Osmanville, France.
Map being used was a GSGS4250. Scale 1:50,000.
D Company 2nd Rangers – Osmanville, France.
Map being used was a GSGS4250. Scale 1:50,000.
E Company 2nd Rangers – Osmanville, France.
Record of events: Advanced to Osmanville. Map being used was a GSGS4250. Scale 1:50,000.
F Company 2nd Rangers – Osmanville, France.
1st Lt. Wintz went from Duty to Detached Service with B Company 2nd Btn.
Pvt. Anderson went from Duty to Hospital.
Map being used was a GSGS4250. Scale 1:50,000.
Medical Detachment 2nd Rangers – Osmanville, France.
Record of events: Map being used was a GSGS4250. Scale 1:50,000.
Headquarters Company 2nd Rangers – Osmanville, France.
Captain Edgar L. Arnold was assigned and joined from B Company 2nd Btn. He assumed Duty as Battalion Commander.
Record of events: Map being used was a GSGS4250. Scale 1:50,000. Advanced to Osmanville, France.

On the 12 June General Eisenhower visited the beaches and then later the battle site at Pointe du Hoc. These press photographs show his landing and arrival at Pointe du Hoc.

Photograph of a 5th Ranger – taken on 10 June in Osmanville. It may be Dick Hathaway from A Company.

Two US Signal Corps photos captioned: 'General "Hap" Arnold, Gen. Dwight Eisenhower, Admiral Ernest King (white cap), and General George Marshall visit the guns moved from Pt du Hoc, Normandy, France, Jun 12, 1944.'

'General "Hap" Arnold, Gen. Dwight Eisenhower, Major General "Cowboy Pete" Corlett (helmet), Gen George Marshall, Lt. General Omar Bradley (pointing), and Admiral Ernest King visit the guns moved from Pt du Hoc, Normandy, France, Jun 12, 1944.'

A post-battle Army Intelligence report covering the US invasion sector found the following weapons to have been in place:

VI.   <u>ENEMY DEFENSES.</u>

Enemy prepared shore defenses against amphibious attack consisted of the following elements:

1. A number of well emplaced coastal and field batteries sited to cover both sea approaches and beach areas.

2. A line of strongpoints along the coast, close enough in good landing areas to provide interlocking fire over beaches and exits. These were supplemented by groups of rocket projectors just inland, which could lay fire on the beach.

3. Quantities of beach obstacles, mines, wire and anti-tank obstructions placed and organized to hold invading troops within areas of fire of the strongpoints.

The function of this trio was to hold the invader on the beach itself until an effective counter attack could be launched. There was comparatively little prepared ground defense in depth except for anti-landing stakes and mines spread over possible inland aircraft landing areas.

<u>BATTERIES.</u>

Batteries were located well inland or on headlands relatively inaccessable from seaward. They were sited to provide a uniform concentration of fire along most of the coastline, except over the Cherbourg sea approaches where the intensity was very high. Numerous radar stations along the coast as well as visual posts provided them with observation. The types of guns used varied from modern German models to captured pieces of equipment; estimates of ranges therefore, were questionable even though the calibers were estimated quite accurately. The most predominant battery pieces in the area were the 105 FGH and the French (type GPF) 155 MM field gun.

All battery positions, except temporary field positions, had underground shelters and living quarters inter-connected with the gun emplacement by well camouflaged communication trenches, and were protected by machine guns

<u>ANNEX B1 - INTELLIGENCE</u>

and anti-tank guns, always surrounded by bands of wire and often with bands of mines. In general the concrete was 6 to 7 feet thick reinforced with $\frac{1}{2}$" round rods spaced 9" on centers horizontally and vertically; the quality of the concrete appeared excellent and the workmanship exceptional; roof slabs were consistently poured onto steel plates which formed the ceilings of the shelters and casemates. In certain cases, for larger caliber guns, roof slabs were as thick as 12'.

Batteries were of the following general types:

(1) Pivot mounted guns in casemates. This comprised the majority of the casemated positions; of the batteries which covered the Assault area, 12 of the 16 positions were casemated or had casemates under construction (actually there were only 15 positions as no. 6A was AA defense for position No. 3) and of these twelve, 7 had pivot mounts, 2 were still under construction but appeared designed for pivot mounts, and 2 positions were not visited.. This also appeared to be the general practice in the area surrounding Cherbourg.

(2) Mobile field guns in casemates. Only the Maisy II battery at 528916 was of this type, however other examples were observed in the Cherbourg area and the casemates at Battery No. 18 may possibly have been for mobile guns.

(3) Mobile guns in open emplacements. Of the positions considered, four were permanent positions (Battery No. 8 was included in this computation although it was partially casemated.) Four positions were temporary awaiting the completion of casemates (No. 9A had log and earth covered underground shelters). There were several additional field positions reported from photographic interpretation, but they were not inspected and there is no definite confirmation that they were occupied at the time of the assault and therefore have not been included in computations for this report.

ANNEX B1 - INTELLIGENCE

POINTE DU HOE BATTERY.

Pointe du Hoe battery was considered the number one priority
in the bombardment plan for it was the only enemy position
which covered both of the beaches and transport areas.
Originally there were six 155 mm guns (French type GPF)
with an estimated range of 25,000 yards, in open concrete
emplacements.   It was strategically located atop a 90 foot
high coastal bluff, remote from any large landing beach,
surrounded by wire and mine fields and extremely well protected on the flanks by prepared strongpoints.   Personnel
and ammunition shelters were underground and constructed
of heavily reinforced mass concrete.   Machine guns position
and communication trenches were well dug in and camouflaged.
The observation and command post on the seaward edge of the
bluff was constructed of heavily reinforced concrete, partially earth banked.

                    ANNEX B1 - INTELLIGENCE

Early in March casemates began to be built near four
of the positions; two guns having been removed from
their emplacements. It was estimated that by D-day
the enemy would probably have two guns in casemates
(sited to fire on UTAH) with 4 guns, possibly only 2
guns, with unrestricted arcs of fire remaining in open
emplacements.

After this position was captured by Rangers it was found
that the guns had been moved from their original positions
and placed along a thickly tree arbored lane, completely
hidden from air reconnaissance about 1000 yards south of
the battery site. The guns were postioned to fire only
on UTAH beach, but retained their observation post and
main ammunition storage on top of the bluff.

Although there were no guns in the completed casemates
(two were ready to receive guns and the other two still
under construction) it was learned from prisoners that
it was the enemy's intention to install new guns, which
were momentarily expected. A captured document from
Admiral Hennike's Headquarters revealed the position was
intended to house 6 - 155 mm guns.

The maximum range was 19,800 yards; minimum range, 1,300
yards. No's 1 and 6 guns were to remain in open emplacements with all around arc of fire. Guns 2 and 3 were to
be in casemates facing 040° and guns 4 and 5 were to be
in casemates facing 330°. Casemated guns would be restricted to 120° traverse. This information coincides identically with intelligence reports.

Pre H-hour air bombardment and naval gunfire completely
disrupted communications and communication trenches, badly
damaged or destroyed open positions, and breached perimeter
wire and mine bands. No serious damage was observed on
underground shelters, O.P. or finished casemates which were
constructed of reinforced concrete, despite many hits.

KNOWN ENEMY BATTERY POSITIONS.

The following tabulation lists the batteries which were
in position on D-day and opposed the landings. No attempt
has been made to list the many unoccupied, dummy or prepared field positions which could not bear on the D-day
assault area.

ANNEX B1 - INTELLIGENCE

For the purpose of this compilation shore reconnaissance
was made on all known battery positions from Port en Bessin
to Cap de la Hague with the exception of some of the temporary prepared postions for mobile guns and several inaccessible positions on the breakwaters at Cherbourg. A
comprehensive detailed analysis of the batteries in the
entire Cherbourg peninsula is being prepared to serve as
an aid to instruction and planning for future operations
and will be disseminated independently to appropriate
authorities. A captured document from Headquarters of the
Commander of the Normandy Sea Frontier has also been used
to confirm and amplify this information.

It must also be noted that this tabulation does not include
the individual gun positions, such as casemated 88's and
 75's which formed strongpoints, as distinguished from
batteries.

No.	GRID	DETAILS AND REMARKS
1	586938	4-155mm guns, Covered under "Pointe du Hoe"
5	533918	4-155 Hows. 1 gun knocked from its emplacement by naval gunfire or air bombardment; the other 3 guns were withdrawn when the enemy retreated.
16 16A	528916 531914	4-105 FGH. 3 guns were in casemates, but had been turned around to fire out of rear entr-ances. 1 casemate was still under construction and the gun was demolished in the open empl-acement at 16A. Casemates were for Mobile guns

INFANTRY STRONGPOINTS.

Beach strongpoints were elaborately constructed groups of
concrete pillboxes, gun casemates and open light gun positions,
connected by tunnels and trenches with underground living
quarters and magazines. Each was surrounded by a band of wire
and mines. Automatic flame throwers were frequently emplaced
outside the perimeter, but none appeared to have been used.

On OMAHA strongpoints were located on the cliffs and behind
the beach at the foot of the cliffs. Most of the pillboxes
and casemates were partially buried in the slope. Positions
were connected by tunnels in the cliffs, and communication

was maintained by means of zinc speaking tubes running between stations. Positions were sited to provide cross-fire exits and over the beach. All exits on OMAHA were blocked by ditches or walls.

The weapons found in beach strongpoints on OMAHA and UTAH were as follows:

1. German 88 mm:
    These were consistently found in concrete casemates three to four feet thick, and sited to fire laterally along the beach. Heavy concrete wing walls protected the openings from gunfire from seaward. The guns were run in from the rear and fired through a narrow slit in front. Some of the casemates had two firing slits, and the gun could be sifted to fire either up or down the beach.

2. 75 mm.
    These were mostly obsolete captured weapons. Some were in casemates similar to the 88's but most of them were in simple open emplacements.

3. German 50 mm.
    These occured on both pivot and field mounts, and in both pillboxes and open positions. In one case on OMAHA a 50mm field gun was hidden underground invisible from aerial view, and was run out only to fire.

4. 47 and 37 MM tank turrets.
    Most of these were old French tank turrets with short barreled weapons. They were mounted over concrete "Torbuk Pits" sunk flush with the ground. On OMAHA they were used rather sparingly, but in UTAH strongpoints there were as many as four or five to a strongpoint. They were located on the dune line and could fire directly on the beach.

5. Infantry mortars, 50mm, 80mm and 81mm.
    The usual emplacement for a mortar was a concrete pedestal in an open Tobruk Pit, though some were fired from shallow bowl shaped concrete emplacements and from other

ANNEX B1 - INTELLIGENCE

open emplacements. Use of a Tobruk Pit had the advantage that personnel were completely below ground. Panoramas of the field of fire were painted around the inside of the coping of such pits so that fire could be laid on a designated spot on the beach without observation. Most of the emplacements used for mortars on OMAHA were so sited that they could have been used for flat trajectory weapons, instead of on reverse slopes as might have been expected; hence many of them were reported before D-day as machine gun positions. Mortar positions were not found to any extent in UTAH strongpoints.

6.   Machine Guns, 50 and 30 cal.
These were found in concrete and timber pillboxes and in open positions. They were sited for direct fire on the beach, for perimeter defense of strongpoints, and for anti-aircraft protection.

Rockets were located several hundred yards behind both beaches in hedgerows. They occurred in groups of 38 firing pits with 4 rockets to a pit. In and near strongpoints on UTAH, and in one strongpoint on OMAHA, were small robot tanks filled with explosive and operated by remote control against boats and troops on the beach. None of these were actually used against landings on American Beaches.

The annotated shoreline sketches show beach defenses as determined by Photo-Interpretation and where possible, after D-day, by shore reconnaissance.

The approximate total number of active beach defense weapons on each beach is shown in the following table:

For OMAHA   -   length 7500 yards.

8   Casemates occupied by 75mm or better.

35   Pillboxes occupied by guns smaller than 75.

4   Open field positions 75mm or better.

18   Anti-tank - 37mm to 75mm.

85   Positions less than 37mm (MG).

<u>ANNEX B1 - INTELLIGENCE</u>

```
6      Mortars (Infantry).
38     Rocket pits bearing on the beach, 4 - 32 cm rockets
       per pit.
```

For UTAH Beach   -   Length 9600 yards.

```
9      Casemates occupied by 75 mm or better.
25     Pillboxes occupied by guns smaller than 75 mm.
2      Open field positions 75 mm or better.
14     Anti-tank guns 37 mm to 75 mm.
65     Positions less than 37 mm (machine guns).
0      Mortars
0      Rocket pits, bearing on the beach.
```

BEACH OBSTACLES

Steel, concrete and timber underwater obstacles were used on both assault beaches, above the 6 foot contour above LLW on OMAHA, and above the 10 foot contour on UTAH. They consisted of irregular rows of stakes, element "C", hedgehogs, wooden ramps, and concrete tetrahedra. Many of them in the seaward rows had Teller mines lashed to the top, and on OMAHA, mines were buried in the sand along the seaward row. Wire occurred between the obstacles in a few places, and captured documents indicate that it was planned to criss-cross the area with wire. The following table shows in general the order and spacing in which obstacles were encountered on each beach. The attached Shoreline Sketches show the exact position of these obstacles.

OMAHA

CONTOUR ABOVE LLW	TYPE	SPACING CENTER TO CENTER	DISTANCE FROM BACK OF BEACH	APPROX. TOTAL NO.
6 to 11 ft.	Element "C"	65 ft.	240 yards	200
8 to 14 ft.	Stakes	70 ft.	225 yards	2000
8 to 15 ft.	Ramps	65 ft.	190 yards	450
12 to 18 ft.	Hedgehogs	30 ft.	130 yards	1050

UTAH

CONTOUR ABOVE LLW	TYPE	SPACING CENTER TO CENTER	DISTANCE FROM BACK OF BEACH	APPROX. TOTAL NO.
10 ft.	Ramps	Single Units	275 yards	12
13 ft.	Tetrahedra	30 to 40 ft.	175 yards	150
14 ft.	Stakes	25 to 30 ft.	160 yards	800
15 ft.	Hedgehogs	30 ft.	145 yards	1350
15 ft.	Stakes	25 to 30 ft.	135 yards	800
16 ft.	Stakes	25 to 30 ft.	125 yards	800
(10 to 12 ft.	Element "C"	Scattered units - not in typical section)		42

ANNEX B1 - INTELLIGENCE

Photographic evidence taken after 9 June confirms that
at least one of the guns had been turned around to face
the rear at La Martinière. Of note is the gunfire damage
to the rear of the casement indicating the direction of
attack taken by some of the Rangers.

The village of Maisy suffered many civilian casualties in
the days following the Allied landings. French funerals
were hastily prepared and the trip to the Maisy village
church was made past many battle damaged buildings.
By 10 June both Ranger Battalions were resting in
Osmanville.

Chapter 11

Medals and Battle Honours

The medals and battle honours awarded to the Rangers for the actions of 6–10 June are impressive. First shown here is the authorisation for the Unit Citation for all of the men from both the 2nd and 5th Battalions for their actions on 6 June.

RESTRICTED

HEADQUARTERS
FIRST UNITED STATES ARMY
APO 230
IN THE FIELD

17 June 1944

GENERAL ORDERS)
           :
NO.   26)

BATTLE HONORS

As authorized by Executive Order No. 9396 (Sec I, Bull. 22, WD, 1943) superseding Executive Order No. 9075 (Sec III, Bull. 11, WD, 1942) citations of the following units by the appropriate commanders, under provisions of section IV, Circular No. 333, War Department, 1943, are approved for extraordinary heroism and outstanding performance of duty in action in the initial assault on the northern coast of Normandy, France, 6 June 1944. Detailed citations will be published in subsequent General Orders of this headquarters.

     8th Infantry
     16th Infantry
     116th Infantry
     501st Parachute Infantry
     502nd Parachute Infantry
     505th Parachute Infantry
     506th Parachute Infantry
     507th Parachute Infantry
     508th Parachute Infantry
     2nd Ranger Infantry Battalion
     3rd Battalion, 22nd Infantry
     5th Ranger Infantry Battalion
     70th Tank Battalion
     741st Tank Battalion
     743rd Tank Battalion
     377th Parachute Field Artillery Battalion
     146th Engineer Combat Battalion
     237th Engineer Combat Battalion
     299th Engineer Combat Battalion
     81st Chemical Battalion (Mtz)
     87th Chemical Battalion (Mtz)
     Headquarters and Headquarters Company, 82nd Airborne Division
     Headquarters and Headquarters Company, 101st Airborne Division
     Company A, 4th Engineer Combat Battalion
     1st Platoon, Company C, 4th Engineer Combat Battalion

By command of the ARMY COMMANDER:

W. B. KEAN,
Brigadier General, G. S. C.,
Chief of Staff.

OFFICIAL:

S. A. MACKENZIE,
Captain, A.G.D.,
Asst Adj General.

DISTRIBUTION:
"C"
Full distribution will be made later   RESTRICTED

Below: The 5th Rangers' Unit Citation.

RESTRICTED

HEADQUARTERS 1ST U.S. INFANTRY DIVISION
APO 1, U.S. Army

GENERAL ORDERS)
:
NO.   36)   13 July 1944

CITATION OF UNIT

    Under the provisions of Section IV, War Department Circular 333, 22 December 1943, the 5th Ranger Infantry Battalion is cited for outstanding performance of duty in action. The citation is as follows:

    "In the invasion of France the 5th Ranger Infantry Battalion was assigned the mission of securing a sector of the beachhead. As the leading assault unit in this sector, the battalion landed on the beach at 'H' hour on 'D' day. This landing was accomplished in the face of tremendous enemy rifle, machine-gun, artillery and rocket fire. In addition, the battalion encountered mines and underwater and beach obstacles. Refusing to be deterred from its mission of securing a beachhead, the 5th Ranger Infantry Battalion faced concentrated enemy fire and hazardous beach obstacles with determination and gallantry. Although subjected to heavy enemy fire during the entire day and despite numerous casualties and fatigue, the courage and esprit de corps of this battalion carried the enemy positions by nightfall, thereby securing the necessary beachhead without which the invasion of the continent could not proceed. The heroic and gallant action of the 5th Ranger Infantry Battalion in accomplishing this mission under unusual and hazardous conditions is in keeping with the highest traditions of the Service."

    By command of Major General HUEBNER:

S. B. MASON
Colonel, G.S.C.
CHIEF OF STAFF

OFFICIAL:

LEONIDAS GAVALAS
Lt. Col., A.G.D.
Adjutant General

RESTRICTED

The award of the Unit Citation for the 2nd Battalion.

As authorized by Executive Order No. 9396 (sec. I, Bul. 22, WD, 1943), superseding Executive Order No. 9075 (sec. III, Bul. 11, WD, 1942), citation of the following unit in General Orders, No. 34, Headquarters 1st Infantry Division, 11 July 1944, as approved by the Commanding General, First Army, is confirmed under the provisions of section IV, Circular No. 333, War Department, 1943, in the name of the President of the United States as public evidence of deserved honor and distinction.   The citation reads as follows:

The 2d Ranger Infantry Battalion is cited for outstanding performance of duty in action.   In the invasion of France the 2d Ranger Infantry Battalion was assigned the mission of securing two separate sectors of the beachhead.   Three companies of the battalion landed on the beach at Pointe du Hoe, Normandy, France, at 0630, 6 June 1944, under concentrated rifle, machine-gun, artillery, and rocket fire of the enemy.   The companies faced not only terrific enemy fire but also mines and hazardous underwater and beach obstacles.   Despite numerous casualties suffered in the landing, these companies advanced and successfully assaulted cliffs 100 feet in height.   By grim determination and extraordinary heroism, large enemy coastal guns which had been interdicting the beach with constant shell fire were reached and destroyed.   At the same time, the remainder of the battalion landed on the beach at Vierville-sur-Mer at 0630, 6 June 1944, directly under withering enemy rifle, machine-gun, artillery, and rocket fire.   These companies suffered heavy casualties.   Yet such was their gallantry and heroism that they would not be stopped in their advance, and despite mines, enemy snipers, and fatigue continued 1 mile inland to destroy a coastal battery of large enemy guns.   This action secured the necessary beachhead for the forces that were to follow.   The outstanding determination and esprit de corps of the 2d Ranger Infantry Battalion, in the face of tremendous odds, are in keeping with the highest traditions of the service.

There is inaccuracy in the above text, which states that they attacked *'large enemy guns which had been interdicting the beach with constant shell fire were reached and destroyed.'* It is a shame because it is an inaccurate addition by someone – and in reality, given the heroism of these men, it was an unnecessary exaggeration.

The US Press Corps reported on the medals to be given to the men of both Rangers Battalions following the D-Day operations. Of particular interest for this work is the highlighted award of the Distinguished Service Cross given to Sgt. Joe Urish, 5th Battalion for orchestrating the surrender of 167 German prisoners from the Maisy II (La Martinière) Battery. However, it says that he won it on 10 June – which is incorrect. It was won with the men of A Company on the morning of the 9th. Why this was recorded inaccurately is a mystery.

Some of the Rangers receiving their DSCs in Normandy. Left to right: Lt. Col Max F. Schneider, Captain George P. Whittington, 1st Lt. Charles H. Parker, 1st Lt. Francis W. Dawson, Sgt. Willie Moody, T5 Howard C. McKissick, Sgt. Denzil O. Johnson, Pfc Alexander W. Barber.

The above US Army photograph is captioned: *'Brief ceremony following the presentation of awards.'*

Shown below is the official US Army Press Release sending information about the Rangers and Lt. Col. Rudder for publication in the US press.

```
                              HEADQUARTERS                    (Censored)
                    EUROPEAN THEATER OF OPERATIONS
                          UNITED STATES ARMY

    FOR IMMEDIATE RELEASE
    NUMBER: 1961
                                                  23 June 1944

        20 UNITED STATES SOLDIERS AWARDED DSC IN FRANCE

        WITH THE U. S. FORCES IN NORMANDY, June 22 (Delayed)-- Twenty officers and
    enlisted men of a Ranger Battalion which landed on the beaches between Vierville
    and Pointe du Hoe in France during the H-Hour assault on D-Day were awarded the
    Distinguished Service Cross in a ceremony before the entire battalion today.
        The award, second highest military honor of the United States, was presented
    to the men by a general officer in recognition of the extraordinary heroism dis-
    played, when under heavy fire, they reorganized and assaulted the cliffs and beach-
    es and put down three enemy counterattacks.
        Receiving the award were:
        Lt. Colonel James E. Rudder, Infantry, of Brady, Texas. Col. Rudder com-
    pletely disregarded his own safety and repeatedly exposed himself in reorganizing
    his unit to assault the cliffs.. As soon as the first elements had scaled the
    cliffs, he moved forward to better direct the attack. His determined leadership
    and dauntlessness inspired his men so that they successfully withstood three enemy
    counterattacks.
        Lt. Colonel Max F. Schneider, Infantry, of Shenandoah, Iowa. According to
    the citation Col. Schneider "led his Ranger Infantry Battalion ashore at H-Hour on
    D-Day in the face of extremely heavy enemy rifle machine gun, mortar, artillery
    and rocket fire. Upon reaching the beach he repeatedly exposed himself while
    reorganizing his unit and led the battalion in the assault on the enemy beach
    positions and after accomplishing this mission led them up a steep incline to
    assault gun emplacements."
        Major Richard P. Sullivan, Infantry, of 30 Pierce Avenue, Dorchester,
    Massachusetts, was presented the award for extraordinary heroism in action from
    6 June 1944 to 10 June 1944 near Vierville-sur-mer and Isigny, France, when he
    personally directed a successful landing operation and led his men across the beach
    under heavy machine gun, artillery and rocket fire.
        Captain Otto Masny, Infantry, of 4 North Vail Avenue, Arlington Heights,
    Illinois. Capt. Masny was wounded in the initial landing but refused to be evacu-
    ated and remained with his company in the narrow and insecure beachhead thus in-
    spiring his men to put down three enemy counterattacks.
        Captain George P. Whittington, Cavalry, of 1717 G Street, Washington, D. C.,
    According to the citation Capt. Whittington "personally supervised the breaching of
    hostile barbed wire and other obstacles, despite the heavy enemy fire, by use of
    bangalores and then led his company and the rest of his battalion through the gap
    he created and directed the scaling of a 100-foot cliff."
        Captain Edgar L. Arnold, Infantry, of 907 6th Avenue, Shenandoah, Iowa.
    Capt. Arnold personally led his Ranger company in an attack against enemy install-
    ations in the face of small arms fire and accurately directed enemy artillery fire
    inspiring his men to advance even though they were suffering large casualties.
        Captain Ralph E. Goranson, Infantry, of 1520 Bryn Mawr Avenue, Chicago,
    Illinois. Capt. Goranson led his company in an advance to force a junction with
    the main body of the assault and though it took 10 hours of the heaviest kind of
    fighting to reach the main body, his men, inspired by his outstanding leadership,
    continuously advanced until the mission was accomplished.
        First Lieutenant Francis W. Dawson, Infantry, of 329 Redwood Street, Pro-
    gress, Pennsylvania. Lt. Dawson personally took charge of the breaching of wire
    entanglements and when a gap was created he led his platoon through it and direct-
    ed them in scaling a 100-foot cliff. Accompanied by one soldier, Lt. Dawson
    rushed forward with a submachine gun and destroyed a German pill box, killing and
    capturing the enemy inside.
        First Lieutenant Charles H. Parker, Infantry, Big Stone City, South Dakota.
    Lt. Parker led his company up the beach under heavy fire overcoming numerous en-
    counters of enemy resistance and succeeded in capturing LePointe du Hoe, the
    battalion objective.
        First Lieutenant Joseph R. Lacy, Chaplain Corps, of 241 Laurel Street, Hart-
    ford, Connecticut. Chaplain Lacy landed on the shores of France with the assault
    units and, completely disregarding his own safety, moved about the beach, while
    under heavy fire, assisting wounded men from the water's edge to the comparative
    safety of a nearby seawall.

                              (Over)
```

-2-

Second Lieutenant George F. Kerchner, Infantry, of 458 South Bentalou Street, Baltimore, Maryland. Lt. Kerchner assumed command of his company when the company commander and other officers of the unit became casualties and by his determined leadership and outstanding heroism led the unit in the successful assault upon 155mm enemy gun positions.

First Sergeant Leonard G. Lomell, Infantry, of Trenton Avenue, Point Pleasant, New Jersey. According to the citation, Sgt. Lomell "led a patrol of men through the heaviest kind of automatic weapons fire to destroy an enemy machine gun nest and later during the same day penetrated through the enemy lines to the rear and discovered five enemy 155mm guns and led his patrol against the enemy, successfully destroying the guns and ammunition."

Technical Sergeant John W. White, Infantry, of 9 Saint Anne Street, Jamaica Plains, Massachusetts. Sgt. White assumed command of machine gun positions when all the officers of his company became casualties in the initial landing on the coast of France, and directed their fire against enemy positions.

Sgt. Joseph W. Urish, Infantry, of 133 Ingram Avenue, Ingram, Pennsylvania. Sgt. Urish, while leading a patrol, voluntarily on a signal given by the enemy moved into the battery alone to persuade them to surrender. After a quarter of an hour, the first of the enemy marched out to surrender. As they did the remainder of the patrol loaded their rifles and the enemy thinking they were to be shot in cold blood, scattered and returned to their post. Instead of attempting to escape and disregarding his own safety, Sgt.Urish continued to persuade them to surrender. One by one they laid down their arms, surrendered and marched out. A total of 167 prisoners were captured from a position that might have held out for days.

Sergeant Julius W. Belcher, Infantry, of Route 1, Swords Creek, Virginia. Sgt. Belcher moved up a beach under heavy fire and scaled a 100-foot cliff to secure toggle ropes to barbed wire on top of the cliff and, though under constant fire, remained at his position to help other men to the top of the cliff.

Sergeant William J. Courtney, Infantry, of 14118 Aspinall Avenue, Cleveland, Ohio. While advancing as the point of a column into a village, Sgt. Courtney met point blank machine gun fire and without hesitation moved forward and destroyed the machine gun. He continued to move forward and engaged the enemy in an uneven fire fight, killing two of them and remaining at this advanced position until the enemy withdrew.

Sergeant Willie W. Moody, Infantry, Route 1, Pine Grove, Portsmouth, Virginia. Sgt. Moody volunteered to attempt to make contact with a battalion that had been cut off and after crawling through enemy minefields, enemy outposts and installations, he finally contacted the unit. He returned to his own unit and started out with a reel of wire unreeling it so that accurate fire could be placed upon enemy positions when mortars were set up.

Sergeant Denzil O. Johnson, Infantry, of 756 Adams Street, Memphis, Tennessee With complete disregard for his personal safety, Sgt. Johnson rushed across fire-swept ground seeking a path through a mine field and finding an escape route, returned to his patrol and led it to a position of safety.

Private First Class William E. Dreher, Jr., Infantry, 1790 W. 48th Street, Cleveland, Ohio. While advancing as the point of a column into a village, Pvt. Dreher met point blank machine gun fire and without hesitation moved forward and destroyed this enemy machine gun. He continued to move forward and killed two enemy riflemen in an uneven fire fight.

Private First Class Alexander W. Barber, Medical Corps, 156 Adams Street, Johnstown, Pennsylvania. Pvt. Barber constantly exposed himself to direct fire of the enemy as he went along the beach administering aid to the wounded and on one occasion took a horse and cart into the middle of an artillery barrage to bring out three men who were wounded.

END

In a number of instances, the actual paper citation issued with the medal expands upon the action taken by the soldier. Here are a couple of these:

Howard D. McKissick – 5th Ranger Infantry Battalion – Distinguished Service Cross

The President of the United States of America, authorized by Act of Congress, July 9, 1918, takes pleasure in presenting the Distinguished Service Cross to Technician Fifth Grade Howard D. McKissick (ASN: 39204430), United States Army, for extraordinary heroism in connection with military operations against an armed enemy while serving with the 5th Ranger Infantry Battalion, in action against enemy forces on 7 June 1944, in France. Technician Fifth Grade McKissick volunteered with another man to make contact with a battalion of Rangers that had been cut off. At midnight, Technician Fifth Grade McKissick moved off and started through the enemy lines. After several hours of crawling through enemy minefields, enemy outposts and enemy installations, he finally reached the isolated battalion. He and his comrade then returned to their own unit and started out again with a reel of wire to a position where they believed their mortars would be set up. He and his companion returned through the enemy lines unreeling the wire so that accurate fire could be placed on the enemy positions once the mortars were set up. Technician Fifth Grade McKissick's intrepid actions, personal bravery and zealous devotion to duty exemplify the highest traditions of the military forces of the United States and reflect great credit upon himself, his unit, and the United States Army.

General Orders: Headquarters, First U.S. Army, General Orders No. 42 (August 6, 1944)
Action Date: 7-Jun-44   Service: Army   Rank: Technician Fifth Grade

Willie W. Moody – 5th Ranger Infantry Battalion – Distinguished Service Cross

The President of the United States of America, authorized by Act of Congress, July 9, 1918, takes pleasure in presenting the Distinguished Service Cross to Sergeant Willie W. Moody (ASN: 33628019), United States Army, for extraordinary heroism in connection with military operations against an armed enemy while serving with the 5th Ranger Infantry Battalion, in action against enemy forces on 7 and 8 June 1944, in France. Sergeant Moody volunteered to attempt to make contact with a battalion of Rangers that had been cut off. At midnight Sergeant Moody moved off and started through the enemy lines. After several hours of crawling through enemy mine fields, enemy outposts and enemy installations, he finally contacted the battalion that had been cut off. He then returned to his own unit, and started out again with a reel of wire to a position where he believed his mortars would be set up. He returned through the enemy lines unreeling the wire so that accurate fire could be placed upon the enemy positions once the mortars had been placed in position. Sergeant Moody's heroic actions, personal bravery and zealous devotion to duty exemplify the highest traditions of the military forces of the United States and reflect great credit upon himself, his unit, and the United States Army.

General Orders: Headquarters, First U.S. Army, General Orders No. 28 (June 20, 1944)
Action Date: 7 & 8-Jun-44   Service: Army   Rank: Sergeant

William J. Courtney – 2nd Ranger Infantry Battalion – Distinguished Service Cross

The President of the United States of America, authorized by Act of Congress, July 9, 1918, takes pleasure in presenting the Distinguished Service Cross to Sergeant William J. Courtney (ASN: 15104744), United States Army, for extraordinary heroism in connection with military operations against an armed enemy while serving with an Infantry Company of the 2nd Ranger Infantry Battalion, in action against enemy forces on 7 June 1944, in France. While advancing as the point of a column into a village, Sergeant Courtney met point-blank machine gun fire. Without hesitation he moved forward and destroyed this enemy machine gun. He continued to move into the village and was suddenly subjected to a barrage of enemy mortar and small arms fire. He engaged the enemy in this uneven fire-fight, killing two enemy riflemen and remained at this advanced position until the enemy withdrew. Sergeant Courtney's intrepid actions, personal bravery and zealous devotion to duty exemplify the highest traditions of the military forces of the United States and reflect great credit upon himself and the United States Army.

General Orders: Headquarters, First U.S. Army, General Orders No. 28 (June 20, 1944)
Action Date: 7-Jun-44   Service: Army   Rank: Sergeant

William E. Dreher, Jr. – 2nd Ranger Infantry Battalion – Distinguished Service Cross

The President of the United States of America, authorized by Act of Congress, July 9, 1918, takes pleasure in presenting the Distinguished Service Cross to Private First Class William E. Dreher, Jr. (ASN: 35051852), United States Army, for extraordinary heroism in connection with military operations against an armed enemy while serving with an Infantry Company of the 2nd Ranger Infantry Battalion, in action against enemy forces on 7 June 1944, in France. While advancing as the point of a column into a village, Private First Class Dreher met point blank machine gun fire. Without hesitation he moved forward and destroyed this enemy machine gun. He continued to move into the village and was suddenly subjected to a barrage of enemy mortar and small arms fire. He engaged the enemy in this uneven fire fight, killing two enemy riflemen and remained at this advanced position until the enemy withdrew. Private First Class Dreher's heroic action, personal bravery and zealous devotion to duty exemplify the highest traditions of the military forces of the United States and reflect great credit upon himself, his unit, and the United States Army.

General Orders: Headquarters, First U.S. Army, General Orders No. 28 (June 20, 1944)
Action Date: 7-Jun-44   Service: Army   Rank: Private First Class

NOT ON THE ABOVE LIST
Gail H. Belmont – 2nd Ranger Infantry Battalion – Distinguished Service Cross

The President of the United States of America, authorized by Act of Congress, July 9, 1918, takes pleasure in presenting the Distinguished Service Cross to Staff Sergeant Gail H. Belmont, United States Army, for extraordinary heroism in connection with military operations against an armed enemy while serving with the 2nd Ranger Battalion, in action against enemy forces on 7 June 1944, at Au Guay, France. On that date, the forward elements of his company were trapped by enemy machine guns on both flanks and to the front. Sergeant Belmont picked up an abandoned enemy machine gun and opened fire against the enemy. Although his position was exposed to and only fifty yards from the enemy, Sergeant Belmont succeeded in his voluntary purpose of drawing the enemy fire on himself, thus allowing his troops to advance. He received first aid for wounds received during the encounter only after the faithful fulfilment of this duty, and while returning to the beach to receive further medical attention, he captured two of the enemy. The extraordinary heroism and courageous actions of Sergeant Belmont reflect great credit upon himself and are in keeping with the highest traditions of the military service.

General Orders: Headquarters, Ninth U.S. Army, General Orders No. 27 (1944)
Action Date: 7-Jun-44   Service: Army   Rank: Staff Sergeant

Theodore A. James – 2nd Ranger Infantry Battalion – Distinguished Service Cross

The President of the United States of America, authorized by Act of Congress, July 9, 1918, takes pleasure in presenting the Distinguished Service Cross to Sergeant Theodore A. James, United States Army, for extraordinary heroism in connection with military operations against an armed enemy while serving with the 2nd Ranger Infantry Battalion, in action against enemy forces on 6 June 1944, in France. On that date, during the initial landings on the beach at Vierville-Sur-Mer, France, Sergeant James took command of his company when all the officers became casualties, and through his superior leadership, enabled many men to successfully cross the beach to their first objective. Here, he reorganized the company and led an assault on a heavily fortified hill to the rear of the beach. Despite being wounded severely in both hands, Sergeant James continued to direct operations and was among the first to reach the crest of the hill. Only after this objective was reached and their position secure would Sergeant James return to the beach to receive medical treatment. His extraordinary heroism and courageous actions exemplify the highest traditions of the military forces of the United States and reflect great credit upon himself, his unit, and the United States Army.

General Orders: Headquarters, Ninth U.S. Army, General Orders No. 27 (1944)
Action Date: 6-Jun-44   Service: Army   Rank: Sergeant

William D. Moody – 2nd Ranger Infantry Battalion – Distinguished Service Cross
Awarded **posthumously** for Actions during World War II

The President of the United States of America, authorized by Act of Congress, July 9, 1918, takes pride in presenting the Distinguished Service Cross (Posthumously) to First Lt. (Infantry) William D. Moody (ASN: 0-1300357), United States Army, for extraordinary heroism in connection with military operations against an armed enemy while serving with the 2nd Ranger Battalion, in action against enemy forces on 6 June 1944, at Normandy, France. On D-Day, First Lieutenant Moody led his platoon, in the face of heavy and intense enemy fire, across the beach to the comparative safety of the cliffs overlooking the beach. He then climbed the cliffs and secured ropes to the top for the ascent of the remainder of his platoon. Without waiting for his men to reach the top, First Lt. Moody valiantly moved to attack and clear the enemy out of his trenches in this vicinity. He was advancing upon an enemy position when he was killed by a sniper. The extraordinary heroism and courageous leadership displayed by First Lt. Moody were an inspiration to the men of his platoon and exemplify the highest traditions of the military forces of the United States, reflecting great credit upon himself, his unit, and the United States Army.

General Orders: Headquarters, First U.S. Army, General Orders No. 70 (October 17, 1944)
Action Date: 6-Jun-44   Service: Army   Rank: First Lieutenant

Denzil O. Johnson – 5th Ranger Infantry Battalion – Distinguished Service Cross

The President of the United States of America, authorized by Act of Congress, July 9, 1918, takes pleasure in presenting the Distinguished Service Cross to Sergeant Denzil O. Johnson (ASN: 38452897), United States Army, for extraordinary heroism in connection with military operations against an armed enemy while serving with a Ranger Infantry Battalion, in action against enemy forces on 7 June 1944, in France. Sergeant Johnson was a scout for a patrol sent out to bring reinforcements to the isolated remnants of a Ranger battalion. The patrol was driven to the edge of a high cliff along the sea by enemy machine gun fire. Led by Sergeant Johnson the patrol worked themselves along the face of the cliff. When the patrol came to the top of the cliff it was stopped by hostile machine gun fire and a minefield. With complete disregard for his own personal safety, Sergeant Johnson rushed across the fire-swept ground seeking a path through the minefield. Finding an escape route, Sergeant Johnson returned to the patrol and led it to a position of safety. His intrepid actions, personal bravery and zealous devotion to duty exemplify the highest traditions of the military forces of the United States and reflect great credit upon himself, his unit, and the United States Army.

General Orders: Headquarters, First U.S. Army, General Orders No. 28 (June 20, 1944)
Action Date: 7-Jun-44   Service: Army   Rank: Sergeant

Charles H. Parker – 5th Ranger Infantry Battalion – Distinguished Service Cross

The President of the United States of America, authorized by Act of Congress, July 9, 1918, takes pleasure in presenting the Distinguished Service Cross to First Lieutenant (Infantry) Charles H. Parker (ASN: 0-1290298), United States Army, for extraordinary heroism in connection with military operations against an armed enemy while Commanding A Company of the 5th Ranger Infantry Battalion, in action against enemy forces on 6, 7, and 8 June 1944, in France. In the invasion of France First Lieutenant Parker led his company up the beach against heavy enemy rifle, machine gun and artillery fire. Once past the beach he reorganized and continued inland. During this advance numerous groups of enemy resistance were encountered. Through his personal bravery and sound leadership this resistance was overcome, and his company succeeded in capturing *******, the Battalion objective. The following morning First Lieutenant Parker led a patrol through enemy-held territory in an effort to establish contact with the balance of the Battalion. First Lieutenant Parker's superior, personal valour and zealous devotion to duty exemplify the highest traditions of the military forces of the United States and reflect great credit upon himself, his unit, and the United States Army.

General Orders: Headquarters, First U.S. Army, General Orders No. 28 (June 20, 1944)
Action Date: 6, 7 & 8-Jun-44   Service: Army   Rank: First Lieutenant

George P. Whittington , Jr. – 2nd Ranger Infantry Battalion (Company B) – Distinguished Service Cross

The President of the United States of America, authorized by Act of Congress, July 9, 1918, takes pleasure in presenting the Distinguished Service Cross to Captain (Cavalry) George P. Whittington, Jr. (ASN: 0-403921), United States Army, for extraordinary heroism in connection with military operations against an armed enemy while serving as Commanding Officer of Company B, 2nd Ranger Infantry Battalion, in action against enemy forces on 6 June 1944, in France. Captain Whittington commanded a Ranger company which landed on the coast of France at "H" hour. The landing was made on the beach against heavy rifle, machine gun, mortar, artillery and rocket fire of the enemy. Despite this fire, he personally supervised the breaching of hostile barbed wire and obstacles by the use of bangalores. He then led his company and the remainder of his battalion through the gap created. He then directed the scaling of a 100-foot cliff by his company. When he reached the top of the cliff he crawled under enemy machine gun fire and destroyed the enemy position. Captain Whittington's bravery, aggressiveness and inspired leadership exemplify the highest traditions of the military forces of the United States and reflect great credit upon himself, his unit, and the United States Army.

General Orders: Headquarters, First U.S. Army, General Orders No. 28 (June 20, 1944)
Action Date: 6-Jun-44   Service: Army   Rank: Captain

Julius W. Belcher – 2nd Ranger Infantry Battalion (Company C) – Distinguished Service Cross

The President of the United States of America, authorized by Act of Congress, July 9, 1918, takes pleasure in presenting the Distinguished Service Cross to Sergeant Julius W. Belcher (ASN: 33213927), United States Army, for extraordinary heroism in connection with military operations against an armed enemy while serving with Company C, 2nd Ranger Infantry Battalion, in action against enemy forces on 6 June 1944, at Verville-Sur-Mer, France. Upon landing with the initial assault Ranger Battalion on the coast of France, Sergeant Belcher immediately moved up the beach under heavy machine gun, mortar and sniper fire, and scaled a 100-foot cliff to secure toggle ropes to barbed wire on top of the cliff. Though under constant fire on top of the cliff, he remained at his position and cleaned out six snipers. Following this, he charged an enemy pillbox and mortar position and destroyed it with grenades. Sergeant Belcher's intrepid actions, personal bravery and zealous devotion to duty exemplify the highest traditions of the military forces of the United States and reflect great credit upon himself and the United States Army.

General Orders: Headquarters, First U.S. Army, General Orders No. 28 (June 20, 1944)
Action Date: 6-Jun-44   Service: Army   Rank: Sergeant

Otto K. Stephens – 2nd Ranger Infantry Battalion (Company C) – Distinguished Service Cross

Private First Class Otto K. Stephens, United States Army, was awarded the Distinguished Service Cross for extraordinary heroism in connection with military operations against an armed enemy while serving with Company C, 2nd Ranger Infantry Battalion, in action against enemy forces on 6 and 7 June 1944, in France. Private First Class Stephens' intrepid actions, personal bravery and zealous devotion to duty exemplify the highest traditions of the military forces of the United States and reflect great credit upon himself, his unit, and the United States Army.

General Orders: Headquarters, First U.S. Army, General Orders No. 69 (1944)
Action Date: 6 & 7-Jun-44   Service: Army   Rank: Private First Class

Lt. Col. James Rudder.

Father Lacy receiving the DSC from Lt. Col. Rudder.

2nd Lt. George Kerchner receives his DSC from Lt. Col. Rudder.

George F. Kerchner – 2nd Ranger Infantry Battalion – Distinguished Service Cross

The President of the United States of America, authorized by Act of Congress, July 9, 1918, takes pleasure in presenting the Distinguished Service Cross to Second Lieutenant (Infantry) George F. Kerchner (ASN: 0-1309569), United States Army, for extraordinary heroism in connection with military operations against an armed enemy while serving with an Infantry Company of the 2nd Ranger Infantry Battalion, in action against enemy forces on 6 June 1944, in France. When the Company Commander and other company officers became casualties from the heavy enemy rifle fire, machine gun and artillery fire upon landing on the coast of France, Second Lieutenant Kerchner assumed command of the company in the successful assault upon and captured the 155-mm enemy gun positions. While engaged in this operation, Second Lieutenant Kerchner and fifteen members of his organization were surrounded and cut off from the main body for two and one-half days. He tenaciously and courageously held his position until relieved and was a constant inspiration to his troops. The outstanding heroism displayed by Second Lieutenant Kerchner during the initial assault and subsequent operations exemplify the highest traditions of the military forces of the United States and reflect great credit upon himself, his unit, and the United States Army.

General Orders: Headquarters, First U.S. Army, General Orders No. 28 (June 20, 1944)
Action Date: 6-Jun-44   Service: Army   Rank: Second Lieutenant

Lt. Col. Max F. Schneider congratulating 1st Lt. Charles H. Parker on his Distinguished Service Cross. Parker is wearing a camouflage cover on his helmet. In his book *Reflections of Courage on D-Day* Parker says*:*

At Maisy…. There were piles of shells on the ground, 8 or 9 inches high, where the Germans had stopped to fire at the paratroopers repeatedly. This was not something we wanted to see. But nevertheless we took advantage of the situation and cut up the parachutes made of camouflage material, covering our helmets with the remnants. We then placed a net over the entire helmet. This broke the helmet's outline.

Ralph E. Goranson – 2nd Ranger Infantry Battalion (Company C) – Distinguished Service Cross

The President of the United States of America, authorized by Act of Congress, July 9, 1918, takes pleasure in presenting the Distinguished Service Cross to Captain (Infantry) Ralph E. Goranson (ASN: 0-1299035), United States Army, for extraordinary heroism in connection with military operations against an armed enemy while serving as Commanding Officer of Company C, 2nd Ranger Infantry Battalion, in action against enemy forces on 6 and 7 June 1944, at Vierville-sur-Mer, France. Captain Goranson landed with his Ranger company at "H" hour on D-Day with the initial assault wave in the invasion of France, in the face of heavy automatic enfilading fire from three different directions and mortar and artillery fire from cliffs overlooking the beach. In spite of extremely heavy casualties, Captain Goranson calmly and courageously reorganized his company and led them in a successful assault upon the enemy positions. He then led his company in an advance to force a junction with the main body of the assault. Though it took ten hours of the heaviest kind of fighting to reach the main body, his men, inspired by his outstanding leadership, continuously advanced until the mission was accomplished. Captain Goranson's heroic actions, personal bravery and zealous devotion to duty exemplify the highest traditions of the military forces of the United States and reflect great credit upon himself, his unit, and the United States Army.

General Orders: Headquarters, First U.S. Army, General Orders No. 28 (June 20, 1944)
Action Date: 6 & 7-Jun-44   Service: Army   Rank: Captain

Alexander W. Barber – 5th Ranger Infantry Battalion (HQ and HQ Co.) – Distinguished Service Cross

The President of the United States of America, authorized by Act of Congress, July 9, 1918, takes pleasure in presenting the Distinguished Service Cross to Private First Class Alexander W. Barber (ASN: 33575048), United States Army, for extraordinary heroism in connection with military operations against an armed enemy while serving as a Medical Aidman with Headquarters and Headquarters Company, 5th Ranger Infantry Battalion, in action against enemy forces on 6 June 1944, in France. Private First Class Barber landed with his medical unit on the coast of France at a time when the beach was under heavy enemy rifle, machine gun and artillery fire. Numerous casualties had already been inflicted by this devastating fire. In spite of this heavy fire, Private First Class Barber constantly exposed himself to the direct fire of the enemy as he went along the beach administering aid to the wounded. On one occasion he took a horse and cart into the middle of an artillery barrage to bring out three men who had been wounded. Private First Class Barber's intrepid actions, personal bravery and zealous devotion to duty exemplify the highest traditions of the military forces of the United States and reflect great credit upon himself, his unit, and the United States Army.

General Orders: Headquarters, First U.S. Army, General Orders No. 28 (June 20, 1944)
Action Date: 6-Jun-44   Service: Army   Rank: Private First Class

Francis W. Dawson – 5th Ranger Infantry Battalion (Company D) – Distinguished Service Cross

The President of the United States of America, authorized by Act of Congress, July 9, 1918, takes pleasure in presenting the Distinguished Service Cross to First Lieutenant (Infantry) Francis W. Dawson (ASN: 0-400036), United States Army, for extraordinary heroism in connection with military operations against an armed enemy while serving with Company D, 5th Ranger Infantry Battalion, in action against enemy forces on 6 June 1944, in France. First Lieutenant Dawson led his Ranger Platoon ashore in the invasion of France against heavy enemy artillery, machine gun, and small arms fire. He then personally took charge of the breaching of wire entanglements. When a gap was created, he led his platoon through it and directed them in scaling a 100-foot cliff. Upon reaching the top of the cliff, he, accompanied by one soldier, rushed forward with a submachine gun and destroyed a German pill box, killing or capturing the enemy located therein. First Lieutenant Dawson's aggressive leadership, personal courage and zealous devotion to duty exemplify the highest traditions of the military forces of the United States and reflect great credit upon himself, his unit, and the United States Army.

General Orders: Headquarters, First U.S. Army, General Orders No. 28 (June 20, 1944)
Action Date: 6-Jun-44   Service: Army   Rank: First Lieutenant

Rex D. Clark – 2nd Ranger Infantry Battalion (Company E) – Distinguished Service Cross

The President of the United States of America, authorized by Act of Congress, July 9, 1918, takes pleasure in presenting the Distinguished Service Cross to Technician Fifth Grade Rex D. Clark, United States Army, for extraordinary heroism in connection with military operations against an armed enemy while serving with Company E, 2nd Ranger Infantry Battalion, in action against enemy forces on 6 June 1944 in France. On that date, Technician Clark was in command of an amphibious vehicle equipped with an extension ladder and mounting three machine guns which was to be used by the assault forces to scale the high cliffs near Pointe du Hoc, France. Then it was found that the vehicle could not reach the cliffs because of the rough terrain, Technician Clark gallantly ordered himself raised on the ladder, and firing his machine gun at the hostile emplacements, effectively diverted the return fire away from the assault troops. Through his intrepid actions, two enemy automatic weapons were neutralized and many of the enemy pinned down, enabling friendly forces to advance on their objective. Technician Clark's heroic actions and unselfish devotion to duty exemplify the highest traditions of the military forces of the United States and reflect great credit upon himself, his unit, and the United States Army.

General Orders: Headquarters, Third U.S. Army, General Orders No. 204 (1945)
Action Date: 6-Jun-44   Service: Army   Rank: Technician Fifth Grade

John W. White – 2nd Ranger Infantry Battalion – Distinguished Service Cross

The President of the United States of America, authorized by Act of Congress, July 9, 1918, takes pleasure in presenting the Distinguished Service Cross to Technical Sergeant John W. White (ASN: 31135430), United States Army, for extraordinary heroism in connection with military operations against an armed enemy while serving with 2nd Ranger Infantry Battalion, in action against the enemy from 6 June 1944 to 8 June 1944 at Vierville and Pointe du Hoc, France. When all the officers of his company became casualties in the initial landing on the coast of France from the devastating enemy fire he assumed command of machine gun positions and directed their fire on the enemy positions. Later he personally acted as the point of the column, which advanced from the beach to Pointe du Hoc. On this advance, Sergeant White exposed himself to the direct rifle and machine gun fire of the enemy as well as sniper fire. Technical Sergeant White's excellent leadership and gallantry under such difficult and hazardous circumstances exemplify the highest traditions of the military forces of the United States and reflect great credit upon himself, his unit, and the United States Army.

General Orders: Headquarters, First U.S. Army, General Orders No. 28 (June 20, 1944)
Action Date: 6–8-Jun-44   Service: Army   Rank: Technical Sergeant

R E S T R I C T E D

HEADQUARTERS
FIRST UNITED STATES ARMY
APO 230

GENERAL ORDERS)
:
NO.   28)   20 June 1944

SECTION
Award of Distinguished-Service Cross------------------------- I
Amendment of General Orders---------------------------------- II

I--AWARD OF DISTINGUISHED-SERVICE CROSS--Under the provisions of AR
600-45, 22 September 1943, and pursuant to authority contained in paragraph
3c, Section I, Circular No. 32, Hq ETOUSA, 20 March 1944, as amended, the
Distinguished-Service Cross is awarded to the following officers and enlisted
men:

Colonel Russell P. Reeder, Jr., 016494, Infantry, United States
Army, for extraordinary heroism in action against the enemy on 7 June
1944, in France. On the morning of 7 June 1944, his unit attacked enemy
fortified positions approximately 500 meters south-west of ************
***** and captured these positions, advancing to *********** where the
attack was temporarily held up by enemy forces in buildings and hedgerows
in that vicinity. Colonel Reeder throughout the attack circulated amongst
his men in the front lines encouraging and urging them forward, exposing
himself continually to enemy small arms and shell fire. His utter disregard for his own personal safety, and his exemplary bravery were largely
responsible for the rapid advance of his troops. Near ************ when
Colonel Reeder noticed that a group of his men were hesitant about crossing an open field on the enemy flank because of small arms fire, he walked
boldly into the open field with complete disregard for his personal safety.
The men immediately got up, crossed the field following Colonel Reeder and
established themselves on the flank of the enemy. This was an outstanding
instance of leadership under fire and was to a great extent responsible
for the swift ejection of the enemy from***********. Colonel Reeder's
extraordinary coolness and personal bravery under fire when personally
inciting his men to further effort were an inspiration to all who served
with him and under him. Entered military service from Kansas.

Colonel James A. Van Fleet, 03847, Infantry, United States Army,
for extraordinary heroism in action against the enemy on 6 - 8 June 1944,
in France. In the initial landing and assault upon the European continent,
Colonel Van Fleet quickly organized his troops and pushed them rapidly
across the beach in an orderly and determined manner, brushing aside
resistance and thereby greatly expediting the early establishment of the
Division beachhead. Colonel Van Fleet was always well forward and on
numerous occasions personally went up to check his battalions. His
superior leadership and personal example of courage aided in clearing the
beach with a minimum of casualties and substantially contributed to the
rapid advance of the division to its D-day objective. On 7 June 1944,
while the enemy was using observed fire to vigorously shell the highways
and avenues of approach in the vicinity of his unit, he displayed cool
leadership and skill in maintaining order under severely trying conditions,

-1- (over)
R E S T R I C T E D

G. O. No. 28. Hq First Army. 20 June 1944 (cont'd)

and did so encourage and inspire confidence in all members of the Combat Team that they followed his example and advanced with no hesitation, and with minimum losses of both men and equipment. This was at a critical time when a failure to procure advanced positions would have endangered the success of the operation. On the morning of 8 June 1944, while visiting his front line battalions, with disregard for his personal safety, he captured an enemy guard and procured important information from him which aided the Regiment in successfully advancing against the enemy's strongly entrenched successive positions. The cool fearlessness, personal bravery, and leadership displayed by Colonel Van Fleet were an inspiration to his men and a great force in their battle success. Entered military service from Florida.

Lieutenant Colonel James E. Rudder, 0294916, Infantry, United States Army, for extraordinary heroism in action on 6 June 1944 at *********** France. Lieutenant Colonel Rudder commanding Force "A" of the Rangers landed on the beach with his unit which was immediately subjected to heavy rifle, machine gun, mortar and artillery fire. Devastating fire was also directed from the cliffs overlooking the beach. Completely disregarding his own safety he repeatedly exposed himself in directing the reorganization of his unit to assault the cliffs. As soon as the first elements had scaled the cliffs, Lieutenant Colonel Rudder immediately scaled the cliffs in order to better direct the attack. Though wounded he refused to be evacuated and continued to direct the attack. By his determined leadership and dauntlessness he inspired his men so that they successfully withstood three enemy counterattacks. Though wounded again he still refused to be evacuated. Lieutenant Colonel Rudder's heroic leadership, courage and complete devotion to duty are in keeping with the highest traditions of the service. Entered military service from Texas.

Lieutenant Colonel Max F. Schneider, 0384849, Infantry, United States Army, for extraordinary heroism in action on 6 June 1944 at ******************* France. In the initial landings in the invasion of France, Lieutenant Colonel Schneider led the 5th Ranger Infantry Battalion ashore at "H" hour on "D" day in the face of extremely heavy enemy rifle, machine gun, mortar, artillery and rocket fire. Upon reaching the beach Lieutenant Colonel Schneider reorganized his unit. During this reorganization he repeatedly exposed himself to enemy fire. He then led his battalion in the assault on the enemy beach positions, and having accomplished this mission led them up a steep incline to assault the enemy gun emplacements on the top of the hill. The destruction of these enemy positions opened one of the vital beach exits, thereby permitting the troops and equipment which had been pinned down to move inland from the beach, with the result that reinforcements could be landed from the sea. By his heroic leadership and personal courage Lieutenant Colonel Schneider set an inspiring example to his command, reflecting the highest traditions of the armed forces. Entered military service from Iowa.

Major Richard P. Sullivan, 0399856, Infantry, United States Army, for extraordinary heroism in action from 6 June 1944 to 10 June 1944 near ****************************** France. Completely disregarding his own safety, he personally directed a successful landing operation and lead his men across the beach covered with machine gun, artillery and rocket fire. After reorganizing his men he immediately resumed his duties as

R E S T R I C T E D

G. O. No. 28, Hq First Army, 20 June 1944 (cont'd)

Battalion Executive officer and was placed in command of two Ranger companies which fought their way inland against fierce opposition to join and relieve the Ranger detachment on ***********. After laying communications through the enemy lines under cover of darkness, Major Sullivan directed the Rangers' progress across country to ************ and ********. In cooperation with United States Infantry an attack was begun on the ***** battery. When certain elements were temporarily halted by artillery fire Major Sullivan, who had been wounded at ***********, calmly and courageously rallied his officers and men, ordered a renewal of the attack, and instead of by-passing the resistance, advanced over heavily mined terrain to capture the ***** battery with a loss of only fifteen (15) men. Eighty six (86) prisoners and several large caliber artillery pieces in concrete bunkers were taken. Attacks by Major Sullivan's command contributed greatly to the success of the entire Corps' operations. By his intrepid direction, heroic leadership and superior professional ability, Major Sullivan set an inspiring example to his command reflecting the highest traditions of the armed forces. Entered military service from Massachusetts.

Captain Edgar L. Arnold, 01286417, Infantry, United States Army, for extraordinary heroism in action on 7 June 1944 at ****************, France. Captain Arnold personally led his Ranger company in an attack against enemy installations in the face of small arms fire and accurately directed enemy artillery fire. Despite this heavy enemy fire, Captain Arnold continued to lead the assault and inspired his men to advance with him even though they were suffering heavy casualties. Captain Arnold's outstanding and courageous leadership is in keeping with the highest traditions of the service. Entered military service from Iowa.

Captain Ralph E. Goranson, O-1299035, Infantry, United States Army, for extraordinary heroism in action on 6 June 1944 and 7 June 1944 at *************, France. Captain Goranson landed with his Ranger company at "H" hour on "D" day with the initial assault wave in the invasion of France, in the face of heavy automatic enfilading fire from three different directions and mortar and artillery fire from cliffs overlooking the beach. In spite of extremely heavy casualties Captain Goranson calmly and courageously reorganized his company and led them in a successful assault upon the enemy positions. He then led his company in an advance to force a junction with the main body of the assault. Though it took ten hours of the heaviest kind of fighting to reach the main body, his men, inspired by his outstanding leadership, continuously advanced until the mission was accomplished. Captain Goranson's heroic action is in keeping with the highest traditions of the service. Entered military service from Illinois.

Captain Otto (NMI) Masny, 01283639, Infantry, United States Army, for extraordinary heroism in action on 6 June 1944 at ********, France. Captain Masny led his company in the face of heavy enemy fire on to the beach at "H" hour on "D" day. Although wounded in this initial landing, he refused to be evacuated and remained with his company on the narrow and insecure beachhead. Captain Masny's action was an example to his men and inspired them to put down three enemy counterattacks. A few days later, still refusing to be evacuated, he voluntarily, despite continuous enemy machine gun fire, led a patrol which destroyed an enemy ammunition dump. Captain Masny's courage and outstanding devotion to duty are in

- 3 - (over)

R E S T R I C T E D

R E S T R I C T E D

G. O. No. 28, Hq First Army, 20 June 1944 (cont'd)

keeping with the highest traditions of the service. Entered military service from Illinois.

Captain George P. Whittington, 0403921, Cavalry, United States Army, for extraordinary heroism in action on 6 June 1944 at ****************, France. Captain Whittington commanded a Ranger company which landed on the coast of France at "H" hour. The landing was made on the beach against heavy rifle, machine gun, mortar, artillery and rocket fire of the enemy. Despite this fire, he personally supervised the breaching of hostile barbed wire and obstacles by the use of bangalores. He then led his company and the remainder of his battalion through the gap created. He then directed the scaling of a 100-foot cliff by his company. When he reached the top of the cliff he crawled under enemy machine gun fire and destroyed the enemy position. Captain Whittington's bravery, aggressiveness and inspired leader- ship are in keeping with the highest traditions of the service. Entered military service from Arkansas.

First Lieutenant Francis W. Dawson, 0400036, Infantry, United States Army, for extraordinary heroism in action on 6 June 1944, at ***************, France. Lieutenant Dawson led his Ranger platoon ashore in the invasion of France against heavy enemy artillery, machine gun, and small arms fire. He then personally took charge of the breaching of wire entanglements. When a gap was created, he led his platoon through it and directed them in scaling a 100-foot cliff. Upon reaching the top of the cliff, he, accompanied by one soldier, rushed forward with a submachine gun and destroyed a German pill box, killing or capturing the enemy located therein. Lieutenant Dawson's heroic action and aggressive leadership are in keeping with the highest traditions of the service. Entered military service from South Carolina.

First Lieutenant Joseph R. Lacy, 0525094, Chaplain Corps, United States Army, for extraordinary heroism in action on 6 June 1944 at ***************, France. In the invasion of France, Chaplain Lacy landed on the beach with one of the leading assault units. Numerous casualties had been inflicted by the heavy rifle, mortar, artillery and rocket fire of the enemy. With complete disregard for his own safety, he moved about the beach, continually exposed to enemy fire, and assisted wounded men from the water's edge to the com- parative safety of a nearby seawall, and at the same time inspired the men to a similar disregard for the enemy fire. Chaplain Lacy's heroic and dauntless action is in keeping with the highest traditions of the service. Entered military service from Connecticut.

First Lieutenant Charles H. Parker, 01290298, Infantry, United States Army, for extraordinary heroism in action on 6, 7 and 8 June 1944 from **** ************ to **************, France. In the invasion of France, Lieutenant Parker led his company up the beach against heavy enemy rifle, machine gun and artillery fire. Once past the beach he reorganized and continued inland. During this advance numerous groups of enemy resistance were encountered. Through his personal bravery and sound leadership this resistance was overcome, and his company succeeded in capturing ************, the Battalion objective. The following morning Lieutenant Parker led a patrol through enemy held territory in an effort to establish contact with the balance of the Battalion. Lieutenant Parker's valor and superior leader- ship are in keeping with the highest traditions of the service. Entered military service from South Dakota.

-4-

R E S T R I C T E D

R E S T R I C T E D

G. O. No. 28, Hq First Army, 20 June 1944 (cont'd)

Second Lieutenant George F. Kerchner, O-1309569, Infantry, United
States Army, for extraordinary heroism in action on 6 June 1944 at *****
*****, France. When the Company Commander and other company officers be-
came casualties from the heavy enemy rifle, machine gun and artillery fire
upon landing on the coast of France, Lieutenant Kerchner assumed command of
the company. By his determined leadership and outstanding heroism he led
the company in the successful assault upon and captured the 155mm enemy gun
positions. While engaged in this operation, Lieutenant Kerchner and fifteen
(15) members of his organization were surrounded and cut off from the main
body for two and one-half (2 ½) days. He tenaciously and courageously held
his position until relieved and was a constant inspiration and source of
encouragement to his troops. The outstanding heroism displayed by Lieutenant
Kerchner during the initial assault and subsequent operations are in keeping
with the highest traditions of the service. Entered military service from
Maryland.

First Sergeant Leonard G. Lomell, 32269677, Infantry, United States
Army, for extraordinary heroism in action 6 June 1944 at ****, France.
First Sergeant Lomell led a patrol of men through the heaviest kind of
automatic weapons fire to destroy an enemy machine gun nest. Later on the
same day while leading another patrol, he penetrated through the enemy lines
to the rear and discovered five (5) enemy 155mm guns which were shelling the
beachhead. Though these guns were well guarded, nevertheless he gallantly
led his patrol against the enemy and successfully destroyed the guns as well
as the ammunition supply. First Sergeant Lomell's bold and outstanding
leadership in the face of superior numbers is in keeping with the highest
traditions of the service. Entered military service from New Jersey.

Technical Sergeant John W. White, 31135430, Infantry, United States
Army, for extraordinary heroism in action from 6 June 1944 to 8 June 1944 at
**** and ****, France. When all the officers of his company became
casualties in the initial landing on the coast of France from the devastating enemy fire he assumed command of machine gun positions and directed
their fire on the enemy positions. Later he personally acted as the point
of the column which advanced from the beach to ****. On this advance
Sergeant White exposed himself to the direct rifle and machine gun fire of
the enemy as well as sniper fire. Technical Sergeant White's excellent
leadership and gallantry under such difficult and hazardous circumstances
is in keeping with the highest traditions of the service. Entered
military service from Massachusetts.

Sergeant Julius W. Belcher, 33213927, Infantry, United States Army,
for extraordinary heroism in action on 6 June 1944 at ****, France. Upon
landing with the initial assault Ranger battalion on the coast of France,
Sergeant Belcher immediately moved up the beach under heavy machine gun,
mortar and sniper fire, and scaled a 100-foot cliff to secure toggle ropes
to barbed wire on top of the cliff. Though under constant fire on top of
the cliff he remained at his position to help other men on to the top of the
cliff. He then moved into the enemy positions and cleaned out six (6)
snipers. Following this he charged an enemy pillbox and mortar position
and destroyed it with grenades. Sergeant Belcher's bravery and heroism is
in keeping with the highest traditions of the service. Entered military
service from Virginia.

-5- (over)

R E S T R I C T E D

R E S T R I C T E D

G. O. No. 28, Hq First Army, 20 June 1944 (cont'd)

Sergeant William J. Courtney, 15104744, Infantry, United States Army, for extraordinary heroism in action on 7 June 1944 at *****, France. While advancing as the point of a column into a village Sergeant Courtney met point blank machine gun fire. Without hesitation he moved forward and destroyed this enemy machine gun. He continued to move into the village and was suddenly subjected to a barrage of enemy mortar and small arms fire. He engaged the enemy in this uneven fire fight, killing two enemy riflemen and remained at this advanced position until the enemy withdrew. Sergeant Courtney's heroic action is in keeping with the highest traditions of the service. Entered military service from Ohio.

Sergeant Denzil O. Johnson, 38452897, Infantry, United States Army, for extraordinary heroism in action on 7 June 1944 at *****, France. Sergeant Johnson was a scout for a patrol sent out to bring reinforcements to the isolated remnants of a Ranger battalion. The patrol was driven to the edge of a high cliff along the sea by enemy machine gun fire. Led by Sergeant Johnson the patrol worked themselves along the face of the cliff. When the patrol came to the top of the cliff it was stopped by hostile machine gun fire and a mine field. With complete disregard for his own personal safety Sergeant Johnson rushed across the fire swept ground seeking a path through the mine field. Finding an escape route Sergeant Johnson returned to the patrol and led it to a position of safety. Sergeant Johnson's heroic and valorous action is in keeping with the highest traditions of the service. Entered military service from Arkansas.

Sergeant Willie W. Moody, 33628019, Infantry, United States Army, for extraordinary heroism in action on 7 June 1944 and 8 June 1944 in France. Sergeant Moody volunteered to attempt to make contact with a battalion of Rangers that had been cut off. At midnight Sergeant Moody moved off and started through the enemy lines. After several hours of crawling through enemy mine fields, enemy outposts and enemy installations, he finally contacted the battalion that had been cut off. He then returned to his own unit, and started out again with a reel of wire to a position where he believed his mortars would be set up. He returned through the enemy lines unreeling the wire so that accurate fire could be placed upon the enemy positions once the mortars had been placed in position. Sergeant Moody's heroic action is in keeping with the highest traditions of the service. Entered military service from Virginia.

Sergeant Joseph W. Urish, 33575265, Infantry, United States Army, for extraordinary heroism in action on 10 June 1944 near ****, France. Just before his company was about to launch an attack on an enemy shore battery, Sergeant Urish, who was leading a patrol, voluntarily, on a signal being given by the enemy, moved into the battery alone to persuade them to surrender. After about a quarter of an hour the first of the enemy marched out to surrender. As they did the remainder of Sergeant Urish's patrol loaded their rifles. The enemy, thinking they were to be shot in cold blood, scattered and returned to their post. Sergeant Urish faced by a now definitely hostile garrison, instead of attempting to escape in the confusion, remained in the battery completely disregarding his own safety in an attempt to further persuade the battery to surrender. Finally after much pleading and promising the enemy, one by one, laid down their arms, surrendered, and marched out. A total of one hundred sixty

-6-

R E S T R I C T E D

R E S T R I C T E D

G. O. No. 28, Hq First Army, 20 June 1944 (cont'd)

seven prisoners were captured from a position that might have held out
for days. Sergeant Urish's heroic and courageous action is in keeping
with the highest traditions of the service. Entered military service
from Pennsylvania.

Private First Class Alexander W. Barber, 33575048, Medical Corps,
United States Army, for extraordinary heroism in action on 6 June 1944 in
France. Private First Class Barber landed with his medical unit on the
coast of France at a time when the beach was under heavy enemy rifle,
machine gun and artillery fire. Numerous casualties had already been inflicted by this devastating fire. In spite of this heavy fire, Private
First Class Barber constantly exposed himself to the direct fire of the
enemy as he went along the beach administering aid to the wounded. On one
occasion he took a horse and cart into the middle of an artillery barrage
to bring out three (3) men who had been wounded. Private First Class
Barber's heroic and gallant action is in keeping with the highest traditions of the service. Entered military service from Pennsylvania.

Private First Class William E. Dreher, Jr., 35051852, Infantry,
United States Army, for extraordinary heroism in action on 7 June 1944
at ****, France. While advancing as the point of a column into a
village, Private First Class Dreher met point blank machine gun fire.
Without hesitation he moved forward and destroyed this enemy machine gun.
He continued to move into the village and was suddenly subjected to a
barrage of enemy mortar and small arms fire. He engaged the enemy in this
uneven fire fight, killing two enemy riflemen and remained at this advanced
position until the enemy withdrew. Private First Class Dreher's heroic
action is in keeping with the highest traditions of the service. Entered
miltary service from Ohio.

II--AMENDMENT OF GENERAL ORDERS--So much of General Orders Number 21,
this headquarters, 30 May 1944, awarding the Soldier's Medal to Technician
Fifth Grade Banks, as reads: "Entered military service from North Carolina",
is amended to read: "Entered military service from Pennsylvania".

By command of the ARMY COMMANDER:

W. B. KEAN,
Major General, G. S. C.
Chief of Staff

OFFICIAL:

R. S. Nourse (signature)

R. S. NOURSE,
Colonel, AGD,
Adjutant General.

DISTRIBUTION:
"C" plus
TAG (Awards & Decorations Br)---3
ETOUSA (Decorations & Awards
        Br AG Mil. Pers)-----2
Central MRU---------------------1

-7-

R E S T R I C T E D

The awards of the Distinguished Service Cross to the Rangers

Directly related to the accounts already shown, these are some of the army's expanded and more detailed versions of the initial Press Corps media releases – for the same actions. Of note is the issue of Joe Urish's DSC for the action and the capture of prisoners at La Martinière.

Pfc Daniel Farley was with A Co. and he fought alongside Joe Urish at La Martinière – this is what he remembered of the incident:

They had this defensive complex with a number of pillboxes covering all sides, but they were barely visible on the surface and at a distance you didn't know where they were firing from. We had to get into the trenches and then we could walk from the trenches... clear up into the main gun positions. We had to fight in the trenches as the Germans were firing at close range and hiding behind things. We were firing and they were firing... it was gun to gun at very close range. They gave up pretty quick initially and we were taking prisoners coaxed out until we got in closer.

Some of them threw down their weapons and we all started shouting at them to come out with their hands up. They had SS officers that were in there and that caused us problems. They tried to calm them down and we were shouting back at them. I watched them shoot one of their own guys in the back for trying to surrender – that was it then as they went back to firing at us and it got harder. I turned a corner in a trench and remember stepping over an SS officer – perhaps a captain, who I thought had killed himself. He had blown his head off with a grenade – it might have been thrown by one of our guys, but my guess is that he killed himself before we got him.

The major issues we had were all down to the SS officers – I think without them being around, we would have had less casualties and it would have been over once we hit their trenches. Perhaps only 30 to 40 minutes had passed and then it all took off again with pistols and machine guns. We then had to keep our heads down and do it slowly... it was a few hours before we got things under control.

Looking a little further into the detail contained in the above awards. Major General (Ret). John Raaen kindly filled in the redacted place names on Major Sullivan's DSC award and it sheds a little more light on the Maisy action. Sullivan was at Les Perruques (Maisy I) whilst at the same time Joe Urish was capturing more prisoners at La Martinière. Major Sullivan and his men captured 86 prisoners at their location.

Under the provisions of AR 600-45,222 September 1943, and pursuant to authority contained in paragraph 3c, Section I, Circular No. 32, HQ ETOUSA, 20 March 1944, as amended, the Distinguished-Service Cross is awarded to the following officers and enlisted men:

Major Richard P. Sullivan – Headquarters – First United States Army
General Orders – 20 June 1944 – Award of Distinguished Service Cross

Major Richard P. Sullivan, O399856, Infantry, [5th Ranger Infantry Battalion,] United States Army, for extraordinary heroism in action from 6 June 1944 to 10 June 1944 near [Vierville-sur-Mer and Maisy,] France. Completely disregarding his own safety, he personally directed a successful landing operation and led his men across the beach covered with machine gun, artillery and rocket fire. After reorganizing his men he immediately resumed his duties as Battalion Executive officer and was placed in command of two Ranger companies which fought their way inland against fierce opposition to join and relieve the Ranger detachment on [Pointe du Hoc]. After laying communications through enemy lines under cover of darkness, Major Sullivan directed the Rangers' progress across country to [Pointe du Hoc] and [Grandcamps-les-Bains]. In cooperation with United States Infantry an attack was begun on the [Maisy] battery. When certain elements were temporarily halted by artillery fire Major Sullivan, who had been wounded at [Omaha Beach], calmly and courageously rallied his officers and men, ordered a renewal of the attack, and instead of bypassing the resistance, advanced over heavily mined terrain to capture the [Maisy] battery with a loss of only fifteen (15) men. Eighty-six (86) prisoners and several large caliber artillery pieces in concrete bunkers were taken.

Attacks by Major Sullivan's command contributed greatly to the success of the entire Corps' operations. By his intrepid direction, heroic leadership and superior professional ability, Major Sullivan set an inspiring example to his command reflecting the highest traditions of the armed forces. Entered military service from Massachusetts.

The original documents had the place names redacted at the time for security reasons. Again as with the award to Joseph Urish, this award was for 9 June. By 10 June the 5th Battalion were stationed in Osmanville.

Leonard G. Lomell – 2nd Ranger Infantry Battalion (Company D)
The citation for the Distinguished Service Cross awarded to S/Sgt. Len Lomell is recorded by the Army officially with slight exaggeration.

Distinguished Service Cross – *Awarded for actions during the World War II.*

The President of the United States of America, authorized by Act of Congress, July 9, 1918, takes pleasure in presenting the Distinguished Service Cross to First Sergeant Leonard G. Lomell (ASN: 32269677), United States Army, for extraordinary heroism in connection with military operations against an armed enemy while serving with Company D, 2nd Ranger Infantry Battalion, in action against enemy forces on 6 June 1944, in France. First Sergeant Lomell led a patrol of men through the heaviest kind of automatic weapons fire to destroy an enemy machine gun nest. Later on the same day, while leading another patrol, he penetrated through the enemy lines to the rear and discovered five enemy 155-mm guns which were shelling the beachhead. Though these guns were well-guarded, nevertheless he gallantly led his patrol against the enemy and successfully destroyed the guns as well as the ammunition supply. First Sergeant Lomell's bold and outstanding leadership in the face of superior numbers is in keeping with the highest traditions of the military forces of the United States and reflect great credit upon himself, his unit, and the United States Army.

General Orders: Headquarters, First U.S. Army, General Orders No. 28 (June 20, 1944)
Action Date: 6-Jun-44   Service: Army   Rank: First Sergeant

Once again it is a shame that some of the above is simply not acurately recorded. Take these lines for example: *'he penetrated through the enemy lines to the rear and discovered five enemy 155-mm guns which were shelling the beachhead. Though these guns were well-guarded, nevertheless he gallantly led his patrol against the enemy and successfully destroyed the guns as well as the ammunition supply.'*

The guns found by Lomell were not firing and they were not well-guarded at that time. It was either Rupinski's patrol that destroyed the ammunition, or the Navy did… so the US Army actually recorded an 'enhanced' version of his heroic actions.

<u>CITATION FOR THE DISTINGUISHED-SERVICE CROSS</u>

Lieutenant Colonel Max F. Schneider, 0384849, Infantry, United States Army. For extraordinary heroism in action on 6 June 1944 at Vierville-sur-Mer, France. In the initial landings in the invasion of France, Lieutenant Colonel Schneider led the 5th Ranger Infantry Battalion ashore at "H" hour on "D" day in the face of extremely heavy enemy rifle, machine gun, mortar, artillery and rocket fire. Upon reaching the beach Lieutenant Colonel Schneider reorganized his unit. During this reorganization he repeatedly exposed himself to enemy fire. He, then, led his battalion in the assault on the enemy beach positions, and having accomplished this mission led them up a steep incline to assault the enemy gun emplacements on the top of the hill. The destruction of these enemy positions opened one of the vital beach exits, thereby permitting the troops and equipment which had been pinned down to move inland from the beach, with the result that reinforcements could be landed from the sea. By his heroic leadership and personal courage Lieutenant Colonel Schneider set an inspiring example to his command, reflecting the highest traditions of the armed forces. Entered military service from Iowa.

The original citation which accompanied the issuing of the Distinguished Service Cross to Lt. Col. Schneider.

William J. Fox, Technician Fifth Grade, U.S. Army
On D-Day, 6 June 1944, Technician Fifth Grade William J. Fox was serving with the 5th Ranger Battalion, Fifth U.S. Army, in the European Theater of Operations. For some reason his name is not included in the above lists for the award of the DSC – however he was awarded that medal. Here is his information:

TEC 5 Fox's 5th Ranger Battalion was in action against German forces when it landed on Omaha Beach at Normandy, France. The 5th Battalion Rangers broke across the sea wall and barbed wire entanglements, and up the pillbox-rimmed heights under intense enemy machine-gun and mortar fire and, with A and B Companies of the 2nd Battalion and some elements of the 116th Infantry Regiment, advanced 4 miles to the key town of Vierville-sur-Mer, France, opening the breach for supporting troops to follow up and expand the beachhead. TEC 5 Fox's courageous actions and extraordinary heroism that day, at the cost of his life, earned him the U.S. Army's second highest award for valor, the Distinguished Service Cross.

Distinguished Service Cross Citation (Synopsis)

Technician Fifth Grade William J. Fox, United States Army, was awarded the Distinguished Service Cross for extraordinary heroism in connection with military operations against an armed enemy, in action against enemy forces during World War II. Technician Fifth Grade Fox's intrepid actions, personal bravery and zealous devotion to duty exemplify the highest traditions of the military forces of the United States and reflect great credit upon himself, his unit, and the United States Army.

General Orders: Headquarters, Fifth U.S. Army, General Orders No.50 (1944)

Technician Fifth Grade William J. Fox is buried at the Normandy American Cemetery and Memorial in Colleville-sur-Mer, Departement du Calvados, Basse-Normandie, France, in Plot J, Row 4, Grave 28.

On the next page is the paperwork relating to the men from the 2nd and 5th Battalions who were awarded the Silver Star.

The award of the Silver Star issued to Joe Vires was the result of his Actions at Maisy II and this was witnessed by A Company medic Jack Burke.

At the time of writing, I do not know why T/4 David Clawson won his Silver Star on 9 June.

The following name is not on the list as a Silver Star winner:

Martin H. Painkin – 5th Ranger Infantry Battalion (V Corps) – Silver Star

The President of the United States of America, authorized by Act of Congress July 9, 1918, takes pleasure in presenting the Silver Star to Private First Class Martin H. Painkin (ASN: 32790566), United States Army, for gallantry in action while serving with the 5th Ranger Infantry Battalion, V Corps, in action on the coast of France for the period 6 June 1944 to 9 June 1944.

General Orders: Headquarters, V Corps, General Orders No. 2A (June 20, 1944)
Action Date: June 6–9, 1944   Service: Army   Rank: Private First Class

CO 5th Ranger Inf. Bn. RESTRICTED

HEADQUARTERS, V CORPS
APO 305

20 June 1944

GENERAL ORDERS)
:
NO. . . . . 2A)

AWARD OF THE SILVER STAR

GO #2A, Hq., V Corps, 20 June 1944, Cont'd.

V.   Under the provisions of AR 600-45, dated 22 September 1943, and Circular No. 66, Headquarters, First United States Army, dated 18 May 1944, the Silver Star is awarded to the following named officers and enlisted men of the 2d Ranger Infantry Battalion:

Captain Walter E. Block, 0483158, MC, United States Army, for gallantry in action on the coast of France for the period 6 June 1944 to 8 June 1944. Entered military service from Illinois.

Captain Harvey J. Cook, 0393475, Infantry, United States Army, for gallantry in action on the coast of France for the period 6 June 1944 to 8 June 1944. Entered military service from Pennsylvania.

Captain Frank H. Corder, 0394557, Infantry, United States Army, for gallantry in action on the coast of France on 6 June 1944. Entered military service from Texas.

Captain Richard P. Merrill, 01295922, Infantry, United States Army, for gallantry in action on the coast of France on 6 June 1944. Entered military service from Massachusetts.

First Lieutenant Robert C. Arman, 01297475, Infantry, United States Army, for gallantry in action on the coast of France for the period 6 June 1944 to 8 June 1944. Entered military service from Indiana.

First Lieutenant Theodore E. Lapres, Jr., 01307833, Infantry, United States Army, for gallantry in action on the coast of France on 6 June 1944. Entered military service from Pennsylvania.

First Lieutenant Sidney A. Salomon, 01302357, Infantry, United States Army, for gallantry in action on the coast of France on 6 June 1944. Entered military service from New Jersey.

First Lieutenant Elmer H. Vermeer, 01103450, CE, United States Army, for gallantry in action on the coast of France for the period 6 June 1944 to 8 June 1944. Entered military service from Iowa.

First Lieutenant Richard A. Wintz, 0463883, Infantry, United States Army, for gallantry in action on the coast of France on 6 June 1944. Entered military service from Nebraska.

Staff Sergeant James K. Patrick, Jr., 13129473, Infantry, United States Army, for gallantry in action on the coast of France on 6 June 1944. Entered military service from Pennsylvania.

Sergeant Charles C. Flanagan, 34132826, Infantry, United States Army, for gallantry in action on the coast of France on 6 June 1944. Entered military service from Mississippi.

VI.   Under the provisions of AR 600-45, dated 22 September 1943, and Circular No. 66, Headquarters, First United States Army, dated 18 May 1944, the Silver Star is awarded to the following named officers and enlisted men of the 5th Ranger Infantry Battalion:

- 3 -

RESTRICTED

R E S T R I C T E D

GO #2A, Hq., V Corps, 20 June 1944. Cont'd.

Captain Hugo W. Heffelfinger, 0416865, Infantry, United States Army, for gallantry in action on the coast of France on 6 June 1944. Entered military service from Nebraska.

Captain Edward S. Luther, 0401752, Infantry, United States Army, for gallantry in action on the coast of France for the period 6 June 1944 to 7 June 1944. Entered military service from Massachusetts.

Captain John C. Raaen, Jr., 025486, CE, United States Army, for gallantry in action on the coast of France on 6 June 1944. Entered military service from Arkansas.

Captain William M. Runge, 0443867, Infantry, United States Army, for gallantry in action on the coast of France on 6 June 1944. Entered military service from Iowa.

Captain Wilmer K. Wise, 01287110, Infantry, United States Army, for gallantry in action on the coast of France on 6 June 1944. Entered military service from Virginia.

First Lieutenant George R. Miller, 01291676, Infantry, United States Army, for gallantry in action on the coast of France on 6 June 1944. Entered military service from Oklahoma.

First Lieutenant Bernard M. Pepper, 01290301, Infantry, United States Army, for gallantry in action on the coast of France on 6 June 1944. Entered military service from Minnesota.

First Lieutenant John J. Reville, 01298289, Infantry, United States Army, for gallantry in action on the coast of France on 7 June 1944. Entered military service from New York.

First Lieutenant Oscar R. Stowe, 01312064, Infantry, United States Army, for gallantry in action on the coast of France on 8 June 1944. Entered military service from Pennsylvania.

First Sergeant Raymond M. Herlihy, 32535294, Infantry, United States Army, for gallantry in action on the coast of France on 6 June 1944. Entered military service from New York.

Technical Sergeant Harold J. Bates, Jr., 32354055, Infantry, United States Army, for gallantry in action on the coast of France on 7 June 1944. Entered military service from New York.

Technical Sergeant Henry M. Klott, 36027949, Infantry, United States Army, for gallantry in action on the coast of France on 7 June 1944. Entered military service from Illinois.

Technician Fourth Grade David L. Clawson, 20726730, MC, United States Army, for gallantry in action on the coast of France on 9 June 1944. Entered military service from Kansas.

- 4 -

R E S T R I C T E D

RESTRICTED

GO #2A, Hq., V Corps, 20 June 1944, Cont'd.

Technician Fifth Grade Joe Vires, 37378745, Infantry, United States Army, for gallantry in action on the coast of France on 9 June 1944. Entered military service from Missouri.

Private First Class Elwood L. Dorman, 33504795, Infantry, United States Army, for gallantry in action on the coast of France on 6 June 1944. Entered military service from Pennsylvania.

Private First Class Ellis E. Reed, Jr., 32763521, Infantry, United States Army, for gallantry in action on the coast of France on 6 June 1944. Entered military service from New Jersey.

Private First Class Albert F. Sweeney, 20109303, Infantry, United States Army, for gallantry in action on the coast of France for the period 6 June 1944 to 8 June 1944. Entered military service from Massachusetts.

Private Warren M. Adams, 20101983, Infantry, United States Army, for gallantry in action on the coast of France on 8 June 1944. Entered military service from Massachusetts.

- 5 -

RESTRICTED

A worthy addition to this list is this posthumous award of the Silver Star issued to Jonathan Harwood. He was a non-graduating member of the U.S. Military Academy at West Point, Class of 1941 and was a member of the 293rd Signal Company attached to the 2nd Rangers at Pointe du Hoc on D-Day.

Jonathan Hartwell Harwood, Jr – 2nd Ranger Infantry Battalion (Attached) – Silver Star

Captain (Field Artillery) Jonathan Hartwell Harwood, Jr. (ASN: 0-464650), United States Army, was awarded the Silver Star (Posthumously) for conspicuous gallantry and intrepidity in connection with military operations against the enemy while serving with the 293rd Signal Company, attached to the 2nd Ranger Battalion, at Normandy, France, on 6 June 1944.

General Orders: Headquarters, 1st Army, General Orders No. 51 (1944)
Action Date: 6-Jun-44   Service: Army   Rank: Captain

Another award for a non-Ranger at Pointe du Hoc, this time the Navy Cross:

Kenneth Sidney Norton – 2nd Ranger Infantry Battalion (Naval Gunfire Liaison Officer) – Navy Cross

The President of the United States of America takes pleasure in presenting the Navy Cross to Lieutenant, Junior Grade Kenneth Sidney Norton, United States Naval Reserve, for extraordinary heroism and distinguished service in the line of his profession as Naval Gunfire Liaison Officer to the 2nd Ranger Battalion, during the assault on Normandy, France, on 6 and 7 June 1944. Lieutenant, Junior Grade, Norton landed with the first wave of Rangers at the base of Pointe Du Hoe. He was one of the first up the cliff. When the Second Ranger Battalion was surrounded by enemy troops in superior numbers, Lieutenant, Junior Grade, Norton called for and adjusted fire in great volume and with marked accuracy and effect throughout the day. Without this accurate fire it is probable that the Rangers could not have survived. On the evening of D-Day, Lieutenant, Junior Grade, Norton's forward observer was killed and Lieutenant, Junior Grade, Norton was wounded. He nevertheless continued his efforts, organized an emergency shore fire control net and successfully directed several additional fire-support missions. After being evacuated and treated on the U.S.S. TEXAS he returned to the battlefield to take up his regular duties. The conduct of Lieutenant, Junior Grade, Norton throughout this action reflects great credit upon himself, and was in keeping with the highest traditions of the United States Naval Service.

General Orders: Bureau of Naval Personnel Information Bulletin No. 334 (January 1945)
Action Date: 6–7-Jun-44   Service: Navy   Rank: Lieutenant Junior Grade

Robert William Leach – Commanding Officer USS *Satterlee* (DD-626) – Silver Star

The President of the United States of America takes pleasure in presenting the Silver Star to Lieutenant Commander Robert William Leach (NSN: 0-72273/1100), United States Navy, for meritorious performance of duty as Commanding Officer of the U.S.S. SATTERLEE (DD-626), in action against German Coastal defenses and German troops on the coast of France on 6 June 1944. Lieutenant Commander Leach pressed his attack with gallantry while his ship was under fire by enemy coastal defenses and machine gun fire by enemy troops. He so skillfully and efficiently handled his ship closing the range to the shore so that his main and heavy machine gun batteries were able to offer effective close fire support to the Rangers who were assaulting enemy fortifications at Pointe du Hoc. His fire silenced numerous enemy machine gun nests and killed many of the enemy troops who were firing on the Rangers. Lieutenant Commander Leach's determination to close the enemy and give close support fire was of invaluable aid to our troops and was in keeping with the highest traditions of the United States Naval Service.

Action Date: 6-Jun-44   Service: Navy   Rank: Lieutenant Commander
[Robert Leach graduated from the U.S. Naval Academy at Annapolis, Class of 1933. He retired as a U.S. Navy Rear Admiral.]

Bennie Berger – Navy – Silver Star

The President of the United States of America takes pleasure in presenting the Silver Star to Lieutenant, Junior Grade Bennie Berger, United States Naval Reserve, for conspicuous gallantry and intrepidity in action while serving as Naval Gunfire Liaison Officer attached to the FIFTH Ranger Battalion during the assault on the coast of Normandy, France, 6 June 1944, and subsequent advance inland 6 June to 15 June 1944. Leading the initial waves under extremely heavy enemy fire, Lieutenant, Junior Grade, Berger displayed great personal bravery and initiative in the direction of cruiser fire in support of the Rangers. Unmindful of his own safety, he remained with the forward patrols assisting the landing force materially with Naval fire support. Later, when juncture with the Second Ranger Battalion had been effected, and on finding no officer with their Shore Fire Control Party, he took charge of both parties and participated in both the advance on Isigny and Grandcamp and was instrumental in the direction of very valuable supporting fires. The actions and initiative of Lieutenant, Junior Grade, Berger during emergencies were in keeping with the highest traditions of the United States Naval Service.

Action Date: 6–15-Jun-44   Service: Navy   Rank: Lieutenant Junior Grade

Jack E. Kuhn – Silver Star

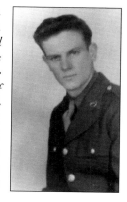

While serving with the Army of the United States, distinguished himself by gallantry in action. From 6 June to 8 June 1944, while on outpost duty at Pointe du Hoe, France, Sergeant Kuhn, together with three other members of his company, protected the battalion command post and aid station. The determination and initiative displayed by these men while performing this duty set an example for the remainder of the company which were engaged in repelling three counterattacks by a numerically superior enemy. Sergeant Kuhn and the three other members of his company held tenaciously to their position against heavy enemy fire thus permitting the safe withdrawal of their men. When finally cut off from the main body, and although without food, water, or medical aid for a period of forty-eight hours, and despite being greatly outnumbered, these heroic men continued to harass the enemy and refused to surrender. On 8 June 1944 the enemy was forced to withdraw making it possible for Sergeant Kuhn and the three others with him to rejoin their unit. The gallantry and courage displayed by these men reflect great credit on themselves and are in keeping with the highest traditions of the military service.

Action Date: 6–8-Jun-44   Service: Army   Rank: Staff Sergeant

Coit M. Coker – Navy

Lt. Coit M. Coker was awarded the Silver Star for working with the Rangers as a naval gunfire liaison officer attached to the 116th Regimental Combat Team.

Awarded for actions during the World War II

The President of the United States of America takes pleasure in presenting the Silver Star to Lieutenant, Junior Grade Coit M. Coker, United States Navy, for gallantry in action as a naval gunfire liaison officer during the invasion of France and the advance inland from 6 to 15 June 1944. Lieutenant, Junior Grade, Coker displayed marked bravery and knowledge in calling for and adjusting fire, which aided materially in the advance on and capture of Grandcamp-les-Bains and Isigny.

General Orders: Bureau of Naval Personnel Information Bulletin No. 334 (January 1945)

Action Date: 6–15-Jun-44   Service: Navy   Rank: Lieutenant Junior Grade

---

HEADQUARTERS
FIFTH RANGER INFANTRY BATTALION
APO 655, U.S. ARMY

GENERAL ORDERS)
            :
NO.   2)   26 August 1944

        1. Under the provisions of AR 600-45, dated 22 September 1943 as ammended, and Circular No. 66, Hq First United States Army dated 18 May 1944, the Purple Heart is awarded to the following enlisted men:

        Staff Sergeant Orvylle A. Rosenblad, 20722145, wounded in action on 6 June 1944 at or near Vierville ser Mer, France.

        Technician 5th Grade Aldus P. Kreider, 33501061, wounded in action on 6 June 1944 at or near Vierville ser Mer, France.

        Technician 5th Grade Edward L. Podkowka, 31186291, wounded in action on 7 June 1944 at or near Vierville ser Mer, France.

        Private First Class Richard T. Sorenson, 31154675, wounded in action on 6 June 1944 at or near Vierville ser Mer, France.

        Private First Class William M. Gardner, 33212796, wounded in action on 11 June 1944 at or near Bois Du Molay, France.

        Private First Class Abbott S. Wittels, 36079191, wounded in action on 7 June 1944 at or near Vierville ser Mer, France.

        Private First Class Carmen W. Montello, 20101950, wounded in action on 7 June 1944 at or near Vierville ser Mer, France.

            By order of Major SULLIVAN:

                                    JOHN L. RAHMLOW
                                    1st Lt., Infantry,
                                    Assist Adjutant.

OFFICIAL:

        JOHN L. RAHMLOW
        1st Lt., Infantry,
        Assist Adjutant.

DISTRIBUTION:
    Individual..................... 1
    AG Decorations & Awards Branch.. 3
    CG ETOUSA...................... 5
    Central MRU, APO 887........... 1
    CG Third United States Army..... 1

Men of the 5th Battalion entitled to the Purple Heart medal.

Other men from the 5th Battalion entitled to the Purple Heart medal (for wounds sustained in combat). Highlighted here are two from Maisy, but the full list of names would have been much greater. To validate this statement, I refer to the F Company diary entries by Hodgson 9 June, as well as the Morning Reports. I also have personal interviews with veterans who were wounded, or witnessed others that had been wounded at Maisy.

RESTRICTED

HEADQUARTERS
FIFTH RANGER INFANTRY BATTALION
APO 230, U.S. ARMY

General Orders)
Number . . . 1)   20 July 1944

1. Under the provisions of AR 600-45, 22 September 1943 as amended, and Cir No. 66 Hqs First United States Army dtd 18 May 1944, the Purple Heart is awarded to the following officers and enlisted men:

MAJOR RICHARD P. SULLIVAN, O-399856, for wounds received in action on June 8, 1944 at or near Pointe Du Hoe, France.

T/Sgt Wilfred F. McGuire, 20721430, for wounds received in action on June 6, 1944 at or near Vierville Sur Mer, France.

S/Sgt James D. Christian, 34361672, for wounds received in action on June 6, 1944 at or near Vierville Sur Mer, France.

Sgt. Edward W. Dickman, 19161568, for wounds received in action on June 6, 1944 at or near Vierville Sur Mer, France.

Sgt. Denzil O. Johnson, 38452897, for wounds received in action on June 9, 1944 at or near Maisy, France.

Sgt. Robert W. Morgan, 35605948, for wounds received in action on June 6, 1944 at or near Vierville Sur Mer, France.

Tec 4 David L. Clawson, 20726730, for wounds received in action on June 8, 1944 at or near Grandcamp, France.

Tec 4 James V. Fitzgerald, 31035200, for wounds received in action on June 6, 1944 at or near Vierville Sur Mer, France.

Cpl Michael G. Zifcak, 31056508, for wounds received in action on June 6, 1944 at or near Vierville Sur Mer, France.

Tec 5 Irvin L. Germain, 36314276, for wounds received in action on June 6, 1944 at or near Vierville Sur Mer, France.

Tec 5 Thomas E. Lanham, 6947405, for wounds received in action on June 6, 1944 at or near Vierville Sur Mer, France.

Tec 5 Andrew L. Spier, 32762678, for wounds received in action on June 9, 1944 at or near Maisy, France.

Pfc John P. Bellows, 11085458 for wounds received in action on June 6, 1944 at or near Vierville Sur Mer, France.

1st Lt. John McKie fought with the 743rd Tank Battalion. Given the description of the action, it is assumed that he was killed during the Maisy battle. He was posthumously given the Bronze Star. His commanding officer wrote up the action.

2. FIRST LIEUTENANT JOHN M. McKIE, O1014369, Infantry, United States Army, for meritorious achievement in military operations against the enemy in Normandy, France, received the Bronze Star (Posthumously). On 9 June 1944, First Lieutenant McKie dismounted from his tank and effectively directed artillery fire on enemy strong points, while intense enemy fire fell all around. His actions resulted in the destruction of the enemy strong points.

STUART G. FRIES
Lieutenant Colonel, Infantry
Commanding

4 Incls:
1. S-2 Journal
2. S-3 Journal
3. Envelope (Supporting Evidence)
4. Map (France)

Chapter 12

After Action Reports – Air Force

Air Force After Action Reports are scarce for the Maisy attacks, primarily because most of the information about individual raids were recorded within Log Books which are now very difficult to find. Here are a few that I am aware of:

The French Air Force
Two French Air Force heavy bomber squadrons of the Allied air forces during World War Two were 346 Squadron and 347 Squadron. They were based at RAF Elvington, York from June 1944 until October 1945.

On 16 May 1944, No. 346 'Guyenne' Squadron RAF was officially formed at Elvington, followed by No. 347 the 'Tunisie' Squadron RAF on 20 June 1944.

'Guyenne' was pronounced operational on 1 June 1944, and attacked the Maisy positions during the night of 5 June, prior to the D-Day Invasion. Jean Carmel, a captain with the unit wrote the following in his book *Night Pilot:*

> *5th Elvington Air Base, York.... That evening at Elvington base no one knew for certain of this operation – at least among the crews. Admittedly, at the general briefing, the particular precautions which were taken for our flight over England rather surprised us. The intelligence officer had warned us that 50 square miles of the coast would be fringed with searchlights rising vertically half a mile apart. We were absolutely forbidden to enter this square.*

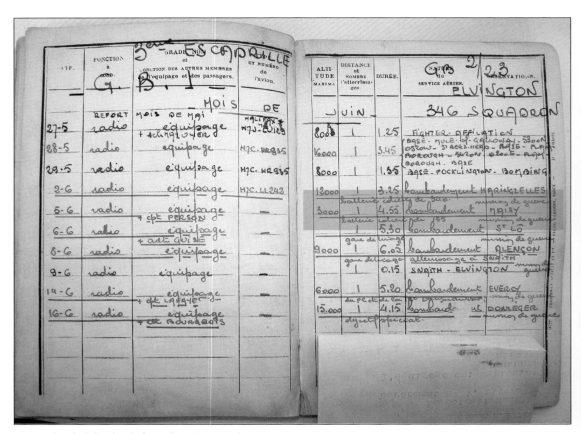

A French pilot's log book from that Maisy raid.

As we learnt later, this was the zone from which aircraft and gliders carrying parachutists took off. Moreover, the target that night was a special one. We were given orders to bombard a heavy German battery installed at the base of the Cotentin Peninsula.

One hundred and fifty bombers were specially detailed for this raid. The disparity between the means and the apparent end were obvious. We easily understood the next day when we learnt that this battery, silenced by our mass raid, had allowed the fleet to sail close in to the shore.

The flight went without incident. England was covered with medium cloud which hid the searchlights. The markers were clearly spotted despite a light mist, which made them less bright than usual. Brion took off in B for Baker. We had a full bomb load because the target was so near home. In actual fact we never had the pleasure of having an easy take-off with a lightly loaded aircraft. If the target was near then it was a full bomb-load, if it was a long way away it was a full load of petrol.'

For the Frenchmen it was finally an opportunity to attack the Germans on their own soil. Something which up to this point they had avoided doing, in case the Germans used any mis-bombing for propaganda purposes. Their bombing undoubtedly created mayhem on the ground in Maisy and assisted the Allied approach to the beaches. For the Frenchmen it was the moment they had waited for – D-Day and the start of the liberation of France.

Dated 17 July 1944 a certificate recognising the men of the Groupes Lourds with the French Military Medal with Bronze Star. Listing them by name and stating: *'in particular they carried out on the night of the 6th of June 1944 a remarkably precise bombardment on an objective of great tactical importance.'*

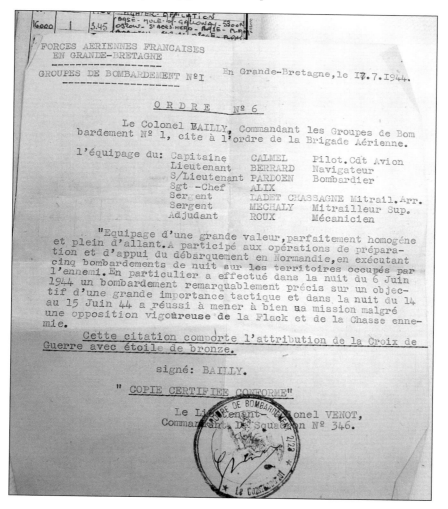

A photograph with Groupes Lourds veterans and the author at their monument in Grandcamp. It was built long before the existence of the Maisy Batteries had been re-established.

Later when the Maisy site opened, the Groupes Lourds veterans and their association installed a second plaque at the Maisy site.

The War Diary of RAF Pocklington records the following:

5th–6th June, 1944 (D-Day)
Maisy, "Heavy Coastal Battery". 26 aircraft. (A Squadron Record). All attacked the target through 3/10 cloud at 5,000ft. No night fighters but some light flak. (On this day Bomber Command flew 1,211 sorties for the loss of 3 aircraft).

RAF Records have the following within the 57th Squadron Operational Records Book:

'4th/5th June 1944. Target – Maisy Gun Emplacement.
15 aircraft were detailed and all took off to attack this target. Owing to poor visibility, little could be seen of the results of the attack. Most crew saw only the glow of Red or Green T.I.'s through cloud and bombed this assisted by navigational aids. Defences very slight. Heavy flak. All aircraft returned safely to base.
Aircraft Type and Number: Lancaster III LM.573.

Crew:	P/O. Owen. N.	Pilot	Sgt. Grice. J.	W/Op
	Sgt. Moore. P.W.L	F/Eng	Sgt. Stevens. M.L	M/U
	F/S Bennett. E.	Nav.	Sgt. Kirwan. K	R/G
	F/S Shaw. E.	A/B		
Up:	01:10		Down:	05:06

Details of Sortie: Sortie Completed. Bomb Load:- 18 x 500lb G.P.'

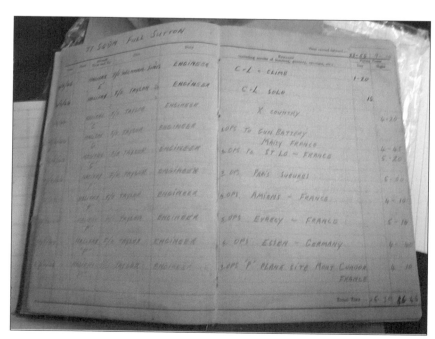

Flying Logbook for Flight Engineer Selwyn Morris – 1861960 RAF.

He took part in the 5 June raids. His logbook reads:

	Aircraft Type	Pilot	Duty	Time
5/6/44	Halifax "G".	Flying Officer Taylor.	Engineer	04.45

Remarks: Operations to Gun Battery – **Maisy**, France.

Next page: A page from the logbook belonging to Pilot Officer Jack Spedding of 109 Reconnaissance Squadron RAF. On 4 June he flew as a pathfinder on the mission.

Year JUNE 1944		AIRCRAFT		Pilot, or 1st Pilot	2nd Pilot, Pupil or Passenger	DUTY (Including Results and Remarks)
Month	Date	Type	No.			
—	—	—	—	—	—	— Totals Brought Forward
JUNE	1.	MOSQUITO XVI	939 NL	SELF	F/L RIMMER.	N.F.T.
	1.	MOSQUITO XVI	NL 939	SELF	F/L RIMMER.	OPERATIONS FERME D'URVILLE.
	2	MOSQUITO XVI	ML939	SELF	F/L RIMMER.	BOMBING WHITTLESEA.
	3.	MOSQUITO XVI	939	SELF	F/L RIMMER.	N.F.T.
	4	MOSQUITO XVI	939	SELF	F/L RIMMER.	N.F.T.
	4	MOSQUITO XVI	ML 939	SELF	F/L RIMMER	OPERATIONS (M) MAISY COASTAL BATTERY
	5.	MOSQUITO XVI	ML 939	SELF.	F/L RIMMER.	N.F.T.
	6.	MOSQUITO XVI	ML 939	SELF	F/L RIMMER	OPERATIONS (M) 3 T·I·R 1·T·I·G. MERVILLE COASTAL BATTERY D·DAY.

A further comment was added on the next page in his book – it confirms the mission to Maisy and that they were also marking a Radio Location Station (which was situated within the centre of the Les Perruques Maisy I site).

(9) 4 June Maisy Coastal Battery + Radio Location Station. marking.

RAF Bomber Command Official War Diary reports further on this particular mission:

4/5 June 1944

*259 aircraft – 125 Lancasters, 118 Halifaxes, 16 Mosquitos – of Nos 1, 4, 5, 6 and 8 Groups to bomb 4 gun positions; 3 of these were deception targets in the Pas de Calais but the fourth battery, at **Maisy**, was in Normandy between what would soon be known as Omaha and Utah Beaches, where American troops would land in less than 36 hours' time. Unfortunately, **Maisy** was covered by cloud and could only be marked by Oboe skymarkers, but it was then bombed by 52 Lancasters of No 5 Group. 2 of the 3 gun positions in the Pas de Calais were also affected by bad weather and could only be bombed through cloud but the position at Calais itself was clear*

and was accurately marked by the Mosquitos and well bombed by Halifaxes and Lancasters of No 6 Group. No aircraft lost on these operations.

Sgt. V. Taggart of the 102nd Squadron RAF were also based at Pocklington and he and his fellow crew members took part in the Maisy Raid.

Once again a simple entry in his log-book for 5 June.

Date	Hour	Aircraft Type and No.	Pilot	Duty	REMARKS (Including results of bombing, gunnery, exercises, etc.)	Flying Times Day	Night
					Time carried forward :—	91·20.	61·30.
2nd June 1944	23·50	Halifax III W DY 616 MZ	Sgt. Bailey	Mid-upper Gunner.	Ops. Coastal Gun Battery Haringzelles		03·10
1st June 1944	01·05	Halifax III W DY 616 MZ	Sgt. Bailey	Mid-upper Gunner.	Ops. Gun battery Boulogne DNCO. Early return. P.O. Engine feathered.		01·45
5 June 1944	01·00	Halifax III W DY 616 MZ	Sgt. Bailey	Mid-upper Gunner.	Ops. Gun battery Maisy.		05·10
6th June 1944	22·40	Halifax III W DY 616 MZ	Sgt. Bailey	Mid-upper Gunner.	Low level Bombing Ops. Communications St. Lô Landed away, Enstone.		04·20
7th June 1944	07·50	Halifax III W DY 616	Sgt. Bailey	Mid-upper Gunner.	Returning from 'Enstone' to Base.	01·05.	
8th June 1944	15·50	Halifax III W DY 616	Sgt. Bailey	Mid-upper Gunner	Air Test.	01·05.	
8th June 1944	22·40	Halifax III W DY 616	Sgt. Bailey	Mid-upper Gunner	Ops. Marshalling yard. Alencon Weather u/s at Base. Diverted to Carnaby.		05·40
9th June 1944	14·05	Halifax III W DY 616 MZ	Sgt. Bailey	Mid-upper Gunner.	Returning from Carnaby to Base.	00·15	
11th June 1944	21·50	Halifax III W DY 616 MZ	Sgt. Bailey	Mid-upper Gunner.	Ops. Marshalling yard. Massy – Palaiseau. (Paris)		04·50
11th June 1944	00·40	Halifax III W DY 616 MZ	Sgt. Bailey	Mid-upper Gunner.	Ops. Panzer Division Evreçy.		05·05
16th June 1944	23·10	Halifax III W DY	Sgt. Bailey	Mid-upper Gunner.	Ops. Synthetic Oil Plant. Sterkrade (Rhur) Early Return R/G. Unit u/s.		03·05.
					TOTAL TIME ...	93·45	94·35
						188·20.	

102. Squadron   Pocklington

Wing Commander Viney commanded a Halifax on D-Day alongside Norman Furness and is mentioned in the above diary entry.

A different entry in the RAF archives confirms further bombing of Maisy.

5/6 June 1944
*1,012 aircraft – 551 Lancasters, 412 Halifaxes, 49 Mosquitos – to bomb coastal batteries at Fontenay, Houlgate, La Pernelle, Longues, **Maisy**, Merville, Mont Fleury, Pointe du Hoc, Ouistreham and St Martin de Varreville. 946 aircraft carried out their bombing tasks. 3 aircraft were lost – 2 Halifaxes of No 4 Group on the Mont Fleury*

Pilot Officer Norman Furness, who flew with 640 Squadron based at RAF Leconfield.

raid and 1 Lancaster of No 6 Group on the Longues raid. Only two of the targets – La Pernelle and Ouistreham – were free of cloud; all other bombing was entirely based on Oboe marking. At least 5,000 tons of bombs were dropped, the greatest tonnage in one night so far in the war.

The history of one particular Handley Page Halifax Mark III bomber from this group, number LV907 (named *Friday the 13th*) was recorded as follows in the *Derby Telegraph*.

*Gradually, the number of bomb tallies applied beneath its title grew and, following a raid on coastal batteries at **Maisy**, Friday was duly adorned with a Swastika over which was superimposed the key of the door signifying this famous Halifax had come of age.*

Hamilton Connolly DFC was from Buderim Pines, Queensland, Australia and he flew with the RAAF 1940–1945. He enlisted in the RAAF in September 1940 and, after operational training on heavy bombers in Britain, he completed his first operational tour in early 1943 in 78 Squadron RAF. He was awarded the Distinguished Flying Cross (DFC) for skillful flying on this tour. His citation reads:

On D-Day, he was the Commanding Officer of 466 Squadron RAAF, which dispatched 13 Halifax bombers as part of an attack on an artillery battery at Maisy, which threatened the Utah and Omaha beaches where American troops were to land. The squadron's aircraft experienced a number of near misses while helping to reduce heavy fire against American forces when they began landing.

No.466 Squadron was a Royal Australian Air Force bomber squadron during World War II. Formed in the United Kingdom in late 1942, the squadron undertook combat operations in Europe until the end of the war, flying heavy bomber aircraft and it converted to the Handley Page Halifax heavy bomber in late 1943. From May 1944 its operations were focused on German infrastructure in France, such as coastal artillery batteries and railway marshalling yards, in preparation for the invasion of Europe.

5th/6th June
Ordered off at 23.45hrs to attack large gun emplacements along various parts of the Normandy coast. This was a maximum effort raid. Sky-full of Lancasters and Halifaxes. My specific target was the Batteries at Maisy. We knocked hell out of these guns and gunners' quarters. Quite a bit of flak. Nothing to speak of. No fighters and landed back at Leconfield at dawn. Got a shock, taxied back to our dispersal followed by petrol and oil bowsers and a Salvation Army van.

*   Joe Viney arrived in a jeep to give us the news that the invasion had now begun.*

The following three pages are taken from the briefing notes for the airmen of the 366th Fighter/Bomber Group USAF for 6 June 1944. The first page is an operating area information sheet – unfortunately the second page is missing. The next page shown is a flight plan for the 391st Bomber Squadron to hit the batteries at Maisy. It shows their route out from England and around the west of the Cherbourg Peninsula, then across overland to attack Maisy from the landward side. Their target was the grid reference 531914 which was the four guns in the open field positions at Foucher's Farm.

SECRET

6 NUNE 1944   1630 B HRS

OPERATIONS ORDER NO. 347

MAPS: NORMAL

1. B. (2) (A)   IX TROOP CARRIER COMMAND IS TOWING GLIDERS AND
                   RESUPPLYING PARACHUTE TROOPS IN FRANCE.
            (B)   MISSION "KEOKUK" AND ELMIRE" "A" AND B" CONSISTS
                   OF APPROX. 108 TUG AND GLIDER COMBINATIONS IN
                   THREE SECTIONS, TOTAL LENGTH OF COLUMN WILL BE
                   APPROX. 40 TO 60 MILES.
            (C)   MISSION "ELMIRE C AND D" CONSISTS OF 100 TUG
                   AND GLIDER COMBINATIONS IN TWO SECTIONS.   TOTAL
                   LENGTH OF COLUMN APPROX. 40 MILES.
2. THIS COMMAND CONDUCTS SWEEPS IN FRANCE IN SUPPORT OF IX TROOP
    CARRIER COMMAND AND DESTROYS E/E.

    ZERO HR AND DATE: 061900 B

3. 71ST FTR BOMBER WING
    A. 366TH F/B GP
       (2) 389 SQDN
       (4) (5) BEACHY HEAD
                LE TREPORT   Z PLUS 170

                SWEEP ZONE
                5000-0130E
                4940-0220E
                4850-0100E
                4920-0030E

                LE TREPORT   Z PLUS 260
                BEACHY HEAD
                BASE
    B. 366TH F/B GP
       (2) 390 SQDN
       (4) (5) BEACHY HEAD
                ETRETAT   Z PLUS 170

                SWEEP AREA
                4920-0030E
                4850-0100E
                4900-0030W
                4825-0000W

                ETRETAT   Z PLUS 260
    C. 366TH F/B GP
       (2) 391ST SQDN
       (4) (5) ST ALBANS HEAD

                SWEEP AREA
                C. FRENET   Z PLUS 170
                4820-0220W
                4825-0020W
                4900-0130W

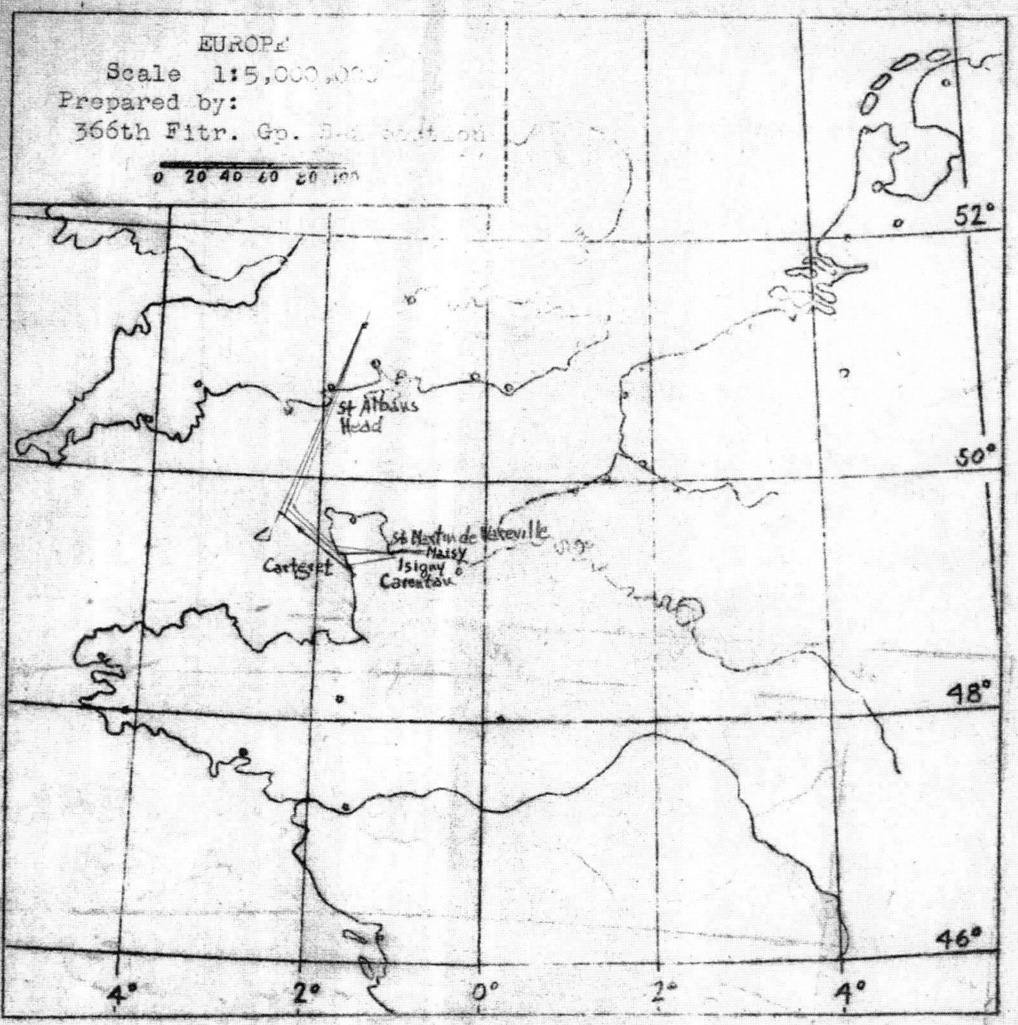

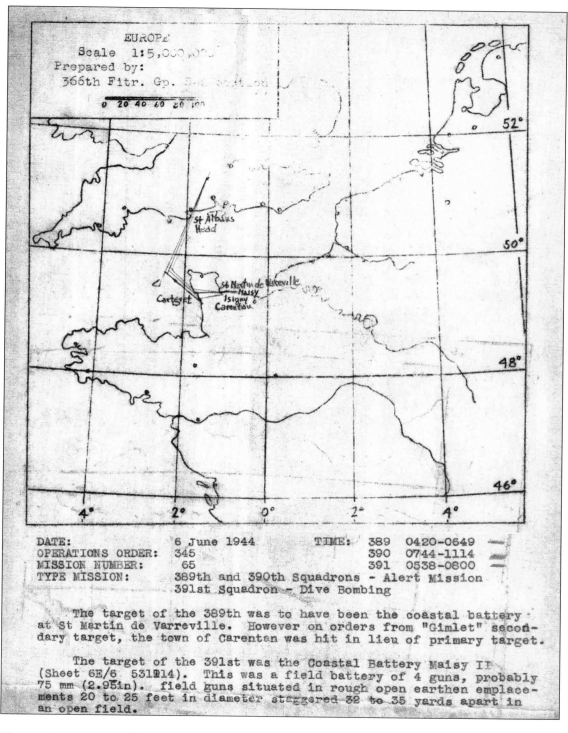

Scale 1:5,000,000
Prepared by:
366th Fitr. Gp.
0 20 40 60 80 100
52°
50°
48°
46°
4°
2°
0°
2°
4°
St Albans Head
St Martin de Varreville
Maisy
Isigny
Carentan
Cartgret

DATE: 6 June 1944 TIME: 389 0420-0649
OPERATIONS ORDER: 345 390 0744-1114
MISSION NUMBER: 65 391 0538-0800
TYPE MISSION: 389th and 390th Squadrons - Alert Mission
391st Squadron - Dive Bombing

The target of the 389th was to have been the coastal battery at St Martin de Varreville. However on orders from "Gimlet" secondary target, the town of Carentan was hit in lieu of primary target.

The target of the 391st was the Coastal Battery Maisy II (Sheet 6E/6 531914). This was a field battery of 4 guns, probably 75 mm (2.95in). field guns situated in rough open earthen emplacements 20 to 25 feet in diameter staggered 32 to 35 yards apart in an open field.

The remaining portion of the mission was to attack Maisy II – La Martinière, for which they used the aerial photograph taken some time prior to D-Day. Of particular interest are the hand written notes on the bottom of the page. *'This battery has been casemated and is now occupied.'* It is likely that this information was provided by the local Resistance.

TARGET - No. 16   Maisy II

MAISY II   Unoccupied field battery   Interservice Target No: 9/J/8

Ref Map: GSGS 4250/GSG/528916
Geographical Coordinates: 49° 22' 26" N.   01° 04' 62" W.
Height above sea level: 20 metres.

Position for 4-gun field troop, unoccupied, probably only temporarily. The original
emplacements have been demolished, and the guns are in the open at 531914
(MAISY IIa).   Interservice Target No: 9/J/39.

This battery has been casemated and is now occupied.

Although both batteries were included in the same mission – the RAF Historical Records simply have it reported as an attack on Maisy Battery II by P-47 fighter bombers on 6 June. Another attack on Maisy II is listed on 7 June by B-26 bombers confirming that it was still operational and had to be silenced. It states that 622.23 tonnes of bombs were dropped on Les Perruques – Maisy I on the evening of the 5th and then later on 6 June.

An odd thing about this particular report is that it says nine B-26s were attacking Pointe du Hoc on 7 June. If that was the case, they would have surely come very close to the Ranger force on the Pointe, and one has to question the purpose of a heavy bomber raid on a gun battery certainly known to have been occupied by Rangers by then.

TABLE VIII			AIR ATTACKS AGAINST COASTAL BATTERIES AFFECTING WESTERN TASK FORCE AREA D - 1 to D ≠ 4							
FUSA TARGET NO.	GRID COORDS	ARM	NAME	DATE OF ATTACK	NO. A/C DESP.	NO. A/C ATTACKING	TYPE A/C	BOMBS DROPPED	TONNAGE DROPPED	TOTAL TONNAGE
1	586938	6-155G	Pt.DeHoe	D-1	36	36	H-B	427x500	106.75	
1	"	"	"	D-1(nite)	115	108	H-B	480x1000MC 697x1000USA 64x500 MC 365x500 GP	695.74	
1	"	"	"	D Day	18	11	B-26	16x2000 4x1000	18	
1	"	"	"	D ≠ 1	16	9	B-26	16x2000	16	836.49
5	533918	4-155G	Maisy I	D-1(nite)	111	105	HB	869x1000MC 7x1000GP 428x500MC 173x500GP	588.23	
5	"	"	"	D Day	17	18(1)	B-26	2x1000 33x2000	34	622.23
16	528916	4-75G	Maisy II	D Day	38	38	P-47	54x500	31.5	
16	"	"	"	D ≠ 1	17	17	B-26	36x1000 33x2000	33	64.5

By way of comparison, here are the tonnage figures of bombs dropped on all of the significant gun batteries affecting the US sector. With a combined bombs dropped weighing a total of 686.73 tonnes, the three positions at Maisy are statistically the second most heavily bombed target in the US landing sector. Longues-sur-Mer is located in the British sector.

	Tonnes dropped.
Pointe du Hoc	836.49
Longues sur Mer	709.5
Maisy I	**622.23**
St. Martin De Varreville	610.5
Crisbecq	609.96
Mont Farville	161.65
La Fosse	104.75
Maisy II & Foucher's Farm	**64.5**
Quinneville	64
Aigremont	63
Gatteville	61
La Pernelle	55
Morsalines	43.50
Azeville	39.25
Géfosse-Fontenay	11.25

Below: Selective excerpts from the US 9th Air Force Operational Report of Invasion Activities:

a.   Mission.

The mission of the Ninth Air Force was described as "to assist the Allied Armies to secure a lodgement on the Continent in the first phase of the operation, and to support the Armies of the First U. S. Army Group in the development of that lodgement in the second phase."

Three other coastal batteries at Pointe du Hoe, just west of Omaha beach, at Maisy I on the eastern shore of the Vire estuary, and at Montfarville, south of Barfleur on the northeast tip to the Cherbourg peninsula were to be attacked by 18 mediums each between H Hour minus 20 and H Hour minus five minutes. All these batteries were capable of interfering with the landings on Utah beach.

In addition the fighter bombers were to attack two coastal batteries in squadron strength. These were Maisy II and Gefosse, both on the eastern shore of the Vire estuary, and both capable of delivering fire on Utah beach. The attacks were to be made between H Hour and H Hour plus 10 minutes.

b.   Intelligence appreciation of assault phase targets.

The nature of these targets is exhibited by Intelligence Section's "Appreciation of Scheduled Targets for 6 June 1944" which follows.

Maisy I

Four emplacements for 155 mm. howitzers consisting of open circular pits 35' in diameter with concrete platform. Attacked 23 May by IX B.C. by blind bombing methods, causing no damage. Casements are under construction in the vicinity.
Weak heavy flak may be encountered.

Pointe du Hoe

Emplacements with six 155 mm. guns. Also casemates under construction. Attacks by IX Bomber Command on 15 April, 22 May and 4 June have damaged all but No. 2 and No. 3 position.
Weak heavy flak may be encountered.

Of the gun batteries listed above as targets, the following have portions of both Utah and Omaha beaches within range:
Maisy I - Maisy II - Gefosse - Pointe du Hoe.
The Barfleur Battery can reach Utah beach.

Maisy II a

Probable 75 mm. field guns in rough open earthen emplacements 20-25 feet in diameter sited in an open field. Range of guns about 13,000 yards.
Weak heavy flak may be encountered.

All of the assignments to IX Bomber Command for the assault phase were carried out. Zero hour had been fixed at 0630. Accordingly the first aircraft involved took off at 0343 hrs.; the last at 0500 hrs. on 6 June. Under these circumstances it was well that much effort had been expended in training flying personnel in formating just before dawn.

The attack on the batteries at Pointe du Hoe, Montfarville and Maisy I, took place between 0625 and 0645 hrs. The results in the first instance were unobserved, in the other two the targets were well covered by the bursts of 1000 and 2000 lb. bombs dropped visually by single boxes accompanied by Pathfinder aircraft.

In attacks against coastal batteries, generally housed in heavy concrete emplacements, hits were reported in the vicinity of the guns, but no physical damage attributable to the bombing was discovered at a later date. It is noteworthy that in all bombing of such targets the effect of other than direct hits may have disrupted controls and communications and demoralized personnel, thus effectively neutralizing the gun position at a critical period.

In addition to their provision of cover and escort the fighter bombers of the Ninth Air Force performed a considerable variety of other missions on D-day. Of the nine special targets assigned to them in the assault phase five were definitely hit. In the remaining cases reports do not exactly specify the target bombed, but indicate that an equivalent target was attacked. The attacks, generally in squadron strength, were delivered between 0550 and 0638 hrs.

The coastal batteries at Maisy II and Gefosse were hit with results reported "good" and "excellent." The attacks were by 18 and 15 aircraft dropping 27 and 20.5 tons respectively.

RAF Bomber Command Reports on Night Operations undertaken on the 5 and 6 June.

SECRET

NIGHT RAID REPORT NO. 625
COPY NO. 44

BOMBER COMMAND REPORT ON NIGHT OPERATIONS

5/6th JUNE 1944 (D-Day)

COASTAL BATTERIES, ETC.

SUMMARY

1.   Over 1,300 aircraft of Bomber Command visited Northern France on the night of the invasion of Western Europe. 1,100 of them attacked coastal batteries between Rouen and Cherbourg; others dropped dummy paratroops, bombed enemy airfields, jammed radar transmissions and posed as naval convoys. 9 bombers and 2 fighters were lost.

5.   Houlgate: Sallennelles: Ouistreham: Mont Fleury: Maisy: Longues OBOE groundmarking with emergency H2S groundmarking. 5 Mosquitos were to mark each target with red T.I. Emergency blind markers either were to release green T.I. on the intersection of an H2S flight line and a GEE lattice line or might release on positive visual identification, if no T.I. were visible. But if T.I. were burning they were to hold their markers. Backers up were to aim green T.I. at the reds, the centre of greens, or the A/P itself if they could identify it visually. Main force crews were to aim at the centre of reds or of greens. H = 0350 at Houlgate; 0030 at Sallennelles; 0505 at Ouistreham; 0435 at Mont Fleury; 0320 at Maisy; and 0420 at Longues. Mosquitos from H-3 to H-1. Emergency blind markers at H-1. Backers up at H+1 and H+2. Main force from H to H+8.

6.   Pointe due Hoe OBOE groundmarking with emergency visual marking. 5 OBOE Mosquitos were to drop red T.I. 5 Group Mosquitos were to back up with green T.I., but if no OBOE markers had been dropped, these Mosquitos were to aim their greens visually at the A/P. The Controller was to assess the accuracy of the markers, and issue a false vector for bombing if necessary. If in force crews were to aim at the centre of their bombsticks at reds or the centre of greens, unless otherwise ordered. H = 0450.

SORTIES

	Desp.	Att.P/A	Abort.	Miss.
La Pernelle	131	115	16	0
Houlgate	116	113	3	0
Mont Fleury	124	113	11	2 (1.6%)
Pointe du Hoc	124	114	10	3 (2.4%)
Maisy	116	112	4	0
Sallennelles	109	88	21	0
Ouistreham	116	114	2	0
Fontenay	101	94	7	0
St.Martin-de-Varreville	100	99	1	0
Longues.....................	99	96	3	1 (1.0%)
TOTAL	1136	1058	78	6 (0.5%)

NARRATIVE OF ATTACKS

11.   Mont Fleury: Maisy: Sallennelles: Fontenay: St.Martin-de-Varrevilles: Longues: Cloud was too dense over these targets for photographs to give any clear poiture of the course of the attacks, but all were reported as fairly well concentrated.

13.   Pointe du Hoc   Reds and greens were well packed around the A/P, and several sticks of bombs were seen to fall across it.

TARGET	GROUP	AIRCRAFT TYPE	SORTIES	A/C REPORTING ATTACK ON		ABORTIVE SORTIES		MISS-ING	D.MAGE				INTERCEPTIONS		RESULTS	
				PRIM. AREA	ALT. AREA	OVER E.T.	NOT OVER E.T.		FLAK	FIGHTER	BRIT. NO. BOMBS	NOT DUE TO E/A	ATTACK-ED	NOT ATTACK-ED	HE.	Inc
POINTE DU HOE	5	Lanc.I	51	47	–	4	–	–	2	–	–	–	2	–	634.8	2.5
		Lanc.III	64	61	–	3	–	3	1	–	–	–	–	3		
		Mosq.IV	4	3	–	1	–	–	–	–	–	–	–	–		
	8	Mosq.IX	3	2	–	1	–	–	–	–	–	–	–	–		
		Mosq.XVI	2	1	–	1	–	–	–	–	–	–	–	–		
POINTE DU HOE			124	114	–	10	–	3	3	–	–	–	2	3		
MAISY	4	Hal.III	93	91	–	–	2	–	1	–	–	1+2AC +1E	1	3	525.2	6.4
		Hal.	13	11	–	–	2	–	–	–	–	–	–	–		
	8	Lanc.III	5	5	–	–	–	–	–	–	–	–	–	–		
		Mosq.XVI	1	1	–	–	–	–	–	–	–	–	–	–		
		Mosq.IX	4	4	–	–	–	–	–	–	–	–	–	–		
MAISY TOTAL			116	112	–	–	4	–	1	–	–	1+2AC +1E	1	3		

A flight direction and mission map titled 'Night Operations 5/6th June 1944 – D-Day.'

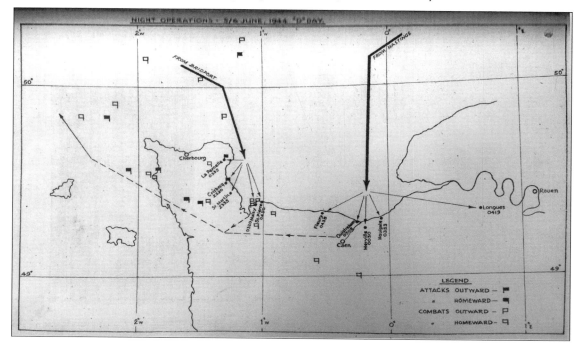

IMMEDIATE.   BY TELEPRINTER.

From:- Headquarters, Bomber Command. 061830/B hrs.

To:- Nos 1 3 4 5 6 8 91 92 93 100 Groups and all Bomber
      Command Stations in those Groups   1 2 3 Bombardment
      Divisions
      Info Admiralty.

BOMBER COMMAND INTELLIGENCE NARRATIVE OF OPERATIONS NO. 818

Covering period 1200 hrs 5th June to 1200 hrs 6th June.

Narrative of Operations.

Day 5th June.   3 Mosquitoes of 8 (P F) Group carried out
     Met. Recce. flights.

Night 5th/6th June.

MAISY C.D.B.   100/106 Halifaxes of 4 Group with 5/5
Lancasters and 5/5 Mosquitoes of 8 (PF) Group bombed the
T.I. which were fairly well concentrated. Weather was good
with 8/10-10/10 cloud at 17/22,000 ft. and 2/10-3/10 at
5/6000 ft.   Opposition was negligible but 2 combats were
reported on the return route. No aircraft are missing.
                                        5/5 Lancasters

Chapter 13

After Action Reports – German

When writing his book – *The Longest Day* – on which the 1962 film was based, author Cornelius Ryan interviewed many of the participants of D-Day from all sides. Within his files are reports which did not make it into his book, yet remain today as first-hand accounts of the men concerned. In this case, here is an interview with Werner von Kistowski. A German officer, who was sent to guard the Maisy Batteries with half of his Flak unit on 5 June. [Author: My thanks go to Ryan's archivist, Doug McCabe, and the staff of Ohio University for all of their help with these, and other Ryan papers.]

Here is another German interview - This is Belt I and it is an interview with Colonel Werner von Kistowski. In 1944 he was age 45. His profession up to 1936 had been that of a naval officer and then he was shifted into the anti-aircraft, the Flak Units. His nickname was "Kisto". He had two young girls and a son. He's tall, well-groomed, erect, even featured, dark blonde hair, blue eyes and must have been quite a dapper colonel in his day.

Kistowski was the commander of a Flak Assault Regiment No. 1 attached to the 3rd Flak Corps. It was fully motorized and it consisted of three artillery groups, the 497th which was a mixed group as was the second one, the 226th and then there was a light anti-aircraft group, the 90th. The two mixed groups had five batteries in all, and the light battery had...or the light group rather had three batteries. Each of the two mixed groups had three batteries apiece. These had in them four 88ths, nine 37ths and twelve 20s. The light battery had 37-mm and 20-mm guns. The entire Flak Regiment had 2,500 men with approximately 600 men to each battery and 100 attached to headquarters and general duties, such as cooks and so on. These men were not all gunners, of course. They were protective infantry which guarded the batteries. Flak Assault Regiment I arrived on the 5th of June in the morning at a place called La Cambe which was their headquarters and it was at the mouth of the Viere at Grandcamp. The light batteries...the light group of batteries was placed at the mouth and the mixed groups were placed at Maisey and stretched across to the outskirts of the town itself of Grandchamps. They had traveled from Trouville on the 3rd, traveling only at night. They dug in on the 5th, just foxholes and camouflaged tents. He was surprised at the move...he wasn't surprised at the move, he was used to it. On one occasion he had actually taken his complete group in by himself into the Caucauses in Russia, so he was quite used to moving suddenly. There'd been no mention of invasion however. He was told he was being moved because of the continual bombing attacks and the planes seemed to be swinging in over Grandcamp as they made their runs into the continent. Anyway, they were tired of invasion alerts and their attitude was "When it comes, it comes." On the evening of the 5th, the Colonel drove to St. Lô to the headquarters of the 84th Corps under the command of Gen. Marcks. He went there for a specific reason. He had been warned that

When looking into German paperwork relating to D-Day, there is not that much available. A lot of the general information we have comes from interviews with German officers from the 352nd Inf. Division, who were part of the opposition to the landings on D-Day. Although relevant, I have decided not to include that much from them because they cover the whole of the Omaha Sector and into the British Sector, on page after page. Therefore I have only included the most relevant and useful German information that can add perspective to this work.

-2-

he should be ready to move again soon and since he had used up all his gasoline he wanted new supplies. He saw the Chief of Staff, a Col. von Criegern and the Quartermaster General and requested gasoline. It was a requirement that he must always have 33,000 litres of gasoline that is enough for a hundred kilometers and his motorized vehicles could not use synthetic gasoline. It had to be the real stuff. The minumum was always 100 kilometers supply. It was about 10 p.m. when he got the okay on the supplies and then he set out for his headquarters at about 11. It was as he was driving back towards La Cambe that he saw the Christmas trees, the flares which had been dropped by aircraft and were hanging in the sky floating down to earth. He said to his engineering officer who was with him, a certain Lt. Col. Busche, "Busche, I think the mess is starting." The bunches of "Christmas trees" hung all the way from Carentan to the mouth of the river at Grandcamp. They drove very slowly as they headed for his headquarters. Then he heard his guns firing and he could see the flashes in the distance. At about 1:43 he sent out a pre-arranged signal to 84th Corps which was "LL" meaning that the invasion had begun. At 1:48 he received a telephone call from the 90th Artillery group that the first POW's paratroopers had been taken. Four had been captured. This was immediately followed by another seventeen near Maisy. These paratroopers fell on a battery between Maisy and Gefoose and Fontenay. He wasn't sure whether these were paratroopers or whether they were bomber crews which had parachuted down to earth. The colonel, who was quite a cool character even though his guns were banging, decided that he had time enough to write to his wife Ruth who lived near Bonne. And since he had rheumatism in his right shoulder he had taken a room in a nearby farmhouse so he wasn't living in a tent. As he wrote, he heard the pounding of the waves of bombers as they flew over and it began to get louder and louder to such an extent that halfway through the letter he wrote "Darling, I must stop now because the bombs are coming too close." So he went out of his farmhouse to his headquarters and shortly after that bombs fell all over. There were reports of paratroopers falling too. He called in the commanding officer...the communications officer, a 1st Lt.Werner Schmidt and he said to him "Schmidt

-3-

send the message." It was then that he sent the message "LL" unquote.

The bombing which then began was described to us by Kistowski as absolutely "hideous". It was just "murder". They cowered in foxholes and the bombs layed a pattern after pattern across their positions. They did not think they could possibly survive the pounding. When they climbed out of these holes, they were absolutely shivering but every time they thought it was going to stop, another wave of planes would come in and no sooner had the air bombardment ceased than the naval bombardment which was much worse, began. All the time in his foxhole he was able to follow the path of the gliders as they were towed in over the mouth of the river Viere passing over Grandcamp. He saw this as he lay in his foxhole cowering under the bombing. And all the time as he lay there he thought to himself "If only this foxhole was smaller". The foxhole itself seemed to him was much too wide and he felt that every shell, every bomb that fell was aimed at him. Instinctively he tried to make himself as small as possible. In fact as he puts it, he was trying to duck and crawl inside his helmet. The moment it let up he lifted his head out of the foxhole and yelled "Schmidt, are you still there"?" Next he called his adjutant, 1st Lt. Gelaubrecht "Are you still alive?" The bombs he remembered which were dropped by the airforces...by the Air Force planes were bombs which detonated just above the ground. They were what is known in our parlance as "Daisy Cutters." He thought how much worse this was than forty days of bombing night after night which he had experienced in Berlin in 1943. And his Communications Officer, Lt. Schmidt, said to him afterwards "Colonel" or no he said to him while the bombers kept going on he called out from his foxhole "Colonel, how I know what my wife is going through in the Ruhr."

When it all stopped the air was filled with the acrid smell of cordite, Both from his own guns and the explosives. Very slowly they came up from their foxholes and even more slowly looked around. The Colonel stood up and one by one saw heads appearing. Everybody was black and covered with dust and everybody was trembling. Some looked around cautiously some were braver than others stood up and stretched. Then everybody got out of the foxholes

-4-

and washed. He got in to his staff and quickly drove to the batteries. The entire Flak Regiment had lost only one man killed and three wounded. He was absolutely amazed. He drove across to Grandchamps and there for the first time he realized the terrible bombard-ment/experienced they because of the huge craters which were all over the ground.

This is the second belt of the interview with Col. Kistowski.

Continuation:

It was while he was at Grandchamps that he happened to look out to sea and there to his amazement he too saw the fleet on the horizon steadily steaming towards the coast. Quickly he drove back to his guns and just as he did the naval bombardment began. Because he had been a former naval officer, he knew how devastating the naval bombardment could be. He knew that it was laid out in squares and that whole areas would automatically be covered so he drove like hell back to his positions. It was during this naval bombardment that one 88-mm gun was destroyed and four or five other smaller ones also, and there was terrific casualties among his men. He forgets now what the casualties were but it was more than a hundred. Now he found that he had no communication except one radio set. He thinks this was due to the "Daisy Cutters" but the real damage was done by the naval shelling. It was different from the air bombardment. It was absolutely "devastating". Now he fully expected the invasion as he watched the fleet come in closer so he ordered his communications officers out on the coast with a small radio as observation posts for his 88-mm guns. The terrible situation which the Colonel found himself in wa s this, that he was caught squarely in the middle, that is he was in along the seam between both Utah and Omaha Beach and his guns could not hit the beaches where the landings were taking place. He could not depress his guns sufficiently to reach these areas and anyway the boats were too far away for his guns to have any effect. He was caught in the middle and he remembers saying to his communications Officer "Damn it if/we were xxxxxxxxxxxxxxxxxxx only a bit to the right or the left we would show them." He never did finish his letter to his wife by the way. He couldn't hear

-5-

his own voice that morning because of the shelling that was taking place. His guns fired right, left and center at the hundreds of planes that came over and by the end of that day he was able to record that his light battery had shot down at 1:38 a B 26, at 1:42 a B 26, at ten minutes past six a lightening, at ten minutes past six another lightening, at 9:15 a thunderbolt; at ten o'clock a thunderbolt, a 4:15 a mustang. To the colonel it was "A very good day , a very good day, indeed, one of the best." One of the planes came down near his own headquarters. There was a terrific fire and the ammunition exploded.

Throughout this morning and the afternoon, the colonel was absolutely on his own with no communications with the 3rd Flak Corps. That was his headquarters and the 84th Corps. General Marcks and the 7th Army had nothing whatsoever to do with them so he never received any orders from them.

On the afternoon of the 6th he decided to move his headquarters to Littry which was the headquarters of the 352nd Division. He had sent one of his officers to Le Mens to telephone to the 3rd Corps to get instructions. Then he set out to move to Littry so as to coordinate his activities with those of the 352nd Division. The night of the...of June 6th he moved out the battery. As I mentioned earlier it didn't worry the colonel to be on his own. He'd once gone into the Caucauses all by himself so it didn't surprise him in the least. So with his battery almost intact and with plenty of ammunition he was ordered out that night. Here again was another case where a group of guns were not used against the invasion fleet. He couldn't move on the 6th because of the strafings but also because he had no gas. ~~gxxxxix~~ His trucks were along a road near St. Germain which was at the very edge of the bomb line apparently. The Allied bombers did not bomb any further inland and so his trucks escaped but the gas didn't arrive until the afternoon of the 6th. He was only able to move one light self-propelled gun that afternoon to a place called Formigny. So here you have a situation well, where five batteries of guns which could have been utilized against the invasion were moved out and were acting without any coordination of orders and were moved out on the afternoon of the 6th but there is one interesting

-6-

point that we should remember about Col. Kistowski's guns and it is simply this. His unit was moved in ~~on the night~~ of the 5th of June and it was his Flak batteries that hit the gliders and the paratrooper planes as they came in over the peninsula and it was this group that caused the paratroopers the U.S.Paratroopers of the 82nd and 101st to be dropped all over the peninsula."

The following report is also written from the German perspective. It was from a 30 January 1947 paper written by Ernst Goettke, Generalleutnant, whilst being interviewed as a prisoner of war – he goes into detail regarding the German defensive operations along the Normandy coast.

MS # B-663   -2-

II. The operational and tactical questions, as well as questions of construction, have been treated by other competent officers, partly with my assistance. I will therefore restrict myself essentially to the subject of army coast artillery.

1. Development

After the occupation of the coast, its artillery protection became necessary. For this purpose, only naval batteries which were yet to be formed were available; their permanent emplacement required considerable time and they were not available in sufficient numbers. They had therefore to be supplemented by army coast batteries which consisted of heavy guns with flat projecting and stationary medium batteries. The originally minor sphere of duties of the coast artillery developed into the following tasks after the plan of landing in Britain had been abandoned:

a. Action against installations on the British coast (only by few heavy flat projecting batteries),

b. Action against enemy convoys,

c. Protection of our own coastal shipping,

d. Action against enemy landing operations,

e. Action against landed enemy,

2. The troops.

The formations of the army coast artillery were newly activated in Zone of Interior. The officers were taken from older classes_____, a few of them having been in the regular army, whilst

MS # B-663   -3-

the majority consisted of former reserve officers of the first world
war who had first to be inducted for this new employment; some were
younger officers no more fit for front service, NCO's and men also
came from older age classes. On account of the severe drain on
manpower to meet the requirements of the field troops and of the new
formations of coast artillery, which latter were now needed for the
entire European coast,--Norway, Denmark, France, Italy, Greece, and
the Mediterranean Isles, Dalmatia, the Black Sea Coast, the Baltic
Sea and the North Sea--the age of the men in the units constantly rose.

It became increasingly difficult to train the physically
deficient and elder men, and also the grades necessary for the many
sided duties in the coast artillery. This service required great
flexibility, since every man had to be trained to serve with two heavy
weapons; as an infantry man and in the signal service, as an observer
or in accountancy service. The numbers of the men in the batteries
had to be kept as low as possible on account of personnel shortage
and totaled no more than 60-90 men, according to the caliber of the
guns.

3. Armament

a. Each battery had 3-6 major guns, 1-4 light rapid
firing guns for use in landward defense, against nearby objectives and
for air defense; 2-6 light or medium machine guns and small arms; and,
furthermore, mortars and mine projectors according to requirements.

b. Vehicles and horses were only assigned for the most
urgent supply service; if it became necessary to render a battery
mobile, emergency means had to be used.

MS # B-663   -4-

        c. The major guns for the entire coast artillery
consisted of a few batteries of 21 cm howitzers (much too slow and
unwieldy for use against sea targets); further of 17 cm, 15 cm, 10.5
cm, and 8.8 cm cannons, and a number of guns, the majority of which
were of small caliber.

        The greater majority of all batteries had to be made
up from captured guns. This resulted in a mixture of all types and
calibers, mostly French 10.5 cm; Russian 12.5 cm and 8.8 cm, and
Italian 10.5 cm cannons.

        d. All guns were constructed for mobile land commitment.
They had to be placed on emergency pivots for fire on sea targets.
Our industry was not able to furnish the essentially necessary
turnable ground platforms before 1944. Since these deliveries were
extremely slow in coming forward, only very few batteries had received
their guns and fire control equipment which rendered them really
capable of firing on sea targets and fast moving landing craft when
invasion began.

    4. Ammunition

        The same applied to the issue of ammunition; the
quantities available were in most cases adequate for battles of long
duration. However, there was practically no armor piercing ammunition for the medium guns since they had originally been intended for
land combat. Hence effective fire on the armor plating of warships
could hardly be expected.

III. During the first stages after the occupation of the coasts, the

MS # B-663   -5-

conduct of battle contemplated was active, i.e., offensive-defense.

That is, it was planned to hold down the attacking fleet with coast

artillery fire and to prevent landing or to pin down the attacks

locally in cooperation with the coastal garrisons until mobile units

of navy and air force could intervene. Later however, when the enemy

gained superiority on the sea and in the air, the preparations had

more and more to be confined to passive defense.

          2. We had no experience in defensive combat on the coast.

Operations and attacks on strong points and single batteries on the

Norwegian, French, and Black Sea coasts in 1941-43, only confirmed

that a superior enemy will always first gain local successes, mainly

by surprise and sudden attack, but that the commitment of local

reserves alone will in most cases beat him back. The successful

enemy landings in Sicily and Italy did not allow for conclusions

applicable to the completely different situation on the French coast

since, when the landing took place south of Rome, defense preparations

on the coast in that region did not ~~correspond with the situation on~~ *answer the requirements of*

defensive combat ~~the French coast~~, from the artillery point of view, in respect of the

stage reached in the development of constructions, or as far as the

garrisoning with troops was concerned.

          3. Two views resulted for the conduct of defensive combat

in case of a major landing:

          a. Strongest development of the coastal fronts with

all technical means on the entire front--mainly so on the Dutch--

Belgian and French north coasts--strong artillery and infantry manning

of defense installations, in order to repel any landing and to immediately clear-up successful penetrations with local reserves.

      b.   Development of good strong points with all-round defense; the main body of troops to be held in reserve, the strong points to tie down the landed enemy forces until the reserves were ready for active intervention. In both these cases the artillery's mission would be action against all floating enemy units, prevention of landing, action against landed enemy with all-round fire in co-operation with and for the support of the land artillery.

      The decision reached for the conduct of battle was according to a.

      4.   The commander's request to keep the army coast batteries mobile, so that transfers could take place from unattacked units to support of attacked units, was futile as firing on sea targets is only possible from fixed emplacements with fire directed from fire direction centers and radio locator stations; furthermore, both materiel and personnel available were quite insufficient for mobile commitment. Also, it was essential to build in the guns as solidly as possible in concrete emplacements on account of the expected severe air attacks and fire from heavy ships artillery, so that mobile commitment was impossible.

      5.   The following had to be requested and was planned for these massive constructions:

      a.   Every battery should be a strong point, a compact combat installation surrounded by strong obstacles and in itself divided up into individual combat installations; every man, including

MS # B-663   -7-

artisans, cooks, and clerks was to be armed and trained for close combat. Considering the age and disabilities of the majority of the men, this was a tall order which could not always be met.

b. Building-in of guns into concrete bunkers, which considerably restricted the angle of traverse. In compensation, light-medium and medium batteries of guns of light construction were assigned to the heavy batteries; these were kept in bomb-proof shelters and were only to be moved in the event of an actual battle, into various gun positions prepared beforehand and committed there for all-round fire.

c. Improvement of bomb proof shelters for troops, medical stations, and ammunition stores.

d. Equipment with mine projectors and mortars, machine guns, small arms, armor piercing ammunition, hand grenades and Panzer-fausts. This equipment made it necessary that every man employed at the battery be trained in the use of several arms besides the major gun, and assigned to man them.

e. Constant maintenance of a big ammunition and ration supply. The stocks requested were: Ammunition supply for 30 days of battle and rations for 50 days, these stocks could often not be fully supplied and their storing encountered considerable difficulties.

f. Underground cable connection within the strong points, and outside to the command agencies and adjacent strong points.

g. Assignment of mobile observers and assault troops for combat against enemy air landings.

MS # B-663   -8-

   h. Preparation for cooperation with the adjacent batteries
and infantry strong points in the case of successful enemy landings.

   i. Preparations for pulling out and improvized mobility
of the medium guns as reinforcement artillery for commitment in other
front sectors.

   j. Preparation of the mutual fire control and observation by fire direction center and radio direction finder stations of
neighboring batteries, with the purpose of exploiting the full range
of fire in flanking fire support.

   6. Since the measures requested and planned in No. 5
only became necessary once, air superiority had definitely passed
over to the enemy powers, execution was only definitely ordered in
1943. The assembly and bringing up of the necessary labor forces,
of the materiel, machines, and equipment and the establishment of the
construction organization required a certain period of time for getting
started. Transport conditions, aggravated by increasing air action
required still more time, so that the stage of construction reached
when invasion began was only adequate with the naval coast batteries
--mainly with the heavy batteries
on the Channel coast,--where construction had started at a much earlier
date. The majority of the army coast batteries were still in field
type positions or construction had reached a more or less advanced
stage. We had to reckon with neutralization or complete destruction
of these batteries by air attacks or enemy ships' artillery, which was
superior as regards range and caliber. This is why the battle directives
and emergency fire direction for each battery were currently adjusted

MS # B-663   -9-

according to the momentary stage of construction.

IV. Command

        1. Up to 1940, coast artillery was the sole concern of the
navy. The rapid expansion of the defense zone over all European
coasts, caused such an increase in artillery requirements that the
navy was hardly able to do more than take over the existing permanent
batteries, reinforcing and supplementing such of them as were at
main centers of gravity. Further reinforcement of the main defense
sectors and of nearly the entire intermediate area was entrusted to
the newly formed coast artillery.

        2. The entire coast artillery was intended essentially for
seaward firing, and hence control had to be centralized in the
naval command authorities, that is with the naval commanders. Their
coast sectors being far too extensive for a centralized control,
groups were formed under the command of Coast Artillery Sector Commanders, the boundaries of which sectors generally corresponded with
the boundaries of divisional sectors; the groups were divided into
sub-groups. Regimental, battalion, and detachment commanders of the
Army and Navy were assigned as group and sub-group commanders. The
groups frequently consisted of combined army and naval battalions and
batteries. Training took place in separate groups of army and naval
artillery in coast artillery schools, under supervision of the General
of the Army coast artillery and the inspector of naval coast artillery.

MS # B-663   -10-

    3. The formation described in No. 2, which only came into effect for all fronts in 1943, guaranteed that, in case of combat on land, as many guns could be turned onto landed enemy by the local coast artillery commander, as the combat situation at sea allowed. The elements of the army coast artillery and of the navy committed landwards, then came under the command of the land army's command authorities.

    4. The combined use of army and naval artillery for the same tasks, led to the following difficulties:

        a. different expressions in the command language of army and navy.

        b. the very unequal standard of training, as the navy was only supplementing its units and was numerically better off than the army, which had to organize everything anew by improvization.

        c. very unequal material equipment. See I no. 2 and 3.

        d. Different kinds of sighting devices, of which those of the army artillery were optically inadequate for firing seawards, as they were only provided for land commitment.

    These difficulties and shortcomings were not completely overcome by the time invasion commenced, however, they were greatly reduced by mutual training courses, detail duties, and joint exercises. The army had to be trained in seaward action, just as the naval artillery had to be newly trained in firing on land targets and in land combat.

    5. The air defense batteries of the Luftwaffe were also incorporated to defensive combat against landed enemy and for this

MS # B-663   -11-

combat task were subordinated to the army command authorities. As

far as their disposition allowed, the batteries of the naval flak

artillery too were incorporated for seaward combat. All antiaircraft

automatic weapons of army and navy were also made available for

commitment in ground combat.

6. In all exercises, map exercises and map maneuvers,

special value was placed on training all commanders, down to battery

commanders, to act independently in any situation, in the event of

communications being severed or if orders failed to arrive; the same

applied to all officers in charge of guns and troops.

In case of encirclement, all battery commanders had the

authority and duties of a fortress commander.

Signed: Ernst Goettke

Generalleutnant

Paragraph 6 of the above report might go some way in answering a point which is regularly raised, that of the operational capabilities of the guns found behind Pointe du Hoc. Those found by Lomell and Rupinski's patrols had not been put into action by their crews, despite it being 9am when they were discovered. Reading between the lines of this report, which describes standard German operational procedures, it could be reasonable to suggest that there may not have been any officers in that area to organise the firing of those guns on 6 June.

The following is an excerpt from a report written by Oberstlb. Ziegelmann, who wrote much about the history of the 352nd Inf. Div. for the US Army. The interesting points here are the mention of the French intelligence operatives sending information via pigeon. He specifically mentions the batteries of the 716th Artillery and Kistowski's Flak Regiment No 1. This is confirmation from the Germans, that close to D-Day the French spies were again telling the Allies of the artillery at Maisy and of the arrival of the Flak unit. This corresponds exactly with the information stated by Jean Marion in his interview with Cornelius Ryan.

II. The Invasion

In the last days of May there was increased activity of enemy air reconnaissance which was also by night (night photography). I myself witnessed the low-level flight of single airplanes on the coast which must have been of importance for reconnaissance (perhaps photographic reconnaissance) because an attack on objectives on the ground did not occur. Messenger pigeon activity, which was more acute than before, is a special chapter, containing mainly statements with regard to rearward installations. They were only of importance for the enemy air force. But one message concerned us. The writer stated he lived in Criqueville south Grandcamps, and gave information about the II Arty Regt 1716; about new anti-aircraft units (anti-aircraft Regt 1); and increases in the construction of coastal zone obstacles near Grandcamp. He did not believe that a landing at Grandcamp would be successful. During the last days of May there were bombing raids on the Army coast battery, on the "Pont de Hoc" (3/1260) and on the positions of the II Arty Regt 1716 which led to partial failure of the artillery; also on the direction finder stations of the Air Forces and Navy so that these were not available for assignment, except to a limited extent.

Chapter 14

After Action Reports – Personal Accounts

Lieutenant Richard Oliphant was onboard USS *Ancon* on D-Day. On 10 July he recorded the following memories of Pointe du Hoc during a post 6 June visit.

INSPECTED POINTE DU HOE

A dusty bumpy ride in an Army truck brought us to Trevieres an absolute junk heap of a monument to our Navy's heavy guns. There were no Germans there only peasants trying with the aid of hand carts to pull what little was left out of their homes and take it God knows where. Brave little flags hung from wrecked windows. The French tricolor, the British and American flags. The American flags were sad little efforts that no more than suggested their intention but for all that, such a welcome sign. Mr. Pommier, mayor of the little town of 900 inhabitants greeted us and posed for a snapshot. He was very much a French offical with his store clothes and straw hat. He had leather shoes on his feet, not make-shift canvas affairs. The police station had been knocked about too, but they were all making the best of it and order was slowly coming out of the wreckage.

Many were sorry for their loss of live stock by which they lived. One man had lost 19 cows. And then, too, the village dead amounted to 20 odd. Still no one seemed to take more than a philosophic, c'est la guerre manner.

Perhaps the most talked of and shattered strongpoint in our sector was the formidable battery installed at Pointe du Hoe. This battery was in a position to sweep our beaches with its heavy guns and so it had to be eliminated and was.

When we got to it, it was discovered that the heavy guns had been removed. Apparently our intentions were suspected beforehand, but the heroism of the Rangers, etc. in going up, the bloody fighting for the defense of that position was in way mitigated by the fact that the guns were moved inland a bit.

I got a ride in a Jeep with a French colonel who had just arrived from London and maintained his French superiority and attitude through out all our conversation. Only a Frenchman can be as superior as a Frenchman when they go at it and nothing can be more irritating. He was critical of our heavy gun fire which had destroyed so many lovely things. Why bother to ask whether it was better to destroy them and save lives and free France. It does no good with that kind. Anyway I was grateful for the ride and though I thanked him for it I felt as though a little thanks might not have been amiss on his part for the American troops had seen to it that he could once more drive in freedom down the roads of Normandy and in an American jeep with an American driver at that.

I found some American signalmen and asked for the location of the battery. There was one they said, not far back in the direction from whence I had come. How to get there? You see that sign saying "Mines" asked the G. I.?

I saw only too well the German sign warning against mines.

"Well, go over to it," he continued, "and go through the field and you will come to the battery."

"What about the mines?" I stammered.

"Weve been over there. You'll find a path. It hasn't been swept yet but they did not go off on us.

Swallowing hard I went over. It was no good turning back now and gingerly through the mine field I made my way to the battery. The field was now well ploughed with craters made by our air and sea bombardment. It no longer looked like land that was tillable but like a dry desert where earthquakes had tossed every living thing into confusion beyond all recognition. The first strong point had been shattered but still stood.

A table in the little dugout behind it bore a knife and fork and mess kits covered over with dirt and debris and live ammunition in broken boxes spilled in every direction. I picked up a shoulder strap of a German non-com. Where the rest of the uniform and the rest of the man in it went, no one knows. Near it a shaving brush and all matter of little personal things were strewn. A water bottle was cast on a crater's edge. Everywhere there were papers and photographs and hand grenades.

Proceeding out to the point, to the heavier an-d heaviest strong points, the story was the same. Though not a long walk, it became one, for the tortuous ascent and descent into craters, stumbling over loose clods of earth was endless. In one place the battery installation was completely buried. In the next, completely blasted to smithereens.

                    SAW EVIDENCE OF RANGERS

The strong point on the outermost position was still very much intact and lying about it were the evidence of recent tenantcy. A half dozen bicycles now solely reduced to wreckage, that not a whole one could have been made from the parts that lay around.

I picked up a gas mask to see the kind Jerry used. I looked and found the legend, made in the US. The Rangers had been there. From there on around the point the story of the Rangers taking that heavily defended position was written everywhere. A low lying ditch to the seaward of the emplacement told its graphic story and first aid bandages and opened rations, partly eaten and lying around with grenades and ammunition. Here under this perilous little shelter the Rangers had stopped for a bit in their heroic advance. Farther on a grappling hook was caught fast in the dirt. Here, then was where the Rangers had succeeded in scaling the bluff. But no, looking farther one came to the frayed end of the rope and Jerry had cut it and dropped any Rangers coming up the ladder back on to the beach.

Sunk below the level of the cliff and pointing its guns out to s-ea was

On 16 July Captain Runge, F Company 5th Battalion Rangers wrote the following letter to his comrade Sgt. Howard McDonald who had been wounded on D-Day. [Author's collection. Some of the names are indistinct in his letter].

16th July 1944
'France'

Dear Mac
I was sure glad to get your letter of the 19th June. I was pretty worried for a while as you were the only one of the Company I couldn't find any trace of. Mac, I don't know how bad you were hit. From what I could find out you were hit in the arm, leg, and maybe chest. I know you'll come out OK so keep on writing. I'll try to tell you a little bit of

another emplacement. In the depression in the cliffs before its guns the Rangers had made their way up. Still trailing down the face of the bluff was the thin ladder they had used. Scattered about the depression below the snub noses of the big guns were first aid supplies. Merciful cans of ether, yards of bandages and miraculous sulfa powders, food knapsacks.

The path of progress led around to the entrance to the concrete emplacement and in it, mixed in unrecognizable confusion, were Jerry and American supplies and equipment. So easy to see, after it was all over, where the marks of the bitter struggle, the hand to hand battle which ended after two days in the relief of the Rangers by our forces. The Rangers had carried out the mission assigned. The struggle was over when I went there but it will always be the high point of the battle in my mind. But the trail of wounded and dying men surging up over the cliff to victory was as plain still in the wreckage left behind them as it had been that first day. As I made my way back to the road the effects of the action slowly disappeared until in the field near the road, but still in sight of Pointe de Hoe, found two French peasants tilling their field. The barn and house were destroyed, but the crops were still being tended and would find their way to the table at the proper time.

the happenings in this letter and some more in following letters. If you have any questions, or anything I can do for you, let me know.

D-Day there were 3 killed and 8 wounded on the beach. They were Bob Miller, Bernard Loboda and Howard Gardner, all by artillery fire were killed. Rosenblad, Minor, Hard, Baker, Sorenson, Ovington, were hit on the beach and Smolich just back of the beach.

D+2 Edward Mapes was wounded when we were advancing down a road.

D+3 Muscatello, Pasuk, and Fogel were wounded when the company attacked an artillery position.

Mac, the company did a great job and you would have really been proud of them. The Btn was awarded the 'Presidential Unit Citation' which I will send you your ribbon when they are issued.

They are the same as every man in the Btn winning the D.S.C. It is a blue ribbon with a gold frame (wood) border worn on the right ride of the blouse.

The 1st Plat. boat was sinking on the way in so we had to cut the motor then we hailed an L.C.T. and came in on it. We landed about a mile to the left of the Btn. Fought there the first two days. Took a hill knocking out 3 pill boxes, and OP and trench system. Capturing 36 Germans, killed eight. Major Street of Army who had been with the 1st Rangers found us the 2nd day and loaded us in a L.C.V.P. and we went down to reinforce 70 men holding the "Point" all that were left of D,E,F of the 2nd. Lt. Reville, Sander(?), Sigambia(?), Gibbons, Pasuk, Mapes, Muscatello, Lewis, and myself went through on a patrol from the Point down the coast and contact the 116th and the XXX(?) coming up the coast, on D+1 night. We did this the next day and the Pointe was completely knocked out. There were no guns there but six big pillboxes.

A,C,F went right down the road into enemy territory – Mapes got hit on the move. Set up a perimeter defence that night. On D+3 we attacked an artillery position with 4 pillboxes and trenches. Captured 86 prisoners there, don't know how many dead. That's about all I can tell you Mac. Lost 2 good men yesterday. Had moved Harris and Rogers to the 1st Plat. Harris stepped on a 'Bouncing Betty' yesterday and was killed. One of the round buck shot broke Roger's leg. That makes 13 out of the 1st Plat. We've got replacements but they're not like the old bunch. The total so far is 4 killed, 13 wounded requiring evacuation, and 3 wounded not requiring evacuation. We suffered less loss than any assault company in either Btn. But even then we've had 30%. Well, Mac don't forget us.

Sincerely yours
Capt. Runge.

PS you should have seen me struggling through the cemetery trying to find you. Muscatello was shot clean through the throat, but didn't hit a thing and I expect him back any day.

Chapter 16

Conclusion

History is the last thing we care about
during operations, and the first thing we
want afterwards. Then it is too little, too
late, and too untrue.

                              W. A. GANOE
                              Colonel, GSC
                              Theater Historian, ETOUSA.

i) Messages and Flares

Winding up all of the new evidence available and straightening it out was never going to be easy. Over the years there have been a great many made-up stories, bogus reports and, as you will see, accounts of things often simply invented by some, about the events of D-Day – especially those events at Pointe du Hoc.

The best place to start is with the Small Unit Actions Report, which was taken primarily from first person interviews with around 120 of the Rangers concerned in that battle; it is said to have been written within one month of the Pointe du Hoc action having taken place. As such, it has to be assumed that it is pretty accurate.

There are areas within it which are worthy of further scrutiny, and I looked at some of it for accuracy and the attention to detail that it contains, especially given new information. All of this helps us have a greater understanding of the events.

For example, a couple of significant lines read: *The main Ranger flotilla, eight companies strong, was following in from the transports, watching anxiously for the signal of success at Pointe du Hoe (two successive flares shot by 60-mm mortars) ….. and later on it continues. By 0700, if no message or signal had come, Colonel Schneider's force was scheduled to adopt the alternate plan of action and land at the Vierville beach.*

Whilst researching for this book, I found the actual radio communications between the landing forces, Pointe du Hoc and USS *Ancon* within the US archives. These are the original messages from that time – just as they were received – and I also found the post-battle 'official' reports, which used these same reports to build up their narrative. As an example, this original radio message was sent at 06 (6 June) 0645hrs to General Gerow from Colonel Talley.

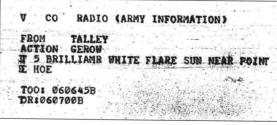

V	CO	RADIO (ARMY INFORMATION)
FROM	TALLEY
ACTION	GEROW
IT 5 BRILLIAMR WHITE FLARE SUN NEAR POINT
IL HOE
TOO: 060645B
DR:060700B

To explain the procedure: when each of the messages arrived on the command ship, they would record the time it was received and responded to – and each message was then stuck onto a page for legibility and filing. The above is an example of this message received in its original format. They are later typed up post-battle into what then becomes the 'official' historical version, as can be seen displayed in most After Action Reports.

These should represent a 100 per cent accurate report of what happened and it makes them of the highest importance historically to anyone looking into the events of the day. I would think that any current serving US Navy officer would agree that these facts are of the utmost importance for historical study after any conflict.

I found it strange that this message was marked as received by USS *Ancon* in their messages list at 0700hrs, some fifteen minutes after it was sent. The strange thing about that is that it was a radio message – so it should have been received instantly the moment that it was sent and not fifteen minutes later. To prove that, here we have both the same messages – the original (previous page) and the later typed-up version shown (below) and yet they do not have matching times.

Also odd is that some of the received messages appear to have changed or been 'dumbed down' in translation, from the original message that was sent, to the final polished and presented product. For example you *could* read Colonel Talley's message to say: '*5 brilliant white flares on / near Pointe du Hoe.*' – a very slight change in the interpretation of the wording – but one which would be very significant to the fate of the Rangers.

The message translated into the 1st Inf. Div. journal reads in the singular '*Brilliant white flare seen near Pointe du Hoe.*' Does this discrepancy mean anything? It may have been of huge importance if the message had been passed back to Schneider's force floating around awaiting news from Pointe du Hoc at 0645hrs. Had they been told of the 'flare' or 'flares', then they almost certainly would have landed at the Pointe – considering that they were waiting for a signal that could come via that very specific method and at that moment in time.

There are often alphabetical spelling mistakes found and accepted in these radio reports – but why does the number 5 appear at the start of the message, if it is not significant to that message. The re-affirming of the number 4 on the repeated message from Talley some time later (also see further below) increases the significance of the 5 to be more accurate at the time. i.e. 4 or 5 flares were seen – and he is confirming that to someone when asked to clarify it.

The USS *Ancon* version which has been retyped *for the record* is changed. Note the time is now recorded and has the message timing as coming in to the *Ancon* at 0700hrs. Coincidentally, this was the very time at which the larger Ranger force was supposed to change direction from landing at PdH and instead go to the beach. The different time potentially puts its significance AFTER the point of no return for Schneider's force to land on the beach.

0700	10	Talley	Brilliant white flare seen near POINTE DE HOE.	Rad	V Corps & J

The message was changed to omit the number of flares seen. By whom and for what reason this change was made, I do not know – but there IS a deliberate amendment/omission to this record. There is no natural explanation I can find for the fifteen minutes' time difference between the two reports. It could be 'fog of war' and someone making a mistake or that someone didn't deliver the message quickly enough because they were 'busy', etc. Indeed, if it were a simple typing error, then this one single mistake knocks out the running order and timing of every other message for the day – and it raises the question: was it done deliberately? Why was this message changed, and who had the ability to do that – and even more importantly, why would they want to change it?

Once I spotted the anomaly on this one radio message, I examined the other Pointe du Hoc / Rangers messages.

From the 0718 entry 'No. 12', on the report is another example. It seems that someone must have queried the number of rocket flares seen by Col. Talley and his response comes back as a definite '*4 Rockets fired*'. By now this entry has no historical significance, because it is indicated in the After Acton Report to have been received at 0718hrs, a time long after the Ranger force started steaming towards Omaha Beach.

It has now become a simple, yet meaningless entry within the log.

0718	12	Talley	4 Rockets fired.	Rad	V Corps & J

But it begs the question, did the Rangers send some flares up from their LCAs whilst they were off course during their navigational error? Certainly something was seen by Col. Talley and he was reporting on what he had witnessed and at what time. It is another example of something which was insignificant to the man in place at the time – yet it turns into potentially a very significant event with a greater historical importance all these years later.

Further evidence of anomalies come forward again, with the timings from the original of the above message. I found reference to the original message in the archives and it was in reality sent at 0629 and not at 0718hrs, when it is marked as being received. In fact it was sent **before** the other message giving more specific details of the flares. The running order of these messages is wrong in the finished, presented report and the timings have been messed around with – or was it simply a mistake in the filing of all these messages, perhaps?

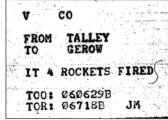

```
V       CO

FROM    TALLEY
TO      GEROW

IT 4 ROCKETS FIRED

TOO: 060629B
TOR: 06718B    JM
```

The historical significance of this should not be underestimated, given that at first glance, someone involved in the recording of these documents appears to have changed some of them later in the official historical records and/or not recorded what happened accurately. Is it conceivable that the Rangers did fire some flares from their LCAs when they realized they were heading to the wrong place (Pointe et Raz de la Percée) – and thus they tried to get the rest of the Ranger force to land sooner, or even ahead of them? That would account for flares being seen at that earlier time of 0629hrs – and that is coincidentally by one minute the exact time when Lt. Col. Rudder was supposed to have landed at the Pointe. He must have been acutely aware that he would not get there on time because of the navigational misdirection of his force, and perhaps he tried to do something about instructing the other group to come in sooner?

It could have taken that long to process the radio report onboard ship and deliver it to those who needed it – but it was a very bad time to have a delay in receiving time-critical operational communications.

That leads us on to a further line of enquiry. If Rudder's party had sent up flares – and they were known about by his superiors and then ignored by them – the consequence of this would guarantee Rudder's main, second force would go into Omaha Beach instead of going to help him.

A further pointer is another G-3 entry which states at 0737hrs *Success signal from Pointe du Hoc reported by V Corps observer on Dukw.* It seems accurate, because coincidentally in the SUA Report it states: *'By 0725, 1st Lt. James W. Eikner had his equipment set up and flashed word by SCR 300 that Colonel Rudder's force had landed.'* But… this message was seen, and not heard by the observer on the DUKW, and then reported in to USS *Ancon.* When you look at the timing of the wording, which is housed within the message (shown below). The "success signal from Pointe du Hoc" comes before the "first wave foundered" message, which is logged in at 0641hrs. Thus suggesting that the DUKW observer also saw the flares that Major Tally did around 0629hrs - and yet nothing was done about it. Therefore we have to question, were the flares sent as a direction signal because a radio message was not physically possible at that time?

| 0737 | 14 | CTF 124 | First wave landed DOG GREEN 0635, second wave 0636, first wave assault group O-1 landed 0635 X One LCA capsized X One LCT (A) sinking with engine room flooded X Success signal from POINTE DU HOE reported by V CORPS observer on DUKW X Unconfirmed report from PC 552 that first wave on FOX GREEN foundered. | Rad | NCWTF & J |

The original message is timed 0737hrs which is 100 per cent correct. So it appears with other messages – standard ones, that 'as normal' came in and were marked with the same time sent as they were received – in the reports. I investigated the normal procedure for messages to be sent and they would have either been sent via Aldis (signal) lamp in Morse Code – which could generate a delay with the Morse Code being translated back into plain English by the receiver – or a signal via radio – which produced simultaneous and matching 'sent and received' times. As you can see from these Radio Reports, these messages were all sent and received by radio and thus would normally have the same matching times on them – but they do not.

```
V EC         VISUAL    P
FROM         CTF 124
TO           NCWTF
FIRST WAVE LANDED DOG GREEN 0635 SECOND WAVE
0636, FIRST WAVE ASSAULT GROUP O-1 LANDED
0635 X ONE LCA CAPSIZED X ONE LCT(A) SINKING
WITH ENGINE ROOM FLOODED X SUCCESS SIGNAL
FROM POINTE DU HOE REPORTED BY V CORPS
OBSERVER ON DUKW X UNCONFIRMED REPORT FROM
PC 552 THAT FIRST WAVE ON FOX GREEN FOUNDEREDX
050737
```

Another example of simplifying and thus changing the contents of an original Rangers-related message historically, is this one. The first version was received at 0945 – exactly and correctly at the same time it was sent – and it says *'Message 49 – Batteries at Maisy completely destroyed.'* It was received by radio and given to the Commanding General (CG).

| 0945 | 49 | Div Bat5 | Btrys at MAISY completely destroyed. | Rad | CG, G-3, J. |

The original of the above message is shown on the next page (before it was rewritten later) and it reads as follows: *'Last report from plane was that Batteries at Maisy were completely destroyed, have been unable to verify from SFCP. Number 1 batteries have not fired at anytime during the night.'*

This says that there was no confirmation on the ground that the batteries had stopped firing, simply that they had not been seen to fire overnight. This message would not have been sent to Rudder, but it also would not have made a difference or had any impact on his force because by 0945hrs – some 45 minutes after the Rangers had destroyed the PdH guns – Rudder and his men should have been long gone from the Pointe and been on their way to Maisy anyway.

The cutting down of the message in the eventual report adds a degree of finality to it, yet it is something which may have left room for doubt, had it been relayed in full, as sent.

There is another strange paragraph in the Small Unit Actions Report from a similar moment, which refers to Schneider's force waiting for messages from the Pointe. It reads: *'By 0700, if no message or signal had come, Colonel Schneider's force was scheduled to adopt the alternate plan of action and land at the Vierville beach. They waited ten minutes beyond the time limit and then received by radio the code word TILT, pre-arranged signal to follow the alternative plan.'*

```
SB              VISUAL

FROM DIV BAT 5
ACTION CTF 124

LAST REPORT FROM PLANE WAS THAT BATTERIES
AT MAISY WERE COMPLETLY DESTROYED HAVE
BEEN UNABLE TO VERIFY FROM SFCP NUMBER      L
ONE BATTERIES HAVE NOT FIRED AT ANYTIME
DURING NIGHT X BT 060945
```

We know that Lt. Col. Rudder did not send that message at that time for the rest of the Rangers to land at Omaha beach – he had lost supplies and equipment on the way in – and he knew he needed their help on the cliff top, so why in fact would he turn them away?

Working on the assumption that this message was not sent by Rudder to Schneider as implied in the SUA Report – I wanted to investigate who had sent this message? We do know that it was received by radio on the LCA belonging to Lt. Col. Schneider and is timed at 0710hrs – which is very precise.

The SUA Report for the same time states: *By 0725, 1st Lt. James W. Eikner had his equipment set up and flashed word by SCR 300 that Colonel Rudder's force had landed. Five minutes later he sent out the code word indicating 'men up the cliff'; the 'Roger' that receipted for this message, again on SCR 300, was Eikner's last communication of D-Day on the Ranger command net. When he sent the message PRAISE THE LORD ('all men up cliff') at 0745, no response was forthcoming.*

Somebody sent Lt. Col. Schneider's group the message 'TILT' at 0710 and it was not Lt. Col. Rudder. As it says in the passage above, he did not have the ability to communicate via radio until 0725hrs, a point which might further indicate that it was Rudder who sent up flares as a signal instead.

When he was able to send a message by radio to confirm that his force had landed, it was too late to affect what was already in motion. Therefore whoever did send the 'TILT' message, did so knowing that they were directing the rest of the Rangers towards the beach and leaving Rudder's smaller force to its fate.

The SUA report is vague in that it does not say who sent the message, but it records it: *'At 0710, as the first craft were grounding under the cliffs, radio silence was broken to send Colonel Schneider the order for landing at Vierville. The message was acknowledged.'*

As a message, it is somewhat obscured by other messages being erroneously recorded late in the official records around the same time. It is true – the message was sent at the exact time the force needed to make their decision – so the question is, did someone take the decision for them, and if so, who was it?

To recap and help to put it into context:

Schneider's force was sailing around in terrible conditions needing direction. It was available to them via the flares but they were not told about them. They were then sent a message to go to the beach at the point in time when Rudder's force actually needed them the most at Pointe du Hoc.

Had these signal flares been seen at the time – they would surely have been most effective as a signal to the rest of the Rangers? Without corroboration, it is difficult to say. But I eventually found the evidence from another source to tell me who sent the the 'TILT' message and it does in some way explain why the information was not available to the writers of the Small Unit Action Report back in 1944.

To understand the lack of communication in both directions, I first looked at the radio equipment carried by Lt. Col. Rudder and his men. To have direct communication with Schneider's group, the Rangers would have needed a radio that could transmit and receive beyond just a couple of miles. The timing of Schneider's force arriving on Omaha Beach goes some way to confirm that they were a distance away, because even after receiving the 'TILT' order, the report states: '*So Colonel Schneider turned in toward Vierville, where the 5th Rangers and A and B of the 2nd landed at 0745.*'. Thus they were 35 minutes away at the time of the message … or were they? It is probable that the men of the US Army, who put together and collated the SUA Report, had not seen or had access to the British Royal Naval After Action Reports.

A small section from the HMS *Prince Charles* After Action Report states that Schneider's force arrived at 0753hrs – a discrepancy of eight minutes. That would mean that potentially the group of craft led by Schneider was further away by perhaps another mile than it was indicated by the Small Unit Action's version of events.

When fully loaded, the LCA had a top speed of 6 knots/6.9 miles per hour – suggesting that Schneider was approximately 5 or 6 miles from the beach – and accounting for the heavy seas, he may have been around 3.5 miles from Pointe du Hoc when he diverted. This is an estimate, as the poor conditions could have pushed or pulled his force and delayed him even further. Therefore, to make a signal work directly between Rudder and Schneider, they needed to have a radio system capable of communicating a number of miles and in poor weather conditions.

From the SUA Report, three types of radio are stated as being used.

SCR 284. The SCR 284 transmitter had a range of hundreds of miles and it comprised a receiver, power unit together with all necessary equipment to make it work – but it weighed more than 100 pounds and it is described as being moved as follows: '*Tech. 4 C. S. Parker and two other communications men hefted the big radio set on a pack board, and managed to get it in and working before the first climbers from 722 reached the top.*'

Although capable of sending the 'TILT' or any other signal to the following Ranger group, it was not set up and operational at a time when the message was received by Schneider. It was simply too big to set up and operate whilst on an LCA at sea.

Next we have the **SCR 300** which is a man-portable back-pack mounted radio. We know the Rangers were using these during the assault because of this paragraph:

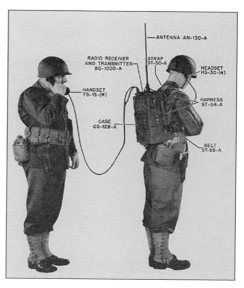

By 0725, 1st Lt. James W. Eikner had his equipment set up and flashed word by SCR 300 that Colonel Rudder's force had landed. Five minutes later he sent out the code word indicating 'men up the cliff'; the 'Roger' that receipted for this message, again on SCR 300, was Eikner's last communication of D-Day on the Ranger command net. When he sent the message PRAISE THE LORD ('all men up cliff') at 0745, no response was forthcoming.

The SCR 300 is (according to its Training Manual) only workable with an operational range of just over 3 miles and less distance if used from a low vantage point.

Colonel Rudder and headquarters personnel remained for the moment below, finding shelter from enfilade fire in a shallow cave at the bottom of the cliff. By 0725, 1st Lt. James W. Eikner had his equipment set up and flashed word by SCR 300 that Colonel Rudder's force had landed.'

Rudder and his HQ men were in a cave at the base of a cliff and it must have been almost impossible to send a sensible message to ships some miles away with this type of equipment.

The other type of radio used was the **SCR 536**, which we know today as a Walkie-Talkie. They have an effective range of 1 to 3 miles and were ideal for the men of the NSFCP who would transmit co-ordinates to the vessels that were close by, to give covering fire to the Rangers. This is confirmed in the paragraph below:

'*Personnel of the fire control party observed results not merely from the Point but from positions inland, sending spotting data back to the Point by SCR 536.*'

This is a piece of kit which could not possibly have been used to contact Schneider's LCA by Rudder. They could have communicated with their relevant fire support ships if close by, or with other Ranger units on the Pointe and then had their message relayed to Schneider perhaps later on: *'At 0728, the* Satterlee *made its first contact with the Naval Shore Fire Control Party…'* so it appears that this was Rudder's forces' first real communication and it was eighteen minutes after the 'TILT' message had been received.

After some searching, I found the answer to the question of who sent the 'TILT' message. Below is part of the After Action Report for HMS *Prince Charles* commanded by Commander Stratford Dennis of the Royal Navy. He states that it was he who ordered Schneider to go to the beach. It is also obvious that he had no knowledge of any flares being seen at the time and he thought it was the most prudent course of action given that there had been no further communication from Rudder. Note also the comment about him expecting to see a 'pyrotechnical signal'.

> success signal BINGO was never received by any ship or craft, nor was the pyrotechnic signal seen. After waiting an extra forty-five minutes after touch down (see operation orders) I decided that there was no option but to send the remaining Rangers to DOG GREEN where they touched down in the face of severe opposition at 0753. This was a hard decision to make, but I could not receive any information from POINT DU HOE, and so had to assume that the landing had been unsuccessful.

Would he have made this same decision if he had been made aware of the flares launched earlier – who knows?

The most surprising thing in this whole situation is that neither Major General Huebner or Major General Gerow made the decision to land the larger Ranger force on Omaha Beach any sooner. USS *Ancon*'s War Diary confirms that both of these generals were onboard ship until the afternoon of D-Day. They were best-placed to know what was happening to all of their men on the beach – and, they could have sent the change of direction order to Schneider. It could certainly be argued that they should have given that order long before Commander Dennis did.

> At 1400, 6 June 1944, Brig. General Hoge, Commanding General Provisional Engineers Special Brigade Group, and his staff left the ship to set up headquarters ashore. At 1705, Lieut. General Bradley came aboard and departed at 1805. At 1715, Major General Heubner, Commanding General 1st Infantry Division, and staff, left the ship for the beach. At 1945, Major General Gerow, Commanding General, V Corps, and staff, left the ship for the beach.

This timing is all the more relevant to the generals for another reason. At 0641 a grim radio message came to them from Omaha Beach stating *'Entire first wave foundered.'* And it was repeated again at 0655. If they needed help on the beach, it was there and then, but they did not initiate the Rangers' Plan B as you might expect – it was left to a member of the Royal Navy.

Below: The 1st Inf. Div. HQ journal pages for 6 June.

HEADQUARTERS 1ST INFANTRY DIVISION
APO #1, U. S. Army

G-3 (JOURNAL*

(From 0001B
Time :
(To — 2400B

Date 6 June 1944

CP Location USS ANCON, English Channel off Coast of France

TIME	NO.	FROM	SYNOPSIS	REC'D VIA	DISPOSITION
0230	1		Arrived in Transport Area at 0230.		
0251	2		Dropped Anchor at 0251.		
0630	3	CG	Land CT 115 at H/4 unless otherwise directed.		Comdr CTF 124
0708	4		1st wave landed 0635, 2nd wave landed 0635.	Rad	J
0830	5		16 Inf and 116 Inf touched down 060635.	Rad	J
0630	6	Talley	1t Y DUKW No one waterborne	Rad	V Corps & J
0636	7	Talley	1t 3 DOG DOGS Launched Saw empty LCT returning.	Rad	V Corps & J
0655	8	PC 552	NK First wave foundered.	Rad	Navy & J
0702	9	Javelin	LCA unit is landing half on DOG GREEN half on CHARLIE.	Rad	Navy & J
0700	10	Talley	Brilliant white flare seen near POINTE DE HOE.	Rad	V Corps & J
0641	11	PC 552	Entire first wave foundered.	Rad	Chase & J
0718	12	Talley	4 Rockets fired.	Rad	V Corps & J

NOTES:
   *Delete one.
   "Rec'd Via" column will indicate how message was transmitted, i.e., Tp — telephone; Rad — radio; Tgp — telegraph; Tpe — teletype.
   #Following abbreviations only will be used in this column, other information will be written out: M — Noted on situation map; J — Appended to journal (applies to Overlays, Msg blanks, written orders, etc.); CG, C/S, etc. — indicates information passed on to Officer indicated; T— indicates information disseminated to units or troops, as indicated in text of message.
Revised 3 Jan. '44)

— 1 —

G-3 Journal* ~~Diary~~* for　6 June 1944　Cont'd.

TIME	NO.	FROM	SYNOPSIS	REC'D VIA	DISPOSITION
0725	13	Prince Charles 1	They are calling in DUKWS now.	Rad	Prince Charles & J
0737	14	CTF 124	First wave landed DOG GREEN 0635, second wave 0636, first wave assault group O-1 landed 0635 X One LCA capsized X One LCT (A) sinking with engine room flooded X Success signal from POINTE DU HOE reported by V CORPS observer on DUKW X Unconfirmed report from PC 552 that first wave on FOX GREEN foundered.	Rad	NCWTF & J
0748	15	3d 16th	Are held up on 7 and 8.	Rad	V Corps & J
0807	16	CTF 124	Does your 060641B refer to Do tanks on FOX GREEN.	Rad	PC 552 & J
0807	17	Thomas Jefferson	Returning boats report floating mines near beach endangering landings. Many boats have swamped because of them. Many persons in water.	Rad	COMTRANSDIV 3 & J.
0807	18	Control Vessel Easy Red	First wave landed 0635. Eighth wave at 075. Unable to determine all waves between them. Believe they were evenly spaced and on time.	Rad	COMFORCE "O" & J
0811	19	3d 16th	Have not landed yet LIS (?). Moving to the right.	Rad	V Corps & J
0750	20	CG 50th Div	69th Inf Brig and 231st Inf Brig First have touched down 0725 BT.	Rad	CG 1st Div & J
0817	21	3d 16th	Have lost all — 11 section lost in water. 2 1/2 moving forward.	Rad	V Corps & J
0827	22	3d Bn	Moving Forward. 1 and 2 sections have not landed yet.	Rad	V Corps & J
0730	23	DC/S V Corps	LCIL 94 and 493 landed 0740. Firing hwy on beach.	Rad	V Corps & J
0838	24	Control Vessel Dog Red	The obstacles are mined. No chance of destroying mines by demolition yet.	Rad	J

— 2 —

Further 'anomalies' exist surrounding the Rangers and Maisy. Remember the radio messages coming in to the USS *Ancon* at 20.40hrs on D-Day from Colonel Talley? Earlier in the day his radio messages are all routinely recorded as incoming and marked TALLEY in the *Ancon* log. It would be natural to assume that the Maisy firing message would be included in the incoming messages for the 1st Inf. Div. command ship that evening.

To repeat the particular point again – there are three pages of messages, sent to and received by the USS *Ancon*. We have those originals before they were put into the After Action Report of radio communication. The problem is that Talley's Maisy messages were NOT put into that report when it was produced post battle. Page one of the three messages reads as follows (again note the time received):

2040hrs 6th June
To : Commanding General 1st Division.
Message reads:- Batteries Number 5, 16 and 16A are firing on Utah Beach, request clearance that it is safe for Uncle Force fire support vessels to fire on these targets........OVER.
(Secret: from HQ Fifth Corp – Action Colonel Talley – info HQ First Division).

We can see the text of the messages stuck down for recording purposes on the original page. But when I asked the 1st Infantry Division Museum in the US if they had a copy of the official USS *Ancon* After Action Report radio log for the late evening of 6 June, they told me that they did not have this page in their archives.

Through my investigation in another US Archive, I found a copy of this page included in papers for Utah Beach (the missing page is shown below). The entries for the time period 2035 and 2135 are shown, and Colonel Talley's radio message above reporting that Maisy was still firing at Utah Beach, is NOT included in this list. So we have the message received at 2040pm on D-Day and landing on USS *Ancon* … but it is then omitted from one of the most important official documents recording events on D-Day?

Remember, this radio document is entitled *Headquarters 1st Infantry Division APO#1, US Army G-3 Journal – From Time: 0001 to 2400. Command Post Location USS ANCON, English Channel off Coast of France.* (Full copy held in the US Archives).

I would love to know why Colonel Talley's message about Maisy firing on Utah Beach at 8.40pm on D-Day does not appear in that radio list as a message having been received – when we have it clearly being received by their radio room. Again I have to ask the question: who would have had the authority to not include this message when the official record of events was typed up? Also, why is it that all of the reports that had been changed, or are missing in the final versions, are ones relating to Maisy, Pointe du Hoc and the Rangers?

ii) The 'Order' to Block the Grandcamp-Vierville Road

Another line that is interesting from the Small Unit Action Report is this: *'It was important, Colonel Rudder thought, to maintain the block on the Grandcamp highway and so deny that vital road to the enemy.'*

This appears to be a direct quote from Lt. Colonel Rudder that he *'thought'* it was important to deny the road usage to the enemy – so it is not an order, but something he thought of? I know of NO evidence that such an order exists prior to D-Day giving him the authority to make that decision – so until such proof is found, it is on his shoulders that this action was taken. By staying to 'guard the highway' he ignored all of his orders, which stated that he was to advance inland.

This was further confirmed by the US Army 1 February order he received, stating *'no major alterations will be made without reference to the Joint Commanders-in-Chief.'* There is no record of that happening and if Lt. Col. Rudder had decided to change his mission, then it would have affected everyone else around him – and someone or some group would have been re-allocated Maisy as a D-Day target. Additionally, from within the same order it states: *'The object will be to capture the towns of St. Mere-Eglise 3495, Carentan 3984, Isigny 5085, Bayeux 7879 and Caen 0368 by the evening of D-Day.'* That could not be done by staying at Pointe du Hoc.

Historians in their hundreds have decided that one of the Rangers' missions was to protect and block the *'Grandcamp-Vierville highway'* – but you have now seen ALL of the intelligence available from the time of the Rangers' training, practice and through all of their many succinct sets of orders, that NO such order of this nature was ever issued.

Let's remember also that a number of veterans said that Lt. Col. Rudder did actually tell his men verbally that they were going to block the highway in the days before they landed. We must ask why he would take that decision and stay at the Pointe and then imply in the SUA Report that he made the decision in the spur of the moment? After all, he was not even supposed to have been on the mission.

If – as has been commonly accepted by historians – there was an order to 'block the highway', then we should easily be able to find copies of this order and additionally, we should also ask ourselves why Lt. Col. Rudder only allocated a single machine gun and a couple of riflemen in each direction of the road to maintain this task. If it was so important, why not dedicate his whole complement to achieving that goal, and use all of the firepower as his disposal? When Len Lomell first reached the highway in the morning of the 6th, he did allocate a number of his men to the task - but this number was reduced later.

Below is the actual disposition map showing the position of the men on the evening of 6 June and into the 7th at a time when arguably the Germans were most likely to counter-attack against the Allied landings. The map once again comes from the SUA Report. As far as I know, it is an accurate positioning of the Rangers fighting under Lt. Col. Rudder in that location, at that time. Highlighted in black is the main road with Pointe du Hoc beyond the top of this map to the north. The two ringed areas show: two men with weapons covering the road going to the west towards Grandcamp (in the direction that Lt. Col. Rudder says he was expecting the Germans to counter-attack) – and on the right, three men covering the road looking back towards Vierville.

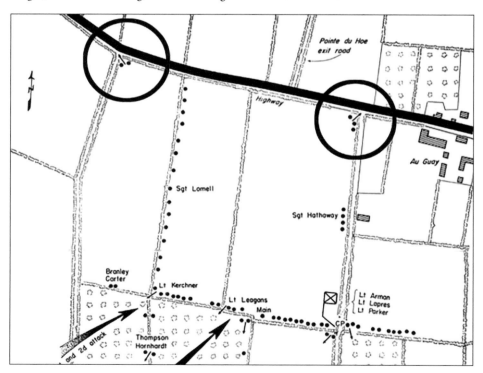

Lt Col. Rudder stated, that he considered that the most likely attack would come along the road, but most of his men were waiting to the south of the road and split from his HQ by the very road they were meant to defend. Thus his deeds were, in my opinion, a contrast to any suggested orders he had to defend the road. He could have achieved both self protection and a blockage of the road by placing his men along the road on its northern edge, ensuring that they were closer to Pointe du Hoc and they could have then covered both eventualities and been able to undertake an orderly retreat to the Pointe if required.

This strange positioning of his men is more striking when you consider that on D-Day, had the Germans sent any type of lightly armoured vehicle down the road against the one machine gun 'road block', the Rangers would have been unable to stop it. The whole position at the Pointe was put in even more peril, not less, by this course of action. Even more so as the men he placed in the fields to the south would have then been cut off from the force at the Pointe if they were attacked via the road. There would have been no way to retreat and they would have been either killed or forced to surrender. This is in part confirmed by this line:

> 'Lapres drew heavy fire from west of the exit road; his attempts in the afternoon were entirely blocked off by Germans who had infiltrated between the two Ranger Groups.'

The 17 May reports showed that the closest German Army armoured units were still some distance away along the French coast. By staying at Pointe du Hoc longer than necessary and not advancing, Rudder risked giving German troops the opportunity to move very close to the front and engage the landings – as they could literally drive straight through the split Rangers force. Had Rudder's group reached Maisy, they would still have been on the same road – just a few miles west. Then the Navy could still have repelled any fresh attackers with heavy gunfire and they could have done it whilst the Germans were held much further away from the landings.

As the map shows, one machine gun and two rifles stood between any German forces using the road and the whole of the Allied flank on Omaha Beach, which I think you will agree was inadequate. With hindsight, we have to consider that this description of events looks more and more like a post-battle excuse and justification for Rudder staying at the Pointe and creating the necessity for a command post and road blockage.

As a result, the problems at Pointe du Hoc became more self-inflicted, the longer he kept his men there.

There is a misconception by many, that the Rangers were beleaguered at Pointe du Hoc during D-Day and had to stay there. Here is a direct quote from the SUA Report: 'At no time were the snipers numerous, and there were periods when the Rangers could move in the open with impunity, anywhere on the Pointe.'

So we surely have to look at all this information with fresh eyes now, and doing so does present an alternative take on things in a way you might not have considered before.

Apparently – although I have been unable to find any concrete evidence for this order – General Huebner ordered all of his senior battalion commanders not to go in on the first wave with their men. The argument (so it is said) was that he did not want any of them 'knocked off in the first round' of the invasion. There could be some merit to this – but was it an actual order or is it just a writer's invention? Perhaps we will never know, unless a senior officer recorded it in the form of a diary or note. But it is very relevant, if Lt. Col. Rudder was originally ordered NOT to go in directly with his men. The biography Rudder: From Leader to Legend (Texas A&M University Press) by Dr Thomas Hatfield states that this was said to Rudder and it is said to have been repeated later by General Bradley in his memoirs - so for the sake of argument, let us assume it is accurate.

I wanted to study in more detail the actions of Lt. Col. Rudder at Pointe du Hoc and I have taken a closer look at the attempted removal of Max Schneider from his position prior to D-Day. As the period documents show, Schneider was a valuable member of the Ranger Force, and we know Schneider's previous war effort was recognized by General Eisenhower when he overruled the attempt by Lt. Col. Rudder to send him home early in 1944.

If Schneider had been removed – then one could argue that Rudder may have had to 'step in' at the last minute to fill the gap he left. We know from the period paperwork that Eisenhower did not allow that to happen. Schneider's contribution to D-Day and the days that followed earned him a well-deserved Distinguished Service Cross. The demand that he should be replaced prior to D-Day was a bad call by Rudder and was seen as such at the time by Eisenhower.

You could argue that if the removal of Schneider was not going to afford Lt. Col. Rudder the opportunity to land with his men on D-Day, then maybe another opportunity might present itself. Or perhaps another one could be created…

By luck, fate or design, on-board ship in Weymouth harbour there was an incident, which created a 'gap' which Lt. Col. Rudder would step into. The basics of it, as it is recounted in most books, go like this: The newly appointed Major Lytle had been promoted from the rank of captain the day before and we were told he had been celebrating his promotion and had been enjoying a little too much to drink. He stood up and told the men that he had found out from reading intelligence reports that there were no guns at Pointe du Hoc. Most contemporary books suggest that he proceeded to disparage the mission to anyone who would listen and he stated this attack would result in the deaths of many Rangers, for no appreciable gain. He was drunk and he told his men that it should not be done.

Apparently Rudder heard about this and had Lytle removed to another room; from there he was sent ashore under guard. The story goes, that Rudder then went to General Huebner in the early hours and stated that if he did not now lead the mission, it stood every chance of failure and thus was born the legend of Lt. Col. Rudder – the leader who stepped in at the last minute to save the day.

In Rudder's biography, Dr Hatfield goes on to suggest that Rudder would probably not have been serious about disobeying Huebner, but he put himself forward to lead the mission at that moment because he could think of no-one better for the job.

Over a long period of time, I have studied this series of events and I do not think that they have been portrayed accurately at all by historians, especially in the light of the new information in the declassified files of the American archives. Firstly, we know that Rudder had designs on removing one of his battalion commanders (Schneider) as head of the 2nd Battalion and failed in his attempt to do so. Yet he does remove Schneider's replacement, Major Lytle, and he does it at a time when he could not receive any argument from his superiors. Thus we must decide if either by design or simply by accident, there was an opportunity created for him to lead the mission.

Dr Hatfield adds further to the detail of this event, and in his book he calls it *'Lytle's dereliction...'* and one assumes for clarity that he means a *'dereliction of duty'* – which is defined in the US Army as follows:

Dereliction of duty *is a specific offense under United States Code Title 10, Section 892, Article 92 and applies to all branches of the US military. A service member who is derelict has willfully refused to perform his duties (or follow a given order) or has incapacitated himself in such a way that he cannot perform his duties.*

Dr Hatfield suggests that the series of events that preceded 'Lytle's dereliction' started a few days before embarkation, Rudder received information – supposed to have originated from the French Resistance – which said that the guns from Pointe du Hoc had been taken away from the site. Dr Hatfield says that the reports were later proved correct, but he implies that Rudder had no way of confirming it that close to the landings, so the Pointe du Hoc mission had to continue.

He states that the Germans had removed the Pointe du Hoc guns after a bombing mission on 25 April 1944 and yet implies that aerial reconnaissance showed that they were probably still in place. (We now know for sure that Rudder knew that this was not the case). He contends that Rudder was not in a position to know that the guns were not there and adds that '*They could be hidden nearby*'.

But by far the most interesting suggestion from the author comes in this sentence:

'Rudder knew the Rangers had a second objective at Pointe du Hoc – to block the coastal road that paralleled the shoreline about a thousand yards inland. Blocking the road would keep the Germans from using it to reinforce their defenses at Omaha.'

He thus in my opinion, suggests that there was no option but for the Rangers to attack the Pointe and make sure the guns were not operational and to block the coastal road. He says: *'Rudder told Lytle, and others who needed to know about the French report. Lytle then tried to persuade Rudder that the assault on Pointe du Hoc was unnecessary and suicidal.'*

But he adds that even if Rudder had believed that the mission was unnecessary, he was not authorized to change the plan and so Lytle's protestations were made in vain.

To take these events under scrutiny is not difficult when using the latest evidence available. To look at these events in more detail, for the purpose of this evaluation, it is assumed that Dr Hatfield had one of the following as the source for his information:

1) It may have come from direct communication between himself and Rudder.
2) It could have originated from surviving men who served under Rudder.
3) The above ideas were formed on assumptions made by him.

He says that Rudder received the information, coming directly from the French Resistance, that there were no longer any guns at Pointe du Hoc. As already shown, the information was indeed available from US intelligence that some guns had been changed, displaced and then removed – and it was available to Rudder long before the first week in June. Although implied that this information was fresh news to Rudder, documentary evidence that we now have shows that these facts would have been very clear and well known to him before that.

iii) The Enigma of the Guns

It is suggested that Rudder had no way of confirming if the Resistance information was true or not. Yet in my view, much of the information was already available from briefings and maps, long before D-Day.

The implication is that by D-Day, aerial intelligence photographs confirmed that the guns were still in their original places. However, the intelligence photographs and reports I have found do not suggest this – quite the opposite in fact. They clearly state that some of the gun positions were 'dismantled' prior to the Neptune Monograph being published in England on 21 April. This intelligence is repeated regularly in the run-up to D-Day, therefore the empty positions at Pointe du Hoc should not have come as a surprise to anyone.

There is a statement, that the Intelligence *interpreters suspected, the enemy had replaced the gun barrels with logs and had camouflaged their emplacements with netting.* Where does this actually come from, I wonder? I can find no evidence suggesting that photo interpreters believed this. Close to D-Day, the French Resistance reported very clearly that there were no guns 'installed' at Pointe du Hoc and we know that the guns previously on the pits would not have fitted inside the unfinished casements. The Germans had not simply moved them inside, but taken them away.

This statement in the book: '*From above or at a distance from the sides, the logs appeared to be the gun barrels*' merits the same answer as above. The logs were known not to be guns because the guns needed for the casements were of a different type and the casements were still being built. The casements are described as empty and under construction (U/C) in the reports – and this was the information which was placed on all maps. This is positive proof that the 'logs' did not fool anyone in England or else they would have stated that the casements were operational. This is further confirmed by the 26 April report, which is one of many that stated that Pointe du Hoc is 'concrete under construction'.

We often hear 'the barrels having been replaced with logs' as an excuse from historians and tour guides. I feel this is being used as a modern-day justification for Rudder's attack on Pointe du Hoc, perhaps because it sounded sensible – and because up until now there has been no other theory. Therefore, this has become a globally accepted truth.

'*He had to make sure …*' Sure of what, one wonders, when the intelligence was accurate and the site was found to have empty casements.

Another line: '*Even if the French report was correct, Rudder could not assume the guns were out of action. So what if they were not in their emplacements? They could be hidden nearby – as they were – and ready to fire.*'

There is a great deal of interpretation as to the way Rudder felt about the possibility of guns remaining at Pointe du Hoc before D-Day, which may have come from Rudder himself, I do not know. Could it be, that Hatfield was trying to nip any accusations in the bud about Rudder knowing – well in advance of the landings – about the guns having been removed. It is easy to say that 'Rudder had to make sure' – and use that to justify the necessity to continue the mission.

However, I think you will agree that all of the available evidence shows that Lt. Col. Rudder was aware that Pointe du Hoc had empty positions. And normally, if something was marked as 'empty' or 'under construction' on intelligence maps, it was NOT deemed a military target. Did the Rangers attack the dummy battery positions to the west of Pointe du Hoc? Or the two dummy batteries north of Maisy? These were equally known about, just like Pointe du Hoc being empty, yet the Rangers didn't attack them to 'make sure' because they 'could have held real guns'. So, this argument is simply not plausible.

Also from the same book is this statement:

'*Rudder knew the Rangers had a second objective at Pointe du Hoc – to block the coastal road that paralleled the shore-line about a thousand yards inland. Blocking the road would keep the Germans from using it to reinforce their defenses at Omaha Beach.*'

This assertion that there was another objective for the Rangers – one of blocking the coastal road behind Pointe du Hoc – is, I believe, a complete fantasy and yet it appears in nearly all modern books on the subject.

The importance of these sentences should not be underestimated. It is continually used in hundreds of books as the reason why Lt. Colonel Rudder did not advance further inland on D-Day. But it is still worth remembering that until Maisy was rediscovered in 2006 – and prior to the latest document releases from the US Archives – it would have made perfect sense for the Rangers to stay at Pointe du Hoc until they were relieved.

We know from Rudder's orders that he had other missions beyond PdH – yet he never mentioned those at all after the war, and the Top Secrecy laws prevented anyone (other than Lytle it seems) ever challenging him then – or afterwards!

Another thing that has always amazed me – in a world where historians and experts can hang on the slightest word of a period document. The 'order' about blocking the roads has mysteriously vanished from EVERY SINGLE piece of paperwork from that time. Seventy-five years later there is STILL no factual evidence anywhere to suggest that this order exists – and if there is, then it needs to be shown. If it cannot be found then this aspect of the Rangers' supposed 'mission' needs to be stopped from being repeated by historians, authors and tour guides. The truth is that it was simply an order given by Rudder to his men on the day and veterans have repeated it.

Let's be 100 per cent clear about this. If the order existed:

1. Why can we not find a copy of it anywhere in the millions of WWII papers now available?
2. Who was given the Maisy batteries as their objective instead of the Rangers? Remember, Maisy is mentioned as a serious target as many times as Pointe du Hoc, in ALL the D-Day-intelligence you have now read.
3. Why did the Rangers train for the Maisy mission at Slapton Sands and have it briefed fully to them in the Neptune Monograph – then forget to go there on D-Day? We have proof that Rudder had the details of the Maisy raid and did not tell his men.
4. Right up until D-Day the missions for the Rangers remained unchanged and they were re-affirmed in every copy of Lt. Col. Rudder's orders. Attacking the batteries at Maisy WAS a D-Day objective given to him. This could never be completed if they stayed to *'block the highway'* instead. These two orders are in direct conflict with each other. We can find full disclosure of a mission to Maisy for the Rangers in a lot of the period paperwork month after month in the run-up to D-Day – and NO mention of a mission to block the highway at Pointe du Hoc EVER appears – other than from verbal orders issued by Rudder. I think you will agree that is a rather strange thing for historians not to have investigated before now.

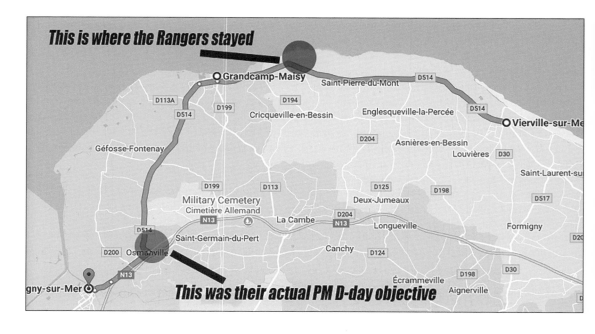

Lt. Col. Rudder did not ever mention this lack of advance in the After Action Reports, nor did he talk about Maisy in any discussions after the war and I believe that by doing so he has diverted historians on a wild goose chase ever since.

Quite simply this fictitious mission at the road is used now as a 'get out of jail free card' to explain the high number of casualties caused by them staying at the Pointe. It is fictional in my opinion, and suits the narrative of events as they unfolded and I can only assume it has seemed sensible to authors, film makers and students of history ever since, so it has become the 'truth'.

The real fact is that Lt. Col. Rudder did not attack Maisy and advance towards Isigny on D-Day to the PM Phase Line as ordered.

It is interesting to see how this one interpretation of events has changed how we all look at the Pointe du Hoc mission and how it made Lt. Col. Rudder into a hero. To be fair to Rudder's biographer, he could well have been told of this 'block the highway' mission from veterans, who said that is what they were ordered to do. Taking their word for it, because there was a lack of evidence to the contrary at the time of his writing might be the reason. In my opinion, the new evidence presented in this book suggests that the whole 'hero' aspect of any Rudder biography is out of step with reality.

We need to ask for a written copy of the original 'block the highway' order when we hear authors talk about it. After all, the history and fame of Lt. Col. Rudder in part revolves around it. If this order cannot be provided and no order can be provided stating that the Rangers were not to go to Maisy, then a lot of people have got this part of US Army D-Day history very wrong.

To be crystal clear – paperwork en-masse over many months exists stating that the Rangers are to attack Maisy. For years, historians told me that this did not exist, yet NO paperwork exists at all, ordering the Rangers to stay at Pointe du Hoc. Fog of war is not applicable here, Lt. Col. Rudder knew long before D-Day that Maisy was his target. If that had changed because of events such as losses at PdH, his men should still have already been told of Maisy during their briefings and undoubtedly they would have told countless historians that post war.

Another example of the manipulation of this historical event is simply explained using the following paragraph from the 2nd Battalion After Action Report. It states that D, E and F (plus others) *and* Lt. Col. Rudder, were to land at H-Hour at Pointe du Hoc… *'with the mission of destroying the six gun coastal battery located thereon and establishing a perimeter 1000 yards inland, so as to protect the landing of the Force "C"…'*

That makes perfect sense at first glance, but it is a document which was written with hindsight and is based on what happened – and yet it is NOT what was actually ordered in writing for the Rangers.

> Force "A"   Companies D/E/F
>
> The Plan of Attack:
>
>   Force "A", comprising Companies D/E/F and the Bn Hq Det with attached Naval Shore Fire Party and Photographic Party, accompanied by two British Official Observers, commanded by Lt Col James E. Rudder, was to land at H-Hour on Beach Charlie (Pointe du Hoe) with the mission of destroying the six gun coastal battery located thereon and establishing a perimeter 1000 yards inland so as to protect the landing of the Force "C". In support were the battleship "Texas", a number of destroyers, and several flights of attack-bombers available on call as long as the Ranger Force remained within the limiting range.

It includes Lt. Col. Rudder by name, in what it suggests were their orders – yet we know he was not supposed to have been with his men at this time on D-Day morning at the Pointe, so he would not possibly have been originally named in those orders in this manner – and at this time. This is a post action write-up. Rudder only became part of the PdH mission in the hours leading up to the mother ships leaving harbour (after the removal of Major Lytle) and this was long after any written Ranger orders were issued. For many years historians have used this document to suggest these were actual orders.

It says that they were to *'protect the landing of the Force 'C'…'* but in other later histories this wording is changed to read *'protect the left flank of the Omaha Sector'*. In my opinion this is history being written afterwards to suit what had happened and this is very obvious once you have seen the actual Rangers' orders sending them further inland.

These post-battle pages deliberately make no mention that the Ranger orders were never completed and the *actual* orders simply vanished for 70 years and were not mentioned again. There is also a strange lack of an After Action Report ever having been filed by the 2nd Battalion Cannon Company, who were involved in the Maisy battle. They must have written one to explain ammunition usage from their 75mm guns and any casualties incurred, etc. But no paperwork has surfaced and they are not mentioned within ANY of the Morning Reports.

Another quote from the SUA Report states: *'There was no alternative but for the Rangers to go in, make certain the guns were out of action, and cut the coastal road.'* I agree that going to Pointe du Hoc was relevant for the purposes of ensuring that no guns would fire from there and that is in the Rangers' orders. It would also put them some miles closer to Maisy and the D-Day Phase Line – and it does also allow for a blocking of the 'highway' – if Lt. Col. Rudder considered that it was such an important a thing to do.

When studied tactically, I feel it would easily have been possible to do both. The D514 (the road historians suggest Rudder was ordered to block) continues along the coast and goes within 100 metres of the Maisy Batteries. Thus any assault on Maisy would have immediately and easily blocked the D514 as well, and it would have been done just a few miles further down the road from the Pointe. It would have killed two birds with one stone.

iv) The Lytle Incident

In his book, Dr Hatfield writes that during the week before the embarkation, Rudder told Lytle and *'others who needed to know'* about the details of the French Resistance report, and that Lytle attempted to persuade Rudder that the Pointe du Hoc attack *'was unnecessary and suicidal'*. He goes on to say that even if Lytle's complaints had been successful, Lt. Col. Rudder was not empowered to change the plan and therefore *'Lytle's protest got him nowhere'*.

This is a strange statement. As I understand it, Lt. Col. Rudder was completely in charge of his mission and could change any aspect of the implementation – this included removing any senior officers who did not agree with the way he was running things. The earlier order only stated that change had to be approved. The fact that Lytle and 'others' were informed about the Rangers' mission complications (i.e. potentially missing guns) in the week before loading is also significant. This was mission-critical information for the men, that was admittedly not given to his senior officers until a week before, yet it had been known to Rudder many weeks before that. This is an acknowledgement that Rudder chose not to tell his officers until they were virtually onboard their ship – and thus by default he had left his officers to continue to brief their men on a mission he knew was flawed. We have to again ask the question of Rudder's motives … was he banking on Lytle complaining about this situation and then he intended to act to relieve him of his command and replace him at the last minute? Because that is actually what happened.

I investigated the particular series of events surrounding Major Lytle in great detail because it has serious historical ramifications and I also felt that I would need to justify what I am suggesting.

I interviewed 2nd Battalion veteran Frank Kennard, who told me he was present on the ship on 3 June 1944 and he was there when Major Lytle discussed the 'situation' as he understood it with the men that night. He remembered Major Lytle standing up and getting the men's attention at dinner. Lytle started to discuss the fact that he now had seen the intelligence relating to the Pointe du Hoc mission and the evidence proved to him that the mission was unnecessary. Instead (according to Kennard) he stated *'we should be attacking a place called Maisy instead.'*

At this point, the battalion doctor 'Doc Block' stood up and grabbed Lytle's shirt, pulling off a button as he tried to get him to sit down. Things got heated and Lytle punched Block. Lytle was led out of the room by two other men to calm down – and that was the last of Lytle and his opinions that the men in the room ever heard. Lytle was widely denounced for being a coward and a bad influence on them and his name has been dragged through the mud ever since in book after book. But I want to question the validity of this, given the evidence I have now uncovered.

Frank Kennard told me in writing *'we didn't know what "Maisy" meant – so it went straight over our heads'*. It would appear that the men in the room thought that Lytle was indeed either drunk and/or a coward.

This is how part of it was relayed to me in Frank's letter in 2014:

> *'The "scoop" was he* (Lytle) *knew about Maisy and talked TOO MUCH about it when on board the troop transport. I have a recollection Lytle was scheduled to be the "ranking" Ranger officer at the Pointe. While Rudder was to be the senior officer in the Ranger Group* (2nd and 5th) *and land later at Vierville. I understand Rudder felt Lytle's Maisy info would "undermine" the confidence of D-E-F personnel, so Rudder fired Lytle while aboard the transport and re-arranged things so he* (Rudder) *landed at the Pte. Ultimately Lytle ended up with some other infantry unit, where I understand he served with distinction.'*

I spoke to veteran Charlie Ryan of C Co. 2nd Battalion on the phone about the same thing – and he told me this: *'We knew there were rumours going around that the big guns had been removed from Pointe du Hoc. We even had an officer removed from the unit for saying it publicly.'*

I am quoting people who were there – these are not my words. The difference with this information and many other versions, is that these men told me this first hand. In the case of Frank Kennard, I also had this particular interview recorded on tape for a TV documentary some years ago and he recalled it all perfectly.

It is highly likely that Doctor Block believed that Lytle was in the wrong and felt strongly enough about it to try and stop him speaking out. This is in part backed up by Block's testimony taken in December 1944 (shortly before he died in combat), that on 7 April he personally was shown the maps and given details of the Pointe du Hoc assault. Before that date he knew nothing about the mission and any objectives and it is clear that he was not briefed at all on the existence of the Maisy Batteries. This has to bring up further questions about Rudder's motives when you consider the vast amount of orders dating prior to 7 April that confirmed Maisy was a target. Block was a senior member of the Rangers team and yet he was also kept from seeing any of these papers by Rudder. It is logical to suggest that he may have formed the wrong opinion of Lytle and what he was talking to the men about that evening.

Major Cleveland Lytle

I tried to look at the 'Lytle incident' in the way that the US military would have done at the time and I found the actual Operation Neptune 1944 standing orders on the subject of the *Demotion for reasons of Moral and Example* – the set of US Army rules which apply exactly to the circumstances discussed here and the reasons offered at the time for the removal of Major Lytle with immediate effect from the Rangers. The orders state the following when being applied to the removal or reclassification of an officer (see next page).

To my knowledge – none of these procedures took place. Indeed what could Lt. Col. Rudder possibly have used as written justification for Lytle's dismissal? He would have had to state honestly that Major Lytle was telling the men about a set of orders that he, as his commanding officer had kept from those same men. He might not have agreed with Lytle telling them – but to remove him from the Rangers for doing it? There had to be more to it than that.

Equally, how could Major Lytle be guilty of any offence by telling the men that intelligence proving that the guns had been removed from Pointe du Hoc actually existed and that this information was within paperwork given to Lt. Col. Rudder some considerable time before D-Day? Would this then ultimately have led to an investigation of Lt. Col. Rudder's motives and actions by his superiors – who knows?

Given the severity of the charges being levelled at Major Lytle, you would imagine the US Army did not look favourably upon him – perhaps they would have locked him up on the eve of D-Day. Cowardice brought on by drunkenness is not something they take lightly in the US Army and for sure, it would certainly not look good when all the evidence was presented in front of a Court Martial.

Yet strangely Major Lytle's removal from his position with the Rangers did

---

Distinguished Service Cross:

"Major CLEVELAND A. LYTLE, 0326170, Infantry, 1st Battalion, **Infantry Regiment, 90th Infantry Division, United States Army. For extraordinary heroism in connection with military operations against an armed enemy. On 20 September 1944 Major LYTLE, Commanding Officer, 1st Battalion, **Infantry Regiment, while at an observation post discovered two soldiers, the survivors of a patrol, marooned on the icebreaker of a demolished bridge which crossed the Moselle River. Although the far shore was strongly manned by the enemy and the approaches to the bridge were covered by enemy machine-guns and mortars, Major LYTLE, under cover of darkness, alone and at the risk of his life, entered the river and attempted to carry a line to the marooned men. After forty-five minutes of vain effort against the swift current and the cold of the river he was forced by fatigue to abandon a relatively safe plan of rescue. Enlisting the voluntary aid of two men he led them out on the undamaged portion of the bridge which he had previously reconnoitered alone. At the approach of the group, the enemy opened heavy fire with mortars, small arms, flares and a fixed machine-gun firing upon the bridge. Despite incessant close bursts of fire Major LYTLE, from an exposed position, directed the rescue work. The marooned men were weak from two days of exposure and barely able to move. Through the sustained and extraordinary heroism, tenacity and leadership of Major LYTLE during eight hours of hazardous, bitterly cold and laborious effort, the two soldiers were rescued. His heroic act was inspirational to all who witnessed it and exemplifies the highest traditions of the military forces of the United States."

Silver Star:

"MAJOR CLEVELAND A. LYTLE, 0326170, Infantry, United States Army. On 18-19 August 1944 Major Lytle, moving with the leading elements of his Battalion, advanced through * * *France, despite a determined enemy resistance, small arms fire and fire from enemy self-propelled guns. Forced to make personal contact between elements of his command in order to maintain control, Major Lytle was further handicapped by dense smoke from several fires raging in the forest which at times enveloped elements of his command. Nevertheless, on 19 August 1944 his Battalion emerged from the forest and captured * * * France. By his heroism, determination and outstanding leadership he not only surmounted an impressive terrain feature but captured the town which was strongly held by the enemy. Entered service from South Carolina."

BIGOT   NEPTUNE

Demotion for Reasons of Morale and Example.

(1)   When an officer in contact with the enemy, or when
      such contact is considered imminent, fails to perform
      satisfactorily the duties of his temporary grade
      under such circumstances that morale and example
      require demotion by the most expeditious means possible,
      his demotion may be requested by written com-
      munication to this headquarters.

(2)   This procedure will be used only when the failure
      occurs under such circumstances as to affect seriously
      the morale of others, or materially to influence others
      from the proper performance of their duties.   This
      method of demotion is not a disciplinary procedure or
      a substitute for disciplinary action.

          Action under these provisions is not applicable
          to those cases in which the current grade of the
          officer concerned is a permanent grade in the
          Regular Army, National Guard, or Officers' Reserve
          Corps. See sub-paragraph b., (1), above.

(3)   Each such request for demotion will contain the follow-
      ing information:

      (a)   Name, branch, and serial number of the officer
            concerned.
      (b)   Present temporary grade will be identified as AUS
            or AUS (AC). In the case of an officer holding a
            temporary Air Corps grade, there will be included
            a statement of any temporary AUS grade held which
            is lower than the temporary Air Corps grade and
            higher than the permanent grade held by the officer
            in the Regular Army, National Guard, or Officers'
            Reserve Corps.

      (c)   Permanent grade in the Regular Army, National Guard,
            or Officers' Reserve Corps, or a statement that
            the officer holds no such appointment.

RECLASSIFICATION OF OFFICERS.

a.   Unit Procedure. Under the provisions of Section I, Circular
No. 95, Headquarters ETOUSA, 6 December 1943, Army headquarters will,
upon receipt of the recommendation for the reclassification of an
officer, immediately issue orders transferring such officer to the
Reclassification Center, ETOUSA.

          Under this procedure the commander recommending re-
          classification of an officer will comply with para-
          graph 7., b., (1), (a), (b), (c), (d), and (f), C.
          1, AR 605-230, 5 November 1943, before forwarding
          the recommendation to this headquarters.

b.   Board Procedure. When the officer concerned appears before it, the ETOUSA Reclassification Board is responsible that the
requirements of paragraph 7., (b), (1), (e) and (g), C. 1, AR 605-
230, 5 November 1943, are fully and completely satisfied. In exceptional circumstances, subject officer will be afforded an opportunity to return to his former station for the purpose of obtaining
additional evidence in his own behalf. The certificate of the
officer will be obtained by the board and attached to the record.

c.   Reclassification Assistance. Reclassification experts have
been appointed to the ETOUSA Reclassification Board for the purpose
of assisting unit officers in preparing reclassification files. One
or more such officers will be attached to Army headquarters to be
available upon call of commanders desiring such assistance. Divisions
will make requests for such assistance direct to Army headquarters.
Requests by other units will be made through this headquarters.

9.   TRANSFERS.

          Transfers of individuals will be made only in the best in-
terests of the service and in accordance with current directives.

not dent his military career at all. Major Cleveland Lytle was reassigned at the same rank from the 2nd Rangers on 23 July. He then took command of 90th Infantry Division HQ and then he transferred to assume command of HQ 1st Bn, on August 2, 1944.

It was while he was with this unit that he won the Distinguished Service Cross.

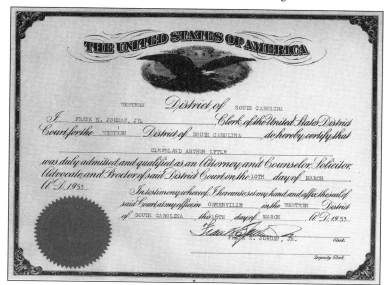

FORT MILL MAJOR HONORED —Brig. Gen. James A. Van Fleet, infantry division commander, is shown above as he awards the Silver Star with Oak Leaf cluster to Maj. Cleveland A. Lytle of Fort Mill, one of his battalion commanders. The award was made for action in France. Maj. Lytle is the son of Mr. and Mrs. T. F. Lytle of Fort Mill, and his wife, the former Miss Kathleen Bradford, teaches school in Fort Mill.

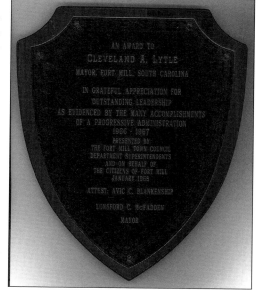

Major Lytle ended his military service at the rank of Lt. Colonel and was awarded the Distinguished Service Cross, the Silver Star with two oak leaf clusters (for three awards), Bronze Star, the Purple Heart with three clusters (he was wounded four times) and he was awarded the Order of Leopold (Belgium).

He then became a lawyer for his state in 1953 and was appointed as Mayor of Fort Mill, where he lived in 1966.

It is a statement of historical fact that Major Lytle was a courageous and valued member of the US Military and also that he did not suffer any of the normal regulatory ramifications as a result of Lt. Col. Rudder's accusations. This is very strange given their severity, which tells us that someone further up the chain of command, i.e. Major General Huebner, Major General Gerow – or even Eisenhower – took the decision to ignore the severity of the allegations against Lytle and keep a lid on things. This despite Major General Huebner having been given a full brief from Lt. Col. Rudder personally about Major Lytle's supposed 'dereliction'.

Is it possible that Major General Huebner did not believe what Rudder had said and decided to place Lytle elsewhere without pressing charges? Or perhaps Major Lytle's 'sideways-move' was done to keep him quiet about what he thought of Rudder's leadership?

To look at all the angles – it could have simply been that Lytle's face did not fit in with the Rangers and Rudder had had enough and wanted him removed in the hours before they left the port. Remember however, that Rudder did not replace Lytle with someone else of similar rank within his men, as would have been normal Army procedure, but he went to Major General Huebner in person, to offer his own services. The way that it appears, Rudder presented Huebner with the 'facts' and left Huebner little or no choice but to grant Rudder permission to go on the mission.

Another interesting piece of this jigsaw starts with the letter below, dated 26 July 1944. The letter is the confirmation of the attempted replacement procedure for Lt. Col. Schneider and it details the process that was started by Rudder's letter in February 1944. It gives the chronology of Rudder's requests to have Schneider removed and it states in Paragraph 1 – 'return officer without replacement'. This is noted on the paperwork as an 'exception to the present rotation policy'. It is documentary proof Lt. Col. Rudder had asked for the return of Lt. Col. Schneider to the US – but also that he had done so without wanting to replace him with anyone else, which was contrary to US Army policy.

Common sense says this would have left the 2nd Battalion without an Executive Officer at a time when they would definitely need one – in the run-up to D-Day. Lt. Col. Rudder wanted him removed, but with no replacement and that can only be viewed as a deliberate and considered decision.

Paragraph 3 is the most revealing part of the story, as this contains details not recorded in the 2nd Battalion diary or Morning Reports. It is also confirmation that the denial of Lt. Col. Rudder's request by Eisenhower's office to the removal of Schneider actually took place in writing to Rudder on 26 March.

On that date, HQ 1st Inf. Div. sent Lt. Col. Rudder a cable stating Lt. Col. Schneider's name should be removed from the list of men to be rotated back to the US. i.e. permission to remove him home was denied and the reason given was that the 'Officer's services could be utilized in initial invasion of the continent.'

In context this is perfectly acceptable, as we know Schneider was a very experienced officer, so the denial of this request at that time was sensible, and at the end of their letter in Paragraph 4, HQ had now (post D-Day) finally approved the return of Schneider to the US. This return order is dated 26 July 1944.

```
C                                                              C
  O                                                              O
    P                                                              P
      Y                                                              Y

AG 201-Schneider, Max P. (O)MPOB        2nd Ind.  S: 26 Aug 44      RSH/MGE/tmg
      (10 July 1944)
Hq, European Theater of Operations, U. S. Army, APO 887, 26 July 1944.

TO:  The Adjutant General, Washington 25, D.C.

     1.  Request an exception be made to the present rotation policy and
authority be granted to return officer without replacement.

     2.  Officer was reported to The Adjutant General for rotation by 4th
indorsement, this headquarters, dated 9 Feb 1944, file as above and authority
for his return granted by AGWAR cable R-9824 Feb 250021Z.

     3.  Request was submitted by cable E-20672, this headquarters, 26 March
1944, to withdraw his name from the rotation report, this being approved by
cable WAR 16751 March 311657Z.  This request was made in order that officer's
services could be utilized in initial invasion of the continent.

     4.  In view of the circumstances it is believed that officer's return would
be to the best interests of the service.

                    By command of General EISENHOWER:


                                              RUSSELL S. HAHN
                                              Lt Col, AGD
                                              Assistant Adjutant General
1 Incl: n/c
```

Looking back at the 26 March entry in the 2nd Battalion diary (shown on the next page), it states that 'coincidentally' on the same day that Rudder was denied permission to remove Schneider until after D-Day, he transferred Schneider out of the 2nd Battalion and put him in charge of the 5th Battalion.

The 5th Battalion were to be the follow-up force in the PdH action and so he replaced Schneider with Captain Lytle and gave Lytle the command of the 2nd Battalion instead. By this action he now had someone else in charge of the 2nd Battalion that he *could* remove at a moment's notice – thus it appears that it was the position he wanted to leave available for himself, and not actually the specific man (Schneider) he wanted to get rid of.

The timing of this change from one man in his cross-hairs running the 2nd Battalion to another, whom he later removes from that exact position, has to be viewed with the utmost suspicion. And as corroboration, this change in battalion leadership happens on exactly the same day he is ordered not to remove Schneider until after D-Day. That is NOT a coincidence! This is clearly premeditated and cynical advanced planning and it is very difficult to explain the coincidence of the HQ letter and the removal of Schneider to another battalion happening on the same day – if they are not connected. Schneider's move was not done as a question of competence, because Lytle was vastly less experienced than Schneider to run the 2nd Battalion. Indeed the roles they previously had were correct given their missions and experience.

Nor can it be suggested that there was a personality clash between Schneider and Rudder at the time, creating a necessity for Schneider to be moved to another battalion, if only for the simple reason that as the new Executive Officer of the 5th Battalion, Schneider would still have to deal with Lt. Col. Rudder on a daily basis in the usual manner. No jurisdictional or chain of command issues would change at all.

It is obvious that Rudder was planning this situation as early as February and when it became clear that he could not remove Schneider, he simply moved him to one side.

Here is the 26 March diary entry again confirming that this happened.

> On 26 March, Major Schneider was relieved of assignment as Executive Officer and assumed command of the 5th Ranger Battalion. Captain Cleveland A. Lytle was appointed Executive Officer on this day.

No paperwork relating to the removal of Major Lytle from the Rangers in June exists or has emerged to date, either from my investigations through the 1st Inf. Division, the US National Archives or after discussion with the Lytle family. There is no other mention of Lytle being in ANY trouble, or any talk of him at all, other than the one line in the Morning Report dated 8 June 1944, which reads:

Headquarters Company 2nd Rangers – *Grandcamp-les-Bains, France.*
Major Cleveland Lytle went from sick in Hospital to relieved of assignment and Duty and assigned to 10th Replacement Depot APO874 as of 7th June 1944 – per SO#159, HQ Southern Base Section, SOS ETOUSA.

It simply states that he was a hospital patient.

Thus nearly ended the career of a brave man who was marked down as being '*sick*' on D-Day. That report entry is dated 7 June – not the 3rd when his removal actually took place. So this is factually inaccurate and yet it also remains as true in US Army records.

Through my contacts with other Ranger veterans, it is clear that the men knew nothing about Maisy or any other missions beyond PdH. They have all stated that they were to guard Pointe du Hoc and that is their story.

We know the mission orders went further than PdH and included Maisy – and Major Lytle was right to try and speak out. Rudder had him removed for this and the men obviously drew their own inevitable conclusions about the events onboard ship. Without any further evidence ever being presented to them, Major Lytle was branded as a coward and he was removed, to be replaced on the mission by Lt. Col. Rudder himself. How much Captain Block was involved, or understood the actual motives behind the removal of Major Lytle is debatable and would be impossible to prove either way now. We do know that he sent Major Lytle to 'hospital' when he was not sick – and he wrote and signed the letter for the attempted removal back to the US of Lt. Col. Schneider earlier in the year. Both are situations which contributed

Captain Walter Block – Ranger Battalion surgeon.

to the positioning of Lt. Col. Rudder on the Pointe du Hoc mission and both are things which Block *could* have been ordered to do by Rudder.

v) The D-Day Phase Line

Irrespective of Maisy as a target, why did Lt. Col. Rudder not tell his men of their orders to reach the D-Day Phase Line on the evening of 6 June? If there was to be any doubt about the significant nature of the 12-mile advance inland to the Phase Line for the Rangers, we must look at the documents that we can prove were provided to Lt. Col. Rudder, in the months before D-Day.

In orders and instructions dating as far back as February 1944 the Rangers are shown to be landing at Vierville, attacking the radar station, simultaneously landing at Pointe du Hoc, going through Grandcamp-les-Bains, attacking the batteries at Maisy – then advancing to the PM D-Day Phase Line. The original of this map below is dated 25 Feb and those objectives are what it shows. A total of 12 miles were to be covered by the Rangers and it is better illustrated here by my adding this modern (grayed) road map overlay. The heavy line measures 12 miles exactly and has been measured using a satellite overlay of that distance. The heavy line coincides with the brief for the objectives at that time and they coincide exactly to ALL the Rangers' orders from February until D-Day, some five months' worth of orders.

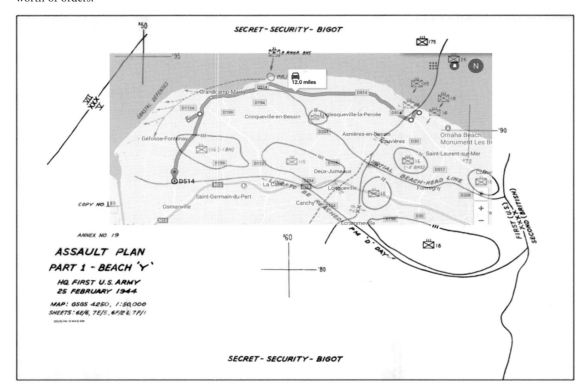

Next, further confirmation of this 12-mile distance having relevance comes from the 4 May Slapton Sands training report where, in the words of Maurice Prince in his 2nd Battalion unit history, they had to march 12 miles after landing. This was deliberate mission-specific training.

> Landing at dawn, 4 May, the Battalion proceeded thru the operation which, after contact with Companies D/E/F was established, lengthened into a forced march of about twelve miles. Burdened as the men were with their complete fighting load, the heat of the day made the march a grueling task. The Battalion was assembled in the evening and Higher Headquarters dictated a non-tactical night.

But it was not just the Rangers who were governed by the necessity to reach the D-Day Line. Here is a portion of a General Staff map belonging to Major General Leonard T. Gerow, which he carried on D-Day onto Omaha Beach. The full map is held within the archives of the Virginia Military Institute, Preston Library, Lexington, Virginia and it too has the line marked, shown here near the bottom right as his objective – 'PM D-DAY'.

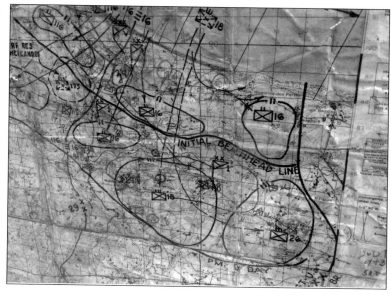

If the motivation of Lt. Col. Rudder was to not mention the Maisy mission to anyone and then hope that the Pointe du Hoc mission was re-vitalised with new guns arriving by the time of D-Day, one can imagine he got worried the closer D-Day came. It is clear that he was the only one fully briefed on Pointe du Hoc and Maisy and perhaps if he told his men, word would get out that the PdH mission should be scrapped. If it was cancelled by his superiors due to its lack of guns, would a standard infantry division be given the job of attacking Maisy – perhaps by direct frontal assault from the Grandcamp Casino beach? An attack of this type would clearly have involved NO cliff climbing at all and it could have relegated the Rangers to a post D-Day landing role.

That could have been motivation enough for Lt. Col. Rudder not to discuss the intelligence with his men and it could help explain why it appears he orchestrated for himself a more prominent role on D-Day when the time came. It also might explain why he was keeping that information quiet until the very last minute. After all, if his actions were deliberate or simply a wild series of coincidences, he did command the D-Day mission. We have to remember also, that in early 1944 he had been handed *'the most important mission on D-Day'* by General Eisenhower.

One thing is for sure, he was guaranteed to retain the top job with the top mission – if he kept quiet about the faltering Pointe du Hoc intelligence.

Some 70+ years later the evidence now tells a version of events that differs from the one saying that he simply *'stepped up'* to get the job done. Was all of his fame achieved at the expense of a valued Ranger officer, Major Lytle, and a good number of men's lives at Pointe du Hoc? Should we now question if it was really worth it?

I hope you will now look at other books on the subject of the Rangers and D-Day and this will make you think twice about what we have all been presented with by historians thus far. We should all now look especially hard at the relevance of the role Lt. Colonel Rudder played in the three-day defence of the empty position at Pointe du Hoc.

Given all of this new evidence, the following questions could be asked about Lt. Col. Rudder:

- Why did he not tell any of his men that part of their orders were to attack Grandcamp and the gun batteries at Maisy on D-Day?
- Why did he not provide his men with any intelligence maps to allow them to adequately train for, and plan an attack on Grandcamp and the Maisy site?
- Why did he not tell his men of the known removal of some of the guns at Pointe du Hoc prior to their assault?
- Why did he then allow groups of his men to attack gun pits which no longer existed?
- Why did he deliberately remove a perfectly competent officer for trying to brief his men of those very facts?
- Why did he not advance inland as his orders directed, and instead stayed put to defend a roadway and empty gun battery at Pointe du Hoc, which was of no strategic value?
- Why did he turn down the offer of Naval firepower on 8 June to assist in the Rangers' advance – at a time when it could have been used to stop the batteries at Maisy firing?
- Why did he create or invent an order to 'block the highway' behind Pointe du Hoc?

- Why did he not mention Maisy after the war and by silence, perpetuate a set of unconfirmed orders?
- Why is he not described in the SUA Report as being in charge and making decisions at Pointe du Hoc?
- Why is Maisy not detailed in Rudder's biography?
- Why was the Maisy site buried after the battle?
- Why do none of the million selling books on the subject of D-Day talk about Maisy's existence?
- Why did General Huebner ignore Rudder's protestations about Lytle being a liability to the US Army and give Lytle a new command of his own? Was it done to stop him talking publicly about Rudder?
- Who ordered the burial of the Maisy site before the land was returned to the local French community?
- Is it justified to suggest that by his actions, Lt. Colonel Rudder endangered not only all the men under his command at Pointe du Hoc, but also those men still landing on Omaha and Utah Beaches?
- Should Lt. Col. Rudder really have been given the DSC?

I have deliberately phrased the above questions in such a way as to challenge the conventional thoughts of historians on this matter.

Some or all of the above points surely would in themselves have been an offence or raised flags in the US military at the time, but much of this would not have been known about until *after* Lt. Col. Rudder had received his Distinguished Service Cross. The DSC awards were issued mid-June and information about them being awarded was sent back to the US for immediate publication by the press. The Army was desperate to fuel the clamour back home for good news about the invasion and the Rangers were able to fulfill that with tales of daring cliff climbing, deprivation, hand-to-hand combat, courage and survival at the Pointe for three days.

I do wonder if the same opinion was upheld by the Army top brass in July, when the Small Unit Actions Report for Pointe du Hoc was compiled. At that time did someone in authority make a conscious decision to order the 'figurative' burial of the Maisy Batteries and omit mention of Maisy and 'other' missions beyond Pointe du Hoc? We know that there is no mention of Maisy in the diaries of the leading generals in the US Army.

We must ask if it is now time that Lt. Col. Rudder's legendary status as a wartime leader should be reviewed. I am NOT on a witch-hunt, but simply presenting the evidence that I have found, and my personal interpretation of it. Unlike many other authors, I have provided my evidence so that it can be seen in its original form. This became very relevant recently, when I tracked down the source of one set of 'Rangers orders' contained in a veteran's book. He had rewritten them (and added grid references, etc) from a book which was published 10 years ago and when I checked, that work referenced a book written in the 1960s as its source. I compared the 1960s book with my own records for the exact orders and I could see that they have been rewritten substantially from the original and the three subsequent authors' interpretations had changed the whole direction of the original document.

Not a single Ranger I have ever met knew anything about the gun batteries at Maisy prior to them being told to attack them on 9 June 1944. At no time were they as individuals or as companies briefed in advance of a planned attack on the Maisy site – nor were they given a site layout or intelligence maps prior to landing.

I feel that we are now moving into a new era in understanding of the role of Maisy and the problems that occurred at Pointe du Hoc – and now we do not need more conjecture, vague rumours or personal verbal post-battle accounts. What we must have from now is an understanding of *actual* written period evidence – and that includes the fact that Maisy was a target – and an honest admission that Rudder did not tell his men about the place.

Equally important now is that ANY evidence must be dated before D-Day, and NOT written up afterwards as nearly every report was. This detail is important for our understanding of these battles, because Maisy has NOT appeared in a single book as a D-Day target for the Rangers, prior to mine. Post battle it vanished historically.

NO Ranger was told in advance by their commanding officer that Maisy existed and so they could all legitimately state that it was NOT one of their targets.

The same I feel can be said of the *'block the highway'* mission, which appears to have been made up to fit the circumstances that eventually happened and was never denied by their commanding officer. Remember the 'block the highway' order ONLY appears in POST D-Day paperwork and in modern books – never before D-Day.

All of the Rangers who survived the war would never have seen their battalion's actual orders for D-Day as they appear in this book – they only knew what they were told and nobody until now has ever said that things were any different.

I am also frankly astonished that nobody has fully researched the original Rangers' orders before now.

Maurice Prince: A Company, 2nd Rangers wrote the following in the 2nd Battalion diary for 30 May:

'These huge guns were casemented in large concrete pillboxes, whose thickness exceeded six to eight feet in depth. These structures were further protected and covered by anti-aircraft defence…. We got so that we knew every angle of the big picture and there wasn't a thing in the entire Army's plan of battle that we weren't familiar with.'

Maurice Prince thought when he wrote the battalion diary that he was fully briefed on the invasion targets – but we know that he was not.

Lt. Col. Rudder could not have known he was going to have problems at Pointe du Hoc BEFORE he got there, yet he did not tell anybody about their missions thereafter – which is very strange. Why the deliberate concealment of the orders from his men?

In my view, continuing the pretence that the PdH mission was still important, allowed Rudder to put himself onto the mission as its leader when the time came. As the Pointe du Hoc mission then became such a mess, you could argue the best thing to do was say nothing about Maisy, talk about guarding the road and thus cover up the problems created by not attacking Maisy.

You might ask, why did his superiors not correct this and sanction him? Perhaps for the same reasons they did nothing about Lytle. What would they do – publicly strip Rudder of his medal, blame him for the mess of Pointe du Hoc and state that he was the cause of Maisy still firing? Of course not, because this would have reflected on them for not monitoring him pre-D-Day.

But perhaps his superiors saved their opinion of Rudder for a little while until all the fuss had died down. Rudder's move to another unit away from the Rangers is not something that I would have normally investigated, as it goes well beyond the remit of this work … but purely as background, I looked into the unit he was reassigned to and it raised a few questions with me.

The following report records how the men of the Rangers, and indeed Rudder himself found out he was being transferred out of the Rangers, some 6 months after D-Day.

US Army Medical Department – Office of Medical History Report based on an Interview with: Major George S. Williams, Commander 2nd Rangers.

HURTGEN FOREST ACTION (23 November–10 December 1944)

2nd Ranger Battalion – "*On 7 December Lt. Col. James E. Rudder, commander of the Rangers, went back to First Army Headquarters on some unknown mission. In his absence Captain George S. Williams, the executive officer, and Captain Harvey Cook, S-2, were called to 8th Division Headquarters where they were given the mission of going to Bergstein. There was little information about the terrain and no one had seen the ground. They wanted the Rangers to attack at 0300 in the morning. Major Williams indicated, however, that "I'm not sure that it isn't better for well trained troops to find their way at night than to hold up and take a chance on being hit by artillery at daylight". However, the Rangers didn't want to attack the place cold (Williams). Trucks were ordered to move towards Kleinhau over a road which had already been reconoitered. The trucks were in a dispersed area and "we had a heck of a time getting them together." Captain Edward Arnold led the truck column to Kleinhau. There the companies detrucked in a defiladed position and began their march to Bergstein. While the companies were moving the Command Post group, led by Lt. Col. Rudder, who had returned from First Army shortly before, and Major Williams proceeded to Brandenberg. There Col. Rudder announced that Major Williams was in command of the battalion. Col. Rudder had just been given command of the 109th Infantry, 28th Division. Captain Arnold pointed out: "It was something of a low blow to George because he knew it was going to be a bad fight and you don't change command in the middle of an operation. It was quite a blow to all the members of the unit to see him go (Williams)."*"

The following text is an evaluation of Rudder's new unit at the very time when he took over his new command and it is taken from the: *Operational Performance of the U.S. 28th Infantry Division, September to December 1944* – Major Geoffrey P. Holt. Published by Pickle Publishing.

"December found the 28th still recovering from its wounds defending a 25 mile front along the Luxembourg-German border. Its assigned frontage was so great that units manned a series of strongpoints instead of a continuous line of resistance. The strongpoints were, for the most part, built around the small villages and towns scattered throughout the sector. This positioning allowed units to rotate soldiers into shelters for rest, minimising exposure to the tough winter conditions. Soldiers also continued to rotate to divisional and corps rest centres further to the rear. Red Cross club mobiles and doughnut wagons made their visits and there was a full schedule of USA shows and dances to help raise morale.

As units began to become effective organisations once more, training activities stepped up. Limited combat missions, primarily intelligence gathering patrols, remained excellent training vehicles to build the experience level of new soldiers and leaders. Units also engaged in foot marches, techniques for assaulting bunkers, and basic infantry skills.

The basic infantry skills training was particularly important, for by this time in the war a large number of the replacements were not infantrymen by training. The insatiable demand for infantry replacements forced the army to convert large numbers of specialty troops into riflemen. Two of the larger sources for such conversions were anti-aircraft artillery units and the airforce. Limited duty soldiers, soldiers who were no longer fit for combat due to medical reasons took the place of the service troops."

It is abundantly clear that Lt. Col. Rudder was removed from the Rangers during an action and given an inferior role to play within another infantry division – this certainly could not in any way be seen as a promotion. This Division was hit hard by the Germans later on, and it gave a very good account of itself. However, at the moment Col. Rudder was transferred to it, it was NOT in the same league as the Rangers.

The evidence presented in the pages of this book – page after page – are not invented. It is not all hearsay, rumour, veterans' remembrances, etc. The facts are here in black and white. Lt. Col. Rudder did not tell his men of the details of their missions before or afterwards. The only reason that I can see for him doing that is because he wanted to lead the Pointe du Hoc mission.

Another strange quote from Prince's history of the 2nd Battalion comes with his admission that his recording of the D-Day mission may not be accurate. One naturally assumes that either he did know all the objectives of the 2nd Battalion as he said early in his report, or he did not, and on this point he later seems suddenly unsure. Logically, why would there be any doubt in his mind as to the mission of the 2nd Battalion? See what you make of this quote from within his narrative, remembering that this was written retrospectively and then dated 30 May.

(Note-due to the high secrets of these documents and maps, plus the danger and hazardness of our mission, these papers had to be destroyed less perchance they fell into enemy hands, so that now my records are very incomplete concerning the plans which were handed down to us about the part our Battalion was to enact in the coming invasion. Please bear with me and forgive me if any discrepencies appear in the following paragraph.)

It certainly suggests to me that he was of the opinion the unit's mission was one thing and ended up being something else. The way he has worded it also appears as though he now does not want to challenge anything said by anyone else. So he plays the middle ground by seeming slightly confused.

Note also the preciseness of his chosen wording *'concerning the plans which were handed down to us about the part our Battalion was to enact in the coming invasion.'* Does this not suggest that his understanding of battalion orders 'handed down' to the 2nd Battalion actually differed from those enacted by his commanding officer on the day – and thus he does not want to contradict anything?

He is clearly trying to fudge his position by apologizing for this. Prince also refers to the guns being casemented, when in actual fact all intelligence stated correctly that there were no guns in the two casements and that there were four under construction. Remember the 'U/C' on the GSGS intelligence maps, the same maps not given out by Lt. Col. Rudder? Remember also, that it could be argued that it suits Lt. Col. Rudder's position post-battle if his men 'thought' that there were guns in the casements just before D-Day. It is no wonder that Prince was confused after the battle when he had to write up a different version of events. Things which were clearly explained as a mission and objectives to him prior to D-Day (and recorded by him at the time) turned out to be nothing of the sort.

The whole of the debate about guns at the Pointe bounces between the Rangers before the assault, thinking they were going after six guns on gun pits – and as individuals and small groups they were each given orders to attack certain guns; then the veterans afterwards are all stating that they were after six guns, others then say four, others say casements, there is chaos, muddled versions, numbers of guns destroyed, etc, and yet, not one of them has mentioned that there was not actually a full six positions at the Pointe capable of holding a gun when they arrived. If you go and look at Pointe du Hoc today – there are NOT actually six operational gun positions there. Yet nobody mentioned in the After Action Report that this intelligence was not given to the men before they arrived?

Post battle, Rangers all talked about casements with wooden guns, six pits with wooden guns, then three casements, etc. Seventy years later the history of PdH is now a series of mixed up versions of individuals' interpretations of events as they understood it. There has never been clarity or correction of the errors from Lt. Col. Rudder about it – and he did not clarify or correct the errors in the SUA Report – either in writing or during interviews after the war. If we are to consider that a lot of the problems are of his own making, then it makes sense not to get drawn into a discussion about gun numbers, objectives or missions. Post war, Rudder was approached (as were most of the Rangers) by Cornelius Ryan and asked to tell his own story of D-Day. Rudder's replies on the questionnaire showed a complete lack of interest in helping, or recording anything historically. Yet, other Rangers wrote many pages of their own personal experiences. All of these interesting accounts are held within the Ohio State University – Ryan Collection.

Below are some quotes taken again directly from the SUA Report, and there are a lot more besides these. Read them and then consider honestly if you think that these quotes convey this action as being a well-led and organized attack with Lt. Col. Rudder in full operational control throughout? He is not mentioned as taking charge, he was not issuing sensible orders and organizing his men in a timely fashion. These comments portray the action in such a way as to suggest that it was leaderless, lacked direction and it was truly a mission saved by the efforts of the junior officers – as it was they who made the command decisions when needed. I believe Lt. Col. Rudder was NOT in charge of this operation – there was a complete lack of control, and no plans for an organized defence of the position were in place.

…Some Rangers of Companies D and E failed to reach the assembly area in time for the next phase of movement, or were kept on the Point to meet unexpected developments.

…one gets a fair reflection of the confusion that existed under the difficulties of this last phase in a night battle. Arman reports that after the opening fire he, Lapres, and the 5th Ranger officers went ahead with the plan to withdraw, already agreed on. Arman had no idea whether Leagans of Company D knew the plan. According to Lieutenant Zelepsky (5th Rangers), there was little or no prearranged plan...

… This led to a hasty decision to withdraw…

…Some of the 5th Ranger men who had been in the Company E line later said that the 2nd Rangers "pulled out and left them there."…

…hasty and informal measures were taken to pass the word around for withdrawal back to the highway and the Pointe. Some Rangers failed to get the notice and were temporarily left behind.

…Noncommissioned officers tried hurriedly to round up their men.…

…some Rangers even believed that the enemy were in the rear of their position, near the blacktop.

…Hathaway stuck his head through the hedgerow and shouted "Hey! What's up? Where you going?"…

…As the parties arrived at the blacktop, there was no sign of any pursuit, and an effort was made to reorganize those Rangers at hand …

… The 5th Ranger men made their way through the completely unfamiliar terrain in scattered parties (and were afterward resentful of their having been cast adrift…

…According to plan or not, a withdrawal took place from the CP area…

…Nevertheless, the advance was still continuing when an order came from the rear to pull back.

…During the day, the D, E, and F parties had co-operated on a more or less informal basis, with co-ordination secured by consultation of the four officers, Lieutenants Kerchner (D), Leagans and Lapres (E), and Arman (F).

When plans had to be made in the morning as to positions for the day, Lieutenant Arman was the senior officer at hand and seems to have made the decisions.

After that he did not consider himself in command in any formal sense. The decision to shorten up and tighten the defenses for the night was taken when Lieutenant Kerchner came over to Arman's post and reported seeing Germans in some strength to the southwest. Arman, Lapres, and Kerchner talked it over and agreed as to readjustment of positions.

… The order had come from some distance and was based on a misapprehension.

I believe it is not justified to suggest that there was confusion created because of the way events unfolded – simply because I feel they unfolded exactly as they would have been expected to do – **if** the mission was to block the road and stay at the Pointe. You would expect to be surrounded, you would have expected to be counter-attacked and you would be cut off until relieved. Everyone would know what they were doing throughout and where they should be.

The whole of the SUA Report reads like a disaster movie from one end to the other. And it *was* a military disaster with hundreds of men killed or wounded by the end.

The current US Army trains its officers to expect the worse and train for every eventuality – and *had* the gun pits and the 'highway' been the Rangers' sole mission objectives, then these events would not have been a surprise to anyone. By leaving his men to flounder in the surrounding fields with NO apparent idea of direction or any orders – while he stayed to create a HQ is not, in my view an example of exemplary leadership. It shows the complete opposite and we need to think about what his superiors would have thought about the mess post battle.

What options did they have? Very few.

Did they discipline him for not completing his missions? NO.

Did they suggest to anyone that this was a mission failure? NO.

Did they cover it all up? Perhaps.

Did Lytle try to tell the men, and did Rudder get rid of him for it? Yes, 100%.

Was Rudder given the DSC for a failed mission? Perhaps, and this was *before* the SUA Report was researched and written. No going back after that.

The list goes on, but the end result is the same. This whole mess has been covered up by inaction and lack of discussion and I can say that with conviction, as many of the documents contained here have never appeared in print before. This all suggests to me that by marking everything Top Secret and allowing flawed After Action Reports to circulate, there was a deliberate effort to let the mists of time gloss over what happened. This was not just an accidental cover-up with a few papers going missing.

Another good example is the award of the DSC to Joe Urish. The official records state it was won by Urish on 10 June – when in fact it was won at Maisy on the morning of the 9th at La Martinière. Why was this error never corrected and Maisy not mentioned within his award? Lt. Col. Rudder will have signed off and/or at least have read his certificate, so he would have known what it was for as he stood with him in-line to receive it. Imagine the scene, when Lt. Col. Rudder is standing with the select number of men who had won the DSC – do you think for one minute that he did not know why each of the men serving under him had won the second highest award in the US Army? It is inconceivable that he did not know why Urish won this DSC – and equally, should we believe that Lt. Col. Rudder knew nothing about Maisy after the war?

Remember also that Major Sullivan won his DSC in part for his actions in capturing prisoners and the position at Maisy. It was also presented at the very same time, on the same day. Yet again are we to believe that Rudder does not know anything about the place. Maisy is not mentioned in Rudder's biography? It is said that Rudder's (and one assumes everyone else's DSCs) were read out in front of the rest of the battalion at a presentation ceremony.

Then there is the 'mystery' order of '*blocking the highway*' which the soldiers were told PRIOR to landing. To a man, they have accepted this as being part of their mission and they have repeated it time and time again.

On this subject – just to address any critical historical analysis of it – this could not have been an order given to Rudder in secret by someone on the day as they left harbour, because Rudder was not supposed to have been on the mission. Major Lytle was removed from his post whilst onboard a ship that was at sea. Any last minute mission changes of that magnitude would have been given to all the senior officers prior to them leaving on 1 June and that did not happen. Additionally they would have briefed their men and it would have been documented as a last minute change in all the copies of plans held by everyone including Major General Huebner.

vi) No Mention of Maisy

Another small evidential example showing a lack of full and open brief for Rudder's men comes by way of a copy of the map carried by Major General John Raaen (Ret). On D-Day he was a captain with HQ Company 5th Rangers and he should have known all there was to know about the Ranger missions, but he was not told the full story either.

At the time of writing this book, he still owns his original D-Day map with his pre-D-Day markings, which he was kind enough to let me photograph. You can see where he marked the Maisy Batteries as numbers – Target

No.5 and 16 on his map, as well as other target numbers along the coastline. He did this based on grid references and he told me that he did so knowing that there was 'something there' and that the low target numbers indicated to him that it was a target of some significance. However, he had ZERO knowledge or briefing of Maisy in advance of the 9 June attack and he simply marked down targets from a written list he had seen. He was also completely unaware of the Maisy part of the Neptune Monograph assault brief and anyone who has had the privilege of knowing John, will confirm that he is not given to making up any part of his D-Day testimony. During the many years that we have corresponded, conducted filming and had discussions, his memory of events has never wavered. He was NOT briefed to attack Maisy in advance of 9 June and nor were the men of the 5th Rangers under him.

In May 1944 the difference between the recorded Army Intelligence and that of the Air Force and Navy starts to become very apparent. In Air Force documents, the question of whether the gun position at Pointe du Hoc should be attacked or not is now being voiced. It is marked as such on the papers – but at the same time the regular Army report paperwork still continues to state that Pointe du Hoc is a 6 x 155mm gun battery. Why the two differences in information when one is 100 per cent correct and the other is factually wrong?

Examining all the intelligence as it approaches D-Day, it is very clear that Pointe du Hoc was known to the Intelligence departments to no longer have six guns – it then is shown as having five, then four – and then quite possibly only three operational closer to D-Day – and these reports then provide those lower figures which are maintained in the run-up to D-Day.

Given everything that appears to have been manipulated during this whole operation, it seems odd that Lt. Col. Rudder did nothing to change the perception that Pointe du Hoc was still the major target with his superiors, and to his men. He was the one receiving all of this intelligence information directly as it was updated daily. I can see no other reason why the intelligence reports reaching Lt. Col. Rudder state a downgrading of Pointe du Hoc, and this is repeated with the Air Force and Navy paperwork which say the same thing. All are coming from the same intelligence sources.

But the regular Army reports being printed out steadfastly continue to state that Pointe du Hoc is a 6 x 155mm gun battery. If the intelligence was gathered and then submitted directly to the Air Force, Navy and simultaneously directly to Lt. Col. Rudder, then went from him and made its way into the Army reports we see today, then we may have our answer. The reports coming out via Rudder maintained that there was a strong position that needed to be attacked at Pointe du Hoc. To other branches of service their versions of the same paperwork suggested that it was not!

Lt. Col. Rudder will have been aware that this was inaccurate intelligence being given out and he said nothing? Once again if looked at cynically, it could suggest that the only person who had everything to gain by this information remaining incorrect was the man himself.

There might be other reasons to 'lose' Maisy from the history books. Here are a few veterans' comments on the subject of Maisy, which include some mention of the large amount of French money found within the site. The amount of money was estimated to have been near to $4.2 million in French currency, which was reported to have been the monthly German payroll for the region. This went unpaid on 6 June because of the invasion. Now this may or may not be relevant to the bigger picture, but all of the money appears to have vanished at the time of the Rangers' assault. Coincidence perhaps and it does not detract from the overall story, but I can find no paperwork confirming that this money was ever handed in at the beach and yet there are comments from Rangers stating that a number of them were taking large amounts of it! I am of the opinion that Rudder had no part in this.

The following comments all come from interviews with veterans filmed by the author.

Frank Kennard HQ 2nd Btn: *I have no knowledge of Maisy. At the invasion staging area all the 2nd Rangers had very large 3-dimensional maps which covered in great detail the Vierville exit and Pointe du Hoc. As far as I can recollect there was no detail of Maisy on it and nor can I recall it ever being named. One could walk on the map and actually see what might be encountered. It wasn't a 2nd Ranger objective and, if all the 2nd & 5th could have come to the Pointe (the initial plan) the Ranger force would have completely 'by-passed' Maisy. I do not recall EVER hearing about Maisy Battery until AFTER V-E Day.*

Pfc Francis Coughlin Intelligence Officer HQ Company 5th Btn: *There is a lot to be desired about Pointe du Hoc – we always argue that what they did there had nothing to do with the war itself. ... there is a lot of history that's lost. I don't remember anything about Maisy from Intelligence at all.*

I heard about the pile of money – some of the guys were saying that they got a lot of money and were splitting it up. Someone said how much and someone else said they don't know how to count. But it's a hell of a lot. They had a lot of money and in fact the guys that got it, they never said anything about it. In-fact if you ask the guys who got it today, there is only about three or four left who were in on it. If you ask them today, they will tell you they had a hell of a good time with it. The guys always said you went to the wrong place and you found guns ... but way back then we argued for an hour and then had a beer.

Jim Wilderson F Company 5th Btn: *When we hit Maisy, I did see three of the gun emplacements and when it was over, we didn't make any big deal over it, we didn't think it was any great big deal. It was just part of the job. I saw many prisoners. Whenever we took prisoners, we had a central stockade to take them to the beach... we would shake them down and take their money. I had a German sergeant and I found out that he was the paymaster for the company. I took this satchel, it was full of money and an officer took it away from me. I know he sent it home. We dug in and waited for replacements before moving out and we were there for the best part of the day. Nobody has ever asked me about Maisy – we didn't realise until afterwards what we had hit. We certainly didn't realise how important it was until afterwards!*

John Reville 1st Lt. F Company 5th: *How could this be a secret for so many years – it didn't make sense that the local people didn't know what was there. Maisy was not any objective of ours. Believe it or not, there is some feeling of resentment between the two battalions... there was that feeling sometimes that nobody stuck up for us.*

Sgt. Len Lomell D Co. 2nd Btn: *(Pointe du Hoc) There were just telephone poles in the casements so we just moved on. We didn't waste two minutes, we were off. We didn't know the difference between any of the guns. We were just looking for guns. We didn't even have a picture of the guns in advance. We were leapfrogging through the hedgerows and I looked out right in front of me were the guns. They were by the hedgerows and they were camouflaged. Not too heavily camouflaged. I told Jack to keep watch.*

There was nobody near the guns – I didn't see anyone with them. The Germans were coming in all directions but not next to the guns. So I said Jack keep your eyes on them and keep your eyes on me. If anyone sees me, kill them. Nobody saw me so I put them out of action. The Germans never even knew we had damaged the guns.

We ran out of grenades so I said we have to go back to the roadblock and get theirs. We all carried one or two to lessen our load as we had so much to carry. I only had two grenades and I took out two howitzers and made them unusable. They just melted into the metal work around the mechanism and working parts. But then I took my submachine gun and wrapped it up in my field jacket and I smashed the sights on the guns so the sights could not be used – or if they were, they would be inaccurate.

So we went back the roadblock at a run. We got the rest of the grenades and stuffed them in our blouses.

We managed to destroy them and get out – as we were getting out of there, the whole place went up – it was the ammunition depot in the other direction and Sgt Rupinski had been looking for guns and destroyed the ammunition.

We had no plan of where everything was. The blast from the ammo was on the other side of the hedgerow and the blast blew up the whole area. We got back to the roadblock. I never heard of Maisy until years after the war until I visited Grandcamp – somebody mentioned Maisy.'

[Author]: In a filmed interview at his home Len Lomell told me this: '*Those guns had not been recently moved to that position. They'd been there a long time. There wasn't one bomb crater near them, therefore they were so well camouflaged that the air force never saw them.*'

This is an interesting comment simply for the fact that so many other books state that the Rangers followed tracks into the lane and this alerted them to the position of the guns. I wonder where those actual quotes comes from as there were only two people who 'followed' these 'tracks' on the day – Len Lomell and Jack Kuhn. Len Lomell told me on camera that there were no tracks.

George Kerchner Lt 2nd Rangers: (talking about PdH) *We felt pretty disappointed when we got there and there were no guns.*

Pfc Daniel Farley A Co. 5th Btn: (talking about Maisy) *One guy from C Company also found a stash of money. We thought there was about $50,000 in francs, in the French notes and I took some of it. The C Company guy and I took a bundle of it and later on took it down to the beach and made out a money order and sent it home. We took advantage of the American taxpayers as we could send it home then. Ace Parker also had a stack of it. Schneider ended up with a bunch of it as well and we all played poker with it later. At the time some guys were wiping their butts with it and lighting their cigars and cigarettes – simply because we didn't know it was any good – then some officer told us it was ok to send it back home in money orders.*

John Raaen: *The money was stacked in 14in square bundles and the Rangers did indeed literally throw it all around. I heard that there was 3 or 4 million francs or dollars total value.*

I didn't send any money home, but my recollection is that if you took the money to any Finance Office it would be converted into dollars. You were then given a money order for the amount and then all you had to do was mail it home. From there we heard that four new millionaires were created through the money orders home!

Dick Hathaway A Co. 5th Btn: (talking about Maisy) *The only thing that surprised me was that the people in Grandcamp didn't know anything about the site. They knew absolutely nothing. The information was really secret, well concealed information.*

Jack Burke A Co. Medic 5th Btn: (talking about Maisy) *It was a tough scene, but we finally got to the top of the hill and started clearing out the trenches and the Germans started to surrender. There was more to taking this battery because it was much larger than we thought. We had never heard of Maisy Battery in our briefings. I remember they told us on board the ship in Weymouth harbour that after we accomplished our initial objective on D-Day we would be going to hook up with the Airborne around Isigny. I would bet my life that the first time I ever heard of Maisy was when we got near it. I did not know we were not going to Isigny as we were told. We were all impressed not only with the size, but the structuring of Maisy - an underground medical area, officer's quarters, and the fire power. They had 88's along with 105's and 155's. There were German SS stationed there.*

Veteran Jack Burke continued more recently: *I have had a question in the back of my mind since June 8th 1944 – always hoping someone will come up with an answer. But it hasn't happened. Let me give you some background. Last week I had my 93rd Birthday therefore I am looking to you for guidance.*

When the 5th Ranger Btn, was getting its briefing on our assignments (primary and secondary) for the period for June 6 thru June 8, we didn't actually meet the time table, but I can vividly remember that after we captured Vierville sur Mer and Pointe du Hoc, we were to strike out for the town of Isigny and link up with paratroopers. This was not done, we went from Pointe du Hoc to Grandcamp and on the 9th the 5th Btn (with NO 2nd Btn) attacked the Maisy Battery.

OK. Why the change from Isigny to Maisy? Why just the 5th Ranger Btn? Where was the 2nd Btn? This was the only time that we were not totally briefed. It was a strange situation. Any help on these questions will be appreciated. Whatever happened to the 2nd Btn?

When Rudder was offered naval gunfire support on 8 June he declined it. I cannot see what possible reason he could have for not accepting this help when Maisy was known to be still operational. Here is a quote from Naval Gunfire Liaison Officer Coit Coker's After Action Report – dated 8 June (US National Archives). '*I volunteered our fire power to the 2nd Rangers, but they had no need for us.*'

Coit Coker thought that it was significant enough to put it into his report.

By way of a further bizarre twist to this whole story, in the weeks running up to their landing Lt. Col. Rudder gave his men specific roles to be undertaken during the Pointe du Hoc assault. I am led to believe that a paper exists drawn by Captain Lytle to this effect (I have not seen it). Orders which we can say with certainty contained elements that Rudder would have known at that time to be unnecessary and this could be why Lytle was so upset with Rudder.

Below is a direct quote – again taken from the Small Unit Actions Report. This is not an account of the Rangers' actual physical orders as a battalion. This is an account of what the individual Rangers told the people writing the report that they were ordered to do by their commanding officer – and these were the orders they tried to carry out on the actual day. There is a big historical distinction between these two points:

> *The first and chief objectives were the gun emplacements and the OP near the end of the Point. Company E had the OP and No.3 position as its assignment; Company D, the western gun emplacements (4, 5, and 6); Company F, guns 1 and 2 and the machine-gun position at the edge of the cliff, just east of the main fortified area. Once these objectives were taken, the plan had been to assemble at a phase line near the south edge of the fortified area. From here, D, F, and most of E would strike inland for the coastal highway about 1,000 yards south, cross it, and establish a road block against enemy movement from the west. A platoon of Company E was to remain on the Point with the headquarters group and arrange for perimeter defence of the captured fortifications.'*

Many of these positions were known in advance to have been emptied, built upon or simply *'dismantled'* by the Germans. From a military leadership perspective, why did Lt. Col. Rudder waste manpower sending his men to attack positions already known to him and allied intelligence to be 100 per cent empty? In the case of pit 5, it had ceased to exist long before 21 April. He would ONLY have done this if he had wished to continue with the pretence that Pointe du Hoc was still operational and the mission was still worthy of the Rangers' involvement.

I must also question why the 'historical records' ie. The Small Unit Actions Report and others which were printed post-battle show aerial photos of a damaged Pointe du Hoc – and onto these pictures someone has re-drawn the round gun positions – as if to indicate where the pits were. This is very misleading from a historical standpoint because it directs the reader to make the assumption that these were all operational targets.

Was it that Lt. Col. Rudder *'had to make sure'* all of the emplacements and surrounding fields were empty as is suggested in his biography? Surely if this was the case, then it is even more bizarre that he then stayed for three days to guard and defend a site full of empty abandoned gun pits, which very obviously offered zero strategic importance to the Germans.

You land, the place is empty, you destroy the guns a mile away and you move on as ordered – and you move especially during the many hours that you have *'no contact with the enemy'*.

Dr Hatfield suggests that a blockage of the road behind Pointe du Hoc would prevent the Germans from using it to bolster their defences at Omaha Beach – and frankly, that sounds like a statement which appears very plausible on the surface, but when you dig deeper, it has very little substance. If the Germans had wanted to go to Vierville, they would have simply bypassed the Pointe du Hoc position completely, moving via the fields or the other shorter routes and carried on their way to the beach landing area. There can be no sensible argument to suggest that by staying at Pointe du Hoc, Rudder's men would in any way protect the landings at Vierville.

The simplest way to prove this is by using a map.

Across fields and side roads, the distance from Isigny-sur-Mer (where the Germans had a moderate troop concentration) to the Omaha landing beach at Vierville is 9 miles.

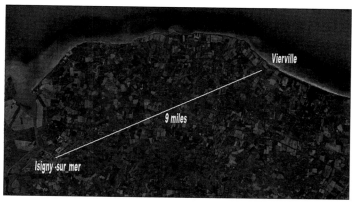

Below: By road – should the Germans wish to drive on a decent surface – there are three routes. The shortest is 12.7 miles and does not go anywhere near Pointe du Hoc and the longest, most direct (and quickest) is 13.3 miles. On the map below, this is called N13, which is a modern road. The old road still exists and runs parallel to the N13. The most time-consuming route German troops could have taken would be the one past Pointe du Hoc. It is a fair guess that Allied Intelligence had noticed that – hence they ordered Lt. Col. Rudder and his men landing at Omaha Beach and at Pointe du Hoc to advance inland far enough to block the D514 just north of Osmanville (on the D-Day Phase Line). They would therefore block ALL three options from being available to the Germans.

If you were a German officer ordered to go to Vierville from Isigny-sur-Mer, which way would you go? And if you were the Allied High Command planning on stopping the Germans from getting to the beach, would you order your men to stay at Pointe du Hoc and leave two other routes open to the Germans, or would you cover all three routes from the same position and order your Rangers to meet at a point where all three routes meet 12 miles inland?

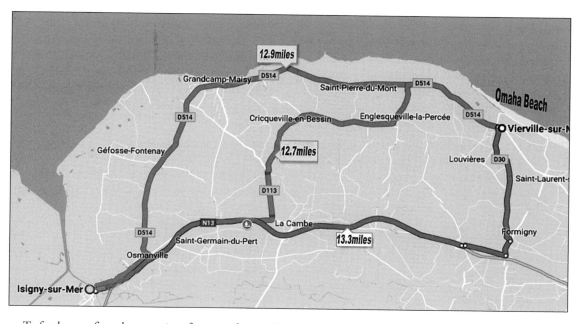

To further confirm the necessity of getting close to Isigny – the intelligence issued on 25 May stated:

"Anytime after the beach crust of defences has been breached, the enemy may counter-attack with battalion size forces: A battalion from ISIGNY Northeast – against elements of 116th RCT.

Anytime after noon of D-Day, the enemy may counter attack northeast from the ISIGNY area with up to an RCT of 91st or 243rd Division."

It was the Rangers' job to stop these forces attacking the beachhead.

The Germans counter-attacked Pointe du Hoc with small forces because that is what they were trained to do. The early garrison figures quoted in other works (which I have not been able to verify) put the number of men first stationed at Pointe du Hoc when it was built at 125 infantry and 85 artillerymen. Another creditable work on Pointe du Hoc puts the figures at 6 officers, 20 NCOs and 120 infantry. But often in reality, well before June 1944, these static units had been stripped of 'decent' men to fight in other combat units, leaving older and less able men in place.

Were there actually that many men at Pointe du Hoc on D-Day? I doubt it. A quick look at the number of soldiers: two per emplacement and then doubled to include overnight defence – and then artillerymen for the guns, observation and range-finding men, etc. probably does come to a figure similar to that. If the site was operational, but as the strongpoint had been packed up and the guns were ready to go, it is logical to suggest that the unit was moving its guns away so that another battery could come in behind them later. The defence on the day does not seem to indicate anywhere near that number of men on or near the cliff tops in the morning. There was no range-finding equipment installed as we have photographs of that, empty. The men were not in their underground 622 personnel shelters sleeping, the infirmary was not occupied by wounded, the observation position was not full of officers, it only had a handful of men. I also think a group of 100+ men motivated to defend Pointe du Hoc, on or near the cliff edge would have finished off the Rangers very quickly once the bombardment had stopped – but they could have only done that if they had been there.

The open gun pits at Pointe du Hoc are of the type used by a German Army Coastal Artillery Battery. The casements being built are more typical of a Kriegsmarine (Navy) Coastal Artillery position and although this is nothing but circumstantial evidence at this time, it makes me wonder if the Germans intended to replace the Army battery stationed at Pointe du Hoc with a Kriegsmarine battery by installing new navy deck-mounted weapons. It would not have been unusual for them to do that and it could account for the lack of soldiers in place when the position was attacked.

German General-Major von Buttlar in an interview with US Intelligence post D-Day stated the following:

> *In the case of land-based naval artillery, the Navy retained control of fire on water-borne targets. This control was not to be transferred to the German Army until there was a definite landing.*
>
> *The regulations for the subordination of the coast artillery, and the directive for its conduct of fire missions, were disapproved by the Army commanders-in-chief in almost all theaters. The Navy, however, cited its combat experiences against naval targets and rejected all compromise. In the face of the very firm stand and bitter opposition of the Navy, it proved impossible to modify the arrangements.*

There was a lot of controversy confirmed to have been encountered by Rommel within the German hierarchy, as to who was responsible for firing upon ships at sea and who could then fire at troops on the beaches. The Kriegsmarine, as stated above, advocated that it was their job to fire at seaborne vessels and the Army were to concentrate on the beaches and inland. It would not be unthinkable to suggest that once the guns had been removed from the Pointe, the gunners reverted to being a land-based artillery unit ordered only to fire at land-based targets. As there were no immediate ground targets for them to attack on D-Day morning – perhaps they were told to wait for further orders?

It is worth remembering also that the batteries at Crisbecq, Maisy and Longues-sur-Mer had the coastal approaches covered by their weapons. Pointe du Hoc was an addition to the coastal defence in the area – not the primary position in the area at that time. One problem we find historically is that many authors have written their works as if PdH had been *the* coastal defence position in the area. It was only when Maisy was 'rediscovered' that people realized there had been another coastal battery position and Pointe du Hoc could have been empty without compromising the integrity of the sector's coastal defence. The main issue is that by the time Maisy appeared from the soil in 2006, most big books had already been written and the tours of Pointe du Hoc had been running for years. That is a difficult historical correction to try and make because opinions have settled in – and authors' reputations for accuracy have already been earned.

Friedrich Ruge was Erwin Rommel's Naval Advisor in 1944 and he accompanied Rommel on his tours of the French coast. Written post war in his dairy entitled *ROMMEL in Normandy*, he confirms the problems of Army and Navy had with their Coastal Artillery.

> *No agreement had been reached regarding the basic principles of placing the artillery on the coast. Probably nobody had made the attempt. Even later in France this was only partially resolved. The navy was of the opinion that only*

by direct sighting methods would they be sufficiently successful against targets moving on the water. Therefore, the navy erected its batteries directly on the coast, accepting the risk that they would be taken under direct fire from the sea. The army, in contrast was of the opinion that the batteries should be camouflaged and stationed in the rear areas with forward-positioned observers directing their fire, since forward positioned artillery could easily be put out of action from the air as well as from the sea.

The batteries stationed in the rear areas could only become effective the moment the enemy's landing craft reached the beach. A well-camouflaged battery several kilometres behind the coast, however, had considerable chance of avoiding early discovery. As a result there was no basic agreement between these opinions either then or later. As early as December 5, 1943 Rommel noted in his daily report: 'Antipathy against the artillery's indirect firing methods seems to be universal in the navy.' [Rommel in Normandy – Published by K. F. Koehler Verlag, Stuttgart, Germany 1979].

Most of the German soldiers mentioned in the SUA Report appear to have already been to the rear at the Pointe – beyond where the guns were found and beyond all the accommodation available at the Pointe – confirming the proposal that they were not staying there. This is proved further because these men were viewed from a distance by 2nd Btn. S/Sgt. Len Lomell and appeared to be getting dressed and changing into their clothes. He saw them whilst he was neutralizing the guns. I have therefore made the assumption that if you were stationed at the Pointe, you would not leave your clothes a mile away and walk back from the Pointe to get dressed each morning?

This is also an indication that the defence of the Pointe on D-Day was commensurate with that of a single coastal observation position with only sentries on duty. I think that a number of the counter-attacks were carried out locally by forces already in the area and not by others having travelled a distance. In my book *Cover Up at Omaha Beach* there is an example of this. I list US Naval strikes called in by spotters on troops advancing towards Pointe du Hoc from the west during daylight. They were travelling from the Maisy village direction across open fields, somewhat proving that they were not eager to travel down open roads during daylight hours.

The German Army practised and promoted the art of counter-attack and it was to be undertaken as soon as possible when an enemy took a position to stop the enemy consolidating their gains. For the German Army it was normal for them to do that – irrespective of the position taken having been an operational site or not. Therefore the reason the Germans counter-attacked the Rangers at Pointe du Hoc was not because the position was of huge importance to them, it was simply tactics that they were trained to employ in situations like this.

We know from the Small Unit Actions report excerpt shown earlier that an order was given by Rudder for men to remain at the Pointe and arrange a *'perimeter defence'*. A number of veterans have said that this order was also issued to them by Lt. Col. Rudder BEFORE the Pointe was attacked. To have instructed his men in advance that they were staying at the Pointe after destroying its guns is a worrying revelation. It shows premeditation on his part not to advance any further and a conscious decision not to follow orders.

The observation post at Pointe du Hoc was not of any military importance, so it could not be used as a justification for him staying there. It is set so low into the cliff-top and it affords a worse observer's view of the coastline than from the upstairs floors of the chateau nearby. Any position on the land locally would give a better perspective on the invasion than what was provided from inside the low-lying observation bunker, not to mention the fact that the Rangers had left Germans inside it for a couple of days. If it was an objective that absolutely had to be stopped from functioning as an observation position – then one assumes the Rangers would simply have blown their way in sooner and not relied on just shooting off the aerials. The Rangers had no way of knowing that the Germans were not still operating conventional telephone communication with other gun batteries from inside the bunker.

The value to the Germans of the observation bunker came from the fact that it was bomb-proof – or relatively so. They could benefit from an unrestricted view of the coastal approaches and do so because it was well-built enough to remain operational during an attack from the air or by naval vessels. It would survive anything other than a direct hit through the front viewing aperture. It could also continue to give ranging information to other batteries if it remained operational, but it was of no real strategic value. Beyond that function, it should have been seen as an incidental objective and more of a nuisance for the Rangers only because they stayed in the area, if for no other reason that it housed a handful of

Germans who could potentially have come out to attack them from behind. The very fact that the Rangers destroyed the aerials on the roof early on, would have indicated to them that they had neutralized it as well as they could, without the necessity of getting inside.

The same could be said for the anti-aircraft gun position to the west of the Pointe, which cost the lives of so many Rangers after 9am. This position was repeatedly attacked in an attempt to destroy it. Sometimes men were ordered to attack it and other times they went about it on their own. Yet it posed little or no direct threat to the troops landing on either Omaha or Utah beaches or to the vessels disembarking craft towards those beaches. At this time on D-Day morning no further air raids were planned for Pointe du Hoc, so it would not have had a lot to do. Why was it not ignored and left impotent in order to get on with the next part of the mission? It almost seems like it was attacked on some occasions to give the men something to do.

To further look at the role that was meant to be played by the Rangers on D-Day, it is worth noting that the Rangers' assaults at Slapton Sands earlier in the year contained a simultaneous cliff-top assault on a gun battery, a beach landing, followed by an advance inland and then further assault on another inland objective. The list of 'mock targets' in the practice area also included a 155mm and a 150mm gun battery and clearly represented Pointe du Hoc and Maisy. It was then to be followed by an advance inland to a designated halt position.

This exercise is a near perfect mimic of all the parts of the Rangers' actual D-Day missions and these were the missions given to the Rangers to be carried out on 6 June – NOT in the days that followed. The Germans needed to be kept at a line which was well behind the beaches – far enough for the Rangers and other units to be advanced and yet still benefit from Naval support, but equally far enough inland to prevent German artillery firing on the landings as they continued. We have seen that on nearly every one of the intelligence maps, the D-Day advancement 'Phase Line' is clearly marked and I feel this has been completely overlooked by historians. By not advancing to Maisy and beyond, Lt. Col. Rudder allowed the potential of a more serious German bombardment of the Omaha Beachhead to be launched from a shorter distance – or even a larger counter-attack of the beaches to build up not far away inland. Frankly, any suggestion that there was an order to stay and 'guard the highway' at Pointe du Hoc is ridiculous because it puts the whole of the western flank of the Omaha Beach landings in jeopardy.

But the status quo has appeared logical to everyone until now and has never been questioned. It stood the test of time and was roundly accepted as being the 'truth'. But the Rangers' orders need to be taken as a whole and the suggestion that the Pointe du Hoc battle was a successful mission does not do that.

Also, if we consider this logically, every other service, the Navy, the Air Forces and the units surrounding the Rangers would have had to have been informed that the Rangers' orders had been changed to remaining to 'guard the highway'. Historians should not only be looking for physical copies of the Rangers' orders to stay at Pointe du Hoc and guard a road – but confirmation of these same orders that would have also been placed with every other Armed service surrounding them. This offers many options beyond just the US Army records for historians to prove me wrong – and lots of other places where they can look for this paperwork. I have personally looked in the archives of the 1st Inf. Div, the US & UK National Archives, the RAF, the USAF, US and Royal Navy, and this change in orders does not exist. No other units around the Rangers were told that they would be staying at the Pointe.

The US generals who planned the Slapton Sands landings were aware that the Rangers had to attack multiple targets – then advance inland to a holding position. They trained and landed the Rangers in as realistic a way as possible to do what they were going to be asked to do later on D-Day. That is common sense and it must have been an important part of their planning. The beachhead needed to remain intact to allow everyone else to land safely.

We know the Royal Navy and Air Force were given the exact same information that allowed them to support and follow the Rangers' advance. This is confirmed by the 8.40pm 6 June radio request for clearance to bombard Targets 5, 16 and 16A. One assumes the request was made as a precaution in case the Rangers were about to reach the area – or in case they had already completed their missions as ordered. In which case they would have been at Maisy and friendly fire could be avoided. Someone was checking it was OK to open fire on Maisy, and the only reason you would check without firing first is if you thought friendly forces were in the area.

Here is a comment from a Situation Report. It is just a simple statement about the Rangers' operations recorded in the British Admiralty War Diary for 6 June. It reads: *The Two Ranger Battalions to secure the Western Flank of Omaha assault area.* The Royal Navy did not have instructions that the Rangers were staying at Pointe du Hoc. The 'Western Flank of Omaha' is to the west of Maisy – not to the east of it!

Guarding a 30ft-wide road 6 miles short of their brief is not quite the same as completing their orders. Had the Germans wanted to attack the beach from that flank by bringing up mobile artillery or rockets miles closer to the beach, they had the opportunity to do it. Fortunately for the Americans continuing to land, the Germans did not exploit that gap, but they could have done because they were left with ample room.

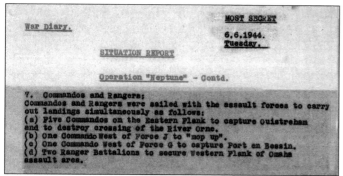

Another purpose for advancing further inland towards Maisy involved passing over the only bridge in the flooded area to the east of Grandcamp. This bridge could have been destroyed at any time by the Germans to prevent a break to the west by American forces towards Grandcamp. If this bridge was not protected, all of the armour landing on the beach would be unable to reach Grandcamp and the Maisy Batteries. By advancing over the bridge as ordered, Rudder and his men would have ensured that it was preserved for other units to use. The Germans did not blow it up and it stayed intact – but this was an obvious error in judgement that could have been costly. Especially when you consider that the attack on Maisy on the 9th was heavily supported by the tanks of the 743rd Tank Battalion and the 2nd Rangers' half-tracks. Without their help, the men of the 5th Btn may have failed to take Maisy on their own.

The way that the Pointe du Hoc assault is portrayed today is one of great daring – and it undoubtedly was. Let there be no doubt that the individual Rangers were rightfully called heroes for their actions. I have had the priviledge to know many Ranger veterans personally and have met many more and their families over the years. They were – and are always going to be – heroes in my eyes, and Maisy is the ONLY site in Europe to fly the Rangers flag for that reason. We have flown their flag for over 10 years – every single day, alongside the Stars and Stripes.

But this story is not just about heroism – it is now about historians telling things as accurately as we can and we owe that to the veterans. It has to be as right as we know it to be. This is in part why I had so much support from Ranger veterans over the history of Maisy. It is a story that they wanted told – yet NOBODY historically was listening to anything other than PdH and Omaha Beach. As veteran Jack Burke put it to me: *'the history of D-Day has been written largely by people who were not there and everyone has believed them…'*

Maisy was more powerful, certainly operational, better defended and put up a longer and more intense fight against the Allies as a whole than Pointe du Hoc – and yet it was buried before it was returned to the local French people. It has been ignored by historians around the world ever since, but, how many times is Maisy mentioned in the D-Day planning papers contained within this book?

I feel that history is not best served defending the actions and reputations of the few at the expense of a great many more heroes.

There needs to be a re-evaluation of what people think is important in the Omaha sector, and I guess that equally needs to start within the current Rangers themselves. I met and discussed this issue separately with two recently retired (post WWII) Ranger officers. They both told me that the Rangers' mission on D-Day was to destroy the PdH gun battery and put a road-block on the road – and that was it. That was exactly what they were taught during their training. I asked them both if they had ever seen any of the Rangers' actual orders in written form as issued – and they said no. Both were knocked off their feet when I showed them order after order over many months, ordering the Rangers to attack Maisy. They had both turned up at Maisy having heard the name and having seen our road sign and they then spent two hours walking around the site trying to figure out why they as Rangers had been told nothing about the place.

To a man on D-Day all the Rangers did exactly what they were ordered to do and, with the exception of Major Lytle, they did not question it. They are brave men for doing that and I believe that Major Lytle was also brave as he attempted to stand up to Rudder and tell him of the necessity to brief his men adequately – in full and in advance. It nearly cost Lytle his rank and liberty for challenging his superior and yet he did try and do this for his men. I doubt it was a decision he took lightly, and I bet there were times post war when he took strength in the fact that he knew he had tried to do the right thing, and yet he was stopped by Rudder.

The American Battlefield Monuments Commission have put up a plaque at Pointe du Hoc in recent years – long after Maisy was rediscovered. It shows the Airborne objectives of St. Marie Eglise, Carentan and St. Marie du Mont on the left, St. Pierre du Mont and Vierville for the 2nd Rangers and the locations where other forces landed, but there is no mention of the 5th Rangers or the Batteries at Maisy – despite Maisy having been the largest concentration of German field guns capable of firing on both Omaha and Utah sectors on D-Day.

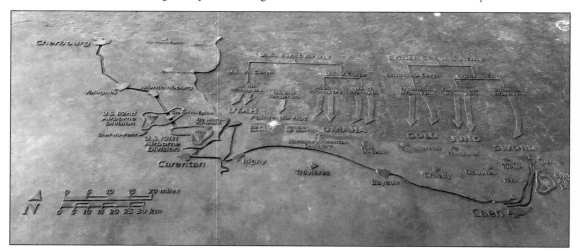

At Pointe du Hoc today there is a sign which states this:

> ## US ARMY RANGER UNITS SUSTAINED HEAVY LOSSES DURING THE NORMANDY LANDINGS.
>
> Of 225 Rangers that left the ships in the first wave to attack Pointe du Hoc, only 90 men were still able to bear arms when the relief force arrived on the morning of June 8. In the larger battle, the 2nd and 5th Ranger Battalions taken together suffered 96 killed, 183 wounded, and 32 missing during the battles for Pointe du Hoc and Omaha Beach.

vii) Counting the Numbers at Pointe du Hoc

To put all the dead and wounded into context for the PdH action and fully understand the numbers of men involved, I have gone back to the period documents and then added up all of the men that made up the attacking force, first wave. The normal figure stated on the plaques at Pointe du Hoc detail the number of Rangers first present at the Pointe at 225. While I do believe this is a slight underestimation, the bigger problem lies elsewhere. This is a serious misrepresentation of the situation, because overall, there were a lot more men fighting at Pointe du Hoc – and not all of them Rangers. And these men have never been given the credit they deserve for their actions... until now.

Why these men have never been included despite there being a clear record of them, I do not know. Perhaps it is just a mistake, and they will change their signs in the future. But the net result is that the actual number of men fighting at the Pointe has been downplayed, therefore the casualty figures have also been underestimated.

I know that's a bold thing to float, so to support that with some statistics, I have broken down the loading figures. They are the numbers of the men who boarded the craft to then land in the first wave of attack at Pointe du Hoc.

We start with the craft that were meant to go in and the number of men known to have been on-board each. This figure is taken from the Loading Schedule. I have assumed this figure is accurate, as it was written down before each craft left harbour with that number of men on board. The only exception to these numbers I know of is the addition of Lt. Col. Rudder, who joined the mission after the boats had left portside in England, and the SUA Report indicates +3, suggesting he took 2 other men with him. Major Lytle is also removed from these figures.

Rudder went on-board LCA 888. This was a logical choice for him, as it was one of the LCAs with the least number of men already allocated to it.

The numbers marked in bold below are the number of troops i.e. Rangers, Commandos, 58th Field Artillery and NSFCP recorded to have been on-board each LCA. Where others, such as the reporters are also known to be on board, they are stated, and the photographers are accounted for later. Further additional men who fought with the PdH group are listed at the end.

LCA 860 Loading schedule states 21 men onboard from D Co.	**21 men**
LCA 914 Supply vessel. Loading schedule lists 3 Rangers from HQ Co.	**3 men**
LCA 862 Loading schedule lists 16 Rangers + 4 Naval Shore Fire Control Party	**20 men**
LCA 722 Loading schedule lists 15 men from E Company and 3 from HQ. (SUA Report states 5 HQ men, so I have used that figure) plus a photographer from *Stars and Stripes,* and 2 British officers – Lieutenant Ronald F. Eades RNVR, and Lt. Col. Thomas Trevor.	**23 men**
LCA 668 Loading schedule lists 22 men from D Company, 1 from HQ Company.	**23 men**
LCA 858 Loading schedule lists 19 men from D Company onboard.	**19 men**
LCA 887 Loading schedule lists 20 men from F Co. and 3 from HQ Co. onboard.	**23 men**
LCA 884 Loading schedule lists 21 men from F. Co. and 4 men from the 58th Field Artillery Battalion.	**25 men**
LCA 861 Loading schedule lists 16 men from E Co. and 5 men from the Naval Shore Fire Control Party.	**21 men**
LCA 883 Loading schedule lists 20 men from F Co. and 5 men from HQ Co. plus Lt. G.K. Hodenfield – *Stars and Stripes* reporter.	**26 men**
LCA 888 Loading schedule lists 15 men from E Co. and 3 from HQ Co. + Lt. Col. Rudder and 2 others.	**21 men**
LCA 1003 Supply vessel. Loading schedule lists 3 men from HQ Co.	**3 men**
4 x DUKWs. Loading schedule states that there were 33 men across the 4 DUKWs.	**33 men**

Thus far we have a **total of 261 men** who were supposed to arrive at Pointe du Hoc.

The Small Unit Actions Report states: *'Among the arrivals were three paratroopers of the 101st Airborne Division, scheduled to drop early that morning north of Carentan, 15 miles away, but dropped instead near Pointe du Hoe.* **+3 men.**

SGT. J. R. DEVOLI, RIGHT
Decorated by Major Gen.
E. N. Harmon for Heroism

L. A. Sergeant Is Ranger Hero

Sergeant Joseph R. Devoli, of 3339 Jeffries avenue, of the Second Rangers Infantry Battalion, participated in the major battles of Europe from D-Day to V-E Day without telling his family that anything unusual had happened. But his sister, Mrs. Victoria Altobelli, of the same address, today received a picture of the Angeleno receiving the Soldier's Medal from Major Gen. E. N. Harmon for heroic action in saving the life of a comrade who lost his life jacket when their invasion craft capsized in the pounding surf of D-Day.

The running total so far is 261 including + 3 paratroopers = 264 men.

A body of men who are rarely ever mentioned within the figures for the Pointe du Hoc attack came from the Royal Navy and British Army, probably because the focus of most works is on the number of Rangers at the Pointe.

There were 12 LCAs altogether. The crew of an LCA consisted of four men. A Sternsheetsman, whose position during Action was at the stern, to help the raising and lowering of the boat from the LSI (Landing Ship Infantry). The next was the stoker/mechanic, who was responsible for keeping the engine running efficiently. The third man was the bowman/gunner, whose position was at the very front of the boat; he was responsible for the opening and closing of the armoured doors, the raising and lowering of the bow ramp and the operation of a Lewis gun sitting behind the armoured shield at the front. Finally, the coxswain sat in the other armoured position in the front steering shelter on the starboard side. He was able to control the use of the rudders and he relayed the control of the engines via the stoker and this was done through a voice pipe and telegraph. Communication with the other craft was done by signal flag and when available, they were fitted with radios.

There are confirmed accounts that many of these men armed themselves with weapons from their own craft and then later with German weapons – and by doing so, they then gave good account of themselves. They are NEVER mentioned as being part of the assault force at Pointe du Hoc – but they were there.

The running total so far is 264 men + 48 Royal Naval crewmen = 312 men.

1st Lieutenant Amos Potts Jr was 30 years old and landed with the 2nd Rangers at Pointe du Hoc with a very different mission to that of the Rangers around him:

> *'I commanded a small unit that suffered 60 per cent casualties [1 KIA, 1 MIA, 1 wounded in the first hours of the Normandy invasion], 60 per cent of this group of five, who were unique in that we did not volunteer for Ranger duty, also came out of it with individual decorations. We were a Photographic Assignment Unit of a Signal Service Battalion borrowed to reinforce the Signal Photographic Company assigned to the First US Army.*
>
> *Around 15 May 1944 we received teletype orders to report to the Second Ranger Battalion. Upon arrival at the Headquarters of the Provisional Ranger Group, we learned that we would have the opportunity to obtain some of the best pictures of the coming invasion of fortress Europe. The Rangers had been training for months while we had been photographing supply activities and we were untrained in cliff-scaling. But the Army had an answer for that; one of the scaling means was fireman's ladders mounted on DUKWs.*
>
> *The 'score' for Photo Assignment Unit A, 850th Signal Service Battalion, attached to the Second Ranger Battalion was as follows:*

Keghan Nigohosian – Killed in Action.	*Herbert J. Stark – Silver Star.*
Irving Lomasky – Missing in Action. [Author: KIA 6 June]	*Amos Potts – Purple Heart.*
Warden F. Lovell – Distinguished Service Cross.	

Warden F. Lovell won the Distinguished Service Cross – this is taken from his official citation.

Sergeant Warden F. Lovell, United States Army, was awarded the Distinguished Service Cross for extraordinary heroism in connection with military operations against an armed enemy while serving with the 165th Signal Photo Company, in action against enemy forces on 6 June 1944, in France. Sergeant Lovell's intrepid actions, personal bravery and zealous devotion to duty exemplify the highest traditions of the military forces of the United States and reflect great credit upon himself, his unit, and the United States Army.

General Orders: Headquarters, First U.S. Army, General Orders No. 92 (1944)
Action Date: 6-Jun-44   **Service:** Army   **Rank:** Sergeant   **Company:** 165th Signal Photo Company

It is abundantly clear that the only reason for the Photographic Unit's involvement in the Pointe du Hoc assault was one of propaganda recording and I am equally sure that Lt. Col. Rudder did not volunteer to have them along. It could only have been under the orders of Eisenhower or Major General Huebner that they were included, as they suddenly appear on the Rangers' Morning Reports without explanation. As was shown by their bravery, these men made every attempt to fight as conventional soldiers and they added to the Rangers' numbers on the day. They are not obviously recorded within the Landing Schedule, but I have assumed that they are already included within the DUKW occupants total.

The running total so far is 312 men = 312

So, this is our starting point for the number of men who could have fought at Pointe du Hoc from the complement commanded by Lt. Col. Rudder. Now we must start to deduct the men as casualties as they happen. From the SUA Report we get a good sense of how the casualties occurred and at what time. A common misconception made by visitors to Pointe du Hoc is to assume that the bulk of the casualties occurred during the cliff assault. You can see from the numbers below, that this is not true. These figures were recorded in chronological order and from interviews with the participants shortly afterwards. Most of the casualties, and all of the names of the men Killed in Action are recorded and are verifiable facts.

The first group we must look at are the boat losses, followed by casualties recorded before or during the Rangers climbing the cliffs. The note in bold below each quote is mine.

LCA 860: *'Eight miles from shore LCA 860, carrying Capt. Harold K. Slater and 20 men of Company D swamped in the 4-foot choppy waves. The personnel were picked up by rescue craft and carried to England.'*

21 men + 4 Navy crew did not get to the Pointe, and were rescued and returned to England. (Running total: 312 - 25 = 287)

LCA 914: *'One of the supply craft sank, with only one survivor.'*

Out of the 7 men on board, 6 died. 1 man survived. (Running total: 287 - 6 = 281)

DUKWs: *'The only serious casualty was a DUKW, hit by 20-mm fire as it neared the target area. Five of the nine men aboard were killed or wounded.'*

5 men killed/wounded. (Running total: 281 - 5 = 276)

LCA 861: *'As the Rangers crossed the strip of cratered sand, grenades were thrown down from above them, or rolled over the cliff edge. These were of the "potato-masher" type, with heavy concussion effects but small fragmentation. They caused two casualties.'*

2 casualties. (Running total: 276 - 2 = 274)

LCA 862: *'The men had no trouble in disembarking, but once on the sand they found themselves exposed to machine-gun fire from eastward of the landing area. One man was killed and one wounded by this fire; two more injured by grenade fragments.'*

1 man killed, 3 wounded. (Running total: 274 - 4 = 270)

LCA 722: *'The only casualty was Pfc. John J. Sillman, wounded three times as the craft came in, hit twice on the beach.'*

1 man wounded. (Running total: 270 - 1 = 269)

'Three of the enemy dropped and the rest disappeared into shelters. Pfc. Frank H. Peterson, lightly wounded on the beach by a grenade, joined up and the three Rangers went off on their mission without waiting for the next climbers.'

1 man wounded. (Running total: 269 - 1 = 268)

LCA 668: *'While 1st Sgt. Leonard G. Lomell was bringing in a box of rope and a hand- projector rocket, he was wounded in the side by a machine-gun bullet but reached shore and kept going.'*

1 man wounded. (Running total: 268 - 1 = 267)

LCA 858: *'Shipping enough water all the way in to keep the Rangers busy, this craft nevertheless kept up fairly well and was only a minute or two behind the others at the beach. The men were put out into a crater and went over their heads in muddy water. Despite the wetting, a bazooka was the only piece of equipment put out of action. Three men were hit by machine-gun fire from the east flank.'*

3 men wounded. (Running total: 267 - 3 = 264)

LCA 887: *'LCA 887 had not been much bothered by either water or enemy action on the trip in. Some enemy fire, including automatic weapons, came from either flank. Two Rangers were wounded.'*

2 men wounded. (Running total: 264 - 2 = 262)

LCA 884: *'This craft, the target for considerable enemy fire from cliff positions on the way to the Point, had replied with its Lewis guns and the BARs of the Rangers.... Three Rangers were hit by fire coming from the left flank.'*

3 wounded. (Running total: 262 - 3 = 259)

Climbing the cliff: The SUA Report states that *'Ranger casualties on the beach totalled about 15, most of them from* the raking fire to their left.' So, we now have 15 casualties recorded during the cliff assault. This is further verified by a radio report received by USS *Ancon,* which also states that exact number. However, if you add up the number from the details above it comes to 17 casualties on the beach [plus 5 on the DUKW and 6 on LCA 914.]

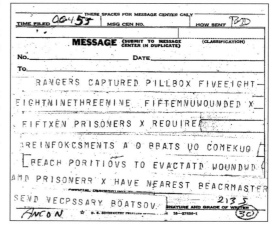

'Rangers captured pillbox 588939 – fifteen wounded x fifteen prisoners. Require reinforcements and boats to come to beach portions to evacuate wounded and prisoners. Have nearest Beach-master send the necessary boats over.' This message was received by USS *Ancon* at what appears to be 0845hrs (although a little indistinct) – and it does fit with the Ranger timeline of them advancing inland, before discovering guns around 9am.

The reports indicate to me that 17 men were casualties on the beach or on their way up the cliff, so I have used that figure, and not 15 as written above via the radio message.

In HMS *Prince Charles*'s After Action Report I have found one of the LCAs from those that made the initial PdH landings showing as having returned to its mother ship on 6 June.

> **0926**   **L.C.A. 858 (AMSTERDAM) reported and proceeded to AMSTERDAM.**

LCA858 made it back to the *Amsterdam* and was hoisted at 0926hrs with its 4-man crew. With a lack of further evidence by way of photographs or direct reports, I have assumed that the rest of the LCAs were not recovered until after 8 June. Thus, by default, the remaining Royal Navy crewmen on board at the start of the day were available to fight as infantry at the Pointe – and some even received awards for their actions.

4 men returned to mother ship. (Running total: 259 - 4 = 255)

To keep the running total as accurate as we can, there were **276 men who reached Pointe du Hoc, of whom 17 were beach casualties and 4 returned to the mother ship = leaving a total of 255 men.**

As the troops move inland and divide up into their individual unit missions, the casualty figures start to rise. The men are now on the top of the Pointe and the casualties are recorded in the order they happen:

> *'The only fighting took place at the tip of the Pointe. Here, the first men up from LCA 861 found themselves about 20 feet to seaward of the massive and undamaged concrete OP. As S/Sgt. Charles H. Denbo and Private Roberts crawled five feet toward a trench, small-arms fire, including machine guns, started up from slits in the OP. The Rangers threw four grenades at the slits, and three went in. The machine gun stopped firing, but Denbo was wounded by a rifle bullet.'*

1 man wounded. (Running total: 255 - 1 = 254)

> *'... three Rangers tried to skirt the OP on the east and get at it from the rear. Cleaves was wounded by a mine.'*

1 man wounded. (Running total: 254 - 1 = 253)

'Near the end of the trench, small-arms fire came at them from some position on the top of the OP which Medeiros could not spot, and Pfc. George W. Mackey was killed; the two others made it safely to the inland side.'

1 man killed. (Running total: 253 - 1 = 252)

'Observation on the Pointe was so limited that no one else had seen the action or any part of it. Ten Rangers had simply disappeared, with Cruz's report and the abandoned weapons as the only indication of their fate. The best guess was that the Germans had attacked by filtering into the area through wrecked trenches connecting the fortified zone with the anti- aircraft gun; as another possibility, they may have emerged from underground shelters on the Pointe.'

10 men MIA. (Running total: 252 - 10 = 242)

'Without waiting for others to arrive, they started along the exit road, taking as much cover as possible in a communications trench along its edge, and keeping in a single file... the Rangers began to meet machine-gun fire from the right flank, and small-arms fire to their left front. They suffered serious casualties in the next few hundred yards: seven killed and eight wounded.'

7 killed & 8 wounded. (Running total: 242 – (7+8) = 227)

'They got to within 20 yards of where they thought the gun position must be, and as Youso half rose to throw a grenade he was shot by a German rifleman.'

1 man wounded. (Running total: 227 - 1 = 226)

'The enemy had spotted their movement, and small- arms fire was covering an open space along the route, wounding one man and slowing progress.'

1 man wounded. (Running total: 226 - 1 = 225)

'The only casualty was a Ranger who fell on a comrade's bayonet as he jumped into the trench.'

1 man wounded. (Running total: 225 - 1 = 224)

The incident with the Ranger falling onto a bayonet was the last significant injury, creating a total of 21 men killed/wounded, as well as 10 MIA on top of the Pointe. The total of all Ranger losses from the beach and on the top, now numbers 48 based on the figures in the SUA Report, a figure drawn directly from the men's own account of the action.

At this moment in time (around 9am) when guns were found 1 mile inland, I calculate **the total number of men still available stands at 224 uninjured,** and this does not include the number of lightly wounded men who were still fit for combat.

A look at some of the injuries sustained by the men above gives an indication that a number of the lightly injured men were still capable of fighting, but for the sake of accuracy I have recorded them on the injured list. The figure of 224 men fit to fight is therefore below the number who were actually still fighting – but it is hard to say how far below.

It is worth noting that ALL other books on this subject suggest that Rudder started with 225 men before landing and this figure went down from there. But the number I have calculated indicates that this was more likely the figure that he had available to him by 9am to continue his mission, after having suffered numerous casualties.

In my opinion, ANY Pointe du Hoc casualties after this moment in time are unquestionably on the shoulders of Lt. Col. Rudder. Remember, the figures stated in this work are all factual numbers based on the SUA and this may be one of the very few books on this subject to have gone into this in such detail.

Approximately at 9am, Lt. Colonel Rudder ordered his men to stay in a position with their backs to the sea – where the Germans could take their time, muster their men and wear down the attacking force over three days, almost to its destruction. Lt. Col. Rudder did not advance any further as ordered – and in an obvious irony, it was most likely the batteries at Maisy which were firing at the Rangers whilst they remained at the Pointe, as this excerpt from the SUA Report suggests.

'German artillery came into action, from somewhere inland. The first rounds were over; the next rounds began to 'creep' back until they bracketed the hedgerow-marked lane which was the axis of the Rangers' attack. There the fire held, right on the lane, 'the prettiest fire I ever saw' (Captain Masny). His attack was smashed in short order; four men were killed and nearly every Ranger in the group was hit. Masny, wounded in the arm, shouted 'Withdraw! Every man for himself!' after the second burst, and the remnants crawled back to the exit road and over to the CP, with snipers killing two more on the way. All its ammunition shot away, the mortar was abandoned at its firing position.'

But beyond this number, there were still further, additional men coming to the Pointe from A Company 5th Battalion on 6 June. Again, told by the SUA Report: *'About 2100, still two hours before dark, a party of 23 men from Company A, 5th Ranger Battalion came into the Ranger lines from the east. Led by 1st Lt. Charles H. Parker, Jr., this force was the 1st Platoon of Company A.'*

This was in part why 1st Lt. Charles Parker received the Distinguished Service Cross.

Thus, the number of men at the Pointe was increased by a further 23 men on the evening of 6 June.

The next day – the 7th – a number of Rangers who had been stranded on Omaha Beach, and others rescued at sea were sent to Pointe du Hoc via two LCVPs. The information for this comes in part from an interview with Frank Kennard who had his now dismounted Cannon company men gathered up for the mission on the first LCVP – along with some men from the 5th Battalion. The USS *Texas* AAR states: *'Two LCVPs were obtained and loaded with provisions and ammunition from the destroyers and the* Texas, *and were sent in to relieve the Rangers.'*

In a letter to the author in 2014, Cannon Company Commander Frank Kennard stated he was on the first one of the two LCVPs: *'at the direction of Major Street from the command ship ANCON, we commandeered a Landing Craft and our group (approx. 8 x 2nd Btn and 12 or more 5th Btn men) motored up to the coast to the Pointe, where we boarded the USS* Satterlee. *Got some food and supplies; then went ashore to join 2nd Rangers there. The ride west (off-shore) was uneventful and I don't recall the Landing Craft showed any damage or blood, etc.'*

The 2nd Battalion After Action Report confirms this for 7 June and states the number of men taken to Pointe du Hoc in the second LCVP:

> Communications: Controlled fire of several destroyers using radio and lamp. Msg to USS Ancon resulted in Major Street, Staff officer, 11 Amphib Force bringing in rations, ammunitions, and equipment. Later, he brought in one officer and 23 EM of the 5th Ranger Bn who had become separated from their Bn on the beach.

Thus, the two LCVPs added another 20 men on the first boat and 24 men on the second boat to the numbers of men at Pointe du Hoc.

Later that same evening, 5th Ranger Howard McKissick and Willie Moody went to PdH with radios and for their heroism they were awarded the DSC.

If you add up the number of men who actually landed at Pointe du Hoc, plus those that arrived later in support, the total number involved in the Pointe du Hoc battle – all one way or another under Lt. Col. Rudder's command – was 341.

I know that this figure is well *above* figures normally stated for the Pointe du Hoc action, but I would suggest that it is closer to being correct. One of the issues is that I cannot find an exact name-to-boat roster for the men who were at Pointe du Hoc. As you can see above, there are only numbers of men given per vessel that departed. So, we have numbers, but not always names allocated to the specific boats. Unless they are mentioned specifically in the SUA Report – or as being wounded or killed with a PdH based unit on the company Morning Reports.

For my own research, I have compiled a list of men who I think were at Pointe du Hoc. I have tried to avoid associating men with a boat simply because their names appear in another author's book; I looked for compelling evidence to state that their presence was correct. Place of death having been at 'Pointe du Hoc' was an obvious indicator they were there.

Taking information from two sets of US Army Archival records, Morning Reports, the SUA Report and AARs – I have tried to compile a sensible list, but I am aware this is not a comprehensive one. Between all the reports, I have found variations of rank, spelling of names and even men listed as being in two companies and two places at the same time, not to mention reports stating WIA – then another KIA entry for the same man, etc. This is particularly also true for Medics, who were transferred in and out of HQ Company to other companies as and when they were needed, and for men who were wounded on one day and died somewhere else on another day.

Therefore, with all of those caveats, I have compiled this list of men whom I consider were *most likely* present at Pointe du Hoc and what their fates were after the battle there. Sadly, this list does not include everyone. It doesn't include all of the names of the 23 men from 1st Lt. Charles Parker's squad from A Co. 5th Btn – 6 June, the men from F Co. 5th under John Reville, who went to PdH on the 7th by LCVP, all those dismounted men from Frank Kennard's 2nd Btn Cannon Company, who also arrived on the 7th. Nor have I included all of the names of the Royal Navy men present, simply because I do not know them. Equally, I have not been able to name all the men of the initial landing force for the same reasons. However, I have endeavoured to include as many as I could.

My reason for doing this list is for historical accuracy and I will continue to pursue it past the completion of this book. Hopefully over time, my research and that of others will add to this to present a 100 per cent complete list, as all of these men deserve to be recognised.

The website for the American Battlefield Monuments Commission states that *'June 6-8: After fighting two days, only about 90 Rangers stood when relieved by Schneider's Rangers and the 29th Division from Omaha Beach.'* I feel that this figure is a little low and here is the evidence:

KEY:
LWA = Lightly Wounded In Action   SWA = Seriously Wounded In Action
WIA = Wounded In Action   KIA = Killed In Action
MIA = Missing In Action   DOW = Died of Wounds – I&O – Intelligence and Operations

Name	Unit	LCA/vessel	Fate if known
Lt. Col. James Rudder	HQ Co.	LCA 888	LWA Wounded
Major George S. Williams	HQ Co.		Survived
Lt. Col. Travis Trevor	British Commando	LCA722	LWA British officer
Lt. Ronald F. Eades	RNVR	LCA722	British officer
Captain Walter E. Block	HQ/Surgeon		Survived
Captain Harvey J. Cook.	HQ Co.		Survived
Captain James A. Malaney	HQ Co.		Survived
Captain Richard P. Merrill	E Co.		Survived
Captain Frederick G. Wilkin	HQ Co.		SWA 6 June
Lt. James R. McCullers	HQ Co.	DUKW	WIA survived
Lt. William Heaney	HQ Co.		Survived
Lt. Elmer Vermeer	HQ Co.		Survived
Lt. G. K. Hodenfield		LCA 883	*Stars and Stripes* reporter – survived
Lt. James W. Eikner	HQ Co.	LCA 888	Survived
1st Sgt. John Erdely	HQ Co.		Survived
M/Sgt. Robert Lemin	HQ Co.	Supply Boat.	KIA 6 June
T/Sgt. Edward Gurney	HQ Co.	Intelligence & Operations – survived	
T/Sgt. Francis J. Roach	HQ Co.	Communications – survived	
S/Sgt. Otto C. Bayer	HQ Co.	LCA 884	Medic – survived
S/Sgt. Colin J. Lowe	D Co.		Survived
S/Sgt. Donald F. Mentzer	HQ Co.		Medic survived
T/3 Randall R. Rinker	HQ Co.		Survived
Sgt. William I. Mollohan Jr.	HQ Co.		KIA 6 June
T/4 Stephen Liscinsky	HQ Co.		Radioman – survived
T/4 Charles S. Parker	HQ Co.	LCA 722	Radioman – survived

Name	Unit	LCA/vessel	Fate if known
T/4 Frank E. South	HQ Co.	LCA 884	Medic – survived
T/5 William C. Clark, Jr	HQ Co.		Survived
T/5 Gerald A. Eberle	HQ Co.	LCA 858	I & O – WIA – survived
T/5 Louis Herman	HQ Co.		Radioman, MIA at sea
T/5 Virgil. A. Hillis	HQ Co.		Survived
T/5 Edward A. Johnson	HQ Co.		SWA. Comm, survived
T/5 Francis Kolodziejczak	HQ Co.	LCA 888	Survived
T/5 Robert C. Lambert	HQ Co.		Medic
T/5 Steven M. Mead	HQ Co.		Transport MIA
T/5 Marcel Miller	HQ Co.		Radioman, survived
Pfc. John R. Ahart	HQ Co.	DUKW	MIA 6 June – survived
Pfc. Thomas J. Armbruster	HQ Co.	DUKW	Survived
Pfc. Eugene C. Doughty	HQ Co.	DUKW	MIA 6 June – survived
Pfc. George A. Hall	HQ Co.	DUKW	Survived
Pfc. Theodore A. Malburg, Jr	HQ Co.		MIA, survived
Pfc. Robert F. Shirey	HQ Co.		Comm, survived
Pfc. Guy C. Shoaf	HQ Co.		Survived
Pfc. Billy Tibbets	HQ Co.	DUKW	Survived
Pfc. John W. Tindell	HQ Co.	DUKW	MIA, survived
Pfc. Kenneth L. Wharff.	HQ Co.		I & O MIA, survived
Pvt. Rolland Revels	HQ Co.	DUKW	KIA. Listed on MR as KIA Vierville
Pvt. Robert K. Roe	HQ Co.		Communications – survived
Pvt. William F. Sluss	HQ Co.	DUKW	Survived
T/4 Harley R. Sampson	HQ Co.		Survived
Pfc. James E. Horn	HQ Co.		Survived

The SUA Report states: 'A Naval Shore Fire Control Party (12 men) and a forward observer of the 58th Armored Field Artillery Battalion were attached to Colonel Rudder's headquarters, who were distributed among the four LCAs carrying Company E.' In fact it was 12 enlisted men and 2 officers.

293rd Joint Assault Signal Company men attached to the Rangers:

Captain Jonathan H. Harwood	KIA 6 June
Lt. Kenneth S. Norton	LWA then KIA
T/5 Edward G. Heineck	Survived
Pfc. Albert Kamente	Survived
Pvt. Charles C. Arvizu	Survived
Pvt. Howard J. Ericson	Survived
Pvt. Arthur E. Gable	Survived
Pvt. John Gallagher	Survived
Pvt. Paul E. Kimbrough	Survived
Pvt. Harold F. Plank	Survived
Pvt. Ramon G. Rolande	Survived
Pvt. Peter P. Simundich	Survived
Pvt. Mitchell H. Goldenstein	Survived
Pvt. Paul Rascon	Survived

Name	Unit	LCA/vessel	Fate if known
165th Signal Photo Company			
Lt. Amos P. Potts			Survived
Sgt. Warden F. Lovell			Survived
T/4 Irving Lomasky			KIA 6 June
Pfc. Keghan Nigohosian			KIA 6 June
Herbert J. Stark			Survived
58th Armored Field Artillery Battalion			
Lt. Johnson Observer 58th Armored Field Artillery Battalion			Survived
D Company LCA 860, LCA 668 and LCA 858			
Captain Harold Slater	D Co.	LCA 860	Survived
Lt. Morten McBride	D Co.	LCA 860	Survived
Lt. George Kerchner	D Co.	LCA 668	Survived
1st Sgt. Leonard G. Lomell	D Co.	LCA 668	LWA 6 June – survived
T/Sgt. Richard Spleen	D Co.	LCA 858	Captured – survived
S/Sgt. Harvey Koenig	D Co.	LCA 668	SWA 6 June – survived
T/Sgt. John Corona	D Co.	LCA 860	MIA – survived
S/Sgt. Jack Kuhn	D Co.	LCA 668	Survived
S/Sgt. Patrick McCrone	D Co.	LCA 668	MIA 6 June – survived
S/Sgt. Francis J. Pacyga	D Co.	LCA 668	SWA 6 June – survived
S/Sgt. Charles Kettering	D Co.	LCA 668	6 June – KIA
S/Sgt. Sigurd Sundby	D Co.	LCA 668	Survived
S/Sgt. Norman Miller	D Co.	LCA 860	KIA 6 June
S/Sgt. Joseph Stevens	D Co.	LCA 860	MIA 6 June – survived
S/Sgt. Melvin W. Sweany	D Co.		Survived
S/Sgt. Joseph Flanagan	D Co.		Survived
S/Sgt. Lawrence Johnson	D Co.		KIA 7 June
S/Sgt. Benjamin Wirtz	D Co.		KIA 6 June
T/Sgt. Lester G. Arthur	D Co.		Survived
Sgt. Michael Branley	D Co.		LWA – survived
Sgt. Robert Austin	D Co.		Survived
Sgt. Kelly Szewczuk	D Co.		KIA 6 June
Sgt. Richard McLaughlin	D Co.		MIA 7 June – survived
Sgt. Harry Fate	D Co.		Survived
Sgt. Emory Jones	D Co.		MIA 7 June
Sgt. Joseph Devoli	D Co.	LCA 860	MIA 6 June – survived
Sgt. Morris N. Webb	D Co.		SWA 6 June – survived
Cpl. Maurice R. Browning	D Co.		Survived
T/5 Robert Wells	D Co.		MIA 6 June – survived
T/5 Raymond Riendeau	D Co.	LCA 860	KIA 6 June – drowned
T/5 Clarence J. Long	D Co.		KIA 6 June
T/5 Clinton Hensley	D Co.		MIA 6 June – survived
T/5 William Vaughan	D Co.	LCA 668	KIA 6 June
T/5 John Clifton	D Co.		KIA 6 June
T/5 Harley R. Huff	D Co.		Survived
T/5 Louis J. Bisek	D Co.		MIA 6 June – survived

Name	Unit	LCA/vessel	Fate if known
T/5 Edwin J. Secor	D Co.		MIA 6 June – survived
T/5 Henry Stecki	D Co.		MIA 7 June – survived
T/5 William A. Walker	D Co.		MIA 6 June – survived
T/5 Gordon Luning	D Co.		Survived
T/5 Thomas Mendenhall	D Co.	LCA 860	KIA 6 June
T/5 George O. Schneller	D Co.		SWA 6 June – survived
Pfc. James Blum	D Co.		MIA 7 June – survived
Pfc. John J. Riley	D Co.	914 (supply boat)	MIA – survived
Pfc. Robert A. Fruhling	D Co.	LCA 860	SWA 6 June – survived
Pfc. John J. Miljavac	D Co.		KIA 6 June
Pfc. William Cruz	D Co.	LCA 858	LWA 6 June – survived
Pfc. Sheldon Bare	D Co.		SWA 6 June – survived
Pfc. James Hudnell	D Co.		MIA 6 June – survived
Pfc. Newton R. Williams Jr.	D Co.		MIA 6 June – survived
Pfc. Harold E. Lester	D Co.	LCA 860	KIA
Pfc. Peter Korpalo	D Co.		MIA, 6 June – survived
Pfc. Wilbur K. Hoffman	D Co.		Survived
Pfc. Dominic Sparaco	D Co.	LCA 860	MIA 6 June – survived
Pfc. Leonard Rubin	D Co.	LCA 668	MIA 7 June – survived
Pfc. John D. Oehlberg	D Co.	914 (supply boat)	KIA 6 June
Pfc. Alvin H. Nance	D Co.	LCA 668	MIA 6 June – survived
Pfc. Anthony J. Ruggiero	D Co.	LCA 860	MIA 6 June – survived
Pfc. Melvin C. Heffelbower Jr.	D Co.		KIA 6 June
Pfc. McCorkle	D Co.		KIA 8 June
Pfc. Lester Harris	D Co.		KIA 6 June
Pfc. John F. Conaboy	D Co.		SWA 6 June – survived
Pfc. Leroy G. Adams	D Co.		SWA 6 June
Pfc Robert C. Carty	D Co.		KIA 7 June
Pfc. Iriving Hoover	D Co.		Survived
Pvt. Henry Sobal	D Co.		Survived
Pfc. Stephen Sczepanski	D Co.		SWA – survived
T/5 William A. Geitz	(HQ Co.)	LCA 668	Attached as a medic – survived
Pfc. Carl Charboneau	D Co.	5th Btn	LWA 7 June

Company E.

Name	Unit	LCA/vessel	Fate if known
1st Lt. Theodore E. Lapres	E Co.	LCA 861	Survived
1st Lt. Joseph E. Leagans	E Co.	LCA 862	KIA 7 June
1st Lt. Gilbert C. Baugh	E Co.	LCA 861	WIA 6 June
1st Sgt. Robert W. Lang	E Co.	LCA 888	Survived
T/Sgt. Clifford E. Mains	E Co.	LCA 858	Captured – survived
T/Sgt. Harold W. Gunther	E Co.	LCA 861	Survived
T/Sgt. Lawrence Lare	E Co.		Survived
T/Sgt. Millard W. Hayden	E Co.		KIA 6 June
T/Sgt. Hayward Robey	E Co.	LCA 722	Survived
T/5 William L. Graham	E Co.		KIA
S/Sgt. Christopher M. Anderson	E Co.		SWA
S/Sgt. Robert S. Pyles	E Co.		SWA
S/Sgt. Robert A. Honhart	E Co.		Survived
S/Sgt. Joseph J. Cleaves	E Co.	LCA 862	SWA

Name	Unit	LCA/vessel	Fate if known
S/Sgt. Charles H. Denbo	E Co.	LCA 861	SWA
S/Sgt. Glen L. Webster	E Co.		Survived
S/Sgt. Curtis A Simmons	E Co.	LCA 861	KIA 6 June
S/Sgt. Frank A. Rupinski	E Co.		Survived
S/Sgt. Rex D. Clark	E Co.	DUKW driver	Survived
S/Sgt. Earl A. Theobald	E Co.		Survived
Sgt. Andrew T. Yardley	E Co.	LCA 861	Survived
Sgt. Anthony P. Catelani	E Co.		Survived
Sgt. Domenick B. Bogetto	E Co.	LCA 888	Survived
Sgt. Alysius S. Nosal	E Co.		Survived
Sgt. Harry G. Fritchman Jr.	E Co.		Survived
Sgt. Theodore M. Pilalas	E Co.	DUKW	MIA 8 June – survived
T/5 Edward P. Smith	E Co.	LCA 722	Survived
T/5 Leroy J. Thompson	E Co.	LCA 862	SWA 7 June – survived
T/5 Mike Milkovich Jr	E Co.		Survived
T/5 George J. Putzek	E Co.	LCA 888	SWA survived
T/5 Albert J. Uronis	E Co.		Survived
T/5 Frank J. LaBrandt	E Co.		Survived
T/5 Kenneth H. Bargmann	E Co.		Survived
T/5 E. G. Colvard	E Co.	LCA 861	KIA 7 June
T/5 Charles G. McCalvin	E Co.		KIA 6 June
T/5 Paul P. Knor	E Co.	DUKW	MIA 8th June – survived
Pfc. John S. Burnett	E Co.	LCA 862	MIA 8 June – survived
Pfc. Paul L. Medeiros	E Co.	LCA 861	SWA – survived
Pfc. Howard Bowens	E Co.		KIA 6 June
Pfc. George W. Mackey	E Co.	LCA 861	KIA 6 June
Pfc. Salva P. Maimone	E Co.		Survived
Pfc. Roy L. Palmer	E Co.		Survived
Pfc. Charles H. Bellows Jr.	E Co.	LCA 862	KIA 6 June
Pfc. Anton Bachleda	E Co.		SWA
Pfc. James R. Shalala	E Co.		Survived
Pfc. Clarence E. Bachman Jr.	E Co.		Survived
Pfc. Frank H. Peterson	E Co.	LCA 722	SWA – survived
Pfc. Nathan C. Reed	E Co.		SWA – survived
Pfc. John J. Sillmon	E Co.	LCA 722	SWA 6 June – survived
Pfc. Harry W. Roberts	E Co.	LCA 861	SWA 8 June – survived
Pfc. Henry A. Wood	E Co		Survived
Pfc. Victor J. Aguzzi	E Co.	LCA 862	Survived
Pfc. George H. Crook	E Co.		Survived
Pfc. Joseph J. Lock	E Co.		Survived
Pfc. Harold D. Main	E Co.		SWA 7 June – survived
Pfc. Woodrow Talkington	E Co.		SWA 7 June – survived
Pfc. Loring L. Wadsworth	E Co.		Survived
Pfc. Jack Lawson Jr	E Co.		Survived
Pfc. Edison W. Crull	E Co.		Survived
Pfc. Francis J. Connolly	E Co.	914 (supply boat)	KIA 6 June
Pfc. Duncan N. Daugherty	E Co.	DUKW	SWA – survived
Pfc. Richard Hubbard	E Co.	DUKW	Survived

Name	Unit	LCA/vessel	Fate if known
Pfc. William D. Bell	E Co.	LCA 861	Survived
Pfc. Charles M. Dunlap	E Co.		Survived
Pfc. Mark A. Keefer Jr.	E Co.		Survived
Pvt. Frank B. Robinson	E Co.		Survived
Pvt. Harold W. Sehorn	E Co.		Survived
Cpl. Louis Lisko	E Co.	LCA 722	Survived
Sgt. Clifford T. Smith	E Co.		Survived
Pfc. Michael J. McDonough		(HQ Co.)	Attached as medic – survived
Pfc. George T. Roberts	E Co.		Survived

Company F. LCA 883, 884 and 887.

Name	Unit	LCA/vessel	Fate if known
Captain Otto Masny	F Co.	LCA 883	LWA 6 June – survived
Lt. Jacob J. Hill	F Co.	LCA 884	KIA – 6 June
Lt. Robert C. Arman	F Co.	LCA 887	Survived
Lt. Richard A. Wintz	F Co.	LCA 883	Survived
1st Sgt. Charles E. Frederick	F Co.		Survived
T/Sgt John W. Franklin	F Co.		WIA 6 June – survived
T/Sgt. Bonnie M. Taylor	F Co.		Survived
T/Sgt. Eugene E. Elder	F Co.		Survived
T/Sgt. William Petty	F Co.	LCA 887	WIA – survived
T/Sgt. John I. Cripps	F Co.	LCA 887	Survived
S/Sgt. Robert G. Youso	F Co.	LCA 883	WIA 6 June – survived
S/Sgt. William Stivison	F Co.	DUKW	Survived
S/Sgt. Carl Bombardier	F Co.	LCA 884	Survived
S/Sgt. Thomas F. Ryan	F Co.	LCA 888	Survived
S/Sgt. Carl Weilage	F Co.		Survived
S.Sgt. James E. Fulton	F Co.	LCA 884	WIA 8 June – survived
S/Sgt. Paul P. Welsch	F Co.		Survived
S/Sgt. Bill L. Thompson	F Co.		Survived
S/Sgt. Leon Otto	F Co.	LCA 884	SWA 6 June – DOW 7th
S/Sgt. Harry J. Ferry	F Co.		Wounded – survived
S/Sgt. Vergil L. Longest	F Co.		Survived
S/Sgt. William H. Simons	F Co.		WIA 6 June – survived
S/Sgt. William J. Uhorczuk	F Co.		Survived
Sgt. Regis McCloskey	F Co.	Supply Boat	MIA survived
Sgt. James R. Alexander	F Co.	LCA 887	MIA 7 June – survived
Sgt. Murrel F. Stinnette	F Co.		Survived
Sgt. Robert G. Roosa	F Co.		Survived
Sgt. Jacob H. Richards	F Co.	LCA 883	KIA 6 June
Sgt. Leonard F. Zajas	F Co.		Survived
Sgt. William M. McHugh	F Co.	LCA 887	Survived
T/5 Glen J. Swafford	F Co.		Survived
T/5 Floyd H. Simkins	F Co.		MIA 7 June – survived.
T/5 Orley R. Jackson	F Co.		Survived
T/5 Herman Stein	F Co.	LCA 883	Survived
T/5 Charles J. Vella	F Co.		Survived
Pfc. William F. O'Keefe	F Co.		Survived
Pfc. Dennis F. Kimble	F Co.		KIA 6 June

Name	Unit	LCA/vessel	Fate if known
Pfc. Garness L. Colden	F Co.	LCA 887	Survived
Pfc. John Bacho	F Co.	LCA 884	WIA 6 June – survived
Pfc. Raymond A. Cole	F Co.	LCA 883	KIA 6 June
Pfc. William D. Walsh	F Co.		WIA 6 June – survived
Pfc. George A. Wieburg	F Co.		KIA 6 June
Pfc. Gerald A. Bouchard	F Co.		WIA 6 June – survived
Pfc. Frederick A. Dix	F Co.	LCA 887	WIA 7 June – survived
Pfc. Alvin E. White	F Co.	LCA 883	WIA 6 June – survived
Pfc. Jack W. Lamero	F Co.		Survived
Pfc Madison B. Cobb	F Co.		MIA/WIA – survived
Pfc. Oscar E. Behrent	F Co.		Survived
Pfc. Walter T. Bialkowski	F Co.		Survived
Pfc. Walter J. Borowski	F Co.		Survived
PFc. William H. Coldsmith	F Co.	LCA 887	Survived
Pfc. William A. Gervais	F Co.		Survived
Pfc. John J. Gilhooly	F Co.	DUKW	Survived
Pfc. Herman W. Kiihnl	F Co.		WIA 6 June – survived
Pfc. Robert G. Landin	F Co.	LCA 887	Survived
Pfc. Robert E. McKittrick	F Co.		Survived
Pfc. Cloise A. Manning	F Co.		Survived
PFc. Edward J. Trombowicz	F Co.		Survived
Pfce. Frank J. Oropello	F Co.		Survived
Pfc. Donald C. Pechacek	F Co.		Survived
Pfc. Rudolph Stefik	F Co.		Survived
Pfc. Jean N. Ver Schave	F Co.		Survived
Pfc. Carl Winsch	F Co.	LCA 887	Survived
Pvt. William E. Anderson	F Co.	LCA 884	Survived
Pvt. James E. Kohl	F Co.		Survived
T/5 Robert E. Gillespie	F Co.		Survived
T/5 Ralph E. Davis	F Co.	LCA 888	Medic – survived
T/5 Charles W. Korb (HQ Co)	F Co.	Supply Boat	Medic – LWA 6 June – survived
S/Sgt. James O. White			Survived
Pvt. Paul Pavey	A Co.	5th Btn	KIA 7 June
Pvt. James Gabaree	A Co.	5th Btn	SWA 7 June – survived
Sgt. Denzil O. Johnson	A Co.	5th Btn	Survived
1st Lt. Charles H. Parker Jr.	A Co.	5th Btn	Survived
Pvt. John Bellows	A Co.	5th Btn	Survived
Pvt. Daniel Farley	A Co.	5th Btn	WIA 7 June – survived
T/5 Howard D. McKissick	C Co.	5th Btn.	Survived
Sgt. Willie W. Moody	C Co.	5th Btn.	Survived
1st Lt. Stanley D. Zelepsky,	A Co.	5th Btn	Survived
S/Sgt. Richard N. Hathaway Jr.	A Co.	5th Bth	Survived
1st Lt. Frank Kennard	HQ Co.		Survived
Lt. John Reville	F Co.	5th Btn	Survived
T/5 Percy C. Hower	A Co.	2nd Btn	KIA 7th June
Pfc. Joseph R. Trainor	A Co.	2nd Btn	KIA 7th June

Name	Unit	LCA/vessel	Fate if known
Leading Seaman Arthur Taylor	Royal Navy		Survived
Stoker First Class William Gordon Ingram	Royal Navy		Survived
Sub Lt. Islwyn Vaughan	Royal Navy		Survived
Sub-lieutenant Alan Lawrence	Royal Navy		Survived
Leading Seaman Arthur Taylor	Royal Navy	LCA1003	Survived
Private Colin Blackmore	Royal Army Service Corps		Survived
Acting Sgt. Joseph John Good	Royal Army Service Corps		Survived

D. COMMENDATIONS.

    I would like to draw attention to the following officers
and ratings whose courage and devotion to duty were exceptional:-

Lieutenant R.D. TURNBULL, S.A.N.F.(V), Flotilla Officer, 501st Flotill

Lieutenant J. JAMES, R.N.V.R., Commanding Officer, M.L. 163

Lieutenant J.M.F. CASSIDY, R.N.V.R., Flotilla Officer, 504th Flotilla.

Lieutenant R.E. DOBSON, R.N.V.R., Flotilla Officer, 522nd Flotilla

Lieutenant E.H. WEST, R.N.V.R., Flotilla Officer, 507th Flotilla

Lieutenant C.W.R. CROSS, R.N.V.R., Flotilla Officer, 520th Fletilla

Sub-Lieutenant J.J. NELSON, R.N.V.R., Divisional Officer, 501st Flotil

Sub Lieutenant H. BENBOW, R.N.V.R., Boat Officer, 501st Flotilla.
       Sub Lieutenant BENBOW's courage and initiative deserve
       special commendation. A further report is being rendered.

Sub Lieutenant H.G.P. KENYON, R.N.V.R., Boat Officer, 501st Flotilla.

Ty Petty Officer H.A. TURTLE, P/JX 159958 CO

Leading Seaman C.E.M. PAYNE, P/JX 328424 CO

Stoker F. CHAMBERLAIN, D/KX 146590 CO

Able Seaman L. DICKENS, C/JX 353617 CO

Able Seaman J. BARCLAY, D/JX 193585 CO (Killed)

Portsmouth Form 15

Ship....SS. BEN MY CHREE..(520th Flotilla)

Date 23rd June 1944

RECOMMENDATION FOR DECORATION OR MENTION IN DESPATCHES

Full Surname .... TAYLOR .... (Poplar, London)

Full Christian Names ..Arthur Thomas....................

Rank or Rating   Leading Seaman....................
(State whether R.N., R.N.R.,
R.N.V.R., R.N.P.S., R.A.N.,
etc.)........R.N. (HO)....................

Official No. and .JX 295440 CO....

Port Division   Portsmouth....

Whether already Decorated   ..No....................
(Give particulars and date of publication of award)

Whether already Mentioned   ..No....................
in Despatches
(Give date of publication of award)

Whether previously recommended   ...No....................
If so, give particulars

Whether now recommended { for Award of Decoration for decoration....................
{ xxMention in Despatches

Whether recommendation is   ....Immediate....................
for Immediate, Operational
or Periodic Award

Description of Services for which Officer or Man is Recommended
Leading Seaman A.T. TAYLOR, Coxswain of L.C.A. 1003, showed skill and
resource in keeping his craft afloat whilst carrying essential ammunition supplies
when taking part in the initial assault on Point du Hoe. Taylor's craft, when
partly swamped by heavy seas and likely to founder was kept afloat by his skill
and courage resulting in the successful landing of ammunition.

Lt. RNVR

Remarks of Intermediate Authority
Concurring. Leading Seaman' Taylor's action and behaviour materially
contributed to the success of the U.S. Rangers at Point du Hoe.

H.M.S. PRINCE CHARLES
26th June 1944

COMMANDER IN CHIEF
29 JUL 1944
PORTSMOUTH

Commander, R.N.,
Commanding Officer, Assault Group 0-4

Remarks of Commander-in-Chief, etc.
Recommended for the award of a Decoration.

Office of A.N.C.X.F.,
c/o Admiralty.
5th August, 1944.

ADMIRAL.

SUA Report: *'Among the arrivals were three paratroopers of the 101st Airborne Division, (one casualty – a paratrooper who got tired of ducking into his fox hole and was hit by the next shell).'*

In addition to the complement of Rangers landing on D-Day, there were many Royal Navy servicemen recognised as having served alongside them.

The Royal Navy recorded their names in despatches because of their bravery. Shown are the names of some, but not all of the men involved.

This list was drawn up by the Commanding Officer of Assault Group O-4 – Commander Stratford Dennis. Unfortunately due to a lack of further available information, it is difficult to track down the name of every other sailor who took part and who was allocated to which LCA.

The contribution given to the Pointe du Hoc action by the men of the Royal Navy has often been overlooked. Leading Seaman Royal Navy Arthur Taylor, for example, was mentioned in despatches as Coxswain of LCA1003 – and he launched from the SS *Ben-My-Chree*.

Another Royal Navy man at Pointe du Hoc:

Stoker First Class William Gordon Ingram Royal Navy
Distinguished Service Medal
STO.1 W.G. Ingram. P/KX. 179183
London Gazette 28 November 1945.

> *For gallantry, skill, determination and undaunted devotion to duty whilst serving in* HMS Ben-My-Chree *during the landing of Allied Forces on the coast of Normandy. He showed conspicuous skill and courage when his craft LCA722 was damaged by enemy action whilst under machine gun fire. Ingram made great efforts to repair his craft's engines; although unsuccessful, his devotion to duty was a great example. This rating had a very difficult task whilst landing U.S. Rangers on Pointe du Hoe.*

> Ben-My-Chree *Sub Lt. Islwyn Vaughan's paperwork reads with typical Royal Navy understatement 'Ability in handling craft… Very good.'. He was with LCA Flotilla 520.*

Stoker First Class Frederick John Chamberlain was on LCA 401. His certificate for the Distinguished Service Medal reads: *Stoker 1st Class Frederick John Chamberlain. Royal Navy No D/KX 146590 from Penryn, Cornwall. Awarded The Distinguished Service Medal for Gallantry, Skill, Determination and Undaunted Devotion to Duty during the landing of Allied Forces on the coast of Normandy.*

This account was kindly provided to me by his son, and I include it simply to demonstrate the hardships undertaken by some of the Royal Navy men. Chamberlain actually landed men from the 5th Ranger Battalion on Omaha Beach:

> *He was Stoker on LCA 401 and manned the engines.* HMS Prince Charles *left Weymouth and picked up 29th Infantry in the Channel. He told me many were sea sick due to bad weather. LCA was first wave and hit Omaha Beach around 0630, a little later than planned, but was hit by mortar fire. When my father crawled on deck through a hatch, all the Americans had gone, the Coxswain and crewman responsible for the landing ramp were dead. He was later picked up by an American landing craft and taken to an American ship. He was therefore listed as missing in action from his own ship.*

2nd photo on the right: Sub-lieutenant Alan Lawrence (second from the left) was in command of LCA 862 and also involved in the Pointe du Hoc operation. His craft was launched from HMS *Amsterdam* and was believed to have landed the nearest to the actual Pointe on the day.

Two men from Motor Launch (ML 204) were also mentioned in Despatches and this was recorded by the Royal Navy. This was a vessel in the LCA convoy. These men did not land at Pointe du Hoc, but nevertheless contributed to the Rangers' landing.

For Operation Neptune – for gallantry and devotion to duty during the landings in Normandy.'

MID – LMtrMch Frank Allum P/MX634493
MID – Tel Eric Midcalf D/JX344151
Other crew members:
Lt. J. Synon-Moss RNVR (Commanding Officer)
SLt A.L. Franklin RNVR
SLt D.W. Vockins RNVR

Private Colin Blackmore and Acting Sgt. Joseph John Good of the Royal Army Service Corps were both recommended for and received the British Military Medal for valour at Pointe du Hoc – a recommendation which was in both cases endorsed by Lt. Col. Rudder.

Both Blackmore and Good joined the Rangers at the top of the cliff as riflemen. As the report says, *'Good and Blackmore scaled the cliffs using rope ladders and fought on the cliff top – and then when ammunition was running low, they returned to the DUKWs and removed their machine guns. The guns and ammunition were then taken back to the top.'*

Included and well mentioned within the Ranger party, there were two British Army officers – Lt. Colonel Trevor and RNVR Lt. Ronald F. Eades, who landed alongside the Rangers at Pointe du Hoc. Lt. Col. Trevor narrowly escaped death from a bullet wound to the side of his head upon landing at the base of Pointe du Hoc and in photographs taken on 8 June, he can be seen wearing a bandage and no helmet. A few weeks after the battle back in England, this letter was received by his family.

Private Blackmore.

(1190) Wt45451/225 110m 1/44 FHD Gp38/10.

Army Form W.3121

Recommendation passed forward

Brigade............... Division............... Corps...............

Unit COXE attached 2nd Ranger Bn, US Army.

Schedule No.............
(To be left blank)

Rank and Army or Personal No. T/76597 Private

Name...............
(Christian names must be stated)

BLACKMORE, Colin Edward.

	Received	Passed
Brigade		
Division		588
Corps		
Army		

| Action for which commended
(Date and place of action must be stated)	Recommended by	Honour or Reward	(To be left blank)
I endorse a report of Lt.Col Rudder on the gallantry shown by Pte. Blackmore in the operations at Points du Hoe on 6th June 1944.
1. Pte.Blackmore navigated and operated a new amphibious device. As this device was still in the development stage it was a dangerous and arduous duty especially in the heavy seas which were running.
2. Pte.Blackmore volunteered for the task well knowing the dangers.
3. After trying every way possible to complete the primary task he scaled the cliffs on rope ladders and joined in the fight as a rifleman. When ammunition ran low he returned to the beach which was still under enemy machine gun fire from the flank and salvaged Vickers machine guns and ammunition from the DUKWS. He again scaled the cliffs and put the machine guns into action.
4. During the fighting Pte.Blackmore was wounded in the foot. After receiving First Aid he evacuated one of the Rangers from the front line under heavy machine gun fire and mortar fire. He volunteered to carry ammunition to the front, repair machine guns and rifles and helped
                                                              .../salvage | | M.M.
M.M
21.12.44
MS.
9.10.44 | M.M
Recommended
D.D. Lennie
Chief of Staff
for Chief of Command Churchii
(absent on duty)
25030 |

(1190) Wt45451/225 110m 1/44 FHD Gp38/10.

Army Form W.3121

Recommendation passed forward

Brigade............... Division............... Corps...............

Unit COXE Attached 2nd Ranger Bn, US Army.

Schedule No.............
(To be left blank)

Rank and Army or Personal No. T/76597 Private

Name...............
(Christian names must be stated)

BLACKMORE, Colin Edward.

	Received	Passed
Brigade		
Division		589
Corps		
Army		

| Action for which commended
(Date and place of action must be stated)	Recommended by	Honour or Reward	(To be left blank)
ammunition from the beach until he was evacuated late on June 7th to the Battleship TEXAS.
5. The work of Pte.Blackmore contributed greatly to the success of the mission of the 2nd Ranger Battalion and reflected credit to himself and to his country.	B.L. Montgomery
Field Marshal
Commander-in-Chief, 21 Army Group | | |

(1190) W45454/225 110m. 1/44 P&D Gp33/10.

Army Form W.3121

recommendation
passed forward

	Received	Passed

Brigade.................. Division.................. Corps

Schedule No..................
(To be left blank)
Unit..COXE..Attached..2nd..Ranger..Bn.
US..Army.

Rank and Army or Personal No...T/113388..Corporal

Name........GOOD,..Joseph..James.
(Christian names must be stated)

	Received	Passed
Brigade		
Division		
Corps		583
Army		

Action for which commended (Date and place of action must be stated)	Recommended by	Honour or Reward	(To be left blank)
I endorse a report of Lt.Col.Rudder on the gallantry shown by Cpl.Good in the operations at Points du Hoc on 6th June 1944. 1. Cpl.Good navigated and operated a new amphibious device. As this device was still in the development stage it was a dangerous and arduous duty especially in the heavy seas which were running. 2. Cpl.Good volunteered for the task well knowing the dangers. 3. After trying every way possible to complete the primary task he scaled the cliffs on rope ladders and joined in the fight as a rifleman. When ammunition ran low he returned to the beach which was still under enemy machine gun fire from the flank and salvaged Vickers machine guns and ammunition from the DUKWS. He again scaled the cliffs and put the machine guns into action. He then remained in action in the front line until the afternoon of June 8th when the Rangers were relieved. 4. The work of Cpl.Good contributed greatly to the success of the mission of the 2nd Ranger Battalion and reflected credit to himself and to his country.		M.M. M.M 21.12.44	

B. L. Montgomery.

Field Marshal,
Commander-in-Chief, 21 Army Group.

He survived his wounds and went on to write a report on the Pointe du Hoc action as it was viewed from his own perspective (dated 12 July). It appears that he too was not in the slightest bit aware of the Rangers' orders to attack Maisy. Had he been told about Maisy by Rudder, then it is logical that this report would have made note of it.

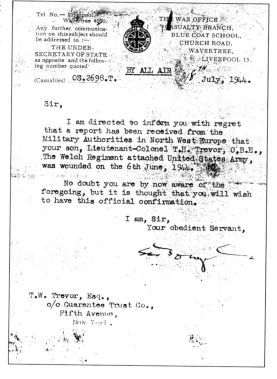

Tel. No.— Liverpool 4200.
Any further communication on this subject should be addressed to :—
THE UNDER-SECRETARY OF STATE
as opposite and the following number quoted"
(Casualties) OS.2698.T.

THE WAR OFFICE
CASUALTY BRANCH,
BLUE COAT SCHOOL,
CHURCH ROAD,
WAVERTREE,
LIVERPOOL 15.

BY ALL AIR 18 July, 1944.

Sir,

I am directed to inform you with regret that a report has been received from the Military Authorities in North West Europe that your son, Lieutenant-Colonel T.H. Trevor, O.B.E., The Welch Regiment attached United States Army, was wounded on the 6th June, 1944.

No doubt you are by now aware of the foregoing, but it is thought that you will wish to have this official confirmation.

I am, Sir,
Your obedient Servant,

T.W. Trevor, Esq.,
c/o Guarantee Trust Co.,
Fifth Avenue,
New York.

SECRET

ASSAULT ON POINTE DU HOE BATTERY

1. The Battery dominated the OMAHA and UTAH beaches and shipping. It was essential, therefore, that the guns be destroyed at the earliest possible moment.

2. The outline plan at the time that I started to work on the project was to land the Rangers on OMAHA beach in the second wave, pass them through the forward troop and then for them to advance along the coast line for 4-5 miles and attack the Battery from the landward (South-East) side. This plan was identical with the plan used to attack the POINTE MATIFOU battery at ALGIERS. There it was demonstrated that even against light opposition it is impossible to reach and reduce the Battery quickly enough to prevent it engaging our shipping to considerable effect. The plan was, therefore, partially abandoned and a landing was sought nearer the objective. That this was right was demonstrated by the fact that neither the balance of the Ranger Group nor the assault Batallions landed at OMAHA, in spite of most violent exertions, covered the 4-5 miles and reached POINTE DU HOE before the evening of D+2. During which time   if the damage done at MATIFOU in a few hours is any criteria   much of our shipping would have been sunk.

3. The search for a nearer landing was complicated by the topography of the coast which, Westward of OMAHA to POINTE DU HOE and on to GRAND CAMP, consists of 90 - 100 ft high cliffs.

4. The second plan consisted of a landing at GRAND CAMP, some two miles to the East of the Battery, and then attacking the Battery from the East. Here, however, there was a large artificial inundation which restricted the line of advance and forced the attack over open country up hill on ground dominated by prepared positions on commanding ground. A careful study of photographs convinced everyone that not only had the enemy foreseen this attack, but that he had made very elaborate preparations to meet it, and had prepared a "killing ground". The object of the inundation being solely to canalise the attackers' advance over this prepared ground. This plan was abandoned. Inspection of the ground and defences later showed that the enemy had, in fact, made the most careful preparations on the above lines and many hitherto unsuspected positions commanding the line of approach were discovered.

5. The right and left attacks having been ruled out, if the battery was to be quickly silenced, there remained only the centre which, as already mentioned, consisted of high vertical cliffs. A plan was produced to scale the cliffs to the East and West of the battery at selected places between the strong points which were sited at regular intervals along the cliff top, and then attack the battery from the East and West by means of a pincer movement.
        This plan offered every prospect of success, if the assault could scale the cliffs under fire. However, when they had done so - no easy task — the defences of the battery still had to be reduced, and these in themselves were formidable.

6. A study of these defences showed that they all faced inland and that the enemy were relying for defence of the battery to seaward on the sheer cliffs. If the assault force had to climb the cliffs under fire it was obviously better to do so and get right into the objective without having to overcome any addirtional obstacles, rather than climb the cliffs and then have to deal with the prepared defences. An additional inducement was the vital impotance of obtaining a quick decision, coupled with the economy of supporting fire which resulted from combining the supporting fire for the attack with the neutralising fire necessary to keep the battery silent during the approach. The final deciding factor was that it was a very bold conception and it is an old dictum that "bold conception and cautious execution leads to quick and favourable decisions". This plan was adopted but unfortunately they hedged by providing for part of the Ranger Group to land at OMAHA and carry out the original plan if the assault of the Battery had not succeeded by H+30. It was, however, the original plan that failed and this "insurance" policy only resulted in the success of this operation not being fully exploited for lack of the necessary follow-up, since the assault did not land until after H+30.

7. The plan of attack having been decided and the route of approach having been chosen, there only remained the technical problem of how to waft two hundred or more men up a vertical cliff. When that problem had been solved a short eight minute film explaining how it was to be done was made, and is included as part of this report.

8. The most prominent event in the execution was that the Rangers were put ashore about 70 minutes instead of 3 minutes after the bombardment ceased. At the time I considered that this alone was enough to render the operation abortive. However, so great was the tactical surprise and such the verve and dash of the troops that it made no difference, the first men being up in about 3 – 4 minutes and the guns captured and destroyed inthirty minutes.

9. The great accuracy of the preliminary bombardment, both by air and sea – the very considerable devastation and the large craters so created were very impressive, but it was of great interest that in spite of this accurate and intnsive concentration of heavy bombs and shells, only one-third of the guns were badly damaged, one-sixth slightly damaged, while half were in perfect order which strikingly confirms the old doctrine that vital objectives must be assaulted if they are to be destroyed with certainty.

10. Throughout the 3 days holding battle that followed the destruction of the guns the supporting fire given by the destroyerswas by its weight and extreme accuracy often the deciding factor it is rather remarkable that much of this fire was controlled from a forward O.P. by Aldous lamp direct to the ship; the wireless sets having become casualties.

11. When the battle was prolonged food and water, both of which we were in need of, were landed by the destroyers in their ships' boats.

12. The lack of landing craft delayed the evacuation of wounded and the value of unit M.Os having blood Plasma and the necessary facilities for blood transfusion was apparent and should never be neglected where there is any likelihood of delayed evacuation.

13. The unseaworthy qualities of the L.C.A. were abnormally apparent in the short lop that ther was during the run in, two out of twelve sank, due to stress of weather, the others were only kept afloat by working all the pumps and every available man bailing with his helmet. Having been for long voyages in the Channel and up the Africa coast in bad weather aboard these craft, without experiencing similar circumstances, I can only suppose that on this occasion the length of the seas was peculiarly unsuited to L.C.A. But it would appear desirable, in view of the above, to consider before employing these craft in the falsely named Pacific.

14. In conclusion I feel that it should be stressed that an operation of this sort against a strongly defended coast is only suitable for bold and skillfull troopss who have had long and careful preparation. Their leaders must combine a courageous spirit in the conception of the plan, with the ability to take infinite pains over minor details of the execution.

12th July 1944

Lieut. Colonel.

A German headquarters report from 4.35am on 6 June stated that an American 1st Lieutenant – a paratrooper – was captured in the early hours at Pointe du Hoc and it confirms the Germans had been alerted to the presence of mis-dropped paratroopers at that location. The original message is shown again here.

4.35 Hours

Report from Gren Regt 916:
An American 1/Lt taken prisoner near St. P le Guay testified that along
with the parachute troops also dummy dolls are being dropped, which explode
when contacting the ground.

All of these extra men do not counterbalance the number of casualties already at the Pointe in any way, but they serve to further emphasise the greater than discussed number of men who were wounded or killed there, because a number of these 'extra men' became casualties themselves before the action finished on the 8th. A good example of that are two 5th Battalion men from A Co. who went to the Pointe from Omaha Beach with 1st Lt. Charles Parker. Pfc James Gabaree was seriously wounded and his friend, Pfc Paul Pavey was killed on the 7th, and yet they do not receive any mention in the SUA Report.

It is safe to say that the number of participants in the PdH battle has been woefully underestimated by historians. There was a large body of men who were added to those numbers at the Pointe at different times, who were not recorded – because they did not come from D, E & F companies of the 2nd Rangers. But in effect, they make the casualty figures for this action far greater than has been previously acknowledged.

The website for the American Battlefield Monuments Commission states that *'After fighting two days, only about 90 Rangers stood when relieved by Schneider's Rangers and the 29th Division from Omaha Beach.'*

I have worked out the figures for the casualties as they appear before 9am on 6 June, leaving **224 men**. At this point, Rudder had more than enough men to continue with his missions in the direction of Maisy – as per his actual orders – but for whatever reason, chose not to. Instead, his decision was to stay at the Pointe and hold that small piece of land. Adding the 69 men that arrived as reinforcements, the total number of men under Rudder's command was **291**. If we believe what historians and tour guides have been telling us for years – that there were 90 men left at Pointe du Hoc who could bear arms when the relieving forces arrived on 8 June – then that leaves us with over **200 casualties** in total that could have been prevented – had Lt. Col. Rudder followed his orders. By their own admission in the SUA, by staying put *'they expected to be the target for heavy concentrations of artillery.'* You must also consider the damage done and the casualties caused by the Maisy guns to both Omaha and Utah sectors, which could have also been prevented by destroying the Maisy Batteries on 6 June – 3 days earlier than was done so in the end.

viii) The Strange Tale of George Klein

You may have noticed that George G. Klein, "one of the last remaining veterans of Pointe du Hoc" is not on the aforementioned list. Sadly, this is not a mistake – George Klein did not fight at Pointe du Hoc. In fact, he was nowhere near Normandy on 6 June, 1944.

During the summers of 2016 and 2017, I was visited at the Maisy Battery by WWII Ranger Veteran, George Klein. Mr Klein was a well-known Ranger, who had visited Normandy many times, often as the special guest of a large historical establishment – and he was also guest of honour at Pointe du Hoc at the annual remembrance ceremony on 6 June for a number of years. He stood next to dignitaries and the US Ambassador to France and he was given the respect his D-Day service demanded.

He handed out flyers during his many talks in Normandy and shown on the next page is the first page of one of his leaflets, which describes his military service and his time with the Rangers.

He gave talks during the evenings whilst in Normandy, and during the daytime he was welcomed everywhere, planting trees and shaking hands. Back in the US he was known for his lengthy and detailed YouTube and TV interviews and personal talks to audiences. A Search for 'George Klein – Ranger Pointe du Hoc' will still show them.

I was working at Maisy and Mr Klein arrived escorted by a French friend of mine. He was very pleasant, but his opening words to me were *'I have read your book and you have got your facts wrong...'*

I don't actually mind being wrong – but I like to be told where and/or how I have got it wrong, so as you can imagine, Mr Klein's opinion interested me. He went on to tell me very specifically, that the Rangers only had

George G. Klein
D.O.B. April 19, 1921

2ᴿᴰ RANGER BATTALION & 5ᵀᴴ INFANTRY DIVISION
U.S. ARMY 1938 - 1945

George Klein joined the Illinois National Guard in 1938 at age 17. He was assigned to the 122ⁿᵈ Field Artillery of the 33ʳᵈ Division. In May of 1942 he attended Officers Candidate School at Fort Sill, Oklahoma (Class 25) and was graduated a 2ⁿᵈ Lieutenant. He was assigned to the 80ᵗʰ Infantry Division prior to applying for the new Army Ranger School at Camp Forrest in Tullahoma, Tennessee. Injured during training, George Klein rejoined the 905ᵗʰ Field Artillery of the 80ᵗʰ Division as a Forward Observer. He later requested Overseas Duty and was reassigned to the 46ᵗʰ Field Artillery battalion of the 5ᵗʰ Infantry Division and was sent to England. It was during a chance encounter on Regent Street in London, England with Colonel James E. Rudder in February 1944 that George Klein was asked to return to the 2ⁿᵈ Ranger Battalion.

Klein rejoined the 2ⁿᵈ Ranger Battalion at their training base at Bude in Cornwall. During the late winter and spring of 1944 the 2ⁿᵈ Ranger Battalion practiced assaulting cliffs in exercises on the Isle of Wight and at locations in southeast England.

On the morning of June 6ᵗʰ platoon leader George Klein and the other members of Fox Company disembarked from HMS Ben Machree onto LCA #884 for the run into Pointe du Hoc between Omaha and Utah beaches. Supported by the battleship USS Texas and the Destroyer USS Satterlee D, E & F Companies were to neutralize six 155mm artillery pieces atop Pointe du Hoc and then establish a roadblock at the Grandcamp Vierville Road to prevent German troops from opposing the American landings later that morning.

After climbing to the top of Pointe du Hoc George Klein engaged the German enemy in close combat for the next several hours. During this he was knifed in the leg by a German bayonet and wounded. He bandaged his wound and continued to fight over the next two days in the initial hedgerow engagements until the wound hindered his mobility. On June 8 he was evacuated via litter down Pointe du Hoc and taken to England for treatment.

After recovering George Klein rejoined the 46th Field Artillery Battalion of the 5ᵗʰ Infantry Division as an air and forward observer. He fought through the Loire Valley and Metz campaigns. In November 1944 he was seriously wounded again due to an explosion by artillery or mines (it was never determined which) as his unit approached the Siegfried Line. Evacuated to England, Klein was hospitalized for three months before joining the 6951ˢᵗ POW Transit Enclosure Unit. For the remainder of the war Klein was involved in the processing of German prisoners of war.

As of this date George Klein is one of the last remaining men of the 2ⁿᵈ Ranger Battalion who is still traveling, meeting the public and carrying forward an eyewitness account of his unit's experiences. He does so as a representative of the men in his unit who are no longer here and in an effort to promote and preserve the legacy and lessons of the Second World War.

two missions on D-Day – '*attack the gun positions at Pointe du Hoc*' and then '*block the Grandcamp-Vierville highway.*' He told me that they had no other missions at all.

He told me that he went to attack '*his objective*', a gun position at the Pointe as ordered with his men of F Company 2nd Battalion – and that he was later wounded by a bayonet.

However, when he spoke, it became obvious that he did not have all the facts. There was no mission to '*guard the highway*' behind Pointe du Hoc and he could give me no specific details. There was no gun on gun pit No. 5 and in his many discussions on film and in person, he was not aware that the pit he said that he attacked had actually been demolished before D-Day. Everything he knew about Pointe du Hoc in detail sounded like he had simply read it in an old book.

Three friends had also noticed a lack of combat detail during their talks with him. They had been to an evening event in Normandy where he was guest speaker and when pushed, he would not divulge parts of his history. It was all very odd, considering he was happy enough to discuss everything in huge detail when the cameras were there.

He also said that once he was wounded, he returned to his original unit (not the Rangers)

The author talking to George Klein at Maisy.

which I felt would not have happened in real life. All the Ranger veterans I had met wanted to return to the Rangers, the 'elite unit'. No other unit would do – so why did Mr Klein not wish to go back to the Rangers? He could not answer that question when I asked.

The people involved in this investigation were Kurt Broddelez, Erwin Leydekkers, Jan Molenaar and myself, and we each decided to look at Mr Klein in more detail. I looked at the Rangers' Morning Reports, which I had on file and could not find any mention of a George Klein being listed as serving at all with the Rangers. Next, I looked at the documents for the issue of the Purple Heart and Silver Star for the action at Pointe du Hoc – again, he was not listed.

The other guys looked at every book available that could document Mr Klein's time with the Rangers. One book mentioned him by name but without any detail – so we considered that this information could have been supplied by Mr Klein himself – and every other book on the market did not discuss him. The guys wrote to Mr Klein a number of times and asked various questions as to why he was not included in any of the books on Pointe du Hoc and where they could find him mentioned. He replied saying that he had not been asked by those particular authors about his experiences during the war. He was also not forthcoming with his promised wartime memoirs.

I found that there were already two lieutenants recorded as being with F Company at Pointe du Hoc; he would have been the third, which was VERY unusual within the Rangers.

I set about acquiring copies of the Morning Reports for the unit he was in prior to his time with the Rangers, and that research was completed in England, when a US researcher (who does not wish to be named) also produced a similar set of papers proving that Klein was with an Artillery Unit in Northern Ireland on D-Day – and nowhere near Pointe du Hoc.

This was the proof needed, and a couple of blunt and very direct phone calls were made to Mr Klein to confirm that his 'D-Day Ranger history' was ALL made up, and his invention. Under direct questioning he admitted it was all a lie, as he had only trained with the Rangers for a short time before an injury, then upon recovery he was sent to another unit, with which he spent the remainder of the war. An internet search for 'George Klein' provides a much longer version of this story, as it was published by a French Historical Association. After being caught out, he admitted to them that he had lied about his military history.

There were times where his story was used to justify crowdfunding to send him back to Normandy and he obtained a lot of goodwill all the way along. He spent years pretending, and made individuals, establishments and even whole countries believe that he was a D-Day hero. As a result, I was often told I was wrong as well – purely based on Mr Klein's stories. After all, who would question the word of someone who was actually there? I feel that he has bent and distorted history for a long time.

Even though some of the organisations that supported him over the years have been trying to delete their internet pages about him since he was outed, his web of lies covering so many years has had an impact on D-Day history.

During the week when he was unmasked, I was stunned to receive a message from a US 'historian' asking that Mr Klein should be left alone and his story be left to die with him. I did not agree, not only because to cover up what he has done to the history of D-Day would be wrong and I was astonished to have been asked to do that, but also to protect the legacy and bravery of the men who actually fought there. Who did the research and due diligence regarding Mr Klein in the US I wonder? The truth about him finally came from a group of like-minded people who quickly realized that something did not add up about his stories.

Mr Klein went on to fight in France later in the war – this time for real – and was awarded the Bronze Star and the Purple Heart for his efforts. He was truly a part of the war effort and that alone is something he deserves respect for – but the rest was unnecessary.

ix) Examining the Evidence on the PdH Guns

The Rangers' mission to neutralize the gun position at Pointe du Hoc was completed – that is a fact. But to put this into a modern context, if a courier was delivering a package to your house and he delivered it to a place a mile away, would you say that he had delivered it to your address or not? The point being that when we read reports of the Rangers finding guns at Pointe du Hoc, they were in reality one mile from Pointe du Hoc – so they were NOT at Pointe du Hoc at all when it was attacked. We must therefore factually state that Pointe du Hoc site was indeed *empty*.

Reports vary between four and five guns having been found inland around one mile from the Pointe. It is certain that the number of guns was NOT six as is often mis-recorded. Len Lomell's personal interviews with me varied with him saying he damaged two and in later talks three, and four of the guns. Rupinski's account is written in other books and they say that he did work on the same guns again, not knowing that Lomell and Kuhn had already been there. So perhaps the higher number of guns is obtained by adding the two incidents together, and it could be that the same guns were counted twice.

Another piece of 'evidence' comes by way of a line from a diary entry from D Company's 2nd Lt. George Kerchner. It was posted online by his son and is said to have been written on 13 June by Kerchner – with help from Kuhn and Arthur. As yet I have been unable to obtain a fuller copy of the account or contact Mr Kerchner's son – but this line does give a little expansion to the PdH action and also indicates that there could have been other men involved.

'I sent Sgt Lomell, Johnson, Kuhn, and Arthur out on patrol and they found and destroyed five 155mm guns, which jerries had pulled out of [Point Du Hoc] 24 hours previous.'

With all the variances of detail, the first-hand accounts of the gun numbers found that are actually stated by the Rangers are inconclusive and it is 100 per cent certain that the guns were not moved *'24 hours previous'.* That will presumably have been Mr Kerchener's personal opinion of what happened.

I think that there were only four guns found to the rear in the trees and I base that opinion on reports from units other than the Rangers.

It is worth remembering that all of the post battle / After Action Reports regarding the mission to Pointe du Hoc recount what Rangers themselves believed to be accurate. *'We went to attack 6 guns'* – *'they had just been moved into trees'* etc. But these are accounts by men that we know were not briefed accurately and were even misled by their commanding officer on the number of guns to expect and where they may or may not be. Many of the men who commented on the guns and their number did not take part in their destruction or even see those guns, so their testimony is more hearsay than fact – even though often these comments came from men who were actually involved in the PdH action nearby.

We must go to contemporary documents, which are not affected by Lt. Colonel Rudder's orders or claims of orders, nor the instructions he gave to his men on the day. These reports could well be the most accurate ones we have and it can be reasonably argued that their authors have no need to make overly bold claims or bend the truth.

The first one shown here is part of a post battle evaluation called *'The First United States Army Report of Operations, 20th August 1943 – 1st August 1944.'* (US National Archives). [It is a long report so I have slimmed down the list].

It makes the following statement about Pointe du Hoc having only four guns, a statement which points out that they were at pains to check with documents from the German headquarters for the region. It seems obvious that they would not have made that statement in that manner, if it was something they had not actually done.

For the purpose of this compilation, shore reconnaissance was made on all known battery positions from Port en Bessin to Cap de la Hague with the exception of some of the temporary prepared positions for mobile guns and several inaccessible positions on the breakwaters at Cherbourg. A comprehensive detailed analysis of the batteries in the entire Cherbourg peninsula is being prepared to serve as an aid to instruction and planning for future operations and will be disseminated independently to appropriate authorities. A captured document from headquarters of the commander of the Normandy sea frontier has also been used to confirm and amplify this information.

It must also be noted that this tabulation does not include the individual gun positions, such as casemated 88.s and 75.s which formed strongpoints, as distinguished from batteries.

No.	Grid.	Details and Remarks.
1	586938	+ 155-mm. guns. Covered under " Pointe du Hoe."
5	533918	4–155 Hows. One gun knocked from its emplacement by naval gunfire or air bombardment; the other three guns were withdrawn when the enemy retreated.
16 16A	528916 531914	4–105-FGH. Three guns were in casemates, but had been turned around to fire out of rear entrances. One casemate was still under construction and the gun was demolished in the open emplacement at 16A. Casemates were for mobile guns.

It reads:

'Target No 1 – 4 x guns 155mm at Pointe du Hoc.'

Their assessment is consistent with the German construction work recorded as being undertaken and the same as was reported by US Intelligence prior to D-Day.

'Target No 5 – 4 x 155mm Howitzers at Les Perruques, 3 removed by retreat and 1 remained.'

The statement about one of the guns being knocked over is backed up by post-battle photographic evidence in the author's collection. I am unsure as to the timing of the removal of the other guns. Veteran accounts mention them – and others do not. I have no evidence to dispute this account as being accurate and I feel that the remaining guns were probably removed from Les Perruques on the evening of the 8th, as there are accounts of them being operational before that. But this also might explain in more detail the accuracy of the events at Pointe du Hoc on D-Day SUA Reports that '*salvos of three*' were being received. '*After finding No.3 casemate, a junk-pile of broken steel and concrete, Lang's group moved south. They began to meet artillery fire, coming in salvos of three, and shifting toward the Pointe with each salvo.*' It would make perfect sense if the remaining three emplaced guns at Les Perruques (Maisy I) were engaging the Rangers at Pointe du Hoc with salvos of three rounds at a time.

'Target No 16 – 4 x 105mm Field Gun Howitzers. Three in casements and one in the open at Target 16A.'

There are three casements at La Martinière, there are photographs of the cannons behind the casements post-battle and 105mm cases have been found there. We have radio reports stating that Target 16A was firing at Utah Beach at 8.40pm on D-Day and aerial and naval attacks continued on the position after that. Wheels for a 150mm German cannon have actually been found at position 16A and we have photographs of the '4th' un-casemented cannon sitting in the open at La Martinière (Target 16) prior to D-Day.

So the question is, did the Germans move this one gun to position 16A or remove other larger calibre guns away during their retreat – or were they all destroyed in their positions before the site was captured and then their remains were removed post war? At this moment with the evidence available, I do not know. But remember by way of backup for this – the GSGS intelligence maps show four guns as being at Target No 16A from 6 March onwards. Those guns remained marked on the maps from that date onwards up until D-Day – so there must have been a reason for them to have remained on the maps, not be deleted and then be the subject of multiple specific bombing missions on D-Day. Not withstanding the fact that all three batteries were reported firing on the evening of D-Day by Col. Talley.

The evidence available to date *implies* all three batteries being operational at the same time on D-Day.

```
              Brief reference may be made to the operation
against POINTE du HOE.  Photographic reconnaissance indicat-
ed the presence of six casemated guns.  On that premise, the
position was subjected to severe air bombing both preceding
and during the operation proper.  Also TEXAS delivered some
250 rounds of 14 inch fire on it.  When the Rangers succeeded
in scaling the cliff, however, they found the casemates empty.
It later developed that four of the guns had been moved and
emplaced in a hedge lane about a mile south.  This new position
was bombarded and knocked out by TEXAS using airspot during
the morning of D day.  Meanwhile, the Rangers found themselves
in a precarious position and were maintained only by their own
efforts and the untiring assistance of SATTERLEE, and later
THOMPSON, HARDING and BARTON.
```

The 1st Infantry Division (post battle) War Diary entries held in the 1st Infantry Division Museum Archives, also report that there were only four guns found at Pointe du Hoc. Again this is evidence coming from a different source than the Rangers.

```
              The Air Plan provided for heavy bombing of specific
targets in the beachhead area on D - 1 day, and subsequently
as necessary to assist Naval gunfire in destroying or neutral-
izing coast defenses.  In addition bombing of the beach de-
fenses was scheduled for delivery between H - 30 minutes and
H hour.  As far as is known, the attacks scheduled for delivery
on D - 1 were carried out.  Visual evidence indicated that dur-
ing this attack, or others carried out intermittently over a
period of months before the actual assault, the enemy battery
on the POINTE du HOE which had caused the Force Commander some
concern was damaged to such an extent that four of its guns
had been removed to a new site about a mile inland.
```

Another comment, this time from Admiral Kirk about there being only 4 guns found behind Pointe du Hoc dated August 1944. It is worth remembering that no guns were discovered actually AT Pointe du Hoc.

SECRET

Narrative by: Rear Admiral Alan G. Kirk, U.S.N., Part II   Film No. 267-1
Recorded: 26 Aug. 1944
Rough: Hatch

There was one battery established on Point du Hoe, by the enemy, that consisted of six 155 mm. guns which we knew commanded the transport area, both areas, O and U This had to be taken out and a contingent of Rangers was assigned to the job. The Air Force bombed these positions very heavily on D minus two and D minus one and the TEXAS, and several other ships put heavy gunfire on the position. The Rangers scaled the palisades by means of scaling ladders and made a most gallant attack. The enemy had withdrawn four of the six guns to inland a little bit and hidden them in the lanes, and concealed them in the bushes but the Rangers carried the position thoroughly.

The following text details the attack on the guns to the rear of Pointe du Hoc – taken from the SUA Report:

Active patrolling was started at once on all sides of the thinly-held positions. About 0900, a two-man patrol from D went down the double-hedgerowed lane that ran south from the highway near Company D's outpost. About 250 yards along the lane, Sergeant Lomell and S/Sgt. Jack E. Kuhn walked into a camouflaged gun position; there, set up in battery, were five of the enemy 155s missing from the Point. They were in position to fire toward Utah Beach, but could easily have been switched for use against Omaha. Piles of ammunition were at hand, points on the shells and charges ready, but there was no indication of recent firing. Not a German was in sight, and occasional sniper fire from a distance could hardly be intended as a defense of the battery. So effective was the camouflage that Lomell and Kuhn, though they could later spot the guns from the highway, had seen nothing until they were right in the position.

With Kuhn covering him against possible defenders, Sergeant Lomell went into the battery and set off thermite grenades in the recoil mechanism of two guns, effectively disabling them. After bashing in the sights of a third gun, he went back for more grenades. Before he could return, another patrol from Company E had finished the job. This patrol, led by S/Sgt. Frank A. Rupinski, had come through the fields and (like Lomell and Kuhn) were in the gun position before they saw it. Failing to notice the fact that some disabling work had already been done, Rupinski's patrol dropped a thermite grenade down each barrel, and removed some of the sights. After throwing grenades into the powder charges and starting a fire, the patrol decided the guns were out of action and withdrew.

For sure the Rangers found a number of guns at the edge of a field – in the hamlet behind Pointe du Hoc – but what of the accuracy of parts of the above quotation. By looking at photographs of General Eisenhower standing next to the guns, taken on 12 June – it is interesting to note that the breech is wide open on the gun in the photograph – and the traversing mechanism is clearly still working as the elevation of the gun barrel differs between both photographs. Someone opened the breech and perhaps the same person changed the elevation of the barrel during the photograph by playing with the gun. The exact detail of events in the excerpt from report above says '*Rupinski's patrol dropped a thermite grenade down each barrel, and removed some of the sights*', is therefore questionable as to the method of destruction for this one gun. The breech

is still operational and so is the traversing mechanism and later it has even had its breech block removed as the gun is being taken away. We can say for sure that it did not have a thermite grenade put down that particular barrel, nor placed on its traversing mechanism.

Author Helmut K. von Keusgen wrote a book about Pointe du Hoc and obtained a quote from a German soldier who was said to have been there prior to D-Day. The quote reads: '*The cannon in emplacement number 5 was totally destroyed and left on its back.*'

If the German numbering of the emplacements is taken to be the same as the US pre-invasion numbering, then I feel this veterans' statement is not only inaccurate – I believe that it is a physical impossibility.

On the previous page is an aerial photograph of gun pit No.5 (taken by the author from a light aircraft). The gun pit can be seen to go under the unfinished casement, rendering it completely incapable of functioning as a gun pit.

Here it is shown as 'No 5' on the Neptune Monograph planning document. The casement is correctly drawn in that document and shown as being

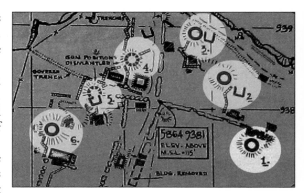

over the pit at that time. The intelligence is a 100 per cent correct match to that which is on the ground.

It would not have been possible for the Germans to continue with the construction of this casement if they had left the damaged gun on the pit in the manner as described above by the German soldier.

If the German account is to be believed, then the Germans numbered their gun positions the opposite way around to the US and pit No.5 was the second from the right (US pit No.2), meaning that not only were there guns missing from pits 4 and 5 prior to D-Day, but there was a further 'dead' gun left upturned in position on (U.S. numbered) pit No.2 after the bombing. Thus, the Rangers' mission to assault only three guns at the Pointe would have been even harder to justify. It is still worth remembering that Lt. Col. Rudder briefed and ordered his men to attack guns on positions 1, 2, 3, 4, 5 & 6 inclusive. He did NOT tell them that some of the pits were not operational and had no weapons.

This veteran's explanation does not really tally with the evidence found in contemporary photographs, which show attempts by the Germans to camouflage the pit by using pieces of wood and camouflage netting. The photographs taken in the days after D-Day do not lie, so one of the two situations stated as fact above must be wrong. Either there was a damaged gun or no gun on the pit. The reality appears to show that wood and netting was found and it appears to prove that there was NO real gun in that place, upside down as described.

Perhaps the answer comes from the Small Unit Actions Report which states: *'Petty and three men had left the cliff edge first, found No.2 gun position destroyed and empty.'* So this seems to confirm that the position the US intelligence maps 'marked No.2' had no gun on it at all.

Below: Here are photographs which are often attributed to Lt. Brandel of the 1st Inf. Division. After investigation with the photographs' owners, these pictures actually came from an Artillery Study undertaken by the 1st infantry Division and post-war they became included in Brandel's papers. They are nevertheless very useful contemporary photographs as they provide visual clarification of the same argument.

They were taken a couple of days after D-Day and not one of these photographs provides evidence of a damaged gun remaining on the gun pit as the German veteran suggests. There is, however, evidence of wood and camouflage having been placed on these gun pits as an attempt to confuse the Allies.

It all seems to show there is no upturned gun on a destroyed gun pit at the Pointe. But then when you read the 2nd Battalion After Action Report in detail it says this (see next page).

This seems to contradict everything else in many ways. It states that a gun was seen destroyed on a gun pit at the Pointe – and more confusingly, it says that at (or after 12 noon) D Co. *'sent out patrol that located the five, destroying*

one, 155mm guns. Later returning with reinforcement, found remaining guns destroyed by patrol from Co. E.'

So if that is accurate then it implies that Len Lomell only destroyed one gun and the members of E Company did the rest – which I do not entirely believe.

In an interview for the website: http://www.historynet. com Len Lomell made this statement: 'as we made our way over to the west side of the Pointe to gun positions 4, 5 and 6. There were no guns there, and we thought, what the hell? What's happened here? There never were any guns here! There was no evidence that there were ever any guns there.'

Lt. Col. Rudder appears to have never made any attempt to correct the historical errors regarding his orders and other statements made about gun numbers at Pointe du Hoc. So it begs the question, why does an intelligent senior officer allow all of those errors to remain in the recording of his crowning moment in the military? These errors are not alone, there are other discrepancies such as this: 'The gun positions, three of them casemated, were partly wrecked; the guns had been removed.' – a direct quote. But there are only two unfinished cannon casements and no guns were ever installed inside them? Another serious error in this historical account. The whole purpose of the Small Unit Actions Report was to report the detail with as much accuracy as possible for future generations and one would have thought that Lt Col. Rudder would have wanted it that way as well. But no corrections were made to it and ALL of the reports from the time remain with conflicting information. It is a real historical mess!

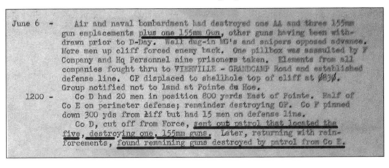

June 6 - Air and naval bombardment had destroyed one AA and three 155mm gun emplacements plus one 155mm Gun, other guns having been withdrawn prior to D-Day. Well dug-in MG's and snipers opposed advance. More men up cliff forced enemy back. One pillbox was assaulted by F Company and Hq Personnel nine prisoners taken. Elements from all companies fought thru to VIERVILLE - GRANDCAMP Road and established defense line. CP displaced to shellhole top of cliff at 0830. Group notified not to land at Pointe du Hoc.

1200 - Co D had 20 men in position 800 yards East of Pointe. Half of Co E on perimeter defense; remainder destroying OP. Co F pinned down 300 yds from cliff but had 15 men on defense line. Co D, cut off from Force, sent out patrol that located the five, destroying one, 155mm guns. Later, returning with reinforcements, found remaining guns destroyed by patrol from Co E.

We have been told in detail of the method of destruction of the guns found to the rear of Pointe du Hoc. These photographs (shown on the previous page) show US infantrymen (not Rangers) taking away one of the guns from behind Pointe du Hoc some time after the battle.

Elevation changed, breech open and then breech block completely removed… which shows no blocking of the barrel, breech or traversing mechanism and on the photograph with the dog, you can see the sighting unit still in place on the top left of the barrel. All of these conflicting statements to do not suggest these reports are very accurate.

I considered the possibility that it could be argued that Lt. Col. Rudder was not fully informed of the Maisy Batteries prior to D-Day – and could this have been the reason why he did not tell his men about the site and other missions. I realized how very ridiculous this was, given the amount of times Maisy is mentioned in his Intelligence briefings – and I am sure that argument will die away once people see these reports. But even the slightest suggestion that he was not receiving intelligence regularly had to be investigated.

For me, the argument is covered well by the following post D-Day US Navy report. It indicates who had been receiving Intelligence information, about what and in what form.

Annex B1.—Intelligence

Due to the proximity of the area chosen for amphibious assault to aircraft bases in England, the demands made on photo-reconnaissance and photo-interpretation were very great. In spite of the comparatively large amount of ground intelligence of the French coast available in the United Kingdom, and the difficulties discussed above, the great majority of the information used by naval forces in both the planning and assault stages of the operation came directly from the study of aerial photographs. Such shore reconnaissance as has been undertaken to date has verified this information as correct.

IV. *Intelligence Disseminated*

In the preparation of the intelligence material, emphasis was placed on graphic, rather than on written material.

During the planning phase the assault force commanders and certain subordinate commands were supplied with basic charts, maps, plans, photographs and rubber models and were kept up to date by the frequent issue of reports, overlays, overprints and pictures covering enemy defenses ; beach, weather and hydrographic data ; enemy order of battle and information on enemy devices and capabilities. A constant plot of enemy defenses was kept on transparent material placed over maps and from these master copies photographic reproductions and overprints were issued frequently to keep planners informed of the details of enemy defenses in the proposed assault areas.

Intelligence material for the actual operation was gathered together in a single illustrated monograph which was widely distributed.

For operational use forces were supplied with shoreline sketches, photo mosaics and the Neptune monograph, together with detailed graphic and written intelligence on enemy defenses, enemy order of battle, weather and hydrographic data and enemy capabilities.

In connection with the preparation and dissemination of intelligence material, constant and direct liaison was maintained with Force Commanders, ANCXF and the First U.S. Army to assure the completeness and accuracy of all material issued. Dissemination included all Allied units concerned with planning and operations.

Intelligence documents of particular value disseminated included the following :—

(1) *Neptune Monograph.*—An attempt was made to include in one convenient volume, in graphic form as far as practicable, a compendium of the intelligence required by ships and craft. Subjects covered by this volume were : weather, sea and surf ; tides, currents and astronomical data, terrain and coast ; beaches ; enemy order of battle and capabilities ; enemy defenses and installations ; small ports in the assault area ; France under German control, and a folio of sketches, charts and maps. The monograph was distributed to forces, groups, ships and craft down to L.C.T.s. Intelligence in the monograph was kept up to date by the dissemination of supplementary intelligence to be inserted in the volume. This included corrections to material previously issued, and new intelligence based on photographic interpretations and revisions and additions to the plans for the operation.

(2) *Shoreline Sketches.*—Produced primarily to guide coxswains and navigators of landing craft to their assigned beaches, the shoreline sketch presented on one 17 by 22 sheet a chart-map of at least half of each of the two assault beaches, a panoramic drawing of the shoreline as seen from seaward, sunlight and moonlight data, beach gradient graphs, inshore current data and tidal curves. They were overprinted with the different beach names and limits and were disseminated to the smallest landing craft. A limited number were overprinted with underwater obstacles and beach minefields immediately before the assault for special distribution to Navy and Army assault forces and demolition crews. The shoreline sketches were thoroughly covered in the intelligence briefing sessions and most landing craft personnel had four or five days to study them before the assault. Four of these sketches covered ' OMAHA ' and ' UTAH ' beaches.

(3) *Annotated Shoreline Sketches and Mosaics.*—To disseminate complete intelligence on beach defenses, based on the latest possible photographic cover, a plot of defenses was kept on transparent acetate placed on a shoreline sketch. This plot with the map beneath was reproduced photographically and bound together with gridded and annotated photographic mosaics of the beach areas to the same scale as the shoreline sketch. At D – 7 these were distributed to force commanders.

(4) *Landing Craft Profiles.*—Printed on transparent material to the same scale and proportion as the beach gradients on the shoreline sketch, these profiles were used with the sketches to estimate where each type of craft would touch down at any stage of tide on either beach. Copies were included in the Neptune monograph.

(5) *Photographic Interpretation Reports.*—A series of photographic reports, based on latest possible cover and including intelligence on all phases of enemy defenses, frequently illustrated with photographs or sketches, was issued as frequently as interpretation of new cover was completed. Copies were sent to the Allied Naval Commander, Expeditionary Force ; Commanding General, First U.S. Army ; and Naval Force Commanders.

Annex B1.—Intelligence

(6) *Bombardment and Gunfire Plan.*—A graphic presentation on a single sheet of enemy heavy batteries in the assault area with their arcs of fire, priorities assigned for neutralization and the plan of attack by aerial bombardment and naval gunfire. Copies were included in the Neptune monograph.

(7) *Inter-Service Information Series.*—Large books prepared by the Inter-Service Topographical Department of the Admiralty, giving detailed information on topography, climate, roads, waterways, maps and pictures of enemy-held territory. Distributed to Force Commanders and large ships.

(8) *Tactical Target Dossiers.*—Large books prepared by the Air Ministry and the U.S. Army Air Forces giving details and aerial photographs of objectives selected because of their importance to ground forces engaged in combined operations and presented to meet the operational requirements of supporting tactical air forces. Distributed to Air Spotters and Support Force ships.

(9) *Annotated Photographic Mosaics.*—Two sets, in addition to those described under 3 above, were ordered for NCWTF by the 21st Army Group. One, to a scale of 1/25,000, was a controlled, gridded and annotated series of 25 sheets covering the entire area of the operation. The other, to a scale of 1/12,500, was an ungridded and unannotated series of 18 sheets covering the area from St. Vaast to Port-en-Bessin to a depth of 12 miles inland. Each set was distributed to gunfire support ships and air spotters. Ground spotters and beach battalion commanders were also issued the 1/25,000 series.

(10) *Annexes to ANCXF Operation Order.*—This series comprised a group of booklets covering assault beach defense maps, texts and diagrams of all batteries in the English Channel area, texts and overlays of coast defenses, aerial photographs (annotated) of all batteries from Honfleur to west of Cherbourg, photographic shoreline silhouettes of the coast from Trouville to Cap de la Hague. These were distributed in selected groups down to L.C.T.s, the distribution lists being gauged to the probable requirements of each group.

(11) *Rubber Models.*—Tweny (20) sets of 1/5,000 rubber models, prepared by the Amphibious Training Command, N.O.B., Norfolk, Va., were distributed to Naval Force commanders and to the First U.S. Army. Their primary use was in connection with briefing.

(12) *Vectographs.*—Vectographic photographs prepared by the Photographic Interpretation Laboratory, Anacostia, for study of the assault areas in three dimensions were distributed to the Assault Force Commanders, primarily for use during briefing.

The report continues:

Batteries

Batteries were located well inland or on headlands relatively inaccessible from seaward. They were sited to provide a uniform concentration of fire along most of the coastline, except over the Cherbourg sea approaches where the intensity was very high. Numerous radar stations along the coast as well as visual posts provided them with observation. The types of guns used varied from modern German models to captured pieces of equipment; estimates of ranges, therefore, were questionable, even though the calibers were estimated quite accurately. The most predominant battery pieces in the area were the 105 FGH and the French (type GPF) 155-mm. field gun.

All battery positions, except temporary field positions, had underground shelters and living quarters, inter-connected with the gun emplacement by well-camouflaged communication trenches, and were protected by machine guns and anti-tank guns, always surrounded by bands of wire and often with bands of mines. In general the concrete was 6 to 7 ft. thick, reinforced with $\frac{1}{2}$-in. round rods spaced 9 in. on centers horizontally and vertically; the quality of the concrete appeared excellent, and the workmanship exceptional; roof slabs were consistently poured onto steel plates, which formed the ceilings of the shelters and casemates. In certain cases, for larger caliber guns, roof slabs were as thick as 12 ft.

Batteries were of the following general types:—

(1) Pivot mounted guns in casemates. This comprised the majority of the casemated positions; of the batteries which covered the Assault area, 12 of the 16 positions were casemated or had casemates under construction (actually there were only 15 positions as No. 6A was AA defense for position No. 3) and of these twelve, seven had pivot mounts, two were still under construction but appeared designed for pivot mounts, and two positions were not visited. This also appeared to be the general practice in the area surrounding Cherbourg.

(2) Mobile field guns in casemates. Only the Maisy II battery at 528916 was of this type. However, other examples were observed in the Cherbourg area, and the casemates at Battery No. 18 may possibly have been for mobile guns.

Pointe du Hoe Battery

Pointe du Hoe Battery was considered the number one priority in the bombardment plan, for it was the only enemy position which covered both of the beaches and transport areas. Originally there were six 155-mm. guns (French type GPF), with an estimated range of 25,000 yards, in open concrete emplacements. It was strategically located atop a 90-ft. high coastal bluff, remote from any large landing beach, surrounded by wire and minefields and extremely well protected on the flanks by prepared strongpoints. Personnel and ammunition shelters were underground and constructed of heavily reinforced mass concrete. Machine gun positions and communication trenches were well dug in and camouflaged. The observation and command post on the seaward edge of the bluff was constructed of heavily reinforced concrete, partially earth banked.

Early in March casemates began to be built near four of the positions; two guns having been removed from their emplacements. It was estimated that by D-Day the enemy would probably have two guns in casemates (sited to fire on UTAH) with four guns, possibly only two guns, with unrestricted arcs of fire remaining in open emplacements.

After this position was captured by Rangers it was found that the guns had been moved from their original positions and placed along a thickly tree-arbored lane, completely hidden from air reconnaissance about 1,000 yards south of the battery site. The guns were positioned to fire only on UTAH beach, but retained their observation post and main ammunition storage on top of the bluff.

Although there were no guns in the completed casemates (two were ready to receive guns and the other two still under construction) it was learned from prisoners that it was the enemy's intention to install new guns, which were momentarily expected. A captured document from Admiral Hennike's headquarters revealed the position was intended to house six 155-mm. guns.

The maximum range was 19,800 yards, minimum range 1,300 yards. Nos. 1 and 6 guns were to remain in open emplacements with all around arc of fire. Guns 2 and 3 were to be in casemates facing 040°, and guns 4 and 5 were to be in casemates facing 330°. Casemated guns would be restricted to 120° traverse. This information coincides identically with intelligence reports.

Pre-H-Hour air bombardment and naval gunfire completely disrupted communications and communication trenches, badly damaged or destroyed open positions, and breached perimeter wire and mine bands. No serious damage was observed on underground shelters, O.P. or finished casemates which were constructed of reinforced concrete, despite many hits.

The last page of this report provides further confirmation from within the US Army that they knew as early as March that the casements were being built and guns had been removed.

The latter paragraphs are also interesting, in particular the sentence *'A captured document from Admiral Hennike's headquarters revealed the position was intended to house six 155mm guns.'*. It seems plausible that the guns that had been removed from the pits (of 155mm calibre) would be going back in the casements (four of them) – and more than likely the other two would be placed back into the two remaining round pits, thus reusing the six guns.

Appearing straightforward enough, when you look at the physical sizes of the guns that were removed – see below – against the size of the internal dimensions of the two nearly finished casements. Then it is not possible that the original 155mm French WWI cannons would be returning, as they do not and could not fit inside the newly constructed casements. Even by removing the wheels and legs, they still would not fit without a huge amount of conversion work and the German army coastal artillery was being upgraded with newer and more powerful weapons than these. It is more likely the casements were being built to house new 10.5cm deck mounted guns and it could be argued they would then be quite possibly manned by a Kriegsmarine (Naval) Coastal Artillery unit.

As an example, the cannon shown here would not fit inside the casements being constructed at the Pointe – thus not all of the guns were going to be returning. Two guns could however, have been placed back into the two remaining open-air pits when the work was finished nearby – just as the Intelligence Report suggests.

This size discrepancy is further proven by studying the internal construction of one of the two casements. Structurally the casement interiors are nearly complete and the inside area steps down to accept the circular steel base mount for a deck-mounted gun. i.e. a gun without wheels or trailing arms of a type used on Navy ships. The shield area in front of the gun would fit into the zig-zag front of the casement to protect the gun crew – and the ammunition would be stored in the area behind. Any suggestion that their removal was a 'temporary measure' is, I feel, incorrect. At what point the new guns would have arrived is difficult to know without period documentation. But if they were due to arrive at

the finish of construction of the fourth casement, then it would have been another couple of months after D-Day before they were operational. The construction of the second pair of casements had not really developed above ground when D-Day interrupted the work. This then leads us to question the permanent removal of the guns from Pit 1 and 2 if they were actually due to stay at the Pointe in the long term…

It is suggested in Rudder's biography that there was another factor which affected both Rudder and Lytle and this came from the French. It is true that reports were given to the Allies which were generated by French spies in the area and transmitted to England. This was undertaken by the Resistance group led by Jean Marion, the then Mayor of Grandcamp-les-Bains.

Below is an interview written up and dated 1958 which comes from a taped and then translated interview with Marion for Cornelius Ryan during his *The Longest Day* book and film research. This paperwork and interview comes from the archives of the Ohio State University, and it lies within the Cornelius Ryan Collection.

Marion confirms that he knew Colonel Kistowski's Flak unit had arrived in Maisy, also that the gun position at Pointe du Hoc was not operational and that the guns at Maisy II (La Martinière) were operational as a fixed costal battery and 'set to fire on Utah'. These were three major factors which would have had a significant influence on the Rangers' mission. If anything, it made their attack on Maisy much more important – rather than less. This is first-hand proof from the man who actually sent the information to London. He had told London before D-Day about Maisy being able to fire on Utah Beach and he said that the guns had been removed from Pointe du Hoc and nothing was installed. Information that remains 100 per cent accurate to this day.

It would be a stretch to believe that this vital information was not given to Lt. Col. Rudder prior to his landing – but for the removal of any doubt, we can prove that it was. Dr Hatfield states in his book that Rudder discussed the PdH French Resistance intelligence with Lytle just *before* embarkation. So there is corroboration that Rudder knew about PdH, and by default Maisy, at that time from the same intelligence source and yet he deliberately withheld the Maisy part of the information from his men.

```
Interview 7/30/58
                                                                Omaha-Utah
Msur Le Mayor

Marie de Grandcamp
Grandcamps - le - Bains
Calvados

Jean Marion, member of municipal, 42, old sailor - Marguerite - no children


Worst days for Grandchamp were 4/5/6 - days when bombers hit bunkers and Kistowski's flak

battery.  He crawled over and wrote down positions of the flak battery.  Couldn't set

pos out.

Flak had taken up positions along small road between Maisy - - Gefosse-Forntenay.  Because

all comm are interrupted.  "I'll forward information by bicycle tomorrow to Andre Farine"

(outside at Letauville where he had cafe.  "What shall we do?"  "Let's get some additional

information and pass it on to Jules Picot (Nievely - la-Fonet).  He would send it to

Nercadier in Bayeux.

Mystery of Pointe de Hoc guns was this.  They had never been mounted.  He had not had

reports that they were mounted.  Guns were immobile; had never been installed.

From beginning of 1944 different calibre of troops.  They were terrorized.  They told the

French people "we're going to be chopped up"

Had spotted Downing's heavy mg batt.  He had informed London.

With exception of 20 Navy men who had a couple of light guns and a line of trenches, there

was nothing else in Grandchamps on 6th.

Had sent info to London about battery set to fire on Utah - set at fixed position covering

mouth of Orne.  Br. destroyer came in afternoon D-Day blew it to hell.  British knowing

way gun was facing came in on blind side.  "Give 'em hell etc" said Marion as he watched.
```

The relief of the men at Pointe du Hoc came on 8 June and this was not without incident. Friendly fire was noted in the 2nd Battalion AAR as coming from US tanks and this cost the lives of a further four Rangers, wounding another three and adding further to the tally of wounded, but this time not from German gunfire.

```
June 8 - Co F sent patrol to stop 116 Inf who were attacking Force on Pointe,
         killing four Rangers and wounding three.
```

Had Lt. Colonel Rudder left Pointe du Hoc as ordered and attacked the gun batteries at Maisy on 6 June then perhaps a vast number of his men who were wounded or killed AFTER 9am that day could have survived. Not to mention many men landing on the beaches, who would not have been shelled by the Maisy Batteries over the three days during which they were operational.

Another area of interest comes in the form of orders to Rudder from his superiors. The headquarters contingent of the 1st Infantry Division finally landed in Normandy on 9 June and set up their base of operations in St. Laurent-sur-Mer. Copies of their very first orders from their new location were issued by them and fresh orders were sent out from this location thereafter. Here is the text from one of their first couple of orders which concerns the Rangers. (1st Inf. Division Museum). (They are actually numbered Order No.1 and 2).

9 June – St. Laurent sur Mer.
At 0617hrs a 'Warning Order' was issued to 1st, 2nd and 29th Infantry Division.

1. *It is contemplated that the advance to the Second Objective will be made with Divisions abreast, 29th, 2nd and 1st Infantry Divisions from right to left at 1200 hours, 9 June. For boundaries and objectives see overlay attached. Order to be issued later.*
2. *2nd Division relieves elements of 1st Division on D-Day position and 2nd Division sector. Time of relief – 0700 hours 9 June.*

By command of Major General GEROW.
Co-signed by *H. J. Matchett Col. Chief of Staff.*

It is a consolidation order by Major General Gerow for the men under his command in the Omaha Sector to change positions and be ready for that change by 0700 hours on 9 June. It can be brought into context in relation to the Rangers when viewed alongside the next second set of orders issued on the same day – numbered 3 and 4 on their original sheet below. Then things become a little clearer.

Order No 3: Delete and substitute the following: 29th Infantry Division will defend D-Day positions in its sector with one regiment (116th) with Ranger Group attached.

Order No 4: Add paragraph. 116th Infantry, with Rangers attached, clear up pockets of resistance in 29th Division sector, move and prepare to defend D-Day line and re-organise.

Simple enough orders – however, on the evening of the 8th – the night before these orders were issued – Lt. Colonel Rudder had effectively already taken nearly all the men of the 2nd Battalion out of combat and put them into rest, leaving only the 5th Battalion to continue to fight. Thus they are now no longer the *'Ranger Group'* as ordered, but less than half of it. As this order includes specific reference to the whole Ranger group – it has to be assumed that Lt. Col. Rudder did not tell his superiors that he had removed the 2nd Battalion from the front line. If he had told them, then they would have no doubt taken that fresh information into account when ordering the remaining Rangers to do other things the next day. One assumes then they would simply have referred to the 5th Battalion and not the

'Rangers'. It is also worth remembering that by the morning of 9 June the men of the 5th had also been in combat for three days.

Below is the Narrative Report for the 2nd Battalion confirming they were removed from the front line and put into rest.

> *Just prior to the Battalion departure from the Pointe at 1600, a Company F patrol located and destroyed a still-active enemy MG firing from a tree-top. Moving out without incident to the Vierville-Grandcamp Road, the Battalion was held up awaiting the return of the contact patrol. Upon the receipt of the patrol information, Lt Col Rudder moved the Battalion into bivouac near au Guay to await the clearing of Grandcamp. Moving out by foot at 1700, the Battalion proceeded to another bivouac area in the Sluice Gate vicinity. Shortly thereafter, the Battalion Supply vehicles were closed into the area and rations, water, ammunition, and bed rolls were distributed. The troops rested during this period with security provided by the "buddy-system", each unit providing its' own rotating sentry. Altho this area was bombed during the night, no casualties occurred.*

It is also confirmed by the actual 2nd Battalion After Action Report for 8 June which states as early as 4pm in the afternoon they were at rest.

> *June 8 -   Moved out at 1600 as Ranger Force Reserve. Bivouaced East of GRANDCAMP. Bed Rolls, C-Rations, and water were brought up.*

We will never know why Lt. Col. Rudder did not put more men (other than one cannon company) from the 2nd Battalion into Action to support the 5th Battalion in the assault on Maisy as ordered. It is worth remembering that he also had men available from the 2nd Battalion who had landed at Omaha Beach, who were unwounded and had not previously fought at Pointe du Hoc.

It appears that Rudder's decision to remove 95 per cent of the 2nd Battalion men from the line was taken without the knowledge of his superiors, and without him knowing how big a defence the Germans would present at Maisy. Common sense (and orders) dictated that the Ranger Group did not completely split up until ALL of its missions were completed. But that is what happened – and the men of the 5th Battalion were left to attack Maisy without any intelligence brief and without a full complement of men or equipment.

Jack Burke, A Co. 5th Battalion: *At Maisy we received artillery fire as we approached our line of departure with A company to attack the front, coming through the swampy area with the beach to our back going up the hill with F Co. attacking from the flank. As we started across the open field we encountered heavy mortar and machine gun fire coming at us. We took some casualties. A Company had about 45 men at this time for the assault because we had lost the remainder on the beach.*

A Company 5th Battalion started the D-Day operations as a 15 per cent over-strength unit deliberately increased to cover expected landing losses. Casualties between the beach and Maisy had reduced their numbers down around 45 men. Any men from the 2nd Battalion would have bolstered the attack and helped guarantee success. Given that the landings were technically still very much in their infancy and that the D-Day objective line was still some miles away and hours from being achieved, it would have seemed prudent for Lt. Col. Rudder to make 100 per cent sure that Maisy was silenced – even if it was three days late.

Another question arises: Perhaps Lt. Colonel Rudder was not aware of German artillery fire from Maisy?

As it is recorded in some After Action Reports and statements – the shelling of Pointe du Hoc and the surrounding area by heavy artillery was in some part coming from the batteries at Maisy. The writers of those documents were aware of where the shelling was coming from, so it is a stretch to think that Lt. Colonel Rudder would not also have been aware that the heavier artillery shells landing on the Pointe were also coming from Maisy. What he thought about that, we will never know, but he took the decision not to advance away from the Pointe and thus his position became completely about defence and in those circumstances, it was almost impossible to avoid incoming heavy artillery.

This stand or lack of advance to complete his missions is something which I consider to be counter to the Ranger ethos as it has been told to me by many Ranger veterans over the years. I discussed this very fact with one of them recently and he read out the Ranger Creed to me, which contains the following sentence:

'Readily will I display the intestinal fortitude required to fight on to the Ranger objective and complete the mission though I be the lone survivor.'

x) Communications at the Pointe

Communication whilst at the Pointe is another interesting topic. The Small Unit Actions Report indicates that on a number of occasions the Rangers were in touch with the Navy or other units. Reading the document in detail, there are plenty of lengths of time when there was no combat with the enemy at all, time in which it can be argued that the Rangers should have advanced out of any potential and latterly expected encirclement.

Rudder's decision to stay at the Pointe was one which he did not attempt to convey to his superiors. In the communications shown below, no mention is made of the Rangers being unable to continue on inland. Yet you would assume his superiors needed to know that he was not advancing and that he would not get to the D-Day phase line? They needed men on that line to guard in case the Germans decided to bring reinforcements to the beach or heavy artillery towards Grandcamp or Maisy – and as things stood, there was *nobody* there.

If the Germans had advanced into that area, the western end of the Omaha beachhead would have been in serious trouble, yet there is NO recorded message or radio communication at ANY time during the three-day period where Lt. Col. Rudder made a single attempt to tell his superiors that he was staying put out of choice.

In so many books covering the Pointe du Hoc action, it is stated with firm conviction that the Rangers were cut off with *'no communications at all'* so perhaps that was the reason. Perhaps Lt. Col. Rudder did not have the ability to transmit this mission-critical message to his superiors. He was helpless with his men, cut off and alone with no communication… or was he?

The following are individual quotes from the Small Unit Action report to help us investigate if he was unable to communicate with anyone:

At 0710, as the first craft were grounding under the cliffs, radio silence was broken to send Colonel Schneider the order for landing at Vierville. The message was acknowledged.

By 0725, 1st Lt. James W. Eikner had his equipment set up and flashed word by SCR 300 that Colonel Rudder's force had landed. Five minutes later he sent out the code word indicating 'men up the cliff'; the 'Roger' that receipted for this message, again on SCR 300, was Eikner's last communication of D-Day on the Ranger command net. When he sent the message PRAISE THE LORD ('all men up cliff') at 0745, no response was forthcoming.

Tech. 4 C. S. Parker and two other communications men hefted the big radio set on a pack board, and managed to get it in and working before the first climbers from 722 reached the top.

The message came on SCR 300, one of the few times that a radio order got through from the CP on the Point to any of the scattered Ranger parties. Colonel Rudder had decided to try naval fire on the cliff strongpoint.

In a footnote from within the SUA Report with regard to the attempted destruction of the anti-aircraft emplacement. The footnote says:

According to testimony by the communications section, this was a British destroyer, with spotting done by Lieutenant Johnson, observer of the 58th Armored Field Artillery Battalion.

Germans were picking up the transmission and using it to register on the CP. Lieutenant Eikner then turned to other means, and made successful contact by signal lamps. These were used with good results during the rest of the day, though radio transmission for fire control was resumed in the afternoon.

If this statement is taken at face value – then Lt. Eikner chose not to use his radio in case the Germans monitored it, quite a distinction historically. So he chose not to use it – rather than being physically unable to contact anyone? The report continues:

> *Personnel of the fire control party observed results not merely from the Point but from positions inland, sending spotting data back to the Point by SCR 536 [radio] for relay to the ships. Targets given the* Satterlee *included inland assembly areas at St-Pierre and Au Guay, road junctions, strongpoints toward Grandcamp, and, especially, the anti-aircraft position west of the Point. By 1723 the* Satterlee *had expended 70 percent (the prescribed maximum) of her ammunition, having fired 164 salvos, plus six minutes of fire for effect, in support of the Rangers since H-Hour. The* Barton *and* Thompson *moved in near the Point to relieve the* Satterlee, *and before dark the NSFCP transmitted data for night fire on road junctions and other targets.*
>
> *Between noon and 1300 Colonel Rudder sent out a message by all available means, SCR 300, SCR 284 (through the* Satterlee) *and pigeon: 'Located Pointe du Hoe mission accomplished need ammunition and reinforcements many casualties.' By 1500 the 116th Infantry replied, stating its inability to decipher the message, which was repeated. About the same time, the destroyer relayed in reply a brief message from the 1st Division commander, General Huebner: 'No reinforcements available.'* [Indicating that they had received and fully understood Rudder's message].
>
> *At 1350, by signal light communication, the destroyer* Barton *was asked to send in a boat to take off the casualties. At 1430, a small motorboat from the* Barton *made the attempt, towing a rubber boat astern.*

This photograph of Rudder was taken on 8 June and a copy of it is held in the US National Archives. It shows a US Army signal lamp set up on a tripod, ready for use at the back of his command post area.

On the next page are copies of a few pages from the USS *O'Brien*'s radio communication log. It lists the contact between the Rangers at Pointe du Hoc and that ship. These three pages are direct person-to-person radio contact undertaken on 7 June between the Rangers at Pointe du Hoc (code name DJX) and USS *O'Brien* (code name RBO). This communication took place over a prolonged period – and it goes some way to question the accepted norm. The historical records simply do not bear out that there was a consistent and extended lack of communication.

Further on the subject of communication, 5th Ranger T/5 Howard D. McKissick won his Distinguished Service Cross for his actions on 7 June. McKissick put both Ranger groups in touch directly by telephone on the evening of the 7th onwards and to my knowledge this communication remained in place until Pointe du Hoc was relieved.

The following is an account of radio contact with the Navy by NSFCP Private Harold F. Plank, who was embedded with the Rangers.

> *Our first priority was to take our radio to a position under the cliffs. We found a kind of alcove, where we could set the radio up and make contact with the ships. We were supposed to be in contact with the battleship* Texas *and the destroyer* Satterlee, *just to let them know that we were ashore. We had been told previously that if we didn't get our objective accomplished within a certain length of time, there was a great number of bombers headed there; and we would just have to look out for ourselves. There was no way that they could take us away. The colonel decided that we had enough guys on top of the cliff and that we had better send word that we had it. Our code phrase for achieving our objective was 'Praise the Lord', and that was sent out over the air, so that the bombers which had been scheduled to drop bombs were diverted to other targets.*
>
> *During that day and evening, I accompanied Rangers on several combat patrols further inland. Every time, we ran into larger German contingents than we could handle; and after a brief fire fight, we would disengage and make our way back to our own area again. This happened several times during the course of the day and the evening. One time, I was given a one-man radio; and we had intended to find a place that we could hide out further inland, where we could spot targets when it came daylight the next day.'*

```
DD725/
                        U. S. S. O'BRIEN

EXCERPTS FROM VOICE LOG SFCP FREQUENCY 7 JUNE 1944

DJX - SECOND RANGER BATTALION

RBO - U.S.S. O'BRIEN (DD725)

2010    NO SIGNALS
2015    RBO V DJX     OVER
        DJX V RBO     OVER
        RBO V DJX     DA 586 930 586 930 DPF CS PF OVER
        DJX V RBO     REPEAT AA NO.
        RBO V DJX     AA NO. DPF CS PF OVER
        DJX V RBO     R OUT
        DJX V RBO     DONT FORGET TO GIVE TARGET BEARING OVER
        RBO V DJX     WILCO GETTING READY
            V DJX     OVER
            V DJX     K
        DJX V RBO     TB 160 OVER
2025    SALVO
        SSS
        RBO V DJX     U1 LF 10 U1 LF 10 OVER
2026        V RBO     R OUT
        SALVO
2027    SSS
        DJX           U LF 10 U LF 10 OVER
2028        V RBO     R OUT
        SALVO
        SSS
        RBO V DJX     U LF10 U LF10 OVER
2029    DJX V RBO     R OUT
        SALVO
        SSS
2030    RBO V DJX     KK RT5 KK RT5 RAPID FIRE 30 SECONDS OVER
        SALVO
        (STEADY FIRE)
2032        V RBO     WE HAVE CHECKED FIRE OVER
2033    RBO V DJX     CEASE FIRE TARGET DESTROYED OVER     V RBO ROGER
2035    RBO V DJX     TA 586931 IXI TA 586931 HLQ DGE CS PF OVER
        DJX V RBO     WE HAVE UR LAST MISSION ROGER OUT
        DJX V RBO     TB 166 OVER
2039    SALVO
        SSS
        RBO V DJX     ZZ OVER
        DJX V RBO     ROGER OUT
        RBO V DJX     U4 KK U4 KK OVER
2040    DJX V RBO     ROGER OUT
2040    DJX V RBO     RG OVER
2041    DJX V RBO     RG OVER
2041    RBO V DJX     R OUT
        DJX V RBO     DO U WANT US TO CONTINUE FIRING
```

```
DD725/
                        U. S. S. O'BRIEN

EXCERPTS FROM VOICE LOG SFCP FREQUENCY 7 JUNE 1944 (continued)

DJX - SECOND RANGER BATTALION

RBO - U.S.S. O'BRIEN (DD725)

2041    RBO V DJX     YES DID U RECEIVE THAT LAST SPOT
        DJX V RBO     AFFIRMATIVE OUT
2044    SALVO
        SSS
        RBO V DJX     D RT10 DRT10 OVER
2044    DJX V RBO     R OUT
        SALVO
2045    SSS
        RBO V DJX     KK RT5 KK RT5 OVER
        DJX V RBO     R OUT
        RBO V DJX     RAPID FIRE ON LAST SPOT 1 MINUTE
2046.5  DJX V RBO     WILCO OUT
            V DJX     ZZ ZZ
2047    DJX V RBO     R OUT
        RBO V DJX     CF M3 CF MS OVER
2049    DJX V RBO     R OUT
2050    NO SIGNALS
2057    RBO V DJX     MSG FOR U TA 579937 CS PF OVER
2058    DJX V RBO     BANKO 2106 OVER
2059    RBO V DJX     SEX RD GM KL OVER
        DJX V RBO     R ALSO WE HAVE UR LAST MISSION OVER
            V DJX     DONT FORGET TARGET BEARING OVER
        DJX V RBO     WE WILL NOT FORGET TARGET BEARING OUT
        DJX V RBO     TB 191 OVER
2100    RBO V DJX     WILL FIRE AS SOON AS RANGE IS CLEAR OVER
2101    RBO V DJX     R OUT
2105    NO SIGNALS
        RBO V DJX     WHAT IS THE DELAY OVER
        DJX V RBO     RANGE WAS FOULED AND IS CLEARING NOW, AS SOON AS IT
                      IS CLEARED WE WILL FIRE OVER
2108    DJX V RBO     TB 200 OUT
        SALVO
2109    SSS
        RBO V DJX     U KK U KK OVER
        DJX V RBO     R OUT
2111        V RBO     SALVO
        SSS
        RBO V DJX     KK LF5 KK LF5 OVER
2112    DJX V RBO     R OUT
        SALVO
2113    SSS
        RBO V DJX     KK LF5 KK LF5 OVER
```

For his heroic actions in keeping radio communication open between the Rangers and the Navy, Private Harold Plank was awarded the Bronze Star. On the next page is the field-written commendation from his commanding officer Kenneth Norton.

Recorded elsewhere regularly in this book and in particular within the After Action Reports, there are numerous occasions when the Navy was in direct contact with the Rangers at the Pointe. You must draw your own conclusions if you think that this is accurately reflected in the statements made in other works about the Rangers being 'completely cut off'.

At the end of the June section of this book there is a photograph of the mound of earth that was dislodged by shelling, prior to the Rangers arriving there on 6 June. The cliff at the Pointe du Hoc site today looks much larger now than it was on D-Day, because all of this debris has washed away over many years, but on D-Day it reduced the Rangers climb by almost half in a number of different places. They had a 50ft cliff to

```
DD725/
                        U. S. S. O'BRIEN

EXCERPTS FROM VOICE LOG SFCP FREQUENCY 7 JUNE 1944 (continued)

DJX - SECOND RANGER BATTALION

RBO - U.S.S. O'BRIEN (DD725)

2114    DJX V RBO     R OUT
        SALVO
        SSS
        RBO V DJX     D KK DKK OVER
2115    DJX V RBO     R OUT
        SALVO
        SSS
        RBO V DJX     D KK D KK OVER
2116    RBO V RBO     BANKO 2120 OVER
        RBO V DJX     R AS
        RBO V DJX     SEX ED GM GK WE WISH CEASE FIRE OVER
            V RBO     IXI
        RBO V DJC     SEX ED GM GK WE WISH TO CEASE FIRE OVER
2120    DJX V RBO     WILCO CEASE FIRE OUT
        RBO V DJX     MSG FOR U TA 576 939 IXI 576 939 MGS CS PF STANDBYE
                      A MOMENT DO NOT GIVE US TB YET WAIT
2125        V RBO     IN THE MEANTIME WE CAN CHECK TARGET WITH U 576 939
                      MG SGMSPF OVER
        RBO V DJX     COMMENCE FIRE ON LAST TARGET INDICATED OVER
2128    DJX V RBO     WILCO COMMENCE FIRE OUT
        DJX V RBO     TB 222 OVER
2130    DJX V RBO     TARGET NOW BEARING 216 OUT
        SALVO
2132    SSS
2133    RBO V DJX     KK KK KK KK RAPID FIRE 30 SECONDS OVER
                      (RAPID FIRE)
        DJX V RBO     WE HAVE CEASED FIRE
        RBO V DJX     CEASE FIRE MISSION SUCCESSFUL OVER
            V RBO     R OUT
        RBO V DJX     NICE JOB OUT
2135        V RBO     TKS OUT
```

climb on the day – not a 100ft one and the SUA Reports that the climb height was even less in another area: "*Picking a spot high on the talus, his men found that one 16-foot section added to a 20-foot section reached the top of the vertical stretch, beyond which a slide of debris had reduced the slope enough to make it negotiable without ropes*". This was a stroke of luck which saved many lives.

RALPH E. HANDLEY, MO M.M.
U.S.S. Y.M.S. - 381
c/o Fleet P.O., New York, N.Y.

2nd Ranger Battalion
APO 230 U.S. Army   June 22, 1944

Subject: Recommendation for Award
To   : Commanding Officer, 2nd Ranger Battalion

1. Under the provisions of A R 600-45
it is recommended that

Harold F. Plank, Private   35 76 18 26
Naval Shore Fire Control   2nd Ranger Battalion

be awarded the
Bronze Star Medal   for

2. bravely assisting in the direction of
Naval gunfire in support of the 2nd Ranger
Battalion landing at Pte du Hoe on June 6, 1944

Private Plank without thought for his own
safety assisted in the control of radio
communications with Naval fire support
ships at sea. This was done from an
observation point constantly under fire
from enemy small arms, mortars, and artillery.

On the night of June 6th, he volunteered
for outpost duty with members of the Ranger
Battalion. This same when his own duty
would permit him to leave it, He
materially assisted in repelling 3 German
counterattacks on the nite of June 6th and
then returned to his post to assist with
further Naval Gunfire support on the following
morning.

His contribution in this capacity made
him outstanding and he carried on until
reinforcements arrived to relieve the Rangers
on the afternoon of June 8th 1944.
Signed Lt. Kenneth S. Norton

Tough Going—But Yank Rangers Make It

Shown above is an example of the actual cliff-climb in one area – it comes from the US National Archives and whilst it is captioned '80-G-45716 Army Rangers at Pointe du Hoc, 6 June 1944' – it is most likely this photograph was taken on the 7th onwards and it could well have been taken during the LCVP re-enforcement and supplies deliveries on that day. The image next to it is a British Newspaper showing how the Rangers made it to the top – the mound is obvious. The last of these images is a French post-war postcard for the area depicting children climbing up ladders to get to the top. (*source: www.Dday.overlord.com*).

xi) Meanwhile at Maisy

On the subject of whether the Maisy Batteries were fully operational on D-Day, we have some evidence to prove what type of artillery was there on 6 June and beyond, through the following photographs.

A post battle photograph of a local farmer who is in the process of removing a set of Schneider 155mm howitzer wheels

(to make a cart) from the first gun pit at Les Perruques. The gun is upturned on pit No.1, just as is described correctly in the After Action Report and on the gun pit today there is a smash / crack, exactly where the barrel hit the wall. These wheels are now on display at The Maisy Battery.

Below: Two photographs of the La Martinière battery. Both of the guns are Czech 100mm weapons – but recovered shell cases on the site have indicated that these guns had been bored out and were firing the larger and more easily available German 10.5cm ammunition. This was a practice undertaken to standardise ammunition sizes at many positions along the Atlantic Wall.

In another US Army Signal Corps photograph captioned *'Ammunition bunker at Maisy'.* The ammunition shown is 155mm in calibre and an Engineer's report stated that *'180 tons of ammunition was removed from this bunker'.* It somewhat challenges the accepted understanding that all of the Atlantic Wall was short of ammunition and it accounts for why the battery was able to continue firing.

In other US Army Signal Corps photographs we have the following captioned picture. *'soldier looking through periscope in bunker – Maisy'.* The markings on the ceiling correspond to those found today on the roof of the Les Perruques 502 Headquarters building.

Further photographs from the same Signal Corps set are: *'Dead German outside dug-out near Maisy France* (above). Maisy village centre on 10 June where the damage from shelling is very evident (right).

I am regularly asked if I can explain why in some reports the Batteries at Maisy had been completely destroyed on D-Day – and yet they were firing again a short time later. The answer is simple – when they were being attacked, gun positions would stop firing and their men would take cover. There are reports from various ships which state *'gun positions destroyed'* only to acknowledge them firing again afterwards. This is quite

It was significant however that at least throughout the first week of the operation, no battery could properly be considered as being destroyed unless captured. There were several instances of positions which were believed on the basis of air and sea observation, to have been destroyed yet guns from these positions subsequently opened fire. In some of these cases it is almost certain that guns were moved and hidden during bombardment, and in others there is evidence that casemates protected the guns against lethal damage although they were rendered in-operative during the bombardment and for many hours thereafter.

well explained in this 21 June dated Utah Beach Naval Report. The 1st Infantry Division's After Action Report states the following on the same subject.

> During the period when the beach is still within range of hostile gunfire but before SFCPs have attained observation on enemy artillery, it is very difficult to search out and eliminate troublesome enemy positions. German artillery has the habit of holding fire when Allied planes are in the vicinity. This accounts for the fact that pilots were sometime unable to locate positions reported by the ground forces.

We know the details of at least one of the units operating the Maisy guns from captured documents. Below is a German *Soldbuch*, which belonged to a Polish national who was fighting with/for the Germans. He was captured at Maisy on 9 June 1944 and later sent to Medicine Hat Concentration Camp in Canada. German Government records report that he died of natural causes long after the war. His last military posting with the German army was to the 8th Battery of the 1716th Artillery, who were stationed at Maisy on D-Day.

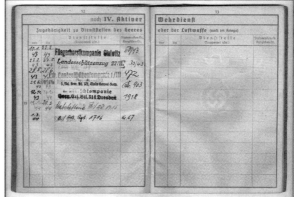

This unit's location at Maisy was further confirmed when we found the skeleton of a German officer in a trench at Les Perruques. His dog tags showed that he was from the 9th Battery 1716th Artillery. He has since been

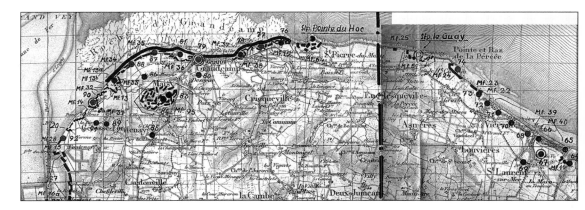

buried with full military honours at the German Cemetery at La Cambe and his service was attended by the German Ambassador to France.

A pre-D-Day German minefield map, captured from the Germans post D-Day by the US Army, can be found today in the US archives. Each of the thick black lines or dots represents a minefield. The Maisy site is surrounded by the largest minefield in the Omaha sector and, when coupled with the knowledge that the German High Command sent half of a flak battalion (some 1,000 men) to guard Maisy from aerial attack on 5 June, it is clear that they considered Maisy to be of some importance.

At 0900 on the morning of D-Day, once guns had been found behind the Pointe, perhaps Lt. Col. Rudder thought that he did not have enough men to continue with the mission to Maisy? I considered that, but quickly concluded that it would be a strange deduction given the Rangers' 'can do' attitude towards missions and also the copies we have of their actual direct orders.

The following reports are relevant to this as a wider question.

A Royal Navy report dated July 1944 says the following:

Commando and Ranger Landings

There is little to add from a naval standpoint to Naval Commander, Eastern Task Force's remarks (N.C.E.T.F.'s Report, paras. 34–37). It was certainly unfortunate that these highly trained troops should have suffered heavy casualties getting ashore (*i.e.*, during a period over which they could have little control). The difficulty of getting ashore bicycles, handcarts and the like from L.C.I. has been stressed many times before, but it is a hard lesson to learn. N.C.E.T.F.'s remarks on the use of L.C.I. (S) in the early phases of a daylight assault are fully concurred in ; a high percentage of these lightly built craft were virtually thrown away and few in consequence were used as planned in the " Build-up " as ferry craft for personnel and as control craft. Similarly in the OMAHA Sector, landings were only effected with considerable loss of craft and casualties to the Rangers. The battery at the POINTE DE HOE upon which so much effort was expended was found to be unoccupied, the guns having been moved to an alternative position to the rear, and the Rangers, after a magnificent feat of cliff scaling, became isolated, and could only be supported with the greatest difficulty.

From Naval Reports it is not possible to judge what these landings achieved, but the crux of the matter was that there were greater Ranger and Commando forces available than there were really suitable tasks for them.

In their opinion at least, the Rangers were not lacking men – but lacking more *'suitable tasks'* to undertake. It is interesting that another combat force would judge the Rangers in this way AFTER the Pointe du Hoc battle had taken place.

On the next page is a post-battle action report of the German 352nd Infantry Division written by the then prisoner of war, Oberstleutnant Fritz Ziegelman, a member of the 352nd Infantry Division Chief of Staff on 6 June. He too had an opinion on the achievements of the advancing US troops and he wrote the following in his report:

The 352. Inf. Div. fulfilled its duty as a unit untiringly, as an extract from the log-book for telephone messages of the Ia shows – (according to the latter there were more than 150 telephone messages given through on the 6. June 1944). (See inclosure No. 18 b .). In spite of the short time it had been in existence – in spite of the enemy's superiority in materiel and finally in spite of the latter's superiority in personnel the Division was in full control of its troops and was no easy pray for the enemy. The reason, why his operational plan, with the objectives laid down for each day after D zero hour, was not carried out – could be, because the enemy had the intention to preserve his forces, his men, or else it might be found in his inability to attack with the ancient soldierlike courage and bravery, so as to get it over with quickly and successfully, or to exploit opportunities which came his way, beyond the daily objective laid down in the plan, a thing which was never done by the 5th (U.S.) Army Corps. It may perhaps not be completely correct to assert, that it probably was the inability to go forward to the attack with courage and bravery, which was the cause of the enemy's operational plan not being executed. With the exception of operations on a fairly small scale the enemy in principle only committed his men in an attack, if he was able to make use of his superiority in materiel before and during such an attack. In newspapers printed for the benefit of the armed forces – (which were found on prisoners of war) – the enemy boasted of successes achieved through the bravery of his troops which, however, in a great many cases were not really successes in a military sense.

Another statement that is a little odd, again comes from the Small Unit Actions Report: *Just why the German guns were thus left completely undefended and unused is still a mystery. One theory, based on the fact that some artillerymen were captured that day on the Pointe, was that bombardment caught them there in quarters, and they were unable to get back to their position. All that can be stated with assurance is that the Germans were put off balance and disorganized by the combined effects of bombardment and assault, to such an extent that they never used the most dangerous battery near the assault beaches, but left it in condition to be destroyed by weak patrols.*

The Germans were in the process of removing their First World War cannons from Pointe du Hoc and replacing most, if not all of them, with deck-mounted naval-style weapons into the new casements. As shown, at least four of them would be of a completely different type of weapons platform and for that matter, a different calibre of ammunition may have been needed. Therefore, the guns behind the Pointe may not have been operational for some time and would not in my view have been returning to be used in the new casements. Two of them could have been going back into open emplacements as discussed. Thus, I think it is more than likely that the guns were placed to the rear ready for collection for use by another unit or they were prepared for transport by their own unit to a new destination.

The SUA Report stated *'there was no sign of the guns or of artillery equipment.'* Remember also the carefully closed up mounts on the empty rangefinder base.

It is perfectly probable that the individual Germans nearby might not have known what to do with the guns in the fields – before they were attacked. It appears that they may not have been set up to fire and may have needed a certain amount of set-up time and one assumes, orders from someone to direct fire for them. There are rumours that the lack of officers was due to an incident when a mine was set off in the days prior to D-Day, and if true, this may have been a contributing factor.

Given all of the evidence now available, it is reasonable to state that the guns represented no material danger to anyone whatsoever in the early hours of D-Day. The German soldiers to the rear were men described as *'not being ready'* at 0900hrs when Lomell and Rupinski's patrols found the guns and saw the Germans getting dressed in the area near the farm. It is ridiculous to believe that the Germans had operational weapons and waited for five hours (from 0400 – to 0900) to get dressed and have them operational. I personally think they were waiting for orders and probably assumed that those orders would come sometime soon. There is also every reason to suspect that they thought someone else above them knew what was going on. This was probably not the case, given the confusion that D-Day caused all along the coast.

As I wrote in my last book *Cover Up at Omaha Beach*: 'It cannot also be argued logically that the gunners behind Pointe du Hoc were surprised by the landings and were simply not ready. German reports, as we have seen, showed the capture of an American Paratrooper Lieutenant in the early hours of 6 June. He is said (in German radio reports) to have given the Germans information relating to the invasion and parachute dummies, etc. This information was sent back to HQ by the men at Pointe du Hoc – by radio, and thus they would have been under no illusions as to the impending landings.' If the guns had been capable of combat readiness, then that would have been the time to give the order for them to prepare to fire on any Allied ships. That order was not given even many hours later, so you have to question why – if it was not deliberate.

Another incident which has not been discussed before in *any* book is the killing of twelve unarmed German prisoners at Pointe du Hoc by a Ranger. I heard about this incident some years ago and discussed it with a couple of Ranger veteran friends recently and one of them spotted that it has been re-published online in the US.

The account of the specific incident reads as follows:

Kills His Prisoners
Ranger Robin [sic.] was a platoon leader, and the last I heard he was still in the Army – I hope so, he's a good guy to have on our side. Anyway, on the second day of the invasion Ranger Robin led a patrol behind the German lines to get prisoners for questioning. He was on his way back with about a dozen of them when the Germans counter-attacked and threatened to chase the Rangers right off the cliffs.*

Ranger Robin and five or six of this men, plus the prisoners, were crouched in a huge shell hole, with German troops all around them. Ranger Robin told his men to take off, one at a time, and get back to our lines as best they could.

His sergeant, the last to leave, asked Robin what he was going to do about the prisoners. 'Don't you worry about that, I'll handle it,' he replied.

When he was alone with the prisoners, Ranger Robin turned his Tommy gun on them and killed them all. Then he made his way back to our command post.

Fighting for Lives: *You could say his act was that of a coward, more than of a hero. But I'll argue with you on that. Ranger Robin was tough, but he was no murderer. He shot down 12 defenceless men in cold blood because he was a Ranger, and the Rangers were fighting for their lives. I got to know him well enough to know that those 12 German prisoners will haunt him as long as he lives.*

If you were there on D-Day you know a dozen stories like this. If you weren't you've heard about them.

D-Day was a terribly personal thing to the men who were there. You fought with a group, but the excitement that was like intoxication, and the fear that was like a clammy chill – those were yours alone.

*[*T/Sgt H. Robey]*

The above account was written by G.K. Hodenfield, a *Stars and Stripes* correspondent who was with the Rangers on D-Day, and it is taken from a newspaper article of Ranger interviews published on 5 June 1959 in the *Gettysburg Times*.

The Small Unit Action Report discusses this same incident in the briefest of detail saying only 'There could be no question of bringing back the prisoners.' which as a euphemism is explained fully in the above interview.

It is widely reported – although I admit, I only have this from other publications – that Lt. Col. Rudder spoke little about his D-Day experiences after the war. He is stated as keeping his own council and it is said that he did not really wish to discuss it. Perhaps that was indeed the nature of a man who did not want the publicity and felt he had done enough. We will never really know, but the evidence available now should make us all rethink at least some of the detail of the Pointe du Hoc battle.

Rangers Fire Rockets With Grapnel Hooks To Scale 100 Foot Cliffs To Reach Germans; Royal Navy Takes Them To Wrong Beach

Editors' Note—Ranger units hit the beach in Normandy at H-Hour on D-Day, 15 years ago Saturday. With them was G. K. Hodenfield, a combat correspondent for Stars and Stripes, now the AP's relaxation writer. Hodenfield, recalls the incredible feats of four Ranger companies in this last of four articles on D-Day.

By G. K. HODENFIELD
Associated Press Staff Writer

The story of four companies of the U. S. 2nd Ranger Battalion and their assault on a heavily fortified position in Normandy on June 6, 7 and 8, 1944, is not the big picture of D-Day. That's for generals and historians.

It's not even the little picture of an isolated action.

Maybe it's not even a story at all—just the things that one man who was with them remembers best from the greatest experience of his life.

The story of D-Day has to be a story of courage. Maybe that's why. Whenever I think of D-Day, I remember Sgt. Bob Young and Pvt. Alvin White.

"Somebody Goofed"

The Ranger assignment on D-Day was to land precisely at H-Hour (6:30 a. m.) on a rocky shelf of beach barely 15 feet wide, scramble up sheer cliffs more than 100 feet high, and destroy six 155mm guns protected by crack German troops and tons of concrete.

But somebody goofed. The guide boat sent along by the Royal Navy headed for the wrong beach. By the time we reached our landing area: (1) we were 36 minutes late; (2) the naval barrage that was supposed to drive the enemy to cover had long since lifted, and (3) German soldiers lined the cliff tops, peppering us with rifle fire and hand grenades.

Fire Grapnel Hooks

As the assault craft crunched to a stop, the Rangers fired a series of rockets that went up and over the cliffs with a loud "whoosh." Attached to the rockets were six pronged grapnel hooks. Attached to the hooks were long rope ladders. The Rangers pulled on the ropes until the grapnel hooks bit into the dirt, then scrambled up the ladders.

The rockets drove the Germans back, but only momentarily. They had returned by the time Young and White were clambering to the cliff top. How those two men made it, I'll never know. But they did, and when they got there they chased the Germans back and made it possible for other Rangers to follow them.

Many Or Die

The big guns were spiked with thermite grenades, then the Rangers dug in for the fight of their lives. There were Germans in front of them, the cliffs and the English Channel behind them, no supplies or reinforcements available. We were going to hang on or get killed trying. It appeared pretty obvious we were all going to get killed.

Which brings me back to Young and White. They were out on the left flank, anchoring one end of a very thin line. About 300 yards away was a German machinegun nest which was cutting our men down every time they showed their heads.

Young and White, armed only with rifles and grenades, went along the machinegunner. To get him they had to snake along in the weeds through a German mine field. One false move and they'd be shot dead or blown to kingdom come.

Wipe Out Nest

Maybe 30 minutes later they were back. Young had been shot through the elbow, White through the knee. But the machinegun nest had been wiped out.

Going up the cliffs, Young and White had shown one kind of courage—the kind born of desperation and excitement. Here they had shown another kind—the cold, calculated courage that overcomes fear of overwhelming odds.

But there's still another kind of courage. I remember Capt. Walter Block, our medic.

Hospital in Dugout

Doc set up a sort of base hospital at a concrete dugout. There was room for about 12 or 16 patients, and that wasn't nearly enough. At times there were so many wounded men that most had to be left outside until some body inside died or was patched up enough to return to battle.

In the afternoon on the first day, Doc was called outside to look at a badly wounded officer. The officer was unconscious, barely breathing.

Abandons Close Friend

Doc took a quick look. "You'll have to leave him out here. There's nothing I can do for him." He walked back into the dugout. The man he left in the unintended and alone was a man who for years had been Doc's closest and dearest friend.

I think it took courage, too, for Ranger Robin to do what he did!

Kills His Prisoners

Ranger Robin was a platoon leader, and the last I heard he was still in the Army. I hope as he's a good guy to have on your side. Anyway, on the second day of the invasion Ranger Robin led a patrol behind the German lines to get prisoners for questioning. He was on his way back with about a dozen of them, when the Germans counterattacked and threatened to chase the Rangers right off the cliff.

Ranger Robin and five or six of his men, plus the prisoners, were crouched in a huge shell hole, with German troops all around them. Ranger Robin told his men to take off, one at a time, and get back to our lines on foot, they could. His sergeant, the last to leave, asked Robin what he was going to do about the prisoners.

"Don't you worry about that, I'll handle it," he replied.

When he was alone with the prisoners, Ranger Robin turned his tommy gun on them and killed them all. Then he made his way back to our command post.

"Fighting For Lives"

You could say his act was that of a coward, more than of a hero. But I'll argue with you on that. Ranger Robin was tough, but he was no murderer. He shot down 12 defenseless men in cold blood because he was a Ranger, and the Rangers were fighting for their lives. I got to know him well enough to know that those 12 German prisoners will haunt him as long as he lives.

If you were there on D-Day you know a dozen stories like this. If you weren't, you've heard about them.

D-Day was a terribly personal thing to the men who were there. You fought with a group, but the excitement that was like intoxication, and the fear that was like a clammy chill—these were yours alone. You couldn't share them, you couldn't talk about them, you couldn't even acknowledge them.

"How You Felt"

And what you remember best are not people, and places, and things.

You remember how you felt. The amazement, on D-Day, when you suddenly realized that, although you had always considered yourself a coward, at this particular time and place you weren't a coward toward stuff, yes, but not a coward.

The resignation on D plus one to death at any moment, and pride that you could accept it without panic.

The anger, outraged and insane, on D plus two, at the men of the U.S. 29th Division who broke through on the left flank and freed first and looked later. They killed two Rangers, wounded 11.

Most of all, when it was all over, the terrible, unshakable loneliness—the sense of deep and personal loss. Of the landing force of 230 Rangers, only 52 were able to walk away.

These things you'll never forget.

A photograph of Les Perruques taken at the end of June 1944. It shows a similar landscape to the one left at Pointe du Hoc after the battle.

xii) Does the existence of the Maisy Batteries Rewrite the History Books?

Prior to D-Day some confusion existed over the calibre and location of the Maisy guns at 16 and 16A. Reports are written with question marks over the calibres and they are estimated at 75mm on some and greater on others. Post D-Day intelligence amendments to the pre-D-Day maps show German Coastal Artillery Ranges for the three batteries confirming that all three were in use at one time or another after the invasion had begun.

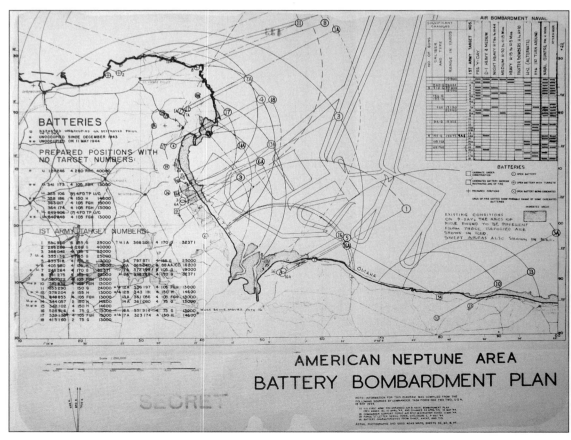

AMERICAN NEPTUNE AREA
BATTERY BOMBARDMENT PLAN

Evidence on the ground has also proved that the three were operational at some point and this is important because it makes the group of batteries a very significant defensive position. If you take the guns from each battery, their ranges and continued capacity to fire – coupled with over 1,000 men and weapons from Colonel Kistowski's Flak battalion – the Maisy Batteries were one of the largest threats to the US invasion plan. No other position to my knowledge in the US invasion sector on D-Day had that many men defending it. So it is again a statement of historical accuracy that Maisy was one of the most heavily fortified German positions engaged by the US Army.

This is further corroborated by the 6 June requests from the Utah Beach land forces to have permission to engage all three numbered positions at Maisy. The US policy on attacking gun positions on D-Day was based upon response. If a position had not fired and had not been seen to fire for some time, then it was left alone in favour of others which were still firing. Therefore, if a request for aerial or naval bombardment was made, it was justified at that time, because that position was still operational and had been seen to have just fired.

Confirmation of this procedure comes from a study of the post-D-Day plan produced by US Naval Intelligence later in June (shown previously and below). It shows an operational range for the Maisy guns as found post battle (targets marked as 5, 16 & 16A) being able to hit the Utah Sector/Beach and Omaha Sector up to the western end of the beach at Vierville. And all the evidence we have confirms that it did fire both to its west and east at targets on differing days.

Perhaps not too visible, but in the box on the top right are amendments (on the original they are coloured in red) – and they record the actual calibre of weapon found at target 16 & 16A as 105mm (post battle) which is consistent with ammunition casings found at the site in more recent years. It is not clear if that is the calibre for one battery at 16 – or both 16 & 16A, as one of the guns could have been moved from 16 to 16A at some point during the first three days of the invasion.

The original map also shows Pointe du Hoc's arc of fire 'in red' (although I apologise that this is reproduced as a black & white image here) and importantly, it is partially marked by a dotted line. The incomplete arc, as has already been discussed, is indicative of a battery under construction, i.e. not operational. Other marks show those ranges accurately recorded by physical observation from the Navy Intelligence team after D-Day. In my opinion, it is the most accurate indication of what was and was not operational on the day. On that basis, it is wholly incorrect to suggest that Pointe du Hoc was an operational six-gun battery – and we know it was not the most dangerous position facing the Americans as they landed. The conditions at Pointe du Hoc were found to be different than those suggested prior to the invasion, but in actual fact they were exactly the same as should have been expected according to the intelligence briefings produced in the weeks leading up to D-Day.

On D-Day, Maisy was a fully functioning Coastal Artillery Battery with a specific section of the coast to cover. No other battery duplicated its role covering that area. Each time you read in one of the reports or radio communications, such as the one below, that Maisy was firing, ask yourself who and what it was firing at. At 0824 when this radio report was recorded, most US units were still on their beaches or at Pointe du Hoc and many of them were under regular artillery bombardment. Obviously not all of this fire would have come from Maisy, but at least some must have done. These reports came from direct Air or Naval observation and as stated, only operational positions seen to have been firing again were ordered to be attacked again.

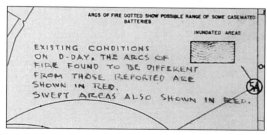

On the morning of 6, 7 and 8 June Maisy was not defending itself from direct land attack and Colonel Kistowski's anti-aircraft guns provided some defence against the repeated air attacks. It is safe to say that Maisy could only have been aiming its guns at two types of target. Either the men landing on the beaches, or the landing ships approaching the beaches – because it could do both.

0824   CTG 124.9 reported that enemy batteries at MAISY apparently still
        in commission and that he was keeping them under fire.

One question regularly comes from people after a visit to the Maisy site. *'How many extra Allied servicemen were killed because the Maisy Batteries continued to fire for days?'* and it is a difficult one to answer. An exact number could only be given by looking at every single casualty between 6 and 9 June and evaluating what killed each man. The problem with that is that many of the statistics gathered during the first three days of the landings did not record where men were actually killed. When their bodies were taken back to the beach, the medical staff did not necessarily know where they had been found prior to them lying on the beach. As a result, many of these men are simply recorded as 'beach casualties' which does distort the real casualty figures, as so many men died inland from the beach.

But the mention of casualties in reports does – in the odd case – tell us something about the operating capabilities of Maisy.

Here is a direct reproduction from the 116th Inf. Div. After Action Report for 7 and 8 June – and it refers to the advance of that unit from Omaha Beach towards Pointe du Hoc.

The US Army publication *American Forces in Action Series BEACHHEAD OMAHA (6 June-13 June 1944)* gives a little more detail on this same action. It clearly states that the 1st Battalion of the 116th lost '*30 or 40 men*' at this time.

After reaching St-Pierre-du-Mont before noon, the relief column planned to push along the coastal highway to the junction of the exit road from Pointe du Hoe. Company A of the 2nd Rangers, forming the column's point, got to a hamlet within 200 yards of the exit road, when heavy interdictory fire from medium howitzers fell on the highway behind them, forcing the tanks to withdraw. Reforming at St-Pierre, the column tried again. This time the tanks got past the exit road, but the 1st Battalion of the 116th was caught by well-directed artillery fire, which blanketed a quarter-mile stretch of the highway, and lost 30 or 40 men. This forced

---

1st Battalion, 116th Infantry and the 5th Ranger Battalion were in the vicinity of St. Pierre-du-Mont. Their advance had been limited by artillery fire from Maisy and numerous strong points. (98)

Situation at Pointe-du-Hoe remained unchanged and the enemy artillery in the vicinity of Grand Camp and Maisy was still active despite all efforts of the Naval fire.

Early the morning of 8 June 44 the 2d and 3d Battalions, 116th Infantry plus two Companies of Tanks moved along the Vierville-Grand Camp road with the 3d Battalion the advance guard. 3d Battalion was in its usual formation.

The advance was uneventful until the head of the column came in sight of Grand Camp and came under fire.

Battalion Commander was formulating his plan of attack when he received orders from Regiment to attack toward Pointe-du-Hoe.

The 1st Battalion and the Rangers were to strike the enemy from the east, and the 3d Battalion, with tanks, from the west. (103)

In order for the 3d Battalion to take up its battle position, the Battalion had to traverse it's steps a 1000 yards under heavy artillery fire.

In the thick of battle, the soldier is busy doing his job. He has the knowledge and confidence that his job is part of a unified plan to defeat the enemy, but he does not have time to survey a campaign from a fox hole. If he should be wounded and removed behind the lines, he may have even less opportunity to learn what place he and his unit had in the larger fight

AMERICAN FORCES IN ACTION *is a series prepared by the War Department especially for the information of wounded men. It will show these soldiers, who have served their country so well, the part they and their comrades played in achievements which do honor to the record of the United States Army.*

G. C. MARSHALL,
Chief of Staff.

another withdrawal. The 58th Armored Field Artillery Battalion and naval guns endeavored to locate the enemy batteries, somewhere to the southwest.

This publication is very detailed and it describes itself in the introduction here (bottom image on previous page).

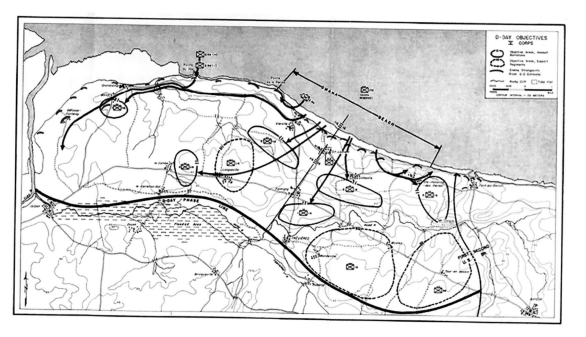

It also describes the objectives of the Rangers, using a map of the Omaha Sector. Note the 2nd Battalion Companies landing at Pointe du Hoc – and the 5th and residue of the 2nd landing on the beach, were both to go through Maisy. As we have seen, the 2nd did not go to Maisy in the end. That publication (which has been around for years) is fully aware of the Rangers' missions and it even displays a map which is based upon those orders? Note: This map is entitled D-DAY OBJECTIVES.

Again, we see the same thing shown on the next page, the Rangers were to land at Pointe du Hoc, advance through Maisy – the Maisy Batteries are ringed as an objective – and then the Rangers were again asked to advance to the D-DAY PHASE LINE. The theme is ALWAYS the same and there were NO orders to stay at Pointe du Hoc.

This was also repeated on the 1 April map overlay in almost identical terms. However, on that version it shows that members of both the 2nd and 5th Battalions were to attack Maisy. From that date onwards at least, Lt. Col. Rudder would have been able to brief his men on Maisy with this detail and yet at their individual unit briefings nothing was said to them.

On the evening of 7 June, the same book states: *'An important aspect of the next day's operation was the prospect of clearing out enemy artillery positions in the Grandcamp-Maisy area, for despite all efforts of naval fire, enemy batteries in this area were still active on the 7 June.'* The use of the plural for batteries is also confirmation that at least two of the batteries were known to be still operational at that time.

In its later pages, it makes further mention of Maisy:

On 9th June, the 116th and Rangers cleaned up the last enemy resistance around Grandcamp, Maisy, and Gefosse-Fontenay.

Elements of the 914th, 915th, and 726th Regiments had been involved in the vain effort to check the 29th Division. Enemy losses in artillery had been considerable, including two horse-drawn batteries of 105-mm guns found deserted near Osmanville on 9 June. One of the most important results of the advance was to deprive the enemy of the coastal defenses and artillery positions between Grandcamp and Isigny, from which fire had been harassing both Omaha and Utah beachheads.

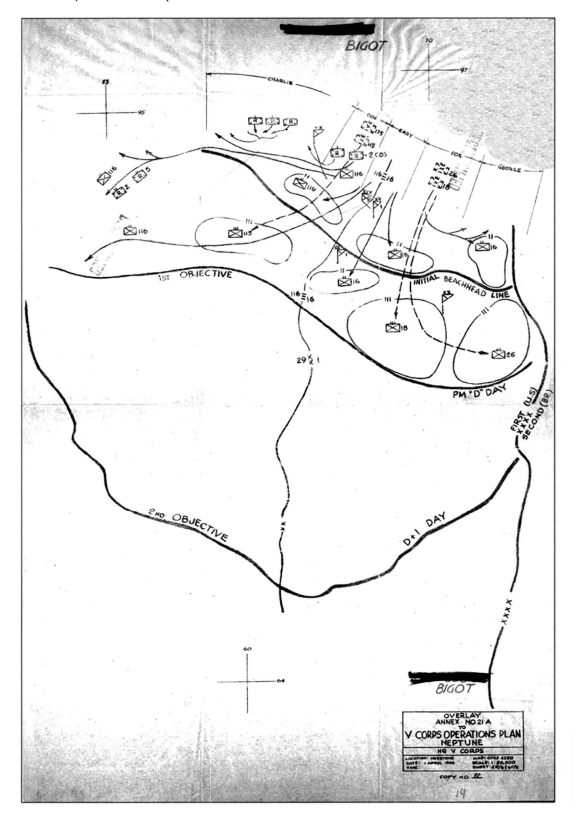

In the action, which some soldiers of the 5th Rangers and 3rd Battalion, 116th, described as more severe than their D-Day fighting, the Germans had lost one of their strongest coastal positions in the V Corps zone.

During this attack along the coastal highway, the 1st Battalion of the 116th was making a wide sweep to the south, not only outflanking Grandcamp but aiming at Maisy. Paced by Company A of the 743rd Tank Battalion, they moved south to Jucoville and then swung west through an area which was practically undefended. Heavy naval guns had torn Maisy to pieces, and the tanks were able to deal easily with resistance from enemy machine guns. Just west of the village an enemy strongpoint blocked the Isigny road and was supported by mortar and 88-mm fire, including interdictory fire behind Maisy, which prevented reinforcement of the leading infantry elements. Since the tanks were running short of fuel, advance was halted for the night. Supporting the 116th on 8 June, the 58th Armoured Field Artillery Battalion fired 123 rounds from positions north of Longueville.

The 116th Infantry, with the Ranger Force attached, engaged in mopping-up operations between Grandcamp and Isigny on 9 June, overcoming final enemy opposition at Maisy and Gefosse-Fontenay; thereafter, it went into division reserve, moving south of the Aure on the afternoon of 11 June.

I leave you with this amusing poster produced post war – it depicts the 743rd Tank Battalion's first few weeks of combat in France. At Maisy, the caption says '*Here 40 krauts surrendered to the maintenance T-2.*'

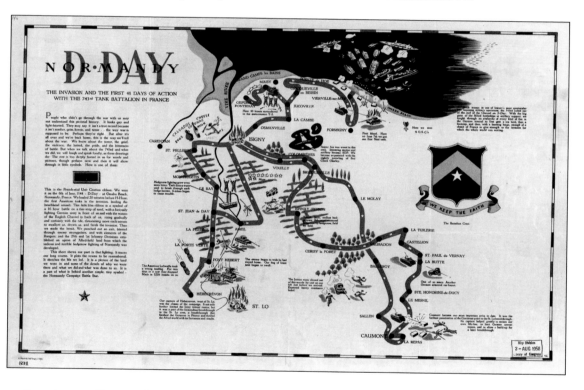

Over the years I have read many opinions about Pointe du Hoc and the Rangers' achievements and some of these go back a long way.

The following statement is taken from Stephen E. Ambrose's book *The Victors: Eisenhower and His Boys: The Men of World War II* – in which Lieutenant Eikner said that '*The Rangers at Pointe-du-Hoc were the first American forces on D-Day to accomplish their mission and we are proud of that.*'

They were not the first to complete their D-Day mission and yet that book has probably sold millions of copies. It is NOT a slight to the honour of a very brave Ranger that said that – for Mr Eikner honestly believed that to be the case.

Below is a copy of a portion of the 1946 Michelin Guide to the battlefields produced post war so that families and veterans could return in peacetime to where their loved ones had fought. This section clearly shows Pointe du Hoc and other gun batteries, but nothing at Maisy, which seems to imply that by 1946 the site had simply 'disappeared' from the collective radar.

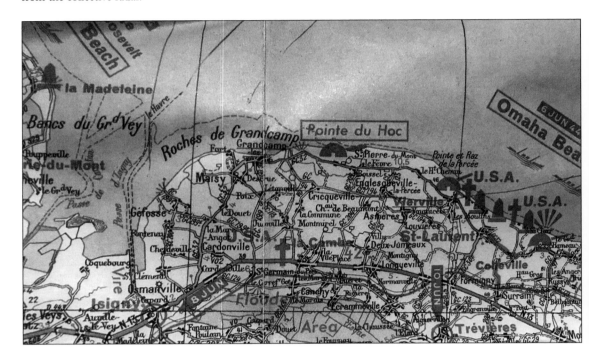

Eleven years ago, when I called a historian at a very large US Museum – I had the phone put down on me when I suggested to the gentleman that I had found a gun battery buried in the Omaha Sector. He put the phone down on me because he simply did not believe me – preferring to tell me that I had *found Pointe du Hoc and we already know about that one...*

Much has changed over the last ten years and the existence of the Maisy Batteries is now well established and I feel this book gives a satisfying answer to the main question I am asked daily: *what did the Allies know about Maisy before D-Day?* You have seen for yourself that at times information was coming in thick and fast for the Rangers on every aspect of their mission and it includes a vast amount of relevant intelligence about the positions at Maisy – in equal measure to references to Pointe du Hoc.

With the greater understanding of the role played on D-Day by the Maisy Batteries, arguments are now slowly changing, which is amusing. A small group of tour guides in Normandy originally started out saying that the Maisy site was *'insignificant'* and *'not important in the local history'* when I first uncovered it, and in my opinion, they took that stance as an excuse to cover why they knew little or nothing about the site.

Over time, when D-Day Ranger veterans came to visit and told their stories, the argument developed to keep pace with reality. Some then said *'Maisy was important – but not as important as Pointe du Hoc or Omaha Beach'* and recently when evidence of the Rangers' actual orders surfaced, including orders to attack Maisy and confirming that there were *NO* orders for Lt. Col. Rudder to stay at Pointe du Hoc and *'block the highway'*, I was told another classic piece of invention by one tour guide. He told me that *'Lt. Col. Rudder had a secret meeting prior to leaving England in which his orders were changed – and he was told to block the Grandcamp-Vierville highway.'* When I asked for any evidence of this 'secret meeting', what its purpose would have been, and who then was assigned to attack Maisy, I was told that it is well known to *'insiders in the tourist business'*. As you can imagine, no evidence at all was ever presented. So – once again the myths and stories are ruining good, solid facts. No *'special meeting'* was ever held to give orders Lt. Col. Rudder to stay at Pointe du Hoc and ignore his orders to go to Maisy. And even if they had been given to him in the last minute – why had he not actually briefed his men about their original orders regarding Maisy prior to leaving England?

The comment was simply a made-up answer to try and justify what had happened with Lt. Col. Rudder all those years ago – by people presented with contradictory factual documentation today. It was an attempt to make a version of events still fit with the new information presented. The guide had no real answer to supply, so he made something up. And I guess it will take a while for these old arguments to die off.

The sad thing is that many of these views are alive and well in Normandy and beyond. People tend to believe their local tour guide or museums' tour-specialist, or the authors of books about D-Day – and I consider myself to be in this category. It is up to you to decide if the information I presented here is made up or if I have actually found something new. Then you can also decide if other books on the subject, and museums running big tours have missed some facts completely. Either way, at the very least I am presenting my argument using period documents and backing it all up by showing over 2.5 kms of original German trenches and bunkers to visitors at Maisy.

I think it is easy to see, given the information supplied in this book, that the information is now readily available, so there is one way we can easily end all of this fantasy. From now on, when someone states one of the old theories about Pointe du Hoc and the highway-blocking order – just ask to see their evidence, ask for their copy of the order.

It is fair to say that a good number of writers have not seen all of the available new evidence and that is understandable. Much of what I have found has only come out of the US National Archives in the last two or three years. However, they are out now, available for anyone to see, so there are no more excuses for ignorance. I have also met many Normandy battlefield guides who have been working for years and yet do not know about Maisy. As a result, they have told hundreds of tourist groups, year on year, a version of events as they understand them, without taking Maisy into account. To their customers, I can only suggest that if you want to know more about what actually happened during the D-Day landings and are planning a tour, then ask your guides what they know about Maisy. If the answer is little, nothing or even scorn, then you will know you will get the same old tour that they have been giving for the last ten or twenty years. With this said, I am happy to say that there are many tour guides who have embraced Maisy from day one and to this day continue to arrive each week, with groups of families, students and history buffs, and to these people I send my thanks. I also fully recommend these passionate guides and their detailed tours to lots of visitors who ask for recommendations.

In a recent correspondence with a reader of my first book from the USA, he told me he had discussed my early findings with 'other authors' (unspecified) – and their opinion was that my having exploited the Maisy site for gain had in some way reduced the credibility of my work. i.e. that I was promoting Maisy beyond its historical value for profit. This was not the first time that I had that levelled at me, and to some extent I have to agree, it is a fine line. But Maisy was never a project motivated by money. When I undertook the work, and bought some 40+ acres of land, I had no way of knowing that I would be allowed to open it to the public. The land was set within a French Nature Reserve, so this alone offered next to zero chance of that happening. The site was unknown and not recorded as existing at that time – so it was also 99 per cent certain that commercial exploitation of it would not gain any traction. After all, who would visit somewhere with no actual D-Day history in an already packed D-Day related tourist area?

I had to dig up the site to prove that it existed because nobody believed me twelve years ago. Once I started the work, I had to keep paying for it – so the site opened to the public. Now we continue to develop the Maisy Battery (Les Perruques) and in the future, we will open more of the other areas. As we do not get any funding from anyone, this has to be self-funded as a project. But in reality, it will probably never pay for itself – nor repay the investment that was put into it to buy the land in the first instance. A look at our online (TripAdvisor, Facebook, Google) reviews says more than we ever could about what you can see at Maisy today, and you can decide for yourself if you think that I should have left it buried or not. I personally feel that we can understand history more by uncovering it – not by leaving it buried.

For me the actual extra motivation to continue my work came sometime after the initial months of exposure. I received a letter from A Co. 5th Ranger veteran Jack Burke, who told me he had fought at Maisy and remembered the battle perfectly. During my visits to the US to interview Jack and over twenty other D-Day Rangers, I realized that it was not just a story about me finding an old battlefield, but it was also about telling their untold story and the role Maisy actually played on D-Day. The veterans all told me that the focus of historians was always on Pointe du Hoc and Omaha Beach. Nobody had EVER asked them about Maisy and yet many of *them* maintained that Maisy was the more important of the two battlefields. That is available for you to read in their own words in my first book, *Cover Up at Omaha Beach*.

The excellent book *Reflections of Courage on D-Day and the Days that Followed* by Marcia Moen and Margo Heinen published in 1999 contains the remembrances of 5th Battalion A Co. Commander Charles 'Ace' Parker. It was written long before I discovered or even knew anything about Maisy, and it goes into detail about the Rangers fighting the SS at Maisy – another fact which is often lost as historians will tell you that the SS were not fighting against US forces in Normandy until 11 June and even then, over 40 miles away.

We have found an SS helmet at Maisy, local people remember the SS arriving to defend the site and they were threatened by them. Rangers discussed the SS with me in detailed filmed interviews, but historians still tell me they were never there. The evidence does seem to suggest that they were!

In correspondence with me a few years ago – Major General (Ret) John Raaen wrote: '*Ace Parker, the A Company Commander, later told me that, as far as he was concerned, the fight at Maisy was far worse than the Omaha Beach landings of four days before.*' John also put this into his own book *"INTACT"*.

Nobody had ever given the Rangers credit for what they had done and this is why we now hold our annual ceremony at the site on 9 June at 11am each year, so that these men and their actions are not forgotten.

I am always interested in more information relating to the Rangers, Maisy, Vierville and Pointe du Hoc on D-Day. If you have anything relating to this sector, then I would love to see it. And I hope that the paperwork contained here has opened up a wider area of interest for you. But in the end, if you are in France, you really should come and see what all the fuss is about.

For a future work, I am collecting photographs of wartime Rangers in their uniforms and any Rangers-related paperwork, badges, medals, etc. If you have any, I would love to hear from you and please do not dismiss the mundane, as it is all part of the Rangers' history. At Maisy, we have for many years been collecting soldiers' personal items for a museum. If you have anything you think we might be interested in – then please get in touch. We are happy to buy original items from WWII and our aim is to put everything we have found at the site, been kindly given to us by veterans or bought locally, on full display for future generations to see.

The author can be contacted via: www.maisybattery.com

Acknowledgements

As with any work of this size, it would have been impossible to complete without the help of my family and many others. I would like to extend my thanks to all those who have assisted in the research for this book. Over a number of years many people have helped and, even if in a small way, all the pieces came together to create a better understanding of the events of 1943 and 1944 and to tell the Rangers' history in a way that has not been done before.

So many people have given up their time and provided information, often without seeking recognition, for which I thank them. Without their contributions and those of the following people, the book would be a lesser work. If I have missed anyone off this list then I apologise.

Thank you to Doug McCabe for allowing me access to the vast amount of research contained within the Cornelius Ryan Collection (Ohio University). I recommend anyone undertaking serious research of the D-Day landings to read copies of the original interviews with the participants.

A very special thank you to Kevin McKernon for his help researching within the US Archives. Without his help, this book would not have been possible.

Chris Spedding for allowing the reproduction of his father's log book; thanks also to Peter Furness for providing information on his grandfather, Pilot Officer Norman Furness RAF.

Jon Plank and the family of Harold F. Plank NSFCP for providing information, and also Brad Lytle and the Lytle family for sharing family history and photographs of Cleveland Lyle.

René Hirsch for his historical perspective, impartial comments and support – and James Schneider for allowing me access to his father's personal papers.

I would like to thank Brian Woolcott and the Bude Heritage Centre for sharing their knowledge of the Bude area and Richard Bass and Neil at Kingfisher Media for their assistance understanding the workings of the ATC at Braunton.

Lt Brandel's Normandy photographs came to me courtesy of Tom at http://www.purplehearts.net/intro.htm

Ron Hudnell and Julie Rankin Fulmer at the www.rangerroster.org for their dedication to preserving the names of all WW2 US Rangers and ensuring the integrity of that list.

Irene Moore, Anita Benko and my son, Dan for their guidance and help editing this book and to Marc Laurenceau, Monique and Yves Sylvain-Huet for their friendship and local knowledge of Calvados.

Paul Bogaert and Suzanne Calmel, along with the Groupes Lourds Association, for their continued support of our work at Maisy, as well as Serg Bigot and the members of the Grandcamp Veterans Association.

Finally, a big thank you to Lisa Hooson and Charles Hewitt at Pen and Sword for their help with everything. Jon Wilkinson for his cover design and Mat Blurton at Mac Style for his unending patience!

The work of Henry Glassman and Maurice Prince must also be recognised as they were given the job of recording the daily activities of their respective battalions. Copies of their work are now declassified and the originals are still held in the US National Archives.

Beyond all others, this book is dedicated to the men of the US Army 2nd and 5th Rangers and their families, who have helped me along the way. Many of the veterans kindly invited me into their homes to talk candidly about their time in England and in Normandy – often in a way which they had not done since the war.

Their bravery during WW2 is without equal and more recently their support and encouragement ensured that I would try and tell their story – good and bad – in as accurate a way as possible.

In the course of my research, it was a privilege to have talked to these men and to the families of a great many others. Thank you.

James Gabaree	Lee Brown	Frank South	James Wilderson	Francis Coughlin
Jack Burke	Cecil Gray	Ralph Goranson	John Hodgson	Charlie Ryan
Daniel Farley	John Bellows	Raymond Tollefson	Frank Kennard	Robert Page Gary
John Raaen	Albert Nyland	John Reville		
Len Lomell	John Perry	Dick Hathaway		

After Action Reports – Navy

Below you will find a number of Royal Navy and US Navy After Action Reports. They played an important role in the Rangers' survival in the opening days of the Normandy campaign and where the Rangers' history has gaps, the Navy records help fill them. Battles are often better told not just from one participant's perspective – and the Naval reports, unlike Army ones, were almost always written immediately after events happened. I am not aware that they have ever been included all together in one work before - so I hope this is of value to other historians.

Naval Commander Western Task Force
Via: Commander Task Force 124.
APA-26/A9-8/A4-3
29 June, 1944

SECRET

6 June, 1944:

    0230 Passed POINT KING. Proceeded to assigned anchorage. 0315 CHASE, followed closely by EMPIRE ANVIL and HENRICO, anchored in assigned positions in Transport Area. Immediately after anchoring, transports commenced lowering assault landing craft. 0635 1st wave of assault units from HENRICO landed on designated beach EASY RED. 0650 Boat Division "B" of the 1st assault wave from EMPIRE ANVIL landed on designated beach, FOX GREEN. 0740 1st wave of assault troops from SAMUEL CHASE landed on designated beach, EASY RED. Following the initial assault waves, succeeding assault waves are believed to have been dispatched and landed on designated beaches on or about scheduled time. Transports reported 100% completion of debarkation of troops, and unloading of equipment, as follows: HENRICO - 1000, CHASE - 1100, and EMPIRE ANVIL - 1200. At 1200 dispatched 15LCVPs from CHASE, and 10 from HENRICO, to beach EASY RED, to assist unloading LCI(L)s and LCTs. 1945 Transferred command of Task Group 124.3 to Deputy Assault Group Commander. 1833 Underway in accordance with orders from COMTRANS DIV THREE, and departed Transport Area, and thence proceeded in convoy formation, via swept channels to Weymouth Bay.

7 June, 1944:

    Proceeding via searched channels to Weymouth Bay. 0536 Anchored in Weymouth Bay. 1500 Underway, proceeding to Portland Harbor, where anchored at 1540.

2.   Reports received clearly indicate that, insofar as landing craft are concerned, this operation was conducted under extremely unfavorable and adverse sea conditions.

3.   Landing craft were severely handicapped in landing operations by shoals, underwater and beach obstacles, mines, rough sea and heavy surf. On approaching the beach, landing craft encountered heavy gun fire and, after beaching and while unloading troops, heavy machine gun and mortar fire.
    The performance of ship-borne craft was generally excellent, except the LCAs, which apparently are very unseaworthy. These craft shipped large quantities of water in the heavy sea, and some were lost by foundering enroute to the beach.

4.   Combat Unit Loading was employed to load transports. For this operation, transports were loaded primarily, and to capacity, with tactical troop units. Army field equipment carried was of a restricted character, and only of such quantity as required and essential to the immediate needs of the assault force. Embarkation and debarkation of troops, and loading and unloading of equipment proceeded generally in accordance with the program, but it was again evident that a considerable amount of confusion existed. It is of the utmost importance that more attention be given in the preliminary planning to priorities in the embarkation and debarkation of troops, the billeting of troops, and the loading and unloading of equipment. It is recommended that a TQM officer, with one or two assistants, be permanently assigned to each transport to serve as liaison officer, and to coordinate the planning for the methodical loading and unloading of individual ships.

5.   Approach to the Transport Area via swept channel was accomplished without incident despite strong tidal currents and without speed signals. Swept channels were well marked. Some buoys marking the channels could not be located, others appeared to have drifted considerably off station.

E. H. FRITZSCHE

A16-3/FB4-36   **DESTROYER DIVISION THIRTY-SIX**

Serial: 0088.

S E C R E T   Care Fleet Post Office,
                                                               New York, N.Y.
                                                               18 June 1944.

From: Commander Destroyer Division THIRTY-SIX.
To :   Naval Commander Western Task Force.
Via :   (1) Commander Destroyer Squadron EIGHTEEN.
           (2) Commander Task Group ONE TWO FOUR POINT NINE.
           (3) Commander Task Force ONE TWO FOUR.

Subject: Narrative of Report of Operations from 1100, 5 June to
                0800 15 June 1944.

Reference: (a) NCWTF dispatch 181212B of June 1944.

        1.   In accordance with reference (a) the following narrative
report is submitted.

        2.   As Commander Task Unit 124.7.3, Commander Destroyer Division
THIRTY-SIX departed Portland, England in SATTERLEE with McCOOK and CARMICK
at 1100, 5 June 1944. Rendezvous with Mine Sweeper Flotilla FOUR, R.N., was
effected at 1700 and the minesweepers escorted down Channel #4 to the Transport
Area. The passage was uneventful except for the sinking of several mines cut
loose by the sweepers. At about 0030, 6 June escorts proceeded to end of Channel #3 and waited for the arrival of Mine Sweeping Flotilla THIRTY-ONE. This
Flotilla was escorted as it swept #3 Gunfire Support Channel. This operation
was completed at H(-) 2 hours 30 minutes. At this time Task Unit 124.7.3 was
disbanded and the destroyers proceeded independently to their assigned stations
in the Close Fire Support Areas.

        3.   At H(-) 40 minutes all destroyers were in assigned positions
and opened fire on their scheduled targets. As Deputy Commander Fire Support
Destroyers Omaha Area in the absence of the Commander I assumed command of
the Fire Support Destroyers Force "O". These destroyers were U.S.S. SATTERLEE,
THOMPSON, McCOOK, CARMICK, EMMONS, DOYLE, BALDWIN, HARDING, and H.M.S. TANATSIDE,
TALYBONT, and MELBREAK. During the period of scheduled fire it was necessary
for nearly all destroyers to temporarily shift fire to artillery or machine gun
nests which opened fire on them. These targets were in the main quickly disposed of and fire was again placed on scheduled targets. During this phase no
destroyers were damaged although all of them were intermittently under some
type of enemy fire.

        Landing boats with Rangers to attack Pointe du Hoe were about
forty five (45) minutes late reaching their beaching point. Due to approach
into bad wind and sea half of their boats foundered before reaching the beach.
TEXAS had ceased fire at Pointe du Hoe on schedule and enemy troops had filtered
back into the fortifications and immediately opened heavy machine gun and rifle
fire on Rangers killing a number and pinning the rest under the cliffs. Directed
SATTERLEE to close Pointe du Hoe and take cliff top under main battery and machine

1

A16-3/FB4-36   **DESTROYER DIVISION THIRTY-SIX**

Serial: 0088.

S E C R E T
                                                    Care Fleet Post Office,

Subject: Narrative of Report of Operations from 1100, 5 June to
                0800 15 June 1944.
- -

gun fire. This fire was delivered accurately and in good volume but in spite
of it a large number of Rangers were killed before a position on this cliff
top could be gained and it was not until noon the next day that the enemy
were cleared out of the immediate vicinity of Pointe du Hoe.

At H plus 1 hour (0730) H.M.S. TALYBONT, and MELBREAK left
Fire Support Area in accordance with previous instructions. At 0820 BALDWIN
received two hits from an 88 millimeter gun. Damage was slight and no personnel casualties occurred. At 0850 H.M.S. TANATSIDE departed in accordance
previous orders. At 0900 Commander Gunfire Support Destroyers arrived in
FRANKFORD and assumed command. At 1550 Commander Fire Support Destroyers
departed to become Area Screen Commander and I again assumed command of destroyers in Fire Support Area.

During remainder of day all destroyers fired at targets in
Close support of the landing troops. Ranges from the beach varied between
eight hundred (800) and twentyfive hundred (2500) yards. Destroyers fired
at targets designated by Shore Fire Control Parties, by me, or at targets of
opportunity. The fire of all destroyers was accurate, effective, and of great
assistance to the landing forces. At 1700 SATTERLEE had fired 70% of her bombardment ammunition, I shifted my pennant to HARDING and directed SATTERLEE
to report to Area Screen Commander for duty in Screen. At 1800 THOMPSON had
depleted her ammunition below 30% and was ordered to depart Fire Support Area
and report to Area Screen Commander. At 2000 CARMICK departed area for same
reason. At 1800 BARTON and O'BRIEN reported and were assigned stations in
Gunfire Support Area.

During the night destroyers fired on targets requested by
Shore Fire Control Parties. There were two enemy air raids. No damage was
experienced by destroyers in Omaha Fire Support Area. During 7 June all destroyers delivered fire as requested by Shore Fire Control Parties. As ammunition was depleted below 30% destroyers were ordered out of the Fire Support
Area and directed to report to Area Screen Commander. These destroyers were
relieved by PLUNKETT and MURPHY.

At 0700 visual contact had been established with Rangers at
Pointe du Hoe and at their request directed HARDING to send her motor whale-
boat in to evacuate casualties. Boat was wrecked attempting to land and LCVP's
were requested from Commander Task Group 124.9

At 1429 HARDING while engaged in bombardment of enemy troops
struck a submerged object in seven (7) fathoms of water off Roches des Grandcamp
damaging her propellers and sound dome. She remained in the Area and continued

2

A16-3/FB4-36   **DESTROYER DIVISION THIRTY-SIX**

Serial: 0088.

S E C R E T   **Care Fleet Post Office,**

Subject: Narrative of Report of Operations from 1100, 5 June to
                  0800 15 June 1944.

- -

Fire Support being able to make a maximum speed of fifteen (15) knots. At 1500
four (4) LCVP's previously requested from Commander Task Group 124.9 reported
and were directed to proceed to the beach just east of Pointe du Hoe to bring
off Ranger casualties and enemy prisoners. As boats returned with casualties
and prisoners they were directed to take them to TEXAS which was anchored about
two miles away. At 1900 HARDING completed shelling Maisy.

          At 1930 DOYLE and BALDWIN departed Fire Support Area and reported
to Commander Area Screen. ELLYSON reported and was assigned BALDWIN's station
and Fire Control Party.

          During night of 7-8 June there were again two enemy air raids.
No destroyers in Omaha Fire Support Area received damage.

          At 0540 on 8 June McCOOK departed to replenish ammunition.
During remainder of day ships in Fire Support Area waited for calls for fire
from Shore Fire Control Parties but none were received.

          At 0800 on 9 June shifted back to SATTERLEE and directed HARDING
proceed Plymouth for repairs. EMMONS also departed to replenish ammunition. At
1800 sent PLUNKETT, BARTON and O'BRIEN to report to Area Screen Commander, retained
MURPHY, ELLYSON and SATTERLEE in Fire Support Area to furnish AA cover during
hours of darkness. At 1900 ELLYSON completed firing at target 646798. To the
best of my knowledge this completed Fire Support by destroyers.

    4.   This situation maintained with an occasional shift in individual
ships from Fire Support Area to Screen and back until 0800 15 June when new Task
Force Organization became effective and I reported to Commander Destroyer Squadron EIGHTEEN for duty in the Area Screen.

    5.   Recommendations:

          (a) That pre-landing bombardment by Naval Forces be for a longer
period than from H (-) 40 minutes to H hour. In this connection it is most
necessary that a ship continue its bombardment until a very short time before
the troops actually touch down. i.e. (TEXAS bombardment of Pointe du Hoe
ceased many minutes before delayed Rangers landed).

          (b) That a much heavier air bombardment be scheduled prior to
and during Naval Bombardment. Omaha area hardly touched by air bombardment
with exception of Pointe du Hoe.

          (c) That special units which are to attack away from the main
beach as the Rangers did; be loaded into a ship which can come closer to
their beach than the regular Transport Area. One of the old converted

3

A16-3/FB4-36   **DESTROYER DIVISION THIRTY-SIX**

Serial: 0088.

S E C R E T
                                        Care Fleet Post Office,
Subject: Narrative of Report of Operations from 1100, 5 June to
                0800 15 June 1944.

- -

four-stack destroyers would have been ideal for this purpose.

    (d) That there be established on the beach or on a control ship an agency which is kept constantly informed of vicinity of front lines and which can pass this information to Fire Support ships who require it. Time after time in this operation destroyers were unable to shoot at excellent targets of opportunity because they could obtain no information as to the location of our own forces in the area in question. This, I believe, was the greatest difficulty the Fire Support destroyers had to contend with.

    (e) That several LCVP's be placed at the disposal of the Fire Support Commander to answer emergency calls for assistance transmitted by Shore Fire Control Parties. It took me nearly eight (8) hours to get some LCVP's to take off Rangers which were desperately wounded and whose only communication with friendly forces was via their Shore Fire Control Party.

    (f) That previous to the touchdown all houses and structures of any description that can allow concealed guns to fire on the beach be knocked down and thoroughly shelled by Naval Bombardment. In this landing too many houses were left standing adjacent to the landing beaches, they should all have been destroyed prior to the first wave landing as numerous casualties by machine gun and rifle fire were caused from them.

    (g) That whenever possible visual communication be established between ships in Fire Support Area and their Shore Fire Control Party or any troops in the vicinity of the beach. SATTERLEE and HARDING established visual communication with Rangers on Pointe du Hoe. This was most satisfactory and enabled ships to repel several enemy attacks which might easily have resulted in extermination of Rangers. It also enabled ships to furnish badly needed ammunition, supplies, water, and to evacuate casualties and prisoners.

M. J. MARSHALL.

HMS *Prince Baudouin*

FROM...Lieutenant E.H.West R.N.V.R. Flotilla Officer, 507th L.C.A. Flotilla.   **9 02735**

DATE...8th June 1944.

TO.....The Commanding Officer, H.M.S. PRINCE BAUDOUIN.   CONFIDENTIAL

Subject: Report on operation ~~Normandy~~
Craft taking part; L.C.A's 1377, 863, 670, 578, 577, 554, 521.
Troops embarked; 5th United States Rangers.

All craft were lowered in Transport Area at 0545 in conditions of heavy swell and choppy seas; but no difficulty was experienced in clearing ship's side. Craft formed up and proceeded, taking up station astern of 504 L.C.A. Flotilla according to operation orders.

2.   The run in towards Dog Green beach was carried out according to plan, speed approximately 5 knots. Difficulty was experienced in keeping station owing to the condition of sea and swell, but under circumstances craft were able to keep fairly good formation.

3.   At 0630 L.C.A. 578 was noticed to be low in the water, owing to swamping, and was quickly left astern. The subsequent report by Coxswain of this craft disclosed that the engines were eventually stopped by flooding and troops were disembarked into passing L.C.T. 88, which was proceeding towards the beach. This craft was taken in tow by an L.C.V.(P), but when engines were restarted, after intensive bailing, she was able to proceed back to ship under own power.

4.   At 0645 signal "Crowbar" was picked up from Charlie Sector, and on reaching position "Queenie" at 0700 the group was stopped by Navigational Leader (M.L.163). As no success signal had been received at 0715 from Charlie Sector, the group continued to Dog Green beach according to orders.

5.   On approach to beach the obstacles expected were seen to line the approaches, and at same time I perceived a certain amount of mortar fire falling amongst the 501st and 504th Flotillas the former being beached to the right, whilst 504th Flotilla was proceeding in well to left of Dog Green beach. I therefore decided that,being unable to await the unbeaching of all craft of their two flotillas, I would take my flotilla into the centre of beach. It was apparent that no clearance of beach obstacles had been made, and therefore there was nothing to choose between any position on beach from navigational point of view.

6.   I deployed the flotilla approximately ½ mile off beach, and after that it was a question of each craft finding its own way into beach independently. Craft had to zig-zag their way through beach obstacles for a matter of 50 yards, and all obstacles had teller mines attached to topmost stakes. I would like to say that officers and coxswains all showed utmost presence of mind and kept a cool head in beaching their craft in these extremely difficult conditions.

7.   All the craft found their way to beach and Rangers were disembarked at 0805 into between one and two feet of water; and I must say that after a very rough passage and a certain amount of sea-sickness the Rangers went ashore in exceptionally good spirits.

8.   As Flotilla touched down there was considerable mortar fire and fairly heavy machine gun fire directed on and across the beach, and an L.C.I. (L), No.91 which had beached just ahead of my craft was hit forward and commenced to burn furiously; this entailed a certain amount of manoeuvering on the part of three of my craft in order to touch down clear of her.

9.   Whilst clearing the beach a number of casualties from L.C.I (L) 91 were picked up by L.C.A's 670, 577 and 521, some being badly burnt. I ordered these craft to return to parent ship at best speed together with L.C.A.554.

10.   In meantime L.C.A. 863 had struck an underwater obstacle which badly holed her forward. The crew commenced bailing and I hailed her coxswain to proceed at maximum speed, hoping that she would be able to rejoin ship. As she commenced to fill up very quickly however, I went alongside with the intention of taking her in tow; but she suddenly began to turn turtle and went down by the head in about threefathoms of water, approximately one mile off the centre of Dog Green beach. All crew were taken on board L.C.A. 1377.

11.   All remaining craft returned to parent ship and were hoisted by 0945.

Lieutenant R.N.V.R.
Flotilla Officer, 507 Flotilla.

CONFIDENTIAL

FROM... The Commanding Officer, H.M.S."Prince Baudouin".

DATE... 9th June, 1944   Ref.No. 14a/555

TO..... Commander, Force"O", through The Commanding Officer, H.M.S."Prince Charles".
     Copies to:-
         Maintenance Captain J, H.M.S."Squid".
         The Commanding Officer, H.M.S."Prince Leopold".

Subject: Report of proceedings during operation ~~████~~ *Normandy* , H.M.S."Prince Baudouin"
          in Force "O".

Enclosed are copies of Flotilla and L.C.S. Officers reports.

2.   Left Portland Area at 1647 on 5th June, 1944. No incidents of interest to report on the passage across, except that there were times when we appeared to be somewhat out of the buoyed channel.

3.   Anchored in Transport Area at 0334 on 6th June, 1944.

4.   Considering the crowded craft and the rough sea I think that the Flotilla did an excellent job of work, and credit for same should be given to all Officers and Coxswains concerned.

5.   Weighed anchor and closed beach at 0808 to pick up L.C.A.'s. Returned and anchored in Transport Area at 1123.

6.   L.C.A.'s which were to have gone to "Thurston" to take a second flight ashore were cancelled, and quite rightly, as the surf on the beaches was just a little too much for the L.C.A.'s. One L.C.A. had to be abandoned on the return trip to the ship, and L.C.S.(M) had also to be abandoned. There was no loss of life.

7.   L.C.A's picked up 15 U.S. Officers and men from a burning L.C.I.(91) and they were subsequently landed in the Isle of Wight Area.

8.   At 1638 weighed anchor, proceeded to the Isle of Wight Area, and arrived there without incident at 2326 and anchored in Area 7, Cowes Roads.

9.   I would like to mention the high morale of the U.S. 5th Rangers and the cheerful way in which they left the ship and subsequently landed

D Jellins

Lieutenant-Commander, R.N.R.
Commanding Officer.

FROM...L.C.S (M) Officer, 507th Assault Flotilla.

DATE...8th June, 1944.

TO.....Commanding Officer, H.M.S. PRINCE BAUDOUIN.

9 02735

CONFIDENTIAL

L.C.S (M) 91 in Operation Normandy

At 0430 the above craft was lowered in Transport Area "Omaha", and after unhooking proceeded on an approximate course of S.60.W. Magnetic for ten minutes at 1500 revs per minute to a position on the starboard wing of the Flotillas of L.C.A., from s.s. "Bem-my-Chree" and s.s. "Amsterdam".

2.   Weather conditions, were far from favourable and the direction of the wind and speed necessary to maintain station were just as much as the craft could stand.

3.   The craft was steered slightly further to starboard than was necessary, to keep station so as to bring her in attacking her objective to a position where she would be running more or less down wind onto her target.

4.   At approximately 0515 one L.C.A. from the starboard column swamped and went down by the head and the L.C.S. had to pass pretty close to the area where her survivors were in the water. Another L.C.A. was dropping astern, obviously in great difficulty, and at approximately 0530 - 0540 she was no longer visible.

5.   At about 0600 with Point du Hoe slightly on the port bow, the Navigating M.L. was seen to alter course to port to bring Point de la Percee dead ahead. This was thought to be due to the fact that De la Percee was wreathed in smoke, whereas Point du Hoe, being bombarded by A.P.Projectiles had much less smoke.

6.   The L.C.S. maintained her original course until it was obvious that the M.L. was committed to her new one, when station was again taken up just astern of the L.C.A's.

7.   Just after the craft had got to within one mile of the beach the L.C.A. Flotillas turned through nearly 160° and made up for the proper beach.

8.   The L.C.S. was turned about and the combination of head sea and the Raz de la Percee was too much for her and she flooded forward. After about five minutes her screws were almost clear of the water and she became unmanageable. Six of the crew got swept into the sea and almost immediately a light machine gun in a cliff position opened up on them. A rapid reply from .5" Vickers and Lewis guns stopped his fire whilst the crew were pulled inboard. Almost as the last one came in a short burst from a heavier weapon (20 m.m ?) hit the craft in three places aft. This gun and the light machine gun supporting it were at once engaged and after about 1,000 rounds of .5", lost all further interest.

9.   The craft slowly drifted down to the boat lines off "Dog Green" after refusing an offer to be taken off by L.C.S. (M) 102.

10.   By keeping all the crew on the shoreward side, lying flat on the deck, danger from odd rounds from rifle armed infantry was reduced, although hits were taken on the after compartment, engine room and upper deck gear.

11.   At approximately 0940 the crew were taken off by M.L. and the stoker, Leading Stoker Atkinson for the first time left his engine room where he had kept his engines running throughout. The craft was left underwater to the mortar well, with screws out of the water.

N.E.Fraser

Lieutenant R.N.V.R.
Commanding Officer, L.C.S (M) 91 507th Flotilla.

11thPHIB/A16-3   ELEVENTH AMPHIBIOUS FORCE

Reg. No.   01798
R. S. No.   9 02735

Serial: 0691

CONFIDENTIAL   11 SEP 1944

FIRST ENDORSEMENT to:
CO HMS PRINCE BAUDOUIN
Conf. ltr., Ref. No.
14a/555 dated 9 June 1944.

From: Commander Eleventh Amphibious Force.
To :   Commander-in-Chief, United States Fleet.

Subject: Report of proceedings during assault on COLLEVILLE-
            VIERVILLE Sector, Coast of NORMANDY.

    1.   Forwarded.

    2.   It is considered that the H.M.S. PRINCE BAUDOUIN performed
very satisfactorily the duties assigned her as a transport in Assault
Group O-4.

    3.   The skill and determination displayed by the 507th LCA
Flotilla in making their way through the underwater obstacles to land
the troops embarked reflects great credit upon their commander, officers
and men. They are also to be commended for their work in rescuing 15
U.S. officers and men from the LCI(L)-91 despite the waterlogged condition of their own craft.

    4.   The Force Commander regrets the loss of the LCA and LCS(M)
but is pleased to note that there was no loss of life aboard either of them.

                                J. L. HALL, Jr.

Copy to:-
    CO PRINCE BAUDOUIN

HMS *Hawkins*

HAWKINS - HAWKINS opened fire promptly when directed,
and her spotting plane reported 18 hits out of
110 rounds on target number 5. Thereafter she
took under fire target number 16 using air spot
and reported 24 hits out of 57 rounds. These
batteries were neutralized and thenceforth caused
no trouble. For the remainder of D Day HAWKINS
fired on targets of opportunity as requested by
air spotting plane and by Shore Fire Control
Parties. HAWKINS area was in territory which was
to be captured by FIFTH Corps troops. She was
not assigned Shore Fire Control Parties attached
to the FIFTH Corps and did not therefore know
in the latter stages of Army advance whether or
not "shoots" could be safely carried out in this
area. It was necessary however that she be
assigned initial targets there and that she
remain on station where targets could be taken
under fire if endangering the landings.

HMS *Prince Charles*

CONFIDENTIAL

FROM: The Commanding Officer, Assault Group O-4, H.M.S. PRINCE CHARLES
DATE: 19th July 1944   No. 1206
TO: The Admiral Commanding 11th Amphibious Force, U.S.S. ANCON,
         c/o U.S. Naval Headquarters, 15 Grosvenor Square, W.1.

                    OPERATION ██████████

     In view of the fact that the U.S. Rangers did not
reach Point du Hoe at the correct time on the 6th June 1944,
the attached report from M.L. 304 is forwarded for information.

                                   [signature]
                              Commander, R.N.,
                              Commanding Officer.

RESTRICTED
CONFIDENTIAL

H.M.S. PRINCE CHARLES

17th June 1944

The Admiral Commanding Force "O".
Copies to: The Naval Commander, Allied Expiditionary Force
             The Naval Commander, Western Task Force
             The Commodore, Force "J"
             The Maintenance Captain, Force "J".
             The Officer Commanding, 5th Ranger Bn.

Sir,

REPORT OF PROCEEDINGS, OPERATION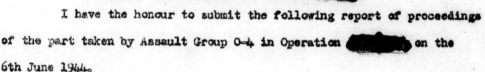

    I have the honour to submit the following report of proceedings
of the part taken by Assault Group O-4 in Operation ▮▮▮▮▮ on the
6th June 1944.

A. GENERAL

    The approach to the Transport Area was carried out according to
operation orders although it was with some difficulty that the rearmost
ships of Convoy Group I were kept in the swept channel. On arrival in
the Transport Area ships were anchored in accordance with my operation
orders (see chronological report).

    Owing to adverse weather, craft were lowered ten minutes earlier
than was ordered, and proceeded to their respective beaches. At "H" hour
no signal was received from the Officer Commanding U.S. Ranger Group
on POINT DU HOE, but at 0709 the signal CROWBAR (touch down) was received.
This indicated that the touch down was thirty-five minutes late. The

/ success signal....

success signal BINGO was never received by any ship or craft, nor was the pyrotechnic signal seen. After waiting an extra forty-five minutes after touch down (see operation orders) I decided that there was no option but to send the remaining Rangers to DOG GREEN where they touched down in the face of severe opposition at C753. This was a hard decision to make, but I could not receive any information from POINT DU HOE, and so had to assume that the landing had been unsuccessful. From later reports (not reliable) I assume that the Rangers did reach the top of the cliffs.

The situation then became more obscure, and the reports from L.C.A. being adverse I decided to close the beaches, and on receiving permission from the Admiral Commanding Force "O", I proceeded with L.S.I.(S) (PRINCE LEOPOLD and PRINCE BAUDOUIN) to within two miles of the beach to recover the craft, many of which were damaged and all of which were waterlogged.   H.M.S. PRINCE CHARLES failed to recover four craft, but hoisted some from other ships and returned to the Transport Area to await instructions, and subsequently sailed for the WIGHT area.

Had the L.S.I.(S) not closed the beaches it is very doubtful if many craft would have been recovered, as most of the returning craft were holed by shell fire and waterlogged.

/ The delay in reaching...

The delay in reaching POINT DU HOE was due to M.L. 304 confusing that beach with POINT DE LA PERCEE, and leading the craft through the tide race off the latter point. During the approach to POINT DU HOE one L.C.A. with troops and one with stores were swamped and lost.

B. LESSONS LEARNT

W/T and R/T communication with L.C.A. proceeding to POINT DU HOE failed due to craft being swamped and the sets being put out of action by salt water.

2. M.L. 304 having made an error in his approach should have broken R/T silence after "H" hour to inform me of the situation.

3. M.L. 163 having received no success signal proceeded to DOG GREEN with resolution and arrived on the correct beach approximately thirty minutes behind schedule.

4. The Ranger assault was not carried out according to the time table for one reason only: the weather and the state of sea.

5. L.C.S.(M) were ineffectual due to the state of the sea, one being swamped and lost.

6. L.C.A. were, in the weather then prevailing, overloaded.

C. CONCLUSIONS.

All personnel under my orders carried out their duties

with resolution and courage and in the highest tradition of the Service. The landing craft crews kept their craft afloat by bailing with their steel helmets and in general did excellent work.

ELEVENTH AMPHIBIOUS FORCE

11thPhib/A16-3
Serial: 00959

S-E-CONFIDENTIAL

21 AUG 1944

FIRST ENDORSEMENT to:
CO HMS PRINCE CHARLES
Secret ltr. No. 1206
of 19 July 1944.

From: Commander Assault Force "O".
To :   Commander-in-Chief, United States Fleet.

Subject: Action Report of H.M.M.L. 304 of Assault on VIERVILLE-
               COLLEVILLE Sector, Coast of NORMANDY.

    1.   Forwarded.

    2.   This report emphasizes the importance of all equipment
being placed in the best possible condition, as the failure of power
supply in this instance was costly. Difficulties of visual recognition
when terrain is obscured by clouds of smoke and dust from naval bombardment are fully recognized. Both QH and radar have given excellent results
when used to assist in beach location.

    3.   If the Rangers had been landed on POINTE DU HOE at H hour
as scheduled, the opposition encountered would probably have been lighter.
The delay in landing gave the enemy time to recover from the shock of
bombardment by the USS TEXAS. The delay in landing also made it impossible
to give the success signal in time to divert to POINTE DU HOE the remainder
of the 2d Ranger Battalion who were to land on DOG GREEN Beach at H/60 if a
success signal was not received from POINTE DU HOE by H/30. The diversion
of this portion of the Ranger Force would have furnished the troops necessary for the exploitation of the success so brilliantly achieved on POINTE
DU HOE by the Ranger elements initially attacking.

                                        J. L. HALL, Jr.

Copy to:
    CO HMML 304
    CO HMS PRINCE CHARLES

H.M.S. PRINCE CHARLES - OPERATION ████

CHRONOLOGICAL REPORT

H.M.S. PRINCE CHARLES sailed at 1645 from Portland on the 5th June 1944 in Convoy O-1. Proceeded by pre-arranged route to OMAHA Transport Area.

6th June 1944

0314   Flares observed bearing Green 90. Flares continued to be dropped intermittently throughout the night.

0328   Anchored in Transport Area.

0353   No.2 craft lowered to embarkation level. Craft took Colonel RUDDER to ARM MY CRAFT.

0405   Nos. 7 and 8 craft to embarkation level.

0417   Fire observed 165°

0427   Nos. 7 and 8 craft with "C" Company Rangers left ship.

0446   No.2 craft returned and hoisted with Lieut. A.P.G. BROWN on board.

0450   Aircraft seen to fall in flames on starboard quarter.

0453   U.S.S. TEXAS started bombardment of POINT DU HOE.

0517   Signalled to L.C.T. "Will lower ten minutes earlier owing to weather".

0518   Hands to Operation Stations.

0525   Craft (other than Nos. 7 and 8) lowered to embarkation level

0537   To M.L. 163 by loud hailer: "Am lowering and want you to take craft in a bit slower. I will come into the beach and pick them up under the lee. Wait till they are formed up before you start off".

0537   Lowered away as ordered.

6

Chronological Report (continued)

0540   All craft clear of ship.

0544   Craft formed up and moved off.

0607   Dropped Dan Buoy.

0750   To H.M.S. PRINCE LEOPOLD and H.M.S. PRINCE BAUDOUIN:
     "Weigh and follow me to beach".

0805   Weighed and closed beach by Bombardment Channel.

0828   L.C.A. 882 (PRINCESS MAUD) hoisted.

0840   L.C.A. 1038 (PRINCE CHARLES) hoisted.

0841   M.L. closed and reported craft returning. One L.C.A.
     from PRINCE BAUDOUIN stranded on beach.

0847   Continued towards beach.

0907   L.C.A. 626 (PRINCE CHARLES) hoisted.

0910   L.C.A. 441 (PRINCE CHARLES) hoisted.

0925   L.C.A. 843 (PRINCESS MAUD) reported and proceeded to
     PRINCESS MAUD.

0926   L.C.A. 858 (AMSTERDAM) reported and proceeded to AMSTERDAM.

0942   L.C.A. 837 (PRINCESS MAUD) hoisted with stretcher case
     (U.S. army).

1000 approx. L.C.A. 421 (PRINCE CHARLES) sighted towing L.C.A. 750
     (PRINCE CHARLES).   M.L. 163 tried to take her in tow, but
     L.C.A. 750 capsized and sank at 1008.

1025   Hoisted L.C.A. 421 (PRINCE CHARLES) and returned to
     Transport Area.

1113   Anchored in Transport Area.

1458   Requested permission by R/T to proceed to Isle of Wight
     area at 1530, and proceeded at 1540.

11thPHIB/A16-3   ELEVENTH AMPHIBIOUS FORCE
Serial: 1756

Reg. No. ___ 1671
R. S. No. ___ 8 02095

CONFIDENTIAL

8 – AUG 1944

FIRST ENDORSEMENT to:
CO., HMS PRINCE CHARLES
Rest. ltr. No. 1158
dated 17 June 1944.

From: Commander Assault Force "O".
To :   Commander-in-Chief, United States Fleet.

Subject: Report of Assault on the COLLEVILLE-VIERVILLE
           Sector, Coast of NORMANDY.

    1.   Forwarded.

    2.   The mistake in beach identification made by ML 304
was costly. The report of HMS TALYBONT indicates that DUKWs
accompanying LCAs were heavily engaged during the run parallel to
the beach from RAZ DE PERCEE to POINTE DU HOE.

J. L. HALL, Jr.

                                        The Commanding Officer,
                                        H.M.M.L. 304,
                                        c/o G.P.O.,
                                        LONDON.
                                        12th June 1944.

The Commanding Officer,
    H.M.S. PRINCE CHARLES,
        Commander, Assault Group O-4

Sir,

    I have the honour to submit the following report of proceedings

on the far shore on the morning of 6th June 1944.

    At H-120 (0430B) I proceeded in accordance with previous instructions

and left the Transport Area with L.C.A. flotillas from L.S.I.'s

"Ben my Chree" and "Amsterdam" formed up astern.

    Course was set for Pointe du Hoe and this was checked by Q.H.2 and Radar

Type 970.   The D.R. position was not considered reliable owing to the

slow speed of advance, the relatively strong effect of wind and tide

and the difficulty of steering an accurate course in the sea which was

running.

    As the light increased and the coastline became more visible, the

problem of identifying Pointe du Hoe arose.   This promised to be

difficult, since the coast was being bombarded heavily by the Gunfire

Support Group and headlands and cliffs were in many places obscured by

thick clouds of smoke.

    At this point, H-60, both the Radar and the Q.H. appeared to be jammed.   Subsequently this was found to be due to a faulty power supply, but from this time onwards they gave no assistance and it was necessary to rely on D.R. and visual recognition.   It was thought that the heavy gun battery on Pointe du Hoe would disclose its own position, but the battery was not firing,

At about three miles from the headland which was thought to be Pointe du Hoe the problem of identification became especially difficult.   The point was smothered in smoke and the bombardment was causing the cliffs to crumble and collapse in many places.   The silhouette of Pointe du Hoe appeared different from the photographs supplied as a result of this bombardment, but a little further to the eastward was another headland which it resembled closely and course was modified to reach it.

At 4000 yards the L.C.T. was instructed to stop and the "Ducks" were launched.

At 1000 yards, when the L.C.A.'s were about to go in, it became apparent that this point was not Pointe du Hoe, since although the appearance coincided with the photographs, there were no concrete emplacements visible.   Accordingly course was modified to reach the original point for which we had steered.   As a result the landing was delayed until H + 30.   No opposition was encountered throughout, save for some light machine-gun fire from the cliffs.   These were engaged with Oerlikon fire and the L.C.S.s also replied with .5 M.G..

The landing was effected without opposition and at this point the top of the cliff became clearly visible.   The smoke had cleared away and several huts and concrete emplacements could be observed.   While the landing was in progress, I engaged these targets with 3 Pdr. and 20 mm. Oerlikon fire at ranges from 700 - 1000 yards.   20 rounds of 3 Pdr. H.E. were fired into the huts and emplacements and 1000 rounds of Oerlikon were used to spray the top of the cliff until the ascent was completed.   A few figures were discerned moving about on the top of the cliff, but these were fired on and appeared to take cover.

Meanwhile an American destroyer came up and assisted in bombarding the cliff top, several hits being observed on the emplacements.

Some counter-fire was opened by a Bofors gun, but the firing was erratic and mostly astern or above us.

The L.C.A.'s were now leaving the beach.   They had shipped a good deal of water owing to the heavy sea and there were several stragglers, for whom I waited.   There was no further opposition from ashore and firing was ceased when the Rangers had gained the top of the cliff.

There appeared to be no underwater obstructions in the immediate vicinity of the point although a little further to the eastward and about 1000 yards offshore where I had gone to engage the light M.G. nests referred to earlier, a minefield was detonated immediately astern without causing us any damage.

When the L.C.A.'s had assembled, course was set for the transport area and I covered their rear until they were out of range of any possible batteries remaining.

It is infinitely regretted that our assistance to the Rangers was of such slight value, especially in the capacity for which we were specifically employed.   While it is thought that Radar Type 970 together with Q.H. would have established definite identification, it is appreciated with great concern that our other resources proved inadequate in the presence of difficulties which it had been impossible to predict.

I have the honour to be, Sir,

Your obedient servant,

Lieutenant, R.N.V.R.

Below is the HMS *Prince Leopold* report written on 7 June by Lt. Cassidy of the Royal Naval Voluntary Reserve. In most other works I have read, Lt. Col. Schneider is described as having made the decision to take the LCA flotilla of 5th Rangers to the east when landing on Omaha Beach – and thus he undoubtedly saved their lives by landing on a less dangerous area of the beach. This is how it is written in the US Army Small Unit Actions Report – *'Approaching shore, Lt. Col. Max F. Schneider got a clear impression of the conditions on Dog Green and ordered the flotilla to swing east.'* – but when reading the Naval report below, it appears that Lt. Cassidy made the decision of where to land – and indeed in Naval combat actions it is always the Coxwain of a vessel who makes such decisions – no matter how small the vessel. (See clarification of Naval seniority over Army earlier in this book).

The SUA Report could be hearsay from Rangers recounting it a month afterwards as they saw it on the day – indeed who knows after all this time? But I think it odd if that was actually the case – by default, why on the 7 June would Lt. Cassidy write it as though he had made the decision if it was not him? From a historical perspective, he would never have known that these few words would be of interest all this time later and on the day he would never have realised that his actions would have such positive consequences for the Rangers. The point is that he appears to have nothing to gain by adding this comment in his report – other than to state things accurately as he remembered them happening.

From: Lieutenant J.McA.F. Cassidy, R.N.V.R., Flotilla Officer, 504 L.C.A. Flotilla.

Date: 7th June 1944.

To: Commanding Officer, H.M.S. PRINCE LEOPOLD.

Subject: Report on movements of 504 L.C.A. Flotilla during operation Normandy
   from time of lowering, 1500 hours.
Forces taking part: L.C.A. 570, 1045, 571, 550, 568, 622 and 623.
Troops carried: 5th U.S. Ranger Battalion.

Craft were lowered at 0500 hours in pairs because of the heavy swell, and formed up in accordance with Assault Group 04 operation orders, astern of H.M.M.L. 163 and proceeded into Dog Green Beach at 5 knots.

Station-keeping was quite good under the conditions, swell and a following sea making it very difficult to control craft.

At 0645 hours we intercepted over R/T the signal "Crowbar" from Charlie Sector, and at 0700 hours heard them pass the signal saying that the DWKS were being called into the beach. After that nothing more was heard from Charlie Sector. At 0715 H.M.M.L. 163 passed to Control that he was carrying on to Dog Green Beach, he disengaged about ¼ mile from the beach and craft carried on. At this time we all came under mortar fire from enemy positions on the beach, the whole of Dog Green Beach was covered by enemy fire from positions by D.1 Exit, and just ahead of where the 501st Flotilla landed. I could see that they could not clear the beach in time for me to land in the same place, they were now under heavy fire from enemy machine-gun positions and mortars around Exit D.1, which covered the beach. Several hits on their craft were seen, so I decided to land 504 Flotilla to the left, because this part of the beach provided more cover from the fire that was sweeping across from the Pill-box and machine-gun positions on the right hand side of the beach, as several D.D. tanks were on the beach. This section of the beach was also covered with smoke.

For the last 30 yards the beaching of each craft became an individual effort for coxswains, who had to weave their craft through well placed obstructions with Teller mines fixed to the top of same, this was made all the more difficult by a swell and following sea.

All coxswains report that the Rangers landed without any casualties, and only had to wade ashore in water up to their knees.

All seven L.C.As managed to get in through these obstructions and out again under very difficult conditions, and it is safe to assume that no craft of this flotilla as much as touched any mines, at times craft were actually alongside stakes with mines fitted to the top, and great praise is due for the extreme coolness and courage with which all officers and coxswains behaved, in order to clear this line of obstruction several seamen were seen to actually fend off craft with their hands from large single stakes that had Teller mines placed on top at an angle of 45 degrees facing inshore. All these mines appeared to be new, no sign of rust being seen.

When clear of the beach, flotilla were collected and we returned to the parent ship in formation, being hoisted at approximately 0930 hours.

The conditions were very bad for small craft, at least two having to bail out some long way off the beach. Craft had pumps going all the time, the short steep sea and swell made conditions for the troops very uncomfortable, but in spite of all these unfavourable conditions their spirits were very high indeed.

On the return to the parent ship we saw one of the DWKS, with fireman's ladder complete, drifting across Dog Green Beach, out of control and with no-one on board. This had come down from Sector Charlie.

Report by officer in command of L.C.S.(M) 102 is attached.

Lieutenant, R.N.V.R.
Flotilla Officer, 504 L.C.A. Flotilla.

CONFIDENTIAL

From: Commanding Officer, H.M.S. PRINCE LEOPOLD.

Date: 7th June 1944.   Ref. 3638/24

To: Commander, Force O,
through Commanding Officer, H.M.S. PRINCE CHARLES.

Copies to: M.C."J", H.M.S. SQUID,
            Commanding Officer H.M.S. PRINCE BAUDOUIN.

SUBJECT: Report of Proceedings - H.M.S. PRINCE LEOPOLD, Group O.4, Force O.

The following report covering assault phase is submitted:

Passage through the Minefield.

2 bouy passed at 2120 appeared to be ½ mile to Eastward of charted position. Convoy, after making a large alteration of course, entered No. 4 Channel and, owing to the fact that many Dan bouys had dragged, zigzagged between Nos. 3 and 4 Channels, becoming very disorganised.

Entered transport area and anchored at 0336.

Assault.

L.C.As were lowered in accordance with plan in a very choppy sea, no difficulty was experienced in unhooking, and craft formed up and proceeded inshore without incident.

Craft were swamped many times on way in, but the Rangers, although soaked, were in very good spirits, and no reports of sea sickness have been received.

C.O., 5th Battalion attempted to contact C.O., 2nd Battalion after intercepting signal from Charlie Sector calling DWKS in, as no reply was received it was agreed that boats must beach on Dog Green, beaching being successfully made at 0800, no casualties to personnel or craft occuring and all Rangers safely disembarked, no casualties being noticed.

Craft withdrew without accident, and two survivors from Empire Javelin Flotilla were picked up.

Recovery of Craft.

Closed beach at 0805 to recover craft. Craft returned to ship in formation and were hoisted, two at a time, on the lee side without difficulty. Signalled 'ready to proceed' to Prince Charles at 0945, and waited in swept channel until returning to transport area at 1030 to await orders for second flight.

Return to United Kingdom.

Weighed at 1620 and returned to Needles under Prince Charles' orders,
arriving at 2210 by Channel No. 1 without incident.

Communications.

U.S. Type SGR 659 was very successful, communication being maintained at on
all stations throughout. Army 18 Sets did not function, the frequency being covered
by an enemy station. All Navigational Aids worked satisfactorarily.

Summary.

The sea conditions were such that loaded L.C.A.s were barely seaworthy and
LC.S.(M) definitely un-seaworthy.

It is apparent that beach obstructions such as were encountered on Dog Green,
consisting of Element C, Teller mines and Hedgehogs, can be avoided by L.C.As by
skilful and cool handling of the craft.

Opposition on beach does not seem to have been such that a lane could not
have been cleared for craft coming in by H + 60. No such lane was seen.

Time Table.

Position A -	1730.
Position X -	1850.
Position Z -	2120.
Anchored.	0336.
Lowered L.C.S.	0445.
Lowered L.C.A.	0530.
L.C.As touched down.	0805.
Weighed and closed shore.	0805.
All craft hoisted.	0945.
Anchored in transport area.	1120.
Weighed and proceeded Needles.	1620.

Lieutenant Commander, R.N.R.
In Command.

From: Commanding Officer, L.C.S.(M) 102.

Date: 7th June 1944.

To: Flotilla Officer, 504 L.C.A. Flotilla, H.M.S. PRINCE LEOPOLD.

OPERATION  *Normandy*

    L.C.S.(M) 102 was lowered at 0415 and proceeded to join 520 and 522
Flotillas alongside S.S. AMSTERDAM. Contact was made at 0430 just as the
Flotillas had formed up on M.L. 194 and L.C.T. 413 and were about to proceed
inshore.
    Steering a S.W. course, the formation steamed inshore at half speed.
Approximately three miles from the transport area an L.C.A. of the starboard
Flotilla was seen to disengage, her stern high; the formation carried on.
    All craft were struggling against the sea and wind. Halfway inshore
L.C.S.(M) 102 reduced speed to slow in order to bail out the forepeak which
was one quarter full, resulting in dropping astern one mile and drifting the
same distance to Port of the formation.
    While closing the formation M.L. 194 was seen to make an approximate
45° degree turn to Port when about three miles from shore, the course was
therefore altered to intercept, contact being made about one mile off shore
at approximately 0640.
    It was at this time that the Senior Officer realised that the M.L. was
approaching the wrong point, and he made to turn to starboard, causing the
formation to run parallel to the shore-line half a mile away, head into the sea.
At this point a machine-gun opened fire on the formation. L.C.S.(M)s 91 and 92
returned the fire, causing the opposition to cease. L.C.S.(M) 91 also fired
three H.E. bombs. Immediately after this, L.C.S.(M) 91 was seen with the stern
out of the water, and bows under ~~to the mortar well~~.
    With the sea in this direction the forepeak of the L.C.S.(M) quickly became
full, also the mortar well cover caved in, in spite of the wooden stretchers and
the mortar and Lewis guns crews supporting it. As the mortar well commenced to
fill, the weight forward became too great and the bow became submerged.
    The craft was then brought round to bring the seas on the quarter while all
hands bailed out. This took some three quarters of an hour to an hour, during
which time the craft drifted down to the right hand edge of Dog Green Beach.
S.C. 322 closed, enquiring whether we were in trouble, but as everything was
under control O.K. was passed.
    During bailing L.C.S.(M) 91 drifted within hailing distance, and he stated
that he had sustained two holes and was going to make for the boat lanes.
    When the craft was on even keel at 0815 she was brought round into the sea
which was found to be still too heavy to make any reasonable speed. As no
opposition could be seen coming from Dog Green Beach, two miles distant, a
course for the transport area was steered at dead slow ahead to rejoin H.M.S.
Prince Leopold.

                                                    W. A. Eccles.
                                   Sub Lieutenant, R.N.V.R.

11thPHIB/A16-3   ELEVENTH AMPHIBIOUS FORCE

Serial: 001025

SECRET   16 SEP 1944

FIRST ENDORSEMENT to:
CO HMS PRINCE LEOPOLD
Conf. ltr., Ref. 3638/24
dated 7 June 1944.

From: Commander Eleventh Amphibious Force.
To :   Commander-in-Chief, United States Fleet.

Subject: Report of Proceedings of Assault on COLLEVILLE-
               VIERVILLE Sector, Coast of NORMANDY.

    1.   Forwarded.

    2.   The H.M.S. PRINCE LEOPOLD performed very satisfactorily
the duties assigned her as a transport in Assault Group O-4.

    3.   The H.M.S. PRINCE LEOPOLD proceeded from PORTLAND Harbor
in company with the ANCON in Convoy Group ONE (O-1). The reasons for
changes of course by this convoy in the swept channel, noted in the basic
letter, have been explained in my action report.

    4.   The Force Commander notes with pleasure the skillful and
determined manner in which LCAs of the 504th LCA Flotilla made their way
through underwater obstacles, landed their personnel, and thereafter cleared
the beach. The successful beaching of all craft in the circumstances prevailing reflects credit upon the skill and courage of the officers and men
involved.

    5.   The classification of this correspondence is hereby
changed to "SECRET".

                                        J. L. HALL, Jr.

Copy to:-
    CO HMS PRINCE LEOPOLD

11thPhib/A16-3   ELEVENTH AMPHIBIOUS FORCE

Serial: 001074

SECRET

SECOND ENDORSMENT to:
Com.Grp 35, LCT-6 Flot
12 ltr., Serial 572 of
14 July 1944.

From: Commander Assault Force "O".
To :   Commander-in-Chief, United States Fleet.

Subject: Action Report of DD Tanks in Assault on COLLEVILLE-
                 VIERVILLE Sector, Coast of NORMANDY.

    1.   Forwarded.

    2.   The question as to who should decide whether to
launch DD Tanks was discussed at length by the Assault Force Commander
with the Commanding General Fifth Corps, U.S. Army and the Commanding
General First Infantry Division, U.S. Army. For the following reasons
it was agreed that the decision should be left to the Senior Army
Officer and Senior Naval Officer of each of the two LCT units carrying
DD Tanks:

         (a)   They had had more experience than any other officers
in the Assault Force in swimming off DD Tanks from LCTs.

         (b)   The decision should be made by someone actually on
the spot where the launching was to take place and embarked on
an LCT rather than on a large vessel. A decision under such
conditions should be sounder than one made on a large vessel
miles away where the sea conditions might have been quite
different.

         (c)   If a decision were to be made elsewhere and action
had to await an order, confusion and delay might result in the
absence of such an order, and it was anticipated that communications might be interrupted by enemy action so that it would be
impossible to transmit orders by radio.

    NOTE: The two unit commanders were to inform each other
by radio of the decisions reached.

11thPhib/A16-3   ELEVENTH AMPHIBIOUS FORCE

Serial: 001074

~~SECRET~~

Subject: Action Report of DD Tanks in Assault on COLLEVILLE-
                  VIERVILLE Sector, Coast of NORMANDY.

- -

        3.   The procedure adopted by Lieutenant D. L. Rockwell,
USNR, and Captain Elder, U.S. Army, in Assault Group O-2 was correct
and their decision sound. Apparently Captain Thornton, U.S. Army,
made the decision to launch the DD Tanks of Assault Group O-1 without
consulting Lt(jg) Barry, USNR, the Senior Naval Officer on the LCT
and the latter tacitly acquiesced in the decision by his failure to
take action to change the order directing the launching. Captain
Thornton's decision was unsound and resulted in the loss of all but
3 of the DD Tanks of Assault Group O-1. These 3 were taken into
the beach by the LCT 600 in which they were embarked after the first
tank launched from that craft had foundered.

        4.   The Force Commander has commented elsewhere, both
in his own report on the landing in NORMANDY and in endorsements to
reports of subordinate commands, on the employment of DD Tanks. His
comments and opinions may be summed up as follows:

        (a)   That because of the vulnerability of its flotation
equipment and the general unseaworthiness of the entire vehicle
the DD Tank is not a practicable weapon for use in assault landings on open beaches. If the flotation equipment were so designed
and constructed that it could be quickly installed in the field,
it might be of value in river crossings where neither bridges
nor boats are available; but as it stands it cannot travel under
its own power to open beaches except under exceptionally good
weather conditions.

        (b)   That under normal circumstances artillery, tanks and
other armored vehicles, which have to be transported in large
landing craft, should not be landed in an assault until the beach
has been cleared of enemy resistance and the vehicles and craft
carrying them will not be exposed to direct aimed artillery fire
during the landing.

        (c)   That if circumstances make it necessary to employ
tanks, artillery or other armored vehicles in the first wave or
other early waves of the assault, they have a far better chance
of reaching the shore in safety if they are transported by landing craft instead of swimming in under their own power.

HMS *Talybont*

Date 24ᵀᴴ June 1944   REF NO: 379/39

TO: The Commander, Assault Force "O" U.S.S. Ancon[i]

Copy   The Commander-in-Chief, Plymouth[ii].
       The Commander, 18ᵗʰ Destroyer Squadron, U.S.S. Frankford.
       The Captain (D), Plymouth.

SUBJECT   REPORT ON THE ASSAULT BOMBARDMENT H.M.S. TALYBONT[iii].

Sir,
I have the honour of forwarding a narrative report on the assault
bombardment carried out by H.M.S. Talybont[iv] on the morning 6ᵗʰ June.

0540	Talybont moved down the fire support channel to take up position to bombard targets 81 and 82. A position was taken up 038 Pointe De Hoe 2.7 m. between U.S.S. Saterlee and U.S.S. Thompson.
0550	Open fire, range 043. No pillboxes or machine gun emplacements could be seen and it was decided to cover the top of the cliff in the target area as thoroughly as possible.
0600 (approx)	Ranger with ML 204 in company passed the ship. It was not realised at the time that they were heading for Raz De Le Percee instead of Pte Du Hoe.
0615	Creased fire
0616	Opened fire on targets 76, 77 range 041.
0630	Creased fire on targets 76, 77. At the time it was noticed that ML 204 and the Rangers had realised their mistake and were making for Pte Du Hoe parallel with the shore at a range of 005 to 010.
0630	Re-opened fire on targets 81 and 82, range 038
0640	Fire was opened on Rangers from the shore with two light machine guns. Three rear DUWKS were being fired on.
0640 ½	Fire was shifted to the cliff face and top in the vicinity of the guns which could not be seen.
0645	Closed range to 021.
0645 ½	Open fire 2-pdr. Pompom to implement 4" fire. Fire from the shore was spasmodic. Two DUKW's were hit - one badly. Shorty afterwards a further 2 L.M.G.'s opened fire from the shore and another DUKW put out of action.
0646-	Fire was maintained on the vicinity of targets 81,82 and the Rangers sustained
0700	No more casualties from these sources.
0700	Ceased fire on targets 81, 82. Rangers were under small arms fire from Pte de Hoe. USS Saterlee was giving close support and I decided not to interfere.
0703	Installations were seen to be standing in the area of targets, 76, 77. A further fifteen salvos were fired which demolished or severely damaged the targets.
0710	Withdrew from Fire Support Area.

CONCLUSION: Targets 67, 77 were evidently completely neutralised or
destroyed. Targets 81, 82 though engaged for 25 minutes prior to "H" hour
were only 60% neutralised. It is considered that up to four L.M.G's were
in action against the Rangers.
The mistake in identification of the target by ML 204 is difficult to
understand as TEXAS fall of shot was obvious. Their course from Raz de le
Percee along the shore to Pte. Du Hoe was suicidal.
After withdrawing Talybont joined the screen area.
                    I have the honour to be, Sir,

                         ??????
                         Lieutenant Commander,
                         Commanding Officer, HMS Talybont

In a letter dated 24 June 1944 Admiral J. L. Hall, Jr. wrote: "*The mistake in beach identification was made by ML304, not ML204, as stated in the basic report. It has been commented on elsewhere by the Force Commander.*" This correction is perhaps in reference to the US Army also erroneously stating a number of times in its reports that the mis-direction away from Pointe du Hoc was undertaken by ML204. (Also a number of times in the the SUA Report).

Task Group 124.9 After Action Report.

PART II - CHRONOLOGICAL ORDER OF EVENTS TASK GROUP 124.9 FOR
PERIOD 3 - 17 JUNE 1944 (Cont'd)

D DAY JUNE 6th, 1944

0035 - Land reported distant 24 miles bearing 241°T.

0040 - Slowed to 10 Knots.

0110 - MELBREAK reported mine off her port beam. Changed course
to avoid.

0115 - Observed heavy AA fire ahead and on starboard hand in vicinity of UTAH Beach followed by numerous flares and heavy
bombing.

0220 - Arrived in Transport Area, OMAHA Beach. GLASGOW and TEXAS
proceeded down West Boat Lane, ARKANSAS, G. LEYGUES and
MONTCALM proceeded via transport area to East Boat Lane.

0300 - TEXAS and GLASGOW anchored in boat lane to await dawn.

0424 - Observed heavy air bombardment on beaches.

0445 - TEXAS & GLASGOW underway proceeding to fire support positions.

0533 - GLASGOW reported communications established with Air Spot.

0538 - ARKANSAS commenced counter battery fire.

0550 - All ships in Fire Support Group opened fire on designated
targets.

0559 - TEXAS reported communications established with Air Spot.

0610 - TEXAS firing rapid fire on assigned targets.

0630 - "H" Hour - All ships cease firing.

0640 - TEXAS anchored.

0730 - TALYBONT detached to proceed on duty assigned.

0740 - TEXAS commenced fire on target 85 with main battery.

0745 - GLASGOW contacted Shore Fire Control Party.

0747 - TEXAS made direct hit on target 85, ceased firing, expended
17 rounds 14/45 H.C.

0810 - TEXAS opened call fire on target 5 with main battery, expended
20 rounds H.C.

PART II - CHRONOLOGICAL ORDER OF EVENTS TASK GROUP 124.9 FOR
PERIOD 3 - 17 JUNE 1944 (Cont'd)

D DAY JUNE 6th, 1944

0825 - GLASGOW reported firing with SFCP No. 1 and Air Spot, unable to contact SFCP No.2.

0900 - Received Red Alert from ANCON - Air attack, planes within 25 miles.

0950 - Enemy firing on Dog Green Beach. Ordered all Fire Support Ships to make determined efforts to locate and silence the enemy battery.

0952 - MONTCALM reported communication established with SFCP.

1033 - **Mobile field battery at 568893** destroyed by TEXAS. 40 rounds 14/45 H.C. expended.

1117 - TEXAS took mobile battery at 618925 under fire with air spot, expended 26 rounds 14/45 H.C. Spotter reported target destroyed.

1215 - TEXAS underway shifting anchorage closer to beach.

1223 - TEXAS commenced firing direct fire to clean out snipers and pill boxes in Exit D1 at Vierville-Sur-Mer.

1300 - Cease firing at shore target and dropped anchor approximately 2 miles off the beach. Expended 6 rounds 14/45 H.C. and 11 rounds 5/51 H.C.

1400 - TEXAS delivered call fire on AA battery west of Vierville-Sur-Mer. Expended 16 rounds 14/45.

1415 - HARDING granted permission to fire on steeple at Vierville-Sur-Mer to dislodge possible spotters for enemy fire on beach. Ceased firing after 1 minute.

1416 - Steeple cut half way down.

1537 - EMMONS requests permission to neutralize mortar battery which is firing on troops on the beach.

1540 - Received word to fire on target 73. Did not commence firing. Pilot of spotting plane was going to bail out due to engine trouble but decided to try to make English Coast.

1550 - CDS 18 in FRANKFORD departed Fire Support Area to establish screen.

1630 - Received message from Rangers ashore through SATTERLEE "Need replacements if you can get them for us".

PART **II** – CHRONOLOGICAL ORDER OF EVENTS TASK GROUP 124.9 FOR
PERIOD 3 – 17 JUNE 1944 (Cont'd)

D DAY JUNE 6th, 1944

1800 – Unable to locate enemy battery harrassing our troops on beach. Suspect it to be located near Port en Bessin.

1801 – Received report heavy batteries firing at ARKANSAS.

1815 – TEXAS commenced firing at battery believed to be one firing on beach and O.P. in church steeple at Vierville-Sur-Mer. Expended 15 rounds 5/51 H.C.

1833 – ARKANSAS commenced firing on two targets vicinity Port-en-Bessin.

1941 – TEXAS commenced firing at target 605877 (cross-roads). Expended 42 rounds 14/45 H.C.

2100 – TEXAS opened fire on target 647885.

2237 – Received word from ANCON to be on alert for E-Boat attack.

2300 – Received word from AUGUSTA for AA battery to assume Condition 1.

D PLUS 1 DAY
JUNE 7, 1944

0304 – BALDWIN opened fire on enemy fortifications at 655855 at request of SFCP #11.

0350 – Received word that friendly convoy approaching area "BASE" through channel No. 9.

0402 – Received report from ARKANSAS that she is being attacked, or attack imminent, from glider bombs.

0415 – Received report that mine was dropped close aboard GHERARDI.

0430 – E-Boats reported by Eastern Task Force patrol who are engaging enemy.

0437 – THOMPSON to commence firing on targets called for by SFCP.

0450 – Received warning from CTF 124 (ANCON) that enemy E-Boats were within 15 miles of Eastern Task Force.

0610 – Requested permission to sail THOMPSON to replenish ammunition. THOMPSON expended all rounds during morning on rapid fire at targets designated by SFCP.

PART II - CHRONOLOGICAL ORDER OF EVENTS TASK GROUP 124.9 FOR
PERIOD 3 - 17 JUNE 1944 (Cont'd)

D PLUS 1 DAY
JUNE 7, 1944

0645 - HARDING commenced firing on orders of SFCP assigned.

0700 - GLASGOW using plane spot opened fire on enemy trucks.

0701 - ARKANSAS opened fire on enemy troops at 645795.

0702 - GLASGOW using air spot firing on mortars at 646866.

0715 - MC COOK opened fire on target 587938, SFCP #1 spotting.

0720 - GLASGOW shifted berth; under enemy fire.

0725 - MC COOK requested permission to open fire on pillbox.

0730 - CARMICK and SATTERLEE released during morning to replenish
       ammunition. Replaced by O'BRIEN and BARTON.

0740 - MC COOK fired at mortars off Point Du Hoe without spot.

0740 - Shell landed astern of GLASGOW.

0741 - PLUNKETT assigned this area by CTG 122.4, CDS 18.

0742 - Spitfire pilot bailed out over OMAHA Beach.

0745 - TEXAS ordered to move out 1500 to 2500 yards to avoid
       enemy fire from beach. GLASGOW underway for same reason.

0750 - ARKANSAS new target 656825 Air Spot.

0752 - ARKANSAS,MONTCALM and DOYLE in touch with own SFCP #13 and
       #7.

0753 - TEXAS underway.

0800 - Received report from BALDWIN that ships are firing vicinity
       own troops.

0804 - TEXAS anchored, bearing 113 degrees, distance 10 miles from
       Ile Du Large St. Marcouf Islands.

0805 - ARKANSAS reported battery 656825 destroyed.

0817 - BARTON ordered to OHIO Beach to assist HARDING.

0840 - TEXAS prepared to fire on target 675857. MONTCALM firing
       at target 695846.

PART II - CHRONOLOGICAL ORDER OF EVENTS TASK GROUP 124.9 FOR
PERIOD 3 - 17 JUNE 1944 (Cont'd)

D PLUS 1 DAY
JUNE 7, 1944

0845 - Reported to CTF 124 that casualties (Rangers) on Pointe Du Hoe should be picked up.

0852 - ARKANSAS reports 2 targets vicinity Trevieres fired on using air spot. Railroad target 40 H.C. expended - Battery target 34 H.C. expended.

0855 - CDD 36 Reports BARTON sent to OHIO Beach being relieved by O'BRIEN.

0900 - TEXAS shifted from target 675857 to 643839 to stop concentration of troops coming out of town of TREVIERES. Commencing 1 hour of deliberate fire, salvo every 2 minutes.

0917 - TEXAS established communication with SFCP.

0940 - TEXAS SFCP shifting position.

0950 - Received Red Alert - Enemy aircraft within 25 miles.

0955 - S. B. ANTHONY hit, presumably mined. All DDS available proceeding to pick up survivors. S. B. ANTHONY sunk at 1012B.

0958 - All Clear received.

1010 - Liberty ship struck mine. Personnel seriously injured who cannot be moved.

1015 - TEXAS ceased firing having expended 25 H.C. on targets.

1035 - Received report from SFCP that our troops are holding COLLEVILLE Sur Mer.

1040 - Received report that enemy in vicinity St. Laurent Sur Mer advancing from FORMIGNY.

1100 - Received report enemy troops advancing north to TREVIERES.

1220 - TEXAS sending provisions and ammunition to Rangers on Pointe Du Hoe. Standing by to receive wounded aboard from the Point.

1255 - TEXAS in communication with SFCPs #15 and #22 through MONTCALM.

1303 - Spotting plane turned over to GLASGOW for spotting on MAISY targets 5 and 16.

PART II - CHRONOLOGICAL ORDER OF EVENTS TASK GROUP 124.9 FOR
PERIOD 3 - 17 JUNE 1944 (Cont'd)

D PLUS 1 DAY
JUNE 7, 1944

1325 - SFCP 15 reports enemy firing on beach from Southeast
of COLLEVILLE Sur Mer.

1327 - Received report Targets 5 and 16 were fired on by GLASGOW.

1350 - Ordered plane to investigate area within 4 miles of Fox
Green Beach; enemy battery reported firing on troops there.

1425 - Ordered TEXAS to stand by to open fire on targets 656869,
656874, 660876. One gun salvo until they are on and then
shift to next target in order.

1430 - Ordered TEXAS not to fire on above targets upon receipt
report that the tanks are British.

1440 - ARKANSAS plane investigating to see whether troops at Target
#1 are German or friendly.

1520 - TEXAS standing by to open fire on target 580880. Intermittent fire for 30 minutes.

1530 - LCVP with ammunition and provisions for Rangers on Pointe
Du Hoe left the TEXAS.

1535 - ENTERPRISE ordered to communicate with GLASGOW and to join
in fire on Targets 5 and 16.

1600 - GLASGOW ceased firing on above targets.

1609 - Received report from ARKANSAS that our troops occupied
TREVIERES. Reported by spotting plane.

1630 - Warning Red West 30.

1635 - Received report LCVP evacuating prisoners and wounded from
Pointe Du Hoe.

1657 - Received All Clear.

1700 - Received request for fire on target 710860 from SFCP #20.
Target approximately 800 yards from front lines. Did not
take under fire for fear of hitting own troops.

1730 - 3 LCVPs alongside TEXAS to discharge casualties and prisoners
taken off Pointe Du Hoe. (Approximately 33 wounded (2 dead),
24 prisoners).

PART II - CHRONOLOGICAL ORDER OF EVENTS TASK GROUP 124.9 FOR
PERIOD 3 - 17 JUNE 1944 (Cont'd)

D PLUS 1 DAY
JUNE 7, 1944

1808 - TEXAS ordered to prepare to open fire on Targets 613902,
619878 with secondary battery (reported enemy troops, tanks
and motor transports).

1816 - TEXAS went to General Quarters.

1820 - TEXAS commenced fire with secondary battery on Targets
613902 and 619878.

1825 - TEXAS secondary battery ceased firing. Expended 6 rounds
5/51 H.C.

1847 - TEXAS standing by to open fire with main battery.

1855 - Received report Hospital Ship struck mine 49°31'N - 00°35'W.

2045 - TEXAS opened fire on target 611809 - Troops & vehicles in
column.

2108 - ANCON instructs all ships anchoring near beach to move
out as necessary to avoid gunfire.

2130 - Transferred prisoners to LCT.

2245 - VIERVILLE-Sur-Mer under very heavy fire by enemy. Large
fires can be seen. Unable to locate enemy battery.

2400 - AA fire observed in area around landing craft.

D PLUS 2 DAYS
JUNE 8, 1944

0045 - Red Alert - West.

0055 - Enemy planes in area.

0143 - TEXAS opened fire with 20mm and 40mm batteries on plane
crossing bow from starboard to port.

0200 - MEREDITH reported mined. All ships ordered to make smoke.

0240 - Received report enemy E-Boats operating within 15 miles of
Eastern Task Force.

0525 - ARKANSAS in contact with air spot.

0535 - MC COOK leaving area to replenish ammunition. ELLYSON
replacing MC COOK in bombarding force.

PART II - CHRONOLOGICAL ORDER OF EVENTS TASK GROUP 124.9 FOR
PERIOD 3 - 17 JUNE 1944 (Cont'd)

D PLUS 2 DAYS
JUNE 8, 1944

0600 - TEXAS underway to anchor in better position for firing on
ISIGNY.

0608 - Received warning Red West.

0626 - Received All Clear.

0700 - ELLYSON relieved HARDING and established communication with
Ranger's SFCP on Pointe Du Hoe.

0708 - TEXAS anchored.

0801 - TEXAS commenced firing on ISIGNY with air spot.

0815 - Plane reports bombs falling in Village Square of ISIGNY.
TEXAS hit railroad station with salvo. Plane reports large
group of motor transports hit in the village square by
TEXAS.

0820 - Plane reports no activity in the village, "Everything
appears to be dead".

0840 - Report of damage done by TEXAS to ISIGNY - Approximately
20 houses destroyed, 3 fires in village, main street wrecked;
barges in canal destroyed.

0844 - HMS BELLONA ordered to report to CTG 124.9 for fire support
duty.

0902 - TEXAS ceased fire. Expended 32 rounds, 14/45 H.C. -
32 rounds, 14/45 A.P.

0950 - RICH and GLENNON reported struck mines off UTAH Beach.

0953 - Battery vicinity Pointe Du Hoe fired on ELLYSON, ELLYSON
silenced battery while shifting berth as Army Forces moved
into this area.

0955 - TEXAS opened fire on enemy tanks at 579938 with secondary
battery - Ceased fire at 1000.

1110 - Our troops occupying Pointe Du Hoe after very heavy fighting
and tank battle which could be observed from the ship.
Hoisted flag on Pointe.

PART II – CHRONOLOGICAL ORDER OF EVENTS TASK GROUP 124.9 FOR
PERIOD 3 – 17 JUNE 1944 (Cont'd)

D PLUS 2 DAYS
JUNE 8, 1944

1130 – ELLYSON moved to Eastern end of OMAHA Beach joining ARKANSAS,
MONTCALM & G. LEYGUES.

1200 – Activity seems to have ceased on Pointe Du Hoe.

1310 – Merchant ship in UTAH Beach presumably struck mine and sank
immediately.

1400 – TEXAS commenced firing at target 643839, near TREVIERES.
Expended 24 rounds 14/45 A.P.

1401 – Noticeable gun splashes on beach at Grandcamp Les Bains.

1435 – Admiral Bryant left ship for conference with CTF 122 in
AUGUSTA.

1515 – Corpse picked up by Hospital Barge close aboard.

1525 – TEXAS sent 33 Ranger casualties to Hospital Ship.

1605 – HMS BELLONA opened fire on target near TREVIERES previously
assigned to TEXAS. TEXAS plane is spotting for GLASGOW.

1645 – Received message from Rangers that they were going to march
on Grandcamp Les Bains.

1710 – HMS BELLONA ceased firing expended 40 rounds.

1731 – Admiral Bryant returned aboard after conference with CTF 122.

1825 – Received report that Dog Green Beach is open.

1940 – ANCXF reports Air Spot grounded for day due to weather.

1950 – Comdr. Marshall, CDD 36, alongside to see Admiral Bryant.

2245 – BELLONA opened fire on target 501856.

2305 – Received warning Red West.

D PLUS 3 DAYS
JUNE 9, 1944

0040 – Enemy bomb attack. Heavy AA fire from all ships. E-Boat
attack driven off by BALDWIN.

ENCL. (B) TO CBD 5
SECRET SERIAL 0042

USS *Harding*:

SYNOPSIS OF EVENTS   7 June 1944

1058B   Machine gun on beach opened fire on HARDING.
1059B   Machine gun ceased fire.
1109B   Sent ammunition replacements and food rations to Rangers in LCT 580.
1131B   Opened fire with 40mm guns at target behind Point Du Hoe.
1132B   Ceased firing.
1249B   Opened fire at various installations in vicinity of target 91. Destroyed target. 100 rounds. This fire requested by Rangers.
1310B   Ceased firing.
1420B   Commenced firing on road behind target 90W on request of Rangers. 44 rounds, **mission reported successful.**
1429B   Ship hit an underwater obstruction, 1500 yards from beach.
1432B   Ship clear of obstruction. Sound gear and both propellers damaged.
1525B   Enemy shore battery opened fire at HARDING. No splashes close.
1558B   Put diver over side to inspect screws. Reported screws badly damaged.
1727B   HARDING landing party returned aboard in LCVP. Reported that MWB wrecked on beach.
2200B   Commenced firing in area behind Point Du Hoe at request of Rangers in vicinity of targets 90-91. Mission successful. 48 rounds.

Ammunition expended - 307 rounds of 5"38 caliber.
Total ammunition expended to date - 764 rounds of 5"38 caliber.

8 June 1944

        Lying off Point Du Hoe, crew at Battle Stations standing easy.
0000B   Enemy Air Raid on beach defenses.
0200B   Air Raid over.
0510B   Commenced jamming. Enemy planes reported in area.
0600B   Commenced patrolling area #3 at slow speeds searching for targets of opportunity.
1433B   Opened fire on waterfront of Grandcamp Les Bains at request of NGLO #3. 160 rounds, **firing unobserved by SFCP #3.**
1440B   Opened fire on **town** of Maisy by request of NGLO #3. 73 rounds.
1815B   On request of NGLO #3 opened fire on Maisy using intermittent fire for one hour.
1900B   Ceased firing.
1920B   NGLO #3 reported fire on Maisy had been highly effective and that our troops were entering the town.
1930B   Closed Texas.
1947B   CDD 36 left ship for Texas.
2010B   Received aboard survivors of Susan B. Anthony.
2043B   CDD 36 returned aboard from Texas.
2100B   Returned to Fire Support Area #3 and lay to.
2332B   Anchored in Fire Support Area #3, Point Du Hoe bearing 240°(T) distant 4500 yards.

        347 rounds of 5"38 caliber ammunition expended.

Photographs kept with the USS *Harding* reports.

6 June: 1533B. U.S.S. HARDING (DD625) assisting Rangers by shelling enemy shore positions
from position off Beach Charlie, Omaha. U.S.S.
LCI(L) 87 alongside to take aboard Army and
Navy flag officers.

13. Same Chateau seen from the front. (Built in 1660).

5. Interior of pillbox shown in No. 2. Note panorama of beach with
ranges to focal points. The 2300 mm range is to the pier off
Grandcamps Sur Mer.

7. Observation post at end of sea wall partially destroyed by 5"
gunfire from U.S.S. HARDING. Also a machine gun emplacement.

Reinforced concrete pillbox commanding the beach on all sides.
Heavy caliber machine gun inside had been demolished by 5" shell
fire of U.S.S. HARDING. On point of land between Pointe du Hoc
and Grandcamps Sur Mer.

Camouflaged barracks 100 yards from the sea wall. This particular
room had about 50 land mines in it which the Germans in their hasty
retreat did not have time to set.

1. Gun emplacement – reinforced concrete. Evidently an unfinished emplacement as there were no signs of a gun there, although in the underground passageways in the rear there were powder cases scattered about indicating gun might have been removed. Powder cases indicated they were for guns of about 6" size. Pointe du Hoc (bombed by air force and shelled by TEXAS 14" guns).

6. Camouflaged trench. The grass over the chicken wire was still green. Many small mortars and plenty of ammunition were in evidence here. This trench ran along the beach to the East of the sea wall shown in Nos. 3 and 8, starting with observation post shown in No. 7.

8. Break in sea wall from 5" shell fired by the U.S.S. HARDING.

11. Sluice gate in sea wall damaged by 5" gunfire.

Naval Commander Western Task Force
Via: Commander Task Force 124.
APA-26/A9-8/A4-3
29 June, 1944

SECRET

6 June, 1944:

0230 Passed POINT KING. Proceeded to assigned anchorage.
0315 CHASE, followed closely by EMPIRE ANVIL and HENRICO,
anchored in assigned positions in Transport Area. Immediately after
anchoring, transports commenced lowering assault landing craft. 0635
1st wave of assault units from HENRICO landed on designated beach
EASY RED. 0650 Boat Division "B" of the 1st assault wave from EMPIRE
ANVIL landed on designated beach, FOX GREEN. 0740 1st wave of assault
troops from SAMUEL CHASE landed on designated beach, EASY RED. Following the initial assault waves, succeeding assault waves are believed
to have been dispatched and landed on designated beaches on or about
scheduled time. Transports reported 100% completion of debarkation of
troops, and unloading of equipment, as follows: HENRICO - 1000, CHASE -
1100, and EMPIRE ANVIL - 1200. At 1200 dispatched 15LCVPs from CHASE,
and 10 from HENRICO, to beach EASY RED, to assist unloading LCI(L)s and
LCTs. 1945 Transferred command of Task Group 124.3 to Deputy Assault
Group Commander. 1833 Underway in accordance with orders from COMTRANS
DIV THREE, and departed Transport Area, and thence proceeded in convoy
formation, via swept channels to Weymouth Bay.

7 June, 1944:

Proceeding via searched channels to Weymouth Bay. 0536 Anchored
in Weymouth Bay. 1500 Underway, proceeding to Portland Harbor, where
anchored at 1540.

2.   Reports received clearly indicate that, insofar as landing craft
are concerned, this operation was conducted under extremely unfavorable and
adverse sea conditions.

3.   Landing craft were severely handicapped in landing operations by
shoals, underwater and beach obstacles, mines, rough sea and heavy surf. On
approaching the beach, landing craft encountered heavy gun fire and, after
beaching and while unloading troops, heavy machine gun and mortar fire.
The performance of ship-borne craft was generally excellent, except
the LCAs, which apparently are very unseaworthy. These craft shipped large
quantities of water in the heavy sea, and some were lost by foundering enroute
to the beach.

4.   Combat Unit Loading was employed to load transports. For this
operation, transports were loaded primarily, and to capacity, with tactical
troop units. Army field equipment carried was of a restricted character, and
only of such quantity as required and essential to the immediate needs of the
assault force. Embarkation and debarkation of troops, and loading and unloading
of equipment proceeded generally in accordance with the program, but it
was again evident that a considerable amount of confusion existed. It is
of the utmost importance that more attention be given in the preliminary
planning to priorities in the embarkation and debarkation of troops, the
billeting of troops, and the loading and unloading of equipment. It is
recommended that a TQM officer, with one or two assistants, be permanently
assigned to each transport to serve as liaison officer, and to coordinate
the planning for the methodical loading and unloading of individual ships.

5.   Approach to the Transport Area via swept channel was accomplished
without incident despite strong tidal currents and without speed signals.
Swept channels were well marked. Some buoys marking the channels could not
be located, others appeared to have drifted considerably off station.

E. H. FRITZSCHE

```
                    U. S. S. LCG(L) 426
A16-3/(sn)          U. S. S. LCG(L) GROUP
Serial 0018.        GUNFIRE SUPPORT CRAFT
                    ELEVENTH AMPHIBIOUS FORCE


S-E-C-R-E-T

                                        27 June 1944.

From:       The Commanding Officer, U.S.S. LCG(L) 426.
To  :       Commander U.S. Naval Forces, Western Task Force.

Via :       (1) Commander Task Unit 124.8.1
            (2) Commander Task Group 124.8
            (3) Commander Task Force 124

Subject:    Operation order ████ - Report on.
```

1.   Weighed anchor from Pool Bay at 0200, 5 June 1944, LCM(3) 18 in tow, passing thru points Baker and Nan (1), cutting thru convoy of Liberty ships. Points Xray, Able (2), (3), (4), (5) and (6), Fox, Nan (2) and Jig (2) passed as per schedule, speed approximately 5 knots. Speed from Jig (2) up to 8 knots at varying times and for considerable periods.

2.   6 June 1944 at about 0300 arrived unknown position astern of LCG(L) 449. Position was determined to be sector Utah. Turned to course 130° True, emergency speed ahead.

3.   Approximately 0610, 6 June survivors sighted to starboard; three (3) American Rangers (one dead) and one (1) British sailor taken aboard. Returned to continue on course and arrived at Omaha area 0745. Commenced seeking targets of opportunity.

4.   Fired upon machine gun nest coordinate no. 64809160 expending 6 rounds H.E. and 6 rounds S.A.P.

5.   At approximately 1600 withdrew to transport area to transfer survivors and dead to U.S.S. APA 45. Returned and cruised until darkness seeking targets. At 0030 fired 250 rounds 20 mm. at enemy plane scoring several bursts. Near bomb misses.

6.   Cruising till 1300, 7 June when proceeded to port En Bessin. Opened fire 1315 at sea wall, small craft and pillbox. Having expended 48 rounds S.A.P. and 7 rounds H.E; also 1100 rounds 20 mm. Thenceforth cruised up and down beach.

7.   8 June, expended 120 rounds 20 mm. at unidentified plane. At 2250 on 8 June port engine completely out. Thereafter anchored and cruised alternately until 13 June at 0700 port engine having been repaired, weighed anchor from transport area in convoy to the United Kingdom.

```
                                R. W. MUELLER,
                                Lieut. (jg) USNR.
```

HMS *Glasgow* After Action Reports:

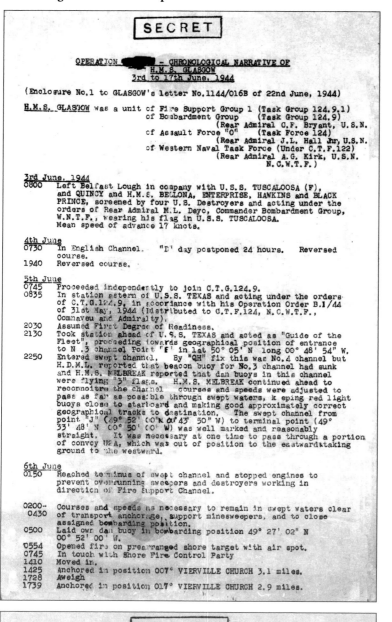

SECRET

OPERATION ▓▓▓▓ – CHRONOLOGICAL NARRATIVE OF
H.M.S. GLASGOW
3rd to 17th June, 1944

(Enclosure No.1 to GLASGOW's letter No.1144/016B of 22nd June, 1944)

H.M.S. GLASGOW was a unit of Fire Support Group 1 (Task Group 124.9.1)
of Bombardment Group   (Task Group 124.9)
(Rear Admiral C.F. Bryant, U.S.N.
of Assault Force "O"   (Task Force 124)
(Rear Admiral J.L. Hall Jnr, U.S.N.
of Western Naval Task Force (Under C.T.F.122)
(Rear Admiral A.G. Kirk, U.S.N.
N.C.W.T.F.)

3rd June, 1944
0800   Left Belfast Lough in company with U.S.S. TUSCALOOSA (F),
and QUINCY and H.M.S. BELLONA, ENTERPRISE, HAWKINS and BLACK
PRINCE, screened by four U.S. Destroyers and acting under the
orders of Rear Admiral M.L. Deyo, Commander Bombardment Group,
W.N.T.F., wearing his flag in U.S.S. TUSCALOOSA.
Mean speed of advance 17 knots.

4th June
0730   In English Channel. "D" day postponed 24 hours.   Reversed
course.
1940   Reversed course.

5th June
0745   Proceeded independently to join C.T.G.124.9.
0835   In station astern of U.S.S. TEXAS and acting under the orders
of C.T.G.124.9, in accordance with his Operation Order B.1/44
of 31st May, 1944 (distributed to C.T.F.124, N.C.W.T.F.,
Comnaveu and Admiralty).
2030   Assumed First Degree of Readiness.
2130   Took station ahead of U.S.S. TEXAS and acted as "Guide of the
Fleet", proceeding towards geographical position of entrance
to N.3 channel Point "F" in lat 50° 05' N long 00° 48' 54" W.
2250   Entered swept channel.   By "QH" fix this was No.4 channel but
H.D.M.L. reported that beacon buoy for No.3 channel had sunk
and H.M.S. MELBREAK reported that dan buoys in this channel
were flying "3" flags.   H.M.S. MELBREAK continued ahead to
reconnoitre the channel   courses and speeds were adjusted to
pass as far as possible through swept waters, keeping red light
buoys close to starboard and making good approximately correct
geographical tracks to destination.   The swept channel from
point "J" (49° 52' 00"N 00° 43' 50" W) to terminal point (49°
33' 48' N 00° 50' 00" W) was well marked and reasonably
straight.   It was necessary at one time to pass through a portion
of convoy U2A, which was out of position to the eastward taking
ground to the westward.

6th June
0150   Reached terminus of swept channel and stopped engines to
prevent overrunning sweepers and destroyers working in
direction of Fire Support Channel.

0200–
0430   Courses and speeds as necessary to remain in swept waters clear
of transport anchorage, support minesweepers, and to close
assigned bombarding position.
0500   Laid own dan buoy in bombarding position 49° 27' 02" N
00° 52' 00' W.
0554   Opened fire on prearranged shore target with air spot.
0745   In touch with Shore Fire Control Party
1410   Moved in.
1425   Anchored in position 007° VIERVILLE CHURCH 3.1 miles.
1728   Aweigh
1739   Anchored in position 017° VIERVILLE CHURCH 2.9 miles.

SECRET

Page 2.

OPERATION ▓▓▓▓ – CHRONOLOGICAL NARRATIVE (cont)

7th June
0720   Under shell fire from shore.   Shifted berth.
1410   Shifted berth to engage targets to westward (Maisy).

For the next four days H.M.S. GLASGOW was supporting
the right flank of the Force landed on "OMAHA" beach;
anchorage was shifted as necessary; hostile aircraft were in
evidence only at night and were engaged only when identified
as hostile.   All bombardment was carried out at anchor.

SECRET

SUBJECT . OPERATION ███████ - CHRONOLOGICAL NARRATIVE REPORT

FROM .... THE COMMANDING OFFICER, H.M.S. GLASGOW.

DATE .... 22nd June, 1944   No.1144/016B.

TO   .... THE COMMANDER TASK FORCE 122
          (via the Commander Task Group 124.9 and
           the Commander Task Force 124).

       Report is herewith submitted in accordance with
N.C.W.T.F.'s message 181212 B June.

    2. It is believed that H.M.S. GLASGOW acted in
accordance with the various written instructions and, it
is hoped, in accordance with Senior Officer's intentions,
and no attempt has therefore been made to give details of
prearranged movements.

COMMENTS

    3. PREPARATIONS
       The many firing practices and communication drills
carried out with aircraft, S.F.C.P. and F.O.B's prior to
Operation ███████ were of the utmost value.

    4. AIRCRAFT SPOTTING
       The results were generally good. There was however,
a slight tendency to observe on a map reference given by the
ship without making certain that there was a target at that
pin point. This was overcome by ordering the pilot to
identify the target before the ship fired. Great keenness
and efficiency was shown by most pilots in seeking targets
of opportunity and in giving accurate map references, though
in some cases they were not provided with maps that covered
a sufficient area in depth.

    5. S.F.C.P.
       Results were most satisfactory though some
communication difficulty was experienced when voice radio
was used on the common channel.

    6. COMMUNICATIONS
       (a) Aircraft - V/H.F. R/T communication with aircraft
on type 86 and 87 was entirely satisfactory. No jamming was
experienced.
       (b) S.F.C.P. - When C.W. channels were used
communication with S.F.C P's was entirely satisfactory. The
results obtained with S.C.R.608 were on the whole disappointing.
To some extent this was due no doubt to lack of technical
experience on the part of the ship, though the set itself
does seem to be somewhat temperamental in it's behaviour.
It appeared that in their anxiety to get on with the job
a number of ships and S.F.C.P's used the common F.M. voice
channel instead of the primary individual frequencies or
C.W. frequencies of S.F.C.P's. It is felt that some means of

SECRET

Page 2.

OPERATION ███████ - CHRONOLOGICAL NARRATIVE REPORT (cont)

Para 6 (b) (cont)
visual communication between S.F.C.P's and the ships would
be extremely valuable in the very early stages of a landing.
Voice communication with S.F.C.P. using S.C.R.284 C.W.
frequency was found to be useful in emergency for ironing out
difficulties.

7.   INFORMATION
It is realized that in the early stages of the
assault the promulgation of information to firing ships
was very difficult and as a result several promising targets
could not be engaged as the position of our own troops was
not known.

8.   NAVIGATIONAL
Outfit "Q.H." was invaluable in the strong tidal
waters.   At no time was jamming experienced of such intensity
that it could not be tuned out by means of the R.F.27 Unit.
During the final approach Radar Identification Chart GR.2613
was used   and gave a good indication of what actually
did present itself on the P.P.I. scan.   "QH." at this stage,
as predicted, was not reliable for distance offshore but
gave good longitude readings.

9.   CONCLUSION
In conclusion I should like to state that I am
sure that the Allied Captains will have been pleased to serve
under the cheerful and inspiring leadership of Rear Admiral
Bryant, U.S.N.; a spirit of enthusiasm and zeal for fighting
efficiency properly infected all the ships of Task Group 124.9.

C.P. Clarke
CAPTAIN

FILE A16-3/OF7
Serial 0036   UNITED STATES ATLANTIC FLEET
                               COMMANDER BATTLESHIP
                                   DIVISION FIVE

SECRET
                                           Care Fleet Post Office,
                                           New York, N. Y.

                                           2 4 JUN 1944

FIRST ENDORSEMENT to:
C.O., HMS GLASGOW ltr.
No.1144/016B of June
22, 1944.

From: The Commander Task Group 124.9.
To :   The Commander Task Force 122.
Via :   The Commander Task Force 124.

Subject: Operation ██████ - Chronological Narrative
             Report (HMS GLASGOW).

     1.   Forwarded. The excellent performance of the
GLASGOW has been made the subject of separate correspondence.

                                        C. F. BRYANT.

SECRET

SUMMARY OF BOMBARDMENTS

(Enclosure No. 2 to GLASGOW's letter No. 1144/016B of 22 June, 1944)

(All map references refer to Map Charts F.1015 and F.1014)

Date and Time	Map Reference	Target	No. of Rounds	Type of Observation	Remarks
6/6 0554	666903 - 668903	Strongpoint at Les Moulins	219	A/c then direct	Prearranged pre H hour - many hits
6/6 0630	649906	Strongpoint	18	A/c	Smoke observed target results not known
6/6 0836	556847	Bridge	39	A/c briefed on this	Target too small for naval fire - no hits
6/6 1035	548848	M/T in wood	69	A/c	M/T mostly destroyed
6/6 1459	550910	Flak battery	27	A/c	Guns destroyed. Hits in target area
6/6 1520	544832	M/T in S.W corner of wood. N.B some were dummies	21	A/c	Fire effective
6/6 1820	657875	Battery firing on beaches	114	Unobserved	Results not known Rock salvoes
6/6 2040	In touch with S.F.C.P. No.2 on W/T (5638 Kc/s).				
7/6 0700	646866	Mortars near Formigny	123	A/c	5 direct hits on mortars, many in target area, fire effective. No more fire from target
7/6 0727	647855	M/T on road	36	A/c	Hits obtained, target disorganised and what remained moved south
7/6 0925	643839	Trevieres	33	A/c	Damage done to town and target
7/6 1000	647867	G.N.F.	39	A/c	1 gun visible. 2 direct hits obtained. Guns silenced
7/6 1042	642838	Troops moving into Trevieres	39	A/c	Ineffective
7/6 1315	553918	Battery at Maisy (target No.5)	63	A/c	Fire effective. Several direct hits Many within 50 yds.
7/6 1450	660875	Battery in action	38	A/c	Results not definite. Some hits observed.
7/6 1527	553918	Maisy battery	48	A/c	Hits obtained. Fire effective.
7/6 1730	665765	G.N.F. near Le Molay	17	A/c	Guns ceased firing after 2 ranging rounds. Hits obtained.
7/6 1750	641881	Enemy reserves C.S.	14	S.F.C.P.	Checked fire due to own troops approaching target. Results not given by S.F.C.P.
7/6 1837	646846	Transport including A/T guns on the move	32	A/c	Many hits. Considerable damage. A/c reports have "Just about had it".
7/6 1900	652838	Gun battery	17	A/c	Ineffective. Smoke made pilots observation impossible.
7/6 1950	612801	Troop concentrations	6	A/c	Ineffective. Pilot R/B after 2 salvoes.
7/6 2110	578918	Suspected Gun battery	18	A/c	No guns seen but direct hits on farm house. Men ran out Net results not known

Page 2.

SUMMARY OF BOMBARDMENTS (cont)

Date and Time	Map Reference	Target	No. of Rounds	Type of Observation	Remarks
8/6 1130	545883	Machine Guns	19	S.F.C.P.24	Hits reported after 1st round M/G's destroyed
8/6 1407	540885	Troops	48	S.F.C.P.24	S.F.C.P. reported mission successful.
8/6 1430	535888	Infantry inter dicting fire	27	S.F.C.P.24	S.F.C.P. reported mission successful
8/6 1455	555932	Troops around Grande amp Les Bains	58	S.F.C.P.2	Results not known
8/6 1600	553930	Water tower being used as Enemy Observation Post	45	Direct	Several near misses. O.P. discovered later to have tripod legs! Observation difficult owing to surrounding woods and buildings
8/6 1715	548884	Machine Guns	34	S.F.C.P.24	S.F.C.P. reports "M.S.5"
8/6 1825	553885	Infantry inter dicting fire	30	S.F.C.P.24	Mission successful
N.B. Bade goodbye to S. C.P.24 at 2000 (out of range)					
10/6 1208	653765	Assembly area (Le Molay area)	6	A/c	Firing stopped owing to uncertainty of position of own troops.
15/6 0725	466809	Bivouac Area	6	S.F.C.P.18	Firing stopped, own troops advancing

USS *LST 372*

Several times during the month of May, LST 372 went out for target practice, spending the remaining time in preparation for the invasion of France. During this time, there were German air raids around Weymouth, but the ship came thru undamaged. On 5 June, 1944, she sailed for Omaha Beach in Normandy, loaded with U.S. Rangers, Engineers, ducks, trucks, and jeeps. The convoy consisted of twenty LST's each protected by two barrage balloons, and escorted by British Corvettes. Having arrived off Dog Red Beach at approximately H/8 hours, the ship was anchored and the "ducks" discharged. Enemy fire on the beach was so intense; however, that the troops were pinned down there, and no vehicles were being landed. Therefore, no other troops or vehicles were unloaded until the next afternoon, when LCT's carried them ashore.

HNLMS *Soemba* After Action Report:

6th June.	0355	Permission granted by SO Escort) in USS BARTON to detach from convoy. Proceeded independently at utmost speed towards Bombarding Area.
	0455	Arrived Transport Area.
		Delay experienced owing to lights on danbuoys being extinguished.
	0540	Reported to SO Bombardment Unit two(CTG/25-8-2) in HM.Cruiser "HAWKINS".
	0610	Opened fire on target 30-545935 and Target 32-538934 in accordance with Appendix Four to Annex Dog to Operation Order 3-44.Para 6.
		Target 30= Defended locality. Infantry position in the built up area of GRANDCAMP.
		Target 32= Defended locality. Infantry position on the open coast west of GRANDCAMP.
	0830	Ceased fire on targets 30 and 32 in accordance with Comfor U despatch 291912 May.

AMMUNITION EXPENDITURE.		RESULT.
0610-0617	15 rounds. Target 30.	Unknown. Hits seen on houses in area.
0620-0622	15 rounds. Target 32.	Unknown. Hits seen on houses in area.
0627-0628	12 rounds. Target 30-gun on pierhead.	Unknown. Smoke & Dust clouds obscured area and fire was ceased.
0632-0635	15 rounds. A.A.Battery firing at planes. East of Pt.de Houe amongst trees.	A.A.Battery ceased fire.
0703-0711	33 rounds. Target 32.	Unknown.
0736-0741	18 rounds. Target 30.	Unknown.
0755-0758	15 rounds. Target 32.	Unknown.
0821-0824	14 rounds. Target 32.	Unknown.
0825-0830	18 rounds. Target 30.	Unknown.

Remained at action stations all day in anticipation of calls for fire.

Refer to DD638/A16-3
Serial   001 (GAM:rks)   U. S. S. HERNDON (638)

SECRET

c/o Fleet Post Office
New York, New York

S E C R E T   21 June 1944.

From: The Commanding Officer.
To :   The Commander-in-Chief, United States Fleet, (Readiness Section).

Via :   Commander Task Group 125.8 (Commander Bombardment Group UTAH).
             Commander Task Force 125(Commander Assault Force UTAH).
             Commander Task Force 122 (N.C.W.T.F.).

Subject: Action Report.

References: (a) CTF 125 Operation Order 3-44 of 15 May 1944.
             (b) U.S. Navy Regulations Art. 712, Art. 874(6).
             (c) Atlantic Fleet Conf. ltr. 13CL-43 (Revised).

1.   In accordance with Annex "Dog" to Commander Task Force 125 Operation
Order 3-44, this vessel, part of Task Unit 125.8.4 (Fire Support Unit Four) proceeded down the boat lane ahead of the first Assault Wave to Fire Support Area
Four on D Day. At 0550 (H minus 40), June 6, 1944, this vessel carried out shore
bombardment to destroy or neutralize the following prearranged enemy shore batteries and defences: Targets 34, 36, 38, 40 and 42. All targets were situated
on the eastern bank of the mouth of the River Vire between Grandcamp Le Bains and
the Carentan Estuary. All targets were classified as defended, localities. Target
#40 consisted of two 105mm guns in open emplacements with one pill box and shelter.
Target #42 consisted of an infantry position with three pill boxes, one casement,
one anti-tank gun, two shelters and two 150mm guns in open emplacements.

2.   Neutralization fire at the rate of eight (8) rounds per minute
was commenced at 0550 (H minus 40). Ceased prearranged fire at 0630 (H hour).
Since preselected targets could not be identified indirect fire was employed
using data supplied by C.I.C. Results of fire could not be positively determined. However, mission was considered satisfactorily accomplished since batteries taken under fire were temporarily neutralized and did not endanger leading assault waves approaching assault beach within their range and arc of fire.

3.   212 rounds of 5"/38 cal. AA common ammunition were expended during
forty minutes of prearranged fire with no casualties.

4.   At 0655 an active AA shore battery in the town of Maisy (T103)
was observed and taken under fire. Ceased firing at 0703 having expended 42
rounds of 5"/38 cal. AA common ammunition. Battery was silenced.

5.   At 0735 T40 and again at 0819 T42 active shore batteries were observed to be firing at the boat lanes. Each target was taken under fire with
neutralization fire. Expended 53 rounds of 5"/38 Cal. AA common ammunition at

- 1 -

Refer to DD638/A16-3   U. S. S. HERNDON (638)
Serial   001 (GAM:rks)

SECRET

S E C R E T

Subject: Action Report (continued).
- -

target T40 and 55 rounds at target T42. Both batteries were neutralized. The
fire from both batteries was slow and erratic. A few splashes were observed in
the vicinity of the boat lane and near this vessel. Apparently local control
was the only method used by the enemy.

6.   Direct fire with direct spotting was employed against each of the
three above mentioned targets of opportunity. Elevation spots were employed to
obtain about 20% air bursts. There were no material or personnel casualties.

7.   During entire bombardment this ship steamed at 5 knots or less in
Fire Support swept channel #4 running east and west approximately 6000 yards
north of Grandcamp Le Bains, France. Firing ranges varied from 6000 to 12,000
yards.

8.   The true bearing of targets of opportunity observed by lookouts
and topside personnel were taken with the torpedo director and transmitted to
C.I.C. for target designation to plot. Communications between C.I.C., Main
Battery, Plot and the bridge were excellent.

G. A. MOORE.

USS *Herndon* also had the same targets as HNLMS *Soemba*.

USS *Ellyson* After Action Report for 8 June includes their helping the Rangers at Pointe du Hoc.

U.S.S. ELLYSON (DD454),
c/o Fleet Post Office,
New York, New York,
8 June 1944.

W-A-R D-I-A-R-Y

1. U.S.S. ELLYSON (DD454), Flagship CDS-10, U.S. Atlantic Fleet, attached temporarily to Task Group 122.4.

2. CTF-122 Operational Plan on West 2.

3. Positions:
    0800: Lat. 49-25-36 N; Long. 00-59-06 W.
    1200: Lat. 49-26-10 N; Long. 00-57-54 W.
    2000: Lat. 49-24-48 N; Long. 00-50-42 W.

4. 0114-"Air Raid warning, Western TF Area. Went to General Quarters. 0129-General air raid over assault area. One plane seen shot down. 0134-Underway. 0201-All ships ordered to "Make Smoke". 0333-Report received that U.S.S. MEREDITH struck a mine and was abandoned. 0341-Secured from General Quarters. 0415-"Commence Smoke". 0520-"Cease Smoke". 0535-U.S.S. ELLYSON was ordered to relieve U.S.S. HARDING in bombarding force, Fire Support Area 3 (KANSAS), OMAHA Beach. Relieved U.S.S. HARDING at 0700 and immediately established visual communications with RANGERS SFCP (Shore Fire Control Party). At about 0800 established voice radio communications. 0918-Anchored 2¼ miles north of Pointe du Hoe to await orders of Fire Control Party. 0929-On orders from RANGERS observation post, bombarded German light gun positions in trees on edge of cliff about 800 yards west of Pointe Du Hoe (LAMBERT grid coordinates 579938). Commenced fire using indirect control from C.I.C. and 5"/38 A.A. Common Projectiles set on safe. Shifted to Director control after Gunnery Officer determined the location of the target. Ceased firing at 0952 after expending 100 rounds. SFCP reported mission successful. 0953-German shore battery in vicinity of target commenced firing at U.S.S. ELLYSON, shells landing short. Returned the fire using Director control and commenced heaving in. 0959-Enemy straddled, 1000-Underway to open range 2000 yards. 1022-Fired 16 rounds at shore battery. Ceased firing on orders from SFCP to allow Army infantry and tanks to move in. Total ammunition expended 124 rounds 5" A.A. common. 1130-American Flag raised over captured position. During remainder of day stood by in areas OREGON and OHIO about two miles off shore awaiting targets from SFCP. 2258-"Air Raid" warning, Western Task Force Area. Took station about 2000 yards to north of U.S.S. ARKANSAS and French cruisers MONTCALM and GEORGES LEYGUES, in northern OHIO area. 2340-"All Clear" Western Task Force Area.

5. Ammunition expended: 124 rounds 5"/38.

Below: Written later in June this is a slightly expanded version of the same events.

DD454/A16
Serial: (069)

CONFIDENTIAL

C-O-N-F-I-D-E-N-T-I-A-L

U.S.S. ELLYSON (DD454),
c/o Fleet Post Office,
New York, New York,
27 June 1944.

From: The Commanding Officer.
To: The Commander in Chief, U.S. Fleet.

Via: (1) Commander Destroyer Squadron TEN.
               (2) Commander Task Group ONE TWO FOUR POINT NINE.
               (3) Commander Task Force ONE TWO TWO.
               (4) Allied Naval Commander in Chief,
                   EXPEDITIONARY FORCE.
               (5) Supreme Commander, ALLIED EXPEDITIONARY FORCE.

Subject: ACTION REPORT -- 8-9, June 1944.

Reference: (a) Art. 712, U.S. Navy Regulations.
               (b) Cinclant Letter 13CL-43 (Revised).
               (c) CO ELLYSON Letter DD454/A15, Serial 005 of
                   June 17, 1944.

    1.   From 0500, June 8, 1944, to 0800, June 15, 1944, this vessel
was a unit of the Bombardment Force, Assault Force "O", off the Normandy
Beachhead in France, and, while thus assigned, conducted three shore
bombardments.

    2.   At 0927, June 8, 1944, while this vessel was anchored
about 2¼ miles north of Pointe du Hoe, a U.S. RANGERS observation post
requested fire on German light gun positions in clumps of trees on edge
of cliff about 800 yards west of Pointe du Hoe (British LAMBERT grid
coordinates 579938). Fire was opened a few minutes later using indirect
control from C.I.C., full salvos and 5"/38 A.A. common projectiles set
on safe. Communiation with the RANGERS was by voice on medium frequency
using the AEF Assault Code. Fire was checked after each salvo to await
spots from observation post. Shore fire control party was having
difficulty spotting. As soon as enemy returned fire his location was
observed by Gunnery Officer and a shift was made to direct fire. At
0952 the observation post ordered "cease fire" and reported "mission
successful". At 0953 a German shore battery in the vicinity of the
target commenced firing at the ELLYSON, shells landing short. Returned
the fire using director control. Stated heaving in. At 0959 the
enemy straddled. At 1000 got underway and opened range about 2000
yards. At 1022 fired 16 rounds at enemy shore battery. Ceased firing
on orders from observation post to allow Army infantry and tanks to
move in. Total ammunition expended 124 rounds 5"/38 A.A. common. At
1130 the American flag was hoisted over the captured position.

CONFIDENTIAL
S-E-C-R-E-T

CHRONOLOGICAL NARRATIVE OF OPERATIONS

June 6-

0000 Underway from Plymouth, England in company with Convoy
"B-2" (Task Group 126.3). Commander Force "B" (CTF 126) in U.S.S.
MALOY. Commander Convoy "B-2" (CTG 126.3) in U.S.S. LCI(L) 414.
Commander Escorts (CTU 126.3.1) in U.S.S. ELLYSON. Convoy consists
of LCI(L) FLOTILLA TWELVE and U.S.S. ACHENAR. Escorts: U.S.S.
ELLYSON, U.S.S. MALOY, H.M.S. AZALEA, H.M.C.S. KITCHNER, U.S.S.
P.C. 1262 and U.S.S. P.C. 1263. 0008 Passed gate. 0100 Convoy
formed up, in two columns, off Eddystone Light. This vessel took
station 3000 yards on port bow of convoy. Convoy followed coastal
route to Portland Bill Light; thence on course 110°(t) to swept
channel #3 north of assault area. Speed of advance 13 knots.
1130 Entered channel #3, course 166°(t). 1424 arrived assault
area. Released from Task Force 126. Reported to Commander Area
Screen for duty. 1851 Anchored in C-30 (DIXIE Grid). 2331 Went
to general quarters. A.A. fire to eastward.

June 7-

0018 Secured from general quarters. 0445 "E-Boat" warning, Western TF Area. Went to general quarters. 0534 Secured from general
quarters. 1634 "Air Raid" warning, Western TF Area. Went to general
quarters. 1658 Secured from general quarters. 1745 Underway. 1800
Took station #25 on DIXIE Line. 1900 Hospital Ship, H.M.S. DINARDS
struck mine in Lat. 49 - 31.0 N., Long. 00 - 35.0 W. Numerous ships
and small craft went to rescue. 2225 Anchored in DIXIE - 25.

June 8-

0114 "Air Raid" warning, Western TF Area. Went to general
quarters. 0129 General air raid over assault area. One plane seen
shot down. 0134 Underway. 0201 All ships ordered to "Make smoke".
0333 Report received that U.S.S. MEREDITH struck a mine and was
abandoned. 0341 Secured from general quarters. 0415 "Commence
smoke". 0520 "Cease smoke". 0535 U.S.S. ELLYSON was ordered to
relieve U.S.S. HARDING in bombarding force, Fire Support Area 3
(KANSAS), OMAHA Beach. Relieved U.S.S. HARDING at 0700 and immediately
established visual communications with RANGERS SFCP (Shore Firecontrol
Party). At about 0800 established voice radio communications. 0918
Anchored 2¼ miles north of Pointe du Hoe to await orders of fire
control party. 0929 On orders from RANGERS observation post, bombarded German light gun positions in trees on edge of cliff about 800
yards west of Pointe du Hoe (LAMBERT grid coordinates 579938).

Page 8-con't

Commenced fire using indirect control from C.I.C. and 5"/38 A.A.
Common Projectiles set on safe. Shifted to Director control after
Gunnery Officer determined the location of the target. Ceased firing at 0952 after expending 100 rounds. SFCP reported mission
successful. 0953 German shore battery in vicinity of target commenced
firing at U.S.S. ELLYSON, shells landing short. Returned the fire
using Director control and commenced heaving in. 0959 Enemy straddled.
1000 Underway to open range 2000 yards. 1022 Fired 16 rounds at shore
battery. Ceased firing on orders from SFCP to allow Army infantry
and tanks to move in. Total ammunition expended 124 rounds 5" A.A.
Common. 1130 American Flag raised over captured position. During
remainder of day stood by in areas OREGON and OHIO about two miles
off shore awaiting targets from SFCP. 2258 "Air Raid" warning,
Western Task Force Area. Took station about 2000 yards to north of
U.S.S. ARKANSAS and French cruisers MONTCALM and GEORGES LEYGUES, in
northern OHIO area. 2340 "All Clear" Western Task Force Area.

June 9-

After Action Report *USS LCG(L) 7*

```
                            U. S. S. LCG(L) NO. 7
                            U. S. S. LCG(L) GROUP
A16-3/(tn)                  GUNFIRE SUPPORT CRAFT
Serial 0033                 ELEVENTH AMPHIBIOUS FORCE

                                      6 July 1944.
```

From: The Commanding Officer, U. S. S. LCG(L) 7.
To: Commander In Chief, United States Fleet.

Via: (1) Commander Task Unit 125.7.1.
                (2) Commander Task Group 125.7
                (3) Commander Task Force 125
                (4) Commander Task Force 122

Subject: Operation Normandy - Report on.

1.   We slipped Salcombe for assault on 3 June at 1430 in convoy U-2A(1). We followed in convoy until dusk of 4 June and were called into Weymouth over night. Never received any notice of postponement. We were anchored at 2335.

2.   Given notice to weigh anchor at 0200, we were on deck and underway at 0245. Rendezvous at 0600 aft "Bill of Portland", and proceeded to assault area in convoy.

3.   We arrived in the assault area at 0545 on D-Day. There was much confusion at this point, and knowing that we were late, I at once proceeded into position at the beginning of the boat lanes. Other ships which were to proceed with us, were now coming on, so with all ahead full speed we proceeded down the boat lanes toward the beach. We had never stopped for a moment.

4.   The boat lanes were crowded with waves of small boats all making good speed. As I was a little out of position, being too close to the center and bearing down on the ship marking mid-channel, I was forced to crowd the LCV(P)'s over into the channel to pass. This I believe was point "X".

5.   On approaching point "Y" the circumstances were unaltered, with these exceptions. The marker ship had apparently struck a mine, and was lying on her side sinking. There were two men standing on the bow, a third man was pulling a fourth from the water. The latter being unable to help himself.

6.   After this position, which I passed to my port, I wanted to near to port and reach the flank of the boat lane. The lanes were still crowded so I peered back to see if there was a chance for me to cross. At this moment a large craft, of the Fire Support Group, made contact with a mine. The craft appeared to have no damage done, and proceeded on. I never glanced back again and so never saw her again. This ship I later discovered was the U. S. LCF 31.

-1-

CONFIDENTIAL

6 July 1944.

From: The Commanding Officer, U. S. S. LCG(L) 7.
To: Commander In Chief, United States Fleet.

Subj: Operation ████ - Report on.
- -

7.   Shortly after this time we opened fire, with both
guns directly over the bow. The first salvo from "B" gun fairly
blasted the crew of "A" gun, so we ordered silence on "B" gun.
We have no way of controlling our fire when shooting over the bow,
because of the design of our ship, however, the range was sufficient
to clear the assault beaches.

8.   At approximately 5,000 yards from the beach, we were
on the left flank of the boat lanes, and opened fire at a home on
the beach. This we fired at until the entire of our beach was obscured
by thick dust and smoke. It was the only object we could see thru
the smoke, at the time.

9.   The order came from Commander Task Unit 125.7.1,
aboard the U. S. S. LCG(L) 893, to proceed to the starboard flank
of the beach head and lend supporting fire there. Upon reaching
that area we sighted a pillbox which was firing on the troops on
the beach. This pillbox was at the end of a long sand-dune. We
immediately took up fire on this target and received several direct
hits. The gun never opened fire again while we were in that area,
the time was approximately 0745.

10.   On completion of that one run, we were ordered, by
Commander Task Group 125.7 aboard the LCH 209, to proceed to our
own area on the port flank, and investigate firing of a gun which
appeared to be mounted in an open casemate, and was firing upon
our tanks, which were approaching it. Our first shells had the
correct range and with one correction we were on the target. The
shots fell square on the emplacement, which we saw to burn most
of the day.

11.   We continued firing at targets of opportunity
such as homes, buildings etc., when we were fired upon by gun
emplacements in Grandcamp, our fire was immediately turned in that
direction. We do not know if we hit our target, nevertheless,
we saw no more firing from that direction.

12.   We continued to cruise up and down the shores of
Grandcamp, shooting at targets, which we thought may contain guns.

-2-

6 July 1944.

From: The Commanding Officer, U. S. S. LCG(L) 7.
To: Commander In Chief, United States Fleet.

Subj: Operation ████████ - Report on.
- -

13.   We had expended all our ready ammunition by 1000
and had pulled out, to the flank of the boat lanes to replenish
from the magazine. At this time we were ordered to the transport
area by Commander Task Group 125.7.

14.   We anchored in the transport area for the whole of
the remaining time.

15.   On the night of 6 June one LCV(P) came alongside,
which had lost its way.

16.   On D/ 1 an air raid accurred, and on each remaining night we were disturbed by the same accurance.

17.   It was D/ 7 when we weighed anchor at 0500 to
return to the United Kingdom.

Comments:

1.   We feel as though our assigned tasks were completed
to the best of our abilty. Our ship held up well under the strain,
however, there were slight damages, such as, lighting fixtures and
systems torn loose, and as the guns were old, the recoil cylinders
began to give us trouble, but we were able to continue fire just
the same.

2.   It is very difficult to keep proper station in
convoy with ships of such different speeds. The speed was far too
slow for this particular ship. Separation of such ships into
different convoys would seem advisable.

3.   Our arc of fire would be greatly increased if our
guns were more elevated, however, we were never at loss because
of this hindrance. Never once during the entire operation were we
urgently called upon to fire dead ahead.

4.   Had we more powerful binoculars it would have been
less difficult to distinguish gun emplacements that were well
camoflaged. The telescopic sights on the guns were much more
powerful then the binoculars on the bridge.

                              R. E. HONE,
                              Lt.(jg) USNR.

USS *Murphy* 8 June

June 8   0100 Using defensive equipment against RGN. 0159 to 0215
Laying smoke to protect heavy units. 0545 Secured from
General Quarters. Awaiting fire mission, attempting to
contact assigned fire control party. 1004 General Quarters.
1025 Under inaccurate fire of small gun at Pointe du Hoe.
1042 Fired two rounds at battery. No fire observed thereafter.
1220 Secured from General Quarters. 2225 Red alert, General

USS *O'Brien* After Action Report:

DD725/ A12-1
Serial 044
(WWO:ejp)

U. S. S. O'BRIEN

C O N F I D E N T I A L   21 June 1944

Subject: Chronological Narrative, June 5 - 17 (inclusive), Operations
U.S.S. O'BRIEN.
- -

June 6   0000 Steaming as before. Firing continued as above. Radar
screen showed few planes on bearing 140° T, range
20,000 yards not closing this convoy. Night action
believed to be friendly patrol vessels engaging "snooper"
aircraft.

          0330 Passed convoy U-3 abeam to port distance about 1000 yards.
U.S.S. MERIDETH was escorting this convoy.

          0503 Entered swept channel 1, proceeding to transport area.

          0720 Passed point K, Red and Green LCI groups proceeded to
assigned areas. Arrived at transport area at H hour
plus 50 minutes. Ten minutes ahead of scheduled time
of arrival. No stragglers or casualties enroute. This
convoy passed all navigational markers in accordance
with the prearranged plan. Squadron Commanders of the
LCI Squadrons kept their ships closed up and in position.
U.S.S. O'BRIEN proceeded to sector SE of transport area
and commenced A/S patrol on various courses at various
speeds as previously directed.

          2157 Shifted patrol sector to area SE of Red LCT anchorage.

          2233 Anchored in 10 fathoms of water on patrol station 4000
yards SE of LCT anchorage.

June 7   0640 Anchored as before. Underway, proceeding to area off
Chateau de le Barren to report to Commander Destroyer
Division 36 in U.S.S. HARDING for Shore bombardment.

          1013 Commenced firing on German Pill Box (coordinates 585964),
Chateau de le Barren, Normandy, France, as directed by
U. S. Army Ranger Fire Control Party # I. Opened fire
at range 2850; fired only one salvo.

DD725/ A12-1
Serial 044
(WWO:ejp)

U. S. S. O'BRIEN

C O N F I D E N T I A L   21 June 1944

Subject: Chronological Narrative, June 5 - 17 (inclusive), Operations
            U.S.S. O'BRIEN.

- -

June 7   1014   Ceased firing as directed by shore fire control group,
                  having expended six rounds 5"/38 caliber AA Common
                  ammunition. Observed enemy soldiers running from location.
                  "Rangers" continued their advance in this area. Standing
                  by for more targets.

          2026   Commenced firing on 2nd German Pill Box (coordinates
                  586931), Chateau de le Barren, Pointe de Hoe, Normandy,
                  France, as directed by U. S. Army Rangers. Opened fire
                  at range 3250 yards. Fired three ranging salvos, then,
                  shifted to rapid continous fire for thirty seconds, as
                  directed by shore fire control party.

          2033   Ceased firing on target, as directed by shore fire control
                  party, having expended 54 rounds of 5"/38 caliber AA
                  Common ammunition. Results not observed by this ship,
                  but shore fire control party reported "target destroyed".

          2035   Commenced firing on German Road Block (coordinates 586931),
                  holding up advance of our troops. Target designated by
                  U. S. Army Ranger fire control group, at Chateau de le
                  Barren, Normandy, France. Opened fire at range 3650
                  yards. Fired three ranging salvos, then, as directed by
                  shore fire control party, shifted to rapid continous fire
                  for one minute.

          2048   Ceased firing on target, as directed by shore fire control
                  party, having expended 86 rounds 5"/38 caliber AA Common
                  ammunition. Results of bombardment not observed but shore
                  fire control party reported "mission successful".

          2128   Commenced firing as directed by U. S. Army Rangers on
                  German Machine Gun Nest (coordinates 579937) at top of
                  100 foot cliff, which was blocking advance of Ranger
                  patrols along beach toward locks, located near Grande
                  Camp - Les Boins, Normandy, France. Opened fire at range
                  2550 yards. Fired one ranging salvo which straddled
                  target, then, shifted to rapid continous fire for thirty
                  seconds, as directed by shore fire control party.

DD725/ A12-1
Serial 044
(WWO:ejp)

U. S. S. O'BRIEN

C O N F I D E N T I A L   21 June 1944

Subject: Chronological Narrative, June 5 - 17 (inclusive), Operations
            U.S.S. O'BRIEN.
- -

June 7	2133	Ceased firing as directed by shore fire control party, having expended 60 rounds 5"/38 caliber AA Common ammunition. Results of bombardment were not available for observation, but shore fire control party reported "mission successful - nice job".
June 8	0000–2200	Lying to two miles to West of Port en Bessin awaiting orders Shore Fire Control Party 22.
	2248	Night air raid by enemy planes. Raid continued.
June 9	0027	Unidentified plane shot down by AA fire from shore batteries.
	0040	Second plane (unidentified) shot down by AA fire from shore batteries.
	0300	Bomb explosions sighted on shore. Went to General Quarters.
	0340	Air raids ceased.
	1030	Lying to in Omaha area awaiting orders from Shore Fire Control Party 18.
	2045	Took anti-E boat patrol on Dixie line station C-5.
	2215	Air raids commenced.
	2256	Unidentified merchant ship in British area bombed.
June 10	0344	Unidentified plane shot down by AA defenses ashore.
	0700	Proceeded and took up patrol as inshore fire support ship in sector North of Port en Bessin.
	2235	Shifted to anchorage about 2 miles west of Port en Bessin as inshore screen and AA support ship.

DD725/ A12-1
Serial 058   **U. S. S. O'BRIEN**

C O N F I D E N T I A L

Subject: Bombardment, Coast of France, by U.S.S. O'BRIEN, June 7,
            1944; Report of.

- -

GUNNERY DATA SHEET

1. Target – Four targets designated by U.S. Army Ranger Shore Firecontrol
            Party.
                Target #1 – German Pillbox (Coordinates 585934).
                    "   #2 – German Pillbox (Coordinates 586931).
                    "   #3 – German Road Block (Coordinates 579937).
                    "   #4 – German Machine Gun Nest (Coordinates 576939).

2. Mean Navigational Range.
                For Target #1 – 2850 yards.
                    "   "   #2 – 3250 yards.
                    "   "   #3 – 3650 yards.
                    "   "   #4 – 2550 yards.

3. Spot – U.S. Army Ranger Shore Firecontrol Party.

4. Method of Fire – Indirect.

5. Battery – 3 5"/38 cal. Dual Purpose Twin Mounts, Mk. 38 Mod. 1.

6. Number of guns firing in salvo – Six.

7. Ammunition for Ranging.
                Target #1 – One salvo (6 rounds 5"/38 cal. AA Common).
                    "   #2 – Three salvos (18 rounds 5"/38 cal. AA Common).
                    "   #3 – Three salvos (18 rounds 5"/38 cal. AA Common).
                    "   #4 – One salvo (6 rounds 5"/38 cal. AA Common).

8. Ammunition for Neutralization.
                Target #1 – Six rounds (One salvo).
                    "   #2 – Thirty-six rounds.
                    "   #3 – Sixty-eight rounds.
                    "   #4 – Fifty-four rounds.

9. Total ammunition expenditure – 206 Rounds 5"/38 cal. AA Common Ammunitio

10. Salvo Analysis – None.

11. Effectiveness – As reported by U.S. Army Rangers to ship.
                Target #1 – No Report.
                    "   #2 – Target Destroyed.
                    "   #3 – Mission Successful.
                    "   #4 – Mission Successful – Nice Shooting.

The full USS *Satterlee* Report:

U.S.S. SATTERLEE (DD626)

Care Fleet Post Office,
New York, N.Y.,
21 June 1944.

SECRET

PART II - COMMENTS AND RECOMMENDATIONS

1. Plans, Planning and Orders.

Plans for the operation were complete and well prepared. The organization of the various plans was adequate and clear. There was no doubt as
to exactly what was required of this ship. It was fortunate that this ship
was in Belfast where the CTF 129 gave orders to open the TOP SECRET and BIGOT
instructions. This gave sufficient time to study the orders and prepare for the
operation, if we had had to wait until receipt of later orders from other
authorities we never would have been able to make the necessary preparations.

It is recommended that one high authority set this date by a general
message which will allow plenty of time for preparations. The fact that the
ships are still operating during this preparation period should be kept in
mind. The briefing conference on the ANCON for Commanding Officers and the
conference for Gunnery Officers in Weymouth were of no value. Too much time
was spent in argument and detailed discussion on subjects which could have been
better left for the small groups concerned to discuss privately. It is recommended that briefing conferences be better planned.

2. Rehearsals.

The rehearsal exercise ▆▆▆▆ and a shore bombardment exercise at
SLAPTON SANDS were of the greatest value in preparing for the invasion. The
general plan and the small details for exercise ▆▆▆▆ were exactly the same
as for operation ▆▆▆▆ for this vessel. During this exercise communications
with the Shore Fire Control Party of the Ranger unit were very good. The
value of this rehearsal cannot be over emphasized. It was extremely well
planned and executed, and provided many valuable lessons.

3. Weather. The Approach to the Assault Area.

The weather was terrible. Station keeping during the approach with
the mine-sweepers was difficult. During the 360° turn, ships and small craft
in channels 3 and 4 became mixed and confused. During this time and again
later near the transport area, the position of the ships supporting the minesweepers was such that they could have offered very little protection against
enemy surface craft. It was fortunate that no opposition or mines were
encountered.

After H-hour, we watched the Ranger units approaching the beach and saw
that the bad weather made it very difficult and caused heavy loss. The weather
delayed the landing past the scheduled time and caused the element of surprise
to be lost and caused a great reduction in the effectiveness of the preparation
firing. When it became obvious (about 0200) that weather would delay the landings,
H-hour should have been delayed. Ammunition available would not permit continuing preparation firing from the scheduled commencement until the delayed time
of arrival of the first waves on the beach.

Page 1 - Part II.

U.S.S. SATTERLEE (DD626)

SECRET

Care Fleet Post Office,
New York, N.Y.,
21 June 1944.

PART II * COMMENTS AND RECOMMENDATIONS (Continued).

4. Beach Identification.

There was very little information concerning the beach defenses around POINTE DU HOE. There was very little material for advance study for identification of targets westward of POINT ET RAZ DE LA PERCEE. As a result it was impossible to locate targets 88 and 89 except by grid coordinates and the direct fire could not be spotted. Later information revealed that these machine gun emplacements were very well camouflaged positions in the face of the cliff. Preparation firing could have been greatly improved if pencil sketches of the face of this cliff had been provided.

5. Naval Gunfire Support.

Many lessons were learned in the gunfire support mission.

Our Shore Fire Control Party came aboard before the Fabius I exercise. We worked with them in a later shore bombardment exercise. We had several communication drills. They came aboard again in Portland just before D-day. There was a complete and intimate understanding between the ship and the Ranger Shore Fire Control Party. As a result, during the close support firing, communications were uniformly excellent. It was as if the Shore Fire Control Party was in our C.I.C.

Incidently, these fine young men were a great source of inspiration to the SATTERLEE. Everyone who had contact with them was greatly impressed by their enthusiasm, determination, and courage. They knew they had a tough assignment and were ready for it. And they had the ship ready to back them. To this one factor can be attributed the success of our mission.

There could be no better method of authentication than to send "Hello, Rocky", and then to hear the familiar voice come back "Hello, Joe, this is Rocky". This should provide a valuable lesson for future operations.

From daylight until the Rangers approached the beach there was no sign of life or activity around POINTE DU HOE. It looked as if the bombardment had knocked them out completely. There were no visible targets. Fire was reduced to conserve ammunition because we did not know for how long the weather would delay the landing. This was a mistake. We should have continued neutralization fire at the scheduled rate against the face of the cliff and we should have called on the TEXAS, who was available, to support us in this mission. As the Rangers hit the beach, the Germans came out of their holes and opened up with their machine guns. From then on we were firing on the Germans directly and on the points where machine-gun fire could be detected. We should never have eased up enough to allow the enemy time enough to get out of their hiding places. This mistake can be attributed to two causes: lack of experience of the Commanding Officer in actual shore bombardment and over-confidence in the effectiveness of the air bombardment. There were no failures of material.

Page 2 - Part II.

Below: part of the **After Action Report from USS** *Shoebrick*.

[Author: This portion of the account is the official record of the *Shoebrick*'s firing. However, I received a written account of this same action some years ago. In that account the guns were placed closer to Maisy and somewhat in line with the co-ordinates for the position at Foucher's Farm. Considering this account seems to be unequivocal in its statement of co-ordinates and will have been taken from gunnery logs, I am now led to believe that the hand written account of this incident I hold, is in error and that these particular guns were further away from Foucher's farm when fired upon. Given the passage of time and the similarity in suggested calibre and location, it is an easy mistake for a veteran to make. That said, it is equally possible that any undamaged guns remaining at Foucher's farm were pulled back by half a mile at some point. At the time of writing this, I do not have the answer.]

From about 0700 occasional two and four gun salvos were seen to land in open water about 4,000 yards to eastward of the boat lane and about the same distance off the beach. The splashes were about the size of those caused by 105mm guns, and since they kept landing in approximately the same location, it was thought this battery had insufficient range to cause any damage. This belief was wrong, for at 0740 salvos commenced landing close aboard. Up to this time, in view of various craft seen to be mined, great care was taken to stay within the swept channel limits, however since these salvos were landing uncomfortably close, it was considered necessary to maneuver outside the swept channel to stay clear. This fire was observed to be coming from near a church tower at approximate coordinates 507899, and at 0746 this battery was taken under fire. Fire was ceased at 0750 as the battery had ceased firing and was thought neutralized. At 0819 a six gun salvo from the same battery again landed close aboard and at 0820 fire was resumed on this target. By this time many loaded landing craft awaiting their turn to go into the beach had drifted with the current down in the area where salvos from this battery had been landing.

Fire was continued on this dangerous target until 0845. Occasional air bursts were used and the salvos were walked across the target many times both in range and deflection. This battery was not seen to fire again and the coordinates of this target were given the GLENNON, on being relieved by her at 1026. A total of 438 rounds of AA common, 50 rounds of common and 2 rounds of white phosphorus projectiles had been expended during the morning shore bombardment.

USS *Texas* After Action Report:

```
BB35/A16-3
Serial 002
```

SECRET
SECRET

23 June 1944.

Subject: Chronological Narrative of Operations of U.S.S.
            TEXAS for period 3 June 1944 - 17 June 1944
            inclusive, Operation ███████

- -

15 June 1944
0630 - Commenced final bombardment for the
period to 17 June, firing enemy troop concentrations in woods near La Rommeire. Army was to
follow this bombardment by an attack which
was successfully accomplished - 24 rounds of
14" HC were expended in 20 single gun and two
2 - gun salvos.

4.   Summary of Bombardments, 3 - 17 June inclusive

MAIN BATTERY

Date & Time	Map Ref.	Target	Type & No. of rounds fired	Type of Spotting	Remarks
6 June 0550-0624	586939	6 155mm guns Pte du Hoe	155 AP 100 HC	Aircraft	Results excellent. Area neutralized. Hits on casemates and emplacements.
6 June 0626-0630	575939	Strong point, MGs and pill boxes	11 AP	Aircraft	Direct hits reported by air spot.
6 June 0742-0747	586932	Fortified position	17 HC	Aircraft	Fire effective reported by air spot.
6 June 0810-0824	533918	Fortified position 4x155mm mortars.	26 HC	Aircraft	Fire effective reported by plane. Several direct hits on emplacement.
6 June 1033-1056	568893	Mobile field battery	40 HC	Aircraft	Fire effective reported by plane.
6 June 1117-1128	618925	Gun position in wooded area	26 HC	Aircraft	Fire effective Gun silenced.

BB35/A16-3
Serial 002

SECRET
SECRET

23 June 1944.

Subject: Chronological Narrative of Operations of U.S.S.
            TEXAS for period 3 June 1944 - 17 June 1944
            inclusive, Operation ████████

- -

Date & Time	Map Ref.	Target	Type & No. of rounds fired	Type of Spotting	Remarks
6 June 1223-1230	646917	Exit D-1, enemy mortar battery behind hedge and wall.	6 HC	Foretop spot	Battery neutralized. Personnel scattered.
6 June 1400-1440	550910	Troop transports, flak station, powerhouse, ammunition dump.	18 HC	Aircraft	Direct hits on ammunition dump and powerhouse. Transports disorganized. Two guns destroyed.
6 June 1941-2011	605877	Troops at crossroads	24 HC	Aircraft	Fire effective. Troops despersed.
6 June 2045-2109	610885	Enemy vehicles	18 HC	Aircraft	Fire effective. Several hits.
7 June 0804-0809	647866	Troops and vehicles at Formigny	10 HC	Aircraft	Buildings razed. Fire effective.
7 June 0841-0901	646866	Troops and vehicles at Formigny	25 HC	Aircraft	Fire effective. Many hits, starting fires.
7 June 0915-1015	643839	Strong point Troops at Trevieres	8 AP 50 HC	Aircraft	Results excellent. Town laid to waste-many fires.
7 June 2048-2110	611809	Troop and vehicle column	26 HC	Aircraft	Fire effective. Dispersed troops.

3B35/A16-3
Serial 002

SECRET

SECRET

23 June 1944.

Subject: Chronological Narrative of Operations of U.S.S.
          TEXAS for period 3 June 1944 - 17 June 1944
          inclusive, Operation ▆▆▆▆▆▆▆

- -

Date & Time	Map Ref.	Target	Type & No. of rounds fired	Type of Spotting	Remarks
8 June 0801-0905	501855	Strong point, troops(Isigny)	32AP 32HC	Aircraft	Very effective. H-it on flak barge in canal. Hit on buildings. Enemy forced to seek cover. Troop movements halted. Many fires started. RR track destroyed.
8 June 0910-0935	501855	Strong point, troops(Isigny)	18AP	Aircraft	Enemy held buildings destroyed and hit on depot. Neutralized area keeping enemy from extingushing many fires.
8 June 1404-1455	643839	Strong point at Trevieres	24AP	SFCP	Buildings destroyed. Enemy movements hampered. Neutralized strong point.
15 June 0630-0700	459816	Strong point Pillboxes Troops	10HC	Aircraft	Fire effective. Neutralized area of target.
15 June 0700-0730	455812	Fortified houses. Strong point.	14HC	Aircraft and SFCP	Fire effective. Houses hit and fire started.

SECONDARY BATTERY

Date & Time	Map Ref.	Target	Type & No. of rounds fired	Type of Spotting	Remarks
6 June 0550-0623	645919	Enemy concentration of pill boxes, anti-tank guns and machine guns.	91HC 99Com.	Foretop	No enemy action observed in area after bombardment completed.

```
BB35/A16-3
Serial 002
SECRET                                          23 June 1944.

SECRET

Subject:        Chronological Narrative of Operations of U.S.S.
                TEXAS for period 3 June 1944 - 17 June 1944
                inclusive, Operation ███████
- - - - - - - - - - - - - - - - - - - - - - - - - - - - - - - - -
```

Date & Time	Map Ref.	Target	Type & No. of rounds fired	Type of Spotting	Remarks
6 June 1223-1226	665906	Pillboxes and snipers in houses Exit D-1.	9 HC	Foretop	Hits in enemy held area, partially neutralizing.
6 June 1231-1235	664905	Exit D-1 Mortar firing & Snipers taking cover in house.	7 HC	Foretop	Several direct hits on house. Enemy guns silenced.
6 June 1815-1820	666903	Exit D-1 Church Steeple used as observation post for mortar fire.	9 HC	Foretop	Fire effective. Direct hits on church steeple.
6 June 1857-1902	665904	Enemy mortar personnel and snipers.	24 HC	Foretop	Fire effective. Direct hits on house and wall concealing snipers.
6 June 1922-1925	668903	Small troop concentration and mortar fire	15 HC	Foretop	Fire effective. Direct hits on house where enemy guns concealed.
7 June 1820-1830	645846	Troop concentration and enemy mortar fire party.	9 HC	Foretop	Mortar neutralized.
8 June 0955-1000	579938	Enemy concentration of tanks firing into our advancing troops.	9 HC	Foretop	One hit reported in area by SFCP.

TABLE OF GUNFIRE SUPPORT, U.S.S. TEXAS

TARGET	Map Grid Ref	Date	ComFire	Cease	AP	HC	Total	Airspot
1. Pt. Du Hoe	586939	6/6	0550	0624	155	100	235	"
2. T88, 89 Fortified Pos.	575939	6/6	0626	0630	11	0	11	"
3. T85 Fortified Pos.	586932	6/6	0742	0747	0	17	17	"
4. T5 Fortified Pos.	533918	6/6	0810	0824	0	26	26	"
5. Mobile Field Batt.	568893	6/6	1033	1056	0	40	40	"
6. Gun Pos in trees	618925	6/6	1117	1128	0	26	26	"
7. Exit D-1	646917	6/6	1223	1250	0	6	6	Foretop Spot
8. Troop transports, Ammu. Dump, Flak. Powerhouse	550910	6/6	1400	1440	0	18	18	Airspot
9. Crossroads	605877	6/6	1941	2011	0	24	24	"
10. Vehicles	610885	6/6	2045	2109	0	18	18	"
11. Formigny	647866	6/7	0804	0809	0	10	10	"
12. Town	646866	6/7	0841	0901	0	25	25	"
13. Trevieres	643839	6/7	0915	1015	8	50	58	"
14. Troop & Vehicle column	611809	6-7	2048	2110	0	26	26	"
15. Isigny	501855	6/8	0801	0905	32	32	64	"
16. Isigny	501855	6/8	0910	0935	18	0	18	"
17. Trevieres	643839	6/8	1404	1455	24	0	24	SFCP
18. House	459816	6/15	0630	0700	0	10	10	Airspot
19. Pillbox, House	455812	6/15	0700	0730	0	14	14	"
				Total	248	442	690	

UNITED STATES ATLANTIC FLEET

U. S. S. TEXAS

File:BB35/A12-1
Serial 089

% Fleet P. O.
New York, N. Y.
June 1944.

CONFIDENDIAL

WAR DIARY

6 June -

    Steaming as before in company with TG 124.9 followed
by Assault Convoy O-1 proceeding down swept channel #3 at
various courses and speeds to conform to buoyed channel.
Several groups of landing craft scheduled to pass down
channel #2 to UTAH Beach were apparently carried to Eastward by the strong tide and were crossing channel #3 ahead
and through formations of Force "O". Individual ships
were maneuvered radically to avoid these craft and to allow
them to pass. By 0100 TG 124.9 was clear of all these
craft and proceeded uneventfully down the remainder of the
Channel arriving in the transport area at 0220. Heavy AA
fire was observed over the beach areas. By 0300 TEXAS and
GLASGOW were maneuvered into Western Fire support lane clear
of the transport area and TEXAS anchored to short stay in
position 092° 11.8 miles from Iles St. Marcouf to await
dawn for scheduled pre H-hour bombardment of assigned targets. Observed heavy air bombardment of 155mm battery
(Target T-1) on Pointe du Hoe and on batteries in Utah
beach. At 0441 underway to take up assigned bombardment
position 12000 yds from shore in the Western Fire Support
Lane.

At 0550 (H-40) commenced main battery bombardment of German Coast defense battery of 6 - 155mm guns on Pointe du Hoe and Secondary Battery bombardment of Strongpoint west of defile leading from Omaha Beach to Vierville-sur-mer (Exit D-1). At 0625 lifted fire from Pointe du Hoe and shifted to strongpoint on cliffs 1000 yds west of Pointe du Hoe. At 0630 (H hour) ceased fire with all batteries and at 0641 anchored to short stay in position 111°true 11 miles from Iles St. Marcouf to await call for fire from SFCP #5 scheduled to land at 0727. Communication with the SFCP was not established at any time on D-day but fire was undertaken on targets of opportunity observed by spotting planes on troop concentrations and batteries well inland clear of the beach heads. A complete table of fire delivered on targets has been prepared and attached hereto. The complete details of fire will not be set forth in this text.

At 0742 opened fire with main battery expending 17 rds of HC ammunition and at 0810 opened fire on howitzer battery expending 20 rds of HC ammunition. At 1033 opened fire with main battery expending 40 rds of HC ammunition and again at 1117 opened fire on new target expending 26 rds of HC. All fire was delivered by air spot and the air spotter reported all targets completely demolished.

During the period the assault of the beach by landing craft was being carried out with a very heavy concentration of fire of all types being delivered on beach heads by special landing craft fitted to deliver rocket and gun fire on strongpoints. The initial landing was accomplished but apparently became stalled by snipers, unreduced pillboxes and strongpoints particularly in area of beach near Exit D-1 at Vierville-sur-mer. The Exit was impossible due to machine guns in houses lining the exit and concealed howitzer battery was delivering deverstating fire on the adjacent beach. At 1207 the TEXAS got underway and moved into position 3000 yds off Exit D-1 to clear out the snipers and machine guns with main battery fire opening fire at 1223. This fire plus that of several destroyers completely demolished all structures in the Exit reducing them to rubble. The steeple of the church in Vierville-sur-mer was neatly sawn off by destroyer fire apparently destroying the German OP as the howitzer fire on the beach slackened and became erratic. At 1313 TEXAS anchored in position bearing 356° distant 2.8 miles from church spire in Vierville-sur-mer. Increased activity was observed on the beach as the Army units previously pinned down by the howitzer fire began to form up and clear the beach. At 1400 delivered main battery fire on AA battery west of Vierville. Delivered 5" fire on suspected OP in Vierville at 1815 and on crossroads SW of Vierville with main battery at 1941. Most of the fire during the afternoon was direct fire on the beach employing top spotters.

At 2230 darkened ship. Air attack developed about dusk and several planes were seen to fall in flames from AA and Flak from transports and landing craft. TEXAS did not engage in fire and was not attacked.

7 June –

Anchored in Baie de la Seine off Vierville-sur-mer, France bearing 356° distant 2.8 miles from church spire in Vierville. Ship in Condition 1E, Material Condition Z. The RGM (Radio Guided Missiles) Counter measure, team reported several bombing signals heard and jammed. Observed heavy air bombardment of enemy positions behind Omaha Beach. At 0750 received orders from CTG 124.9 to shift berth clear of beach to avoid falling enemy shells and to clear range for GLASGOW which was anchored about 1000 yds outboard of us. At 0808 anchored in position bearing 113° distant 10 miles from Ile du Large, Iles St. Marcouf. At 0841 delivered main battery fire on the town of Surrain and at 0915 shifted fire to the town of Trevieres for one hour of fire against enemy troop concentrations in the town.

At 1607 secured crew from General Quarters after more than 42 hrs at Battle Stations. The system of feeding personnel on stations developed during training period in Belfast proved quite successful and at least two hot meals were served the crew every day during Condition 1E.

Word was received from destroyers close inshore at Pointe du Hoe that the Ranger Battalion which had landed there at H hour on D day was still isolated from our own troops. They were running low on provisions and ammunition and had a number of prisoners and casualties to be evacuated. Two LCVP's were obtained by CTG 124.9 and loaded with provisions and ammunition from the destroyers and the TEXAS and sent in to relieve the Rangers. At 1730 the LCVP's returned with 28 German prisoners (including one officer and several Italians from a labor battalion) and 34 wounded Rangers. The prisoners were fed and then questioned by several officers proficient in German. Questioning revealed that the assault had been entirely unexpected, at least in this area, and that no warning or alert had been sounded. The first real warning of the attack was the sight of the assault force covering the Baie de la Seine at daybreak of the 6th. The prisoners were transferred to LST 266 for further transportation to England.

The wounded Rangers were given medical attention and for the most part were suffering from minor wounds. One Ranger died during the night from very severe abdominal wounds.

At 1815 sent crew to General Quarters preparatory to opening fire and at 1820 opened fire with Secondary battery firing only 6 rds due to difficulty in controlling the 5" 51 guns for indirect fire. At 2048 opened fire with main battery at suspected position of mortar which was shelling the beach.

8 June -

Anchored in Baie de la Seine off Vierville-sur-mer in
position 10 miles bearing 113° from Iles St. Marcouf. Ship
in condition IE, Material Condition Z. At 0015 got underway to shift berth on suspicion that our position may have
been spotted and reported. At 0045 anchored in position
9.8 miles bearing 104° from Ile du Large, Iles St. Marcouf.
Received air raid warning for Western Task Force Area. RGM
team reported bombing signals received and jammed. At 0140
enemy planes sighted in area flying just below overcast.
Observed heavy AA fire over transport area with several
planes falling in flames. At 0143 Opened fire with 20mm
and 40mm AA batteries at plane approaching on starboard
quarter altitude about 500 ft. Plane sheared off and crossed stern through heavy flak and disappeared off the port
quarter. No visible damage done. 208 rds of 40mm and 538
rds of 40mm ammunition expended. At 0208 the destroyer
screen reported possible presence of "E" boats but no action
developed. At 0552 underway to take up position to fire
on town of Isigney in accordance with request from Army
to destroy the town. At 0707 anchored in position 7.5 miles
bearing 116° from Iles St. Marcouf. At 0801 opened fire
with main battery, fire continuing until 0935. Nearly all
the major installations of the town were reported destroyed
by air spotters. At 0955 fired with secondary battery on
enemy shore battery ceasing fire at 1000 and secured from
General Quarters at 1115 and set Condition II M. At 1404
commenced firing on town of Trevieres under direction of
SFCP. At 1455 lost communication with SFCP and ceased fire.
At 2221 underway to shift berth for night anchoring at 2250
in position bearing 043°t distant 9400 yds from Pointe du
Hoe. Sent crew to General Quarters and set condition IE
for the night. No enemy air or surface activity in area.

9 June -

Anchored in Baie de la Seine in position 043° distant
9400 yds from Pointe du Hoe near Omaha Beach. Weather
overcast with light rain. At 0005 heard many planes passing overhead and saw heavy AA fire in transport area. At
0045 saw gun fire flashes bearing 310°t and received word
from destroyer screen that "E" boats were trying to break
through into Utah Area. Engagement continued intermittently
until dawn as the destroyers turned back every attempt to
break through. At 0630 received orders for TEXAS to leave
the Assault Area and proceed to Plymouth, England to replenish fuel and ammunition, leaving the area at about
0900. At 0850 Rear Admiral C.F. BRYANT, USN, CTG 124.9
transferred his flag to the ARKANSAS and at 0900 TEXAS got
underway proceeding via swept channel #34 to Pt Z thence
via British war channels to Plymouth.

USS *Ancon* (Flagship) After Action Report:

ACTION REPORT
ASSAULT ON VIERVILLE-COLLEVILLE SECTOR
COAST OF NORMANDY

PART II
CHRONOLOGICAL RECORD OF EVENTS

The following is a chronological record of events from the time of sortie of Assault Force "O" on 5 June until the return of the Flagship to Devonport, England on 29 June.

5 June (D-1)

1600	Convoy O-1 of Assault Force "O" (CTF 124) USS ANCON, guide, commenced sortie from Portland Harbor, Portland, Dorset.
1743	Ordered FRANKFORD to return to USS CHARLES CARROLL, ascertain cause of delay in sortie, and report steps being taken to correct.
1912	Commander Destroyer Squadron 18 reported all transports out of Portland Harbor and directed all ships to close up in convoy formation at best speed.
2152	USS ANCON altered course to starboard by emergency turn to clear floating mine.
2312	Senior Officer, 4th Minesweeping Flotilla, reported completion of minesweeping.
2350	Observed A.A. fire on starboard bow.

6 June (D day)

0115	Observed anti-aircraft fire on starboard bow.
0208	ComBatDiv 5 reported his force delayed by minesweepers ahead.
0251	Anchored with 45 fathoms of chain in transport area. Position USS ANCON 41° 29' N 00° 42' W.
0325	Observed heavy enemy A.A. fire ashore.
0355	MS 104 reported that center boat lane was danned.
0400	Heavy A.A. fire and bombing ashore in OMAHA Area.
0410	MS 104 reported Western Fire Support Channel swept with negative results.
0522	CinC Portsmouth reported E-boat activity suspected north of Cap Levi.
0605	HMS SCYLLA reported 3 enemy destroyers bearing 072 distance 9 miles from position 49° 24' N 00° 14' W on course 210.
0606	Senior Officer, 31st Minesweeping Flotilla reported sweep of Approach Channel 3 and Transport Area 34 Completed.
0614	Senior Officer, 167th Minesweeping Flotilla reported sweep of Western Fire Support Channel completed.
0632	Ordered CTG 124.4 to land the 115th R.C.T. at H/4 hours unless otherwise directed.

6 June (D-day)

0635	First wave landed on DOG GREEN; first wave landed on EASY RED.
0636	Second wave landed on DOG GREEN.
0638	Second wave landed EASY GREEN.
0641	PC 552 reported that DD tanks for EASY GREEN foundered.
0644	Com LCT Flot 19 reported LCT 2041 about to be abandoned at sea.
0645	Ordered Control Vessels to report time of landings on all beaches.
0647	LCC 50 reported one LCA with troops capsized on the right flank of DOG GREEN.
0705	HMS TALYBONT reported targets 82 and 83 still 50% active.
0729	USS SATTERLEE reported she had established communications with Rangers ashore at Pointe du Hoe.
0745	Granted permission to CTG 124.6 to close beach by swept channel to assist damaged LCAs.
0805	HMS TANATSIDE reported completion of all bombardment missions (100% of her bombardment ammunition expended).
0807	8th wave landed on EASY RED. Control vessel EASY RED unable to distinguish all waves between first at 0635 and eighth but believes they are evenly spaced and on time. Boats returning to USS THOMAS JEFFERSON report mines near beach endangering landings and many boats swamped as a result of obstacles and seas.
0817	CTG 124.13 ordered to send 5 rescue boats to the vicinity of beach for rescue work.
0824	CTG 124.9 reported that enemy batteries at MAISY apparently still in commission and that he was keeping them under fire.
0840	15th wave landed on EASY RED.
0843	Senior Officer 167th Minesweeping Flotilla reported no mines found in sweeps completed so far.
0845	HMS TANATSIDE reported to CTF 124 that all targets were successfully bombarded.
0849	Report received that First Battalion of 116th Infantry had landed but were being retarded by machine gun fire.
0859	CTG 124.4 reported that obstacles not cleared and heavy machine gun fire on beach DOG GREEN.
0900	Army observer in boat 100 yards off DOG RED beach reported several companies of 16th Infantry were on EASY RED and FOX RED beaches, enemy artillery and machine gun fire still effective, about 30 LCTs standing by to land, obstacles appeared thicker than in photographs, LCI 85 hit and burning after unloading, 2 LCTs burning and landing resuming on DOG beaches.
0909	Ordered CTG 124.9 to locate and silence an enemy battery back of DOG GREEN which was firing on beach.
0915	CTG 124.8 reported that he could find no targets of opportunity without endangering own troops and requested information on likely targets for LCGs.

6 June (D-day)

0921	CTF 124 ordered MS 31 to sweep OHIO, OREGON, and KANSAS areas outside of boat lanes and 104th MMS to make magnetic sweep in same areas.
0928	CTG 124.4 reported that enemy gunfire on exit at DOG GREEN and battery behind DOG GREEN were hindering landing.
0930	HMS PRINCE LEOPOLD reported that Rangers had landed safely but against heavy opposition. Beach obstructions not cleared.
0930	CTF 124 informed CTG 124.4 that there were DUKWs in distress between his position and the beach.
0941	CTF 124 informed 124.9 of a target near exit of DOG GREEN which was believed to be causing trouble.
0945	ComBatDiv 5 relayed a report from plane that batteries at MAISY were completely destroyed but that he was unable to have report verified by Shore Fire Control Party.
0951	LCC 40 reported very few LCTs landing on DOG GREEN, and no sign of DUKWs.
0955	CTG 124.3 reported many wounded at DOG RED needing evacuation.
1001	CTG 124.4 reported that tanks at exit DOG ONE were held up by cross fire by machine guns.
1002	USS TEXAS reported enemy battery at MAISY knocked out.
1006	Informed ComBatDiv 5 that fighter bombers had reported MAISY batteries destroyed.
1016	Informed CTG 124.9 of many reports of machine gun and mortar fire on DOG GREEN, and ordered him to render all assistance possible.
1020	Com LCT(A) Flot reported for ferry service. Instructed to report to Assault Group Commanders.
1026	Informed USS ARKANSAS and CTG 124.9 of heavy shell fire on DOG RED and ordered them to endeavor to locate and destroy enemy batteries.
1030	CTG 124.4 reported that underwater obstacles no longer visible due to rising tide and gaps on DOG GREEN and CHARLIE not marked. Beachmaster EASY RED reported little progress made by LCTs landing on FOX and EASY RED beaches.
1032	CTG 124.4 reported machine gun fire on right flank of DOG GREEN.
1040	CTG 124.4 reported DOG GREEN beach not favorable for landing due to mines.
1100	Headquarters V Corps reported to headquarters First Army aboard USS ACHERNAR that DOG WHITE and DOG GREEN beach obstacles not breached by 060910; FOX GREEN and EASY RED beaches not clear of enemy fire by 1010; LCT and LCI(L) unable to unload on these beaches; 116th Infantry Division moving along slowly; General Wyman instructed to reinforce with the 18th Infantry where needed.
1100	LCIs 408, 409, 411, 412, 554 reported landing on EASY RED; met by some artillery fire.
1100	Control Vessel EASY RED reported "Conditions of beaches opposite exits still critical. Beaches between exits drawing occasional artillery and mortar fire.

6 June (D day)

1110   CTF-122 informed CTF-124 that he desired transports to depart for
        UK or move south of DIXIE line by 1600 at which time he expected
        to form the area screen.

1120   CTG-124.4 reported large number of landing craft lying off DOG
        Beaches because of heavy gun fire on EASY GREEN, DOG WHITE and
        DOG RED; stated that more gun fire required on exit DOG GREEN
        and behind EASY GREEN.

1128   Beachmaster EASY RED informed division commander aboard ANCON
        that enemy holding vigorously.

1130   PC-552 informed CTF-124 that because so many craft were waiting
        to land on FOX GREEN it was holding up all further waves at line
        of departure at 1230. CTG-124.3 directed that waves proceed to
        beach.

1137   USS THOMAS JEFFERSON informed Transport Division 3 that Germans
        leaving post and surrendering to American Soldiers. Fire support
        on EASY GREEN reported excellent.

1140   V Corps observer informed CG V Corps that troops were advancing up
        West slope of exit EASY ONE. "Thanks due Destroyers".

1144   Informed CTG-124.8 and CTG-124.9 that more gun fire was required
        on exit DOG GREEN and behind EASY GREEN.

1145   CTG-124.5 informed CTF-124 that he estimated completion of
        unloading of Assault Group O-3 by 1530.

1146   Ordered control vessels O-1, O-2, O-3 to rush all infantry
        elements to beach.

1153   1st Battalion informed 116th Infantry that help was needed along
        beach.

1157   CTG-124.6 informed CTF-124 that all ships and craft of Assault
        Group O-4 were unloaded.

1202   Control Vessel EASY RED informed USS DIX that FOX GREEN Beach
        was not yet securely held.

1208   ComBatDiv 5 informed CTF-124 that he was moving in close to
        beaches in order to keep in touch with situation.

1210   Inquired of CTG-124.6 if all Rangers had landed on POINTE DU HOE.
        Reply that only two companies of Rangers had landed at POINTE
        DU HOE, remainder on DOG GREEN.

1211   Order CTG-124.4 to instruct his beachmasters to request fire
        through Shore Fire Control Party, if possible.

1225   CTG-124.4 informed CTF-124 that debarkation of troops from
        transports of Assault Group O-2 was completed.

1228   Deputy Assault Commander O-1 reported he was sending LCMs to
        assist in landing 18th Infantry in case needed.

1230   Control Vessel EASY RED informed LCH-87 that Chief of Staff of
        1st Division was aboard and requested LCH-87 to advise on
        condition of gaps and beach obstacles.

6 June (D day)

1230 Commander LCT Flot 19 relayed report that Beach EASY RED was closed by enemy fire and inquired if he should continue to beach LCTs or if CTF-124 intended to shell the beach.

1235 Requested information from USS SATTERLEE on whereabouts of Rangers. Reply that Rangers were at position 586934.

1239 Control Vessel DOG GREEN informed CTF-124 that he had no Rhino ferries on hand at line of departure and that beach was temporarily closed due to congestion.

1240 CTF-124 advised CTF-122 that he expected transport unloading to be nearly complete by 061600; that they would sail as soon as possible and that he considered it inadvisable to shift their positions at this time.

1246 CTG-124.3 forwarded to CTF-124 a combined summary of Boat Officers reports as follows: Situation at FOX GREEN and EASY RED Beaches extremely critical heavy machine gun fire; unloading of LCI and LCT delayed by lack of channels through beach obstacles; only one DD tank reported landing on EASY RED; first wave of EMPIRE ANVIL LCA reported foundered; strong currents causing landing craft to land on wrong beaches.

1250 V Corps observer informed CG V Corps that enemy artillery firing on craft on beach EASY RED. Observer believed craft could be seen from VIERVILLE Church Spire.

1255 ComTransDiv 3 reported following information with reference to DOG GREEN waves: five boats of second wave beached 3 minutes late, one boat sinking due to underwater obstacles; 8 boats of 4th wave beached 5 minutes late and one 20 minutes late; craft in great difficulty in passing through obstacles; 5 boats of 5th wave beached 15 minutes late; beach appeared heavily mined; 6 craft lost.

1256 CTF-124 ordered PC-552 to give priority in landing to craft carrying infantry.

1300 Assistant Div. Comdr. 1st Div. informed CG 1st Div. that 16th Infantry had taken COLLEVILLE at 061233.

1328 Ordered CTG-124.8 to direct LCG to fire on church steeple in VIERVILLE.

1334 V Corps observer informed CG V Corps of a general advance up slope EASY RED and continued advance up FOX RED with some men moving on ridge towards PORT EN BESSIN at 1200.

1341 CTG-124.9 informed CTF-124 that DOG Beaches were clear of opposition and ready for landing troops; no opposition on EASY Beaches and troops ashore apparently awaiting infantry reinforcements; and that all fire support ships were awaiting target assignments from Army.

6 June (D-day)

1345   LCI 86 informed CTF 124 that DOG RED and EASY GREEN beaches were
       only beaches being used; that much congestion existed near beach;
       and that he was moving LCTs and Rhinos back to primary control
       vessel.

1400   Brig. Gen. Hoge, CG Prov. Eng. Spec. Brig. Group, and party left
       USS ANCON to set up headquarters on the beach.

1417   Secondary Control Vessel DOG RED informed ComTransDiv 3 that DOG
       RED and EASY GREEN were being shelled again; situation difficult;
       any help in gunfire support would be appreciated. This informa-
       tion passed to CTG 124.8 and CTG 124.9.

1430   ComLCIGroup 34 asked CTF 124 if disabled ships should return to
       Portland. Reply affirmative.

1430   Com Force B reported to CTF 124 with convoy BAKER TWO.

1431   CTG 124.4 informed CTF 124 that he estimated transports would be
       ready to proceed as follows: TransDiv 1, 1700; TransDiv 3, 1500;
       TransDiv 97, 1700.

1443   CTG 124.9 informed CTF 124 that church steeple VIERVILLE destroyed.

1445   Control Vessel DOG GREEN informed CTF 124 that he had been unable
       to unload Rhino Ferries on DOG GREEN or DOG RED beaches due to
       heavy enemy fire.

1458   Assigned anchorages to Com Force B and Com Convoy Group O-3 and
       ordered Deputy Assault Group Commanders O-1, O-2, and O-3 to
       bring in craft to unloading anchorages as required for expeditious
       unloading.

1500   Ordered CTF 126 (Commander Force B) to land troops in accordance
       with plan and to use LCVPs to unload from LCI as necessary.

1500   CTG 124.6 requested permission from CTF 124 to proceed to ISLE OF
       WIGHT area at 1530. Reply, affirmative.

1523   CTF 122 asked CTF 124 where and when he proposed to unload OCEANWAY.

1526   OCEANWAY requested orders from CTF 124.

1530   V Corps observer informed CG V Corps that 1st Div. CP being set up
       at Exit EASY ONE; 29th Div. CP near exit DOG THREE; COLLEVILLE taken,
       ST LAURENT partially occupied.

1534   Ordered CTG 124.5 to send 200 litter units to EASY RED.

1540   CTF 124 ordered OCEANWAY to proceed to FOX GREEN beach and discharge
       LCMs as near beach as possible.

1542   CG 1st Army relayed report of destroyer that troops on cliff near
       target one urgently required reinforcements.

1603   CTF 124 informed CTF 122 that the OCEANWAY had been instructed to
       close FOX GREEN.

1626   CTG 124.9 relayed following message from Rangers ashore at POINT du
       HOE to CTF 124. "Need replacements urgently, can you get them
       ashore?"

1633   CG 1st Division informed Commanding Officer Ranger Force. "All
       Rangers have landed DOG GREEN. No other troops available."

<u>6 June (D-day)</u>

1645   CTF 124 sent situation report No. 1 to CTF 122: 16th Infantry has reported taking COLIEVILLE and advancing to eastward. Strong point and exit taken at VIERVILLE but no indication as yet that 116th Infantry has moved inland. Some portions of the beach still under fire. Rangers have taken POINTE DU HOE. Unloading as of 1230: Total personnel unloaded 18772, vehicles unloaded 1,033, remaining personnel to be unloaded 15,801, remaining vehicles to be unloaded 2,474; all APAs and LSIs except DIX are completely unloaded. Information on LSTs, LCTs and LCIs very incomplete. A large number of personnel and vehicles are standing off the beaches and cannot be moved forward, and landed because of the inability of the troops already landed to move forward. Craft casualties as of 1600: sunk or in damaged condition, LCT 294, Dispatch Boat 350; damaged, LST 375, LCIs 487, 553, 85, LCT 2043, 210, 25, 2041, 2037, 538, 2307, Dispatch Boat 320, LCA 25, 418, unknown number of LCVPs.

1655   Commander Destroyer Squadron 18 informed CTF 122 and CTF 124 that he had been released from Fire Support duties and was ready as Commander Area Screen.

1700   CTG 124.5 informed CTF 124 that Assault Group O-3 had completed unloading except for LST 375.

1700   CTF 124 requested CTF 127 to sail ARL-4 to OMAHA Assault Area in earliest convoy.

1705   Lieut. General Omar Bradley, Commanding General, 1st Army came aboard USS ANCON.

1715   Major General Huebner, CG 1st Inf. Div., and Staff left USS ANCON to establish headquarters on the beach.

1721   V Corps observer sent following summary of beach conditions to CG, V Corps: "Enemy action against beach is slight. Beach area free of small arms. Beach condition will permit vehicular traffic over most of the area below high water line. Cratering due to bombing and shell fire light. Beach difficulties should soon be corrected and work on beach is progressing in orderly fashion".

1723   Message received from 1st Battalion 116th Infantry "We do not want naval fire as it is falling amongst friendly troops".

1735   CTG 124.4 informed CTF 124 that heavy gun fire on all DOG beaches was destroying beached landing craft and help was needed badly.

1745   CTG 124.4 reported DOG RED, EASY GREEN, DOG GREEN under intense shell fire.

1800   ComTransDiv 3 reported to CTF 124 that all transports were ready to proceed and requested permission to proceed. Granted. CG, 1st Div. requested of CG, V Corps that 26th Inf. be landed as quickly as possible.

6 June (D-day)

1815   Lieut. General Bradley left USS ANCON.

1822   Ordered CTG 124.9 to order any ship that might be firing on DOG GREEN beach to stop firing immediately, due to repeated requests from the beach to cease naval fire.

1824   ComDesRon 60 informed CTF 122 that Rangers at POINTE DU HOE had captured pillbox, had 10 to 15 wounded and about 15 prisoners and that they required reinforcements and boats for wounded and prisoners immediately.

1835   LCI(L) 86 informed CTF 124 that his beaches under heavy gun fire, beach full of vehicles half burned and that he considered any vehicles put ashore would be a total loss unless enemy fire was reduced.

1914   OCEANWAY reported all craft discharged and believed that all tanks landed on beach.

1928   CTF 124 ordered LCI 86 to send 2 LCVPs to POINT DU HOE to take off wounded Rangers and prisoners.

1945   Major General Gerow and V Corps personnel left USS ANCON for head-quarters on beach.

1954   Ordered CTF 126 to land 26th Inf. as soon as practicable over scheduled beaches.

1959   Ordered CTF 126 and Deputy Commanders Assault Group O-1 and O-2 to give priority to unloading to tank and artillery units aboard LCTs and LSTs of Force BAKER.

2100   CTF 126 informed CTF 124 that landing of 26th Infantry was completed.

2319   One enemy plane dove overhead USS ANCON, very low and fired 2 shots. This plane not picked up by radar and no warning received of approach.

2320   Observed heavy A.A. fire on port bow.

2322   Red Alert. General Quarters.

2325   Plane shot down starboard quarter of ANCON, 3,000 yards.

2329   Large bombs being dropped in transport area, ANCON firing at observed plane.

2334   Bombs dropped off port bow of ANCON, distance 500 yards.

2336   Bomb dropped 200 yards off port beam of ANCON. Ships in area firing at planes.

2336   USS ANCON shot down enemy plane on port beam by 40mm gun.

7 June (D/1)

0024   Control Vessel DOG GREEN relayed message to CTF 124 of beachmaster DOG GREEN that there was urgent need for gasoline and that tanks were stopped for lack of it.

7 June (D⁄1 day)

0045	CG, V Corps informed CTF 124 that his present line was generally along road from VIERVILLE - ST. LAURENT - one mile south of COLLEVILLE and that he was attacking with the Beachhead line as his objective.
0236	CTF 124 requested CTF 127 to send special equipment for NCDU parties by quickest available means.
0250	Observed plane crash on beach - identity unknown.
0552	CTF 124 ordered CTF 126 and Deputy Assault Group Commanders 0-1 and 0-2 to land 175th Infantry on DOG GREEN at scheduled time.
0724	CG, VII Corps relayed message from Rangers at POINT DU HOE to CG, V Corps that there were many casualties and support was needed.
0758	Beachmaster DOG WHITE relayed request from CG, 29th Division to CTF 124 that remaining regimental combat teams and division troops be landed on DOG WHITE immediately.
0800	LCH 492 informed CTF 124 that convoy group 0-4 had arrived at 0750.
0800	Ordered CTF 126 and Deputy Assault Group Commanders 0-1 and 0-2 to land 175th Regimental Combat Team and Division Troops of Force "B" on beach DOG WHITE as they were urgently needed.
0804	CTF 128 requested permission of CTF 124 to carry out Operation MULBERRY commencing with survey of GOOSEBERRY and survey of MULBERRY. Reply affirmative.
0820	SUSAN B. ANTHONY struck mine requested CTF 124 to send landing craft to remove troops.
0832	Control Vessel DOG GREEN relayed request of CG, V Corps that 175th Infantry landed immediately at DOG GREEN Beach.
0845	CTF 124 ordered LCI 86 to send LCVP to POINT DU HOE to evacuate litter cases.
0900	ComDesRon 18 informed CTF 124 that wreck of SUSAN B. ANTHONY was located 49° 29' 30"N 00° 42' 00"W in about 12 fathoms of water.
0907	CG, V Corps informed CTF 124 that 175th RCT should land at once according to plan and assemble in vicinity of ST. LAURENT; 2nd Division should begin landing upon arrival. Informed Deputy Commander Assault Group 0-2 that 175th Infantry be landed immediately on DOG GREEN.
0930	CG, 1st Army informed CG, V Corps that Rangers at POINTE DU HOE urgently needed reinforcements and ammunition and asked if naval gunfire support could be provided them.
1020	AT 90 informed CTF 124 that troops aboard SUSAN B. ANTHONY (AP 72) evacuated to LCT 624, LCT 625, LCI 924 and HMS MENOP with a few unidentified small craft.
1035	Informed CTF 122 that SUSAN B. ANTHONY sunk by mine nine miles 013 degrees from PORT EN BESSIN; survivors on numerous small ships.

7 June (D ≠ 1)

1042	Again directed LCH-86 and LCH-492 that 175th RCT should be landed at once according to plan.
1111	Ordered LCI-86, LCI-492 and Transports BORINQUEN, GOETHALS, SIMONDS to land Second Division at earliest possible time.
1125	Informed CG V Corps that CTF-124 would transport troops to vicinity POINTE DU HOE in LCTs and land them in LCVPs to assist Rangers if desired.
1140	LCI-86 informed CTF-124 that 175th RCT had begun to land.
1202	Ordered USS ANCON to send two boats to POINTE DU HOE to remove wounded men.
1210	CTF-122 directed CTF-124 to use every effort to evacuate wounded from beaches.
1220	Ordered Task Group 124.9 not to engage targets inside British area.
1225	HMS ENTERPRISE informed CTF-124 that she had been attached to CTF 124 by CTG-125.8.
1400	CTG-124.8 informed CTF-124 that he had observed British Fire Support Ships fire on PORT EN BESSIN; that he had 9 fully loaded rocket ships and 5 gun ships available for close neutralizing fire and requested instructions.
1405	Boats left ANCON for USS TEXAS on mission to carry reinforcements to Rangers at POINTE DU HOE and evacuate casualties.
1410	Ordered HMS ENTERPRISE to report to CTG-124.9.
1437	Informed Commander Force "G" that CTF-124 had 9 rocket ships available for fire on PORT EN BESSIN if desired.
1515	CG First Army issued situation report on OMAHA Beach as of 071000B:- 1st Div. and 2 regiments of 29th Div. extend from ST. HONORINE DES PERTES, GOOS LE HAMEL, LOUVIERS, GRUCHY. Landings opposed by 4 German regiments who were alert and waiting. Estimated casualties 116th Inf. 30%, 16th Inf. 40%, 26th Inf. 10%; snipers and machine gun fire still being placed on beach directly north of SAN LAURENT and sporadic fire still landing on beach. Attack will continue according to plan; Obstacles on beach continue to delay craft. Rhino ferries working well.
1612	Requested CTF-122 to assign six PCs immediately for duty as Control Vessels.
1633	Red Alert; General Quarters.
1657	Secured from General Quarters. No attack developed.
1705	CTG-124.9 informed CTF-124 that British were firing into PORT EN BESSIN.
1725	CTF-127 informed CTF-124 that special demolition equipment for underwater obstacles is being shipped via PT-521.
1807	CTF-122 informed WESTERN NAVAL TASK FORCE that Shuttle Control would become effective at 081100 and that prior to that time latest information could be obtained from CTF-124 and CTF-125.

7 June (D ≠ 1)

1830	MT 233 informed CTF 124 that she had struck two mines while coming into anchorage and requested that troops be removed.
1927	ANCXF advised that 2 squadrons of Spitfires would escort 6 Stirlings carrying out an airborne supply mission tomorrow.
1929	Informed CTG 122.3 that MT 233 had been damaged by mine and unloading of troops and cargo would require approximately 2 days.
2059	CTF 122 directed CTF 124 to send LSTs and other vessels farther out from beach in OHIO Area due to heavy gunfire near the beach.
2103	Beachmaster DOG RED reported heavy gunfire directed at MULBERRY.
2107	Ordered ships and craft anchored near beach to move out as necessary to avoid gunfire.
2126	CTF 122 reported heavy shelling off GOOSEBERRY TWO and directed CTF 124 to move large ships and LSTs out about two miles.
2140	Ordered GOETHALS, BORINQUEN and SIMONDS to get underway with escort. Requested assistance of CG V Corps in locating battery firing on shipping.
2156	CTF 122 authorized CTF 124 to retain five PCs for control, all above that number to be returned to Area Screen prior to sunset.
2212	CTG 124.9 informed CTF 124 that two cruisers had come to his area to aid in fire support and that he had been using them since their arrival. He inquired whether they should be returned to UTAH Area in compliance with dispatch orders of CTG 125.8.
2229	Ordered CTG 124.9 to direct HAWKINS and ENTERPRISE to carry out orders. Requested information on needs for additional fire support ships.
2310	CTF 122 informed CTF 124 that he believed it desirable for battleships to shift berths due to possibility that enemy aircraft had spotted exact positions.
2322	Observed flares, heavy anti-aircraft fire in beach area.
2336	CTG 124.9 inquired concerning position of front lines to assist him in locating batteries firing on beaches. CTF 122 informed CTF 124 that the enemy should be expected to have excellent observation of our dispositions; that large ships should not be concentrated and their position should be changed frequently.
2342	Informed CTG 124.9 that it was advisable to shift berths because of probability that enemy aircraft had spotted exact positions for bombing runs.

8 June (D ≠ 2)

0015	Observed bombing and strafing on beach.
0105	Red Alert. General Quarters.
0125	Heavy AA fire in transport area.

8 June (D ∕ 2)

0130	Plane apparently attempting bombing run over transport area, driven off by very heavy A.A. fire.
0158	Secured from General Quarters.
0345	CG V Corps urgently requested CTF 124 that one BB be put in position to fire ISIGNY at first light June 8.
0445	Planes believed to have laid mines in anchorage area. Splashes observed in area and position noted 49° 29' N - 00° 55' W.
0450	Radio warning of enemy "E" Boats operating in Western Transport Area.
0515	Informed CG V Corps that request for BB fire on ISIGNY was not received until 080400 and that it might be necessary to substitute a cruiser due to range and depth of water. CTF 124 directed compliance if possible.
0625	CTF 124 informed CG V Corps that BB would be in position to fire by 080630.
0644	CTF 122 ordered HMS BELLONA to report to CTG 124.9 for fire support duty.
0716	Informed C.G. Shore Party that compliance with requests for priority of unloading could be expedited if information were supplied as to ships in which cargo embarked; CTF 124 did not have information on loading of follow-up convoys.
0717	Informed CTG 124.9 that he was authorized to request fire support by AUGUSTA direct to CTF 122.
0850	Beachmaster EASY WHITE reported he was having trouble with prisoners and requested information on what craft were available to remove them.
0955	Informed CTF 127 that extensive damage to ferry craft had occurred during early stage of operation and requested immediately five spare Rhinos complete with bulldozers and tugs and other spare equipment.
1012	Com LST Group 30 informed CTF 124 that Convoy Group O-3 unloaded except for LST 309 and LST 75; requested permission to proceed without these two vessels.
1030	CG V Corps informed CTF 124 that landing was proceeding very slowly and that he was anxious to expedite arrival second division per priority set. Assistance in expediting unloading requested.
1035	USS ARKANSAS commenced firing on shore installations.
1050	HMS Hospital Ship NAUSHON informed CTF 124 that there appeared to be a delay in casualty evacuation and requested that evacuation be expedited.
1100	CG 1st Army made situation report as of 072400 as follows: Beach condition improving, casualties V Corps fairly heavy, no contact with British 50th Division on left, contact made with Rangers at ST. PIERRE DU MONT. West edge of PORT EN BESSIN entered at 1630 but not held. 2nd Division commences landing at 1530 and moves to assembly area vicinity of VIERVILLE. Beach obstacles and wreckage of many craft delayed unloading schedule and V Corps one tide behind.

8 June (D ≠ 2)

1119 Informed TF 124 that at 081100 Commander Shuttle Control (CTG 122.7) in HMS CAPETOWN began to function and that after that time all matters pertaining to arrival and sailing of convoys, escorts and assignments of anchorages for Western Task Force Area would be handled by him.

1224 ARL-4 ADONIS reported for duty to CTF 124.

1405 USS TEXAS commenced firing on shore installations.

1445 CTG 124.8 submitted preliminary report to CTF 124 on gunfire support craft losses: three LCP lost at sea enroute; three LCP sunk, one badly damaged on beach, one sinking, now under tow to beach, one in sinking condition alongside salvage tug. One LCF minor damage. All other gunfire craft operational.

1520 French Cruiser MONTCALM commenced firing on shore installations.

1631 CTF 122 ordered USS TEXAS to sail at 090900 to PLYMOUTH to replenish ammunition and return to OMAHA area before 112100.

1727 Informed CTG 124.9 of a prisoner of war report that naval gunfire on evening of D-day killed 125 of 150 men in German company at PORT EN BESSIN and hit all vessels in the harbor.

1800 USS BALDWIN enroute to Area Screen reported for duty to CTF 124.

1805 CTU 122.3.1 (Aboard USS ANCON) ordered PINTO, ARIKARA and ATR-2 to proceed without further orders to move any loaded damaged craft toward beaches, requesting assistance if necessary, and to move unloaded crippled craft in condition for towing to UK to mooring at position GEORGE 26; those in imminent danger of sinking to be beached.

1902 CTG 126.2 informed Commander Force "O" that 5522 personnel and 1230 vehicles of Convoy BAKER ONE had been unloaded as of 8 June.

1952 CTF 126 informed CTF 124 that 45 LCTs of his force had been unloaded.

2032 ANCON shifted anchorage to position 49° 24' N - 00° 47' W in ten (10) fathoms of water.

2255 Red Alert. General Quarters.

2335 Secured from General Quarters. No attack developed. Observed heavy gun flashes in beach area.

USS *Barton*:

DD72/A16-3
Serial: 038.   JWC/jg

U. S. S. BARTON (DD722)

C-O-N-F-I-D-E-N-T-I-A-L   c/o Fleet Post Office,
                                       New York, New York.

                                       28 June 1944.

From: The Commanding Officer.
To   :   The Commander Task Force ONE TWENTY-SEVEN.

Via :   (1) Commander Destroyer Squadron SIXTY.
            (2) Commander Task Force ONE TWENTY-FIVE.
            (3) Commander Task Force ONE TWENTY-TWO.

Subject: Narrative of U.S.S. BARTON (DD722) for the
            period 3-17 June 1944 for the invasion of
            France.

Reference: (a) Commander Task Force 127 secret desp.
                161212B of June 1944.

    1.   In accordance with reference (a) the following
narrative of movements of the U.S.S. BARTON (DD722) from
3-17 June 1944 is hereby submitted:

3 June 1944

    The BARTON was operating in accordance with Operation
Order Number 3-44 of Assault Force "U", Western Naval Task
Force, Allied Expeditionary Force, as Task Group 125.6. The
BARTON was assigned to escort Convoy U2A2 from United Kingdom to Transport Area, Utah Beach, Baie De La Seine, France
together with the LAFFEY (DD724). Commander Escort, Commander Destroyer Squadron SIXTY, was in the BARTON. BARTON
and LAFFEY joined first section of LCT Convoy at point af-
firm eight miles from Plymouth Harbor. Remainder of the convoy joined off Dartmouth. Departed from there at 2115B at
a speed of five knots. The weather throughout the day was
very good. The wind increased in force during the evening.

4 June 1944

    Wind force continued increasing throughout hours of
darkness. The convoy kept excellent station. At 0800B despatch from Naval Commander Allied Expeditionary Force postponed "H" hour 24 hours. Convoy reversed course and proceeded toward Plymouth. Increasing wind force and moderate
seas caused difficulty in station keeping for small craft.

DD722 /A16-3   JWC/jg
Serial: 038

U. S. S. BARTON (DD722)

C-O-N-F-I-D-E-N-T-I-A-L   c/o Fleet Post Office,
                                           New York, New York.

                                           28 June 1944.

Subject: Narrative of U.S.S. BARTON (DD722) for the
            period 3-17 June 1944 for the invasion of
            France.

- -

4 June 1944 (Cont'd)

It should be emphasized, however, that in spite of these obstacles the LCTs kept excellent formation. At 1630B, having
just passed the Bill of Portland a despatch directed the convoy to proceed to Weymouth Harbor. Convoy again reversed
course and started for Weymouth. After the reversal of course
had been effected BARTON received a visual signal from the
LAFFEY stating that LCT 2498 was taking water and was in danger of sinking. LCT 2498 was carrying U.S. Army personnel,
thirty-one of whom were transferred from the LCT to the BARTON
by the ship's motor whaleboat. The remainder being taken aboard
the BANNOCK. The crew of the craft remained aboard and it was
in tow by the BANNOCK. It sunk before reaching Weymouth. All
personnel were removed safely. The convoy entered Weymouth
Harbor at 2320.

5 June 1944

    Visibility was somewhat better and wind force had de-
creased to 1-15 knots when convoy got underway from Weymouth
at daylight. It was necessary for the escorting ships to
spend two to three hours rounding up the LCTs and forming
them. After all the craft had been formed it was found that
because of the distance between two groups safe passage and a
timely arrival could be better insured by escorting them separately. BARTON escorting the leading group and LAFFEY the
second. Weather during passage to Point "HE" off Point De
Barfleur was good. At 1755B in latitude 50°12'N longitude
01°12'W a U.S. minesweeper near the convoy struck a mine and
sank with seven reported casualties. Difficulty was experienced in locating swept channel number two to Transport Area
as the lighted buoys that had been laid at the entrance had
been extinguished. The entire convoy was in channel two proceeding to the Transport Area by 2330B.

DD722/A16-3
Serial: 938

JWC/jg

U. S. S. BARTON (DD722)

C-O-N-F-I-D-E-N-T-I-A-L

c/o Fleet Post Office,
New York, New York.

28 June 1944

Subject: Narrative of U.S.S. BARTON (DD722) for the
period 3-17 June 1944 for the invasion of
France.

- -

6 June 1944

Convoy U2A2 arrived in Transport Area, Utah Beach at
0602B. BARTON took screening station to northwest of Transport Area and patrolled until H/5 hour at which time BARTON
was ordered to relieve the HERNDON in Utah Five Support Station Number Four. HERNDON was not on station when BARTON
arrived. 1230B relieved HERNDON on station #4, off Point
Du Hoe. 1300B personnel observed on cliff, taking cover
from enemy fire. Communications established, party identified as 2nd Ranger Battalion. 1435B Motor whaleboat left
ship to pick up casualties. 1519B Motor whaleboat returned
to ship holed by machine gun fire, one casualty. Unable to
reach beach. 1522B Opened fire on enemy machine gun positions, as directed by 2nd Rangers. 1625B ceased fire, having expended 43 round 5"/38 AA Common. 1902B Opened fire on
enemy concentration southeast of Grandcamp Les Bains. 1925B
ceased fire, having expended 44 rounds 5"/38 AA Common. 1930B
proceeded to night station #4, off Port En Bessin.

7 June 1944

0730B patrolling station #4, off Point Du Hoe. 0745B
opened fire on targets designated by 2nd Rangers, directed by
Lieutenant JOHNSON. 0900B (About) ceased fire, having expended
185 rouns 5"/38 AA Common. Ordered to close flagship to receive new assignment. BARTON went close aboard the TEXAS
at which time Commander Destroyer Squadron SIXTY in BARTON was
placed in charge of destroyers in the Ohio Area. The ship then
took station in the Ohio Area acting as fire support. There
was one air alert in the afternoon but the chief interest was
the large and numerous flights of friendly bombers passing
over. At 2055B heavy gunfire on the Ohio Beaches began. The
ships had no success in locating the enemy battery at first..
It was directing an accurate and effective fire into the landed craft on the beach and landing craft along the shore line.

DD722 A16-3/A9
Serial: 004.

JWC/do

U. S. S. BARTON (DD722)

CONFIDENTIAL

c/o Fleet Post Office,
New York, New York.

CONFIDENTIAL

28 June 1944.

From: The Commanding Officer.
To :   The Commander in Chief, United States Fleet.
Via :   (1) The Commander Destroyer Squadron SIXTY.
          (2) The Commander Task Force ONE TWENTY-NINE.
          (3) The Commander Task Force ONE TWENTY-TWO.

Subject: Bombardment of Enemy Positions, Baie De La
          Seine, June 6-10, 1944 - report of.

Reference: (a) Cominch and CNO serial 7152 of 29 October
               1943.

     1.   This action report is submitted in accordance
with reference (a).
                 All times are zone -2.
     2.   During the period 6-10 June 1944, BARTON oper-
ated with Task Groups 124.9 and 125.8, furnishing supporting fire for the assault on the enemy held beaches in the
Baie De La Seine. Numerous targets were engaged, at ranges
varying from 1800 yards to 18000 yards, both with and without shore fire control spotting.

     3.   On 6 June, BARTON relieved U.S.S. HERNDON (DD
638) on station #4, off Point Du Hoe. As her shore fire
control party could not be contacted, BARTON patrolled station, awaiting targets of opportunity. Shortly thereafter,
a party of the 2nd Ranger Battalion was observed, taking
shelter from German fire beneath the lip of the cliff. A
number of German prisoners had been taken, and were under
guard on the beach. Communications were established by
flashing light, and in response to a request for a boat to
evacuate several wounded, the motor whaleboat was sent in.
This boat, under the command of the First Lieutenant,
reached a point twenty yards from the beach before being
forced to retire by heavy and accurate machine gun fire
from nearby enemy positions. The boat was holed several
times, BACON, Garnet Lee, 620 31 84, PhM2c, V6, USNR, was
wounded in the hip, and a soldier (previously recovered
from an unseaworthy LCT) was struck squarely on the helmet
while returning the fire. He was stunned but uninjured.

DD722/A16-3/A9
Serial: 004.

JWC/dc

CONFIDENTIAL   U. S. S. BARTON (DD722)

~~S-E-C-R-E-T~~
~~CONFIDENTIAL~~

28 June 1944.

Subject: Bombardment of Enemy Positions, Baie De La
Seine, June 6-10, 1944 - report of.

- -

BARTON thereupon opened fire on these enemy positions, spots
being received by light from the Shore Fire Control Parties
of Lieutenant NORTON, USN, and Lieutenant JOHNSON, USA, operating with the 2nd Rangers. Several positions were neutralized or destroyed, and the enfillading fire which had harassed
the group ceased.

4.   Following the destruction of these targets, radio
communication was established on a common frequency, and BAR-
TON continued to fire on targets designated by this party.
An enemy counterattack on the road west of Grandcamp Les Bains
(556912) was engaged, after which fire was shifted to a concentration southest of this town (567924). The SFCP reported
to the BARTON "Good shooting" BARTON was ordered to return to
her night station off Port En Bessin at 1930.

5.   On 7 June, BARTON was again assigned station #4.
As no word had yet been received from her own SFCP, she continued to work with Lieutenant JOHNSON'S party, still isolated
near the beach. Lieutenant NORTON'S SFCP had managed to work
its way inland during the night, and was directing the fire of
the TEXAS, as originally scheduled. During this period BARTON
took various targets under fire. The first mission was a
strong machine gun position, which was also being bombed and
strafed by a strong flight of Thunderbolts. Following its
neutralization, fire was shifted to a chateau, occupied by the
enemy. As friendly troops were in the foreground, the shells
were placed above the second floor. This target was observed
severely damaged, and the salvos were then walked right through
a grove of trees harboring snipers. The proximity of friendly
units forbade the use of air bursts, but a shell was seen to
strike a branch and detonate, with evident shrapnel effect.
Several unidentified strongpoints were next engaged, with excellent results, and a second chateau was heavily hit and rendered useless to the enemy. The Rangers then moved inland.
BARTON was ordered to return to station off Port En Bessin.

DD722/A16-3/A9   JWC/do
Serial: 004.

CONFIDENTIAL   U. S. S. BARTON (DD722)

CONFIDENTIAL
                                        28 June 1944.

Subject: Bombardment of Enemy Positions, Baie De La
            Seine, June 6-10, 1944 - report of.

- -

    6.   From 7 to 16 June, BARTON was available for sup-
porting fire, but was called only once, on 10 June. This
target was a road junction, range 18500 yards, firing from
1500 yards off the beach near Port En Bessin. The last spot
received was "out 400." This was applied, and several salvos
fired with unknown results.

    7.   Chronological order of events pertinent to shore
bombardment:

6 June 1944.

    1230   Relieved U.S.S. HERNDON on station #4, off
            Pointe Du Hoe.
    1300   Personnel observed on cliff, taking cover from
            enemy fire. Communications established, party
            identified as 2nd Ranger Battalion.
    1435   Motor whaleboat left ship to pick up casualties.
    1519   Motor whaleboat returned to ship holed by machine
            gun fire, one casualty. Unable to reach beach.
    1522   Opened fire on enemy machine gun positions, as
            directed by 2nd Rangers.
    1625   Ceased fire, having expended 130 rounds 5"/38 AA
            Common.
    1645   Opened fire on road east of Grandcamp Les Bains.
    1700   Ceased fire, having expended 43 rounds 5"/38 AA
            Common.
    1902   Opened fire on enemy concentration southeast of
            Grandcamp Les Bains.
    1925   Ceased fire, having expended 44 rounds 5"/38 AA
            Common.
    1930   Proceeded to night station #4, off Port En Bessin.

7 June 1944.

    0730   Patrolling station #4, off Pointe Du Hoe.
    0745   Opened fire on targets designated by 2nd Rangers,
            directed by Lieutenant JOHNSON.
    0900   (about) Ceased fire, having expended 185 rounds
            5"/38 AA Common. Ordered to close flagship to
            receive new assignment.

The ordnance installation performed well, with no major casualties. On 6 June, an open firing circuit on Mount #2 necessitated percussion firing, but in no way affected the performance of the battery.

Direct fire was used on the majority of targets, as the range was usually below 3000 yards, and the target visible. By introducing target angle and target speed until the line of sight and regenerated range remained on the target, the effect of strong and variable currents was nullified. When the target itself was not visible, the director was trained on a prominent object in the close vicinity, and spots applied to place the MPI where required.

On some targets, such as the chateaux, hitting was delayed in the interests of safety. As our own forces were immediately in front of the buildings, it was necessary to apply arbitrary out spots on the initial salvos. The spot was then reduced until the second story of the building was hit.

Ammunition performed excellently throughout, all observed detonations being high order. The projectiles seemed to have a satisfactory effect on both unfortified positions and stone buildings. According to instructions, ammunition was husbanded carefully, and two-gun salvos used the greater part of the time.

DD722/A16-3/A9
Serial: OO4.

JWC/do

CONFIDENTIAL

U. S. S. BARTON (DD722)

~~CONFIDENTIAL~~

28 June 1944.

Subject: Bombardment of Enemy Positions, Baie De La
Seine, June 6-10, 1944 - report of.

- -

AMMUNITION WAS EXPENDED AS FOLLOWS:

    6 June   217   AA Common
    7 June   185   AA Common
    10 June   55   AA Common
    TOTAL   457   AA Common 5"/38

12.   No damage was sustained by BARTON during this
period.

13.   The following despatch was received from ComDes
Ron SIXTY:

On June 18 ComDesRon SIXTY inspected beach area
and sectors behind beach including a number of targets
which were fired on by ships of DesDiv 119. The fire
support rendered was very effective as evidenced by the
destruction observed and statements of both Army and
Navy personnel who were involved in operations ashore.
Convey this information to your entire crews including
my personal gratification over their excellent performance in assisting our land forces in clearing and securing the beachhead in the most complicated and extensive
amphibious operation ever undertaken.

14.   All radar equipment functioned exceptionally well
with no casualties or interruptions. It is recommended that,
in waters with strong and variable currents, direct fire using
any object as point of aim and introducing arbitrary spots be
used as much as possible (an offset). It is extremely difficult to navigate with pinpoint accuracy at all times in such
times in such waters and the offset method seems to give a
satisfactory answer.

15.   Personnel performance was excellent throughout.
One casualty was suffered: BACON, G.L., PhM2c, was wounded
in hip by a .30 caliber enemy machine gun bullet while in the
ship's whaleboat which was attempting to assist wounded Rangers
on the beach.

Below: Task Force 124.7.3 After Action Report:

ENCLOSURE "A"

Part I – <u>General Narrative</u>.

1.   As Commander Task Unit 124.7.3, Commander Destroyer Division THIRTY-SIX, in SATTERLEE with McCOOK and CARMICK departed Portland, England at 1100, 5 June, 1944. (D minus 1 day). The mission of this Task Unit was to escort and protect from enemy action the Mine Sweepers which were to sweep Approach Channel #4, the Omaha Transport Area, and Gunfire Support Channel #3 in Omaha Area, Operation ▬▬▬. Rendezvous with British Mine Sweeper Flotilla FOUR was effected at 50° 05' N 0° 46' W at 1700 B (H minus 13 hours 30 minutes). Shortly thereafter the sweepers formed up and commenced sweeping and buoying Approach Channel #4. This Task Unit escorted the sweepers down the Approach Channel and into the Omaha Transport Area. The passage was uneventful except for the sinking by gunfire of several mines cut loose by the sweepers. No enemy forces were encountered. At 0030 6 June (H minus 6 hours) proceeded to southern end of Approach Channel #3 and waited for British Mine Sweeping Flotilla ONE SIX SEVEN and one (1) division of Mine Sweeping Flotilla ONE ZERO FOUR to commence sweeping Gunfire Support Channel #3. Escorted these sweepers down the Gunfire Support Channel until leading sweep had turned north at which time stationed escorts on western edge of channel and waited for sweepers to pass. Sweeping operation was completed at 060400 B (H minus 2 hours 30 minutes). At this time directed escorts to proceed independently to their assigned Fire Support Stations.

2.   In the absence of Commander Destroyer Gunfire Support Group, Force "O", who was also Screen Commander, as Deputy Commander I assumed command of the Gunfire Support Destroyers. This Group of eleven (11) destroyers was constituted as follows:

<u>Fire Support Area #3</u>	<u>Fire Support Area #4</u>
U.S.S. SATTERLEE	H.M.S. TANATSIDE
H.M.S. TALYBONT	U.S.S. EMMONS
U.S.S. THOMPSON	U.S.S. BALDWIN
U.S.S. McCOOK	U.S.S. HARDING
U.S.S. CARMICK	U.S.S. DOYLE
	H.M.S. MELBREAK

Ships were arranged in this order from west to east so as to avoid crossfire on assigned targets. The mission of this Destroyer Fire Support Group was to deliver scheduled fire on assigned targets before H hour, to deliver close supporting fire at targets of opportunity during and after the landing, and to deliver call fire for Shore Fire Control Parties as soon as parties had become established on the beach. Each destroyer had previously held numerous drills and conferences with their own Shore Fire Control Party. This proved invaluable as each ship and Shore Fire Control Party was used to and familiar with the procedure and peculiarities of its individual opposite.

3.   All destroyers had been previously directed to be in their assigned Fire Support station and ready to open fire at H minus 40 minutes, but to be prepared to use counter-battery fire at any time after passing Transport Area if fired upon by the enemy. Destroyers entering Fire Support Area #3 were not fired upon prior to opening fire but those proceeding down Fire Support Channel #4 were taken under fire by German Coastal Batteries at 0535 (H minus

55 minutes). Fire was promptly returned by BALDWIN, HARDING, and EMMONS. The battery which appeared through the smoke to be located at or near Port en Bessin was temporarily silenced at 0552. Several enemy salvos landed quite close to the destroyers but none suffered material damage or casualties.

4.   At H minus 40 minutes (0550 B) or shortly thereafter all destroyers opened fire on their assigned targets. Coastal artillery immediately answered the fire and from then on until late the next day all destroyers were under intermittent fire by enemy coastal defenses, mortars and heavy machine guns. During the period of scheduled fire from H minus 40 minutes to H hour it was necessary for the destroyers to occasionally shift fire from their assigned target to some enemy gun that was shooting at them. In most of these instances a few salvos were sufficient to temporarily silence these enemy guns and fire was then immediately shifted back to scheduled targets. The fire of all destroyers during this period was fast and accurate. There were no material or personnel casualties during this phase of the Support Fire although many enemy shells fell close aboard the destroyers. As the first wave closed the beach the Fire Support destroyers preceded them closing the beach to from one thousand (1000) to two thousand (2000) yards. At 0617 (H minus 13 minutes) LCT(R)'s commenced firing rockets drenching the area just inland from the beaches. Fire from this beach was temporarily silenced and the entire area covered with heavy smoke and dust. Troops landed and proceeded up the beach into the smoke.

5.   From the landing of the troops until the establishment of Shore Fire Control Parties the Fire Support Destroyers fired on targets of opportunity. It is considered that the support of destroyers during this phase was not utilized to over twenty (20) percent of their possibilities. There was no communication with the beach and on numerous occasions destroyers could not fire on targets which should have been fired on because they did not know the location of our own troops. This is a most crucial period in the assault and some method of communication between troops and Fire Support Ships must be devised. The Destroyers acquited themselves well indeed whenever a target presented itself. Numerous guns firing on the beaches were detected by their flashes and were destroyed by the Fire Support Ships. The destroyers closed to less than a thousand (1000) yards from the beach, the fire of each ship being directed by the Commanding Officer.

At 0730 H.M.S. TALYBONT departed in accordance with previous instructions and at 0850 H.M.S. TANATSIDE left the Fire Support Area. At 0821 BALDWIN was hit by two (2) 105 millimeter shells. These caused but minor material damage and no personnel casualties.

6.   At 0710 (H plus 40 minutes) the first boat of the 2nd Rangers which were to attack Pointe du Hoe landed just to the east of the point. These boats were forty minutes late in arriving at their beach. This was due to two (2) reasons (1) additional distance from transports to Pointe du Hoe and (2) slow progress by the heavily loaded boats into wind and sea. Wind was from the West force ten - fifteen (10 - 15) knots, sea was from the west waves two - four (2 - 4) feet high and moderate swells from North North West. Five (5) or six (6) out of the ten (10) boats foundered before they reached the beach. Fortunately this occured in shallow water between one (1) and two (2) hundred yards from the beach. Most of the Rangers from these boats reached the beach although there were a few casualties by drowning at this time.

2

ENCLOSURE "A"

The fortifications at Pointe du Hoe had been under heavy fire by
TEXAS from H minus 40 minutes to H minus 05 minutes. However this fire had been
lifted according to schedule and when the Rangers landed fortyfive (45) minutes
later the Germans had filtered back into the fortifications and were waiting for them
with machine guns, mortars, rifles, and hand grenades. At this point the cliffs
rise abruptly from the water to a height of approximately one hundred (100) feet.
As the Rangers landed they found themselves pinned under the cliffs and were being
rapidly cut to pieces by enemy fire. I immediately ordered SATTERLEE to close the
point and take the cliff tops under main battery and machine gun fire. This was
done. Her fire control was excellent and the Rangers were enabled to establish a
foothold on the cliff top. 40 millimeter machine gun fire was very effective
against troops driven out of their trenches by 5" guns. The Rangers had brought
some rockets with grapnels and rope ladders attached to shoot over the cliff and
provide a means of ascent. These novel gadgets did not appear to be particularly
successful. By 0728 SATTERLEE had established communication with the Ranger fire
control party and the situation had improved slightly. At that nearly sixty (60)
percent of these Rangers were killed in the first two (2) hours of the battle.
As their Shore Fire Control Party advanced inland the remainder of the Rangers
established communication with SATTERLEE by light and were thus enabled to rapidly
call for close support fire. By this means SATTERLEE and later THOMPSON and
HARDING were able to repel several enemy counter-attacks which otherwise would
have wiped out this Ranger Battalion to a man. The gallant fight of this 2nd
Battalion of our Rangers against tremendous odds and difficulties was an inspiration
to all naval personnel fortunate enough to witness this phase of the battle. The
Rangers were magnificent.

7.   At 0900(H plus 2 hours 30 minutes) Commander Destroyer Fire Support
Group in FRANKFORD (Commander Destroyer Squadron EIGHTEEN) entered Fire Support
Area and assumed command of Fire Support destroyers until 1600, at which time he
departed to assume command of Area Screen and I again assumed command of Force
"O" Fire Support Destroyers.

8.   During the remainder of the day Fire Support Destroyers fired at
targets as directed by Shore Fire Control Parties, Commander Destroyer Squadron
EIGHTEEN, Commander Task Group 124.9, and by their own commanding officers. (For
individual ship targets and ammunition expenditure on each target see Reports of
Action by Ships). At 1750 SATTERLEE had fired over seventy (70) percent of her
bombardment ammunition. Directed THOMPSON to relieve her in support of Rangers
and shifted my pennant and staff to HARDING. SATTERLEE departed Fire Support Area
to report to Area Screen Commander. At 1800 BARTON (Commander Destroyer Squadron
SIXTY) and O'BRIEN reported to Fire Support Area and were assigned stations and
Shore Fire Control Parties. At 2000 directed CARMICK to report to Area Screen
Commander she having expended over seventy (70) percent of her bombardment ammunition. Omaha beaches were under sporadic but heavy shelling during most of the
afternoon and evening of D day. This fire came from sources Fire Support Ships
had great difficulty in locating. However it was evidently controlled by observers
watching the beaches. There were numerous houses behind the beaches and on adjacent hills and cliffs overlooking the beaches which had not been thoroughly shelled
even at this late date. I believe that this was a costly error on our part and
for future landing operations I strongly advocate the demolishment of all structures,
houses, Churches, etc., that could possibly house light artillery, machine guns,

3

SECRET   ENCLOSURE "A"

mortars and/or observation and communication posts prior to and immediately after the landing of troops. This could have readily been done by the destroyers but by the time we realized this our troops were advancing and we were unable to obtain permission to shell any but a few of the most obvious. It was most galling and depressing to lie idly a few hundred yards off the beaches and watch our troops, tanks, landing boats, and motor vehicles being heavily shelled and not be able to fire a shot to help them just because we had no information as to what to shoot at and were unable to detect the source of the enemy fire. Advancing troops must have some visual means to call for immediate fire support from close Fire Support Ships. A mortar shell with a distinctively colored smoke would have been most effective and would have insured immediate destruction of a target so designated.

    9. During the hours of darkness destroyers answered call fire from Shore Fire Control Parties. THOMPSON was especially busy repelling German counter-attacks on the 2nd Rangers at Pointe du Hoe.

    At 2330 B 6 June the first enemy air raid began. Heavy AA fire by numerous ships in Transport Areas was almost as dangerous to adjacent ships as to enemy planes. Fire discipline on merchant ships and landing craft was not satisfactory.

    10. 7 June 1944.

    At 0100 B AA firing ceased and air raid was over for the night. There were no casualties to Fire Support Bestroyers. At 0630 HARDING relieved THOMPSON in support of Rangers and THOMPSON departed to replenish ammunition having expended over eighty (80) percent of her bombardment ammunition.

    During the day destroyers fired on targets as requested by Shore Fire Control Parties and as the troops moved further inland the calls became fewer. At 0740 directed HARDING to send motor whale-boat to beach at Pointe du Hoe to evacuate Ranger casualties. Boat was wrecked in landing. Requested LCVP's from Commander Task Group 124.9 (Commander Battleship Division FIVE) and furnished list of ammunition and supplies Rangers needed which they had trans-mitted to me by flashing light from the beach.

    At 1100 commandeered a passing LCT and placed ammunition, food, and water for Rangers on board. LCT attempted to make beach but was unsuccess-ful due to state of tide. I then sent LCT to transport pool with orders to trans-fer supplies to an LCVP and have it return to me. At 1200 PLUNKETT reported for duty in Fire Support Area and was assigned station and Shore Fire Control Party. At 1429 HARDING struck an underwater obstruction about fifteen hundred (1500) yards north of Roches des Grandcamp. Chart showed water to be between seven (7) and eight (8) fathoms deep at present state of tide. Sound dome and pro-pellers damaged. Ship cleared at 1432 and was able to make twelve (12) to fifteen (15) knots, without excessive vibration. Retained ship in Fire Support Area as she had only expended fifty (50) percent bombardment ammunition.

    At 1500 two (2) LCVP's reported for duty. Sent them to Ranger Beach to evacuate casualties. At 1600 two (2) more LCVP's reported one containing supplies earlier furnished by HARDING and other with supplies furnished by TEXAS.

4

SECRET   ENCLOSURE "A"

Sent them to Ranger beach at Pointe du Hoe. LCVP's returned with wounded and prisoners and were directed to take them to TEXAS.

          At 1730 DOYLE having expended seventy (70) percent ammunition de-
parted with orders to report to Area Screen Commander. At 2240 MURPHY reported
for duty in Fire Support Area and was assigned station and Shore Fire Control Party.

     11.   8 June 1944.

          At 0000 enemy air raid on beach defenses and shipping commenced.
Large volumes of AA fire from beach and ships. Saw only two (2) enemy planes
shot down. No destroyers suffered damage during raid. Destroyers in Ohio area
smoke screened ARKANSAS and French Cruisers. Destroyers in Oregon area failed
to receive word to make smoke. At 0206 MEREDITH reported being hit by glider
bomb in Utah area. 0215 AA fire ceased and area reported clear of enemy planes.
At 0540 McCOOK departed from area having expended over seventy (70) percent of
her bombardment ammunition and ELLYSON (Commander Destroyer Squadron TEN) reported
for duty in Fire Support Area and was assigned station and Shore Fire Control
Party.

          During the day destroyers stood by to deliver fire on call from
Shore Fire Control Parties but there were not many calls as troops had advanced
inland beyond range of destroyer guns in a number of areas. At 1433 HARDING
called on to shell waterfront buildings in Grandcamp des Bains and at 1815 fired
on town of Maisy for fortyfive (45) minutes intermittent fire as requested by
Shore Fire Control Party. At 1900 lifted fire and troops entered town. At 1930
directed BALDWIN to report to Area Screen Commander for duty in screen. In accordance with instructions from Commander Task Group 124.9 Fire Support Destroyers
were directed to anchor after darkness in position best suited for AA protection
of shipping. This was done to reduce hazard of hitting mines dropped by enemy
aircraft in night air raids. Unless called by Shore Fire Control Party I attempted
to keep destroyers anchored during morning until adjacent areas had been swept
for mines.

     12.   9 June 1944.

          At 0010 enemy air raid started. Heavy AA fire from all merchant
ships and landing craft. Saw only one (1) enemy plane shot down. BALDWIN reported
she saw five (5) shot down. ELLYSON reported four (4) rocket bombs fell close
to her but no damage sustained. Planes using "window" to jam air search radars.
Numerous mines or delayed action bombs fell in area. 0100 Air raid over. At
0625 more enemy aircraft reported over area but did not see or hear of any bombs
falling. At 0705 SATTERLEE returned from England having replenished ammunition.
Shifted pennant and staff back to SATTERLEE and directed HARDING proceed to Plymouth for repairs in accordance with her previous orders. Very little fire support was required of destroyers during the day. At 1900 ELLYSON completed
firing on target 646798. This was the last time Shore Fire Control Parties called
for destroyer fire support. Directed PLUNKETT, BARTON and O'BRIEN to report to
Area Screen Commander for duty in screen retaining only ELLYSON, MURPHY and
SATTERLEE in Fire Support Area to furnish AA support during hours of darkness.

<u>SECRET</u>   ENCLOSURE "A"

13.   10 - 15 June 1944.

        No more fire support was required of destroyers by Shore Fire
Control Parties and all but three (3) destroyers were detached from Fire Support
Area and turned over to Area Screen Commander. This situation maintained with
an occasional shift of an individual ship from Fire Support Area to Screen and
back until 0800 15 June when new Task Organization became effective, Destroyer
Fire Support Group, Force "O" was disbanded, and I reported to Commander Destroyer
Squadron EIGHTEEN for duty in Area Screen.

Part II - <u>Chronological Order of Events.</u>

<u>5 June 1944.</u>

1100   Task Unit 124.7.3 departed Portland England.
1200   Rendezvoused with British Mine Sweeping Flotilla FOUR at 50° 05' N,
        0° 46' W and proceeded down Approach Channel #4 escorting minesweepers.

<u>6 June 1944.</u>

0030   Arrived Omaha Transport Area proceeded to Channel #3 awaiting arrival
        Mine Sweeping Flotilla ONE SIX SEVEN and ONE ZERO FOUR.
0145   Rendezvoused with Mine Sweeping Flotilla ONE SIX SEVEN and ONE ZERO
        FOUR and escorted them as they swept Gunfire Support Channel #3
        Omaha Area.
0400   Sweeping Operations completed directed destroyers to proceed in-
        dependently to Fire Support Stations.
0535   German Shore Batteries commenced firing on destroyers in Ohio Fire
        Support Area.
0537   BALDWIN, HARDING, EMMONS returned fire on enemy Coastal batteries.
0550   Fire Support Destroyers commenced fire on assigned targets. Deputy
        Commander Fire Support Destroyers, Force "O", (Commander Destroyer
        Division THIRTY-SIX) in SATTERLEE assumed command Fire Support Des-
        troyers.
0617   LCT(R)'s commenced firing rockets at beach.
0710   First boat of 2nd Rangers arrived Pointe du Hoe beach.
0728   SATTERLEE established first communication with Shore Fire Control
        Party.
0730   H.M.S. TALYBONT departed in accordance with previous orders.
0821   BALDWIN hit by two (2) 105 millimeter shells.
0850   H.M.S. TANATSIDE departed in accordance with previous orders.
0900   Commander Destroyer Squadron EIGHTEEN in FRANKFORD entered area
        and assumed command of Fire Support Destroyers.
0930   H.M.S. MELBREAK departed in accordance with previous orders.
1600   Commander Destroyer Squadron EIGHTEEN in FRANKFORD departed to
        take command of Area Screen and Commander Destroyer Division
        THIRTY-SIX again assumed command Fire Support Destroyers.
1750   Shifted Pennant and Staff to HARDING.
1800   BARTON and O'BRIEN reported for duty in Fire Support Area and were
        assigned stations and Fire Control Party.
2000   SATTERLEE having expended seventy-five (75) percent of her bombard-
        ment ammunition departed Fire Support Area to report for duty in Area
        Screen.

6

ENCLOSURE "A"

2000	Directed CARMICK to report to Area Screen Commander she having expended over seventy (70) percent of her bombardment ammunition.
2330	Enemy air raid commenced. Heavy AA fire by merchant ships and landing craft. Very poor fire discipline.

7 June 1944.

0100	Area clear of enemy aircraft.
0630	THOMPSON departed for England to replenish ammunition.
0740	HARDING sent motor whale-boat to Pointe du Hoe in attempt to evacuate Ranger wounded. Boat wrecked on beach.
1200	PLUNKETT reported for duty in Fire Support Area and was assigned station and Shore Fire Control Party.
1429	HARDING struck submerged object off Roches des Grandcamp damaging sound dome and both propellers.
1432	HARDING cleared obstruction. Now able to make twelve to fifteen (12 to 15) knots without excessive vibration. Retained her in Fire Support Area.
1500	Two (2) LCVP's reported for duty and were directed proceed to Ranger beach and evacuate casualties.
1600	Two (2) more LCVP's reported with ammunition replacements, food, and water for Rangers. Directed them to proceed to Ranger beach at Pointe du Hoe.
1730	DOYLE departed to report to Area Screen Commander having expended over seventy (70) percent of her bombardment ammunition.
2240	MURPHY reported for duty in Fire Support Area and was assigned station and Shore Fire Control Party.

8 June 1944.

0000	Enemy air raid on beach and shipping commenced. Two (2) enemy planes shot down. Destroyers in Ohio area smoke screened ARKANSAS and French Cruisers. Destroyers in Oregon area did not receive orders to make smoke.
0206	MEREDITH reported being hit by glider bomb.
0215	AA fire ceased, area reported clear of enemy planes.
0540	McCOOK departed for England to replenish ammunition and ELLYSON reported for duty in Fire Support Area. Assigned her station and Shore Fire Control Party.
1430	Directed BALDWIN depart and report to Area Screen Commander.
2000	Directed Destroyers in Fire Support Area to anchor after dark.

9 June 1944.

0010	Enemy air raid commenced. Five planes shot down. Rocket bombs fell close to ELLYSON but no damage sustained.
0100	Area reported clear of enemy planes.
0625	Enemy air raid reported. Did not see any planes or bombs.
0630	SATTERLEE returned to area and Commander Destroyer Division THIRTY-SIX shifted pennant and staff to SATTERLEE.
0730	HARDING departed Area for Plymouth for repairs and replenishment of ammunition.
1900	ELLYSON completed fire on target 646798. This completed destroyer fire support in Omaha area.

7

SECRET   ENCLOSURE "A"

1930   Directed PLUNKETT, BARTON, and O'BRIEN to report to Area Screen
        Commander. Retained ELLYSON, MURPHY and SATTERLEE in Fire Support
        Area to furnish AA support during hours of darkness.

10 - 15 June 1944

Three (3) destroyers retained in Fire Support Area others in Area
Screen. At 0800 15 June new Task Organization became effective.
Fire Support Destroyers disbanded and I reported to Area Screen
Commander (Commander Destroyer Squadron EIGHTEEN) for duty in the
Screen.

The area chart, Enclosure (B), is not a track chart but is for
ready reference and shows the positions of the Fire Support Destroyers, Force
"O", at H hour on 6 June 1944. Ship tracks are shown on charts submitted with
action report of individual ships.

Part III - Performance of Ordnance Material.

The performance of all ordnance material was uniformly excellent.
No ordnance casualties occured which could not be expeditiously repaired by ship's
force. The only factor that limited the fire support these destroyers could give
was the amount of ammunition the ships could carry.

The photographs of Enclosure (C) show the effectiveness of the
5"/38 cal. gun against various types of beach defenses. AA common is not suitable for use against concrete positions, but of course this statement is no news.
In an assault such as Operations ███████ against prepared beach defenses I believe
the percentage of common should be much higher than the forty (40) rounds per gun
we carried. I suggest at least one hundred (100) rounds per gun. It is further
suggested that twenty - twentyfive (20 - 25) rounds per gun of white phosphorus
be carried for incendiary use against houses as well as for smoke screens. Very
few duds were noted and as all AA common was set on safe when firing at fortifications no air bursts were noted. When firing against troops fuses were set on
advanced range and the usual percent of air bursts obtained. This method was
highly effective against troops. In one instance HARDING walked salvos down a
road well behind the beach and dispersed or killed a body of German troops advancing along the road to attack the flank of our troops. The road was not visible
from the ship and range used was optical range to beach plus chart range from
beach to road.

When used the 40 millimeter was highly effective against troops.
These guns should have been used more as almost all the destroyers were within
effective 40 millimeter range of the beach most of the first three (3) days of
the assault.

For ammunition expenditures see individual ship action reports.

8

ENCLOSURES "A"

Part IV – Battle Damage

    1.   Own ships damage.

        At 0820 B 6 June the BALDWIN received two (2) direct hits from enemy 105 millimeter shells. Size of shell was calculated from curvature of shrapnel fragments.

1. Two projectiles. Estimated type – common, weight – about 30 pounds, diameter – 105 millimeter – fuzes – instantaneous.
2. Range – relative bearing of enemy battery, 2500 – 3000 yards. relative bearing 215°.
3. Location of impact: First projectile hit after bitt, port side, frame 40. Second projectile inboard boat gripe and after starboard side of port motor whale-boat (rigged out from port davits), frames 74-75.
4. Path of projectiles through ship; both projectiles exploded on impact.
5. Thicknesses penetrated; 3/16" plating and lesser thicknesses penetrated by shrapnel.
6. Distance from point of impact to detonations: apparently instantaneous detonations.
7. Type of detonation; low order detonation; fragments varying from approximately $\frac{1}{2}$" to 1" x $2\frac{1}{2}$".
8. Brief description of damage:
   (a) Impact effect negligible.
   (b) Direct effects: 1. First projectile made 8" x 12" hole in forecastle deck (frames 35-36), dented deck and bitt. 2. Second projectile demolished after starboard side of motor whale-boat, causing hole about 7 feet long extending from keel to gunwale at widest point.
   (c) Fragment effect: 1. Shrapnel from 1st projectile made five other smaller holes in vicinity and cut two oil lines in Gun. No. 1, which was trained in direction of beach, penetrating plating 3/16" at a distance of 5-7 feet. 2. Shrapnel from second projectile made 36 holes varying from $\frac{1}{2}$" to 1" x 4", penetrating plating 3/16" at distance of about 38-40 feet. Supply cables to bridge under overhead above C.I.C. outside deck were cut in 1 M.C. and navigational light systems.
   (d) Incendiary effects on subsequent explosions: none.
   (e) Path and effects of flash or flame; not noticed; effects negligible.
9. Noxious gases or fumes; not noticed.
10. Action taken: Damage was local and not serious. All necessary repairs were made shortly by ship's force.

        At 1429 B 7 June HARDING struck submerged object with Pointe du Hoe bearing 140° (t) and right hand Church of Grandcamp des Bains bearing 133° (t). The sound dome and both propellers were badly damaged. It is believed HARDING struck a recently sunk ship or an uncharted wreck as the water at this

point showed seven (7) fathoms on the chart for the stage of tide obtaining at
the time. Several of our landing craft and larger ships had been sunk in this
general area on D-day and their exact location was then and still is unknown.
As the ship could make twelve to fifteen (12 - 15) knots without excessive
vibration I retained her in the Fire Support Area as she had only expended about
fifty (50) percent of her ammunition at that time.

    2.   Enemy damage.

        It is impossible to assess full amount of damage inflicted on the
enemy by the Fire Support Destroyers. The inspecting officer who made photographs of Enclosure (C) stated that he saw no gun emplacements, machine gun nests,
etc., which had not been at least partially destroyed. I am unable to estimate
the number of enemy troops killed and wounded by our fire.

Part V - A. Special Comments.

    1.   Communications.

        Communications on the whole were satisfactory. The original eight
(8) U. S. Destroyers in the Fire Support Group were equipped with SCR 608 for
voice communications with Shore Fire Control Parties. However when BARTON,
O'BRIEN, and ELLYSON arrived they were not equipped with this set and had to
work Shore Fire Control Parties by CW. One of these destroyers used the basic
fire control channel 4300 kcs. as a voice channel. This did not cause as much
confusion as might have been expected but still is not considered to be good
practice. BARTON and O'BRIEN also did not have the destroyer frequency crystal
for their TBS sets (66.25 mc) and had only a TBY on board for this frequency.
As usual the TBY turned out to be thoroughly unsatisfactory. We must stop
kidding ourselves that the TBY can be used in battle. These sets should be
removed from combatant vessels and replaced by the SCR 608 or 609 both of which
have been used by ships of this squadron with complete satisfaction. Destroyer
Squadron EIGHTEEN is also equipped with SCR 624 and ships of this squadron were
never at a loss for a circuit by which to talk to each other. The SCR 608 has
20 receiving and 10 transmitting channels and 96 crystals, the SCR 609 2 channels
and 4 crystals and the SCR 624 7 channels and 14 crystals.

        Visual communications were established by at least two destroyers
with troops ashore and proved to be most valuable both in soliciting fire support, requesting removal of casualties, and replacement of ammunition, food,
etc. Such communication would be most valuable immediately after the landing
and before Shore Fire Control Parties have become established on the beach.
Several destroyers did not establish communications with their Shore Fire Control
Parties until late afternoon of D day. These ships could readily have delivered
fire requested by light or any other means.

        We still do not take full advantage of our splendid TBS sets. Al-
though each combatant ship and many of the transports had four or five crystals
for the TBS only two channels were in use in the Western Task Force Area, 66.25 mc
for the Fire Support Ships and 72.5 mc for all other uses. This overloaded both
of these channels while three unused crystals rested peacefully in their con-
tainers.

SECRET   ENCLOSURE "A"

There must be some way to improve the air-raid warning system. Destroyers were not allowed to use their air-search radars and usually their first warning was the explosion of the first bomb. Perhaps radar picket ships stationed away from the Area is a partial answer.

2.   Food distribution at General Quarters.

Prior to sortie from England ships of Destroyer Squadron EIGHTEEN were directed to procure three (3) days supply of K rations. All Fire Support ships were constantly at General Quarters for the first three (3) days of the assault and the food distribution problem was greatly simplified by use of these K rations. Most ships served hot soup and coffee at least once a day in addition to the K rations. The preparation and serving of the soup and coffee presented no problem and in conjunction with the K rations made a most satisfactory diet for the crew and officers. A three (3) day supply of K rations is admittedly bulky and presents a problem in stowage, however the simplification of food distribution thus furnished more than paid for the slight difficulty in stowing the rations. It is only necessary to procure these rations shortly before the sortie.

B. Recommendations.

1.   That pre-landing bombardment by Naval Forces be for a longer period than from H minus 40 minutes to H hour. In this connection it is most necessary that a ship continue its bombardment until a very short time before the troops actually touch down. i.e. (TEXAS bombardment of Pointe du Hoe ceased forty-five (45) minutes before delayed Rangers landed).

2.   That a much heavier air bombardment be scheduled prior to and during Naval Bombardment. Omaha area was hardly touched by air bombardment with the exception of Pointe du Hoe.

3.   That special units which are to attack away from the main beach as the 2nd Rangers did; be loaded into a ship which can come closer to their beach than the regular Transport Area. One of the old converted four-stack destroyers would have been ideal for this purpose. Such a ship should also carry ammunition replacements for its assault party.

4.   That there be established on the beach or on a control ship an agency which is kept constantly informed of vicinity of front lines and which can pass this information to Fire Support Ships who require it. Time after time in this operation destroyers were unable to shoot at excellent targets of opportunity because they could obtain no information as to the location of our own forces in the area in question. This, I believe, was the greatest difficulty with which the Fire Support destroyers had to contend.

5.   That several LCVP's be placed at the disposal of the Fire Support Commander to answer emergency calls for assistance transmitted by Shore Fire Control Parties. It took me nearly eight (8) hours to get some LCVP's to take off Rangers who were desperately wounded and whose only communication with friendly forces was via their Shore Fire Control Party and by flashing light to one destroyer

11

ENCLOSURE "A"

6.   That whenever possible visual communication be established between ships in Fire Support Area and their Shore Fire Control Party or any troops in the vicinity of the beach. SATTERLEE and HARDING established visual communication with Rangers on Pointe du Hoe. This was most satisfactory and enabled ships to repel several enemy attacks which might easily have resulted in extermination of Rangers. It also enabled ships to furnish badly needed ammunition, supplies, water, and to evacuate casualties and prisoners.

7.   That a mortar shell having a smoke of distinctive color be used by troops when they desire immediate fire support on any target so designated.

8.   That at least one destroyer be stationed in the boat lane where an unobstructed view of the beach may be obtained. Targets of opportunity will thus be observed that could not be seen from positions outside the boat lanes.

9.   That previous to the touchdown and before the troops have advanced too far inland every structure, House and Church adjacent to the beaches or overlooking the beaches that could house any artillery, machine guns, mortars, and/or communication and observation posts be demolished. One destroyer in each Fire Support Area should be assigned this mission during the pre-landing Naval bombardment and all Fire Support Ships should assist while waiting for targets of opportunity.

10.   That for an operation against prepared coastal defenses the number of 5"/38 common be increased to one hundred rounds per gun. AA common is not satisfactory for use against gun emplacements and concrete pillboxes.

11.   That twenty (20) to twenty-five (25) rounds per gun of white phosphorus be carried for use as incendiaries against houses and other beach structures as well as to provide smoke screens for our own troops.

12.   That TBY's be replaced by SCR 608 or SCR 609.

13.   That all Channels of TBS be assigned before assignment of less reliable voice set channels is made.

Part VI - Personnel, performance and casualties.

All personnel behaved in a manner in keeping with the Highest Traditions of the U.S. Naval Service. Morale was exceptionally good. Although kept at General Quarters for several days at a time and with only brief periods of rest at their battle stations there was no grumbling and no decrease in the desire to meet the enemy at every opportunity.

I cannot too highly praise the bravery and superb fighting ability displayed by the 2nd Ranger Battalion in its attack on the fortifications at Pointe du Hoe. If any group deserves a Unit Citation for this battle these Rangers should get it.

12

ENCLOSURE "A"

All the destroyers of this Fire Support Group were under intermittent enemy fire from artillery, mortars, and machine guns for the first three (3) days of the assault. Most ships had many near misses, one was hit by two (2) 105 millimeter shells, and several hit by machine gun fire but not a single personnel casualty caused by enemy action was experienced in the Destroyer Fire Support Group, Force "O".

Recommendations for awards to Naval Personnel have been made the subject of separate correspondence.

13

Shore bombardment on the 7th of June was much more satisfying than the previous day, as several targets were designated by SFCP on which excellent results were obtained. As our own troops were advancing toward Quienville from the eastward, we were in a good position to support them and were most anxious to do so.

About 0900, SFCP 34 commenced designating targets, firing on target #5 (4 gun, 155mm battery);

USS *Thompson* After Action Report:

```
OF6-18/A16-3              DESTROYER SQUADRON EIGHTEEN
Serial: 0048

S-E-C-R-E-T                              Care Fleet Post Office,
                                         New York, N. Y.,
                                         8 July 1944.
SECOND ENDORSEMENT to
THOMPSON ltr. DD627/A16-
3/Dg. (019) of 21 June 1944.


From:        Commander Task Group ONE TWENTY-FOUR POINT SEVEN, Commander
             Destroyer Fire Support Group, Force "O", and Commander
             Task Group ONE TWENTY-TWO POINT FOUR (CDS 18).
To  :        The Commander in Chief, United States Fleet.
Via :        (1) Commander Task Group ONE TWENTY-FOUR POINT NINE.
             (2) Commander Task Force ONE TWENTY-FOUR.
             (3) Commander Task Force ONE TWENTY-TWO.
             (4) Commander U.S. Naval Forces, EUROPE.

Subject:     Action Report, U.S.S. THOMPSON - 5 - 17 June, 1944.

     1.      The passage of Convoy O-1, the main assault convoy, from Portland,
England, to the Assault Area in the Baie de la Seine was uneventful and without
incident.  Orders for the escort of this convoy and for the mine sweeping flotilla
support groups are in my Operation Order 5-44; also see my serial 075 of 1 July
1944.

     2.      The action of the Force "O" Destroyer Gunfire Support Group
(DesRon 18 less ENDICOTT plus EMMONS, H.M.S. TANATSIDE, MELBREAK and TALYBONT)
may be divided into three phases:

             (a) Scheduled pre-landing shore bombardment.
             (b) Firing at targets of opportunity on D day.  This action con-
                 sisted in disposing the destroyers close along the beaches,
                 generally within 1000 yards or less.  In many places enemy
                 light guns, mortars and machine guns were pinning our troops
                 to the beaches.  The destroyers therefore assumed the role of
                 close mobile artillery in direct support of the troops and,
                 by watching for enemy gun flashes, spent the day in silencing
                 these guns.  The action gave the destroyers the unique ex-
                 perience of participating in a land battle at close range and
                 of seeing German troops, driven from their guns by destroyer
                 gun fire, surrender to United States troops on the beaches, who
                 were thus enabled to advance.
             (c) Firing call fire as requested by shore fire control parties.
                 In general, most of this fire was subsequent to D day.

     3.      Due to my duties as Commander Area Screen (CTG 122.4) FRANKFORD
was in the fire support area only between 0920 and 1600 on D day - see paragraph
2 (b).  At other times Commander W.J. Marshall, ComDesDiv 36 was in active com-
```

mand of the Force "O" gunfire support destroyers under Commander Task Group 124.9 in accordance with my Operation Order 7-44.

4.   THOMPSON's performance during the E boat action of 11 June was interesting and effective. I had managed to vector two British steam gunboats (H.M.S. GREY WOLF, GREY GOOSE) into contact with two E boats which were approaching the screen from the north. Both British and Germans opened fire on each other at about 1200 yards range and at a distance from the screen of about 9000 yards. THOMPSON, observing the action, fired star shells beyond the retreating E boats and provided good illumination for the steam gunboats. Details of this action are in other correspondence.

5.   THOMPSON's general performance of duty during ███████ - escorting, gunfire support and as a unit of the Western Task Force area screen - was excellent.

Harry Sanders

HARRY SANDERS

11thPHIB/A16-3   **ELEVENTH AMPHIBIOUS FORCE**
Serial: 00904

SECRET

S-E-C-R-E-T

8 - AUG 1944

FOURTH ENDORSEMENT to:
CO USS THOMPSON Secret
ltr., A16-3, Serial 019
dated 21 June 1944.

From: Commander Assault Force "O".
To :   Commander-in-Chief, United States Fleet.

Subject: Report of Assault on COLLEVILLE-VIERVILLE Sector,
             Coast of NORMANDY.

1.   Forwarded.

2.   The fire of the THOMPSON was of particular assistance during the early morning of D ≠ 1 in enabling the Rangers to maintain their positions on POINTE DU HOE.

J L Hall Jr

J. L. HALL, Jr.

U.S.S. THOMPSON (DD627)
c/o Fleet Post Office
New York, N. Y.

U.S.S. THOMPSON (DD627) - OPERATIONS 5 - 17 JUNE 1944

5 JUNE 1944

1806   Underway from Portland, England in accordance with operation
~~——~~ and CTF-124 operation order BB-44. Escorting convoy
O-1 consisting of transports and landing craft. Escort commander CTG-124.7 (CDS-18 in FRANKFORD). THOMPSON station
3000 yards astern of convoy, as rear escort.

2204   Passed through point "Zebra". Changed course to 180°T. Left
standard searched channels and entered special operations
channel.

2240   General Quarters. Condition "Able" set. Four boilers on
main steam line.

2330   Experiencing some congestion resulting from another convoy
group closing in from northeastward and mingling with O-1.
White flares on horizon 250°T.

2332   Red and green flares, 205°T.

2335   Anti-aircraft fire, 210°T.

2345   White flares on horizon, 200°T.

6 JUNE 1944

0000   Proceeding down FS channel #3 astern of landing craft of convoy O-1. Intermittent AA flashes and frequent flares along
French coast to southward.

0245   Arrived Omaha transport area. Proceeding through convoy at
slow speed to attain favorable position to depart for FS area
off Point de la Percbe.

0330   Intense illumination of Seine Bay by aerial flares over Utah
transport area.

0430   Left transport area to take FS station off Point de la Percbe.
Became unit of TG-124.9. (CTG-124.9 Rear Admiral Bryant in
U.S.S. TEXAS.) Intense aerial bombardment of Point du Hoc
area taking place. Shore line completely obscured by smoke
and dust.

0458	Plane exploded and crashed, 180°T.
0530	Arrived assigned FS position with Point de la Perœe bearing 180°T, 2200 yards.
0530	Battleships commenced firing at shore installations.
0550	Commenced firing on target 74 with 5" battery.
0620	Shifted fire to target 75. Target 74 apparently destroyed. 107 rounds ammunition expended. (55 rounds common and 52 rounds AA common.)
0635	Landing craft moving in toward beach.
0638	Landing craft at beach, rocket barges firing at beachline.
0646	Checked fire due to dense smoke and dust covering coastline.
0700	Resumed fire on target 75.
0710	Ceased firing on target 75, target destroyed. Expended 56 rounds ammunition. (26 rounds common and 30 rounds AA common expended.)
0716	Field gun observed firing on beachhead from approximately 636928. Commenced firing on above gun.
0755	Ceased fire on above target. Target destroyed. All cover in vicinity reduced. Expended 106 rounds ammunition. (60 rounds common and 46 rounds AA common.)
0757	Shifted fire to clump of trees approximately 634939 which appears to be good cover for field battery.
0810	Landing craft continued to land on beach. 1 L.C.I. on fire from shell hit.
0812	Ceased fire on suspected artillery cover. 68 rounds expended. (36 common and 32 AA common.) Cover demolished.
0813	Lying to, watching for enemy gun fire.
0835	Proceeding westward toward Point du Hoe searching for targets of opportunity.

Overleaf: The 1032hrs onwards targeting of the Radar Station had such a comprehensive effect, it ensured its destruction by the time the Rangers arrived there.

0905   Area air alert.

0912   Area air "all clear".

0913   Attempting to establish communications with SFCP # 16 and 18.

1029   Commenced firing at position 625934. Target is Giant Wurtz-
        burg Radar.

1032   Target destroyed. 20 rounds AA common ammunition expended.
        Shifted fire to second Giant Wurtzburg, position 632936.

1036   Target destroyed. 30 rounds AA common ammunition expended.

1037   Commenced firing on third Radar and buildings, position 632934.

1043   Ceased firing. 24 rounds ammunition expended. Building ex-
        ploded causing series of detonations toward cliff's edge, as
        though ammunition dump had been hit.

1052   Standing toward "Easy Red" beach.

1151   Commenced firing on suspected fortified house at "Easy Red"
        beach.

1155   Ceased fire. 10 rounds ammunition expended. Shots observed
        to hit, effect unknown. Rocket Guns observed firing on beach-
        head from about 678893. Shifted fire to that target imme-
        diately.

1213   Ceased firing. 30 rounds ammunition expended. (4 rounds com-
        mon and 26 rounds AA common.) Target completely silenced.

1215   Landing force attempting to use Dog Green Exit apparently
        stopped by unlocated snipers or batteries. THOMPSON moving
        over toward Dog Green Exit.

1223   Commenced demolition of all houses and structures commanding
        Dog Green Exit.

1250   Ceased fire. Effect of fire indeterminate. Tanks still re-
        fusing to use Dog Green Exit. 47 rounds AA common expended.

1300   Lying to watching for targets.

1311   Established contact with SFCP #16. Ordered to standby. Lying
        to off Dog Green beach.

- 3 -

CONFIDENTIAL

1403	Resumed fire at Dog Green Exit concentrating on all structures and possible sniper nests.
1437	Ceased firing at Dog Green Exit. 71 rounds AA common expended. Effect of fire not determinable. Battleships shooting at same area.
1730	Unlocated Field Battery causing extreme damage to forces assembling on beachhead. 7 tanks and 3 LST's afire from direct hits, personnel casualties apparently high. Destroyers closing in to 1500 yards and using every facility to locate battery.
1812	Commenced firing at church concealed in gulley behind "Easy Red" beach.
1822	Ceased Fire. 23 rounds AA common ammunition expended. Effect not observed. Shifted target to red roof building to the right of Vierville church.
1827	Target blew up. Ceased fire. 24 rounds AA common expended.
1836	Shifted fire to slot on Point de la Percee cliff face.
1838	Ceased fire. Slot caved in. 12 rounds AA common expended.
1839	Ordered by CTG-124.9 to exchange stations with USS SATTERLEE off Point du Hoe and to take her SFCP.
1904	Relieved USS SATTERLEE and standing by for target designation.
1930	Received visual dispatch from Ranger group on Point du Hoe requesting boat to evacuate wounded. Relayed same to CTF-124 by radio.
1954	Commenced firing at first target (fortified house), Chateau de M. le Baron. First salvo a direct hit, target destroyed. 8 rounds AA Common expended.
2015	Commenced firing at fortified house 500 yards east of Chateau de M. le Baron.
2029	Ceased firing at above target. Fire ineffective. 24 rounds AA common expended.
2030	Commenced firing on SFCP target 593928 - Pillbox. 12 rounds AA common expended. Fire not effective.
2033	Shifted fire to 575935 - Pillbox. 43 rounds AA common expended, fire effective.

⑧

- 4-

CONFIDENTIAL

2043	Shifted fire to 583932 - Railroad. 21 rounds AA common expended, fire effective.
2054	Ceased firing.
2222	Commenced firing at targets 91 amd 93.
2225	Ceased firing - Target destroyed. Target consisted of machine guns, howitzers, shelters, and flak guns. 26 rounds AA common expended.
2230	Received visual dispatch from Point du Hoe Rangers giving coordinates of 7 targets to be called for by blinker during night.

7 JUNE 1944.

0440	Commenced firing at blinker designated targets 1 and 2. Coordinates 574932 and 572935.
0450	Ceased fire. 66 rounds ammunition expended, effect not reported.
0457	Commenced firing at targets # 5 and 6, coordinates 590920 and 580926.
0505	Ceased firing. 84 rounds AA common expended, effect not reported.
0508	Commenced fire at target # 3, coordinate 581932, consisting of 6 AA guns.
0510	Ceased fire. 40 rounds AA common expended. Effect not reported.
0525	Commenced fire on AA battery at 565935.
0527	Checked fire. Ensign on foretruck fouled,on SG antenna.
0536	Resumed fire on same target.
0547	Ceased fire. 30 rounds AA common expended. Target destroyed.
0600	Commenced fire on AA Battery at 575938.
0603	Ceased firing. 20 rounds AA common expended. Fire effective. 70% of ammunition now expended.

- 5 -

ENCLOSURE (A)

CNFIDENTIAL

0606	Relieved on station by USS HARDING. Remaining targets of those received by blinker from Point du Hoe Rangers turned over to USS HARDING.
0645	Set course for Portland, England, in accordance with verbal instructions of CDS-18. Proceeding various courses and speeds conforming to channel 34 and THOMPSON 070755B.
0750	Secured from General Quarters, set condition II-M.
1246	Anchored in Weymouth Bay to take on fuel and ammunition.

8 JUNE 1944

0034	Completed fueling and loading ammunition to capacity. Underway in company with USS SATTERLEE for Omaha area in accordance SATTERLEE's 072115B and FOINC, Portland dispatch 072218. Set condition II.
0625	Arrived Omaha area, reported to CTG-122.4 and assumed screening station Dixie 48. Nothing to report throughout remainder of day.

9 JUNE 1944

0042	Went to General Quarters.
0044	E-Boat attack developed from Point Barfluer. Ships in screen commenced firing. This vessel held fire because range was fouled by other screening ships. E-Boats successfully driven off, retiring northeastward at high speed.
0245	Target re-appeared at 028°. Range again fouled. Fired 1 starshell at range of 10,000 yards.
0430	Screen resumed normal formation.
0545	Set condition II.
1617	Provisioned USS PC-1225.
2154	Area air alert.
2200	Went to General Quarters.

- 6 -

Utah Beach Gunfire Support Summary:
HMS *Hawkins* and HMS *Enterprise* were in touch with the Rangers by radio on 7 June.

```
SECRET-OPERATION ▓▓▓▓▓
ANNEX "GEORGE" to
FORCE "U" OPERATION REPORT
Serial: 00198

    GUNFIRE SUPPORT SUMMARY    6 June 1944

        Coastal defense batteries opened fire on Bombarding Force at 0523
    in Fire Support Channel One.  Ships returned fire, engaging targets as
    called for in Gunfire Annex of CTF 125 Op. Plan 3-44.

        Fire continued by Bombarding Force throughout day upon known targets
    and upon call from Shore Fire Control Parties.  Air spot and air recon-
    naisance was used and results were fair.

        Enemy gunfire was accurately directed at the beach area.

        Following results of counterbattery fire and air bombing during D-
    day were reported:

        BATTERY    1A   Camouflaged and undamaged
           "       7A   Six casemates undamaged
           "       17   Four casemates damaged
           "        9   Four casemates still intact
           "        8   Four casemates undamaged

    Improvement in air spotting obviously very necessary.

                        7 June 1944

        Bombarding ships resumed original fire support stations.  HMS
    HAWKINS and HMS ENTERPRISE set Force "O" common frequency channel on
    SCR 608's to assist Ranger Shore Fire Control Party in vicinity of Point
    Du Hoc.  Heavy shelling of Red and Green Beach continued throughout day.
    Air reconnaisance and air spotting available.  Great improvements in re-
    sults.

    Reports received from Air Spotting Planes.
```

TARGET	SHIP	SPOTTER COMMENT
5	HAWKINS	18 hits
16	HAWKINS	24 hits
13A	QUINCY	Hits in Area
	TUSCALOOSA	Effective
	NEVADA	No further activity
	BLACK PRINCE	Effective
14	BLACK PRINCE	Neutralized
3	BLACK PRINCE	Effective
	NEVADA	Neutralized
	QUINCY	Neutralized
	GLENNON	Results effective
5	HAWKINS	Silenced
	ENTERPRISE	Shoot effective
7A	QUINCY	Numerous hits
	NEVADA	Hits
7B	QUINCY	Done for
3	NEVADA	Silenced
9	NEVADA	Silenced, 6 casemates destroyed
15	BLACK PRINCE	Effective
8A	BLACK PRINCE	Effective
20	NEVADA	Neutralized
17	NEVADA	Destroyed
26	QUINCY	Direct hit

```
                        -1-
```

After Action Reports USS *McCook*:

```
                         U.S.S. Mc COOK (DD496)

C-DD496/A12-1/A16-3                          Care of Fleet Post Office,
Serial 028                                      New York, New York,
                                                  24 July 1944


C-O-N-F-I-D-E-N-T-I-A-L

Subject:        War Diary - Month of June 1944.
- - - - - - - - - - - - - - - - - - - - - - - - - - - - - - - - - - - -


6 June 1944

   00-04
        Steaming in company with U.S.S. SATTERLEE and U.S.S. CARMICK in
column formation astern of advance minesweepers of Force "O", steaming
on various courses and speeds enroute Invasion area between Le Havre
and Cherbourg. OTC ComDesDiv 36 in U.S.S. SATTERLEE. Ship at General
Quarters; ship darkened. All boilers on main and auxiliary lines. 0056
Heaved to, to wait for minesweepers to pass through bombardment area.
0140 Stood out of channel 4 on orders OTC, standing towards channel 3
at slow speed. 0205 19900 yards from Point Du Hoe. 0229 14000 yards from
Point Du Hoe. 0253 Advance minesweepers, Force "O" commenced return
from bombardment area. 0320 Bombing of beach and water in front of beach
commenced. 0329 Chandelier flares and heavy bomb explosions seen in
direction of Cherbourg beach. 0352 Chandelier flares and bombs dropped
on port quarter.

   04-08
        Steaming as before, moving slowly towards assigned bombardment
area. 0447 Heavy bombing of beach defenses commenced. Continuous flares,
bomb blasts, explosions and AA fire. 0501 Beach bombing ceased. 0527
Approached within 3200 yards of beach off Vierville-Sur-Mer. Beach quiet;
no fire or counter fire. 0533 Beach batteries opend fire on British units
to Eastward, drawing counter fire from ships. 0538 U.S. Battleships open-
ed fire. H.M.S.  GLASGOW opened fire. 0550 H-40. U.S.S. Mc COOK opened
fire on assigned targets on beach to seaward of Vierville-Sur-Mer church.
0600 First two assigned targets neutralized, shifted to third. 0603 Re-
ceived two near misses off fantail, believed from 105mm or 155mm shore
battery. 0604 Received near miss 1000 yards off starboard beam, believed
from 155mm shore battery or mortar. 0608 220 rounds 5"/38 cal. project-
iles expended in rapid continuous fire. 0614 Automatic weapons commenced
firing. 0615 Ceased firing automatic weapons due to excessive range. 0616
All assigned targets neutralized. Shifted targets of opportunity. 0638
First landing craft containing men and material made landing on beach.
Enemy fire severe from unknow points. 0642 Ceased firing, having expended
320 rounds 5"/38 cal. projectiles. 0645 Fighter protection in large numbers
arrived over bombardment area. 0650 fired starshell salvo to clear guns.
Endeavoured to contact SFCP without success. 0715 Received report U.S.S.
CORRY hit repeatedly by Target 86 (anti-tank gun). 0745 Commenced firing
on target then under fire by U.S.S. THOMPSON.
```

U.S.S. Mc COOK (DD496)

C-DD496/A12-1/A16-3   Care of Fleet Post Office,
Serial 028   New York, New York,
                                            24 July 1944.

C-O-N-F-I-D-E-N-T-I-A-L

Subject: War Diary - Month of June 1944.
- -

6 June 1944 (Cont'd)

08-12
        Steaming as before. 0807 LCT hit by mortar fire, burned at edge
of beach. 0815 Target under fire demolished. Ceased fire. Believed target
to be enemy battery. 0839 Commenced firing on pillbox which was delivering
fire against beach. 0852 Ceased firing - range fouled by PC. 0854 Commenced firing. 0858 Ceased firing. Pillbox demolished by direct hits. Two
beach guns destroyed in addition. 0904 Contacted U.S. Naval shore liaison
officer; unable to contact SFCP proper. 0908 Received air raid warning via
radio. 0914 Received all clear from air raid warning. 0915 Total 5"/38 cal.
projectiles expended to this time: 503 rounds. 0933 Commenced firing on
two guns which were set into cliff and were enfilading beach. 0937 Ceased
firing on orders from ComDesDiv 36. 0940 Commenced firing on previous targets. 0946 Ceased firing. Batteries destroyed. One gun emplacement plunged from cliff, other flew into air. 0956 Received "Well Done" from ComDes-
Ron 18 and Admiral Bryant (ComTaskFor 124.7). 1000 Score to date: 3 pillboxes, 6 beach batteries in addition to assigned targets. Resumed fire on
targets of opportunity. Ceased firing. 1024 Resumed firing. Commenced
moving in close to beach at Vierville-Sur-Mer. Distance from beach now 1300
yards. Target gun on cliff about beam. 1043 Received TBS report that infantry was advancing. One gun on cliff destroyed. 1055 Received TBS report
that our infantry was halted in advance in Colleville area. 1111 Sprayed
Cliff abeam with 40mm fire. 1112 Ceased firing - ineffective. 1115 PC-586
moved within 500 yards of beach to take individual houses under fire. 1120
Continuing intermittent fire. 1135 Under mortar fire from undisclosed beach
position; shells dropped 500 yards short. No automatic weapon fire from
beach at any time. 1138 Commenced moving along beach. 1149 Sighted flashes
from enemy battery bearing 300° relative. 1150 Sighted rocket gun battery
in draw; took under fire. 1153 Rocket gun emplacement demolished. Score to
this time: 3 pillboxes, 8 gun emplacements in addition to initially assigned targets.

12-16
        Steaming as before, firing intermittently on tagets of opportunity.
1200 Opened fire on enemy pillbox on cliffside. 1203 Pillbox demolished by
direct hits. 1205 Total 5"/38 cal. ammunition expended to this time: 640
rounds. 1217 Commenced firing on numerous houses and emplacements in gully
leading seaward from Vierville Sur-Mer Church. Destroyed 6 houses (one
three story) and stone wall housing snipers and beach guns. 1250 5"/38 cal.
projectiles expended to this time: 771 rounds.

U.S.S. Mc COOK (DD496)

C-DD496/A12-1/A16-3
Serial 028

Care of Fleet Post Office,
New York, New York,
24 July 1944.

C-O-N-F-I-D-E-N-T-I-A-L

Subject: War Diary - Month of June 1944.

- -

6 June 1944 (Cont'd)

20-24

Steaming as before. 2014 Fired on and demolished remainder of
targets in gully leading seaward from Vierville-Sur-Mer church. 2020
Assigned SFCP formerly assigned to U.S.S. CARMICK. Unable to contact
any SFCP. 2245 Darkened ship. Commenced maneuvering at very slow speed
in bombardment area off Vierville-Sur-Mer beach, watching for targets.
2330 Heavy air raids in vicinity of Force "O" transport area; counted
two ships hit by bombs, fire aircraft shot down in flames. 2350 JU-88
German bomber passed overhead, not identified in time to open fire.
2359 Total score to this time: 6 pillboxes, 8 gun emplacements, 10 stone
houses, in addition to regularly assigned targets.

7 June 1944

00-04

Steaming slowly in company with other ships of assualt bombardment
force of Force "O". 2000-3000 yards of Dog Red and Dog Green beaches to
Eastward of Cap du Hoe, to seaward of Vierville-Sur-Mer, awaiting targets
of opportunity and daylight communication with assigned SFCP. OTC Admiral
Bryant in U.S.S. TEXAS (ComTaskFor 124.7), immediate OTC ComDesDiv 36 in
U.S.S. SATTERLEE. Ship at General Quarters. All boilers on main and auxiliary lines; ship darkened. Intermittent air raids and AA fire. Beach areas
under intermittent mortar fire from Vierville-Sur-Mer area.

04-08

Steaming as before. 0445 U.S.S. SATTERLEE, U.S.S. THOMPSON, U.S.S.
CARMICK departed bombardment area for Portland, England, to replenish
ammunition and fuel. ComDesDiv 36 shifted flag to U.S.S. HARDING. 0500
5"/38 cal. ammunition expended to this time: 936 rounds. 0558 Sunrise.
Lighted ship. No communication with SFCP. 0645 Allied heavy bombers and
fighters concentrated bombing and strafing of beach area and area in
rear of beach, in support of troops. 0710 Allied medium bombers made concentrated runs on shore batteries near tip of Pt. Du Hoe. 0724 Detected
AA fire from Eastward radar station pill box on bluffs East of Pt. Du Hoe.
Commenced firing on pill box. 0738 Ceased firing on orders ComTaskFor 124.7.
Pill box neutralized, gaint **Wuerz** buerger radar demolished. 0745 5"/38 cal.
ammunition expended to this time: 971 rounds. No AA common remaining.

U.S.S. Mc COOK (DD496)

C-DD496/A12-1/A16-3   Care of Fleet Post Office,
Serial 028   New York, New York,
                                                     24 July 1944.

C-O-N-F-I-D-E-N-T-I-A-L

Subject: War Diary - Month of June 1944.
- -

<u>6 June 1944 (Cont'd)</u>

12-16 Cont'd
     1400 Ordered by Admiral Bryant to relieve troops at waters edge who
were under fire by enemy snipers hidden in buildings behind breakwater at
Vierville-Sur-Mer. 1410 Moved into position and commenced firing. 1411
Ceased firing momentarily to avoid PC-586. 1412 Resumed firing, having demolished 4 stone houses believed to contain A/T guns. 1455 Firing on one
camouflaged anti-air craft position on cliff. Destroyed pillbox and gun.
1537 Total 5"/38 cal. ammunition expended to this time: 836 rounds. Reported ammunition expenditure to ComDesRon 18. Total score to this time:
5 pillboxes, 8 gun emplacements, 10 stone houses, in addition to regularly
assigned targets.

16-20
     Steaming as before. 1630 Moved up beach to Eastward in accordance 1620
directive of liaison officer on beach. 1635 Fired four salvos indirect fire,
firing into cliff positions. Group of German soldiers coming out of cliff
partially buried, remainder showed white flag and endeavoured to signal
ship by flashing light and semaphore. 1635-1735 Trying to signal German
troops in German and English. Troops could not receive or transmit legibly
until advised in English that ship was resuming pointblank fire. Received
message "cease fire, friendly". Ordered troops to march to Eastward and
surrender. Cliff appeared to be honey-combed with passages and emplacements.
1741 Took under rapid continuous fire and destroyed houses in gully which
were subjecting beach troops and landing craft to murderous automatic
weapon fire. German troops to Westward commenced moving East with hands up,
and were taken prisoner by Rangers. 1810 Commenced firing on stone tower
on hill in back of beach, which was delivering rapid fire against beach.
Demolished tower on second salvo. 1836 Received report heavy fire against
beach originating in Formigny, reported by Major W.B. Benson, U.S.A. Commenced barage fire against supposed target located in heavy grove to Eastward of Vierville-Sur-Mer. 1840 5"/38 cal. ammunition expended to this
time: 931 rounds. Ordered to hold church under strict surveillance as possible source of fire and spotting center. 1850 Received message in flashing light from beach "Extremely urgent to evacuate casualties". Relayed
message to TEXAS. 1855 Resumed intermittent fire at supposed targets.

U.S.S. Mc COOK (DD496)

C-DD496/A12-1/A16-3
Serial 028

Care of Fleet Post Office,
New York, New York,
24 July 1944.

C-O-N-F-I-D-E-N-T-I-A-L

Subject: War Diary - Month of June 1944.

- -

6 June 1944 (Cont'd)

20-24

Steaming as before. 2014 Fired on and demolished remainder of
targets in gully leading seaward from Vierville-Sur-Mer church. 2020
Assigned SFCP formerly assigned to U.S.S. CARMICK. Unable to contact
any SFCP. 2245 Darkened ship. Commenced maneuvering at very slow speed
in bombardment area off Vierville-Sur-Mer beach, watching for targets.
2330 Heavy air raids in vicinity of Force "O" transport area; counted
two ships hit by bombs, fire aircraft shot down in flames. 2350 JU-88
German bomber passed overhead, not identified in time to open fire.
2359 Total score to this time: 6 pillboxes, 8 gun emplacements, 10 stone
houses, in addition to regularly assigned targets.

7 June 1944

00-04

Steaming slowly in company with other ships of assualt bombardment
force of Force "O". 2000-3000 yards of Dog Red and Dog Green beaches to
Eastward of Cap du Hoe, to seaward of Vierville-Sur-Mer, awaiting targets
of opportunity and daylight communication with assigned SFCP. OTC Admiral
Bryant in U.S.S. TEXAS (ComTaskFor 124.7), immediate OTC ComDesDiv 36 in
U.S.S. SATTERLEE. Ship at General Quarters. All boilers on main and auxiliary lines; ship darkened. Intermittent air raids and AA fire. Beach areas
under intermittent mortar fire from Vierville-Sur-Mer area.

04-08

Steaming as before. 0445 U.S.S. SATTERLEE, U.S.S. THOMPSON, U.S.S.
CARMICK departed bombardment area for Portland, England, to replenish
ammunition and fuel. ComDesDiv 36 shifted flag to U.S.S. HARDING. 0500
5"/38 cal. ammunition expended to this time: 936 rounds. 0558 Sunrise.
Lighted ship. No communication with SFCP. 0645 Allied heavy bombers and
fighters concentrated bombing and strafing of beach area and area in
rear of beach, in support of troops. 0710 Allied medium bombers made concentrated runs on shore batteries near tip of Pt. Du Hoe. 0724 Detected
AA fire from Eastward radar station pill box on bluffs East of Pt. Du Hoe.
Commenced firing on pill box. 0738 Ceased firing on orders ComTaskFor 124.7.
Pill box neutralized, gaint Wusrz buerger radar demolished. 0745 5"/38 cal.
ammunition expended to this time: 971 rounds. No AA common remaining.

U.S.S. Mc COOK (DD496)

C-DD496/A12-1/A16-3   Care of Fleet Post Office,
Serial 028   New York, New York,
                                                 24 July 1944.

C-O-N-F-I-D-E-N-T-I-A-L

Subject: War Diary - Month of June 1944.
- -

7 June 1944 (Cont'd)

    08-12
        Steaming as before, firing intermittently on targets of opportunity.
Total score to this time: 7 pillboxes, 8 gun emplacements, 10 stone houses,
in addition to regularly assigned targets.

    12-16
        Steaming as before. 1200 Contacted SFCP No. 3. 1300 Received targets
from SFCP, relayed to U.S.S. TEXAS so that own airspot could be employed.
U.S.S. TEXAS directed H.M.S. GLASGOW to open fire with salvoes of 7.5's.
1314 Targets neutralized, U.S.S. GLASGOW ceased firing. SFCP moved to
position forward. 1315 Observed numerous large explosions in "U" force
transport area, believed to be mines or 255mm battery reported in area
backing Cap Du Hoe. 1325 Heavy and Medium Allied bombers began "shuttle-
bombing" of area back of assualt beaches. 1430 Regained contact with SFCP
No. 3; no targets available.

    16-20
        Steaming as before. 1835   Reconnaisance determined Pt. Du Hoe to be
in Allied hands. LCVP went inshore to evacuate seriously wounded at point
and discharge ammunition, water and small arms. 1855 Received SOS from SS
DINARD, (hospital ship), position 000-35' W; 49°-34' N. Ship hit mine.
1856 SFCP came in, reported no assistance needed at this time. 1911 Departed
bombardment area for screen area on orders Admiral Deyo; acting as courier
to U.S.S. FRANKFORD. Steaming on various courses and speeds.

    20-24
        Steaming as before. 2005 Reached transport area. Transmitted message
to U.S.S. FRANKFORD by flashing light. 2034 Received report hospital ship
SS DINARD still afloat. 2037 Departed transport area for bombardment area,
steaming on various courses and speeds. 2040 SFCP Reported they were subjected to heavy fire: requested fire support. Transmitted message to U.S.S.
TEXAS. U.S.S. TEXAS provided support requested. 2112 SFCP Reported enemy
fire neutralized. 2130 Received target designation from SFCP. 2148 Arrived
in bombardment area approximately 2500 yards to seaward from Cap Du Hoe,
opened fire, using indirect fire. 2158 Ceased firing; no information as to
effectiveness of fire. SFCP Order cease fire. 2207 SFCP Secured for night.
Total 5"/38 cal. projectiles expended at this time: 1013 rounds.

U.S.S. Mc COOK (DD496)

C-DD496/A12-1/A16-3
Serial 028

Care of Fleet Post Office,
New York, New York,
24 July 1944.

C-O-N-F-I-D-E-N-T-I-A-L

Subject: War Diary - Month of June 1944.
- -

7 June 1944 (Cont'd)

   20-24 (Cont'd)
      2255 Army signal unit on Western extremity of Vierville-Sur-Mer
beach made signal by flashing light; designated target. Enemy fire detected from vicinity of beach fires in Vierville-Sur-Mer target area.
2257 U.S.S. McCOOK selected by Admiral Bryant (ComTaskFor 124.7) to fire
on source of enemy fire because of ship's firecontrol. Commenced firing.
2303 Ceased firing, having started three brilliant fires accompanied by
explosions in area to rear of and Westward of Vierville-Sur-Mer. No
further enemy fire notice from this area. Requested more explicit data
from Army signal station, received no reply. 2350 Enemy bombing commenced.
Moderate AA fire. 2400 Moved Westward along beach to assume night bombardment patrol in vicinity of Pt. Du Hoe. Total score to this time: 7 pill
boxes, 8 gun emplacements, 10 stone houses, in addition to regularly assigned targets first day: one shore battery not confirmed.

U.S.S. Mc COOK (DD496)

C-DD496/A12-1/A16-3
Serial 028

Care of Fleet Post Office,
New York, New York,
24 July 1944.

C-O-N-F-I-D-E-N-T-I-A-L

Subject: War Diary - Month of June 1944.
- -

8 June 1944 (Cont'd)

   04-08 (Cont'd)
      Total score during initial phase of assualt, June 6 to June 8:   7
pillboxes, 8 gun emplacements, 10 stone houses, in addition regularly assigned targets, and one shore battery believed neutralized but not seem to be
destroyed. Original assigned targets consisted of three pillboxes, 13 machine gun nests and three shore guns.

U.S.S. Mc COOK (DD496)

S-E-C-R-E-T

PART II

At 1101B 5 June 1944, this vessel got underway from Weymouth Harbor in company with U.S.S. SATTERLEE and U.S.S. CARMICK. 1720 Rendezvoused with minesweepers and proceeded at slow speed across the English Channel. At 2200 the ship went to General Quarters. Just prior to midnight, bombing, flares, and A.A. fire were observed on the Cherbourg Penisula. 0056 Heaved to, to wait for minesweepers to pass through bombardment area. 0140 Stood out of Channel 4 on orders OTC, stood towards Channel 3 at slow speed. 0205 19,900 yards from Point Du Hoe. 0229 14,000 yards from Point Du Hoe. 0253 Advance mine-sweepers, Force "O" commenced return from bombardment area. 0320 Bombing of beach and water in front of beach commenced. 0329 Chandelier flares and heavy bomb explosions were seen in direction of Cherbourg beach. 0352 Chandelier flares and bombs dropped on port quarter. 0447 Heavy bombing of beach defences commenced. Continuous flares, bomb blasts, explosions and A.A. fire were seen. 0501 Beach bombing ceased. 0527 Approached within 3200 yards of beach off Vierville Sur Mer. Beach was quiet; no fire or counter fire. 0533 Beach batteries opened fire on British units to Eastward, drawing counter fire from ships. 0538 U.S. Battleships opened fire. H.M.S. CLASGOW opened fire. 0550 H Hour-40. U.S. Mc COOK opened fire on assigned targets on beach to seaward of Vierville Sur Mer church. 0600 First two assigned targets neutralized, shifted to third. 0603 Received two near misses off fan-tail, believed from 155 mm shore battery or mortar. 0608 220 rounds 5"/38 cal. projectiles expended in rapid continuous fire. 0614 Automatic weapons commenced firing. 0615 Ceased firing automatic weapons due to excessive range. 0616 All assigned targets appeared neutralized. Shifted to targets of opportunity. 0638 First landing craft containing men and material made landing on beach. Enemy fire severs from unknown points. 0642 Ceased firing, having a total of 320 rounds 5"/38 cal. projectiles. 0645 Fighter protection in large numbers arrived over bombardment area. 0650 Fired starshell salvo to clear guns. Endeavoured to contact SFCP without success. 0715 Received report U.S.S. CORRY hit repeatedly by target 86 (anti-tank gun). 0745 Commenced firing on target then under fire by U.S.S. THOMPSON. 0807 LCT hit by mortar fire, burned at edge of beach. 0815 Target under fire demolished. Ceased fire. Believed target to be enemy battery. 0839 Commenced firing on pillbox which was delivering fire against beach. 0852 Ceased firing on pillbox - range fouled by Patrol craft. 0854 Commenced firing. 0858 Ceased firing. Pillbox demolished by direct hits. Two beach guns destroyed in addition. 0903 Contacted U.S. Naval Shore Liaison Officer; unable to contact SFCP proper. 0908 Received air raid warning via radio. 0914 Received all clear from air raid warning. 0915 Total 5"/38 cal. projectiles expended to this time: 503 rounds.

U.S.S. Mc COOK (DD496)

S-E-C-R-E-T

PART II - CONT'D

0933 Commenced firing on two guns which were set into cliff and were enfilading beach. 0937 Ceased firing on orders from ComDesDix 36. 0940 Commenced firing on previous targets. 0946 Ceased firing. Batteries appeared destroyed. One gun emplacement plunged from cliff, other flew into air. 1000 Resumed fire on targets of opportunity. 1003 Ceased firing. 1024 Resumed firing. Commenced moving in close to beach at Vierville Sur Mer. Distance from beach now 1300 yards. Target, gun on cliff, about abeam. 1043 Received TBS report that infantry was advancing. One gun on cliff destroyed. 1055 Received TBS report that infantry was halted in advance in Colleville area. 1111 Sprayed cliff abeam with 40 mm fire. 1112 Ceased 40 mm fire - ineffective. 1115 PC 568 moved within 500 yards of beach to take individual houses under fire. 1120 Continuing intermittent fire. 1135 Under mortar fire from undisclosed beach position; shells dropped 500 yards short. No automatic weapon fire from beach at any time. 1138 Commenced moving along beach. 1149 Sighted flashes from enemy battery bearing 300° relative. 1150 Sighted rocket gun battery in draw; took battery under fire. 1153 Rocket gun emplacement demolished. Score to this time: 3 pillboxes, 8 gun emplacements in addition to initially assigned targets. 1200 Opened fire on enemy pillbox in cliffsides. 1203 Pillbox demolished by direct hits. 1205 Total 5"/38 cal. ammunition expended to this time: 640 rounds. 1217 Commenced firing on numerous houses and emplacements in gully leading seaward from Vierville Su Mer. church. Destroyed 6 houses (one three story) and stone wall housing snipers and beach guns. 1250 5"/38 cal. projectiles expended to this time: 771 rounds. 1400 Ordered by Admiral Bryant to relieve troops at waters edge who were under fire by enemy snipers hidden in buildings behind breakwater at Vierville Sur Mer. 1410 Moved into position and commenced firing. 1411 Ceased firing momentarily to avoid PC 568. 1412 Resumed firing. 1416 Ceased firing, having demolished 4 stone houses believed to contain A/T guns. 1455 Fired on one camouflaged anti-aircraft gun position on cliff. Destroyed pillbox and gun. 1537 Total 5"/38 cal. ammuntion expended to this time: 836 rounds. 1630 Moved up beach to Eastward in accordance 1620 voice directive of liaison officer on beach. 1635 Fired four indirect fire; firing into cliff positions. Group of German soldiers coming out of cliff partially buried; remainder showed white flag and endeavoured to signal ship by flashing light and semaphore. 1635-1735 Trying to signal German troops in German and English. Troops could not receive or transmit legibly until advised in English that ship was resuming pointblank fire. Received message Ceize Fire. Ordered troops to march to Eastward and surrender. Cliff appeared to be homey-combed with passages and emplacements. 1741 Took under rapid continuous fire and destroyed houses in gully which were subjecting beach and landing craft to murderous automatic weapon fire. German troops to Weatward commenced moving East with hands up, and were taken prisoner by Rangers.

U.S.S. Mc COOK (DD496)

S-E-C-R-E-T

PART II - CONT'D

1810 Commenced firing on stone tower on hill in back of beach, which
was delivering rapid fire against beach. Demolished tower on second
salvo. 1836 Received report heavy fire against beach originating in
Formigny, reported by Major W.B. Benson, U.S.A. Commenced barrage fire
against supposed target located in heavy grove to Eastward of Vierville Sur Mer. 1840 5"/38 cal. ammunition expended to this time: 931
rounds. Ordered to hold church under strict surviellance as possible
source of fire and spotting center. 1850 Received message in flashing
light from beach "Extremely urgent to evacuate casualties". Relayed
message to TEXAS. 1855 Resumed intermittent fire at supposed targets.
2014 Fired on and demolished remainder of targets in gully leading seaward from Vierville Su Mer church. 2020 Assigned SFCP formerly assigned
to U.S.S. CARMICK. Unable to contact any SFCP. 2245 Darkened ship.
Commenced maneuvering at very slow speed in bombardment area off Vierville Sur Mer beach, watching for targets. 2330 Heavy air raids in
vicinity of Force "O" transport area; counted two ships hit by bombs,
five aircraft shot down in flames. 2350 JU-88 German bomber passed
overhead; not identified in time to open fire.

7 JUNE 1944: Steaming slowly 2000-3000 yards off "DOG RED" and "DOG
GREEN" beaches, to Eastward of Cap Du Hoe, to seaward of Vierville Sur
Mer, awaiting targets of opportunity and daylight communications with
assigned SFCP. 0445 ComDesDiv 36 shifted flag to U.S.S. HARDING. 0500
5"/38 cal. ammunition expended to this time: 936 rounds. 0558 Sunrise.
0645 Allied heavy bombers and fighters concentrated bombing and strafing
of beach area and area in rea of beach, in support of troops. 0710
Allied medium bombers made concentrated runs on shore batteries near
tip of Point Du Hoe. 0724 Detected A.A. fire from Eastward of radar
station pillbox on bluffs east of Point Du Hoe. Commenced firing on
pillbox. 0738 Ceased firing on orders ComTaskFor 124.7. Pillbox neutralized; giant radar demolished. 0745 5"/38 cal. ammunition expeneded to
this time: 971 rounds. No. A.A. common remaining. 1200 Contacted SFCP
No. 3. 1300 Received targets from SFCP, relayed to U.S.S. TEXAS so that
own airspot could be employed. U.S.S. TEXAS directed H.M.S. GLASGOW to
open fire. 1314 Targets neutralized. H.M.S. GLASGOW ceased firing. SFCP
moved to position further forward. 1315 Observed numerous large explosions in "U" force transport area, believed to be mines or 255 mm battery
reported in area backing Cap Du Hoe. 1325 Heavy and Medium Allied bombers began "shuttle-bombing" of area back of assault beaches. 1430 Regained contact with SFCP No. 31 no targets available. 1835 Air recon-
naisance determined Point Du Hoe to be in Allied hands. LCVP went inshore to evacuate seriously wounded at point and discharge ammunition,
water and small arms. ·

U.S.S. Mc COOK (DD496)

S-E-C-R-E-T

PART II - CONT'D

1855 Received SOS from SS DINARD (hospital ship), position 00°-35';
49°-34' N. Ship hit mine. 1856 SFCP came in, reported no assistances
needed at this time. 1911 Departed bombardment area for screen area on
orders Admiral Deyo; acting as courier to U.S.S. FRANKFORD. Steaming
various courses and speeds. 2005 Reached transport area. 2027 Transmitted messages to U.S.S. FRANKFORD by flashing light. 2034 Received
report hospital ship SS DINARD still afloat. 2037 Departed transport
area for bombardment area. 2040 SFCP reported they were subjected to
heavy fire: requested fire support. Transmitted message to U.S.S. TEXAS.
U.S.S. TEXAS provided support requested. 2112 SFCP reported enemy fire
neutralized. 2130 Received target designation from SFCP. 2148 Arrived
in bombardment area approximately 2500 yards to seaward from Cap Du
Hoe; opened fire, using indirect fire. 2158 Ceased firing; no information
as to effectiveness of fire. SFCP ordered ceased fire. 2205 SFCP secured
for night. Total 5"/38 cal. projectiles expended to this time: 1013
rounds. 2255 Army signal unit on western extremity of Vierville Sur Mer
beach made signal by flashing light; designated target. Enemy fire
detected from vicinity of beach fire in Vierville Sur Mer target area.
2257 U.S.S. Mc COOK selected by Admiral Bryant (ComTaskFor 124.7) to
fire on source of enemy fire. Commenced firing. 2303 Ceased firing,
having started three brilliant fires accompanied by explosions in area
to rear and westward of Vierville Sur Mer. No further enemy fire noticed
from this area. Requested more explicit data from Army signal station, received no reply. Targets assumed neutralized or destroyed: 7 pillboxes,
8 gun enplacements, and numerous houses.

After Action Report – Commander Destroyer Squadron Sixty.

COMMANDER DESTROYER SQUADRON SIXTY

OF6-60/A12-1/A16-3   C/O FLEET POST OFFICE   (lw)
Serial 003   ~~SAN FRANCISCO CALIFORNIA~~
                            New York, New York

SECRET

                                              24 June 1944.

Subject: Narrative and Report of Operations by Comdesron SIXTY
            in Operation ▮▮▮▮▮▮ (3 June 1944 to 17 June 1944).
- -

0945 - Comtaskfor 125 directed assignment of one DD to fire support
       station 1. WALKE was designated.

1145 - Comtaskfor 125 directed that one DD be designated to relieve
       the HERNDON in fire support area. BARTON was designated
       and proceeded via swept channels to that station.

1215 - Comdesron 60 in BARTON arrived on station and advised HERNDON
       that BARTON was her relief. The latter stated she was unable
       to contact shore fire control party by radio. The BARTON was
       also unsuccessful, so she was directed to patrol along the
       section of OMAHA Beach, searching shoreline for targets of
       opportunity.

1350 - A signal light was sighted on top of a cliff just east of
       Point de Hoe. A detachment of U. S. Soldiers in a pill box
       or gun emplacement recessed into the top of the face of the
       cliff were signalling for assistance. They were Rangers, and
       requested the BARTON to send boat for casualties and first aid.

1430 - Directed BARTON to send in boat with pharmacist mate, one
       officer, and soldiers which were removed from the sunken
       LCT. This boat went in towing a rubber boat astern.

1445 - The SATTERLEE just to the east of the BARTON, shelling shore
       positions with other U. S. ships, began firing in the vicinity
       of the American soldiers and near the landing spot of the
       BARTON boat. She was directed to cease firing on the BARTON
       boat.

1455 - Machine gun fire from the cliff was observed and was directed
       at the BARTON boat. The boat turned and headed back for the
       ship.

1517 - BARTON boat returned and reported gun emplacement was held by
       a detachment of about 15 rangers. There were about 7 wounded
       Americans and about 15 German prisoners who were assembled
       at the bottom of the cliff. The boat returned because of
       German machine gun fire and a rocky beach on which a landing
       could not be made. The pharmacist mate had been wounded, but
       not seriously, by a .30 caliber machine gun bullet.

Below: The 1700hrs request for gunfire support was directed at the troop concentration in the lane to the rear of where the guns were discovered. This is probably the accommodation buildings for the unit in charge of the guns that were found by Lomell and Rupinski.

COMMANDER DESTROYER SQUADRON SIXTY

OF6-60/A12-1/A16-3   C/O FLEET POST OFFICE   (1w)
Serial 003
                          New York, New York

SECRET

24 June 1944.

Subject: Narrative and Report of Operations by Comdesron SIXTY
            in Operation ▓▓▓▓ (3 June 1944 to 17 June 1944).

- -

1521 - Ranger Detachment by light requested fire support. It
       appeared that they were surrounded by German machine gun
       nests recessed in the cliff and by Germans in the area
       inland from the shore line. They also desired immediate
       reinforcements.

       I directed the BARTON to support the Rangers and fire was
       opened on a machine gun position 2000 yards east of the gun
       emplacement. Other positions further to the eastward were
       fired on also, with good results reported by the Rangers. All
       spotting was done by visual signalling.

1625 - Ranger Detachment requested that a LCA be sent to remove
       prisoners and wounded. This message was relayed to Comtaskfor
       122 and Comtaskgroup 125.8.

1640 - A radio antenna was sighted at the gun emplacement and com-
       munication established with the Rangers on 4300 kcs. for
       fire control on their assigned call of HVS. This station was
       evidently in communication by wire or radio with their
       battalion shore fire control party.

1700 - The Rangers requested fire support in a grid position of
       581925, and BARTON was directed to comply.

1726 - It was desired to authenticate requests from this station for
       fire support. However, the Ranger detachment advised that
       they had no verification tables with them. Lt. Gately, attached
       to the staff of Comtaskfor 122, who was attached to my staff
       for temporary duty in connection with fire support matters,
       authenticated the Rangers' request after discussion with the
       party by radio and upon learning the names of various officers
       involved in their shore fire control party.

1745 - SATTERLEE advised that she had to leave area and requested
       BARTON take over her fire support of the Rangers. BARTON was
       directed to do so. BARTON continued to support the Ranger
       detachment in gun emplacement.

1823 - Sent despatch to Comtaskfor 122 giving co-ordinate position of
       Ranger detachment and requesting that assistance be sent, as
       well as reinforcements. BARTON continued fire support of
       Rangers until 1918.

COMMANDER DESTROYER SQUADRON SIXTY

OF6-60/A12-1/A16-3
Serial 003

C/O FLEET POST OFFICE

~~XXXWXXXXXCXXXEXXXXXXXX~~
New York, New York

(1w)

SECRET

24 June 1944.

Subject: Narrative and Report of Operations by Comdesron SIXTY
in Operation ███████ (3 June 1944 to 17 June 1944).

- -

1853 - Comdesdiv 36 advised the BARTON that she was to proceed to
OMAHA area for fire support.

1920 - BARTON arrived in Western OMAHA Area off Point de la Perce
but could not obtain radio communication with shore fire
control party in that area.

7 June 1944.

0153 - Comtaskfor 122 directed by despatch that BARTON and O'BRIEN
replace the CARMICK and SATTERLEE in fire support group of
Force "O".

0345 - Received despatch from Comtaskfor 125 directing WALKE,
MEREDITH, and BARTON to take stations in UTAH area, with
BARTON in station 4. Since the BARTON could not be in the
OMAHA Fire Support Group and also on station 4 in the UTAH
area, she was directed to be in station 4 at sunrise.

0600 - Upon arriving in station 4, Rangers requested fire support
from the BARTON.

0650 - Comtaskfor 124 directed BARTON to proceed to inshore fire
support area in OHIO area and report to Commander Bombardment
Group of Force "O".

Comtaskfor 124 advised that he was sending 2 LCVPs to
Ranger position to remove wounded and prisoners.

0656 - Comtaskgroup 124.9 asked if BARTON had a shore fire control
party contact. He was advised in the affirmative and that
she had a target for a Ranger group requiring immediate
assistance.

0730 - Rangers attempted to evacuate their wounded down the face
of the cliff under fire of German machine guns. This
evacuating was covered by BARTON's firing on positions designated by Rangers.

0900 - Comdesron 60 received orders from Comtaskfor 124 via TEXAS
for BARTON to proceed to OHIO area.

COMMANDER DESTROYER SQUADRON SIXTY

OF6-60/A12-1/A16-3   C/O FLEET POST OFFICE   (1w)
Serial 003   ~~SAN FRANCISCO, CALIFORNIA~~
                            New York, New York

SECRET   24 June 1944.

Subject: Narrative and Report of Operations by Comdesron SIXTY
            in Operation ▬▬▬▬▬ (3 June 1944 to 17 June 1944).

- -

0901 – Advised Comdesdiv 36, who appeared to be a representative of
        Comtaskgroup 124.9, that BARTON had orders from Comtaskfor 125
        to take fire support station 4 in Prairie Area.

0912 – Advised Comtaskgroup 124.9 that BARTON had been ordered to
        Station 4 by Comtaskfor 125 to relieve SATTERLEE. Also advised
        that BARTON had radio contact with a shore fire control party
        of Rangers and was now covering evacuation of wounded, and
        in view of situation did he still desire BARTON to proceed to
        OHIO Area. An immediate reply was received stating that
        orders to proceed to the OHIO Area came from Comtaskfor 125
        and that they should be carried out.

0930 – BARTON arrived in OHIO area, but could not obtain contact with
        a shore fire control party.

1128 – Received orders from Comtaskgroup 125.8 for BARTON to return
        to Station 4 in Prairie Area.

1200 – BARTON returned to Station 4 and received a message again from
        the Rangers requesting a landing barge for removal of wounded
        and prisoners. Comdesron 18 and MC COOK near by stated they
        had also requested the landing barge.

1212 – Received a despatch from Comtaskgroup 124.9 for Comdesron 60
        to report to Admiral Bryant in TEXAS. This was later modified
        to come within hailing distance.

1228 – BARTON closed TEXAS. Comdesron 60 was informed by Comtaskgroup
        124.9 that orders to the OHIO Area came from the highest
        authority and that the BARTON now belonged to Force "O" and
        was under his direction. Comtaskgroup 124.9 directed
        Comdesron 60 to return to OHIO Area and take charge of inshore
        fire support group in that area.

1320 – Arrived with BARTON in OHIO Area and took charge of the fire
        support group consisting of BARTON, BALDWIN, DOYLE, and EMMONS.
        BARTON and EMMONS could make no contact with a fire control
        party of that section.

1420 – Received despatch from ARKANSAS ordering all DDs to cease
        firing into British area. No destroyers of this fire support
        group had fired into the British area.

COMMANDER DESTROYER SQUADRON SIXTY

OF6-60/A12-1/A16-3   C/O FLEET POST OFFICE   (lw)
Serial 003   ~~SAN FRANCISCO, CALIFORNIA~~
                       New York, New York

SECRET   24 June 1944.

Subject: Narrative and Report of Operations by Comdesron SIXTY
             in Operation ▓▓▓▓▓ (3 June 1944 to 17 June 1944).
- -

1630 - Comdesron 60 finally succeeded in establishing radio contact
       with fire control headquarters with the Commander of the
       4th Army Division, and was advised that ships not firing should
       stand by for a call when support was required.

1802 - DOYLE advised that she had been ordered to join the area screen
       and that EMMONS was taking over her fire control party.

2104 - Ordered BARTON, BALDWIN and EMMONS to remain underway in area
       during night subject to call from fire control parties.

2318 - As an air raid alarm was received, directed the BARTON,
       BALDWIN and EMMONS to screen the ARKANSAS and the cruisers,
       MONTCALM and GEORGES LEYGUES.

8 June 1944.

0118 - Received despatch from Comtaskgroup 125.8 directing Comdesron 60
       to take station near him in the UTAH Area to screen the heavy
       ships. An attempt to obtain communication with Comtaskgroup
       125.8 by TBS to advise him in regard to our inability to
       screen him was not successful.

0128 - BARTON fired on an unidentified plane flying at 1500 feet
       from the eastward to westward over OMAHA anchorage. It was
       brought down in flames after 20 rounds of 5" firing with full
       radar control.

0200 - Destroyers made smoke and covered heavy ships after orders
       were received to execute smoke plan No. 1.

0230 - Stopped smoke on orders from Comtaskfor 122.4.

0415 - Destroyers were again ordered to make smoke in accordance
       with Plan No. 1, which was terminated by orders received at
       0527.

0528 - Ships moved into fire support area and BALDWIN received a
       firing assignment.

0600 - Received orders from Comtaskgroup 125.8 for BARTON to return
       to fire support station 4 in UTAH Area prior to sunrise.

COMMANDER DESTROYER SQUADRON SIXTY

OF6-60/A12-1/A16-3   C/O FLEET POST OFFICE   (1w)
Serial 003   ~~SAN FRANCISCO, CALIFORNIA~~
                            New York, New York

SECRET   24 June 1944.

Subject: Narrative and Report of Operations by Comdesron SIXTY
            in Operation ████ (3 June 1944 to 17 June 1944).

- -

0830 - Advised Comtaskgroup 125.8 that Comtaskgroup 124.9 had
       directed BARTON to remain with fire support group in Eastern
       OHIO Area.

0925 - O'BRIEN reported for duty with fire support group in Eastern
       OHIO area.

1335 - Intercepted an attempt by Shore Fire Control Party 31 to
       contact BARTON by radio to Comtaskgroup 125.8. Shore Fire
       Control Party 31 was advised that BARTON was not in their
       area. This was apparently due to the confusion over the
       assignment of destroyers between Forces "U" and "O".

1935 - BALDWIN advised she had orders to proceed to the screen and
       was being relieved by EMMONS.

2005 - Directed destroyers in OHIO Fire Support Area to remain under-
       way during darkness and screen ARKANSAS and French cruisers
       in event of air or surface raids.

2048 - Requested Comtaskfor 124 to send landing boat alongside
       BARTON to remove the 31 soldiers removed from the sinking
       LCT, all men being fit for duty. Comtaskfor 124 advised
       landing barge would be alongside BARTON in the morning.

2155 - Comdesron 10 in ELLYSON arrived in OHIO Fire Support Area
       and joined fire support group.

9 June 1944.

0819 - BARTON received fire support assignment which was cancelled
       by the Army because of poor visibility.

0907 - O'BRIEN advised that she was proceeding to establish com-
       munication with Shore Fire Control Party 18, but didn't know
       its location since the target given was in the Western OMAHA
       Area (Prairie). In view of instructions given by Comtaskgroup
       124.9, he was asked whether or not the O'BRIEN should proceed
       to the Prairie Area to cover the assignment. Comtaskgroup
       124.9 directed that the O'BRIEN proceed and carry out fire
       support request.

Below: USS *Navy* D-Day evaluation report paragraph.

> It appeared that the enemy battery expected to be at Pointe du Hoe either did not exist there or was neutralized by the combined efforts of the Army, Navy, and Rangers. Batteries Maisy, Asnieres, Formigny and Le Molay continued to be effective throughout the day.

Below: Destroyer Fire Support Group report.

It is interesting that the writer of this report makes such statements as '60% of the Ranger force was killed in the first 2 hours'… a statement which is simply not true.

Part I - General Narrative.

1.   As Commander Task Unit 124.7.3, Commander Destroyer Division THIRTY-SIX, in SATTERLEE with McCOOK and CARMICK departed Portland, England at 1100, 5 June, 1944. (D minus 1 day). The mission of this Task Unit was to escort and protect from enemy action the Mine Sweepers which were to sweep Approach Channel #4, the Omaha Transport Area, and Gunfire Support Channel #3 in Omaha Area, Operation ███████. Rendezvous with British Mine Sweeper Flotilla FOUR was effected at 50° 05' N 0° 46' W at 1700 B (H minus 13 hours 30 minutes). Shortly thereafter the sweepers formed up and commenced sweeping and buoying Approach Channel #4. This Task Unit escorted the sweepers down the Approach Channel and into the Omaha Transport Area. The passage was uneventful except for the sinking by gunfire of several mines cut loose by the sweepers. No enemy forces were encountered. At 0030 6 June (H minus 6 hours) proceeded to southern end of Approach Channel #3 and waited for British Mine Sweeping Flotilla ONE SIX SEVEN and one (1) division of Mine Sweeping Flotilla ONE ZERO FOUR to commence sweeping Gunfire Support Channel #3. Escorted these sweepers down the Gunfire Support Channel until leading sweep had turned north at which time stationed escorts on western edge of channel and waited for sweepers to pass. Sweeping operation was completed at 060400 B (H minus 2 hours 30 minutes). At this time directed escorts to proceed independently to their assigned Fire Support Stations.

2.   In the absence of Commander Destroyer Gunfire Support Group, Force "O", who was also Screen Commander, as Deputy Commander I assumed command of the Gunfire Support Destroyers. This Group of eleven (11) destroyers was constituted as follows:

Fire Support Area #3	Fire Support Area #4
U.S.S. SATTERLEE	H.M.S. TANATSIDE
H.M.S. TALYBONT	U.S.S. EMMONS
U.S.S. THOMPSON	U.S.S. BALDWIN
U.S.S. McCOOK	U.S.S. HARDING
U.S.S. CARMICK	U.S.S. DOYLE
	H.M.S. MELBREAK

Ships were arranged in this order from west to east so as to avoid crossfire on assigned targets. The mission of this Destroyer Fire Support Group was to deliver scheduled fire on assigned targets before H hour, to deliver close supporting fire at targets of opportunity during and after the landing, and to deliver call fire for Shore Fire Control Parties as soon as parties had become established on the beach. Each destroyer had previously held numerous drills and conferences with their own Shore Fire Control Party. This proved invaluable as each ship and Shore Fire Control Party was used to and familiar with the procedure and peculiarities of its individual opposite.

3.   All destroyers had been previously directed to be in their assigned Fire Support station and ready to open fire at H minus 40 minutes, but to be prepared to use counter-battery fire at any time after passing Transport Area if fired upon by the enemy. Destroyers entering Fire Support Area #3 were not fired upon prior to opening fire but those proceeding down Fire Support Channel #4 were taken under fire by German Coastal Batteries at 0535 (H minus

1

ENCLOSURE "A"

55 minutes). Fire was promptly returned by BALDWIN, HARDING, and EMMONS. The
battery which appeared through the smoke to be located at or near Port en
Bessin was temporarily silenced at 0552. Several enemy salvos landed quite
close to the destroyers but none suffered material damage or casualties.

4.   At H minus 40 minutes (0550 B) or shortly thereafter all destroyers
opened fire on their assigned targets. Coastal artillery immediately answered
the fire and from then on until late the next day all destroyers were under
intermittent fire by enemy coastal defenses, mortars and heavy machine guns. During
the period of scheduled fire from H minus 40 minutes to H hour it was necessary
for the destroyers to occasionally shift fire from their assigned target to some
enemy gun that was shooting at them. In most of these instances a few salvos
were sufficient to temporarily silence these enemy guns and fire was then immediately shifted back to scheduled targets. The fire of all destroyers during
this period was fast and accurate. There were no material or personnel casualties
during this phase of the Support Fire although many enemy shells fell close aboard
the destroyers. As the first wave closed the beach the Fire Support destroyers
preceded them closing the beach to from one thousand (1000) to two thousand (2000)
yards. At 0617 (H minus 13 minutes) LCT(R)'s commenced firing rockets drenching
the area just inland from the beaches. Fire from this beach was temporarily
silenced and the entire area covered with heavy smoke and dust. Troops landed
and proceeded up the beach into the smoke.

5.   From the landing of the troops until the establishment of Shore
Fire Control Parties the Fire Support Destroyers fired on targets of opportunity.
It is considered that the support of destroyers during this phase was not utilized
to over twenty (20) percent of their possibilities. There was no communication
with the beach and on numerous occasions destroyers could not fire on targets
which should have been fired on because they did not know the location of our
own troops. This is a most crucial period in the assault and some method of
communication between troops and Fire Support Ships must be devised. The Destroyers acquited themselves well indeed whenever a target presented itself.
Numerous guns firing on the beaches were detected by their flashes and were destroyed by the Fire Support Ships. The destroyers closed to less than a thousand
(1000) yards from the beach, the fire of each ship being directed by the Commanding Officer.

At 0730 H.M.S. TALYBONT departed in accordance with previous
instructions and at 0850 H.M.S. TANATSIDE left the Fire Support Area. At 0821
BALDWIN was hit by two (2) 105 millimeter shells. These caused but minor material
damage and no personnel casualties.

6.   At 0710 (H plus 40 minutes) the first boat of the 2nd Rangers which
were to attack Pointe du Hoe landed just to the east of the point. These boats
were forty minutes late in arriving at their beach. This was due to two (2) reasons (1) additional distance from transports to Pointe du Hoe and (2) slow progress
by the heavily loaded boats into wind and sea. Wind was from the West force ten
- fifteen (10 - 15) knots, sea was from the west waves two - four (2 - 4) feet
high and moderate swells from North North West. Five (5) or six (6) out of the
ten (10) boats foundered before they reached the beach. Fortunately this occured
in shallow water between one (1) and two (2) hundred yards from the beach. Most
of the Rangers from these boats reached the beach although there were a few casualties by drowning at this time.

The fortifications at Pointe du Hoe had been under heavy fire by
TEXAS from H minus 40 minutes to H minus 05 minutes. However this fire had been
lifted according to schedule and when the Rangers landed fortyfive (45) minutes
later the Germans had filtered back into the fortifications and were waiting for them
with machine guns, mortars, rifles, and hand grenades. At this point the cliffs
rise abruptly from the water to a height of approximately one hundred (100) feet.
As the Rangers landed they found themselves pinned under the cliffs and were being
rapidly cut to pieces by enemy fire. I immediately ordered SATTERLEE to close the
point and take the cliff tops under main battery and machine gun fire. This was
done. Her fire control was excellent and the Rangers were enabled to establish a
foothold on the cliff top. 40 millimeter machine gun fire was very effective
against troops driven out of their trenches by 5" guns. The Rangers had brought
some rockets with grapnels and rope ladders attached to shoot over the cliff and
provide a means of ascent. These novel gadgets did not appear to be particularly
successful. By 0728 SATTERLEE had established communication with the Ranger fire
control party and the situation had improved slightly. At that nearly sixty (60)
percent of these Rangers were killed in the first two (2) hours of the battle.
As their Shore Fire Control Party advanced inland the remainder of the Rangers
established communication with SATTERLEE by light and were thus enabled to rapidly
call for close support fire. By this means SATTERLEE and later THOMPSON and
HARDING were able to repel several enemy counter-attacks which otherwise would
have wiped out this Ranger Battalion to a man. The gallant fight of this 2nd
Battalion of our Rangers against tremendous odds and difficulties was an inspiration
to all naval personnel fortunate enough to witness this phase of the battle. The
Rangers were magnificent.

7.   At 0900(H plus 2 hours 30 minutes) Commander Destroyer Fire Support
Group in FRANKFORD (Commander Destroyer Squadron EIGHTEEN) entered Fire Support
Area and assumed command of Fire Support destroyers until 1600, at which time he
departed to assume command of Area Screen and I again assumed command of Force
"O" Fire Support Destroyers.

8.   During the remainder of the day Fire Support Destroyers fired at
targets as directed by Shore Fire Control Parties, Commander Destroyer Squadron
EIGHTEEN, Commander Task Group 124.9, and by their own commanding officers. (For
individual ship targets and ammunition expenditure on each target see Reports of
Action by Ships). At 1750 SATTERLEE had fired over seventy (70) percent of her
bombardment ammunition. Directed THOMPSON to relieve her in support of Rangers
and shifted my pennant and staff to HARDING. SATTERLEE departed Fire Support Area
to report to Area Screen Commander. At 1800 BARTON (Commander Destroyer Squadron
SIXTY) and O'BRIEN reported to Fire Support Area and were assigned stations and
Shore Fire Control Parties. At 2000 directed CARMICK to report to Area Screen
Commander she having expended over seventy (70) percent of her bombardment ammunition. Omaha beaches were under sporadic but heavy shelling during most of the
afternoon and evening of D day. This fire came from sources Fire Support Ships
had great difficulty in locating. However it was evidently controlled by observers
watching the beaches. There were numerous houses behind the beaches and on adjacent hills and cliffs overlooking the beaches which had not been thoroughly shelled
even at this late date. I believe that this was a costly error on our part and
for future landing operations I strongly advocate the demolishment of all structures,
houses, Churches, etc., that could possibly house light artillery, machine guns,

3

SECRET   ENCLOSURE "A"

mortars and/or observation and communication posts prior to and immediately
after the landing of troops. This could have readily been done by the destroyers but
by the time we realized this our troops were advancing and we were unable to obtain
permission to shell any but a few of the most obvious. It was most galling and
depressing to lie idly a few hundred yards off the beaches and watch our troops,
tanks, landing boats, and motor vehicles being heavily shelled and not be able to
fire a shot to help them just because we had no information as to what to shoot at
and were unable to detect the source of the enemy fire. Advancing troops must have
some visual means to call for immediate fire support from close Fire Support Ships.
A mortar shell with a distinctively colored smoke would have been most effective
and would have insured immediate destruction of a target so designated.

9.   During the hours of darkness destroyers answered call fire from Shore
Fire Control Parties. THOMPSON was especially busy repelling German counter-
attacks on the 2nd Rangers at Pointe du Hoe.

At 2330 B 6 June the first enemy air raid began. Heavy AA fire by
numerous ships in Transport Areas was almost as dangerous to adjacent ships as
to enemy planes. Fire discipline on merchant ships and landing craft was not
satisfactory.

10.   7 June 1944.

At 0100 B AA firing ceased and air raid was over for the night.
There were no casualties to Fire Support Destroyers. At 0630 HARDING relieved
THOMPSON in support of Rangers and THOMPSON departed to replenish ammunition
having expended over eighty (80) percent of her bombardment ammunition.

During the day destroyers fired on targets as requested by Shore
Fire Control Parties and as the troops moved further inland the calls became
fewer. At 0740 directed HARDING to send motor whale-boat to beach at Pointe
du Hoe to evacuate Ranger casualties. Boat was wrecked in landing. Requested
LCVP's from Commander Task Group 124.9 (Commander Battleship Division FIVE) and
furnished list of ammunition and supplies Rangers needed which they had transmitted to me by flashing light from the beach.

At 1100 commandeered a passing LCT and placed ammunition, food,
and water for Rangers on board. LCT attempted to make beach but was unsuccessful due to state of tide. I then sent LCT to transport pool with orders to transfer supplies to an LCVP and have it return to me. At 1200 PLUNKETT reported for
duty in Fire Support Area and was assigned station and Shore Fire Control Party.
At 1429 HARDING struck an underwater obstruction about fifteen hundred (1500)
yards north of Roches des Grandcamp. Chart showed water to be between seven
(7) and eight (8) fathoms deep at present state of tide. Sound dome and propellers damaged. Ship cleared at 1432 and was able to make twelve (12) to
fifteen (15) knots, without excessive vibration. Retained ship in Fire Support
Area as she had only expended fifty (50) percent bombardment ammunition.

At 1500 two (2) LCVP's reported for duty. Sent them to Ranger Beach
to evacuate casualties. At 1600 two (2) more LCVP's reported one containing
supplies earlier furnished by HARDING and other with supplies furnished by TEXAS.

4

ENCLOSURE "A"

Sent them to Ranger beach at Pointe du Hoe. LCVP's returned with wounded and prisoners and were directed to take them to TEXAS.

At 1730 DOYLE having expended seventy (70) percent ammunition departed with orders to report to Area Screen Commander. At 2240 MURPHY reported
for duty in Fire Support Area and was assigned station and Shore Fire Control Party.

11.   8 June 1944.

At 0000 enemy air raid on beach defenses and shipping commenced.
Large volumes of AA fire from beach and ships. Saw only two (2) enemy planes
shot down. No destroyers suffered damage during raid. Destroyers in Ohio area
smoke screened ARKANSAS and French Cruisers. Destroyers in Oregon area failed
to receive word to make smoke. At 0206 MEREDITH reported being hit by glider
bomb in Utah area. 0215 AA fire ceased and area reported clear of enemy planes.
At 0540 McCOOK departed from area having expended over seventy (70) percent of
her bombardment ammunition and ELLYSON (Commander Destroyer Squadron TEN) reported
for duty in Fire Support Area and was assigned station and Shore Fire Control
Party.

During the day destroyers stood by to deliver fire on call from
Shore Fire Control Parties but there were not many calls as troops had advanced
inland beyond range of destroyer guns in a number of areas. At 1433 HARDING
called on to shell waterfront buildings in Grandcamp des Bains and at 1815 fired
on town of Maisy for fortyfive (45) minutes intermittent fire as requested by
Shore Fire Control Party. At 1900 lifted fire and troops entered town. At 1930
directed BALDWIN to report to Area Screen Commander for duty in screen. In accordance with instructions from Commander Task Group 124.9 Fire Support Destroyers
were directed to anchor after darkness in position best suited for AA protection
of shipping. This was done to reduce hazard of hitting mines dropped by enemy
aircraft in night air raids. Unless called by Shore Fire Control Party I attempted
to keep destroyers anchored during morning until adjacent areas had been swept
for mines.

12.   9 June 1944.

At 0010 enemy air raid started. Heavy AA fire from all merchant
ships and landing craft. Saw only one (1) enemy plane shot down. BALDWIN reported
she saw five (5) shot down. ELLYSON reported four (4) rocket bombs fell close
to her but no damage sustained. Planes using "window" to jam air search radars.
Numerous mines or delayed action bombs fell in area. 0100 Air raid over. At
0625 more enemy aircraft reported over area but did not see or hear of any bombs
falling. At 0705 SATTERLEE returned from England having replenished ammunition.
Shifted pennant and staff back to SATTERLEE and directed HARDING proceed to Plymouth for repairs in accordance with her previous orders. Very little fire support was required of destroyers during the day. At 1900 ELLYSON completed
firing on target 646798. This was the last time Shore Fire Control Parties called
for destroyer fire support. Directed PLUNKETT, BARTON and O'BRIEN to report to
Area Screen Commander for duty in screen retaining only ELLYSON, MURPHY and
SATTERLEE in Fire Support Area to furnish AA support during hours of darkness.

5

ENCLOSURE "A"

13.   10 - 15 June 1944.

        No more fire support was required of destroyers by Shore Fire
Control Parties and all but three (3) destroyers were detached from Fire Support
Area and turned over to Area Screen Commander. This situation maintained with
an occasional shift of an individual ship from Fire Support Area to Screen and
back until 0800 15 June when new Task Organization became effective, Destroyer
Fire Support Group, Force "O" was disbanded, and I reported to Commander Destroyer
Squadron EIGHTEEN for duty in Area Screen.

Part II - Chronological Order of Events.

5 June 1944.

1100   Task Unit 124.7.3 departed Portland England.
1200   Rendezvoused with British Mine Sweeping Flotilla FOUR at 50° 05' N,
         0° 46' W and proceeded down Approach Channel #4 escorting minesweepers.

6 June 1944.

0030   Arrived Omaha Transport Area proceeded to Channel #3 awaiting arrival
         Mine Sweeping Flotilla ONE SIX SEVEN and ONE ZERO FOUR.
0145   Rendezvoused with Mine Sweeping Flotilla ONE SIX SEVEN and ONE ZERO
         FOUR and escorted them as they swept Gunfire Support Channel #3
         Omaha Area.
0400   Sweeping Operations completed directed destroyers to proceed in-
         dependently to Fire Support Stations.
0535   German Shore Batteries commenced firing on destroyers in Ohio Fire
         Support Area.
0537   BALDWIN, HARDING, EMMONS returned fire on enemy Coastal batteries.
0550   Fire Support Destroyers commenced fire on assigned targets. Deputy
         Commander Fire Support Destroyers, Force "O", (Commander Destroyer
         Division THIRTY-SIX) in SATTERLEE assumed command Fire Support Des-
         troyers.
0617   LCT(R)'s commenced firing rockets at beach.
0710   First boat of 2nd Rangers arrived Pointe du Hoe beach.
0728   SATTERLEE established first communication with Shore Fire Control
         Party.
0730   H.M.S. TALYBONT departed in accordance with previous orders.
0821   BALDWIN hit by two (2) 105 millimeter shells.
0850   H.M.S. TANATSIDE departed in accordance with previous orders.
0900   Commander Destroyer Squadron EIGHTEEN in FRANKFORD entered area
         and assumed command of Fire Support Destroyers.
0930   H.M.S. MELBREAK departed in accordance with previous orders.
1600   Commander Destroyer Squadron EIGHTEEN in FRANKFORD departed to
         take command of Area Screen and Commander Destroyer Division
         THIRTY-SIX again assumed command Fire Support Destroyers.
1750   Shifted Pennant and Staff to HARDING.
1800   BARTON and O'BRIEN reported for duty in Fire Support Area and were
         assigned stations and Fire Control Party.
2000   SATTERLEE having expended seventy-five (75) percent of her bombard-
         ment ammunition departed Fire Support Area to report for duty in Area
         Screen.

.T

2000	Directed CARMICK to report to Area Screen Commander she having expended over seventy (70) percent of her bombardment ammunition.
2330	Enemy air raid commenced. Heavy AA fire by merchant ships and landing craft. Very poor fire discipline.

7 June 1944.

0100	Area clear of enemy aircraft.
0630	THOMPSON departed for England to replenish ammunition.
0740	HARDING sent motor whale-boat to Pointe du Hoe in attempt to evacuate Ranger wounded. Boat wrecked on beach.
1200	PLUNKETT reported for duty in Fire Support Area and was assigned station and Shore Fire Control Party.
1429	HARDING struck submerged object off Roches des Grandcamp damaging sound dome and both propellers.
1432	HARDING cleared obstruction. Now able to make twelve to fifteen (12 to 15) knots without excessive vibration. Retained her in Fire Support Area.
1500	Two (2) LCVP's reported for duty and were directed proceed to Ranger beach and evacuate casualties.
1600	Two (2) more LCVP's reported with ammunition replacements, food, and water for Rangers. Directed them to proceed to Ranger beach at Pointe du Hoe.
1730	DOYLE departed to report to Area Screen Commander having expended over seventy (70) percent of her bombardment ammunition.
2240	MURPHY reported for duty in Fire Support Area and was assigned station and Shore Fire Control Party.

ENCLOSURE "A"

Part III – <u>Performance of Ordnance Material</u>.

The performance of all ordnance material was uniformly excellent. No ordnance casualties occured which could not be expeditiously repaired by ship's force. The only factor that limited the fire support these destroyers could give was the amount of ammunition the ships could carry.

The photographs of Enclosure (C) show the effectiveness of the 5"/38 cal. gun against various types of beach defenses. AA common is not suitable for use against concrete positions, but of course this statement is no news. In an assault such as Operations ▬▬▬▬ against prepared beach defenses I believe the percentage of common should be much higher than the forty (40) rounds per gun we carried. I suggest at least one hundred (100) rounds per gun. It is further suggested that twenty - twentyfive (20 - 25) rounds per gun of white phosphorus be carried for incendiary use against houses as well as for smoke screens. Very few duds were noted and as all AA common was set on safe when firing at fortifications no air bursts were noted. When firing against troops fuses were set on advanced range and the usual percent of air bursts obtained. This method was highly effective against troops. In one instance HARDING walked salvos down a road well behind the beach and dispersed or killed a body of German troops advancing along the road to attack the flank of our troops. The road was not visible from the ship and range used was optical range to beach plus chart range from beach to road.

When used the 40 millimeter was highly effective against troops. These guns should have been used more as almost all the destroyers were within effective 40 millimeter range of the beach most of the first three (3) days of the assault.

For ammunition expenditures see individual ship action reports.

8

ENCLOSURES "A"

Part IV - Battle Damage

    1.   Own ships damage.

          At 0820 B 6 June the BALDWIN received two (2) direct hits from
enemy 105 millimeter shells. Size of shell was calculated from curvature of
shrapnel fragments.

1. Two projectiles. Estimated type - common, weight - about
   30 pounds, diameter - 105 millimeter - fuzes - instantaneous.
2. Range - relative bearing of enemy battery, 2500 - 3000 yards.
   relative bearing 215°.
3. Location of impact: First projectile hit after bitt, port
   side, frame 40. Second projectile inboard boat gripe and
   after starboard side of port motor whale-boat (rigged out
   from port davits), frames 74-75.
4. Path of projectiles through ship; both projectiles exploded
   on impact.
5. Thicknesses penetrated; 3/16" plating and lesser thicknesses
   penetrated by shrapnel.
6. Distance from point of impact to detonations: apparently
   instantaneous detonations.
7. Type of detonation; low order detonation; fragments varying
   from approximately $\frac{1}{2}$" to 1" x $2\frac{1}{2}$".
8. Brief description of damage:
   (a) Impact effect negligible.
   (b) Direct effects: 1. First projectile made 8" x 12" hole in
       forecastle deck (frames 35-36), dented deck and bitt.
       2. Second projectile demolished after starboard side of
       motor whale-boat, causing hole about 7 feet long extending
       from keel to gunwale at widest point.
   (c) Fragment effect: 1. Shrapnel from 1st projectile made five
       other smaller holes in vicinity and cut two oil lines in
       Gun. No. 1, which was trained in direction of beach, pene-
       trating plating 3/16" at a distance of 5-7 feet.
       2. Shrapnel from second projectile made 36 holes varying
       from $\frac{1}{2}$" to 1" x 4", penetrating plating 3/16" at distance
       of about 38-40 feet. Supply cables to bridge under over-
       head above C.I.C. outside deck were cut in 1 M.C. and
       navigational light systems.
   (d) Incendiary effects on subsequent explosions: none.
   (e) Path and effects of flash or flame; not noticed; effects
       negligible.
9. Noxious gases or fumes; not noticed.
10. Action taken: Damage was local and not serious. All necessary
    repairs were made shortly by ship's force.

          At 1429 B 7 June HARDING struck submerged object with Pointe du
Hoe bearing 140° (t) and right hand Church of Grandcamp des Bains bearing 133°
(t). The sound dome and both propellers were badly damaged. It is believed
HARDING struck a recently sunk ship or an uncharted wreck as the water at this

ENCLOSURE "A"

point showed seven (7) fathoms on the chart for the stage of tide obtaining at
the time. Several of our landing craft and larger ships had been sunk in this
general area on D-day and their exact location was then and still is unknown.
As the ship could make twelve to fifteen (12 - 15) knots without excessive
vibration I retained her in the Fire Support Area as she had only expended about
fifty (50) percent of her ammunition at that time.

   2.   Enemy damage.

          It is impossible to assess full amount of damage inflicted on the
enemy by the Fire Support Destroyers. The inspecting officer who made photographs of Enclosure (C) stated that he saw no gun emplacements, machine gun nests,
etc., which had not been at least partially destroyed. I am unable to estimate
the number of enemy troops killed and wounded by our fire.

Part V - A. Special Comments.

   1.   Communications.

          Communications on the whole were satisfactory. The original eight
(8) U. S. Destroyers in the Fire Support Group were equipped with SCR 608 for
voice communications with Shore Fire Control Parties. However when BARTON,
O'BRIEN, and ELLYSON arrived they were not equipped with this set and had to
work Shore Fire Control Parties by CW. One of these destroyers used the basic
fire control channel 4300 kcs. as a voice channel. This did not cause as much
confusion as might have been expected but still is not considered to be good
practice. BARTON and O'BRIEN also did not have the destroyer frequency crystal
for their TBS sets (66.25 mc) and had only a TBY on board for this frequency.
As usual the TBY turned out to be thoroughly unsatisfactory. We must stop
kidding ourselves that the TBY can be used in battle. These sets should be
removed from combatant vessels and replaced by the SCR 608 or 609 both of which
have been used by ships of this squadron with complete satisfaction. Destroyer
Squadron EIGHTEEN is also equipped with SCR 624 and ships of this squadron were
never at a loss for a circuit by which to talk to each other. The SCR 608 has
20 receiving and 10 transmitting channels and 96 crystals, the SCR 609 2 channels
and 4 crystals and the SCR 624 7 channels and 14 crystals.

          Visual communications were established by at least two destroyers
with troops ashore and proved to be most valuable both in soliciting fire support, requesting removal of casualties, and replacement of ammunition, food,
etc. Such communication would be most valuable immediately after the landing
and before Shore Fire Control Parties have become established on the beach.
Several destroyers did not establish communications with their Shore Fire Control
Parties until late afternoon of D day. These ships could readily have delivered
fire requested by light or any other means.

          We still do not take full advantage of our splendid TBS sets. Al-
though each combatant ship and many of the transports had four or five crystals
for the TBS only two channels were in use in the Western Task Force Area, 66.25 mc
for the Fire Support Ships and 72.5 mc for all other uses. This overloaded both
of these channels while three unused crystals rested peacefully in their con-
tainers.

ENCLOSURE "A"

B. Recommendations.

1.   That pre-landing bombardment by Naval Forces be for a longer period than from H minus 40 minutes to H hour. In this connection it is most necessary that a ship continue its bombardment until a very short time before the troops actually touch down. i.e. (TEXAS bombardment of Pointe du Hoe ceased forty-five (45) minutes before delayed Rangers landed).

2.   That a much heavier air bombardment be scheduled prior to and during Naval Bombardment. Omaha area was hardly touched by air bombardment with the exception of Pointe du Hoe.

3.   That special units which are to attack away from the main beach as the 2nd Rangers did; be loaded into a ship which can come closer to their beach than the regular Transport Area. One of the old converted four-stack destroyers would have been ideal for this purpose. Such a ship should also carry ammunition replacements for its assault party.

4.   That there be established on the beach or on a control ship an agency which is kept constantly informed of vicinity of front lines and which can pass this information to Fire Support Ships who require it. Time after time in this operation destroyers were unable to shoot at excellent targets of opportunity because they could obtain no information as to the location of our own forces in the area in question. This, I believe, was the greatest difficulty with which the Fire Support destroyers had to contend.

5.   That several LCVP's be placed at the disposal of the Fire Support Commander to answer emergency calls for assistance transmitted by Shore Fire Control Parties. It took me nearly eight (8) hours to get some LCVP's to take off Rangers who were desperately wounded and whose only communication with friendly forces was via their Shore Fire Control Party and by flashing light to one destroyer

11

ENCLOSURE "A"

6.   That whenever possible visual communication be established between ships in Fire Support Area and their Shore Fire Control Party or any troops in the vicinity of the beach. SATTERLEE and HARDING established visual communication with Rangers on Pointe du Hoe. This was most satisfactory and enabled ships to repel several enemy attacks which might easily have resulted in extermination of Rangers. It also enabled ships to furnish badly needed ammunition, supplies, water, and to evacuate casualties and prisoners.

7.   That a mortar shell having a smoke of distinctive color be used by troops when they desire immediate fire support on any target so designated.

8.   That at least one destroyer be stationed in the boat lane where an unobstructed view of the beach may be obtained. Targets of opportunity will thus be observed that could not be seen from positions outside the boat lanes.

9.   That previous to the touchdown and before the troops have advanced too far inland every structure, House and Church adjacent to the beaches or overlooking the beaches that could house any artillery, machine guns, mortars, and/or communication and observation posts be demolished. One destroyer in each Fire Support Area should be assigned this mission during the pre-landing Naval bombardment and all Fire Support Ships should assist while waiting for targets of opportunity.

10.   That for an operation against prepared coastal defenses the number of 5"/38 common be increased to one hundred rounds per gun. AA common is not satisfactory for use against gun emplacements and concrete pillboxes.

11.   That twenty (20) to twenty-five (25) rounds per gun of white phosphorus be carried for use as incendiaries against houses and other beach structures as well as to provide smoke screens for our own troops.

12.   That TBY's be replaced by SCR 608 or SCR 609.

13.   That all Channels of TBS be assigned before assignment of less reliable voice set channels is made.

Part VI - Personnel, performance and casualties.

All personnel behaved in a manner in keeping with the Highest Traditions of the U.S. Naval Service. Morale was exceptionally good. Although kept at General Quarters for several days at a time and with only brief periods of rest at their battle stations there was no grumbling and no decrease in the desire to meet the enemy at every opportunity.

I cannot too highly praise the bravery and superb fighting ability displayed by the 2nd Ranger Battalion in its attack on the fortifications at Pointe du Hoe. If any group deserves a Unit Citation for this battle these Rangers should get it.

SECRET   ENCLOSURE "A"

　　　　All the destroyers of this Fire Support Group were under
intermittent enemy fire from artillery, mortars, and machine guns for the first
three (3) days of the assault. Most ships had many near misses, one was hit
by two (2) 105 millimeter shells, and several hit by machine gun fire but not
a single personnel casualty caused by enemy action was experienced in the Destroyer Fire Support Group, Force "O".

　　　　Recommendations for awards to Naval Personnel have been made
the subject of separate correspondence.

Also from the same author:

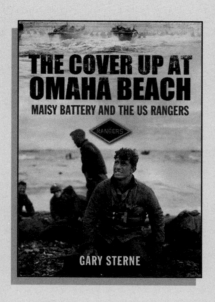

Using personal interviews with the surviving US Army Ranger veterans who fought on the beach, Pointe du Hoc and at Maisy - this is an exceptionally detailed work which offers fresh historical research. The Rangers tell their story in their own words and the reader is led into the heart of the action in a very personal way.

The Maisy Battery had been lost from the historical radar for the previous 63 years and many historians had already finished their books about Pointe du Hoc and the Operation Neptune landings. By putting the history of the Maisy Battery together from evidence found on site - including the discovery of the remains of a German soldier - personal equipment and maps, the author was able to tell a remarkable story which had not been told before. The Maisy Battery is now one of the major Omaha Sector tourist attractions and it has over 2.5 kms of trenches, cannons and bunkers which are open to the public.

All these elements combined make this a fascinating addition to any D-Day library.

Signed copies are available from www.maisybattery.com